PERSPECTIVES: AN OPEN INVITATION TO CULTURAL ANTHROPOLOGY

Edited by Nina Brown, Laura Tubelle de González, and Thomas McIlwraith

(cc) 2017 American Anthropological Association

American Anthropological Association
2300 Clarendon Blvd, Suite 1301
Arlington, VA 22201

ISBN: 978-1-931303-55-2

http://www.perspectivesanthro.org

This book is a project of the Society for Anthropology in Community Colleges (SACC) http://sacc.americananthro.org/ and our parent organization, the American Anthropological Association (AAA). Please refer to the website for a complete table of contents and more information about the book.

PREFACE TO PERSPECTIVES: AN OPEN INVITATION TO CULTURAL ANTHROPOLOGY

Welcome to *Perspectives* and open access anthropology!

We are delighted to bring to you this novel textbook, a collection of chapters on the essential topics in **cultural anthropology**. Different from other introductory textbooks, this book is an edited volume with each chapter written by a different author. Each author has written from their experiences working as an anthropologist and that personal touch makes for an accessible introduction to cultural anthropology.

Our approach to cultural anthropology is **holistic**. We see the interconnectedness of cultural practices and, in all of the chapters, we emphasize the comparison of cultures and the ways of life of different peoples. We start with Laura Nader's observation that cultural differences need not be seen as a problem. In our complicated world of increasing migration, nationalism, and climate challenges, cultural diversity might actually be the source of conflict resolution and new approaches to ensuring a healthier world. Indeed, as Katie Nelson reminds us, anthropology exposes the familiarity in the ideas and practices of others that seem bizarre. Robert Borofsky advocates for anthropology's ability to empower people and facilitate good. Borofsky calls on anthropologists to engage with a wider public to bring our incredible stories and important insights to helping resolve the most critical issues we face in the world today. This book brings Nader, Nelson, Borofsky, and many others together to demonstrate that our anthropological understandings can help all of us to improve the lives of people the world over. We need you, as students, to see the possibilities. As instructors, we want to help you share anthropological knowledge and understanding easily. We want all readers to be inspired by the intensely personal writings of the anthropologists who contribute to this volume.

WHY THIS BOOK?

For students, we promise readable and interesting writing on topics that will be covered in your first year anthropology course. The chapters contain links to support your use and enjoyment of the book. They are designed to help learn the material. Use this book, even if it is not your course text, and then ask your instructor tough questions! Use social media to ask us questions or to send us comments—the details are below.

For instructors, we invite you to build your own book, the perfect book for your course. The available chapters mirror the lecture topics in many first-year courses. The chapters form a whole and they can also stand-alone. Choose the ones you need, assigning some of these chapters and not others. We know that there is some overlap in the chapters. This is a consequence of multiple authors writing about topics which, obviously and necessarily, do not exist without reference to other topics in cultural anthropology. This overlap is teachable because it reinforces the holistic approach used by cultural anthropologists to understand the people with whom we work.

In addition to the chapters, the Perspectives website (http://www.perspectivesanthro.org) provides teaching resources, including a collection of video lectures as well as reflections on the importance of anthropology from well-known members of our discipline. The interviews explain how these scholars became anthropologists and what they see as the importance and relevance of anthropology today. We hope you will use this textbook with your students, either as a stand alone text or in conjunction with other textual and digital materials.

ABOUT THE SOCIETY FOR ANTHROPOLOGY IN COMMUNITY COLLEGES

This book is produced by the Society for Anthropology in Community Colleges (SACC). SAC-Cers, as we call ourselves, are teaching anthropologists who work in community colleges and universities across North America. We teach first year students – like you —many of whom have never taken an anthropology course. We believe strongly in the importance of learning about cultural diversity and we assert that the ideas and skills of anthropologists can inform work in any career. SACC has been building this book since 2012. We have assembled a terrific writing team of authors who teach in colleges and senior anthropologists who share our commitment to creating an open and accessible textbook. SACC tweets @SACC_L and is on Facebook. We encourage you to tweet at us or post on our Facebook page when you are using this book. SACC is an official section of the American Anthropological Association.

WHY OPEN ACCESS?

This book was motivated by SACC's long-standing interest in supporting a diversity of anthropology students, including first generation college learners and students with lower incomes. Frequently, these are the students we teach. Further, SACCers have an interest in progressive social values and believe in the power of education in anthropology to improve the living conditions and situations of people abroad and at home. We want these messages to find their ways to as many people as possible, even if students aren't formally enrolled in an anthropology course.

This book is published under a creative commons license (CC-BY-NC) which grants permission to instructors to copy, distribute, or remix the chapters to suit your educational needs as long as you credit the original author and the original source of the material. The contents of this book may not be used for commercial purposes, meaning it cannot be sold in any form.

THE COVER DESIGN

We put considerable thought into **the cover** of *Perspectives*. We wanted a cover that provokes discussion without stereotyping. We chose a design that prompts reflection and classroom engagement, while remaining friendly and inviting. We invite instructors to use the cover as a teaching tool. Consider discussing that the cover is a story that may be told in many ways. Consider the possibilities of this scene: Who are these people? Where are they in this snapshot and where are they off to? What did they have for breakfast and who will they meet in the course of their day? Similarly, examine this cover along with other recent and past covers of a range of Cultural Anthropology textbooks. What are the messages being sent by the different types of images that represent Cultural Anthropology?

We aren't sure the cover is quite perfect yet, so please teach its strengths and its limitations for understanding what anthropology is – and then let us know what you decide in your class.

Please be in touch with us via **social media or email** if you have suggestions or questions. If you would like to be involved with this project by writing a chapter or creating ancillary materials, please contact us. The dynamic nature of an open access book means that there is always room to add new chapters or other materials.

Thank you for adopting *Perspectives*.

Nina Brown
Thomas McIlwraith
Laura Tubelle de González

ACKNOWLEDGEMENTS

This book would not have been possible without the generous contributions of many people. We would like to thank the Executive Board of the Society for Anthropology in Community Colleges for their support of this project starting in 2012 as well as SACC members who contributed their time and expertise. Jeanne Thompson (Cypress College), and Philip L. Stein (Pierce College) served on the editorial committee and played a central role in shaping the book from the beginning. We also appreciate the assistance of Janine Chiappa McKenna, Director of Publishing for the American Anthropological Association, who helped us develop this book as an open access publishing project.

We would like to express our gratitude to Robert Borofsky (Hawaii Pacific University and Center for a Public Anthropology), who championed this project from its earliest stages and elevated our efforts through his outreach to authors and willingness to share resources. His commitment to a public anthropology that seeks to address the central issues of our time while engaging broad audiences was a central inspiration for our work.

In addition, we thank the following people for their expertise.

Peer Reviewers

Jessica Amato, Napa Valley College
Anthony Balzano, Sussex County Community College
Beverly Bennett, Wilbur Wright College, City Colleges of Chicago
Lin Bentley Keeling, El Paso Community College
Ronald Castanzo, University of Baltimore
Chuck Ellenbaum, College of DuPage
Carol Hayman, Austin Community College
Jeffrey Hoelle, University of California, Santa Barbara
Danielle James, Community College of Baltimore County
Angela Jenks, University of California, Irvine
Diane Levine, Pierce College
Brandon Lundy, Kennesaw State University
Bob Muckle, Capilano University

Carol Mukhopadhyay, San Jose State University
Karen Muir, Columbus State Community College
Philip Naftaly, State University of New York, Adirondack
Christian Palmer, Windward Community College, University of Hawaii
Anastasia Panagakos, Cosumnes River College
Philip Stein, Pierce College
Tim Sullivan, Richland College
Jeanne Thompson, Cypress College
Andrew Walsh, University of Western Ontario

Book Design and Production

Stacy Dreyer, Natalie Karst, and Janet Keller, copyeditors
Stuart Williams, cover design
Grapevine Publishing Services, page design and typesetting

THE DEVELOPMENT OF ANTHROPOLOGICAL IDEAS

Laura Nader, The University of California, Berkeley

LEARNING OBJECTIVES

- Identify the central concepts of cultural anthropology and describe how each of these concepts contributed to the development of the discipline.

- Describe the role anthropologists play in examining cultural assumptions and explain how the anthropological perspective differs from both ethnocentrism and American exceptionalism.

- Explain the relationship between early anthropology and colonialism and assess the ways in which the demise of colonialism changed the practice of anthropology.

- Evaluate the topical or thematic specializations that exist within contemporary anthropology as examples of the range of questions and concerns anthropologists address.

Anthropology is the study of humankind, otherwise known as *Homo sapiens*, the wise primate. It is about our history, our prehistory before written records, our biology, our language, our distribution of peoples all over the planet, and the cultural and social aspects of our existence. The methods we use on this journey are varied and eclectic—an unusual discipline. What is perhaps unique about anthropology is its global quality, its comparative potential, and its integrative possibilities, which result from its examination of histories, biologies, languages, and socio-cultural variations. As a discipline, it is unusual because it is both soft and hard, including science as well as the humanities, between nature and culture, the past and the present, searching for new ways to understand the human condition. We are an academic discipline with porous boundaries that has refused to specialize and as a result can claim to have made enormous contributions to understanding what it means to be human. Anthropology is a young discipline, in only its fourth generation, one of the first of the new sciences along with ecology.

In the nineteenth century, archaeology challenged short chronologies of biblical origin with longer time depth, while biological and cultural anthropology questioned stereotyped thinking about race and ethnicity. Socio-cultural anthropology moved from armchair theorizing to first-hand fieldwork and, with the concept of cultural relativism, challenged predominant theories of the day, including scientific theories. We know that science is created by humans so it is bound to have human limitations, human error, human ignorance. Such realizations made us think about how knowledge is created and challenge the idea that western ways of thinking are the only source of truth. Early climate predictions were available in Peru before the arrival of European colonizers.

CENTRAL CONCEPTS

Culture

A central concept in our discipline is the idea of culture, a concept that changed how we explain human differences. Edward Burnett Tylor (1832–1917) was an English Quaker who, because of religious prejudice, could not enroll in any English universities and so went to work in his father's business. However, in his mid-twenties he became ill, and his doctor recommended rest and travel. Tylor traveled first to Cuba and then to Mexico for six months. While the idea of culture was not new, Tylor used the concept to make sense of what he learned from his travels. In his 1871 book, *Primitive Culture*, he defined the idea: "Culture or civilization, taken in its ethnographic sense, is that complex whole which includes knowledge, beliefs, art, morals, law, custom, and any other capabilities and habits acquired by man as a member of society."[1] We are all human, something that Columbus was not so sure about in 1492 when he first encountered the Caribs or, more generally, the Amerindians. Before Tylor, differences were explained as due to climate differences or even as God's choice, wrong-headed ideas about difference. Tylor's cross-cultural approach opened new vistas in nineteenth-century anthropology.

In North America, Lewis Henry Morgan (1818–1881), a lawyer who had grown up amid the Iroquois, wrote *League of the Iroquois* in 1851. He noticed that their terms for kinfolk were not classified in the same way as English terms. Terminology for cousins was different depending on whether the maternal or fraternal line was credited. As a lawyer for the New York Central Railroad, he had noticed other differences among speakers of other languages as well. Morgan began to collect kinship terminologies from all over the world, and in 1871 he published his master work, *Systems of Consanguinity and Affinity*, which would influence French anthropologist Claude Lévi-Strauss.

New questions arose. Could terminology be a key to understanding the social organization of small societies? The Iroquois were matrilineal; membership in a clan was determined by female links only, and one's father and his sisters and brothers belonged to a different clan. Without going into further detail, it should be clear that the invention of the concept of culture paved the way for explaining differences among peoples. Culture differentiates peoples, but in the process, we need to remember we are all members of the same species. We might identify others according to their color, but all peoples everywhere share the need to survive disease. Every society has primary groups, such as families, whose primary function is to have and raise children.

Holism

Another important founding father of American anthropology was German-born Franz Boas (1858–1942), a scholar originally trained in physics. He turned to anthropology after a year-long expedition to Baffin Island, land of the Inuit in the Canadian Arctic. He began to study their language. He came to the United States, where he is recognized as the father of cultural anthropology. More than anyone, Boas framed the discipline around the concept of **holism:** taking a broad view of the historical and cultural foundations of behavior rather than attributing differences to biology dismantling the concept of race. Although he stressed cultural differences, he explained such differences in terms of the historical development of each culture. In his book *Race, Language, and Culture* (1940), he stressed the idea that there is *no necessary correlation* between race, language, and culture, that one's physical appearance does not determine one's culture or ability to learn any language.

Boas is also noted for his development of the concepts of **cultural relativism** and **cultural determinism**—that all behavioral differences among peoples result from cultural, not racial or genetic causes. It was Boas who grounded the discipline in four fields and founded the American Anthropological Association. The four fields—archeological, cultural, linguistic, and physical anthropology—defined most departments in the United States until more recently when four became five with medical anthropology. Throughout the development of anthropology in the United States, there was a fear of fragmentation for holistic thinkers. As Boas noted in 1905, "there are indications of [anthropology] breaking up. The biologic, linguistic, and ethnologic-archeological methods are so distinct."[2] It must be noted that Boas trained many women anthropologists such as Margaret Mead and Ruth Benedict, knowing that diversifying fieldworkers by including people of all genders was important to successful fieldwork.

Plasticity

Talking about biologically superior and inferior races was common to colonialists who carried the notion of the "white man's burden," in which it was their mission to civilize the savages or, among some groups, to classify groups according to their perceived slots, as for example, the idea that some "races" were thought to be biologically intended to be solely servants! The scientific study of race has often floundered in confusion and misunderstanding over the past 200 years even though anthropologists have repeatedly stressed the observation that people can be equally endowed without being alike. In spite of our efforts, race bigots are alive and well. It is apparently comforting to believe that "we" are the best, a belief that is not restricted to Euro-Americans. After all, Navajo means people and many groups think they are superior to others. Thus, Boas' assessment was that all healthy individuals of the *Homo sapiens* species had the capacity to learn any language or culture, that **plasticity** is part of our species.

In the contemporary world, difference is treated as if it were a problem. Why? Some say it is due to the movement of cheap labor, debates over racism and tolerance in the midst of refugee crises, the power of the Islamic "scarf." In other words, to colonialist language in modern garb, state management of diversity and far-right politics, institutionalized racism, and the primacy of difference, especially in the context of Europe and the United States. In early 2001, a volume by historian Elisabeth Lasch-Quinn was published. *Race Experts, Etiquette, Sensitivity Training, and New Age Therapy Hijacked the Civil Rights Revolution* examined the racial-problem industry and racial-solution industry that have flourished and have had difficulty acknowledging that any differences between people may be superficial compared with what they have in common. The concept of race also avoids discussion of class and inequality associated with poverty. Such social-engineering is deeply interested in difference as a problem. The pursuit of homogeneity by state structures is something that has been observed all over Europe and the western worlds, especially at the contemporary moment when refugees are pouring into western countries from North Africa and the Middle East.

Participant Observation

With European colonization of peoples around the globe, more anthropological research around the planet began to happen. Better data collection came to be referred to as **participant observation** meaning that the ethnographers participated in the daily lives of the people they studied, learned their languages, and became immersed in the ordinary workings of others' societies. A Polish anthropologist, Bronislaw Malinowski (1884–1942), is often credited with setting the standard for ethnography with wide-angled vision. Malinowski had studied in London, and during World War I, he found himself in the Trobriand Islands, then a British dependency. Although he was a Pole, he was allowed to remain in the Trobriands. He had to learn the language—had to because the local people were his only companions. He moved among native people, speaking to them in their language. He studied their gardens, magic, science, law—all with the tools of participant observing. Malinowski wrote a number of ethnographies based on his work there: *Argonauts of the Western Pacific* (1922) on trade and the economy involving multiple sites, *The Sexual Life of the Savages* (1929) about kinship and sexuality, *Coral Gardens and their Magic* (1935) on gardens and farming, and *Crime and Custom in a Savage Society* (1926) dealt with problems of law and social order. Malinowski set a very high standard for participatory ethnographic fieldwork that stands to this day, a standard in which ethnography was theory, not mere description. The ethnography itself, as well as its explanatory uses, is a theoretical endeavor, a combination of loose and strict thinking.[3]

The invention of new technologies facilitates new frontiers of ethnography. In linguistic anthropology, the appearance of the cassette tape recorder and "shotgun" microphones in the early 1970s, of video cameras in the early 1980s, and of the internet and other electronic inventions in the past 25 years has allowed people to seek connections hitherto unnoticed. Similarly, geographic information systems, so important to archeologists and ecological anthropologists, are also used to locate the people we study. In the process, fieldworkers have lost the possibility of immersion in other cultures with little contact from home sites. Technological innovations connect us all, for better or for worse.

Area Studies and Beyond

By the mid-twentieth century, the major concepts were in place for the discipline—*culture, comparison,* and ethnography as participation *fieldwork.* The organizing concept is **area studies.** Anthropology departments commonly organize their curriculums around area studies courses taught about Africa, the Middle East, East Asia, China, Latin America, Europe, and so forth. Students learn about the geography and history and delve into specific topics such as religion, kinship, minorities, and language—subjects that equip them for a general understanding of a particular geographic area. Area specialties are useful for gaining funding, job searching, and hires especially in large departments.

In more recent times, critical research has investigated the origins of area studies in museums and in association with the military. It was American imperialist, Alfred Thayer Mahan, who first called the area between Europe and India the Middle East. Area studies are useful, but they can cause intellectual blindness that limits the anthropological analysis and imagination. At times, those who go beyond the boundaries of a region have been censored, raising the question: Can we be both area scholars and comparativists searching for similarities and differences between cultures, or even diffusionists who study the spread of cultural ideas from one area to another. The study of the colonized and not the colonizers still haunts our work. In 1989, Sir Edmund Leach had to reiterate that social systems are open, not bounded. We live in a globalized world, and, as Sidney Mintz reminded us in his 1996 distinguished lecture to the American Anthropological Association, we have been globalized for a very long time.[4]

The subject matter of anthropological research was expanding from isolated locales to the urban ethnography of cities such as S. F. Nadel's ethnography of urban Nigeria in *A Black Byzantium* (1942) and Cora Du Bois' investigation of the link between culture and personality and Euro-American colonialism in *The People of Alor* (1944). In 1949, Clyde Kluckhohn published *Mirror for Man—The Relation of Anthropology to Modern Life*. It was time to use the study of others to examine their own cultures and to test assumptions that might be ethnocentric. Margaret Mead had already published *Coming of Age in Samoa* (1928) in which she examined the adolescence problem as originating in culture, not as a physical and inevitable result of hormones as commonly thought in the United States at the time. Thus, through the comparative method we may learn that while human populations face some common problems, such as growing up, each addresses those problems in different ways. Mead's findings were considered controversial by some; thus, it is not surprising that some years later John and Beatrice Whiting carried out a controlled comparison of *Six Cultures: Studies of Child Rearing* (1963) one of which was in New England.

Gradually, anthropology was no longer the study of "savages" or "primitives;" it became the study of all human cultures. As Ruth Benedict pointed out in her bestselling *Patterns of Culture* (1934), people of different cultures interpret life differently. Her observation implied that one cannot judge one culture as superior to another. Both Boas and Malinowski elaborated on cultural relativism. Boas in particular pushed hard against the common tendency to judge others by one's own culture rather than by the basic assumptions of the culture being studied. He was fighting the phenomenon called **ethnocentrism**, seeing the world through one's own glasses. Ethnocentrism allowed people to see or categorize others as somehow less than or inferior, as "primitive" and in need of aid or development.[5]

Examining Cultural Assumptions

The fight against ethnocentrism—what in the United States today is sometimes called exceptionalism (we are always better)—is what motivates anthropologists to examine assumptions commonly used by Americans for example, or even embedded in the work of anthropologists themselves. Indeed, as fieldworkers, anthropologists must understand themselves, understand the eyes doing the recording of others. Does an anthropologist's gender influence what he or she "sees"? Does an aversion to conflict affect the record, the choice of research interests? Do the bilingual or bicultural characteristics of anthropologists increase sensitivity in the field? The ethnographies that we produce are, in the final analysis, the theory of what we do and why, and what the people we study do and why: a *Mirror for Man*.

A frequently cited example of analyzing the underlying premises is E. E. Evans-Pritchard (1902–1973), a British anthropologist who published *Witchcraft, Oracles, and Magic among the Azande* (1937), a work of ethnography as theory. His study of the Azande of the southern Sudan was meant to indicate why and how Azande beliefs in magic and witchcraft made perfect sense according to Azande premises (and to many peoples everywhere who wanted to understand human ills such as disease and death). He avoided ethnocentric notions like "they are ignorant primitives." His point was that their beliefs made sense given their premises, and that they were as logical as any other people. The main reason the Azande work is so much cited is that the main discovery is that we are all caught in our premises, our unchallenged assumptions. This idea applies to any thought including western science, as for example, the "nuclear religion"—the belief that President Eisenhower's atoms for peace made up for dropping nuclear bombs on Japan during World War II, in spite of scientists' inability to deal with nuclear waste and other associated problems. In Evans-Pritchard's case, he was writing not merely about the Azande or, later, about the Nuer herdsmen; he was also writing about how a particular ethnography is theoretically comparative, raising issues about our ingrained premises.

By mid-century, ethnographies had begun to include power as with *The Political Systems of High-land Burma* by Sir Edmund Leach (1954). Although there was general agreement in anthropology, scholars in academia were hesitant to deal with the phenomenon of power in anything but abstract terms. Also around the same time, Gregory Bateson's *Naven* was re-issued (1958) and ethnographers began to understand the many different lenses useful for interpreting the lives and rituals of people under study. By the 1960s, the unease in American academia began to be affected by the Civil Rights Movement, the war in Vietnam, the American Indian Movement, and sexual and gender liberations.

Dell Hymes edited a book (1972) called *Reinventing Anthropology* which called anthropologists to a revised or reinvented anthropology, one that took into consideration race, newly independent states, and what might be called the vertical slice. Laura Nader wrote "Up the Anthropologist: Perspectives Gained from Studying Up," a thought piece about the need to study up, down, and sideways as a way to liberate anthropologists from narrow concerns and exclusions. For example, she argued for studying the colonizers as well as the colonized, for understanding poverty and ghettos in connection with bank's redlining practices, which were essentially illegal, for understanding the enormous role corporations play in raising our children through the foods they prepare or the technologies required of children as part of their normal schooling. Today, some anthropologists study up while others study up, down, and sideways simultaneously.[6]

Moving into the twenty-first century, anthropologists had major intellectual interests in political economy, gender, representation, the Cold War, the Native American Grave Protection and Repatriation Act (NAGPRA), the anthropology of science, colonialism, tourism and more. The story of how the study of humankind advanced over a century does not move in steady progression. Science is prickly and contentious, and anthropology, more than most disciplines, is not only contentious but also self-reflexive. Indeed, the self-critical tradition has helped us adapt to the incoherent conditions of accelerated history and the new technologies that have come with it. So one might conclude that what changed least was what scholars in 1929 called "the anthropological attitude," which values both detachment and involvement as a mode of rethinking assumptions, while the changed relationship between those who study and those being studied forced anthropologists to reconsider the conditions under which their knowledge had been acquired. In addition, anthropology has increasingly become a worldwide discipline.

THE FALL OF COLONIALISM AND THE RISE OF NEWLY INDEPENDENT STATES

About 500 years ago, the first major colonization movements by western Europeans were a result of Portugal, Spain, and England looking for new resources. Colonies were implanted in Africa, Asia, and the New World. A second major colonial movement arose after the Industrial Revolution, motivated in part by a search for cheap labor and resources. By the end of the nineteenth century, Britain, France, Belgium, and Germany had divided up Africa, and Britain, France, and the United States were acquiring territories in the Pacific. Especially in Britain and France, ethnographic research was encouraged as a function of colonialism. Thus, well into the 1950s, anthropologists were employed by colonial offices. The demise of colonialism and emergence of new independent states gave rise to issues such as plundering of resources, and the new nations produced their own ethnographers whose approaches to anthropology were different from the approaches used by the Euro-American colonial powers. Anthropologists from Mexico, Brazil, and the Indian subcontinent primarily studied their own people. Only the travelers from these former colonial countries thought about the colonialists as their "other." In part, these post-colonial anthropologists set about correcting previously set anthropological agendas. More or less quiet debates are now occurring as to what a "global anthropology" should entail.

Colleagues outside of the Anglo-American world have criticized our biases and ethnocentrisms. Their polite admonishments underscored the need for self-awareness and the calibration of the instrument—in this instance, the anthropologist. Anthropologists in France, the Middle East, India, Pakistan, and elsewhere are pointing to Anglo-Americans' difficulty in coming to terms with power. The French fieldwork tradition sees research as inherently fraught with power relations. Our foreign colleagues are raising questions about scientific validity. The small social groups that classical anthropologists examined as stable or static units are now recognized as part of larger worlds that reconstitute them and are reconstituted in turn: The World Bank, the International Monetary Fund, and trade deals such as the North American Free Trade Agreement (NAFTA) and trade deals with Europe and the Asian-Pacific.

Akbar Ahmed, an anthropologist from Pakistan who trained in Britain, indicates what new dimensions can be gleaned by non-Anglo-American anthropologists in *The Thistle and the Drone: How America's War on Terror Became a Global War on Islam* (2013). Ahmed's work, the third in a trilogy, combines ethnographic analysis with history and comparison and uses his wide-ranging experience, which includes work as a Pakistani government agent and later as ambassador to Waziristan. Ahmed is also a poet, a playwright, a film producer, and an inexhaustible public speaker. He is presently the Ibn Khaldun chair for Islamic Studies at the American University of Washington, D.C. He is what some call a public anthropologist—someone whose work is accessible to anthropologists as well as to the public in general.

In his book, Ahmed includes the tribal peoples, the state, the American empire, and technology to understand the problems that began with European colonization and continued through the post-colonial period of nation-building, when the periphery became attached or connected to a state that gave them few rights. Ahmed's book reflects a paradigm shift in the twenty-first century—contemporary analyses of states and empires as well as the tribes, which were the traditional subject for ethnography. Thus, he includes not only the tribes, but also Osama bin Laden, the president of Pakistan, the president of the American empire, and the agonies of the anthropologist who discovers the horrors and hurts. Ahmed is a humanist anthropologist arguing for mutual respect and co-existence. Perhaps he can be thought of as an Islamic anthropologist in contrast to a Christian or Jewish anthropologist: he is objective and subjective and includes "us" and "them." The book discusses 40 examples of peripheral Islamic groups and their relations with state authorities to illustrate the relationship between center and periphery from Waziristan to Yemen Somalia and across North Africa to Indonesia and the Philippines. Ahmed concludes that drone strikes and cruel invasions by the central government will not work towards peace and mutual respect given that brutal revenge attacks from the periphery will continue in reaction to state and empire aggressions. Experts on terrorism ignore both culture and historical context. When anthropologists have dealt with the periphery, we have too often supported state assimilation, maneuvered the creation of reservations, and sometimes closed our eyes to mass killings.

The new dimensions mentioned above must not detract from the solid contributions of anthropologists of the British **functionalist** schools to our understanding of political and social processes in Africa, New Guinea, Burma, and elsewhere. In Africa, they were the first to address problems of order in societies of tens of thousands of people with no government, no police, and no constabulary—places where social control was achieved by means of social relationships. The concept of cross-linkage was used to understand African modes of maintaining peace through feuding, another piece of the picture of order in stateless societies that might be useful to the United Nations. The British focus was more on the concept of social organization than culture, on the colonized rather than the colonizers.

SPECIALIZATION—A WIDE RANGE

In the mid-twentieth century, Norwegian anthropologist Fredrik Barth (1928–2016) challenged the British school's work on Africa and their position that social systems transcended individual actors. On the contrary, Barth argued that political systems were generated by individual actors seeking to maximize their positions. In his ethnography on the Swat Pathans in northern Pakistan, Barth (1959) was moving away from the functionalist equilibrium analysis toward examinations of processes of change. Others followed suit in their arguments. According to Talal Asad, the notion that individuals strategize to maximize power is a distortion of history. In *Anthropology and the Colonial Encounter* (1973), Asad notes that Barth's conclusions were accelerated by British colonial practices in India and the northern frontier. Asad's critique made a critical point: the political system must be seen as part of a wider system that is based on a historical perspective that also includes class as an important variable but does not nullify individual choices. Control is both political and economic. The conversations about Barth's work were to continue later in the work of Pakistani anthropologist Akbar Ahmed. Anthropology can now be said to be a cosmopolitan dialogue.

As the number of anthropologists expanded so did the number of specialties, especially in large departments. Indeed the small departments are most likely to teach anthropology from a generalist point of view. While kinship and religion were the major specialties more than half a century ago, we now find professors specialized in fields like tourism, political economics, law, gender, folklore, as well as areas such as the Middle East, for example, or southern Africa, or Mexico (previously Mesoamerica), and so forth. In addition, there are many kinds of anthropology, such as applied and practicing. These specializations are found in dedicated journals for cognitive anthropology, law and politics, and musicology while general reports may be found in the British journal *Anthropology Today* or in *Anthropology News* in the United States, and in journals such as *American Anthropologist* or *JRAI*, the journal of the Royal Anthropological Institute. The following examples give some insight into the general range of questions being addressed.

Political Economy

A political economy approach contextualizes the world as an open system, as process not statis. To understand how power works in the world today requires comparison, paying attention to the intersection of power and culture. One example of this approach is found in the work of Ashraf Ghani, whose research focused on the history of power, particularly in Afghanistan, and who later became president of Afghanistan.[7] To understand how power works requires attention to disintegration as well as integration, on a local and global levels, which are then compared in terms of process, not essentialized societies. Work in this area has brought radical changes to traditional ethnography. An economic system such as corporate capitalism is treated as a type of economy that may change in particular context, such as contemporary China, in direct contrast to **world system theorists** who track the distribution of a system across the globe. There are many kinds of capitalism—penny capitalism, regional capitalism, and corporate capitalism. In *Worked Over: The Corporate Sabotage of an American Community*, for example, Dimitra Doukas (2003) covered dramatic changes in northern New York mill towns in the Mohawk River Valley with the move from regional to corporate or global capitalism. She documented the impact of hit-and-run corporate capitalism on the American workers on whose back American industry was built. Over 100 years, these vibrant industrial centers had become impoverished deindustrialized communities. Earlier still, Anthony F. C. Wallace, in his underappreciated book *Rockdale* (1978) wrote the story of Rockdale: "An account of the coming of the machines, the making of a new way of life in the mill hamlets, the triumph of evangelical capitalists over socialists and infidels, and the transformation of the workers into Christian soldiers in a cotton-manufacturing district in Pennsylvania in the years before and during the Civil War."

Power and Politics

Continuing examination of power centered on control as the dynamic of power. Laura Nader's early study, "Controlling Processes" (1997), focused on means of exercising power, a catalyst for analyzing the role of free will in power relations in American society. Examples were taken from the alternative dispute-resolution movement in U.S. law, which diminished the civil justice system in the United States and then went global, the standardization of definitions of beauty, which has spread globally, or the content of museum exhibits, or examining how marketing firms influence teenagers' perceptions of parental authority. The study of controlling processes enabled readers to understand control as indirect means to power and to recognize the fragility of both culture and its human carriers. In *Buddha is Hiding – Refugees, Citizenship, The New America*, Aihwa Ong (2003) followed the everyday lives of Cambodian refugees in California as they dealt with American values that contradicted Cambodian values in a story of Cambodian Americans experiencing American citizenship, a bottom up study about the impact of U.S. medical, social welfare, judicial, religious, and economic institutions of citizen making. This ethnography is about Cambodian Americans and about the types of controls operating across American institutions seeking to mold a certain type of citizen and the book is a tour-de-force examination of the reconfiguring of citizenship in a world of wars and movements.

World events are critical to academic pursuits, and anthropology had successes in World War II because of previous anthropological work in areas that became war zones. The Cold War following World War II also wrought critical changes. The number of anthropologists expanded, as did funding, and access to military technology revolutionized our methodologies in all fields, although differently. For socio-cultural anthropologists, the Cold War raised issues of race, war, genocide, counterinsurgency, and natural resources. We realized that anthropology was not an autonomous pursuit; instead, all of academia was embedded in politics. Anthropologists such as Hugh Gusterson (1996) and Joseph Masco (2006) began to write about nuclear laboratory cultures.[8]

During a decade in which nuclear and alternative energy systems have played critical roles in world events, a wide-angled anthropology was a requirement. Anthropology has integrated holism, appreciation of history and the depth of time, and the consequences arising from how language frames thought. The discourse of energy specialists, for example, was rooted in models of growth that assumed an unlimited supply of natural resources and undervalued ecosystems. The idea that energy experts might be part of the problem was novel, as was the idea that energy problems have human dimensions, a theme explored in works such as *The Energy Reader* (Nader 2010), *Cultures of Energy: Power, Practices, and Technologies* (Strauss, Rupp and Love 2013), and "Energopolitics and the Anthropology of Energy" (Boyer 2011). All of us were influenced by campus struggles in the 1960 and 1970s over militarism, multi-national capitalism, scientific racism, and the politics of gender. But a larger question remains: What makes people human?

Subdividing and Specializing

Expanded funding in the four basic fields and in medical anthropology led to specializations and topical expertise. In socio-cultural anthropology, these include specializations in the law, politics, the economy, religion, ecology, medical issues, art, and education. Anthropologist Eric Wolf (1923–1999) was critical of the tendency to specialize: "We subdivide and subdivide and call it anthropology."[9] The history of anthropology now goes far beyond disciplinary boundaries to include the impact of national policies, militarism, and priorities in funding. Credit goes to David Price, who singlehandedly examined the history of anthropology in its widest context in his book *Anthropological Intelligence: The Deployment and Neglect of American Anthropology in the Second World War* (2008). After all, our nationalities are reflected in the work we do. However, as anthropologists specialized, the concept of culture spread beyond the discipline to sociology, psychology, business schools, law schools, and beyond. Culture as a concept was loose on the streets! We now have cultural sociology, cultural psychology, cultural geography, cultural law. Changes in the field, which included fascination with French philosophers such as Michel Foucault and Jacques Derrida and French anthropologist Pierre Bourdieu, stimulated vigorous critiques. Others used the changes to enrich ethnography. People built on June Nash's ethnography of a Bolivian tin mine, *We Eat the Mines and the Mines Eat Us* (1979), which followed industrial mining that came with Spanish conquest, still causing internal problems today since controls continue to operate on Bolivia from beyond its borders. Some call this global development theory.

Because of all of this intellectual ferment, we now realize that anthropology has much to say about our own lives. Our ethnographies are written about the Shanghai stock market and the invention of derivatives on Wall Street.[10] Examinations of law and finance have moved from the earlier intersections of anthropology and law primarily associated with resolution of disputes in small locales to connecting legal knowledge (that is, state-level knowledge) to global financial markets and their legal and regulatory practices in which traders deal with probabilities and legal fictions.[11] Also in the vein of banking is the interest in Islamic banking. Though Islam forbids collecting interest, Islamic financial concerns operate in some 70 countries and have assets in the range of $200 billion.[12] Studies of the alternative currencies of Islamic banks are part and parcel of law, economics, and finance and the anthropologist's subject goes beyond the tribe, village, state, and even geographic region. The anthropology of policy worlds is an emerging field that covers the politics of financialization, the rise of audit cultures and their impacts on culture and society, and the spread of diseases such as cholera epidemics.[13] In *Global Assemblages, Technology, Politics, and Ethics as Anthropological Problems* (2005), Aihwa Ong and Stephen Collier integrate issues that are globalizing, including concern with ethics. Anthropologists are asking, for example, why some informants waste time with anthropologists and what exactly the collaborative engagement of anthropologists and subjects is in terms of ethics.

New concerns with dichotomies of nature and culture led to studies of mythologies of menopause in Japan and North America and the pharmaceutical business. Can menopause really be a disease if it happens to all women? Similar questions are asked of aging in India.[14] The examination of energy use in culture and society is rapidly expanding along with studies of emerging industrial businesses that use bio-power for commercial and regulatory purposes.[15] Thus, anthropologists like Nancy Scheper-Hughes and Loïc Wacquant, are are studying the buying, selling, and theft of human body parts, the significance of the concept of "brain dead," and who owns the body in books like *Commodifying Bodies* (2002). Building on ethics and human rights issues are decades of research by Nancy Scheper-Hughes. In *Death without Weeping* (1992), she addressed violence in everyday life and how violence and even death become normal and routine. She has made her work public by sharing with journalists wherever possible, testifying in court regarding crimes against humanity, and working hand in hand with Israeli colleagues. The work is multi-sited, sometimes conducting research undercover while examining criminal networks and transplant tourism. Though power need not be the central theme for all anthropology, it is critical for understanding central dogmas.

Audiences for Anthropology

Our audiences are unpredictable. Anthropologists who speak to a public wider than members of the discipline often have a greater immediate impact outside the discipline than in it. When I began writing and speaking about **coercive harmony**, interest among anthropologists was slow to develop (for reasons I examine elsewhere) while those who had felt the sting of being coercively harmonized—our public—quickly recognized its power in the workplace with quality circles, with "facilitators" in environmental movements at loggerheads with Clinton-style negotiation, and on Native American reservations when dealing with negotiations over nuclear waste. Grade schools regularly taught **harmony ideology** dispute-resolution and in global arenas lawyers were up against new international negotiators selling psychology rather than the rule of law.[16] And in the 2016 presidential election, the Republican candidate used language that would be considered uncivil under the harmony model but received positive responses from voters.

If we remain ignorant of debates outside of academia, we will increasingly find ourselves talking mainly to each other, trapped in a diminished space and working in cramped quarters.[17] It took an anthropologist, David Graeber, to notice that debt was on the mind of many, especially economically insecure Americans and the young who were in heavy debt for their costs in higher education.[18] Graeber's book *Debt: The First 5000 Years* (2011) was an instant bestseller worldwide. Debt is a problem that affects all societies that employ money. His analysis helps us understand the present economic situation by means of a long-term perspective. In similar critical efforts, Graeber has moved to other issues on people's minds. In 2001, he published *Toward an Anthropological Theory of Value* (2001) and more recently he explored political ideologies and exotic practices by self-destructive tribes in *The Utopia of Rules: On Technology, Stupidity, and the Secret Joys of Bureaucracy* (2015). Though Graeber is thought of as a specialist in studies of the Occupy Wall Street movement, his initial fieldwork was conducted in Madagascar.

Some of the most distinguished anthropologists in the nineteenth and twentieth centuries were effective spokespeople for the demarcation of science from other forms of knowledge such as magic and religion. As represented by Boas and Malinowski, who were trained in physics and mathematics, anthropological work in the late twentieth century was grounded in the ethnographic study of the practice of science, which did not always privilege western science. Modern scientists are crossing paths with indigenous peoples; biologists are side by side with indigenous peoples whose ecological knowledge they covet. Rapid globalization makes considerations of intermingling of knowledge systems inevitable. There is power in juxtaposing how traditional knowledge is produced in very different cultures, such as comparing our own culture with that of the Inuit or with peoples of the Amazon. We study not only Amazonians' indigenous plants and Pacific marine biology (and their appropriation of that knowledge) but physics and biotechnology laboratories and immunologists as well. Malinowski wrote about magic, science, and religion among the Trobrianders; we (following Leach's advice) examine magic, science, and religion in national laboratories.

Science

Emerging ethnographies of science are having as powerful an effect on contemporary anthropology as earlier studies of political economy and colonialism. Comparison of American high-energy physicists with Japanese high-energy physicists or Japanese and American primatologists show that science is not free of culture but, rather, is full of it.[19] Meanwhile, anthropologists working in African agriculture have noted the devastating effects of a cultural preference for universal explanations that override ecological particularism and site-specific knowledge.[20] It sounds counterintuitive, but "based on measures of energy expended per calorie of food produced, industrial agriculture is the most inefficient form of food production in the history and prehistory of humankind."[21] The principles of a physical model may not be true at all times or in all places since, even in Europe, there are many scientific traditions. When western approaches and technologies are transferred elsewhere, there can be downsides. In *Naked Science – Anthropological Inquiry into Boundaries, Power, and Knowledge* (1996), Laura Nader discusses the power of western science over other sciences around the world, revealing a cultural framework for understanding "what science is really like." Ethno-science and techno-science are examined comparatively rather than hierarchically.

Even the science of race has changed dramatically in the past 50 years. During the post-Civil Rights movement, many scholars and scientists thought of race as nothing more than a social construction. By the twenty-first century, race as a social, legal, and medical category had been explored as a result of the Human Genome Project. Degrees of variation came to be debated. One example is Ian Whitmarsh and David Jones' *What's the Use of Race – Modern Governance and the Biology of Difference* (2010), which examines the uses of race in the courtroom, law enforcement, and scientific views in attempts to address human diversity in relation to inequities in health and disease without using race as a basis for discrimination. Matters of race are not settled yet. Forensics, ancestry, testing, and medicine are hopefully innovating pathways to better medical treatments and health outcomes—and simultaneously advancing our conversations about "race" as a useful category.

Anthropological contributions to science debates can be critical in relocating and rethinking the future of western science traditions for variations exist there as well. The issues relate to the function of western science, its cultural ascendancy, its ethnocentricity, and its universality as they pertain to the charting of more-productive science paradigms.[22] As previously mentioned, anthropologists working in African agriculture have observed the devastating effects of a scientific preference for universal explanations that override ecological particularisms and site-specific subsistence knowledge. The assumption that western science functions autonomously is contradicted by findings in archaeology and ethnology, such as the observation that science does not develop independent of the influence of non-scientists. Is the anthropology of science a scientific effort or a humanistic one? Does it matter since "humanistic" and "scientific" are adjectives of convenience that are not mutually exclusive? The notion that people in a particular political context could consciously construct a cultural tradition should be important to the structurally minded, along with conscious linguistic code-switching for those interested in the consequences of differences in school settings.

Violence and War

The search for explanations for violence—especially the kind of intercommunal violence seen in places like Rwanda, Northern Ireland, Israel, Sri Lanka, and the former Yugoslavia and now seen throughout the Islamic world in the Middle East—involves the understanding of a holistic ethnography. Does it relate to competition for scarce resources, such as oil in the 2003 U.S. war on Iraq, or to dislocation of colonial legacies as seen in Waziristan in northern Pakistan? How do such forces translate into violence? Some scholars have invoked identity politics as a prerequisite to intercommunal violence, the implication being that it depends on identity formation that contrasts with another group. An alternative approach might be to examine the role of the international arms industry and of regimes that encourage hostilities. What kept Iraq together under Saddam Hussein? In a word, nationalism. When Saddam Hussein was at war with Iran, all Iraqi citizens—Shia, Sunni, Kurdish, and Christian fought together as one Iraqi people. After the U.S. invasion of Iraq in 2003, American forces used the old colonial technique of divide and conquer by pitting Shia against Sunni. A decade later, we have seen the rise of an Islamic Caliphate (ISIS) waging war on Iraq and Syria. Gillian Tett refers to the peril of expertise as *The Silo Effect* (2015)—an inability to "connect the dots" as one consequence of the 2003 American invasion of Iraq.

Certainly, no agreement has been reached among anthropologists on issues of violence and aggression, especially between those who stress biological origins of aggressive behavior and those who note that humans are not uniformly aggressive and warlike. Human populations can be peaceful or almost continuously engaged in aggressive encounters. The violence between East and West Germany, for example, is explained not by old antagonisms but by new phenomena—the ideologies associated with the Cold War and the Soviet Union. A nation can change from warlike to peaceful in a remarkably short period. Consider Sweden, which, particularly under Gustavus Adolphus, was the scourge of Europe but now has been largely peaceful for many decades. France under Napoleon was the most feared country in Europe, but a century later, the aggressive position had shifted to Germany. On the other hand, however, humans can also learn to be aggressive, as the record of feuds, raids, tortures, and wars amply testifies. There is no empirical evidence that individuals in warlike nations are genetically more aggressive than individuals in peaceful nations, and the complex institutions of war, which depend on uniquely human organizations, cannot be understood in terms of individual aggression (although conflicts in animal societies can be so understood). Only human animals make war, and only human animals kill themselves.

The current violence in the Middle East cannot be explained without implicating states and history. Afghanistan was invaded first by the British Empire, then by the Soviets, and by the Americans in 2001. All three stated that they wanted to bring development to the Afghans, a better life. What followed instead was violence continuing to this day in the case of American invasion. Thousands have died and sectarian violence has erupted. The word jihad is commonly used in reference to the Islamic state and is sometimes translated as holy war. Perhaps all of the contemporary wars in the Middle East from Afghanistan to Somalia are holy wars—Islamic, Christian, and Jewish—all monotheistic religions emanating from the Middle East. What we may be experiencing in the early twenty-first century are religious wars posing as secular for Christians and Jews and as jihad holy wars for Muslims.

It behooves anthropologists to unveil the contemporary scene that has been appropriated by politicians and pundits because the consequences of failing to do so are so great in terms of mass killings and destruction. For some Arabs, Israel is a western beachhead in the Middle East; for some Israelis, it is a return and compensation for the Nazi killings of Jews in World War II. In 2001, President George W. Bush referred to a "crusade" against terrorism. Terrorism is a general word, not specific, but used in carrying out American drone strikes in Waziristan, Somalia, Yemen, and Palestinian Gaza. Explanations such as resource wars have been generally avoided, except in joking that if Iraq grew broccoli instead of having oil we would not have invaded. As comparatists, anthropologists are well-equipped to contribute to the public's understanding of these issues by connecting the dots.[23]

Law

In the 1960s, anthropological research on law and anthropology involved ethnographies of particular peoples such as the Barotse, Tiv, and Arusha in Africa, the Cheyenne in the United States, the Trobrianders in Melanesia, and the Ifugao in the Philippines. The first generation of scholars—Bronislaw Malinowski, Max Gluckman, Paul Bohannan, Philip Gulliver, Karl Llewellyn, and E. Adamson Hoebel—had a local world view. They examined the functions of law, its presence or absence, processes of negotiation, mediation, adjudication, or retaliation. The generation that followed wanted to increase the number of quality ethnographies and local ethnographies such as those on the Zapotec of Oaxaca, Mexico, or the Zinacantan of Chiapas, Mexico, and new locales from Africa to New Guinea and Hawaii.[24] Variation was examined within these places but, when teaching anthropology of law in the early years, the central core was ethnography in place.[25]

However, as peoples who had been colonized by European powers gained independence, the number of new states worldwide increased rapidly, and those states were incorporating the local people into state law. Attention turned to globalization, the diffusion of legal ideologies such as the rule of law to new states and law and modernization. Research and teaching changed and by the latter part of the twentieth century and particularly after the end of the Cold War, students were eager to learn about the new states, legal imperialism, military law, and legal rights. The war on terror was also on their minds after the U.S. invasions of Afghanistan and Iraq in terms of due process, fairness, and imposition of foreign laws. Thus, teaching law and anthropology in 2016 bore little resemblance to such teachings in the 1960s although documentary films such as *Little Injustices* (1981) and *Losing Knowledge* (2012), give students a sense of how much has changed with the loss of local sovereignty. Assigned readings have also changed. One of the favorites is Leach's *Custom, Law, and Terrorist Violence* (1977).

One anthropologist who has tried to analyze the fantasy sources of terror wars is Joseba Zulaika, a Basque anthropologist, author of many books on terrorism. His most recent is *Terrorism – the Self-Fulfilling Prophecy* (2009). Well into his argument about counter-terrorism producing terrorism, Zulaika refers to a medieval component of U.S. policy. He invokes the fear of witches prevalent historically in Europe to understand current counter-terrorism behavior and a premodern type of thinking that denies contrary evidence and sees all as either black or white, as good or evil. Zulaika refers to Evans-Pritchard's *Witchcraft, Oracles, and Magic among the Azande* (1937) to help us understand the belief in the mystical power of some individuals to harm others. Finally, he notes that what was normal and unquestionable in medieval Europe gave way to skepticism.

Wherever anthropologists have studied witchcraft and witch-hunting, fear is present—fear of sickness, fear of violence.[26] In contemporary Africa, according to Elizabeth Colson, witchcraft accusations have increased along with apparently unexplainable HIV deaths.[27] Questions of "Why me? Why us?" must be answered. In explaining the fear of "terrorism" in the United States, some have argued that connecting those dots may be a new challenge for anthropologists working in the West. Witch-hunting in more-complex settings require broader contexts than that of pre-literate societies in which witchcraft may be taken for granted. In complex societies such as the United States, beliefs based on irrational or illogical thinking are not accepted as part of being modern, or so it is said.

Urban Anthropology

The interest in violence and war might be connected to the growing interest in urban spaces. The proportion of the world's population living in urban areas has been increasing over the past 200 years, starting, some would say, with the Industrial Revolution. In 1800, only about 3 percent of all humans lived in cities. By 1900, 13 percent lived in urban areas. A mere 80 years later, the proportion had risen to 40 percent, and today it stands at more than 50 percent. The percentages of urban dwellers are highest in highly developed societies. One source suggests that in 1900 the world had only 16 cities with more than a million inhabitants, while by 2015, the number had grown to over 300 such cities and still increasing. New cities are being built as in Brasília.[28] Thus, it is not surprising that there has been comparable growth in urban anthropology. A stunning find in urban archaeology is that of Cahokia, a city of 83 hectares at the convergence of the Missouri, Mississippi, and Illinois rivers, a city once occupied by some 20,000 people, larger in the eleventh and twelfth centuries than London and Paris.[29]

Urban anthropology has both theoretical and applied dimensions and the topics range from immigration, poverty, class, ethnicity, drugs, and urban violence and investigates societies in Canada, the United States, Africa, Brazil and other locales. The work is comparative as well as deeply ethnographic and documents the bringing of rural customs to cities and urban traits to rural areas. For instance, Erik Harms' *Saigon's Edge—On the Margins of Ho Chi Min City* (2011) shows how people live in zones of urban-rural divides in the wasteland of urban industrial expansion, between worlds and transformations linked to global markets. Los Angeles has the largest Samoan immigrant population anywhere outside of the Pacific region. Different customs influence questions of law, such as individuals who commit crimes when *In Search of Respect*, the title of an ethnography of crack dealers in Harlem, New York, by Philippe Bourgois (1995). Gangs and gang violence make headlines and inspire applied anthropologists, as do new interests in drug and sex trafficking and widespread stress caused by debt and inequalities.

Health and Medicine

As the reader can see, all behaviors, institutions, and ideas related to human populations are of interest. For example, all societies construct beliefs about the causes of illnesses and systems for preserving health. The sub-specialty of medical anthropology includes anthropologists from all sub fields. In many areas of the world colonialism, warfare, diseases, and changes in diet contribute to health problems. Hunter-gatherer societies have been relatively isolated from other groups and have not suffered from the epidemics of infectious diseases that have affected agrarian and urban societies, especially in this age of widespread travel. The spread of malaria, for example, has been linked to population growth and changes associated with food production. Obesity and diabetes have spread with economic development and globalization, and diseases such as HIV infections appear more in Africa than in other parts of the world.[30] Cultural factors enter as HIV spreads more often among men who are circumcised than those who are not. Then there are emotional diseases such as *susto*, an illness caused by anxiety or fright, or widespread stress caused by debt and inequalities. Underlying explanations of human behavior are based on unstated assumptions.

CONCLUSION

What is anthropology? The question can be answered in many ways depending on the particular anthropologist-author. A linguistic anthropologist might start with a reference to Boas' student, Edward Sapir, whose work on *Language* (1921) is as good today as it was when he wrote it. Sapir's work spanned the subjects of Amerindian languages and their connections and distributions as they pertain to anthropology, the interdisciplinary nature of the study of language from earliest times to the contemporary use of speech. Language and culture studies encompass both technical aspects of language and socio-linguistics—the study of language in context.[31] The founding of the Summer Institute of Linguistics in the 1930s also played an important role in educating anthropologists of all stripes in the techniques of linguistic study whether we were specialists or not. Such broad education would include folklorists for whom language is key. Forever forward-thinking, Alan Dundes demonstrated the important but disputed point that folklore is not necessarily transmitted and expressed orally, particularly folklore of the electronic age.[32]

For all of anthropologists' divergences and disagreements, we share the "anthropological attitude," which values both detachment and involvement as modes of rethinking existing assumptions. Such shared values have not changed much since the nineteenth century, nor have the social prejudices that anthropologists have challenged: ethnocentrism, racism, sexism, and inadequate measures of human worth. What has changed is the world around us, a world that affects who we are, what we study, and what consequences result, forcing us to question why we take the stands we do. Factors external to the profession that have been a critical part of doing anthropology in the United States are still with us and merit remembering. Anthropology, more than any other discipline, has the capacity to generate the kind of introspection that can influence the future role of human beings on earth—to impart the lessons of history, the experience of *Homo sapiens* on the planet.

DISCUSSION QUESTIONS

1. Laura Nader explains that examining cultural assumptions is the main motivation for anthropologists. Why is this kind of examination important? What does she mean when she says that anthropologists should study "up, down, and sideways"?
2. This chapter describes several specializations, or areas of expertise, that have developed in anthropology, including investigations of both science and law. In what ways can science and law be analyzed as products of culture?
3. In the conclusion, Laura Nader writes that anthropology "values both detachment and engagement." Why is this particularly challenging in a profession that relies on participant observation research?

GLOSSARY

Area studies: a way of organizing research and academic programs around world regions such as Africa, the Middle East, East Asia, China, Latin America, and Europe.

Coercive harmony: an approach to dispute resolution that emphasizes compromise and consensus rather than confrontation and results in the marginalization of dissent (**harmony ideology**) and the repression of demands for justice.

Cultural determinism: the idea that behavioral differences are a result of cultural, not racial or genetic causes.

Cultural relativism: the idea that we should seek to understand another person's beliefs and behaviors from the perspective of their own culture and not our own.

Ethnocentrism: the tendency to view one's own culture as most important and correct and as the stick by which to measure all other cultures.

Functionalist: an approach developed in British anthropology that emphasized the ways that the parts of a society work together to support the functioning of the whole.

Holism: taking a broad view of the historical, environmental, and cultural foundations of behavior.

Participant observation: a type of observation in which the anthropologist observes while participating in the same activities in which her informants are engaged.

Plasticity: refers to the human capacity to learn any language or culture.

World Systems Theory: an approach to social science and history that involves examination of the development and functioning of the world economic system.

ABOUT THE AUTHOR

Laura Nader is a Professor of sociocultural anthropology at the University of California, Berkeley. Nader's current work focuses on how central dogmas are made and how they work in law, energy science, and anthropology. She has published several books on conflict resolution and the law including *Harmony Ideology: Justice and Control in a Mountain Zapotec Village* (1990) and *The Life of the Law: Anthropological Projects* (2002). She has also conducted research in the anthropology of science, with a particular focus on energy. Her books *Naked Science: Anthropological Inquiry into Boundaries, Power, and Knowledge* (1996) and *The Energy Reader* (2010) are two examples of her work on these topics. She has also produced ethnographic films, including the 2012 film *Losing Knowledge: 50 Years of Change*, which explores the ways in which indigenous knowledge is vanishing. Dr. Nader is a member of the American Academy of Arts and Sciences and has received numerous awards and honors including the CoGEA Award from the American Anthropological Association and the Harry J. Kalven, Jr. award from the Law and Society Association.

BIBLIOGRAPHY

Ahmed, Akbar. *The Thistle and The Drone: How America's War on Terror Became a Global War on Tribal Islam.* Washington, D.C.: Brookings Institution Press, 2013.

Asad, Talal. *Anthropology and the Colonial Encounter.* London: Ithaca Press, 1973.

Asquith, Pamela. "Japanese Science and Western Hegemonies: Primatology and the Limits Set to Questions." In *Naked Science: Anthropological Inquiry into Boundaries, Power and Knowledge*, edited by Laura Nader, 239–258. New York: Routledge, 1996.

Auge, Marc. *A Sense for the Other: The Timeliness and Relevance of Anthropology*, Translated by A. Jacob. Stanford: Stanford University Press, 1998.

Barth, Fredrik. *Political Leadership Among Swat Pathans*. London: The Athlone Press, 1995.

Bateson, Gregory. *Naven: A Survey of the Problems Suggested by a Composite Picture of the Culture of a New Guinea Tribe Drawn from Three Points of View*. Stanford: Stanford University Press, 1958.

Benedict, Ruth. *Patterns of Culture*. Boston: Houghton Mifflin, 1934.

Boas, Franz. "The History of Anthropology." In *Congress of Arts and Science, Universal Exposition St. Louis*, Vol. 5, edited by H.J. Rogers, 468–482. New York: Houghton Mifflin, and Company, 1905.

———. *Race, Language, and Culture*. Chicago: University of Chicago Press, 1940.

Bourgois, Philippe. *In Search of Respect: Selling Crack in El Barrio*. New York: Cambridge University Press, 1996.

Boyer, Dominic. "Energopolitics and the Anthropology of Energy." *Anthropology News* 52, no. 5 (2011): 5–7.

Briggs, Charles and Clara Mantini-Briggs. *Stories in Time of Cholera: Racial Profiling During a Medical Nightmare*. Berkeley: University of California Press, 2003.

Coco, Linda. "Mortgaging Human Potential: Student Indebtedness and the Practices of the Neoliberal State." *Southwestern Law Review* 42, no. 3 (2013).

Cohen, Lawrence. *No Aging in India: Alzheimer's, the Bad Family, and Other Modern Things*. Berkeley: University of California Press, 1998.

Collier, Jane F. *Courtship and Marriage in Zinacantan, Chiapas, Mexico*. New Orleans: Middle American Research Institute, 1968.

Colson, Elizabeth. "The Social History of an Epidemic: HIV/AIDS in Gwembe Valley, Zambia." In *Morality, Hope and Grief: Anthropologies of AIDS in Africa*, edited by Hansjorg Dilger and Ute Luig, 127–147. New York, NY: Berghahn Books, 2010.

Du Bois, Cora. *The People of Alor: A Social-Psychological Study of an East Indian Island*. Minneapolis: The University of Minnesota Press, 1944.

Doukas, Dimitra. *Worked Over: The Corporate Sabotage of an American Community*. Ithaca, NY: Cornell University Press, 2003.

Evans-Pritchard, E.E. *Witchcraft, Oracles, and Magic among the Azande*. Oxford: The Clarendon Press, 1937.

Gonzalez, Roberto and Laura Nader. *Losing Knowledge: 50 Years of Change*. Film. Produced and Directed by Roberto Gonzalez and Laura Nader. Berkeley, CA: Berkeley Media, 2012.

Graeber, David. *Debt: The First 5,000 Years*. New York: Melville House, 2011.

———. *Toward an Anthropological Theory of Value: The False Coin of our Own Dreams*. New York: Palgrave, 2001.

———. *The Utopia of Rules: On Technology, Stupidity, and the Secret Joys of Bureaucracy*. Brooklyn, NY: Melville House, 2015.

Harms, Erik. *Saigon's Edge: On the Margins of Ho Chi Min City*. Minneapolis, MN: University of Minnesota Press, 2011.

Hertz, Ellen. *The Trading Crowd: An Ethnography of the Shanghai Stock Market*. Cambridge: Cambridge University Press, 1998.

Holston, James. *The Modernist City: An Anthropological Critique of Brasilia*. Chicago: Chicago University Press, 1989.

Hymes, Dell, ed. *Reinventing Anthropology*. New York: Pantheon Books, 1972.

Kehoe, Alice B. *The Land of Prehistory: A Critical History of American Archeology*. New York: Routledge, 1998.

Kluckhohn, Clyde. *Mirror for Man: The Relation of Anthropology to Modern Life*. New York: Whittlesey House, 1949.

Lasch-Quin, Elisabeth. *Race Experts: How Racial Etiquette, Sensitivity Training and New Age Therapy Hijacked the Civil Rights Revolution*. New York: W. W. Norton & Company, 2001.

Leach, Edmund. *The Political Systems of Highland Burma: A Study of Kachin Social Structure*. Cambridge, MA: Harvard University Press, 1954.

Lock, Margaret. *Encounters with Aging: Mythologies of Menopause in Japan and North America*. Berkeley, CA: University of California Press, 1993.

Malinowski, Bronislaw. *Argonauts of the Western Pacific*. London: Routledge and Kegan Paul Ltd., 1922.

———. *Coral Gardens and Their Magic*. New York: American Book Co., 1935.

———. *Crime and Custom in a Savage Society*. New York: Harcourt, Brace and Company, 1926.

———. *The Sexual Life of the Savages in Northwestern Melanesia*. New York: Harcourt, Brace and World, 1929.

Masco, Joseph. *The Nuclear Borderlands: The Manhattan Project in Post-Cold War New Mexico*. New Jersey: Princeton University Press, 2006.

Maurer, Bill. *Mutual Life, Limited: Islamic Banking, Alternative Currencies, Lateral Reason*. Princeton: Princeton University Press, 2005.

Mead, Margaret. *Coming of Age in Samoa*. New York: Blue Ribbon Books, 1928.

Merry, Sally. *Colonizing Hawai'i: The Cultural Power of Law*. Princeton: Princeton University Press, 2002.

Mintz, Sidney. "'Sows' Ears and Silver Linings:' The 1996 AAA Distinguished Lecture," *Current Anthropology* 41, no. 2 (2000): 169–89.

Morgan, Lewis Henry. *League of the Ho-dé-no-sau-nee, or Iroquois*. New York: Sage & Brother, 1851.

———. *Systems of Consanguinity and Affinity of the Human Family*. Washington, D.C.: Smithsonian Institution, 1871.

Nadel, S.F. *A Black Byzantium: Kingdom of Nupe in Nigeria*. Oxford: Oxford University Press, 1942.

Nader, Laura. "The ADR Explosion: The Implications of Rhetoric in Legal Reform," in *Windsor Yearbook of Access to Justice*, 269–291. Ontario: University of Windsor, 1989.

———. "Civilization and Its Negotiators." In *Understanding Disputes: The Politics of Law*, edited by Pat Kaplan. Oxford: Berg Publishers, 1995.

———. "Controlling Processes: Tracing the Dynamic Components of Power and Knowledge." *Current Anthropology* 38, no. 5 (1997): 711–737.

———. *Culture and Dignity*. New York: Wiley-Blackwell Publishers, 2013.

———. *The Energy Reader*. Oxford: Wiley-Blackwell Publishers, 2010.

———. *Harmony Ideology: Justice and Control in a Zapotec Mountain Village*. Stanford: Stanford University Press, 1990.

———. *The Life of the Law: Anthropological Projects*. Berkeley, CA: University of California Press, 2002.

———. *Naked Science: Anthropological Inquiry into Boundaries, Power and Knowledge*. New York: Routledge, 1996.

———. "Up the Anthropologist: Perspectives Gained from Studying Up." In *Reinventing Anthropology*, edited by Dell H. Hymes, 284–311. New York: Pantheon Books, 1972.

———. *What the Rest Think of the West: Since 600 A.D.* Oakland: University of California Press, 2015.

Nash, June. *We Eat the Mines and the Mines Eat Us: Dependency and Exploitation in Bolivian Tin Mines*. New York: Columbia University Press, 1979.

Ong, Aihwa. *Buddha Is Hiding: Refugees, Citizenship, the New America*. Berkeley, CA: University of California Press, 2003.

Ong, Aihwa and Stephen J. Collier, eds. *Global Assemblages: Technology, Politics, and Ethics as Anthropological Problems*. Oxford: Blackwell Publishing, 2005.

Ou, Jay. "Native Americans and the Monitored Retrievable Storage Plan for Nuclear Wastes: Hate capitalism, Negotiation, and Controlling Processes." In *Essays on Controlling Processes*, edited by Laura Nader. Kroeber Anthropological Society Papers, No. 80, 1996.

Pauketat, Timothy R. *Cahokia: Ancient America's Great City on the Mississippi*. New York: Viking-Penguin, 2009.

Price, David. *Anthropological Intelligence: The Deployment and Neglect of American Anthropology in the Second World War*. Durham, NC: Duke University Press, 2008.

Richards, Paul. *Indigenous Agricultural Revolution: Ecology and Food Crops in West Africa*. London: Westview Press, 1985.

Riles, Annelise. *Collateral Knowledge: Legal Reasoning in the Global Financial Markets*. Chicago: Chicago University Press, 2011.

Sapir, Edward. *Language: An Introduction to the Study of Speech*. New York: Harcourt, Brace and Company, 1921.

Scheper-Hughes, Nancy. *Death Without Weeping: The Violence of Everyday Life in Brazil*. Berkeley, CA: University of California Press, 1992.

Scheper-Hughes, Nancy and Loïc Wacquant, eds. *Commodifying Bodies*. Thousand Oaks: Sage Publications Inc., 2002.

Shore, Chris and Susan Wright, eds. *Anthropology of Policy: Critical Perspectives on Governance and Power*. New York: Routledge, 1997.

Strauss, Sarah, Stephanie Rupp and Thomas Love, eds. *Cultures of Energy: Power, Practices, and Technologies*. Walnut Creek: Left Coast Press, 2013.

Stryker, Rachel and Roberto Gonzales. *Up, Down and Sideways: Anthropologists Trace the Pathways of Power*. New York: Berghahn Books, 2014.

Tambiah, Stanley. *Magic, Science, Religion and the Scope of Rationality*. Cambridge: Cambridge University Press, 1990.

Tett, Gillian. *Fool's Gold: The Inside Story of J.P. Morgan and How Wall Street Greed Corrupted Its Bold Dream and Created a Financial Catastrophe*. New York: Free Press, 2010.

——. *The Silo Effect: The Peril of Expertise and the Promise of Break Down Barriers*. New York: Simon & Schuster, 2015.

Thu, Kendall and E. Paul Durrenberger, eds. *Pigs, Profits, and Rural Communities*. Albany: State University of New York, 1998.

Traweek, Sharon. *Beamtimes and Lifetimes: The World of High Energy Physicists*. Cambridge: Harvard University Press, 1988.

Tylor, Edward. *Primitive Culture*. London: John Murray, 1871.

Wallace, Anthony F.C. *Rockdale: The Growth of an American Village in the Early Industrial Revolution*. New York: Knopf, 1978.

Warde, Ibrahim. *Islamic Banking in the Global Economy*. Edinburgh: Edinburgh University Press, 2000.

Whitehead, Neil and Sverker Finnstrom, eds. *Virtual War and Magical Death: Technologies and Imaginaries for Terror and Killing*. Durham, NC: Duke University Press, 2013.

Whiting, Beatrice B. and John W.M. Whiting. *Six Cultures: Studied of Child Rearing*. New York: Wiley, 1963.

Whitmarsh, Ian and David Jones, eds. *What's the Use of Race? Modern Governance and the Biology of Difference*. Cambridge, MA: MIT Press, 2010.

Wolf, Eric R. "They Divide and Subdivide, and Call It Anthropology," *The New York Times*, November 30, 1980, E9.

Zulaika, Joseba. *Terrorism: The Self-fulfilling Prophecy*. Chicago: University of Chicago Press, 2009.

NOTES

1. Edward Burnett Tylor, *Primitive Culture* (London: John Murray, 1871), 1.

2. Franz Boas, "The History of Anthropology," in *Congress of Arts and Science, Universal Exposition St. Louis*, Vol. 5 (New York: Houghton, Mifflin and Company, 1905), 451.

3. Laura Nader, *Culture and Dignity* (New York: Wiley-Blackwell, 2013), 51.

4. Sidney Mintz, "'Sows' Ears and Silver Linings:' The 1996 AAA Distinguished Lecture," *Current Anthropology* 41 (2): 169–89.

5. Antonio De Lauri, *The Politics of Humanitarianism: Power, Ideology and Aid* (London: Tauris, 2015).

6. See for example Rachel Stryker and Roberto Gonzales, *Up, Down and Sideways: Anthropologists Trace the Pathways of Power* (New York: Berghahn Books, 2014).

7. See for example Ashraf Ghani, "Writing a History of Power: An Examination of Eric R. Wolf's Anthropological Quest" in *Articulating Hidden Histories: Exploring the Influence of Eric R. Wolf*, ed. Jane Schneider and Rayna Rapp (Berkeley: University of California Press, 1995).

8. See for example Hugh Gusterson, *Nuclear Rites: A Weapons Laboratory at the End of the Cold War* (Berkeley, CA: University of California Press, 1996) and Joseph Masco, *The Nuclear Borderlands: The Manhattan Project in Post-Cold War New Mexico* (New Jersey: Princeton University Press, 2006).

9. Eric R. Wolf, "They Divide and Subdivide, and Call It Anthropology," *The New York Times*, November 30, 1980, E9.

10. See for example Ellen Hertz, *The Trading Crowd: An Ethnography of the Shanghai Stock Market* (Cambridge: Cambridge University Press, 1998) and Gillian Tett, *Fool's Gold: The Inside Story of J.P. Morgan and How Wall Street Greed Corrupted Its Bold Dream and Created a Financial Catastrophe* (New York: Free Press, 2010).

11. Annelise Riles, *Collateral Knowledge: Legal Reasoning in the Global Financial Markets* (Chicago: Chicago University Press, 2011).

12. See for example Bill Maurer, *Mutual Life, Limited: Islamic Banking, Alternative Currencies, Lateral Reason* (Princeton: Princeton University Press, 2005) and Ibrahim Warde, *Islamic Banking in the Global Economy.* Edinburgh: Edinburgh University Press, 2000).

13. Charles Brigg and Clara Mantini-Briggs. *Stories in the Time of Cholera: Racial Profiling during a Medical Nightmare* (Berkeley: University of California Press, 2003) and Chris Shore and Susan Wright, eds., *Anthropology of Policy: Critical Perspectives on Governance and Power* (New York: Routledge, 1997).

14. Margaret Lock, *Encounters with Aging: Mythologies of Menopause in Japan and North America* (Berkeley: University of California Press, 1993) and Lawrence Cohen, *No Aging in India: Alzheimer's, the Bad Family, and Other Modern Things* (Berkeley: University of California Press, 1998).

15. Laura Nader, *The Energy Reader* (Oxford: Wiley-Blackwell Publishers, 2010).

16. The examples here come from several publications by Laura Nader. See Laura Nader, "The ADR Explosion: The Implications of Rhetoric in Legal Reform," in *Windsor Yearbook of Access to Justice* (Ontario: University of Windsor, 1989), 269–291; *Harmony Ideology: Justice and Control in a Zapotec Mountain Village* (Stanford: Stanford University Press, 1990); "Civilization and Its Negotiators" in *Understanding Disputes: The Politics of Law*, ed. Pat Kaplan (Oxford: Berg Publishers, 1995); "Controlling Processes: Tracing the Dynamic Components of Power and Knowledge" *Current Anthropology* 38 (1997): 711–737. For further discussion of Native American negotiations with the government over nuclear waste, see Jay Ou, "Native Americans and the Monitored Retrievable Storage Plan for Nuclear Wastes: Hate Capitalism, Negotiation, and Controlling Processes," in *Essays on Controlling Processes*, ed. Laura Nader. (Kroeber Anthropological Society Papers, No. 80, 1996).

17. Marc Auge, *A Sense for the Other: The Timeliness and Relevance of Anthropology*, A. Jacob, trans. (Stanford: Stanford University Press, 1998).

18. Linda Coco, "Mortgaging Human Potential: Student Indebtedness and the Practices of the Neoliberal State," *Southwestern Law Review*, 42 (3) 2013.

19. The two examples cited here are Sharon Traweek, *Beamtimes and Lifetimes: The World of High Energy Physicists* (Cambridge, MA: Harvard University Press, 1988) and Pamela Asquith, "Japanese Science and Western Hegemonies: Primatology and the Limits Set to Questions," in *Naked Science: Anthropological Inquiry into Boundaries, Power and Knowledge*, ed. Laura Nader (New York: Routledge, 1996).

20. Paul Richards, *Indigenous Agricultural Revolution: Ecology and Food Crops in West Africa* (London: Westview Press, 1985).

21. Kendall Thu and E. Paul Durrenberger, eds. *Pigs, Profits, and Rural Communities* (Albany: State University of New York Press, 1998), 2.

22. Stanley Tambiah, *Magic, Science, Religion and the Scope of Rationality* (Cambridge: Cambridge University Press, 1990).

23. Laura Nader, *What the Rest Think of the West: Since 600 A.D.* (Berkeley: University of California Press, 2015).

24. Discussion of Oaxaca, Mexico is found in Laura Nader, *Harmony Ideology: Justice and Control in a Zapotec Mountain Village* (Stanford: Stanford University Press, 1990). The Chiapas, Mexico example is from Jane F. Collier, *Courtship and Marriage in Zinacantan, Chiapas, Mexico* (New Orleans: Middle American Research Institute, 1968). Analysis of these dynamics in Hawaii is found in Sally Merry, *Colonizing Hawaii': The Cultural Power of Law* (Princeton: Princeton University Press, 2000).

25. Laura Nader, *The Life of the Law: Anthropological Projects* (Berkeley: University of California Press, 2002).

26. Neil Whitehead and Sverker Finnstrom, eds. *Virtual War and Magical Death: Technologies and Imaginaries for Terror and Killing* (Durham: Duke University Press, 2013).

27. See for example Elizabeth Colson, "The Social History of an Epidemic: HIV/AIDS in Gwembe Valley, Zambia," in *Morality, Hope and Grief: Anthropologies of AIDS in Africa*, ed. Hansjorg Dilger and Ute Luig, 127–147 (New York: Bergahn Books, 2010). Additional perspectives on Colson's work can be found in Elizabeth Colson, "Anthropology and a Lifetime of Observation," an oral history conducted in 2000–2001 by Suzanne Reiss. Regional Oral History Office (The Bancroft Library: University of California, Berkeley, 2002).

28. James Holston, *The Modernist City: An Anthropological Critique of Brasilia* (Chicago: Chicago University Press, 1989).

29. For more information about Cahokia, see Alice Kehoe, *The Land of Prehistory: A Critical History of American Archeology* (New York: Routledge, 1998) and Timothy R. Pauketat, *Cahokia: Ancient America's Great City on the Mississippi* (New York: Viking-Penguin, 2009).

30. Paul Farmer, *Aids and Accusation: Haiti and the Geography of Blame* (Berkeley: University of California Press, 1992).

31. See for example Dell Hymes, ed., *Reinventing Anthropology.*

32. See for example Alan Dundes, *The Study of Folklore* (Englewood Cliffs: Prentice-Hall, 1965) and *International Folkloristics: Classical Contributions by the Founders of Folklore* (Lanham MD: Rowman and Littlefield, 1999).

THE CULTURE CONCEPT

Emily Cowall, McMaster University
cowallee@mcmaster.ca
Priscilla Medeiros, McMaster University
medeirp@mcmaster.ca

LEARNING OBJECTIVES

- Compare and contrast the ideas of ethnocentrism and cultural relativism.
- Describe the role that early anthropologists Sir James Frazer and Sir E. B. Tylor played in defining the concept of culture in anthropology.
- Identify the differences between armchair anthropology and participant-observer fieldwork and explain how Bronislaw Malinowski contributed to the development of anthropological fieldwork techniques.
- Identify the contributions Franz Boas and his students made to the development of new theories about culture.
- Assess some of the ethical issues that can arise from anthropological research.

THOUGHTS ON CULTURE OVER A CUP OF COFFEE

Do you think culture can be studied in a coffee shop? Have you ever gone to a coffee shop, sat down with a book or laptop, and listened to conversations around you? If you just answered yes, in a way, you were acting as an anthropologist. Anthropologists like to become a part of their surroundings, observing and participating with people doing day-to-day things. As two anthropologists writing a chapter about the culture concept, we wanted to know what other people thought about culture. What better place to meet than at our community coffee shop?

Our small coffee shop was filled with the aroma of coffee beans, and the voices of people competed with the sound of the coffee grinder. At the counter a chalkboard listed the daily specials of sandwiches and desserts. Coffee shops have their own language, with vocabulary such as *macchiato* and *latte*. It can feel like entering a foreign culture. We found a quiet corner that would allow us to observe other people, and hopefully identify a few to engage with, without disturbing them too much with our conversation. We understand the way that anthropologists think about culture, but we were also wondering what the people sitting around us might have to say. Would having a definition of culture really mean something to the average coffee-shop patron? Is a definition important? Do people care? We were very lucky that morning because sitting next to us was a man working on his laptop, a service dog lying at his feet.

Meeting Bob at the Coffee Shop

Having an animal in a food-service business is not usually allowed, but in our community people can have their service dogs with them. This young golden retriever wore a harness that displayed a sign stating the owner was diabetic. This dog was very friendly; in fact, she wanted to be touched and would not leave us alone, wagging her tail and pushing her nose against our hands. This is very unusual

1

because many service dogs, like seeing eye dogs, are not to be touched. Her owner, Bob, let us know that his dog must be friendly and not afraid to approach people: if Bob needs help in an emergency, such as a diabetic coma, the dog must go to someone else for help.

We enjoyed meeting Bob and his dog, and asked if he would like to answer our question: what is culture? Bob was happy to share his thoughts and ideas.

Bob feels that language is very important to cultural identity. He believes that if one loses language, one also loses important information about wildlife, indigenous plants, and ways of being. As a member of a First Nations tribe, Bob believes that words have deep cultural meaning. Most importantly, he views English as the language of commerce. Bob is concerned with the influence of Western consumerism and how it changes cultural identity.

Bob is not an anthropologist. He was just a person willing to share his ideas. Without knowing it though, Bob had described some of the elements of anthropology. He had focused on the importance of language and the loss of tradition when it is no longer spoken, and he had recognized that language is a part of cultural identity. He was worried about globalization and consumerism changing cultural values.

With Bob's opinions in mind, we started thinking about how we, two cultural anthropologists, would answer the same question about culture. Our training shapes our understandings of the question, yet we know there is more to culture concepts than a simple definition. Why is asking the culture concept question important to anthropologists? Does it matter? Is culture something that we can understand without studying it formally?

In this chapter, we will illustrate how anthropology developed the culture concept. Our journey will explore the importance of storytelling and the way that anthropology became a social science. This will include learning about the work of important scholars, how anthropology emerged in North America, and an overview of the importance of ethics.

STORIES AS A REFLECTION ON CULTURE

Stories are told in every culture and often teach a moral lesson to young children. Fables are similar, but often set an example for people to live by or describe what to do when in a dangerous situation. They can also be a part of traditions, help to preserve ways of life, or explain mysteries. Storytelling takes many different forms such as tall tales and folktales. These are for entertainment or to discuss problems encountered in life. Both are also a form of cultural preservation, a way to communicate morals or values to the next generation. Stories can also be a form of social control over certain activities or customs that are not allowed in a society.

A fable becomes a tradition by being retold and accepted by others in the community. Different cultures have very similar stories sharing common themes. One of the most common themes is the battle between good and evil. Another is the story of the quest. The quest often takes the character to distant lands, filled with real-life situations, opportunities, hardships, and heartaches. In both of these types of stories, the reader is introduced to the anthropological concept known as *the Other*. What exactly is *the Other*? **The Other** is a term that has been used to describe people whose customs, beliefs, or behaviors are different from one's own.

Can a story explain the concept of the Other? Jonathan Swift's *Gulliver's Travels* is about four different voyages that Gulliver undertakes. His first adventure is the most well-known; in the story, Lemuel Gulliver is a surgeon who plans a sea voyage when his business fails. During a storm at sea, he is shipwrecked, and he awakens to find himself bound and secured by a group of captors, the Lilliputians, who are six inches tall. Gulliver, having what Europeans consider a normal body height,

Figure 1: Travel writer Lemuel Gulliver is captured and tied down by the Lilliputians.

suddenly becomes a giant. During this adventure, Gulliver is seen as an outsider, a stranger with different features and language. Gulliver becomes the Other.

What lessons about culture can we learn from *Gulliver's Travels*? Swift's story offers lessons about cultural differences, conflicts occurring in human society, and the balance of power. It also provides an important example of the Other. The Other is a matter of perspective in this story: Gulliver thinks the Lilliputians are strange and unusual. To Gulliver, the Lilliputians are the Other, but the Lilliputians equally see Gulliver as the Other—he is a their captive and is a rare species of man because of his size.

The themes in *Gulliver's Travels* describe different cultures and aspects of storytelling. The story uses language, customary behaviors, and the conflict between different groups to explore ideas of the exotic and strange. The story is framed as an adventure, but is really about how similar cultures can be. In the end, Gulliver becomes a member of another cultural group, learning new norms, attitudes, and behaviors. At the same time, he wants to colonize them, a reflection of his former cultural self.

Stories are an important part of culture, and when used to pass on traditions or cultural values, they can connect people to the past. Stories are also a way to validate religious, social, political, and economic practices from one generation to another. Stories are important because they are used in some societies to apply social pressure, to keep people in line, and are part of shaping the way that people think and behave.

Anthropologists as Storytellers

People throughout recorded history have relied on storytelling as a way to share cultural details. When early anthropologists studied people from other civilizations, they relied on the written accounts and opinions of others; they presented facts and developed their stories, about other cultures based solely on information gathered by others. These scholars did not have any direct contact with the people they were studying. This approach has come to be known as **armchair anthropology**. Simply put, if a culture is viewed from a distance (as from an armchair), the anthropologist tends to measure that culture from his or her own vantage point and to draw comparisons that place the anthropologist's culture as superior to the one being studied. This point of view is also called ethnocentrism. **Ethnocentrism** is an attitude based on the idea that one's own group or culture is better than any other.

Early anthropological studies often presented a biased ethnocentric interpretation of the human condition. For example, ideas about racial superiority emerged as a result of studying the cultures that were encountered during the colonial era. During the colonial era from the sixteenth century to the mid–twentieth century, European countries (Britain, France, Germany, Belgium, Dutch Republic, Spain, Portugal) asserted control over land (Asia, Africa, the Americas) and people. European ideas of wrong and right were used as a measuring stick to judge the way that people in different

cultures lived. These other cultures were considered primitive, which was an ethnocentric term for people who were non-European. It is also a negative term suggesting that indigenous cultures had a lack of technological advancement. Colonizers thought that they were superior to the Other in every way.

Armchair anthropologists were unlikely to be aware of their ethnocentric ideas because they did not visit the cultures they studied. Scottish social anthropologist Sir James Frazer is well-known for his 1890 work *The Golden Bough: A Study of Comparative Religions*. Its title was later changed to *A Study in Magic and Religion*, and it was one of the first books to describe and record magical and religious beliefs of different culture groups around the world. Yet, this book was not the outcome of extensive study in the field. Instead, Frazer relied on the accounts of others who had traveled, such as scholars, missionaries, and government officials, to formulate his study.

Figure 2: Sir James Frazer is among the founders of modern anthropology.

Another example of anthropological writing without the use of fieldwork is Sir E. B. Tylor's 1871 work *Primitive Culture*. Tylor, who went on to become the first professor of anthropology at Oxford University in 1896, was an important influence in the development of sociocultural anthropology as a separate discipline. Tylor defined **culture** as "that complex whole which includes knowledge, belief, art, law, morals, custom, and any other capabilities and habits acquired by man as a member of society."[1] His definition of culture is still used frequently today and remains the foundation of the culture concept in anthropology.

Tylor's definition of culture was influenced by the popular theories and philosophies of his time, including the work of Charles Darwin. Darwin formulated the theory of evolution by natural selection in his 1859 book *On the Origin of Species*. Scholars of the time period, including Tylor, believed that cultures were subject to evolution just like plants and animals and thought that cultures developed over time from simple to complex. Many nineteenth century anthropologists believed that cultures evolved through distinct stages. They labeled these stages with terms such as savagery, barbarism, and civilization.[2] These theories of **cultural evolutionism** would later be successfully refuted, but conflicting views about cultural evolutionism in the nineteenth century highlight an ongoing nature versus nurture debate about whether biology shapes behavior more than culture.

Both Frazer and Tylor contributed important and foundational studies even though they never went into the field to gather their information. Armchair anthropologists were important in the development of anthropology as a discipline in the late nineteenth century because although these early scholars were not directly experiencing the cultures they were studying, their work did ask important questions that could ultimately only be answered by going into the field.

Figure 3: Drawing of a Mother and Child in Malaysia from *Anthropology: An Introduction to the Study of Man and Civilization*, E.B. Tylor, 1904

Anthropologists as Cultural Participants

The armchair approach as a way to study culture changed when scholars such as Bronislaw Malinowski, Alfred Radcliffe-Brown, Franz Boas, and Margaret Mead took to the field and studied by being participants and observers. As they did, fieldwork became the most important tool anthropologists used to understand the "complex whole" of culture.

Bronislaw Malinowski, a Polish anthropologist, was greatly influenced by the work of Frazer. However, unlike the armchair anthropology approach Frazer used in writing *The Golden Bough*, Malinowski used more innovative ethnographic techniques, and his fieldwork took him off the veranda to study different cultures. The off the veranda approach is different from armchair anthropology because it includes active **participant-observation**: traveling to a location, living among people, and observing their day-to-day lives.

What happened when Malinowski came off the veranda? *The Argonauts of the Western Pacific* (1922) was considered the first modern ethnography and redefined the approach to fieldwork. This book is part of Malinowski's trilogy on the Trobriand Islanders. Malinowski lived with them and observed life in their villages. By living among the islanders, Malinowski was able to learn about their social life, food and shelter, sexual behaviors, community economics, patterns of kinship, and family.[3]

Malinowski went "native" to some extent during his fieldwork with the Trobriand Islanders. **Going native** means to become fully integrated into a cultural group: taking leadership positions and assuming key roles in society; entering into a marriage or spousal contract; exploring sexuality or fully participating in rituals. When an anthropologist goes native, the anthropologist is personally

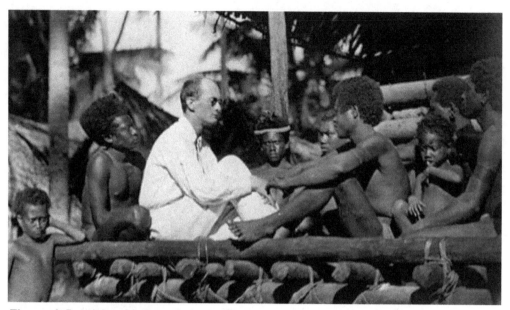

Figure 4: Bronislaw Malinowski in the Trobriand Islands, 1915–1918

involved with locals. In *The Argonauts of the Western Pacific*, Malinowski suggested that other anthropologists should "grasp the native's point of view, his relations to life, to realize his vision of his world."[4] However, as we will see later in this chapter, Malinowski's practice of going native presented problems from an ethical point of view. Participant-observation is a method to gather ethnographic data, but going native places both the anthropologist and the culture group at risk by blurring the lines on both sides of the relationship.

THE DEVELOPMENT OF THEORIES OF CULTURE

Anthropology in Europe

The discipline of cultural anthropology developed somewhat differently in Europe and North America, in particular in the United States, during the nineteenth and early twentieth centuries with each region contributing new dimensions to the concept of culture. Many European anthropologists were particularly interested in questions about how societies were structured and how they remained stable over time. This highlighted emerging recognition that culture and society are not the same. Culture had been defined by Tylor as knowledge, beliefs, and customs, but a society is more than just shared ideas or habits. In every society, people are linked to one another through social institutions such as families, political organizations, and businesses. Anthropologists across Europe often focused their research on understanding the form and function of these social institutions.

European anthropologists developed theories of **functionalism** to explain how social institutions contribute to the organization of society and the maintenance of social order. Bronislaw Malinowski believed that cultural traditions were developed as a response to specific human needs such as food, comfort, safety, knowledge, reproduction, and economic livelihood. One function of educational institutions like schools, for instance, is to provide knowledge that prepares people to obtain jobs and make contributions to society. Although he preferred the term **structural-functionalism**, the British anthropologist A.R. Radcliffe-Brown was also interested in the way that social structures functioned to maintain social stability in a society over time.[5] He suggested that in many societies it was the family that served as the most important social structure because family relationships determined much about an individual's social, political, and economic relationships and these patterns were repeated from one generation to the next. In a family unit in which the father is the breadwinner and the mother stays home to raise the children, the social and economic roles of both the husband and the wife will be largely defined by their specific responsibilities within the family. If their children grow up to follow the same arrangement, these social roles will be continued in the next generation.

In the twentieth century, functionalist approaches also became popular in North American anthropology, but eventually fell out of favor. One of the biggest critiques of functionalism is that it views cultures as stable and orderly and ignores or cannot explain social change. Functionalism also struggles to explain why a society develops one particular kind of social institution instead of another. Functionalist perspectives did contribute to the development of more sophisticated concepts of culture by establishing the importance of social institutions in holding societies together. While defining the division between what is cultural and what is social continues to be complex, functionalist theory helped to develop the concept of culture by demonstrating that culture is not just a set of ideas or beliefs, but consists of specific practices and social institutions that give structure to daily life and allow human communities to function.

Anthropology in the United States

During the development of anthropology in North America (Canada, United States, and Mexico), the significant contribution made by the American School of Anthropology in the nineteenth and twentieth centuries was the concept of **cultural relativism**, which is the idea that cultures cannot be objectively understood since all humans see the world through the lens of their own culture. Cultural relativism is different than ethnocentrism because it emphasizes understanding culture from an insider's view. The focus on culture, along with the idea of cultural relativism, distinguished cultural anthropology in the United States from social anthropology in Europe.

The participant-observation method of fieldwork was a revolutionary change to the practice of anthropology, but at the same time it presented problems that needed to be overcome. The challenge was to move away from ethnocentrism, race stereotypes, and colonial attitudes, and to move forward by encouraging anthropologists to maintain high ethical standards and open minds.

Franz Boas, an American anthropologist, is acknowledged for redirecting American anthropologists away from cultural evolutionism and toward cultural relativism. Boas first studied physical science at the University of Kiel in Ger-

Figure 5: Franz Boas, one of the founders of American anthropology, 1915

many. Because he was a trained scientist, he was familiar with using empirical methods as a way to study a subject. Empirical methods are based on evidence that can be tested using observation and experiment.

In 1883, Franz Boas went on a geographical expedition to Baffin Island in the Canadian Arctic. *The Central Eskimo* (1888) details his time spent on Baffin Island studying the culture and language of the central Eskimo (Inuit) people. He studied every aspect of their culture such as tools, clothing, and shelters. This study was Boas' first major contribution to the American school of anthropology and convinced him that cultures could only be understood through extensive field research. As he observed on Baffin Island, cultural ideas and practices are shaped through interactions with the natural environment. The cultural traditions of the Inuit were suited for the environment in which they lived. This work led him to promote cultural relativism: the principle that a culture must be understood on its own terms rather than compared to an outsider's standard. This was an important turning point in correcting the challenge of ethnocentrism in ethnographic fieldwork.[6]

Boas is often considered the originator of American anthropology because he trained the first generation of American anthropologists including Ruth Benedict, Margaret Mead, and Alfred Kroeber. Using a commitment to cultural relativism as a starting point, these students continued to refine the concept of culture. Ruth Benedict, one of Boas' first female students, used cultural relativism as a starting point for investigating the cultures of the American northwest and southwest. Her best-selling book *Patterns of Culture* (1934) emphasized that culture gives people coherent patterns for thinking and behaving. She argued that culture affects individuals psychologically, shaping individual personality traits and leading the members of a culture to exhibit similar traits such as a tendency toward aggression, or calmness.

Benedict was a professor at Columbia University and in turn greatly influenced her student Margaret Mead, who went on to become one of the most well-known female American cultural anthropologists. Mead was a pioneer in conducting ethnographic research at a time when the discipline was predominately male. Her 1925 research on adolescent girls on the island of Taʻū in the Samoan Islands, published as *Coming of Age in Samoa* (1928), revealed that teenagers in Samoa did not experience the same stress and emotional difficulties as those in the United States. The book was an important contribution to the nature versus nurture debate, providing an argument that learned cultural roles were more important than biology. The book also reinforced the idea that individual emotions and personality traits are products of culture.

Alfred Louis Kroeber, another student of Boas, also shared the commitment to field research and cultural relativism, but Kroeber was particularly interested in how cultures change over time and influence one another. Through publications like *The Nature of Culture (1952),* Kroeber examined the historical processes that led cultures to emerge as distinct configurations as well as the way cultures could become more similar through the

Figure 6: Ruth Benedict, 1936

spread or diffusion of cultural traits. Kroeber was also interested in language and the role it plays in transmitting culture. He devoted much of his career to studying Native American languages in an attempt to document these languages before they disappeared.

Anthropologists in the United States have used cultural relativism to add depth to the concept of culture in several ways. Tylor had defined culture as including knowledge, belief, art, law, morals, custom, capabilities and habits. Boas and his students added to this definition by emphasizing the importance of **enculturation**, the process of learning culture, in the lives of individuals. Benedict, Mead, and others established that through enculturation culture shapes individual identity, self-awareness, and emotions in fundamental ways. They also emphasized the need for **holism**, approaches to research that considered the entire context of a society including its history.

Kroeber and others also established the importance of language as an element of culture and documented the ways in which language was used to communicate complex ideas. By the late twentieth century, new approaches to symbolic anthropology put language at the center of analysis. Later on, Clifford Geertz, the founding member of postmodernist anthropology, noted in his book *The Interpretation of Cultures* (1973) that culture should not be seen as something that was "locked inside people's heads." Instead, culture was publically communicated through speech and other behaviors. **Culture**, he concluded, is "an historically transmitted pattern of meanings embodied in symbols, a system of inherited conceptions expressed in symbolic forms by means of which men communicate, perpetuate, and develop their knowledge about and their attitudes toward life."[7] This definition, which continues to be influential today, reflects the influence of many earlier efforts to refine the concept of culture in American anthropology.

ETHICAL ISSUES IN TRUTH TELLING

As anthropologists developed more sophisticated concepts of culture, they also gained a greater understanding of the ethical challenges associated with anthropological research. Because participant-observation fieldwork brings anthropologists into close relationships with the people they study, many complicated issues can arise. Cultural relativism is a perspective that encourages anthropologists to show respect to members of other cultures, but it was not until after World War II that the profession of anthropology recognized a need to develop formal standards of professional conduct.

The Nuremberg trials, which began in 1946 Nuremberg, Germany, were conducted under the direction of France, the Soviet Union, the United Kingdom, and the United States, prosecuted members of the Nazi regime for war crimes. In addition to military and political figures, physicians and scientists were also prosecuted for unethical human experimentation and mass murder. The trials demonstrated that physicians and other scientists could be dangerous if they used their skills for abusive or exploitative goals. The Nuremberg Code that emerged from the trials is considered a landmark document in medical and research ethics. It established principles for the ethical treatment of the human subjects involved in any medical or scientific research.

Because of events such as the Nuremberg trials, many universities embraced research ethical guidelines for the treatment of human subjects. Anthropologists and students who work in universities where these guidelines exist are obliged to follow these rules. The American Anthropological Association (AAA), along with many anthropology organizations in other countries, developed codes of ethics describing specific expectations for anthropologists engaged in research in a variety of settings. The principles in the AAA code of ethics include: do no harm; be open and honest regarding your work; obtain informed consent and necessary permissions; ensure the vulnerable populations in every study are protected from competing ethical obligations; make your results accessible; protect and preserve your records; and maintain respectful and ethical professional relationships. These principles sound simple, but can be complicated in practice.

Bronislaw Malinowski

The career of Bronislaw Malinowski provides an example of how investigations of culture can lead anthropologists into difficult ethical areas. As discussed above, Malinowski is widely regarded as a leading figure in the history of anthropology. He initiated the practice of participant-observation fieldwork and published several highly regarded books including *The Argonauts of the Western Pacific*. Following his death, the private diary he kept while conducting fieldwork was discovered and published as *A Diary in the Strictest Sense of the Term* (1967). The diary described Malinowski's feelings of loneliness and isolation, but also included a great deal of information about his sexual fantasies as well his some insensitive and contemptuous opinions about the Trobriand Islanders. The diary provided valuable insight into the mind of an important ethnographer, but also raised questions about the extent to which his personal feelings, including bias and racism, were reflected in his official conclusions.

Most anthropologists keep diaries or daily notes as a means of keeping track of the research project, but these records are almost never made public. Because Malinowski's diary was published after his death, he could not explain why he wrote what he did, or assess the extent to which he was able to separate the personal from the professional. Which of these books best reflects the truth about Malinowski's interaction with the Trobriand Islanders? This rare insight into the private life of a field researcher demonstrates that even when anthropologists are acting within the boundaries of professional ethics, they still struggle to set aside their own ethnocentric attitudes and prejudices.

Napoleon Chagnon

A more serious and complicated incident concerned research conducted among the Yanomami, an indigenous group living in the Amazon rainforest in Brazil and Venezuela. Starting in the 1960s, the anthropologist Napoleon Chagnon and James Neel, a geneticist, carried out research among the Yanomami. Neel was interested in studying the effects of radiation released by nuclear explosions on people living in remote areas. Chagnon was investigating theories about the role of violence in Yanomami society. In 2000, an American journalist, Patrick Tierney, published a book about Chagnon and Neel's research: *Darkness in El Dorado: How Scientists and Journalists Devastated the Amazon*. The book contained numerous stunning allegations, including a claim that the pair had deliberately infected the Yanomami with measles, starting an epidemic that killed thousands of people. The book also claimed that Neel had conducted medical experiments without the consent of the Yanomami

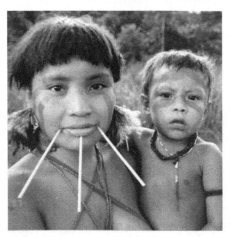

Figure 7: Yanomami Woman and Child, 1997

and that Chagnon had deliberately created conflicts between Yanomami groups so he could study the resulting violence.

These allegations were brought to the attention of the American Anthropological Association, and a number of inquiries were eventually conducted. James Neel was deceased, but Napoleon Chagnon steadfastly denied the allegations. In 2002, the AAA issued their report; Chagnon was judged to have misrepresented the violent nature of Yanomami culture in ways that caused them harm and to have failed to obtain proper consent for his research. However, Chagnon continued to reject these conclusions and complained that the process used to evaluate the evidence was unfair. In 2005, the AAA rescinded its own conclusion, citing problems with the investigation process. The results of several years of inquiry into the situation satisfied few people. Chagnon was not definitively pronounced guilty, nor was he exonerated. Years later, debate over this episode continues.[8] The controversy demonstrates the extent to which truth can be elusive in anthropological inquiry. Although anthropologists should not be storytellers in the sense that they deliberately create fictions, differences in perspective and theoretical orientation create unavoidable differences in the way anthropologists interpret the same situation. Anthropologists must try to use their toolkit of theory and methods to ensure that the stories they tell are truthful and represent the voice of the people being studied using an ethical approach.

BACK IN THE COFFEE SHOP

This chapter has looked at some historic turning points in the way anthropologists have defined culture. There is not one true, absolute definition of culture. Anthropologists respect traditions such as language; the development of self, especially from infancy to adulthood; kinship; and the structure of the social unit, or the strata of a person within their class structure; marriage, families, and rites of passage; systems of belief; and ritual. However, anthropologists also look at change and the impact it has on those traditions.

With globalization moving at a dramatic pace, and change unfolding daily, how will emerging trends redefine the culture concept? For example, social media and the Internet connect the world and have created new languages, relationships, and an online culture without borders. This leads to the question: is digital, or cyber anthropology the future? Is the study of online cultures, which are encountered largely through reading text, considered armchair or off the veranda research? Is the cyber world a real or virtual culture? In some ways, addressing online cultures takes anthropology back to its roots as anthropologists can explore new worlds without leaving home. At the same time, cyberspaces and new technologies allow people to see, hear, and communicate with others around the world in real time.

Back in the coffee shop, where we spent time with Bob, we discovered that he hoped to keep familiar aspects of his own culture, traditions such as language, social structure, and unique expressions of values, alive. The question, what is culture, caused us to reflect on our own understandings of the cultural self and *the cultural Other*, and on the importance of self and cultural awareness.

Emily

My cultural self has evolved from the first customary traditions of my childhood, yet my life with the Inuit caused me to consider that I have similar values and community traits as my friends in the North. My childhood was focused on caring, acceptance, and working together to achieve the necessities of life. Life on the land with the Inuit was no different, and throughout the years, I have seen how much we are the same, just living in different locations and circumstances. My anthropological training has enriched my life experiences by teaching me to enjoy the world and its peoples. I have also experienced being *the cultural Other* when working in the field, and this has always reminded me that *the cultural self* and *the cultural Other* will always be in conflict with each other on both sides of the experience.

Priscilla

Living with different indigenous tribes in Kenya gave me a chance to learn how communities maintain their traditional culture and ways of living. I come from a Portuguese- Canadian family that has kept strong ties to the culture and religion of our ancestors. Portuguese people believe storytelling is a way to keep one's traditions, cultural identity, indigenous knowledge, and language alive. When I lived in Nairobi Province, Kenya, I discovered that people there had the same point of view. I found it odd that people still define their identities by their cultural history. What I have learned by conducting cultural fieldwork is that the meanings of culture not only vary from one group to another, but that all human societies define themselves through culture.

Our Final Reflection

Bob took us on a journey to understand what is at the heart of the culture concept. Clearly, the culture concept does not follow a straight line. Scholars, storytellers, and the people one meets in everyday life have something to say about the components of culture. The story that emerges from different voices brings insight into what it is to be human. Defining the culture concept is like putting together a puzzle with many pieces. The puzzle of culture concepts is almost complete, but it is not finished…yet.

DISCUSSION QUESTIONS

1. How did the armchair anthropology and the off the veranda approaches differ as methods to study culture? What can be learned about a culture by experiencing it in person that cannot be learned from reading about it?
2. Why is the concept of culture difficult to define? What do you think are the most important elements of culture?
3. Why is it difficult to separate the "social" from the "cultural"? Do you think this is an important distinction?
4. In the twenty-first century, people have much greater contact with members of other cultures than they did in the past. Which topics or concerns should be priorities for future studies of culture?

GLOSSARY

Armchair anthropology: an early and discredited method of anthropological research that did not involve direct contact with the people studied.

Cultural determinism: the idea that behavioral differences are a result of cultural not racial or genetic causes.

Cultural evolutionism: a theory popular in nineteenth century anthropology suggesting that societies evolved through stages from simple to advanced. This theory was later shown to be incorrect.

Cultural relativism: the idea that we should seek to understand another person's beliefs and behaviors from the perspective of their own culture and not our own.

Enculturation: the process of learning the characteristics and expectations of a culture or group

Ethnocentrism: the tendency to view one's own culture as most important and correct and as the stick by which to measure all other cultures.

Functionalism: an approach to anthropology developed in British anthropology that emphasized the way that parts of a society work together to support the functioning of the whole.

Going native: becoming fully integrated into a cultural group through acts such as taking a leadership position, assuming key roles in society, entering into marriage, or other behaviors that incorporate an anthropologist into the society he or she is studying.

Holism: taking a broad view of the historical, environmental, and cultural foundations of behavior.

Kinship: blood ties, common ancestry, and social relationships that form families within human groups.

Participant observation: a type of observation in which the anthropologist observes while participating in the same activities in which her informants are engaged.

Salvage anthropology: activities such as gathering artifacts, or recording cultural rituals with the belief that a culture is about to disappear.

Structuralism: an approach to anthropology that focuses on the ways in which the customs or social institutions in a culture contribute to the organization of society and the maintenance of social order.

The Other: a term that has been used to describe people whose customs, beliefs, or behaviors are "different" from one's own

ABOUT THE AUTHORS

Dr. Emily Cowall is a cultural anthropologist and instructor in the department of Anthropology at McMaster University, Canada; Medical Historian; and former regulated health practitioner in Ontario. Her primary academic research interests are focused on the cultural ethno-history of the Canadian Arctic. Emily moved to the Eastern Arctic in the 1980s, where she became integrated into community life. Returning for community-based research projects from 2003 to 2011, her previous community relationships enabled the completion of a landmark study examining the human geography and cultural impact of tuberculosis from 1930 to 1972. From 2008 to 2015, her work in cultural resource management took her to the Canadian High Arctic archipelago to create a museum dedicated to the Defense Research Science Era at Parks Canada, Quttinirpaaq National Park on Ellesmere Island. When she is not jumping into Twin Otter aircraft for remote field camps, she is exploring cultural aspects of environmental health and religious pilgrimage throughout Mexico.

Priscilla Medeiros is a PhD candidate and instructor at McMaster University, Canada, and is defending her thesis in fall 2017. Her primary research interests center on the anthropology of health. This involves studying the biocultural dimensions of medicine, with a particular emphasis on the history and development of public health in developed countries, sickness and inequalities, and gender relationships. Priscilla began her community-based work in prevention, care, and support of

people living with HIV and AIDS seven years ago in Nairobi Province, Kenya, as part of her master's degree. Her current research focuses on the absence of gender-specific and culturally appropriate HIV prevention initiatives and programs for women in the Maritime Provinces, Canada, and is funded by the Canadian Institutes of Health Research. When she is not working in rural areas or teaching in the classroom, Priscilla is traveling to exotic destinations to learn to prepare local cuisine, speak foreign languages, and explore the wonders of the world. In fact, she is the real-life Indiana Jane of anthropology when it comes to adventures in the field and has many great stories to share.

BIBLIOGRAPHY

Benedict, Ruth. *Patterns of Culture*. Boston: Houghton and Mifflin Company, 1934.

Boas, Franz. *Race, Language, and Culture*. Chicago: University of Chicago Press, 1940.

Darwin, Charles. *On the Origin of Species*. London: John Murray, Albemarle Street, 1859.

Kroeber, Alfred. *The Nature of Culture*. Chicago: University of Chicago Press, 1952.

Malinowski, Bronislaw. *Argonauts of the Western Pacific*. London: Routledge and Sons, 1922.

Mead, Margaret. *Coming of Age in Samoa: A Psychological Study of Primitive Youth for Western Civilization*. New York: William Morrow and Company, 1928.

Swift, Jonathan. *Gulliver's Travels into Several Remote Nations of the World*. London: Benjamin Motte, 1726.

Tylor, Edward B. *Primitive Culture: Researches into the Development of Mythology, Philosophy, Religion, Language, Art, and Customs*. London: Cambridge University Press. 1871.

NOTES

1. Edward B. Tylor, *Primitive Culture: Researches into the Development of Mythology, Philosophy, Religion, Language, Art, and Customs* (London: Cambridge University Press, 1871), preface.

2. Lewis Henry Morgan was one anthropologist who proposed an evolutionary framework based on these terms in his book *Ancient Society* (New York: Henry Holt, 1877).

3. The film *Bronislaw Malinowski: Off the Veranda*, (Films Media Group, 1986) further describes Malinowski's research practices.

4. Bronislaw Malinowski. *Argonauts of the Western Pacific* (London: Routledge & Keegan Paul, 1922), 290.

5. For more on this topic see Adam Kuper, *Anthropology and Anthropologists: The Modern British School* (New York: Routledge, 1983) and Alfred Radcliffe-Brown, *Structure and Function in Primitive Society* (London: Cohen and West, 1952).

6. Boas' attitudes about cultural relativism were influenced by his experiences in the Canadian Arctic as he struggled to survive in a natural environment foreign to his own prior experience. His private diary and letters record the evolution of his thinking about what it means to be "civilized." In a letter to his fiancé, he wrote: "I often ask myself what advantages our 'good society' possesses over that of the 'savages' and find, the more I see of their customs, that we have no right to look down upon them … We have no right to blame them for their forms and superstitions which may seem ridiculous to us. We 'highly educated people' are much worse, relatively speaking." The entire letter can be read in George Stocking, ed. *Observers Observed: Essays on Ethnographic Fieldwork* (Madison, WI: University of Wisconsin Press, 1983), 33.

7. Clifford Geertz, *The Interpretation of Culture* (New York: Basic Books, Geertz 1973), 89.

8. For more information about the controversy, see Thomas Gregor and Daniel Gross, "Guilt by Association: The Culture of Accusation and the American Anthropological Associations Investigation of Darkness in El Dorado." *American Anthropologist* 106 no. 4 (2004):687-698 and Robert Borofsky, *Yanomami: The Fierce Controversy and What We Can Learn From It* (Berkley: University California Press, 2005). Napoleon Chagnon has written his rebuttal in *Noble Savages: My Life Among Two Dangerous Tribes—The Yanomamo and the Anthropologists* (New York: Simon and Schuster, 2013).

DOING FIELDWORK: METHODS IN CULTURAL ANTHROPOLOGY

#3

Katie Nelson, Inver Hills Community College
ktanelson@gmail.com
knelson@inverhills.mnscu.edu
http://kanelson.com/

LEARNING OBJECTIVES

- Discuss what is unique about ethnographic fieldwork and how it emerged as a key strategy in anthropology.

- Explain how traditional approaches to ethnographic fieldwork contrast with contemporary approaches.

- Identify some of the contemporary ethnographic fieldwork techniques and perspectives.

- Discuss some of the ethical considerations in doing anthropological fieldwork.

- Summarize how anthropologists transform their fieldwork data into a story that communicates meaning.

FINDING THE FIELD

My first experience with fieldwork as a student anthropologist took place in a small **indigenous** community in northeastern Brazil studying the Jenipapo-Kanindé of *Lagoa Encantada* (Enchanted Lake). I had planned to conduct an independent research project on **land tenure** among members of the indigenous tribe and had gotten permission to spend several months with the community. My Brazilian host family arranged for a relative to drive me to the rural community on the back of his motorcycle. After several hours navigating a series of bumpy roads in blazing equatorial heat, I was relieved to arrive at the edge of the reservation. He cut the motor and I removed my heavy backpack from my tired, sweaty back. Upon hearing us arrive, first children and then adults slowly and shyly began to approach us. I greeted the curious onlookers and briefly explained who I was. As a group of children ran to fetch the *cacique* (the chief/political leader), I began to explain my research agenda to several of the men who had gathered. I mentioned that I was interested in learning about how the tribe negotiated land use rights without any private land ownership. After hearing me use the colloquial term "*índio*" (Indian), a man who turned out to be the *cacique's* cousin came forward and said to me, "Well, your work is going to be difficult because there are no Indians here; we are only Brazilians." Then, abruptly, another man angrily replied to him, stating firmly that, in fact, they were Indians because the community was on an Indian reservation and the Brazilian government had recognized them as an indigenous tribe. A few women then entered the rapid-fire discussion. I took a step back, surprised by the intensity of my first interaction in the community. The debate subsided once the *cacique* arrived, but it left a strong impression in my mind. Eventually, I discarded my original research plan to focus instead on this disagreement within the community about

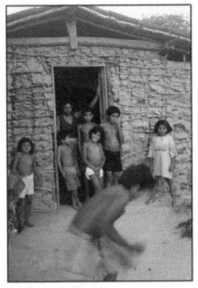

Figure 1: Children playing outside a home on the Jenipapo-Kanindé Reservation, 2001.

who they were and were not. In anthropology, this type of conflict in beliefs is known as **contested identity**.

I soon learned that many among the Jenipapo-Kanindé did not embrace the Indian identity label. The tribe members were all monolingual Portuguese-speakers who long ago had lost their original language and many of their traditions. Beginning in the 1980s, several local researchers had conducted studies in the community and had concluded that the community had indigenous origins. Those researchers lobbied on the community's behalf for official state and federal status as an indigenous reservation, and in 1997 the Funai (*Fundação Nacional do Índio* or National Foundation for the Indian) visited the community and agreed to officially demarcate the land as an indigenous reservation. More than 20 years later, the community is still waiting for that demarcation. Some in the community embraced indigenous status because it came with a number of benefits. The state (Ceará), using partial funding from Funai, built a new road to improve access to the community. The government also constructed an elementary school and a common well and installed new electric lines.

Despite those gains, some members of the community did not embrace indigenous status because being considered Indian had a pejorative connotation in Brazil. Many felt that the label stigmatized them by associating them with a poor and marginalized class of Brazilians. Others resisted the label because of long-standing family and inter-personal conflicts in the community.

Fieldwork is the most important method by which cultural anthropologists gather data to answer their research questions. While interacting on a daily basis with a group of people, cultural anthropologists document their observations and perceptions and adjust the focus of their research as needed. They typically spend a few months to a few years living among the people they are studying.

Figure 2: Author Katie Nelson (center) with her Brazilian host family, 2001.

Figure 3: A young Jenipapo-Kanindé boy shows off his grass skirt prior to a community dance, 2001.

The "field" can be anywhere the people are—a village in highland Papua New Guinea or a supermarket in downtown Minneapolis. Just as marine biologists spend time in the ocean to learn about the behavior of marine animals and geologists travel to a mountain range to observe rock formations, anthropologists go to places where people are.

> **Doing Anthropology:**
>
> In this short film, Stefan Helmreich, Erica James, and Heather Paxson, three members of the Massachusetts Institute of Technology's Anthropology Department, talk about their current work and the process of doing fieldwork.

Making the Strange Familiar and the Familiar Strange

The cultural anthropologist's goal during fieldwork is to describe a group of people to others in a way that makes strange or unusual features of the culture seem familiar and familiar traits seem extraordinary. The point is to help people think in new ways about aspects of their own culture by comparing them with other cultures. The research anthropologist Margaret Mead describes in her monograph *Coming of Age in Samoa* (1928) is a famous example of this. In 1925, Mead went to American Samoa, where she conducted ethnographic research on adolescent girls and their experiences with sexuality and growing up. Mead's mentor, anthropologist Franz Boas, was a strong proponent of cultural determinism, the idea that one's cultural upbringing and social environment, rather than one's biology, primarily determine behavior. Boas encouraged Mead to travel to Samoa to study adolescent behavior there and to compare their culture and behavior with that of adolescents in the United States to lend support to his hypothesis. In the foreword of *Coming of Age in Samoa*, Boas described what he saw as the key insight of her research: "The results of her painstaking investigation confirm the suspicion long held by anthropologists that much of what we ascribe to human nature is no more than a reaction to the restraints put upon us by our civilization."[1]

Mead studied 25 young women in three villages in Samoa and found that the stress, anxiety, and turmoil of American adolescence were not found among Samoan youth. Rather, young women in Samoa experienced a smooth transition to adulthood with relatively little stress or difficulty. She documented instances of socially accepted sexual experimentation, lack of sexual jealousy and rape, and a general sense of casualness that marked Samoan adolescence. *Coming of Age in Samoa* quickly became popular, launching Mead's career as one of the most well-known anthropologists in the United States and perhaps the world. The book encouraged American readers to reconsider their own cultural assumptions about what adolescence in the United States should be like, particularly in terms of the sexual repression and turmoil that seemed to characterize the teenage experience in mid-twentieth century America. Through her analysis of the differences between Samoan and American society, Mead also persuasively called for changes in education and parenting for U.S. children and adolescents.

Another classic example of a style of anthropological writing that attempted to make the familiar strange and encouraged readers to consider their own cultures in a different way is Horace Miner's *Body Ritual among the Nacirema* (1956). The essay described oral hygiene practices of the Nacirema ("American" spelled backward) in a way that, to cultural insiders, sounded extreme, exaggerated, and out of context. He presented the Nacirema as if they were a little-known cultural group with strange, exotic practices. Miner wrote the essay during an era in which anthropologists were just beginning to expand their focus beyond small-scale traditional societies far from home to large-scale post-industrial societies such as the United States. He wrote the essay primarily as a satire of how anthropologists often wrote about "the Other" in ways that made other cultures seem exotic and glossed over features that the Other had in common with the anthropologist's culture. The essay also challenged U.S. readers in general and anthropologists in particular to think differently about their own cultures and re-examine their cultural assumptions about what is "normal."

Emic and Etic Perspectives

When anthropologists conduct fieldwork, they gather data. An important tool for gathering anthropological data is **ethnography**—the in-depth study of everyday practices and lives of a people. Ethnography produces a detailed description of the studied group at a particular time and location, also known as a "**thick description**," a term coined by anthropologist Clifford Geertz in his 1973 book *The Interpretation of Cultures* to describe this type of research and writing. A thick description explains not only the behavior or cultural event in question but also the context in which it occurs and anthropological interpretations of it. Such descriptions help readers better understand the internal logic of why people in a culture behave as they do and why the behaviors are meaningful to them. This is important because understanding the attitudes, perspectives, and motivations of cultural insiders is at the heart of anthropology.

Ethnographers gather data from many different sources. One source is the anthropologist's own observations and thoughts. Ethnographers keep field notebooks that document their ideas and reflections as well as what they do and observe when participating in activities with the people they are studying, a research technique known as **participant observation.** Other sources of data include informal conversations and more-formal interviews that are recorded and transcribed. They also collect documents such as letters, photographs, artifacts, public records, books, and reports.

Different types of data produce different kinds of ethnographic descriptions, which also vary in terms of perspective—from the perspective of the studied culture (**emic**) or from the perspective of the observer (**etic**). Emic perspectives refer to descriptions of behaviors and beliefs in terms that are meaningful to people who belong to a specific culture, e.g., how people perceive and categorize their culture and experiences, why people believe they do what they do, how they imagine and explain things. To uncover emic perspectives, ethnographers talk to people, observe what they do, and participate in their daily activities with them. Emic perspectives are essential for anthropologists' efforts to obtain a detailed understanding of a culture and to avoid interpreting others through their own cultural beliefs.

Etic perspectives refer to explanations for behavior made by an outside observer in ways that are meaningful to the observer. For an anthropologist, etic descriptions typically arise from conversations between the ethnographer and the anthropological community. These explanations tend to be based in science and are informed by historical, political, and economic studies and other types of research. The etic approach acknowledges that members of a culture are unlikely to view the things they do as noteworthy or unusual. They cannot easily stand back and view their own behavior objectively or from another perspective. For example, you may have never thought twice about the way you brush your teeth and the practice of going to the dentist or how you experienced your teenage years. For you, these parts of your culture are so normal and "natural" you probably would never consider questioning them. An emic lens gives us an alternative perspective that is essential when constructing a comprehensive view of a people.

Most often, ethnographers include both emic and etic perspectives in their research and writing. They first uncover a studied people's understanding of what they do and why and then develop additional explanations for the behavior based on anthropological theory and analysis. Both perspectives are important, and it can be challenging to move back and forth between the two. Nevertheless, that is exactly what good ethnographers must do.

TRADITIONAL ETHNOGRAPHIC APPROACHES

Early Armchair Anthropology

Before ethnography was a fully developed research method, anthropologists in the nineteenth and early twentieth centuries used techniques that were much less reliable to gather data about people throughout the world. From the comfort of their homes and library armchairs, early scholars collected others' travel accounts and used them to come to conclusions about far-flung cultures and peoples. The reports typically came from missionaries, colonists, adventurers, and business travelers and were often incomplete, inaccurate, and/or misleading, exaggerated or omitted important information, and romanticized the culture.

Early scholars such as Wilhelm Schmidt and Sir E. B. Tylor sifted through artifacts and stories brought back by travelers or missionaries and selected the ones that best fit their frequently pre-conceived ideas about the peoples involved. By relying on this flawed data, they often drew inaccurate or even racist conclusions. They had no way of knowing how accurate the information was and no way to understand the full context in which it was gathered.

The work of Sir James Frazer (1854–1941) provides a good example of the problems associated with such anthropological endeavors. Frazer was a Scottish social anthropologist who was interested in myths and religions around the world. He read historical documents and religious texts found in libraries and book collections. He also sent questionnaires to missionaries and colonists in various parts of the world asking them about the people with whom they were in contact. He then used the information to draw sweeping conclusions about human belief systems. In his most famous book, *The Golden Bough*, he described similarities and differences in magical and religious practices around the world and concluded that human beliefs progressed through three stages: from primitive magic to religion and from religion to science. This theory implied that some people were less evolved and more primitive than others. Of course, contemporary anthropologists do not view any people as less evolved than another. Instead, anthropologists today seek to uncover the historical, political, and cultural reasons behind peoples' behaviors rather than assuming that one culture or society is more advanced than another.

The main problem with Frazer's conclusion can be traced back to the fact that he did not do any research himself and none of the information he relied on was collected by an anthropologist. He never spent time with the people he was researching. He never observed the religious ceremonies he wrote about and certainly never participated in them. Had he done so, he might have been able to appreciate that all human groups at the time (and now) were equally pragmatic, thoughtful, intelligent, logical, and "evolved." He might also have appreciated the fact that how and why information is gathered affects the quality of the information. For instance, if a colonial administrator offered to pay people for their stories, some of the storytellers might have exaggerated or even made up stories for financial gain. If a Christian missionary asked recently converted parishioners to describe their religious practices, they likely would have omitted non-Christian practices and beliefs to avoid disapproval and maintain their positions in the church. A male traveler who attempted to document rite-of-passage traditions in a culture that prohibited men from asking such questions of women would generate data that could erroneously suggest that women did not participate in such activities. All of these examples illustrate the pitfalls of armchair anthropology.

Off the Veranda

Fortunately, the reign of armchair anthropology was brief. Around the turn of the twentieth century, anthropologists trained in the natural sciences began to reimagine what a science of humanity should look like and how social scientists ought to go about studying cultural groups. Some of those anthropologists insisted that one should at least spend significant time actually observing and talking to the people studied. Early ethnographers such as Franz Boas and Alfred Cort Haddon typically traveled to the remote locations where the people in question lived and spent a few weeks to a few months there. They sought out a local Western host who was familiar with the people and the area (such as a colonial official, missionary, or businessman) and found accommodations through them. Although they did at times venture into the community without a guide, they generally did not spend significant time with the local people. Thus, their observations were primarily conducted from the relative comfort and safety of a porch—from their *verandas*.

Polish anthropologist Bronislaw Malinowski's (1884–1942) pioneering method of participant observation fundamentally changed the relationship between ethnographers and the people under study. In 1914, he travelled to the Trobriand Islands and ended up spending nearly four years conducting fieldwork among the people there. In the process, he developed a rigorous set of detailed ethnographic techniques he viewed as best-suited to gathering accurate and comprehensive ethnographic data. One of the hallmarks of his method was that it required the researcher to get off the veranda to interact with and even live among the natives. In a well-known book about his research, *Argonauts of the Western Pacific* (1922), Malinowski described his research techniques and the role they played in his analysis of the Kula ceremony, an exchange of coral armbands and trinkets among members of the social elite. He concluded that the ceremonies were at the center of Trobriand life and represented the culmination of an elaborate multi-year venture called the Kula Ring that involved dangerous expeditions and careful planning. Ultimately, the key to his discovering the importance of the ceremony was that he not only observed the Kula Ring but also participated in it. This technique of participant observation is central to anthropological research today. Malinowski did more than just observe people from afar; he actively interacted with them and participated in their daily activities. And unlike early anthropologists who

Figure 4: Bronislaw Malinowski (center) with Trobriand Islanders circa 1918

worked through translators, Malinowski learned the native language, which allowed him to immerse himself in the culture. He carefully documented all of his observations and thoughts. Malinowski's techniques are now central components of ethnographic fieldwork.

Salvage Ethnography

Despite Malinowski's tremendous contributions to ethnography and anthropology generally, he was nevertheless a man of his time. A common view in the first half of the twentieth century was that many "primitive" cultures were quickly disappearing and features of those cultures needed to be preserved (salvaged) before they were lost. Anthropologists such as Malinowski, Franz Boas, and many of their students sought to document, photograph, and otherwise preserve cultural traditions in "dying" cultures among groups such as Native Americans and other traditional societies experiencing rapid change due to modernization, dislocation, and contact with outside groups. They also collected cultural artifacts, removing property from the communities and placing it in museums and private collections.

Others who were not formally trained in the sciences or in anthropology also participated in salvage activities. For instance, in his "documentary" film *Nanook of the North* (1922), Robery Flaherty filmed the life of an Inuit man named Nanook and his family in the Canadian Arctic. In an effort to preserve on film what many believed was a traditional way of life soon to be lost, Flaherty took considerable artistic license to represent the culture as he imagined it was in the past, including staging certain scenes and asking the Inuit men to use spears instead of rifles to make the film seem more "authentic."

Photographers and artists have likewise attempted to capture and preserve traditional indigenous life in paintings and photographs. Renowned painter George Catlin (1796–1872), for example, is known to have embellished scenes or painted them in ways that glossed over the difficult reality that native people in the nineteenth century were actively persecuted by the government, displaced from their lands, and forced into unsustainable lifestyles that led to starvation and warfare. Photographer Edward S. Curtis (1868–1952) has been criticized for reinforcing romanticized images of "authentic" native scenes. In particular, he is accused of having perpetuated the problematic idea of the **noble savage** and, in the process, distracted attention from the serious social, political, and economic problems faced by native people.[2]

Today, anthropologists recognize that human cultures constantly change as people respond to social, political, economic, and other external and internal influences—that there is no moment when a culture is more authentic or more primitive. They acknowledge that culture is fluid and cannot be treated as isolated in time and space. Just as we should not portray people as primitive vestiges of an earlier stage of human development, we also should not romanticize a culture or idealize another's suffering as more authentic or natural.

Holism

In the throes of salvage ethnography, anthropologists in the first half of the twentieth century actively documented anything and everything they could about the cultures they viewed as endangered. They collected artifacts, excavated ancient sites, wrote dictionaries of non-written languages, and documented cultural traditions, stories, and beliefs. In the United States, those efforts developed into what is known today as the four-field approach or simply as general anthropology. This approach integrates multiple scientific and humanistic perspectives into a single comprehensive discipline composed of cultural, archaeological, biological/physical, and linguistic anthropology.

A hallmark of the four-field approach is its holistic perspective: anthropologists are interested in studying everything that makes us human. Thus, they use multiple approaches to understanding humans throughout time and throughout the world. They also acknowledge that to understand people fully one cannot look solely at biology, culture, history, or language; rather, all of those things must be considered. The interrelationships between the four subfields of anthropology are important for many anthropologists today.

Linguistic anthropologists Edward Sapir and Benjamin Whorf, for instance, examined interrelationships between culture, language, and cognition. They argued that the language one speaks plays a critical role in determining how one thinks, particularly in terms of understanding time, space, and matter. They proposed that people who speak different languages view the world differently as a result. In a well-known example, Whorf contrasted the Hopi and English languages. Because verbs in Hopi contained no future or past tenses, Whorf argued that Hopi-speakers understand time in a fundamentally different way than English-speakers. An observation by an English-speaker would focus on the difference in time while an observation by a Hopi-speaker would focus on validity.[3]

Figure 5: A chart from a 1940 publication by Whorf illustrates differences between a "temporal language" (English) and a "timeless" language (Hopi).

In another example, Peter Gordon spent many years living among the Pirahã tribe of Brazil learning their language and culture. He noted that the Pirahã have only three words for numbers: one, two, and many. He also observed that they found it difficult to remember quantities and numbers beyond three even after learning the Portuguese words for such numbers.[4]

Pirahã Numerical Terms:

In this short film, linguist Daniel Everett illustrates Pirahã numerical terms.

Although some scholars have criticized Whorf and Gordon's conclusions as overly deterministic, their work certainly illustrates the presence of a relationship between language and thought and between cultural and biological influences. Words may not force people to think a particular way, but they can influence our thought processes and how we view the world around us. The holistic perspective of anthropology helps us to appreciate that our culture, language, and physical and cognitive capacities for language are interrelated in complex ways.

ETHNOGRAPHY TODAY

Anthropology's Distinctive Research Strategy

Ethnography is cultural anthropology's distinctive research strategy. It was originally developed by anthropologists to study small-scale, relatively isolated cultural groups. Typically, those groups had relatively simple economies and technologies and limited access to larger, more technologically advanced societies. Early ethnographers sought to understand the entirety of a particular culture. They spent months to years living in the community, and in that time, they documented in great detail every dimension of people's lives, including their language, subsistence strategies, political systems, formation of families and marriages, and religious beliefs. This was important because it helped researchers appreciate the interconnectedness of all dimensions of social life. The key to the success of this ethnographic approach was not only to spend considerable time observing people in their home settings engaged in day-to-day activities but also to participate in those activities. Participation informed an emic perspective of the culture, something that had been missing in earlier social science research.

Because of how useful the ethnographic research strategy is in developing an emic perspective, it has been adopted by many other disciplines including sociology, education, psychology, and political science. Education researchers, for example, use ethnography to study children in classrooms to identify their learning strategies and how they understand and make sense of learning experiences. Sociologists use ethnography to study emerging social movements and how participants in such movements stay motivated and connected despite their sometimes-conflicting goals.

New Sites for Ethnographic Fieldwork

Like the cultures and peoples studied, anthropology and ethnography are evolving. Field sites for ethnographic research are no longer exclusively located in far-flung, isolated, non-industrialized societies. Increasingly, anthropologists are conducting ethnographic research in complex, technologically advanced societies such as the United States and in urban environments elsewhere in the world. For instance, my doctoral research took place in the United States. I studied identity formation among **undocumented** Mexican immigrant college students in Minnesota. Because some of my informants were living in Mexico when my fieldwork ended, I also traveled to Veracruz, Mexico, and spent time conducting research there. Often, anthropologists who study migration, **diasporas**, and people in motion must conduct research in multiple locations. This is known as multi-sited ethnography.

Anthropologists use ethnography to study people wherever they are and however they interact with others. Think of the many ways you ordinarily interact with your friends, family, professors, and boss. Is it all face-to-face communication or do you sometimes use text messages to chat with your friends? Do you also sometimes email your professor to ask for clarification on an assignment and then call your boss to discuss your schedule? Do you share funny videos with others on Facebook and then later make a Skype video call to a relative? These new technological "sites" of human interaction are fascinating to many ethnographers and have expanded the definition of fieldwork.

Problem-oriented Research

In the early years, ethnographers were interested in exploring the entirety of a culture. Taking an **inductive** approach, they generally were not concerned about arriving with a relatively narrow pre-defined research topic. Instead, the goal was to explore the people, their culture, and their homelands and what had previously been written about them. The focus of the study was allowed to emerge gradually during their time in the field. Often, this approach to ethnography resulted in rather general ethnographic descriptions.

Today, anthropologists are increasingly taking a more **deductive** approach to ethnographic research. Rather than arriving at the field site with only general ideas about the goals of the study, they tend to select a particular problem before arriving and then let that problem guide their research. In my case, I was interested in how undocumented Mexican immigrant youth in Minnesota formed a sense of identity while living in a society that used a variety of dehumanizing labels such as illegal and alien to refer to them. That was my research "problem," and it oriented and guided my study from beginning to end. I did not document every dimension of my informants' lives; instead, I focused on the things most closely related to my research problem.

Quantitative Methods

Increasingly, cultural anthropologists are using quantitative research methods to complement qualitative approaches. **Qualitative** research in anthropology aims to comprehensively describe human behavior and the contexts in which it occurs while **quantitative** research seeks patterns in numerical data that can explain aspects of human behavior. Quantitative patterns can be gleaned from statistical analyses, maps, charts, graphs, and textual descriptions. Surveys are a common quantitative technique that usually involves closed-ended questions in which respondents select their responses from a list of pre-defined choices such as their degree of agreement or disagreement, multiple-choice answers, and rankings of items. While surveys usually lack the sort of contextual detail associated with qualitative research, they tend to be relatively easy to code numerically and, as a result, can be easier to analyze than qualitative data. Surveys are also useful for gathering specific data points within a large population, something that is challenging to do with many qualitative techniques.

Anthropological nutritional analysis is an area of research that commonly relies on collecting quantitative data. Nutritional anthropologists explore how factors such as culture, the environment, and economic and political systems interplay to impact human health and nutrition. They may count the calories people consume and expend, document patterns of food consumption, measure body weight and body mass, and test for the presence of parasite infections or nutritional deficiencies. In her ethnography *Dancing Skeletons: Life and Death in West Africa* (1993), Katherine Dettwyler described how she conducted nutritional research in Mali, which involved weighing, measuring, and testing her research subjects to collect a variety of quantitative data to help her understand the causes and consequences of child malnutrition.

Mixed Methods

In recent years, anthropologists have begun to combine ethnography with other types of research methods. These mixed-method approaches integrate qualitative and quantitative evidence to provide a more comprehensive analysis. For instance, anthropologists can combine ethnographic data with questionnaires, statistical data, and a media analysis. Anthropologist Leo Chavez used mixed methods to conduct the research for his book *The Latino Threat: Constructing Immigrants, Citizens, and the Nation* (2008). He started with a problem: how has citizenship been discussed as an identity marker in the mainstream media in the United States, especially among those labeled as Latinos. He then looked for a variety of types of data and relied on ethnographic case studies and on quantitative data from surveys and questionnaires. Chavez also analyzed a series of visual images from photographs, magazine covers, and cartoons that depicted Latinos to explore how they are represented in the American mainstream.

Mixed methods can be particularly useful when conducting problem-oriented research on complex, technologically advanced societies such as the United States. Detailed statistical and quantitative data are often available for those types of societies. Additionally, the general population is usually literate and somewhat comfortable with the idea of filling out a questionnaire.

ETHNOGRAPHIC TECHNIQUES AND PERSPECTIVES

Cultural Relativism and Ethnocentrism

The guiding philosophy of modern anthropology is **cultural relativism**—the idea that we should seek to understand another person's beliefs and behaviors from the perspective of their culture rather than our own. Anthropologists do not judge other cultures based on their values nor view other cultural ways of doing things as inferior. Instead, anthropologists seek to understand people's beliefs within the system they have for explaining things.

Cultural relativism is an important methodological consideration when conducting research. In the field, anthropologists must temporarily suspend their own value, moral, and esthetic judgments and seek to understand and respect the values, morals, and esthetics of the other culture on their terms. This can be a challenging task, particularly when a culture is significantly different from the one in which they were raised.

During my first field experience in Brazil, I learned firsthand how challenging cultural relativism could be. Preferences for physical proximity and comfort talking about one's body are among the first differences likely to be noticed by U.S. visitors to Brazil. Compared to Americans, Brazilians generally are much more comfortable standing close, touching, holding hands, and even smelling one another and often discuss each other's bodies. Children and adults commonly refer to each other using playful nicknames that refer to their body size, body shape, or skin color. Neighbors and even strangers frequently stopped me on the street to comment on the color of my skin (It concerned some as being overly pale or pink—Was I ill? Was I sunburned?), the texture of my hair (How did I get it so smooth? Did I straighten my hair?), and my body size and shape ("You have a nice bust, but if you lost a little weight around the middle you would be even more attractive!").

During my first few months in Brazil, I had to remind myself constantly that these comments were not rude, disrespectful, or inappropriate as I would have perceived them to be in the United States. On the contrary, it was one of the ways that people showed affection toward me. From a culturally relativistic perspective, the comments demonstrated that they cared about me, were concerned with my well-being, and wanted me to be part of the community. Had I not taken a culturally relativistic view at the outset and instead judged the actions based on my cultural perspective, I would have been continually frustrated and likely would have confused and offended people in the community. And offending your informants and the rest of the community certainly is not conducive to completing high-quality ethnography! Had I not fully understood the importance of body contact and physical proximity in communication in Brazil, I would have missed an important component of the culture.

Another perspective that has been rejected by anthropologists is **ethnocentrism**—the tendency to view one's own culture as most important and correct and as a stick by which to measure all other cultures. People who are ethnocentric view their own cultures as central and normal and reject all other cultures as inferior and morally suspect. As it turns out, many people and cultures are ethnocentric to some degree; ethnocentrism is a common human experience. Why do we respond the way we do? Why do we behave the way we do? Why do we believe what we believe? Most people find these kinds of questions difficult to answer. Often the answer is simply "because that is how it is done." They believe what they believe because that is what one normally believes and doing things any other way seems wrong.

Ethnocentrism is not a useful perspective in contexts in which people from different cultural backgrounds come into close contact with one another, as is the case in many cities and communities throughout the world. People increasingly find that they must adopt culturally relativistic perspectives in governing communities and as a guide for their interactions with members of the community. For anthropologists in the field, cultural relativism is especially important. We must set aside our innate ethnocentrisms and let cultural relativism guide our inquiries and interactions with others so that our observations are not biased. Cultural relativism is at the core of the discipline of anthropology.

Objectivity and Activist Anthropology

Despite the importance of cultural relativism, it is not always possible and at times is inappropriate to maintain complete objectivity in the field. Researchers may encounter cultural practices that are an affront to strongly held moral values or that violate the human rights of a segment of a population. In other cases, they may be conducting research in part to advocate for a particular issue or for the rights of a marginalized group.

Take, for example, the practice of female genital cutting (FGC), also known as female genital mutilation (FGM), a practice that is common in various regions of the world, especially in parts of Africa and the Middle East. Such practices involving modification of female genitals for non-medical and cultural reasons range from clitoridectomy (partial or full removal of the clitoris) to infibulation, which involves removal of the clitoris and the inner and outer labia and suturing to narrow the vaginal opening, leaving only a small hole for the passage of urine and menstrual fluid Anthropologists working in regions where such practices are common often understandably have a strong negative opinion, viewing the practice as unnecessary medically and posing a risk of serious infection, infertility, and complications from childbirth. They may also be opposed to it because they feel that it violates the right of women to experience sexual pleasure, something they likely view as a fundamental human right. Should the anthropologist intervene to prevent girls and women from being subjected to this practice?

Anthropologist Janice Boddy studied FGC/FGM in rural northern Sudan and sought to explain it from a culturally relativistic perspective. She found that the practice persists, in part, because it is believed to preserve a woman's chastity and curb her sexual desire, making her less likely to have affairs once she is married. Boddy's research showed how the practice makes sense in the context of a culture in which a woman's sexual conduct is a symbol of her family's honor, which is important culturally.[5]

Boddy's relativistic explanation helps make the practice comprehensible and allows cultural outsiders to understand how it is internally culturally coherent. But the question remains. Once anthropologists understand why people practice FGC/FGM, should they accept it? Because they uncover the cultural meaning of a practice, must they maintain a neutral stance or should they fight a practice viewed as an injustice? How does an anthropologist know what is right?

Unfortunately, answers to these questions are rarely simple, and anthropologists as a group do not always agree on an appropriate professional stance and responsibility. Nevertheless, examining practices such as FGC/FGM can help us understand the debate over objectivity versus "activism" in anthropology more clearly. Some anthropologists feel that striving for objectivity in ethnography is paramount. That even if objectivity cannot be completely achieved, anthropologists' ethnography should be free from as much subjective opinion as possible. Others take the opposite stance and produce anthropological research and writing as a means of fighting for equality and justice for disempowered or voiceless groups. The debate over how much (if any) activism is acceptable is ongoing. What is clear is that anthropologists are continuing to grapple with the contentious relationship between objectivity and activism in ethnographic research.

Science and Humanism

Anthropologists have described their field as the most humanistic of the sciences and the most scientific of the humanities. Early anthropologists fought to legitimize anthropology as a robust scientific field of study. To do so, they borrowed methods and techniques from the physical sciences and applied them to anthropological inquiry. Indeed, anthropology today is categorized as a social science in most academic institutions in the United States alongside sociology, psychology, economics, and political science. However, in recent decades, many cultural anthropologists have distanced themselves from science-oriented research and embraced more-humanistic approaches, including symbolic and interpretive perspectives. Interpretive anthropology treats culture as a body of "texts" rather than attempting to test a hypothesis based on deductive or inductive reasoning. The texts present a particular picture from a particular subjective point of view. Interpretive anthropologists believe that it is not necessary (or even possible) to objectively interrogate a text. Rather, they study the texts to untangle the various webs of meaning embedded in them. Consequently, interpretive anthropologists include the context of their interpretations, their own perspectives and, importantly, how the research participants view themselves and the meanings they attribute to their lives.

Anthropologists are unlikely to conclude that a single approach is best. Instead, anthropologists can apply any and all of the approaches that best suit their particular problem. Anthropology is unique among academic disciplines for the diversity of approaches used to conduct research and for the broad range of orientations that fall under its umbrella.

Science in Anthropology:

For a discussion of science in anthropology, see the following article published by the American Anthropological Association: AAA Responds to Public Controversy Over Science in Anthropology.

Ethnographic Techniques

Observation and Participant Observation

Of the various techniques and tools used to conduct ethnographic research, observation in general and participant observation in particular are among the most important. Ethnographers are trained to pay attention to everything happening around them when in the field—from routine daily activities such as cooking dinner to major events such as an annual religious celebration. They observe how people interact with each other, how the environment affects people, and how people affect the environment. It is essential for anthropologists to rigorously document their observations, usually by writing field notes and recording their feelings and perceptions in a personal journal or diary.

As previously mentioned, participant observation involves ethnographers observing while they participate in activities with their informants. This technique is important because it allows the researcher to better understand why people do what they do from an emic perspective. Malinowski noted that participant observation is an important tool by which "to grasp the native's point of view, his relation to life, to realize *his* vision of *his* world."[6]

To conduct participant observation, ethnographers must live with or spend considerable time with their informants to establish a strong rapport with them. Rapport is a sense of trust and a comfortable working relationship in which the informant and the ethnographer are at ease with each other and agreeable to working together.

Participant observation was an important part of my own research. In 2003, I spent six months living in two Mayan villages in highland Chiapas, Mexico. I was conducting ethnographic research on behalf of the Science Museum of Minnesota to document changes in *huipil* textile designs. *Huipiles* (pronounced "we-peel-ays") are a type of hand-woven blouse that Mayan women in the region weave and wear, and every town has its own style and designs. At a large city market, one can easily identify the town each weaver is from by the colors and designs of her *huipiles*. For hundreds of years, *huipil* designs changed very little. Then, starting around 1960, the designs and colors of *huipiles* in some of the towns began to change rapidly. I was interested in learning why some towns' designs were changing more rapidly than other towns' were and in collecting examples of *huipiles* to supplement the museum's existing collection.

I spent time in two towns, Zinacantán and San Andrés Larráinzar. Zinacantán was located near the main city, San Cristóbal de las Casas. It received many tourists each year and had regularly established bus and van routes that locals used to travel to San Cristóbal to buy food and other goods. Some of the men in the town had worked in the United States and returned with money to build or improve their family homes and businesses. Other families were supported by **remittances** from relatives working in the United States or in other parts of Mexico. San Andrés, on the other hand, was relatively isolated and much further from San Cristóbal. Most families there relied on subsistence farming or intermittent agricultural labor and had limited access to tourism or to outside communities. San Andrés was also the site of a major indigenous revolt in the mid-1990s that resulted in greater autonomy, recognition, and rights for indigenous groups throughout Mexico. Politically and socially, it was a progressive community in many ways but remained conservative in others.

I first asked people in Zinacantán why their *huipil* designs, motifs, and colors seemed to change almost every year. Many women said that they did not know. Others stated that weaving was easy and could be boring so they liked to make changes to keep the *huipiles* interesting and to keep weaving from getting dull. When I asked people in San Andrés what they thought about what the women in

Zinacantán had said, the San Andrés women replied that "Yes, perhaps they do get bored easily. But we in San Andrés are superior weavers and we don't need to change our designs." Neither response seemed like the full story behind the difference.

Though I spent hundreds of hours observing women preparing to weave, weaving, and selling their textiles to tourists, I did not truly understand what the women were telling me until I tried weaving myself. When I watched them, the process seemed so easy and simple. They attached strings of thread vertically to two ends of the back-strap looms. When weaving, they increased and decreased the tension on the vertical threads by leaning backward and forward with the back strap and teased individual threads horizontally through the vertical threads to create the desired pattern. After each thread was placed, they pushed it down with great force using a smooth, flat wooden trowel. They did the entire process with great ease and fluidity. When I only watched and did not participate, I could believe the Zinacantán women when they told me weaving was easy.

When I began to weave, it took me several days simply to learn how to sit correctly with a back-strap loom and achieve the appropriate tension. I failed repeatedly at setting up the loom with vertically strung threads and never got close to being able to create a design. Thus, I learned through participant observation that weaving is an exceptionally difficult task. Even expert weavers who had decades of experience sometimes made mistakes as half-finished weavings and rejected textiles littered many homes. Although the women appeared to be able to multi-task while weaving (stoking the fire, calling after small children, cooking food), weaving still required a great deal of concentration to do well.

Through participant observation, I was able to recognize that other factors likely drove the changes in their textiles. I ultimately concluded that the rate of change in *huipil* design in Zinacantán was likely related to the pace of cultural change broadly in the community resulting from interactions between its residents and tourists and relatively frequent travel to a more-urban environment. Participant observation was an important tool in my research and is central to most ethnographic studies today.

Conversations and Interviews

Another primary technique for gathering ethnographic data is simply talking with people—from casual, unstructured conversations about ordinary topics to formal scheduled interviews about a particular topic. An important element for successful conversations and interviews is establishing rapport with informants. Sometimes, engaging in conversation is part of establishing that rapport. Ethnographers frequently use multiple forms of conversation and interviewing for a single research project based on their particular needs. They sometimes record the conversations and interviews with an audio recording device but more often they simply engage in the conversation and then later write down everything they recall about it. Conversations and interviews are an essential part of most ethnographic research designs because spoken communication is central to humans' experiences.

Gathering Life Histories

Collecting a personal narrative of someone's life is a valuable ethnographic technique and is often combined with other techniques. Life histories provide the context in which culture is experienced and created by individuals and describe how individuals have reacted, responded, and contributed to changes that occurred during their lives. They also help anthropologists be more aware of what makes life meaningful to an individual and to focus on the particulars of individual lives, on the tenor of their experiences and the patterns that are important to them. Researchers often include life histories in their ethnographic texts as a way of intimately connecting the reader to the lives of the informants.

The Genealogical Method

The genealogical (kinship) method has a long tradition in ethnography. Developed in the early years of anthropological research to document the family systems of tribal groups, it is still used today to discover connections of **kinship**, descent, marriage, and the overall social system. Because kinship and genealogy are so important in many nonindustrial societies, the technique is used to collect data on important relationships that form the foundation of the society and to trace social relationships more broadly in communities.

When used by anthropologists, the genealogical method involves using symbols and diagrams to document relationships. Circles represent women and girls, triangles represent men and boys, and squares represent ambiguous or unknown gender. Equal signs between individuals represent their union or marriage and vertical lines descending from a union represent parent-child relationships. The death of an individual and the termination of a marriage are denoted by diagonal lines drawn across the shapes and equal signs. Kinship charts are diagramed from the perspective of one person who is called the Ego, and all of the relationships in the chart are based on how the others are related to the Ego. Individuals in a chart are sometimes identified by numbers or names, and an accompanying list provides more-detailed information.

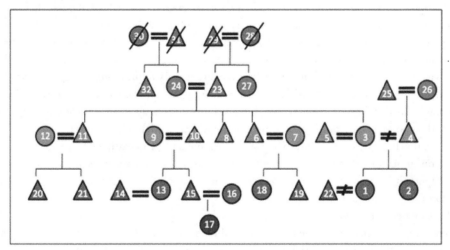

Figure 6: Anthropological kinship chart created by one of Katie Nelson's cultural anthropology students.

Key Informants

Within any culture or subculture, there are always particular individuals who are more knowledgeable about the culture than others and who may have more-detailed or privileged knowledge. Anthropologists conducting ethnographic research in the field often seek out such cultural specialists to gain a greater understanding of certain issues and to answer questions they otherwise could not answer. When an anthropologist establishes a rapport with these individuals and begins to rely more on them for information than on others, the cultural specialists are referred to as key informants or key cultural consultants.

Key informants can be exceptional assets in the field, allowing the ethnographer to uncover the meanings of behaviors and practices the researcher cannot otherwise understand. Key informants can also help researchers by directly observing others and reporting those observations to the researchers, especially in situations in which the researcher is not allowed to be present or when the researcher's presence could alter the participants' behavior. In addition, ethnographers can check information they obtained from other informants, contextualize it, and review it for accuracy. Having a key informant in the field is like having a research ally. The relationship can grow and become enormously fruitful.

A famous example of the central role that key informants can play in an ethnographer's research is a man named Doc in William Foote Whyte's *Street Corner Society* (1943). In the late 1930s, Whyte studied social relations between street gangs and "corner boys" in a Boston urban slum inhabited by first- and second-generation Italian immigrants. A social worker introduced Whyte to Doc and the two hit it off. Doc proved instrumental to the success of Whyte's research. He introduced Whyte to his family and social group and vouched for him in the tight-knit community, providing access that Whyte could not have gained otherwise.

Field Notes

Field notes are indispensable when conducting ethnographic research. Although making such notes is time-consuming, they form the primary record of one's observations. Generally speaking, ethnographers write two kinds of notes: field notes and personal reflections. Field notes are detailed descriptions of everything the ethnographer observes and experiences. They include specific details about what happened at the field site, the ethnographer's sensory impressions, and specific words and phrases used by the people observed. They also frequently include the content of conversations the ethnographer had and things the ethnographer overheard others say. Ethnographers also sometimes include their personal reflections on the experience of writing field notes. Often, brief notes are jotted down in a notebook while the anthropologist is observing and participating in activities. Later, they expand on those quick notes to make more formal field notes, which may be organized and typed into a report. It is common for ethnographers to spend several hours a day writing and organizing field notes.

Ethnographers often also keep a personal journal or diary that may include information about their emotions and personal experiences while conducting research. These personal reflections can be as important as the field notes. Ethnography is not an objective science. Everything researchers do and experience in the field is filtered through their personal life experiences. Two ethnographers may experience a situation in the field in different ways and understand the experience differently. For this reason, it is important for researchers to be aware of their reactions to situations and be mindful of how their life experiences affect their perceptions. In fact, this sort of reflexive insight can turn out to be a useful data source and analytical tool that improves the researcher's understanding.

The work of anthropologist Renato Rosaldo provides a useful example of how anthropologists can use their emotional responses to fieldwork situations to advance their research. In 1981, Rosaldo and his wife, Michelle, were conducting research among the Ilongots of Northern Luzon in the Philippines. Rosaldo was studying men in the community who engaged in emotional rampages in which they violently murdered others by cutting off their heads. Although the practice had been banned by the time Rosaldo arrived, a longing to continue headhunting remained in the cultural psyche of the community.

Whenever Rosaldo asked a man why he engaged in headhunting, the answer was that rage and grief caused him to kill others. At the beginning of his fieldwork, Rosaldo felt that the response was overly simplistic and assumed that there had to be more to it than that. He was frustrated because he could not uncover a deeper understanding of the phenomenon. Then, on October 11, 1981, Rosaldo's wife was walking along a ravine when she tripped, lost her footing, and fell 65 feet to her death, leaving Rosaldo a grieving single father. In his essay "Grief and a Headhunter's Rage," Rosaldo later wrote that it was his own struggle with rage as he grieved for his wife that helped him truly grasp what the Ilongot men meant when they described their grief and rage.

> Only a week before completing the initial draft of an earlier version of this introduction, I rediscovered my journal entry, written some six weeks after Michelle's death, in which I made a vow to myself about how I would return to writing anthropology, if I ever did so, by writing Grief and a Headhunter's Rage . . . My journal went on to reflect more broadly on death, rage, and headhunting by speaking of my wish for the Ilongot solution; they are much more in touch with reality than Christians. So, I need a place to carry my anger – and can we say a solution of the imagination is better than theirs? And can we condemn them when we napalm villages? Is our rationale so much sounder than theirs? All this was written in despair and rage.[7]

Only through the very personal and emotionally devastating experience of losing his wife was Rosaldo able to understand the emic perspective of the headhunters. The result was an influential and insightful ethnographic account.

ETHICAL CONSIDERATIONS

Ethical Guidelines

From the earliest days of anthropology as a discipline, concern about the ethical treatment of people who take part in studies has been an important consideration. Ethical matters are central to any research project and anthropologists take their ethical responsibilities particularly seriously. As discussed throughout this chapter, anthropologists are oriented toward developing empathy for their informants and understanding their cultures and experiences from an emic perspective. Many also have a sense of personal responsibility for the well-being of the local people with whom they work in the field.

The American Anthropological Association has developed a Code of Ethics that all anthropologists should follow in their work. Among the many ethical responsibilities outlined in the code, doing no harm, obtaining informed consent, maintaining subjects' anonymity, and making the results of the research accessible are especially important responsibilities.

Do No Harm

First and foremost, anthropologists must ensure that their involvement with a community does not harm or embarrass their informants. Researchers must carefully consider any potential harm associated with the research, including legal, emotional, political, economic, social, and cultural dimensions, and take steps to insulate their informants from such harm. Since it is not always possible to anticipate every potential repercussion at the outset, anthropologists also must continually monitor their work to ensure that their research design and methods minimize any risk.

Regrettably, the proscription to do no harm is a deceptively complex requirement. Despite their best efforts, anthropologists have run into ethical problems in the field. Work by Napoleon Chagnon among an isolated indigenous tribe of the Amazon, the Yanomami, is a well-known example of ethical problems in anthropological research. In his groundbreaking ethnography *Yanomamö: The Fierce People* (1968), Chagnon portrayed the Yanomami as an intensely violent and antagonistic people. The ethnography was well received initially. However, not long after its publication, controversy erupted. Anthropologists and other scholars have accused Chagnon of encouraging the violence he documented, staging fights and scenes for documentary films and fabricating data.

Today, Do No Harm is a central ethical value in anthropology. However, it can be difficult to predict every challenge one may encounter in the field or after the work is published. Anthropologists must continually reevaluate their research and writing to ensure that it does not harm the informants or their communities. Before fieldwork begins, researchers from universities, colleges, and institutions usually must submit their research agendas to an institutional review board (IRB). IRBs review research plans to ensure that the proposed studies will not harm human subjects. In many cases, the IRB is aware of the unique challenges and promise of anthropological research and can guide the researcher in eliminating or mitigating potential ethical problems.

Obtain Informed Consent

In addition to taking care to do no harm, anthropologists must obtain informed consent from all of their informants before conducting any research. Informed consent is the informant's agreement to take part in the study. Originally developed in the context of medical and psychological research, this ethical guideline is also relevant to anthropology. Informants must be aware of who the anthropologist is and the research topic, who is financially and otherwise supporting the research, how the research will be used, and who will have access to it. Finally, their participation must be *optional* and not coerced. They should be able to stop participating at any time and be aware of and comfortable with any risks associated with their participation.

In medical and psychological research settings in the United States, researchers typically obtain informed consent by asking prospective participants to sign a document that outlines the research and the risks involved in their participation, acknowledging that they agree to take part. In some anthropological contexts, however, this type of informed consent may not be appropriate. People may not trust the state, bureaucratic processes, or authority, for example. Asking them to sign a formal legal-looking document may intimidate them. Likewise, informed consent cannot be obtained with a signed document if many in the community cannot read. The anthropologist must determine the most appropriate way to obtain informed consent in the context of the particular research setting.

Maintain Anonymity and Privacy

Another important ethical consideration for anthropologists in the field is ensuring the anonymity and privacy of informants who need such protection. When I did research among undocumented Mexican immigrant college students, I recognized that my informants' legal status put them at considerable risk. I took care to use pseudonyms for all of the informants, even when writing field notes. In my writing, I changed the names of the informants' relatives, friends, schools, and work places to protect them from being identified. Maintaining privacy and anonymity is an important way for anthropologists to ensure that their involvement does no harm.

Make Results Accessible

Finally, anthropologists must always make their final research results accessible to their informants and to other researchers. For informants, a written report in the researcher's native language may not be the best way to convey the results. Reports can be translated or the results can be converted into a more accessible format. Examples of creative ways in which anthropologists have made their results available include establishing accessible databases for their research data, contributing to existing databases, producing films that portray the results, and developing texts or recommendations that provide tangible assistance to the informants' communities. Though it is not always easy to make research results accessible in culturally appropriate ways, it is essential that others have the opportunity to review and benefit from the research, especially those who participated in its creation.

WRITING ETHNOGRAPHY

Analysis and Interpretation of Research Findings

Once all or most of the fieldwork is complete, ethnographers analyze their data and research findings before beginning to write. There are many techniques for data analysis from which to choose based on the strategy and goals of the research. Regardless of the particular technique, data analysis involves a systematic interpretation of what the researcher thinks the data mean. The ethnographer reviews all of the data collected, synthesizes findings from the review, and integrates those findings with prior studies on the topic. Once the analysis is complete, the ethnographer is ready to write an account of the fieldwork.

Ethnographic Authority

In recent years, anthropologists have expressed concern about how ethnographies should be written in terms of ethnographic authority: how ethnographers present themselves and their informants in text. In a nonfiction text, the author is a mediator between readers and the topic and the text is written to help readers understand an unfamiliar topic. In an ethnography, the topic is people, and people naturally vary in terms of their thoughts, opinions, beliefs, and perspectives. That is, they have individual voices. In the past, anthropologists commonly wrote ethnographic accounts as if they possessed the ultimate most complete scientific knowledge on the topic. Subsequently, anthropologists began to challenge that writing style, particularly when it did not include the voices of their informants in the text and analysis. Some of this criticism originated with feminist anthropologists who noted that women's experiences and perspectives frequently were omitted and misrepresented in this style of writing. Others believed that this style of writing reinforced existing global power dynamics and privileges afforded to Western anthropologists' voices as most important.

Polyvocality

In response to criticisms about ethnographic authority, anthropologists have begun to include polyvocality. A polyvocal text is one in which more than one person's voice is presented, and its use can range from ensuring that informants' perspectives are presented in the text while still writing in the researcher's voice to including informants' actual words rather than paraphrasing them and co-authoring the ethnography with an informant. A good example of polyvocality is anthropologist Ruth Behar's book *Translated Woman: Crossing the Border with Esperanza's Story* (1993). Behar's book documents the life story of a Mexican street peddler, Esperanza Hernández, and their unique friendship. Large sections of the book are in Esperanza's own words and discuss issues that are important to her. Behar also includes pieces of her own life story and an anthropological analysis of Esperanza's story.

By using polyvocality, researchers can avoid writing from the perspective of the ultimate ethnographic authority. A polyvocal style also allows readers to be more involved in the text since they have the opportunity to form their own opinions about the ethnographic data and perhaps even critique the author's analysis. It also encourages anthropologists to be more transparent when presenting their methods and data.

Reflexivity

Reflexivity is another relatively new approach to ethnographic research and writing. Beginning in the 1960s, social science researchers began to think more carefully about the effects of their life experiences, status, and roles on their research and analyses. They began to insert themselves into their texts, including information about their personal experiences, thoughts, and life stories and to analyze in the accounts how those characteristics affected their research and analysis.

Adoption of reflexivity is perhaps the most significant change in how ethnography is researched and written in the past 50 years. It calls on anthropologists to acknowledge that they are part of the world they study and thus can never truly be objective. Reflexivity has also contributed to anthropologists' appreciation of the unequal power dynamics of research and the effects those dynamics can have on the results. Reflexivity reminds the ethnographer that there are multiple ways to interpret any given cultural scenario. By acknowledging how their backgrounds affect their interpretations, anthropologists can begin to remove themselves from the throne of ethnographic authority and allow other, less-empowered voices to be heard.

DISCUSSION QUESTIONS

1. If you were to conduct anthropological fieldwork anywhere in the world, were would you go? What would you study? Why? Which ethnographic techniques would you use? What kinds of ethical considerations would you likely encounter? How would you disseminate your research?
2. What is unique about ethnographic fieldwork and how did it emerge as a key strategy in anthropology?

3. How do traditional approaches to ethnographic fieldwork contrast with contemporary approaches?
4. What are some of the contemporary ethnographic fieldwork techniques and perspectives and why are they important to anthropology?
5. What are some of the ethical considerations in doing anthropological fieldwork and why are they important?
6. How do anthropologists transform their fieldwork data into a story that communicates meaning? How are reflexivity and polyvocality changing the way anthropologists communicate their work?

GLOSSARY

Contested identity: a dispute within a group about the collective identity or identities of the group.

Cultural relativism: the idea that we should seek to understand another person's beliefs and behaviors from the perspective of their own culture and not our own.

Deductive: reasoning from the general to the specific; the inverse of inductive reasoning. Deductive research is more common in the natural sciences than in anthropology. In a deductive approach, the researcher creates a hypothesis and then designs a study to prove or disprove the hypothesis. The results of deductive research can be generalizable to other settings.

Diaspora: the scattering of a group of people who have left their original homeland and now live in various locations. Examples of people living in the diaspora are Salvadoran immigrants in the United States and Europe, Somalian refugees in various countries, and Jewish people living around the world.

Emic: a description of the studied culture from the perspective of a member of the culture or insider.

Ethnocentrism: the tendency to view one's own culture as most important and correct and as the stick by which to measure all other cultures.

Ethnography: the in-depth study of the everyday practices and lives of a people.

Etic: a description of the studied culture from the perspective of an observer or outsider.

Indigenous: people who have continually lived in a particular location for a long period of time (prior to the arrival of others) or who have historical ties to a location and who are culturally distinct from the dominant population surrounding them. Other terms used to refer to indigenous people are aboriginal, native, original, first nation, and first people. Some examples of indigenous people are Native Americans of North America, Australian Aborigines, and the Berber (or Amazigh) of North Africa.

Inductive: a type of reasoning that uses specific information to draw general conclusions. In an inductive approach, the researcher seeks to collect evidence without trying to definitively prove or disprove a hypothesis. The researcher usually first spends time in the field to become familiar with the people before identifying a hypothesis or research question. Inductive research usually is not generalizable to other settings.

Key Informants: individuals who are more knowledgeable about their culture than others and who are particularly helpful to the anthropologist.

Kinship: blood ties, common ancestry, and social relationships that form families within human groups.

Land tenure: how property rights to land are allocated within societies, including how permissions are granted to access, use, control, and transfer land.

Noble savage: an inaccurate way of portraying indigenous groups or minority cultures as innocent, childlike, or uncorrupted by the negative characteristics of "civilization."

Participant observation: a type of observation in which the anthropologist observes while participating in the same activities in which her informants are engaged.

Qualitative: anthropological research designed to gain an in-depth, contextualized understanding of human behavior.

Quantitative: anthropological research that uses statistical, mathematical, and/or numerical data to study human behavior.

Remittances: money that migrants laboring outside of the region or country send back to their hometowns and families. In Mexico, remittances make up a substantial share of the total income of some towns' populations.

Thick description: a term coined by anthropologist Clifford Geertz in his 1973 book *The Interpretation of Cultures* to describe a detailed description of the studied group that not only explains the behavior or cultural event in question but also the context in which it occurs and anthropological interpretations of it.

Undocumented: the preferred term for immigrants who live in a country without formal authorization from the state. Undocumented refers to the fact that these people lack the official documents that would legally permit them to reside in the country. Other terms such as illegal immigrant and illegal alien are often used to refer to this population. Anthropologists consider those terms to be discriminatory and dehumanizing. The word undocumented acknowledges the human dignity and cultural and political ties immigrants have developed in their country of residence despite their inability to establish formal residence permissions.

ABOUT THE AUTHOR

Katie Nelson, PhD is a professor of anthropology at Inver Hills Community College. Her current research focuses on identity, belonging and citizenship(s) among migrant and undocumented populations in the U.S., Mexico and Morocco. She is particularly interested in examining how migrants forge a sense of identity and belonging in the contexts of national discourses that problematize their presence. She serves as the incoming Chair-elect of the Teaching Anthropology Interest Group, a part of the General Anthropology Division of the American Anthropological Association. She is fluent in the Spanish and Portuguese languages and is currently learning French and Arabic. Katie received her BA in Anthropology and Latin American Studies from Macalester College, her MA in Anthropology from the University of California, Santa Barbara, an MA in Education and Instructional Technology from the University of Saint Thomas and her PhD from CIESAS Occidente

(Centro de Investigaciones y Estudios Superiores en Antropología Social – Center for Research and Higher Education in Social Anthropology), based in Guadalajara, Mexico.

BIBLIOGRAPHY

Behar, Ruth. *Translated Woman: Crossing the Border with Esperanza's Story*. Boston, MA: Beacon Press, 1993.

Boddy, Janice. *Civilizing Women: British Crusades in Colonial Sudan*. Princeton, NJ: Princeton University Press, 2007.

Chagnon, Napoleon. *Yanomamö: The Fierce People*. New York: Holt, Rinehart and Winston, 1968.

Chavez, Leo. *The Latino Threat: Constructing Immigrants, Citizens and the Nation*. Stanford: Stanford University Press, 2008.

Dettwyler, Katherine A. *Dancing Skeletons: Life and Death in West Africa*. Long Grove, IL: Waveland Press, 2014

Frazer, James. *The Golden Bough: A Study in Comparative Religion*. London: Macmillian Press, 1894.

Geertz, Clifford. *The Interpretation of Cultures: Selected Essays*. New York: Basic Books, 1973.

Gordon, Peter. "Numerical Cognition without Words: Evidence from Amazonia." *Science* 306 no. 5695 (2004): 496–499.

Malinowski, Bronislaw. *Argonauts of the Western Pacific: An Account of Native Enterprise and Adventure in the Archipelagoes of Melanesian New Guinea*. London: Kegan Paul 1922.

Mead, Margaret. *Coming of Age in Samoa: A Psychological Study of Primitive Youth for Western Civilization*. New York: William Morrow and Company, 1928.

Miner, Horace. "Body Ritual Among the Nacirema." *American Anthropologist* 58 no. 3 (1956): 503-507.

Nelson, Katherine. 2015. *Between Citizenship and Alienage: Flexible Identity Among Informally Authorized Mexican College Students in Minnesota*, USA. PhD diss., CIESAS Occidente (Centro de Investigaciones y Estudios Superiores en Antropología Social – Institute for Research and Higher Education in Social Anthropology).

Rosaldo, Renato. "Grief and a Headhunter's Rage" in *Violence in War and Peace,* edited by Nancy Scheper-Hughes and Philippe I. Bourgois, 150-156. Malden, MA: Blackwell, 2004.

Scheper-Hughes, Nancy. *Saints, Scholars, Schizophrenics: Mental Illness in Rural Ireland*. Los Angeles, CA: University of California Press, 1979.

Whorf, Benjamin Lee. "Science and Linguistics." *MIT Technology Review*: 42 (1940): 229–248.

Whyte, William Foote. *Street Corner Society: The Social Structure of an Italian Slum*. Chicago: University of Chicago Press, 1993[1943].

NOTES

1. Franz Boas, "Foreward," in *Coming of Age in Samoa* by Margaret Mead (New York: William Morrow, 1928).
2. Examples of Curtis' photography can be found in Edward Curtis, *The North American Indian: The Photographic Images* (New York: Aperture, 2005).
3. Benjamin Lee Whorf, "Science and Linguistics," *MIT Technology Review* 42 (1940): 229–248.
4. Peter Gordon, "Numerical Cognition Without Words: Evidence from Amazonia," Science 306 no. 5695 (2004): 496–499.
5. Janice Bodd, *Civilizing Women: British Crusades in Colonial Sudan* (Princeton NJ: Princeton University Press, 2007).
6. Bronislaw Malinowski, *Argonauts of the Western Pacific: An Account of Native Enterprise and Adventure in the Archipelagoes of Melanesian New Guinea* (London: Kegan Paul, 1922), 25.
7. Renato Rosaldo, "Grief and a Headhunter's Rage," in *Violence in War and Peace*, ed. Nancy Scheper-Hughes and Philippe I. Bourgois (Malden, MA: Blackwell, 2004), 171.

LANGUAGE #4

Linda Light, California State University, Long Beach
Linda.Light@csulb.edu

LEARNING OBJECTIVES

- Explain the relationship between human language and culture.

- Identify the universal features of human languages and the design features that make them unique.

- Describe the structures of language: phonemes, morphemes, syntax, semantics, and pragmatics.

- Assess the relationship between language variations and ethnic or cultural identity.

- Explain how language is affected by social class, ethnicity, gender and other aspects of identity.

- Evaluate the reasons why languages change and efforts that can be made to preserve endangered languages.

THE IMPORTANCE OF HUMAN LANGUAGE TO HUMAN CULTURE

Students in my cultural anthropology classes are required to memorize a six-point thumbnail definition of culture, which includes all of the features most anthropologists agree are key to its essence. Then, I refer back to the definition as we arrive at each relevant unit in the course. Here it is—with the key features in bold type.

> Culture is:
> 1. An integrated system of *mental elements* (beliefs, values, worldview, attitudes, norms), the *behaviors* motivated by those mental elements, and the *material items* created by those behaviors;
> 2. A system shared by the members of the society;
> 3. 100 percent learned, not innate;
> 4. Based on symbolic systems, the most important of which is language;
> 5. Humankind's most important adaptive mechanism, and
> 6. Dynamic, constantly changing.

This definition serves to underscore the crucial importance of language to all human cultures. In fact, human language can be considered a culture's most important feature since complex human culture could not exist without language and language could not exist without culture. They are inseparable because language encodes culture and provides the means through which culture is shared and passed from one generation to the next. Humans think in language and do all cultural activities using language. It surrounds our every waking and sleeping moments, although we do not usually think about its importance. For that matter, humans do not think about their immersion in culture either, much as fish, if they were endowed with intelligence, would not think much about the water that surrounds them. Without language and culture, humans would be just an-

1

other great ape. Anthropologists must have skills in linguistics so they can learn the languages and cultures of the people they study.

All human languages are symbolic systems that make use of symbols to convey meaning. A **symbol** is anything that serves to refer to something else, but has a meaning that cannot be guessed because there is no obvious connection between the symbol and its referent. This feature of human language is called **arbitrariness**. For example, many cultures assign meanings to certain colors, but the meaning for a particular color may be completely different from one culture to another. Western cultures like the United States use the color black to represent death, but in China it is the color white that symbolizes death. White in the United States symbolizes purity and is used for brides' dresses, but no Chinese woman would ever wear white to her wedding. Instead, she usually wears red, the color of good luck. Words in languages are symbolic in the same way. The word *key* in English is pronounced exactly the same as the word *qui* in French, meaning "who," and *ki* in Japanese, meaning "tree." One must learn the language in order to know what any word means.

THE BIOLOGICAL BASIS OF LANGUAGE

The human anatomy that allowed the development of language emerged six to seven million years ago when the first human ancestors became bipedal—habitually walking on two feet. Most other mammals are quadrupedal—they move about on four feet. This evolutionary development freed up the forelimbs of human ancestors for other activities, such as carrying items and doing more and more complex things with their hands. It also started a chain of anatomical adaptations. One adaptation was a change in the way the skull was placed on the spine. The skull of quadrupedal animals is attached to the spine at the back of the skull because the head is thrust forward. With the new upright bipedal position of pre-humans, the attachment to the spine moved toward the center of the base of the skull. This skeletal change in turn brought about changes in the shape and position of the mouth and throat anatomy.

Humans have all the same organs in the mouth and throat that the other great apes have, but the **larynx**, or voice box (you may know it as the Adam's apple), is in a lower position in the throat in humans. This creates a longer **pharynx**, or throat cavity, which functions as a resonating and amplifying chamber for the speech sounds emitted by the larynx. The rounding of the shape of the tongue and **palate**, or the roof of the mouth, enables humans to make a greater variety of sounds than any great ape is capable of making (see Figure 1).

Speech is produced by exhaling air from the lungs, which passes through the larynx. The voice is created by the vibration of the vocal folds in the larynx when they are pulled tightly together, leaving a narrow slit for the air to pass through under pressure. The narrower the slit,

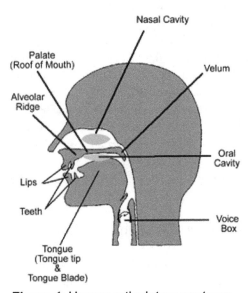

Figure 1: Human articulatory anatomy.

the higher the pitch of the sound produced. The sound waves in the exhaled air pass through the pharynx then out through the mouth and/or the nose. The different positions and movements of the articulators—the tongue, the lips, the jaw—produce the different speech sounds.

Along with the changes in mouth and throat anatomy that made speech possible came a gradual enlargement and compartmentalization of the brain of human ancestors over millions of years. The modern human brain is among the largest, in proportion to body size, of all animals. This development was crucial to language ability because a tremendous amount of brain power is required to process, store, produce, and comprehend the complex system of any human language and its associated culture. In addition, two areas in the left brain are specifically dedicated to the processing of language; no other species has them. They are Broca's area in the left frontal lobe near the temple, and Wernicke's area, in the temporal lobe just behind the left ear.

Language Acquisition in Childhood

Linguist Noam Chomsky proposed that all languages share the properties of what he called **Universal Grammar (UG)**, a basic template for all human languages, which he believed was embedded in our genes, hard-wiring the brains of all human children to acquire language. Although the theory of UG is somewhat controversial, it is a fact that all normally developing human infants have an innate ability to acquire the language or languages used around them. Without any formal instruction, children easily acquire the sounds, words, grammatical rules, and appropriate social functions of the language(s) that surround them. They master the basics by about age three or four. This also applies to children, both deaf and hearing, who are exposed to signed language.

If a child is not surrounded by people who are using a language, that child will gradually lose the ability to acquire language naturally without effort. If this deprivation continues until puberty, the child will no longer be biologically capable of attaining native fluency in any language, although they might be able to achieve a limited competency. This phenomenon has been called the **Critical Age Range Hypothesis**. A number of abused children who were isolated from language input until they were past puberty provide stark evidence to support this hypothesis. The classic case of "Genie" is an example of this evidence.[1] Found at the age of almost 14, Genie had been confined for all of her life to her room and, since the age of two, had been tied to a potty chair during the day and to a crib at night with almost no verbal interaction and only minimal attention to her physical needs. After her rescue, a linguist worked with her intensively for about five years in an attempt to help her learn to talk, but she never achieved language competence beyond that of a two-year old child. The hypothesis also applies to the acquisition of a second language. A person who starts the study of another language after puberty will have to exert a great deal of effort and will rarely achieve native fluency, especially in pronunciation. There is plenty of evidence for this in the U.S. educational system. You might very well have had this same experience. It makes you wonder why our schools rarely offer foreign language classes before the junior high school level.

The Gesture Call System and Non-Verbal Human Communication

All animals communicate and many animals make meaningful sounds. Others use visual signs, such as facial expressions, color changes, body postures and movements, light (fireflies), or electricity (some eels). Many use the sense of smell and the sense of touch. Most animals use a combination of two or more of these systems in their communication, but their systems are **closed systems** in that they cannot create new meanings or messages. Human communication is an **open system** that can easily create new meanings and messages. Most animal communication systems are basically innate; they do not have to learn them, but some species' systems entail a certain amount of learning. For example, songbirds have the innate ability to produce the typical songs of their species, but most of them must be taught how to do it by older birds.

Great apes and other primates have relatively complex systems of communication that use varying combinations of sound, body language, scent, facial expression, and touch. Their systems have therefore been referred to as a **gesture-call system**. Humans share a number of forms of this gesture-call, or non-verbal system with the great apes. Spoken language undoubtedly evolved embedded within it. All human cultures have not only verbal languages, but also non-verbal systems that are consistent with their verbal languages and cultures and vary from one culture to another. We will discuss the three most important human non-verbal communication systems.

Figure 2: Chimpanzees and other great apes use gesture-call communication systems.

Kinesics

Kinesics is the term used to designate all forms of human body language, including gestures, body position and movement, facial expressions, and eye contact. Although all humans can potentially perform these in the same way, different cultures may have different rules about how to use them. For example, eye contact for Americans is highly valued as a way to show we are paying attention and as a means of showing respect. But for the Japanese, eye contact is usually inappropriate, especially between two people of different social statuses. The lower status person must look down and avoid eye contact to show respect for the higher status person.

Facial expressions can convey a host of messages, usually related to the person's attitude or emotional state. Hand gestures may convey unconscious messages, or constitute deliberate messages that can replace or emphasize verbal ones.

Proxemics

Proxemics is the study of the social use of space, specifically the distance an individual tries to maintain around himself in interactions with others. The size of the "space bubble" depends on a number of social factors, including the relationship between the two people, their relative status, their gender and age, their current attitude toward each other, and above all their culture. In some cultures, such as in Brazil, people typically interact in a relatively close physical space, usually along with a lot of touching. Other cultures, like the Japanese, prefer to maintain a greater distance with a minimum amount of touching or none at all. If one person stands too far away from the other according to cultural standards, it might convey the message of emotional distance. If a person invades the culturally recognized space bubble of another, it could mean a threat. Or, it might show a desire for a closer relationship. It all depends on who is involved.

Paralanguage

Paralanguage refers to those characteristics of speech beyond the actual words spoken. These include the features that are inherent to all speech: pitch, loudness, and tempo or duration of the sounds. Varying pitch can convey any number of messages: a question, sarcasm, defiance, surprise, confidence or lack of it, impatience, and many other often subtle connotations. An utterance that is shouted at close range usually conveys an emotional element, such as anger or urgency. A word or syllable that is held for an undue amount of time can intensify the impact of that word. For example, compare "It's beautiful" versus It's beauuuuu-tiful!" Often the latter type of expression is further emphasized by extra loudness of the syllable, and perhaps higher pitch; all can serve to make a part of the utterance more important. Other paralinguistic features that often accompany speech might be a chuckle, a sigh or sob, deliberate throat clearing, and many other non-verbal sounds like "hm," "oh," "ah," and "um."

Most non-verbal behaviors are unconsciously performed and not noticed unless someone violates the cultural standards for them. In fact, a deliberate violation itself can convey meaning. Other non-verbal behaviors are done consciously like the U.S. gestures that indicate approval, such as thumbs up, or making a circle with your thumb and forefinger—"OK." Other examples are waving at someone or putting a forefinger to your lips to quiet another person. Many of these deliberate gestures have different meanings (or no meaning at all) in other cultures. For example, the gestures of approval in U.S. culture mentioned above may be obscene or negative gestures in another culture.

> Try this: As an experiment in the power of non-verbal communication, try violating one of the cultural rules for proxemics or eye contact with a person you know. Choosing your "guinea pigs" carefully (they might get mad at you!), try standing or sitting a little closer or farther away from them than you usually would for a period of time, until they notice (and they will notice). Or, you could choose to give them a bit too much eye contact, or too little, while you are conversing with them. Note how they react to your behavior and how long it takes them to notice.

HUMAN LANGUAGE COMPARED WITH THE COMMUNICATION SYSTEMS OF OTHER SPECIES

Human language is qualitatively and quantitatively different from the communication systems of all other species of animals. Linguists have long tried to create a working definition that distinguishes it from non-human communication systems. Linguist Charles Hockett's solution was to create a hierarchical list of what he called **design features**, or descriptive characteristics, of the communication systems of all species, including that of humans.[2] Those features of human language not shared with any other species illustrate exactly how it differs from all other species.

> ### Hockett's Design Features
>
> The communication systems of all species share the following features:
>
> 1. **A mode of communication** by which messages are transmitted through a system of signs, using one or more sensory systems to transmit and interpret, such as vocal-auditory, visual, tactile, or kinesic;

2. **Semanticity**: the signs carry meaning for the users, and

3. **Pragmatic function**: all signs serve a useful purpose in the life of the users, from survival functions to influencing others' behavior.

Some communication systems (including humans) also exhibit the following features:

4. **Interchangeability**: the ability of individuals within a species to both send and receive messages. One species that lacks this feature is the honeybee. Only a female "worker bee" can perform the dance that conveys to her hive-mates the location of a newly discovered food source. Another example is the mockingbird whose songs are performed only by the males to attract a mate and mark his territory.

5. **Cultural transmission**: the need for some aspects of the system to be learned through interaction with others, rather than being 100 percent innate or genetically programmed. The mockingbird learns its songs from other birds, or even from other sounds in its environment that appeal to it.

6. **Arbitrariness**: the form of a sign is not inherently or logically related to its meaning; signs are symbols. It could be said that the movements in the honeybees' dance are arbitrary since anyone who is not a honeybee could not interpret their meaning.

Only true human language also has the following characteristics:

7. **Discreteness**: every human language is made up of a small number of meaningless discrete sounds. That is, the sounds can be isolated from each other, for purposes of study by linguists, or to be represented in a writing system.

8. **Duality of patterning** (two levels of combination): at the first level of patterning, these meaningless discrete sounds, called **phonemes,** are combined to form words and parts of words that carry meaning, or **morphemes**. In the second level of patterning, morphemes are recombined to form an infinite possible number of longer messages such as phrases and sentences according to a set of rules called **syntax**. It is this level of combination that is entirely lacking in the communication abilities of all other animals and makes human language an open system while all other animal systems are closed.

9. **Displacement**: the ability to communicate about things that are outside of the here and now made possible by the features of discreteness and duality of patterning. While other species are limited to communicating about their immediate time and place, we can talk about any time in the future or past, about any place in the universe, or even fictional places.

10. **Productivity/creativity**: the ability to produce and understand messages that have never been expressed before or to express new ideas. People do not speak according to prepared scripts, as if they were in a movie or a play; they create their utterances spontaneously, according to the rules of their language. It also makes possible the creation of new words and even the ability to lie.

A number of great apes, including gorillas, chimpanzees, bonobos and orangutans, have been taught human sign languages with all of the human design features. In each case, the apes have been able to communicate as humans do to an extent, but their linguistic abilities are reduced by the limited cognitive abilities that accompany their smaller brains.

UNIVERSALS OF LANGUAGE

Languages we do not speak or understand may sound like meaningless babble to us, but all the human languages that have ever been studied by linguists are amazingly similar. They all share a number of characteristics, which linguists call **language universals.** These language universals can be considered properties of the Universal Grammar that Chomsky proposed. Here is a list of some of the major ones.

1. All human cultures have a human language and use it to communicate.
2. All human languages change over time, a reflection of the fact that all cultures are also constantly changing.
3. All languages are systematic, rule driven, and equally complex overall, and equally capable of expressing any idea that the speaker wishes to convey. There are no primitive languages.
4. All languages are symbolic systems.
5. All languages have a basic word order of elements, like subject, verb, and object, with variations.
6. All languages have similar basic grammatical categories such as nouns and verbs.
7. Every spoken language is made up of **discrete** sounds that can be categorized as vowels or consonants.
8. The underlying structure of all languages is characterized by the feature **duality of patterning**, which permits any speaker to utter any message they need or wish to convey, and any speaker of the same language to understand the message.

DESCRIPTIVE LINGUISTICS: STRUCTURES OF LANGUAGE

The study of the structures of language is called descriptive linguistics. Descriptive linguists discover and describe the phonemes of a language, research called **phonology**. They study the **lexicon** (the vocabulary) of a language and how the morphemes are used to create new words, or **morphology.** They analyze the rules by which speakers create phrases and sentences, or the study of **syntax.** And they look at how these features all combine to convey meaning in certain social contexts, fields of study called **semantics** and **pragmatics**.

The Sounds of Language: Phonemes

A **phoneme** is defined as the minimal unit of sound that can make a difference in meaning if substituted for another sound in a word that is otherwise identical. The phoneme itself does not carry meaning. For example, in English if the sound we associate with the letter "p" is substituted for the sound of the letter "b" in the word *bit*, the word's meaning is changed because now it is *pit*, a different word with an entirely different meaning. The human articulatory anatomy is capable of producing many hundreds of sounds, but no language has more than about 100 phonemes. English has about 36 or 37 phonemes, including about eleven vowels, depending on dialect. Hawaiian has only five vowels and about eight consonants. No two languages have the same exact set of phonemes.

Linguists use a written system called the International Phonetic Alphabet (IPA) to represent the sounds of a language. Unlike the letters of our alphabet that spell English words, each IPA symbol always represents only one sound no matter the language. For example, the letter "a" in English can represent the different vowel sounds in such words as *cat, make, papa, law,* etc., but the IPA symbol /a/ always and only represents the vowel sound of *papa* or *pop*.

The Units That Carry Meaning: Morphemes

A **morpheme** is a minimal unit of meaning in a language; a morpheme cannot be broken down into any smaller units that still relate to the original meaning. It may be a word that can stand alone, called an **unbound morpheme** (*dog, happy, go, educate*). Or it could be any part of a word that carries meaning that cannot stand alone but must be attached to another morpheme, **bound morphemes**. They may be placed at the beginning of the root word, such as *un-* ("not," as in *unhappy*), or *re-* ("again," as in *rearrange*). Or, they may follow the root, as in *-ly* (makes an adjective into an adverb: *quickly* from *quick*), *-s* (for plural, possessive, or a verb ending) in English. Some languages, like Chinese, have very few if any bound morphemes. Others, like Swahili have so many that nouns and verbs cannot stand alone as separate words; they must have one or more other bound morphemes attached to them.

The Structure of Phrases and Sentences: Syntax

Rules of syntax tell the speaker how to put morphemes together grammatically and meaningfully. There are two main types of syntactic rules: rules that govern word order, and rules that direct the use of certain morphemes that perform a grammatical function. For example, the order of words in the English sentence "The cat chased the dog" cannot be changed around or its meaning would change: "The dog chased the cat" (something entirely different) or "Dog cat the chased the" (something meaningless). English relies on word order much more than many other languages do because it has so few morphemes that can do the same type of work.

For example, in our sentence above, the phrase "the cat" must go first in the sentence, because that is how English indicates the subject of the sentence, the one that does the action of the verb. The phrase "the dog" must go after the verb, indicating that it is the dog that received the action of the verb, or is its object. Other syntactic rules tell us that we must put "the" before its noun, and "–ed" at the end of the verb to indicate past tense. In Russian, the same sentence has fewer restrictions on word order because it has bound morphemes that are attached to the nouns to indicate which one is the subject and which is the object of the verb. So the sentence *koshka [chased] sobaku*, which means "the cat chased the dog," has the same meaning no matter how we order the words, because the *–a* on the end of *koshka* means the cat is the subject, and the *–u* on the end of *sobaku* means the dog is the object. If we switched the endings and said *koshku [chased] sobaka*, now it means the dog did the chasing, even though we haven't changed the order of the words. Notice, too, that Russian does not have a word for "the."

Conveying Meaning in Language: Semantics and Pragmatics

The whole purpose of language is to communicate meaning about the world around us so the study of meaning is of great interest to linguists and anthropologists alike. The field of **semantics** focuses on the study of the meanings of words and other morphemes as well as how the meanings of phrases and sentences derive from them. Recently linguists have been enjoying examining the multitude of meanings and uses of the word "like" among American youth, made famous through the film *Valley Girl* in 1983. Although it started as a feature of California English, it has spread all across the country, and even to many young second-language speakers of English. It's, like, totally awesome dude!

The study of **pragmatics** looks at the social and cultural aspects of meaning and how the context of an interaction affects it. One aspect of pragmatics is the **speech act.** Any time we speak we are performing an act, but what we are actually trying to accomplish with that utterance may not be interpretable through the dictionary meanings of the words themselves. For example, if you are at the dinner table and say, "Can you pass the salt?" you are probably not asking if the other person is capable of giving you the salt. Often the more polite an utterance, the less direct it will be syntactically. For example, rather than using the imperative syntactic form and saying "Give me a cup of coffee," it is considered more polite to use the question form and say "Would you please give me a cup of coffee?"

LANGUAGE VARIATION: SOCIOLINGUISTICS

Languages Versus Dialects

The number of languages spoken around the world is somewhat difficult to pin down, but we usually see a figure between 6,000 and 7,000. Why are they so hard to count? The term **language** is commonly used to refer to the idealized "standard" of a variety of speech with a name, such as English, Turkish, Swedish, Swahili, or Urdu. One language is usually considered to be incomprehensible to speakers of another one. The word **dialect** is often applied to a subordinate variety of a language and the common assumption is that we can understand someone who speaks another dialect of our own language.

These terms are not really very useful to describe actual language variation. For example, many of the hundreds of "dialects" spoken in China are very different from each other and are not mutually comprehensible to speakers of other Chinese "dialects." The Chinese government promotes the idea that all of them are simply variants of the "Chinese language" because it helps to promote national solidarity and loyalty among Chinese people to their country and reduce regional factionalism. In contrast, the languages of Sweden, Denmark, and Norway are considered separate languages, but actually if a Swede, a Dane, and a Norwegian were to have a conversation together, each could use their own language and understand most of what the others say. Does this make them dialects or languages? The Serbian and Croatian languages are considered by their speakers to be separate languages due to distinct political and religious cultural identities. They even employ different writing systems to emphasize difference, but they are essentially the same and easily understandable to each other.

So in the words of linguist John McWhorter, actually "dialects is all there is."[3] What he means by this is that a continuum of language variation is geographically distributed across populations in much the same way that human physical variation is, with the degree of difference between any two varieties increasing across increasing distances. This is the case even across national boundaries. Catalan, the language of northeastern Spain, is closer to the languages of southern France, Provençal and Occitan than any one is to its associated national language, Spanish or French. One language variety blends with the next geographically like the colors of the rainbow. However, the historical influence of colonizing states has affected that natural distribution. Thus, there is no natural "language" with variations called "dialects." Usually one variety of a language is considered the "standard," but this choice is based on the social and political prestige of the group that speaks that variety; it has no inherent superiority over the other variants called its "dialects." The way people speak is an indicator of who they are, where they come from, and what social groups they identify with, as well as what particular situation they find themselves in, and what they want to accomplish with a specific interaction.

How Does Language Variation Develop?

Why do people from different regions in the United States speak so differently? Why do they speak differently from the people of England? A number of factors have influenced the development of English dialects, and they are typical causes of dialect variation in other languages as well.

Settlement patterns: The first English settlers to North America brought their own dialects with them. Settlers from different parts of the British Isles spoke different dialects (they still do), and they tended to cluster together in their new homeland. The present-day dialects typical of people in various areas of the United States, such as New England, Virginia, New Jersey, and Delaware, still reflect these original settlement sites, although they certainly have changed from their original forms.

Migration routes: After they first settled in the United States, some people migrated further west, establishing dialect boundaries as they traveled and settled in new places.

Geographical factors: Rivers, mountains, lakes and islands affected migration routes and settlement locations, as well as the relative isolation of the settlements. People in the Appalachian mountains and on certain islands off the Atlantic coast were relatively isolated from other speakers for many years and still speak dialects that sound very archaic compared with the mainstream.

Language contact: Interactions with other language groups, such as Native Americans, French, Spanish, Germans, and African-Americans, along paths of migration and settlement resulted in mutual borrowing of vocabulary, pronunciation, and some syntax.

Have you ever heard of "Spanglish"? It is a form of Spanish spoken near the borders of the United States that is characterized by a number of words adopted from English and incorporated into the phonological, morphological and syntactic systems of Spanish. For example, the Spanish sentence *Voy a estacionar mi camioneta,* or "I'm going to park my truck" becomes in Spanglish *Voy a parquear mi troca*. Many other languages have such English-flavored versions, including Franglais and Chinglish. Some countries, especially France, actively try to prevent the incursion of other languages (especially English) into their language, but the effort is always futile. People will use whatever words serve their purposes, even when the "language police" disapprove. Some Franglais words that have invaded in spite of the authorities protestations include the recently acquired *binge-drinking, beach, e-book,* and *drop-out*, while older ones include *le weekend* and *stop*.

Region and occupation: Rural farming people may continue to use archaic expressions compared with urban people, who have much more contact with contemporary life styles and diverse speech communities.

Social class: Social status differences cut across all regional variations of English. These differences reflect the education and income level of speakers.

Group reference: Other categories of group identity, including ethnicity, national origin of ancestors, age, and gender can be symbolized by the way we speak, indicating in-group versus out-group identity. We talk like other members of our groups, however we define that group, as a means of maintaining social solidarity with other group members. This can include occupational or interest-group jargon, such as medical or computer terms, or surfer talk, as well as pronunciation and syntactic variations. Failure to make linguistic accommodation to those we are speaking to may be interpreted as a kind of symbolic group rejection even if that dialect might be relatively stigmatized as a marker of a disrespected minority group. Most people are able to use more than one style of speech, also called **register,** so that they can adjust depending on who they are interacting with: their family and friends, their boss, a teacher, or other members of the community.

Linguistic processes: New developments that promote the simplification of pronunciation or syntactic changes to clarify meaning can also contribute to language change.

These factors do not work in isolation. Any language variation is the result of a number of social, historical, and linguistic factors that might affect individual performances collectively and therefore dialect change in a particular speech community is a process that is continual.

Try This: Which of these terms do you use, *pop* versus *soda* versus *coke*? *Pail* versus *bucket*? Do you say "vayse" or "vahze" for the vessel you put flowers in? Where are you from? Can you find out where each term or pronunciation is typically used? Can you find other regional differences like these?

What Is a "Standard" Variety of a Language?

The standard of any language is simply one of many variants that has been given special prestige in the community because it is spoken by the people who have the greatest amount of prestige, power, and (usually) wealth. In the case of English its development has been in part the result of the invention of the printing press in the sixteenth-century and the subsequent increase in printed versions of the language. This then stimulated more than a hundred years of deliberate efforts by grammarians to standardize spelling and grammatical rules. Their decisions invariably favored the dialect spoken by the aristocracy. Some of their other decisions were rather arbitrarily determined by standards more appropriate to Latin, or even mathematics. For example, as it is in many other languages, it was typical among the common people of the time (and it still is among the present-day working classes and in casual speech), to use multiple negative particles in a sentence, like "I *don't* have *no* money." Those eighteenth-century grammarians said we must use either *don't* or *no*, but not both, that is, "I don't have any money" or "I have no money." They based this on a mathematical rule that says that two negatives make a positive. (When multiplying two signed negative numbers, such as -5 times -2, the result is +10.) These grammarians claimed that if we used the double negative, we would really be saying the positive, or "I have money." Obviously, anyone who utters that double-negative sentence is not trying to say that they have money, but the rule still applies for standard English to this day.

Non-standard varieties of English, also known as **vernaculars**, are usually distinguished from the standard by their inclusion of such stigmatized forms as multiple negatives, the use of the verb form *ain't* (which was originally the normal contraction of *am not*, as in "I ain't," comparable to "you aren't," or "she isn't"); pronunciation of words like *this* and *that* as *dis* and *dat*; pronunciation of final "–ing" as "–in;" and any other feature that grammarians have decreed as "improper" English.

The standard of any language is a rather artificial, idealized form of language, the language of education. One must learn its rules in school because it is not anyone's true first language. Everyone speaks a dialect, although some dialects are closer to the standard than others. Those that are regarded with the least prestige and respect in society are associated with the groups of people who have the least amount of social prestige. People with the highest levels of education have greater access to the standard, but even they usually revert to their first dialect as the appropriate **register** in the context of an informal situation with friends and family. In other words, no language variety is inherently better or worse than any other one. It is due to social attitudes that people label some varieties as "better" or "proper," and others as "incorrect" or "bad." Recall Language Universal 3: "All languages are systematic, rule driven, and equally complex overall, and equally capable of expressing any idea that the speaker wishes to convey."

In 1972 sociolinguist William Labov did an interesting study in which he looked at the pronunciation of the sound /r/ in the speech of New Yorkers in two different department stores. Many people from that area drop the /r/ sound in words like *fourth* and *floor* (*fawth, floah*), but this pronunciation is primarily associated with lower social classes and is not a feature of the approved standard for English, even in New York City. In two different contexts, an upscale store and a discount store, Labov asked customers what floor a certain item could be found on, already knowing it was the fourth floor. He then asked them to repeat their answer, as though he hadn't heard it correctly. He compared the first with the second answers by the same person, and he compared the answers in the expensive store versus the cheaper store. He found 1) that the responders in the two stores differed overall in their pronunciation of this sound, and 2) that the same person may differ between situations of less and more self-consciousness (first versus second answer). That is, people in the upscale store tended to pronounce the /r/, and responders in both stores tended to produce the standard pronunciation more in their second answers in an effort to sound "higher class." These results showed that the pronunciation or deletion of /r/ in New York correlates with both social status and context.[4]

There is nothing inherently better or worse in either pronunciation; it depends entirely on the social norms of the community. The same /r/ deletion that is stigmatized in New York City is the prestigious, standard form in England, used by the upper class and announcers for the BBC. The pronunciation of the /r/ sound in England is stigmatized because it is used by lower-status people in some industrial cities.

It is important to note that almost everyone has access to a number of different language variations and registers. They know that one variety is appropriate to use with some people in some situations, and others should be used with other people or in other situations. The use of several language varieties in a particular interaction is known as **code-switching.**

> **Try This:** To understand the importance of using the appropriate register in a given context, the next time you are with a close friend or family member try using the register, or style of speech, that you might use with your professor or a respected member of the clergy. What is your friend's reaction? I do not recommend trying the reverse experiment, using a casual vernacular register with such a respected person (unless they are also a close friend). Why not?

Linguistic Relativity: The Whorf Hypothesis

In the 1920s, Benjamin Whorf was a graduate student studying with linguist Edward Sapir at Yale University in New Haven, Connecticut. Sapir, considered the father of American linguistic anthropology, was responsible for documenting and recording the languages and cultures of many Native American tribes, which were disappearing at an alarming rate. This was due primarily to the deliberate efforts of the United States government to force Native Americans to assimilate into the Euro-American culture. Sapir and his predecessors were well aware of the close relationship between culture and language because each culture is reflected in and influences its language. Anthropologists need to learn the language of the culture they are studying in order to understand the world view of its speakers. Whorf believed that the reverse is also true, that a language affects culture as well, by actually influencing how its speakers think. His hypothesis proposes that the words and the structures of a language influence how its speakers think about the world, how they behave, and ultimately the culture itself. (See our definition of culture above.) Simply stated, Whorf believed that human beings see the world the way they do because the specific languages they speak influence them to do so. He developed this idea through both his work with Sapir and his work as a chemical engineer for the Hartford Insurance Company investigating the causes of fires.

One of his cases while working for the insurance company was a fire at a business where there were a number of gasoline drums. Those that contained gasoline were surrounded by signs warning employees to be cautious around them and to avoid smoking near them. The workers were always careful around those drums. On the other hand, empty gasoline drums were stored in another area, but employees were more careless there. Someone tossed a cigarette or lighted match into one of the "empty" drums, it went up in flames, and started a fire that burned the business to the ground. Whorf theorized that the meaning of the word *empty* implied to the worker that "nothing" was there to be cautious about so the worker behaved accordingly. Unfortunately, an "empty" gasoline drum may still contain fumes, which are more flammable than the liquid itself.

Whorf's studies at Yale involved working with Native American languages, including Hopi. The Hopi language is quite different from English, in many ways. For example, let's look at how the Hopi language deals with time. Western languages (and cultures) view time as a flowing river in which we are being carried continuously away from a past, through the present, and into a future. Our verb systems reflect that concept with specific tenses for past, present, and future. We think of this concept of time as universal, that all humans see it the same way. A Hopi speaker has very different ideas and the structure of their language both reflects and shapes the way they think about time. The Hopi language has no present, past, or future tense. Instead, it divides the world into what Whorf called the manifested and unmanifest domains. The manifested domain deals with the physical universe, including the present, the immediate past and future; the verb system uses the same basic structure for all of them. The unmanifest domain involves the remote past and the future, as well as the world of desires, thought, and life forces. The set of verb forms dealing with this domain are consistent for all of these areas, and are different from the manifested ones. Also, there are no words for hours, minutes, or days of the week.

Native Hopi speakers often had great difficulty adapting to life in the English speaking world when it came to being "on time" for work or other events. It is simply not how they had been conditioned to behave with respect to time in their Hopi world, which followed the phases of the moon and the movements of the sun. In a book about the Abenaki who lived in Vermont in the mid-1800s, Trudy Ann Parker described their concept of time, which very much resembled that of the Hopi and many of the other Native American tribes. "They called one full day a sleep, and a year was called a winter. Each month was referred to as a moon and always began with a new moon. An Indian day wasn't divided into minutes or hours. It had four time periods—sunrise, noon, sunset, and midnight. Each season was determined by the budding or leafing of plants, the spawning of fish or the rutting time for animals. Most Indians thought the white race had been running around like scared rabbits ever since the invention of the clock."[5]

The **lexicon**, or vocabulary, of a language is an inventory of the items a culture talks about and has categorized in order to make sense of the world and deal with it effectively. For example, modern life is dictated for many by the need to travel by some kind of vehicle—cars, trucks, SUVs, trains, buses, etc. We therefore have thousands of words to talk about them, including types of vehicles, models, brands, or parts.

The most important aspects of each culture are similarly reflected in the lexicon of its language. Among the societies living in the islands of Oceania in the Pacific, fish have great economic and cultural importance. This is reflected in the rich vocabulary that describes all aspects of the fish and the environments that islanders depend on for survival. For example, in Palau there are about 1,000 fish species and Palauan fishermen knew, long before biologists existed, details about the anatomy, behavior, growth patterns and habitat of most of them—in many cases far more than modern biologists know even today. Much of fish behavior is related to the tides and the phases of the moon. Throughout Oceania, the names given to certain days of the lunar months reflect the likelihood of successful fishing. For example, in the Caroline Islands, the name for the night before the new moon is *otolol*, which means "to swarm." The name indicates that the best fishing days cluster around the new moon. In Hawai`i and Tahiti two sets of days have names containing the particle `ole or `ore; one occurs in the first quarter of the moon and the other in the third quarter. The same name is given to the prevailing wind during those phases. The words mean "nothing," because those days were considered bad for fishing as well as planting.

Parts of Whorf's hypothesis, known as **linguistic relativity**, were controversial from the beginning, and still are among some linguists. Yet Whorf's ideas now form the basis for an entire sub-field of cultural anthropology: cognitive or psychological anthropology. A number of studies have been done that support Whorf's ideas. Linguist George Lakoff's work looks at the pervasive existence of metaphors in everyday speech that can be said to predispose a speaker's world view and attitudes on a variety of human experiences.[6] A metaphor is an expression in which one kind of thing is understood and experienced in terms of another entirely unrelated thing; the metaphors in a language can reveal aspects of the culture of its speakers. Take, for example, the concept of an argument. In logic and philosophy, an argument is a discussion involving differing points of view, or a debate. But the conceptual metaphor in American culture can be stated as ARGUMENT IS WAR. This metaphor is reflected in many expressions of the everyday language of American speakers: I *won* the argument. He *shot down* every point I made. They *attacked* every argument we made. Your point is *right on target*. I had a *fight* with my boyfriend last night. In other words, we use words appropriate for discussing war when we talk about arguments, which are certainly not real war. But we actually think of arguments as a verbal battle that often involve anger, and even violence, which then structures how we argue.

To illustrate that this concept of argument is not universal, Lakoff suggests imagining a culture where an argument is not something to be won or lost, with no strategies for attacking or defending, but rather as a dance where the dancers' goal is to perform in an artful, pleasing way. No anger or violence would occur or even be relevant to speakers of this language, because the metaphor for that culture would be ARGUMENT IS DANCE.

LANGUAGE IN ITS SOCIAL SETTINGS: LANGUAGE AND IDENTITY

The way we speak can be seen as a marker of who we are and with whom we identify. We talk like the other people around us: where we live, our social class, our region of the country, our ethnicity, and even our gender. These categories are not homogeneous. All New Yorkers do not talk exactly the same; all women do not speak according to stereotypes; all African-Americans do not speak an African-American dialect. No one speaks the same way in all situations and contexts, but there are some consistencies in speaking styles that are associated with many of these categories.

Social Class

As discussed above, people can indicate social class by the way they speak. The closer to the standard version their dialect is, the more they are seen as a member of a higher social class because the dialect reflects a higher level of education. In American culture, social class is defined primarily by income and net worth, and it is difficult (but not impossible) to acquire wealth without a high level of education. However, the speech of people in the higher social classes also varies with the region of the country where they live, because there is no single standard of American English, especially with respect to pronunciation. An educated Texan will sound different from an educated Bostonian, but they will use the standard version of English from their own region. The lower the social class of a community, the more their language variety will differ from both the standard and from the vernaculars of other regions.

Ethnicity

An ethnicity, or ethnic group, is a group of people who identify with each other based on some combination of shared cultural heritage, ancestry, history, country of origin, language, or dialect. In the United States such groups are frequently referred to as "races," but there is no such thing as biological race, and this misconception has historically led to racism and discrimination. Because of the social implications and biological inaccuracy of the term "race," it is often more accurate and appropriate to use the terms ethnicity or ethnic group. A language variety is often associated with an ethnic group when its members use language as a marker of solidarity. They may also use it to distinguish themselves from a larger, sometimes oppressive, language group when they are a minority population.

A familiar example of an oppressed ethnic group with a distinctive dialect is African-Americans. They have a unique history among minorities in the United States, with their centuries-long experience as captive slaves and subsequent decades under Jim Crow laws. (These laws restricted their rights after their emancipation from slavery.) With the Civil Rights Acts of 1964 and 1968 and other laws, African-Americans gained legal rights to access public places and housing, but it is not possible to eliminate racism and discrimination only by passing laws; both still exist among the white majority. It is no longer culturally appropriate to openly express racism, but it is much less frowned upon to express negative attitudes about African-American Vernacular English (AAVE). Typically, it is not the language itself that these attitudes are targeting; it is the people who speak it.

As with any language variety, AAVE is a complex, rule-driven, grammatically consistent language variety, a dialect of American English with a distinctive history. A widely accepted hypothesis of the origins of AAVE is as follows. When Africans were captured and brought to the Americas, they brought their own languages with them. But some of them already spoke a version of English called a **pidgin.** A pidgin is a language that springs up out of a situation in which people who do not share a language must spend extended amounts of time together, usually in a working environment. Pidgins are the only exception to the Language Universal number 3 (all languages are systematic, rule driven, and equally complex overall, and equally capable of expressing any idea that the speaker wishes to convey).

There are no primitive languages, but a pidgin is a simplified language form, cobbled together based mainly on one core language, in this case English, using a small number of phonemes, simplified syntactic rules, and a minimal lexicon of words borrowed from the other languages involved. A pidgin has no native speakers; it is used primarily in the environment in which it was created. An English-based pidgin was used as a common language in many areas of West Africa by traders interacting with people of numerous language groups up and down the major rivers. Some of the captive Africans could speak this pidgin, and it spread among them after the slaves arrived in North America and were exposed daily to English speakers. Eventually, the use of the pidgin expanded to the point that it developed into the original forms of what has been called a Black English plantation **creole**. A creole is a language that develops from a pidgin when it becomes so widely used that children acquire it as one of their first languages. In this situation it becomes a more fully complex language consistent with Universal number 3.

All African-Americans do not speak AAVE, and people other than African-Americans also speak it. Anyone who grows up in an area where their friends speak it may be a speaker of AAVE like the rapper Eminem, a white man who grew up in an African-American neighborhood in Detroit. Present-day AAVE is not homogeneous; there are many regional and class variations. Most variations have several features in common, for instance, two phonological features: the dropped /r/ typical of some New York dialects, and the pronunciation of the "th" sound of words like *this* and *that* as a /d/ sound, *dis* and *dat*. Most of the features of AAVE are also present in many other English dialects, but those dialects are not as severely stigmatized as AAVE is. It is interesting, but not surprising, that AAVE and southern dialects of white English share many features. During the centuries of slavery in the south, African-American slaves outnumbered whites on most plantations. Which group do you think had the most influence on the other group's speech? The African-American community itself is divided about the acceptability of AAVE. It is probably because of the historical oppression of African-Americans as a group that the dialect has survived to this day, in resistance to the majority white society's disapproval.

Language and Gender

In any culture that has differences in gender role expectations—and all cultures do—there are differences in how people talk based on their sex and gender identity. These differences have nothing to do with biology. Children are taught from birth how to behave appropriately as a male or a female in their culture, and different cultures have different standards of behavior. It must be noted that not all men and women in a society meet these standards, but when they do not they may pay a social price. Some societies are fairly tolerant of violations of their standards of gendered behavior, but others are less so.

In the United States, men are generally expected to speak in a low, rather monotone pitch; it is seen as masculine. If they do not sound sufficiently masculine, American men are likely to be negatively labeled as effeminate. Women, on the other hand, are freer to use their entire pitch range, which they often do when expressing emotion, especially excitement. When a woman is a television news announcer, she will modulate the pitch of her voice to a sound more typical of a man in order to be perceived as more credible. Women tend to use **minimal responses** in a conversation more than men. These are the vocal indications that one is listening to a speaker, such as *m-hm, yeah, I see, wow,* and so forth. They tend to face their conversation partners more and use more eye contact than men. This is one reason women often complain that men do not listen to them.

Deborah Tannen, a professor of linguistics at Georgetown University in Washington, D.C., has done research for many years on language and gender. Her basic finding is that in conversation women tend to use styles that are relatively cooperative, to emphasize an equal relationship, while men seem to talk in a more competitive way in order to establish their positions in a hierarchy. She emphasizes that both men and women may be cooperative and competitive in different ways.[7]

Other societies have very different standards for gendered speech styles. In Madagascar, men use a very flowery style of talk, using proverbs, metaphors and riddles to indirectly make a point and to avoid direct confrontation. The women on the other hand speak bluntly and say directly what is on their minds. Both admire men's speech and think of women's speech as inferior. When a man wants to convey a negative message to someone, he will ask his wife to do it for him. In addition, women control the marketplaces where tourists bargain for prices because it is impossible to bargain with a man who will not speak directly. It is for this reason that Malagasy women are relatively independent economically.

In Japan, women were traditionally expected to be subservient to men and speak using a "feminine" style, appropriate for their position as wife and mother, but the Japanese culture has been changing in recent decades so more and more women are joining the work force and achieving positions of relative power. Such women must find ways of speaking to maintain their feminine identities and at the same time express their authority in interactions with men, a challenging balancing act. Women in the United States do as well, to a certain extent. Even Margaret Thatcher, prime minister of England, took speech therapy lessons to "feminize" her language use while maintaining an expression of authority.

The Deaf Culture and Signed Languages

Deaf people constitute a linguistic minority in many societies worldwide based on their common experience of life. This often results in their identification with a local Deaf culture. Such a culture may include shared beliefs, attitudes, values, norms, and values, like any other culture, and it is invariably marked by communication through the use of a sign language. It is not enough to be physically deaf (spelled with a lower case "d") to belong to a Deaf culture (written with a capital "D"). In fact, one does not even need to be deaf. Identification with a Deaf culture is a personal choice. It can include family members of deaf people or anyone else who associates with deaf people, as long as the community accepts them. Especially important, members of Deaf culture are expected to be competent communicators in the sign language of the culture. In fact, there have been profoundly deaf people who were not accepted into the local Deaf community because they could not sign. In some deaf schools, at least in the United States, the practice has been to teach deaf children how to lip read and speak orally, and to prevent them from using a signed system. They were expected to blend in with the hearing community as much as possible. This is called the **oralist approach** to education, but it is considered by members of the Deaf community to be a threat to the existence of their culture. For the same reason, the development of cochlear implants, which can restore hearing for some deaf children, has been controversial in U.S. Deaf communities. The members often have a positive attitude toward their deafness and do not consider it to be a disability. To them, regaining hearing represents disloyalty to the group and a desire to leave it.

According to the World Federation of the Deaf, there are over 200 distinct sign languages in the world, which are not mutually comprehensible. They are all considered by linguists to be true languages, consistent with linguistic definitions of all human languages. They differ only in the fact that they are based on a gestural-visual rather than a vocal-auditory sensory mode. Each is a true language with basic units comparable to phonemes but composed of hand positions, shapes, and movements, plus some facial expressions. Each has its own unique set of morphemes and grammatical rules. American Sign Language (ASL), too, is a true language separate from English; it is not English on the hands. Like all other signed languages, it is possible to sign with a word-for-word translation from English, using finger spelling for some words, which is helpful in teaching the deaf to read, but they prefer their own language, ASL, for ordinary interactions. Of course, Deaf culture identity intersects with other kinds of cultural identity, like nationality, ethnicity, gender, class, and sexual orientation, so each Deaf culture is not only small but very diverse.

LANGUAGE CHANGE: HISTORICAL LINGUISTICS

Recall the language universal stating that all languages change over time. In fact, it is not possible to keep them from doing so. How and why does this happen? The study of how languages change is known as **historical linguistics**. The processes, both historical and linguistic, that cause language change can affect all of its systems: phonological, morphological, lexical, syntactic, and semantic.

Historical linguists have placed most of the languages of the world into **taxonomies**, groups of languages classified together based on words that have the same or similar meanings. Language taxonomies create something like a family tree of languages. For example, words in the Romance family of languages, called sister languages, show great similarities to each other because they have all derived from the same "mother" language, Latin (the language of Rome). In turn, Latin is considered a "sister" language to Sanskrit (once spoken in India and now the mother language of many of India's modern languages, and still the language of the Hindu religion) and classical Greek. Their "mother" language is called "Indo-European," which is also the mother (or grandmother!) language of almost all the rest of European languages.

Let's briefly examine the history of the English language as an example of these processes of change. England was originally populated by Celtic peoples, the ancestors of today's Irish, Scots, and Welsh. The Romans invaded the islands in the first-century AD, bringing their Latin language with them. This was the edge of their empire; their presence there was not as strong as it was on the European mainland. When the Roman Empire was defeated in about 500 AD by Germanic speaking tribes from northern Europe (the "barbarians"), a number of those related Germanic languages came to be spoken in various parts of what would become England. These included the languages of the Angles and the Saxons, whose names form the origin of the term Anglo-Saxon and of the name of England itself—Angle-land. At this point, the languages spoken in England included those Germanic languages, which gradually merged as various dialects of English, with a small influence from the Celtic languages, some Latin from the Romans, and a large influence from Viking invaders. This form of English, generally referred to as **Old English**, lasted for about 500 years. In 1066 AD, England was invaded by William the Conqueror from Normandy, France. New French rulers brought the French language. French is a Latin-based language, and it is by far the greatest source of the Latin-based words in English today; almost 10,000 French words were adopted into the English of the time period. This was the beginning of **Middle English**, which lasted another 500 years or so.

The change to **Modern English** had two main causes. One was the invention of the printing press in the fifteenth century, which resulted in a deliberate effort to standardize the various dialects of English, mostly in favor of the dialect spoken by the elite. The other source of change, during the fifteenth and sixteenth centuries, was a major shift in the pronunciation of many of the vowels. Middle English words like *hus* and *ut* came to be pronounced *house* and *out*. Many other vowel sounds also changed in a similar manner.

None of the early forms of English are easily recognizable as English to modern speakers. Here is an example of the first two lines of the Lord's Prayer in Old English, from 995 AD, before the Norman Invasion:

> *Fæder ūre, ðū ðē eart on heofonum,*
> *Sī ðīn nama gehālgod.*

Here are the same two lines in Middle English, English spoken from 1066 AD until about 1500 AD. These are taken from the Wycliffe Bible in 1389 AD:

> *Our fadir that art in heuenes,*
> *halwid be thi name.*

The following late Middle English/early Modern English version from the 1526 AD Tyndale Bible, shows some of the results of grammarians' efforts to standardize spelling and vocabulary for wider distribution of the printed word due to the invention of the printing press:

> *O oure father which arte in heven,*
> *halowed be thy name.*

And finally, this example is from the King James Version of the Bible, 1611 AD, in the early Modern English language of Shakespeare. It is almost the same archaic form that modern Christians use.

> *Our father which art in heauen,*
> *hallowed be thy name.*[8]

Over the centuries since the beginning of Modern English, it has been further affected by exposure to other languages and dialects worldwide.[9] This exposure brought about new words and changed meanings of old words. More changes to the sound systems resulted from phonological processes that may or may not be attributable to the influence of other languages. Many other changes, especially in recent decades, have been brought about by cultural and technological changes that require new vocabulary to deal with them.

> **Try This**: Just think of all the words we use today that have either changed their primary meanings, or are completely new: mouse and mouse pad, google, app, computer (which used to be a person who computes!), texting, cool, cell, gay. How many more can you think of?

GLOBALIZATION AND LANGUAGE

Globalization is the spread of people, their cultures and languages, products, money, ideas, and information around the world. Globalization is nothing new; it has been happening throughout the existence of humans, but for the last 500 years it has been increasing in its scope and pace, primarily due to improvements in transportation and communication. Beginning in the fifteenth-century, English explorers started spreading their language to colonies in all parts of the world. English is now one of the three or four most widely spoken languages. It has official status in at least 60 countries, and it is widely spoken in many others. Other colonizers also spread their languages, especially Spanish, French, Portuguese, Arabic, and Russian. Like English, each has its regional variants. One effect of colonization has often been the suppression of local languages in favor of the language of the more powerful colonizers.

In the past half century, globalization has been dominated by the spread of North American popular culture and language to other countries. Today it is difficult to find a country that does not have American music, movies and television programs, or Coca Cola and McDonald's, or many other artifacts of life in the United States, and the English terms that go with them.

In addition, people are moving from rural areas to cities in their own countries, or they are migrating to other countries in unprecedented numbers. Many have moved because they are refugees fleeing violence, or they found it increasingly difficult to survive economically in their own countries. This mass movement of people has led to the on-going extinction of large numbers of the world's languages as people abandon their home regions and language in order to assimilate into their new homes.

Language Shift, Language Maintenance, and Language Death

Of the approximately 6,000 languages still surviving today, about half the world's more than seven billion people speak only ten. These include Mandarin Chinese, two languages from India, Spanish, English, Arabic, Portuguese, Russian, Japanese, and German. Many of the rest of the world's languages are spoken by a few thousand people, or even just a few hundred, and most of them are threatened with extinction, called **language death**. It has been predicted that by the end of this century up to 90 percent of the languages spoken today will be gone. The rapid disappearance of so many languages is of great concern to linguists and anthropologists alike. When a language is lost, its associated culture and unique set of knowledge and worldview are lost with it forever. Remember Whorf's hypothesis. An interesting website shows short videos of the last speakers of several endangered languages, including one speaking an African "click language."

Some minority languages are not threatened with extinction, even those that are spoken by a relatively small number of people. Others, spoken by many thousands, may be doomed. What determines which survive and which do not? Smaller languages that are associated with a specific country are likely to survive. Others that are spoken across many national boundaries are also less threatened, such as Quechua, an indigenous language spoken throughout much of South America, including Colombia, Ecuador, Peru, Chile, Bolivia, and Argentina. The great majority of the world's languages are spoken by people with minority status in their countries. After all, there are only about 193 countries in the world, and over 6,000 languages are spoken in them. You can do the math.

The survival of the language of a given speech community is ultimately based on the accumulation of individual decisions by its speakers to continue using it or to abandon it. The abandonment of a language in favor of a new one is called **language shift.** These decisions are usually influenced by the society's prevailing attitudes. In the case of a minority speech community that is surrounded by a more powerful majority, an individual might keep or abandon the native language depending on a complex array of factors. The most important factors will be the attitudes of the minority people toward themselves and their language, and the attitude of the majority toward the minority.

Language represents a marker of identity, an emblem of group membership and solidarity, but that marker may have a downside as well. If the majority look down on the minority as inferior in some way and discriminates against them, some members of the minority group may internalize that attitude and try to blend in with the majority by adopting the majority's culture and language. Others might more highly value their identity as a member of that stigmatized group, in spite of the discrimination by the majority, and continue to speak their language as a symbol of resistance against the more powerful group. One language that is a minority language when spoken in the United States and that shows no sign of dying out either there or in the world at large, is Spanish. It is the primary language in many countries and in the United States it is by far the largest minority language.

A former student of mine, James Kim (pictured in Figure 3 as a child with his brother), illustrates some of the common dilemmas a child of immigrants might go through as he loses his first language. Although he was born in California, he spoke only Korean for the first six years of his life. Then he went to school, where he was the only Korean child in his class. He quickly learned English, the language of instruction and the language of his classmates. Under peer pressure, he began refusing to speak Korean, even to his parents, who spoke little English. His parents

Figure 3: James Kim with his brother.

tried to encourage him to keep his Korean language and culture by sending him to Korean school on Saturdays, but soon he refused to attend. As a college student, James began to regret the loss of the language of his parents, not to mention his relationship with them. He tried to take a college class in Korean, but it was too difficult and time consuming. After consulting with me, he created a six-minute radio piece, called "First Language Attrition: Why My Parents and I Don't Speak the Same Language," while he was an intern at a National Public Radio station. He interviewed his parents in the piece and was embarrassed to realize he needed an interpreter.[10] Since that time, he has started taking Korean lessons again, and he took his first trip to Korea with his family during the summer of 2014. He was very excited about the prospect of reconnecting with his culture, with his first language, and especially with his parents.

The Korean language as a whole is in no danger of extinction, but many Korean speaking communities of immigrants in the United States, like other minority language groups in many countries, are having difficulty maintaining their language and culture. Those who are the most successful live in large, geographically coherent neighborhoods; they maintain closer ties to their homeland by frequent visits, telephone, and email contact with relatives. There may also be a steady stream of new immigrants from the home country. This is the case with most Spanish speaking communities in the United States, but it is less so with the Korean community.[11]

Another example of an oppressed minority group that has struggled with language and culture loss is Native Americans. Many were completely wiped out by the European colonizers, some by deliberate genocide but the great majority (up to 90 percent) by the diseases that the white explorers brought with them, against which the Native Americans had no immunity. In the twentieth-century, the American government stopped trying to kill Native Americans but instead tried to assimilate them into the white majority culture. It did this in part by forcing Native American children to go to boarding schools where they were required to cut their hair, practice Christianity, and speak only English. When they were allowed to go back home years later, they had lost their languages and their culture, but had not become culturally "white" either. The status of Native Americans in the nineteenth and twentieth-centuries as a scorned minority prompted many to hide their ethnic identities even from their own children. In this way, the many hundreds of original Native American languages in the United States have dwindled to less than 140 spoken today, according to UNESCO. More than half of those could disappear in the next few years, since many are spoken by only a handful of older members of their tribes. However, a number of Native American tribes have recently been making efforts to revive their languages and cultures, with the help of linguists and often by using texts and old recordings made by early linguists like Edward Sapir.

Revitalization of Indigenous Languages

A fascinating example of a tribal language revitalization program is that of the Wampanoag tribe in Massachusetts. The Wampanoag were the Native Americans who met the Puritans when they landed at Plymouth Rock, helped them survive the first winter, and who were with them at the first Thanksgiving. The contemporary descendants of that historic tribe still live in Massachusetts, but bringing back their language was not something Wampanoag people had ever thought possible because no one had spoken it for more than a century.

Figure 4: Jessie Little Doe Baird with daughter Mae. Photo courtesy of Cultural Survival and Make Peace Productions.

A young Wampanoag woman named Jessie Little Doe Baird (pictured in Figure 4 with her daughter Mae) was inspired by a series of dreams in which her ancestors spoke to her in their language, which she of course did not understand. She eventually earned a master's degree in Algonquian linguistics at Massachusetts Institute of Technology in Boston and launched a project to bring her language back from the dead. This process was made possible by the existence of a large collection of documents, including copies of the King James Bible, written phonetically in Wampanoag during the seventeenth and eighteenth-centuries. She also worked with speakers of languages related to the Algonquian family to help in the reconstruction of the language. The community has established a school to teach the language to the children and promote its use among the entire community. Her daughter Mae is among the first new native speakers of Wampanoag.[12]

How Is the Digital Age Changing Communication?

The invention of the printing press in the fifteenth-century was just the beginning of technological transformations that made the spread of information in European languages and ideas possible across time and space using the printed word. Recent advances in travel and digital technology are rapidly transforming communication; now we can be in contact with almost anyone, anywhere, in seconds. However, it could be said that the new age of instantaneous access to everything and everyone is actually continuing a social divide that started with the printing press.

In the fifteenth-century, few people could read and write, so only the tiny educated minority were in a position to benefit from printing. Today, only those who have computers and the skills to use them, the educated and relatively wealthy, have access to this brave new world of communication. Some schools have adopted computers and tablets for their students, but these schools are more often found in wealthier neighborhoods. Thus, technology is continuing to contribute to the growing gap between the economic haves and the have-nots.

There is also a digital generation gap between the young, who have grown up with computers, and the older generations, who have had to learn to use computers as adults. These two generations have been referred to as digital natives and digital immigrants.[13] The difference between the two groups can be compared to that of children versus adults learning a new language; learning is accomplished much more easily by the young.

Computers, and especially social media, have made it possible for millions of people to connect with each other for purposes of political activism, including "Occupy Wall Street" in the United States and the "Arab Spring" in the Middle East. Some anthropologists have introduced computers and cell phones to the people they studied in remote areas, and in this way they were able to stay in contact after finishing their ethnographic work. Those people, in turn, were now able to have greater access to the outside world.

Facebook and Twitter are becoming key elements in the survival of a number of endangered indigenous languages. Facebook is now available in over 70 languages, and Twitter in about 40 languages. For example, a website has been created that seeks to preserve *Anishinaabemowin*, an endangered Native American language from Michigan.

The language has 8,000-10,000 speakers, but most of the native speakers are over 70 years old, which means the language is threatened with extinction. Modern social media are an ideal medium to help encourage young people to communicate in their language to keep it alive.[14]

Clearly, language and communication through modern technology are in the forefront of a rapidly changing world, for better or for worse. It's anybody's guess what will happen next.

DISCUSSION QUESTIONS

1. How do you think modern communication technologies like cell phones and computers are changing how people communicate? Is the change positive or negative?
2. How is language related to social and economic inequality? Do you think that attitudes about language varieties have affected you and/or your family?
3. How has the use of specific terms in the news helped to shape public opinion? For example, what are the different implications of the terms *terrorist* versus *freedom fighter*? *Downsizing* versus *firing* staff at a company? Euphemistic terms used in reference to war include *friendly fire, pacification, collateral damage*? Can you think of other examples?

4. Think about the different styles you use when speaking to your siblings and parents, your friends, your significant other, your professors, your grandparents. What are some of the specific differences among these styles? What do these differences indicate about the power relationships between you and others?

GLOSSARY

Arbitrariness: the relationship between a symbol and its referent (meaning), in which there is no obvious connection between them.

Bound morpheme: a unit of meaning that cannot stand alone; it must be attached to another morpheme.

Closed system: a form of communication that cannot create new meanings or messages; it can only convey pre-programmed (innate) messages.

Code-switching: using two or more language varieties in a particular interaction.

Creole: a language that develops from a pidgin when the pidgin becomes so widely used that children acquire it as one of their first languages. Creoles are more fully complex than pidgins.

Critical age range hypothesis: research suggesting that a child will gradually lose the ability to acquire language naturally and without effort if he or she is not exposed to other people speaking a language until past the age of puberty. This applies to the acquisition of a second language as well.

Cultural transmission: the process by which aspects of culture are passed from person to person, often generation to generation; a feature of some species' communication systems.

Design features: descriptive characteristics of the communication systems of all species, including that of humans, proposed by linguist Charles Hockett to serve as a definition of human language.

Dialect: a variety of speech. The term is often applied to a subordinate variety of a language. Speakers of two dialects of the same language do not necessarily always understand each other.

Discreteness: a feature of human speech that can be isolated from others.

Displacement: the ability to communicate about things that are outside of the here and now.

Duality of patterning: at the first level of patterning, meaningless discrete sounds of speech are combined to form words and parts of words that carry meaning. In the second level of patterning, those units of meaning are recombined to form an infinite possible number of longer messages such as phrases and sentences.

Gesture-call system: a system of non-verbal communication using varying combinations of sound, body language, scent, facial expression, and touch, typical of great apes and other primates, as well as humans.

Historical linguistics: the study of how languages change.

Interchangeability: the ability of all individuals of the species to both send and receive messages; a feature of some species' communication systems.

Kinesics: the study of all forms of human body language.

Language: an idealized form of speech, usually referred to as the standard variety.

Language death: the total extinction of a language.

Language shift: when a community stops using their old language and adopts a new one.

Language universals: characteristics shared by all linguists.

Larynx: the voice box, containing the vocal bands that produce the voice.

Lexicon: the vocabulary of a language.

Linguistic relativity: the idea that the structures and words of a language influence how its speakers think, how they behave, and ultimately the culture itself (also known as the Whorf Hypothesis).

Middle English: the form of the English language spoken from 1066 AD until about 1500 AD.

Minimal response: the vocal indications that one is listening to a speaker.

Modern English: the form of the English language spoken from about 1500 AD to the present.

Morphemes: the basic meaningful units in a language.

Morphology: the study of the morphemes of language.

Old English: English language from its beginnings to about 1066 AD.

Open system: a form of communication that can create an infinite number of new messages; a feature of human language only.

Oralist approach: an approach to the education of deaf children that emphasizes lip reading and speaking orally while discouraging use of signed language.

Palate: the roof of the mouth.

Paralanguage: those characteristics of speech beyond the actual words spoken, such as pitch, loudness, tempo.

Pharynx: the throat cavity, located above the larynx.

Phonemes: the basic meaningless sounds of a language.

Phonology: the study of the sounds of language.

Pidgin: a simplified language that springs up out of a situation in which people who do not share a language must spend extended amounts of time together.

Pragmatic function: the useful purpose of a communication. Usefulness is a feature of all species' communication systems.

Pragmatics: how social context contributes to meaning in an interaction.

Productivity/creativity: the ability to produce and understand messages that have never been expressed before.

Proxemics: the study of the social use of space, including the amount of space an individual tries to maintain around himself in interactions with others.

Register: a style of speech that varies depending on who is speaking to whom and in what context.

Semanticity: the meaning of signs in a communication system; a feature of all species' communication systems.

Semantics: how meaning is conveyed at the word and phrase level.

Speech act: the intention or goal of an utterance; the intention may be different from the dictionary definitions of the words involved.

Standard: the variant of any language that has been given special prestige in the community.

Symbol: anything that serves to refer to something else.

Syntax: the rules by which a language combines morphemes into larger units.

Taxonomies: a system of classification.

Universal grammar (UG): a theory developed by linguist Noam Chomsky suggesting that a basic template for all human languages is embedded in our genes.

Unbound morpheme: a morpheme that can stand alone as a separate word.

Vernaculars: non-standard varieties of a language, which are usually distinguished from the standard by their inclusion of stigmatized forms.

ABOUT THE AUTHOR

Linda Light has been a lecturer in linguistic and cultural anthropology at California State University Long Beach since 1995. During much of that period she also taught as adjunct professor at Cypress College, Santa Ana College, Rancho Santiago College, and Golden West College, all in Orange County, California. She was a consultant to Coastline Community College District in the production of thirty-five educational videos that were used in three series, including the cultural anthropology series *Our Diverse World.* Her main areas of interest have been indigenous language loss and maintenance, language and gender, and first language attrition in the children of immigrants.

NOTES

1. You can find a documentary film about Genie via Google or YouTube under the title *Genie, Secret of the Wild Child*, a NOVA production.
2. Adapted here from Nick Cipollone, Steven Keiser, and Shravan Vasishth, *Language Files* (Columbus: Ohio State University Press 1998), 20-23.
3. John McWhorter, *The Power of Babel: A Natural History of Language* (New York: Times Books, Henry Holt, 2001), 53.
4. William Labov, The Social Stratification of English in New York City (Cambridge, UK: Cambridge University Press, 1964).
5. Trudy Ann Parker, *Aunt Sarah, Woman of the Dawnland* (Lancaster, NH, Dawnland Publications 1994), 56.
6. George Lakoff and Mark Johnson, *Metaphors We Live By* (Chicago and London: The University of Chicago Press, 1980), 4-5.
7. For more information see Deborah Tannen, *Gender and Discourse* (Oxford, UK: Oxford University Press, 1996). Or, Deborah Tannen, *You Just Don't Understand: Women and Men in Conversation* (New York: Harper Collins, 2010).
8. From Wikipedia: History of the Lord's Prayer in English.
9. You can hear the entire prayers in Old English and Middle English read out loud in YouTube files: The Lord's Prayer in Old English from the Eleventh Century, and The Lord's Prayer/Preier of Oure Lord in Recorded Middle English.
10. You can hear the 6-minute piece at http://www.scpr.org/programs/offramp/2012/04/05/25912/first-language-attrition-why-my-parents-and-i-dont/
11. From François Grosjean, *Life with Two Languages: An Introduction to Bilingualism* (Cambridge, Mass: Harvard University Press, 1982), chapter two.
12. Filmmaker Anne Makepeace created a documentary of the story, called *We Still Live Here: Âs Nutayuneân*, which PBS broadcast in 2010. You can watch the clips from the video online.
13. Terms first coined by John Palfrey and Urs Gasser, *Born Digital: Understanding the First Generation of Digital Native* (New York, Basic Books, 2008).
14. Lydia Emmanouilidou, For Rare Languages, Social Media Provide New Hope. http://www.npr.org/sections/alltechconsidered/2014/07/26/333732206/for-rare-languages-social-media-provide-new-hope

SUBSISTENCE

Isaac Shearn, Community College of Baltimore County
ishearn@ccbcmd.edu
http://ccbcmd.academia.edu/IsaacShearn

LEARNING OBJECTIVES

- Identify the four modes of subsistence and describe the major activities associated with obtaining food in each system.

- Explain the difference between wild and domesticated resources and how plants and animals are domesticated.

- Explain the relationship between the subsistence system used in a society and the amount of private property or wealth differences that develop.

- Assess the ways in which subsistence systems are linked to expectations about gender roles.

- Categorize the social and economic characteristics associated with agriculture and describe the benefits and drawbacks of the agricultural subsistence system.

- Analyze the ways in which the global agricultural system separates producers from consumers and contributes to wealth differences.

- Appraise the ways in which human intervention in the environment has made it difficult to separate the "natural" from the human-influenced environment.

Think about the last meal you ate. Where did the ingredients come from? If it was a cheeseburger, where did the cow live and die? Now think about all the food you consume in a normal week. Can you identify the geographic origin of all the ingredients? In other words, how much do you know about the trip your food took to arrive at your plate? How much you know about where your food comes from would tell an anthropologist something about the **subsistence system** used in your community. A subsistence system is the set of practices used by members of a society to acquire food. If you are like me and you cannot say much about where your food comes from, then you are part of an agricultural society that separates food production from consumption, a recent development in the history of humans. People who come from nonagricultural societies have a more direct connection to their food and are likely to know where 100 percent of their food comes from.

Finding food each day is a necessity for every person no matter where that person lives, but food is not just a matter of basic survival. Humans assign symbolic meaning to food, observing cultural norms about what is considered "good" to eat and applying taboos against the consumption of other foods. Catholics may avoid meat during Lent, for instance, while Jewish and Islamic communities forbid the consumption of certain foods such as pork. In addition to these attitudes and preferences, every society has preferred methods for preparing food and for consuming it with others. The cultural norms and attitudes surrounding food and eating are known as **foodways**. By studying both the subsistence system used by a society to acquire food and the foodway associated with consuming it, anthropologists gain insight into the most important daily tasks in every society.

STUDYING SUBSISTENCE SYSTEMS

Since the need to eat is one of the few true human universals, anthropologists have studied subsistence systems from a variety of perspectives. One way to think about the importance of food for human populations is to consider the number of calories an individual must obtain every day in order to survive. Anthropologists use the term **carrying capacity** to quantify the number of calories that can be extracted from a particular unit of land to support a human population. In his 1798 publication *An Essay on the Principle of Population,* Thomas Malthus argued, "the power of population is indefinitely greater than the power in the earth to produce subsistence for man."[1] He suggested that human populations grow at an exponential rate, meaning the population climbs at a rate that is constantly increasing. However, the availability of resources in the environment increases at only an arithmetic rate, which means that left unchecked human populations would soon outstrip the environment's ability to provide sustenance. Malthus famously argued that war, famine, and disease were "good" or at least "functional" in the sense that they kept populations from growing too large.

Figure 1: Carrying Capacity: The area in the orange box, which is not under cultivation, might provide enough resources for a family of four to survive for a year. An equivalent area, marked by the blue box, could provide enough resources for a significantly larger population under intensive agricultural cultivation.

While Malthus presented a grim view of humanity's future, research suggests that the rate of human population growth, currently about one percent per year, is actually slowing. It is also not necessarily true that population growth has an entirely negative impact on human communities. The Danish economist Ester Boserup, for example, argued that human history reveals a connection between population growth and cultural innovation, particularly innovation in farming techniques. Because necessity is the mother of invention, she reasoned, the pressure of having more mouths to feed could be the dynamic that drives societies to develop new solutions.[2]

Modern anthropological studies of subsistence systems draw on insights and perspectives from several different fields, including biology, chemistry, and ecology, as well as a range of ethnographic techniques. This interdisciplinary perspective allows for cross-cultural comparison of human diets. In several decades of anthropological research on subsistence systems, anthropologists have observed that the quest for food affects almost every aspect of daily life. For instance, every person plays a role in society as a producer, distributor, or consumer of food. In the journey of a fish from the sea to the plate, for instance, we can see that in some societies, the same person can fill more than one of those roles, while in other societies there is more specialization. In a small fishing village, the same person might catch the fish, distribute some extra to friends and family, and then consume the bounty that same day. In a city, the consumer of the fish at a fancy restaurant is not the same person who caught the fish. In fact, that person almost certainly has no knowledge of who caught, cleaned, distributed, and prepared the fish he or she is consuming. The web of social connections that we can trace through subsistence provide a very particular kind of anthropological insight into how societies function at their most basic level.

Figure 2: These images show how fish are harvested in two different subsistence systems. Consider the amount of investment and labor that went into the development of technologies that make mass fish farming, or aquaculture, possible compared to fishing with simple nets.

MODES OF SUBSISTENCE

Like all human systems, a society's subsistence system is intricately linked to other aspects of culture such as kinship, politics, and religion. Although we can study these systems in isolation, it is important to remember that in the real world all aspects of culture overlap in complex ways. Consider harvest rituals, for example, which are religious ceremonies focused on improving the food supply. These rituals are shaped by religious beliefs as well as the demands and challenges of obtaining food. Likewise, subsistence systems are the economic base of every society. Working to put food on the table is the essential task of every family or household, and this work is the basis of a **domestic economy** that interacts with the modes of production and modes of exchange described in the Economics chapter.

When anthropologists first began to examine subsistence systems, they started like all scientists do, with classification. Early on, anthropologists saw the benefit of grouping similar societies into types, or categories, based on the range of practices they used in the quest for food. These groupings allowed for comparisons between cultures. At a basic level, societies can be divided into those that have an **immediate return system** for finding food and those that have a **delayed return system**. The residents of a small fishing village who eat the fish they catch each day have an immediate return on their labor. Farmers who must wait several months between the time they plant seeds and the time they harvest have a delayed return system.

Beyond this basic division, anthropologists recognize four general types of food system known as **modes of subsistence**. The four modes of subsistence are foraging, pastoralism, horticulture, and agriculture. Each mode is defined by the tasks involved in obtaining food as well as the way members of the society are organized socially to accomplish these tasks. Because each mode of subsistence is tailored to particular ecological conditions, we can think of each culture's subsistence system as an adaptation, or a set of survival strategies uniquely developed to suit a particular environment. Because culture shapes the way we view and interact with the environment, different societies can adapt to similar environments in different ways. **Foraging**, sometimes known as hunting and gathering, describes societies that rely primarily on "wild" plant and animal food resources. **Pastoralism** is a subsistence system in which people raise herds of domesticated livestock. **Horticulture** is the small-scale cultivation of crops intended primarily for subsistence. **Agriculture**, the subsistence system used in the United States, involves the cultivation of domesticated plants and animals using technologies that allow for intensive use of the land. Can all societies be categorized neatly into one of these modes? No. In fact, almost every society combines one or more of these strategies into their subsistence practices. For example, in the United States there are individuals who participate in all of these subsistence modes, including foraging. When anthropologists analyze a subsistence system, they look for the dominant mode of subsistence, or the most typical way that members of a society procure food. So, while some people in the United States grow their own food or hunt wild animals, the dominant mode of subsistence is agriculture, and people obtain food primarily by purchasing it.

Foraging

"Why should we plant, when there are so many mongongos in the world?"
—/Xashe, !Kung forager[3]

Foraging is a mode of subsistence defined by its reliance on wild plant and animal food resources already available in the environment rather than on domesticated species that have been altered by human intervention. Foragers use a remarkable variety of practices to procure meals. Hunting for animal protein is central to the foraging lifestyle and foragers capture and consume a wide variety of animals, from squirrels caught with a bow and arrow or blow dart to buffalo once killed by the dozens in communal hunts. Fishing for marine resources forms the basis for acquiring protein in many foraging communities and includes a range of practices from exploiting coastal shellfish and crab, to harvesting offshore resources such as deep sea fish and marine mammals such as whales and seals. Augmenting the protein from hunting or fishing, gathered wild plant resources, such as fruits, nuts, roots, tubers, and berries typically provide a large percentage of the calories that go into any meal. Gathering requires expert knowledge of where plant resources can be found, when they will be best to harvest, and how to prepare them for consumption. Foraging is the only immediate return subsistence system.

Foraging societies tend to have what is called a **broad spectrum diet**: a diet based on a wide range of resources. Many of the foods regularly eaten by foragers, such as insects and worms, would not necessarily be considered edible by many people in the United States. For example, many people do not know that earthworms are a good source of iron and high-quality protein, roughly equivalent to eggs, but that is exactly what anthropologists learned by studying the diet of foraging societies in Venezuela.[4] Foragers are scientists of their own ecosystems, having acquired extensive knowledge of the natural world through experience that allows them to exploit many kinds of food resources. The Aché, a foraging group living in the subtropical rainforest in Paraguay, eat 33 different kinds of mammals, more than 15 species of fish, the adult forms of 5 insects, 10 types of larvae, and at least 14 kinds of honey. This is in addition to finding and collecting 40 species of plants.[5] The !Kung foragers, who live in the Kalahari Desert in southern Africa, treasure the mongongo nut, which is tasty, high in protein, and abundant for most of the year, but they also hunt giraffes, six species of antelope, and many kinds of smaller game like porcupine.[6]

In general, foraging societies are small, with low population densities of less than 5 people per square mile. Large families and communities are not necessarily desirable since more mouths to feed can equate to increased pressure to find food. Another factor that contributes to a lower population density is the fact that it is more difficult for the young and the elderly to participate in food procurement. Children only gradually acquire the skills necessary to successfully find food and generally do not make significant contributions to the group until their teenage years. Likewise, elders who can no longer produce enough food themselves expect to be cared for by others.[7]

One important hallmark of foraging societies is their egalitarian social structure. Stark differences in wealth, which characterize many societies, are rare in foraging communities. One reason for this is that foragers have a different perspective on private property. Foraging societies tend to move their camps frequently to exploit various resources, so holding on to a lot of personal possessions or "wealth" is impractical. Foragers also place a high cultural value on generosity. Sharing of food and other resources is a social norm and a measure of a person's goodness. Those who resist sharing what they have with others might be ridiculed, or could even become social outcasts.[8] Over the long term, daily habits of giving and receiving reinforce social equality. This practice is also an important survival strategy that helps groups get through times of food scarcity.

Though foragers have high levels of social equality, not everyone is treated exactly the same. Gender inequality exists in many communities and develops from the fact that work among foragers is often divided along gender lines. Some jobs, such as hunting large animals, belong to men whose success in hunting gives them high levels of respect and prestige. While women do hunt in many communities and often contribute the majority of the group's food through gathering, their work tends not to be as socially prestigious.[9] Likewise, elders in foraging communities tend to command respect and enjoy a higher social status, particularly if they have skills in healing or ritual activities.

Rule-Breaking Foragers

Nomadic lifestyles are the norm for most foragers, but there have been some societies that have broken this rule and developed large-scale sedentary societies. This was possible in areas with abundant natural resources, most often fish. Historically, fishing formed the foundation of large-scale foraging societies in Peru, the Pacific Northwest (the Kwakwa̱ka̱'wakw), and Florida (the Calusa). These societies all developed advanced fishing technologies that provided enough food surplus that some people could stop participating in food procurement activities.

The Kwakwa̱ka̱'wakw of the Pacific Northwest provide an excellent example. In that region, the salmon that spawn in the rivers are so abundant that they could support sedentary populations of a size that would normally be associated with intensive agriculture. Because there was a surplus of food, some members of society were able to pursue other full-time occupations or specializations such as working as artisans or even becoming "chiefs." This led to wealth differences and social inequality that would not normally be found in a foraging community. Conscious of the corrosive effect of wealth and status differences on their community, the Kwakwa̱ka̱'wakw developed a tradition of potlatch, a kind of "extreme gift-giving" to neutralize some of these tensions.

Assessing the Foraging Lifestyle

In 1651, the English philosopher Thomas Hobbes became one of the first scholars to comment on foragers, describing their lifestyle as "nasty, brutish, and short." We now realize that his viewpoint was colored by ethnocentrism and, more specifically, Eurocentrism. Hobbes, as well as many scholars that came after him, viewed Western societies as the pinnacle of social evolution and viewed less technologically advanced societies as deficient, antiquated, or primitive, a perspective that persisted well into the twentieth century.

In the 1960s, the anthropological perspective on foragers changed when Marshall Sahlins suggested that these communities were "the original affluent society." He argued that foragers had an idyllic life, in which only a small percentage of the day was spent "working," or acquiring resources, and most of the day was spent in leisure and socializing, leading to stronger community and family bonds:

> Hunter-gatherers consume less energy per capita per year than any other group of human beings. Yet when you come to examine it the original affluent society was none other than the hunter's—in which all the people's material wants were easily satisfied. To accept that hunters are affluent is therefore to recognize that the present human condition of man slaving to bridge the gap between his unlimited wants and his insufficient means is a tragedy of modern times.[10]

Today anthropologists recognize that foraging, far from being primitive, is one of the most effective and dynamic subsistence systems humans have ever developed, yet Sahlins' conception of the original affluent society is overly romantic. Foraging is a challenging lifestyle; some groups spend up to 70 hours per week collecting food. The amount of leisure time and relative comfort of the foraging lifestyle vary significantly based on differences in the availability of food and environmental conditions.[11]

Contemporary studies of foraging also recognize that foragers have rarely lived in isolation. Throughout the world, foragers have lived near farming populations for hundreds or even thousands of years. Conflicts and competition for resources with non-foraging societies have characterized the foraging experience and foragers, with their relatively small population size and limited technology, have often been on the losing end of these confrontations. Government policies containing foragers to small "reservation" areas or forcing them to settle in towns have had catastrophic effects on foragers, as has the destruction through agricultural and industrial development of the ecosystems on which many groups once depended. A sad worldwide pattern of exploitation and marginalization is the reason that many foragers today live in dwindling communities in marginal ecological zones.[12]

The Built Environment and Domesticated Landscapes

None of us live in a natural environment. Current research on the causes of global climate change have demonstrated that humans are having a profound effect on the Earth and its ecosystems, but it would be a mistake to conclude that human effects on the environment are a recent development. Humans have been making environmental alterations for a long time and we have been engaged in a process of domesticating the planet for several thousand years. For this reason, no part of the planet can really be considered 100 percent "natural." When anthropologists study subsistence, they gain a window into the ways in which cultures have co-evolved with their environments, a field of study known as **historical ecology**. Analysis of the ways in which cultures and the environment are mutually interconnected, demonstrates that there is no way to separate the "natural" world from the human-influenced world, or what anthropologists refer to as the **built environment**.

This can be seen by considering the historical ecology of the Nukak, a group of foragers who live in the Amazon rainforest near the headwaters of the Rio Negro along the southern border between Colombia and Venezuela and whose subsistence demonstrates the blurry line between foraging and agriculture and "natural" and "domesticated." The Nukak are a small linguistic and ethnic group who are part of the larger culture known as Makú. The Nukak were the last among the Makú to be contacted by the outside world and perhaps owing to this fact, they practice the most "traditional" way of life. The Nukak were not known to the public at large until 1988, when a group of 41 individuals came in contact with a school in the rural town of Calamar, in southeastern Colombia.

The Nukak are a highly mobile group of foragers who make an average of between 70 and 80 residential moves a year. The frequency of their moves changes seasonally: infrequent short-distance moves in the wet season, and more frequent long-distance moves occurring in the dry season. Anthropologist Gustavo Politis, who spent years living with the Nukak, observed that the Nukak will never occupy the same camp twice, even if they are moving to an area where an old camp is still in good shape. When they establish a camp, they remove all the light brush and some of the medium-sized trees, leaving a few medium-sized trees and all the large trees intact.

Due to the selective nature of the forest clearing, a habitat, which can most readily be described as a "wild orchard," is produced. This wild orchard offers nearly perfect conditions for the germination and growth of seeds because the large trees provide enough shade to prevent the invasion of vines and shrubs. As the Nukak use the camp and consume fruit they have gathered, they discard the uneaten portions, including the seeds. Significantly, the kinds of fruit the Nukak tend to eat in their camps are the ones that have hard outer seed cases. Once discarded in a Nukak campsite, these seeds have a higher chance of germinating and growing in the abandoned camp than they do in other parts of the rainforest. The result is that Nukak territory is peppered with wild orchards that have high concentrations of edible plants, and the forest reflects a pattern of human intervention long after the Nukak have departed.[13]

The Nukak are an important case study in the Amazon for a number of reasons. They are a testament to the ability of small foraging groups to domesticate landscapes in active ways that greatly increase the productivity of the environment. They do this even though they are not "farmers" and will not always utilize the resources they help create. In addition, the Nukak demonstrate that no place in the Amazon can be considered *pristine* if a group such as the Nukak have ever lived there. The same can be said for the rest of the planet.

The Domestication of the Dog and Cooperative Hunting

Although the transition from foraging to agriculture is often described as the Agricultural Revolution, archaeological evidence suggests this change took a long time. The earliest species humans chose to domesticate were often not staple crops such as wheat, corn, rice, or cows, but utilitarian species. For instance, bottle gourds were domesticated for use as water containers before the invention of pottery. Dogs were domesticated as early as 15,000 years ago in eastern Asia from their wild ancestor the wolf. Although it is unlikely that dogs were an important source of food, they did play a role in subsistence by aiding humans who relied on hunting the Ice Age megafauna such as wooly mammoths. Dogs played such a critical role in hunting that some archaeologists believe they may have contributed to the eventual extinction of the woolly mammoths.[14] Dogs were also valued for their role as watchdogs capable of protecting the community from predators and invaders.

Figure 3: The woolly mammoth was hunted to extinction in North America at the end of the last ice age. It is possible that dogs played a role in hunting these and other large game animals.

Pastoralism

"To us, a co-wife is something very good, because there is much work to do. When it rains . . . the village gets mucky. And it's you who clears it out. It's you who . . . looks after the cows. You do the milking . . . and your husband may have very many cows. That's a lot of work. . . . So Maasai aren't jealous because of all this work."
—Maiyani, Maasai woman [15]

Pastoralism is a subsistence system that relies on herds of domesticated livestock. Over half of the world's pastoralists reside in Africa, but there are also large pastoralist populations in Central Asia, Tibet, and arctic Scandinavia and Siberia. The need to supply grazing fields and water for the livestock requires moving several times a year. For that reason, this subsistence system is sometimes referred to as nomadic pastoralism. In Africa, for instance, a nomadic lifestyle is an adaptation to the frequent periods of drought that characterize the region and put stress on the grazing pastures. Pastoralists may also follow a nomadic lifestyle for other reasons such as avoiding competition and conflict with neighbors or avoiding government restrictions.

Pastoralists can raise a range of different animals, although most often they raise herd animals such as cows, goats, sheep, and pigs. In some parts of South America, alpaca and llama have been domesticated for centuries to act as beasts of burden, much like camels, horses, and donkeys are used in Asia and Africa. Pastoralists who raise alpacas, donkeys, or camels, animals not typically considered food, demonstrate an important point about the pastoralist subsistence system. The goal of many pastoralists is not to produce animals to slaughter for meat, but instead to use other resources such as milk, which can be transformed into butter, yogurt, and cheese, or products like fur or wool, which can be sold. Even animal dung is useful as an alternate source of fuel and can be used as an architectural product to seal the roofs of houses. In some pastoral societies, milk and milk products comprise between 60 and 65 percent of the total caloric intake. However, very few, if any, pastoralist groups survive by eating only animal products. Trade with neighboring farming communities helps pastoralists obtain a more balanced diet and gives them access to grain and other items they do not produce on their own.

Figure 4: A Typical Maasai Herd: Although women do most of the work of tending the herd, only men are allowed to own cattle

A community of animal herders has different labor requirements compared to a foraging community. Caring for large numbers of animals and processing their products requires a tremendous amount of work, chores that are nonexistent in foraging societies. For pastoralists, daily chores related to caring for livestock translate into a social world structured as much around the lives of animals as around the lives of people.

The Maasai, a society of east African pastoralists whose livelihood depends on cows, have been studied extensively by anthropologists. Among the Maasai, domestic life is focused almost entirely around tasks and challenges associated with managing the cattle herds. Like many pastoralist communities, the Maasai measure wealth and social status according to the number of animals a person owns. However, raising cattle requires so much work that no one has the ability to do these jobs entirely on his or her own. For the Maasai, the solution is to work together in family units organized around polygynous marriages. A household with multiple wives and large numbers of children will have more labor power available for raising animals.

Pastoralism and Gender Dynamics

The example of the Maasai demonstrates the extent to which a subsistence system can structure gender roles and the division of labor between the sexes. In Maasai society, women do almost all of the work with the cows, from milking several times each day to clearing the muck the cows produce. Despite doing much of the daily work with cattle, Maasai women are not permitted to own cattle. Instead, the cattle belong to the men, and women are given only "milking rights" that allow them to use the products of the female animals and to assign these animals to their sons. Men make all decisions about slaughtering, selling, and raising the cattle. Lack of cattle ownership means that women do not have the same opportunities as men to build wealth or gain social status and the woman's role in Maasai society is subordinate to man's. This same pattern is repeated in many pastoralist societies, with women valued primarily for the daily labor they can provide and for their role as mothers.

While women lack the political and economic power enjoyed by Maasai men, they do exercise some forms of power within their own households and among other women. They support each other in the daily hard work of managing both cattle and domestic responsibilities, for instance sharing in childcare, a practice based on the belief that "men care about cattle while women care about children."[16] Because most marriages are arranged by elders, it is common for women to engage in love affairs with other men, but women keep each other's secrets; telling anyone about another woman's adultery would be considered an absolute betrayal of solidarity. Women who resist their husband's authority by having love affairs are also resisting larger claims of male authority and ownership over them.[17]

Pastoralism and Private Property

As discussed previously, foragers tend to have little private property. Obtaining food from the natural environment and living a highly mobile lifestyle does not provide the right conditions for hoarding wealth, while the strong value on sharing present in foraging communities also limits wealth differences. Pastoralists, in contrast, have a great deal of personal property: most of it in the form of animals, a kind of "money on legs," but also in the form of household objects and personal items like clothing or jewelry that pastoralists can keep more easily than foragers because they do not move as frequently.

Ownership of the grazing land, water supply, and other resources required for livestock is a trickier matter. Generally, these natural resources are treated as communal property shared by everyone in the society. Pastoralists may range over hundreds of miles throughout the year, so it would be highly impractical to "own" any particular plot of land or to try fencing it to exclude outsiders as is commonly done by agriculturalists. Sharing resources can lead to conflict, however, both within pastoralist societies and between pastoralists and their neighbors. In an influential essay, *Tragedy of the Commons* (1968), Garrett Hardin pointed out that people tend not to respect resources they do not own. For instance, pastoralists who have a personal interest in raising as many cattle of their own as possible may not be particularly motivated to preserve grass or water resources in the long term. Do pastoralists destroy the environments in which they live? Evidence from anthropological studies of pastoralist communities suggests that pastoralists do have rules that regulate use of land and other resources and that these restrictions are effective in conserving environmental resources.

The Maasai, for instance, have a complex land-management system that involves rotating pastures seasonally and geographically to preserve both grass and water. Research conducted in Kenya and

Tanzania suggests that these grazing practices improve the health and biodiversity of the ecosystem because grazing cattle cut down the tall grasses and make habitats for warthogs, Thomson's gazelle, and other species. In addition, the large swaths of community land managed by the Maasai stabilize and support the vast Serengeti ecosystem. Ecologists estimate that if this land were privately owned and its usage restricted, the population of wildebeest would be reduced by one-third. Since thousands of tourists visit the Serengeti each year to view wildlife, particularly the migration of the wildebeest, which is the largest mammal migration in the world, the Maasai's communal land management is worth an estimated $83.5 million to the tourist economies of Kenya and Tanzania.[18]

Despite the sophistication of their land and animal management techniques, pastoralists today face many pressures. The growth of the tourism industry in many countries has led to increased demand for private land ownership to support safari centers, wild game parks, and ecolodges. The steady growth of human populations and intensive agriculture has also led to the widespread encroachment of cities and farms into traditional pastoralist territories. Persistent drought, famine, and even civil war threaten some pastoralist groups, particularly in central Africa. Meanwhile, pastoralists continue to experience tense relationships with their agricultural neighbors as both groups compete for resources, disputes that are intensifying as global warming leads to more intense heat and drought in many world regions.

Horticulture

"Yams are persons with ears. If we charm they hear."
—Alo, Trobriand Island farmer[19]

Have you ever grown a garden in your backyard? How much time did you put into your garden? How much of your diet did the garden yield? People whose gardens supply the majority of their food are known as **horticulturalists.** Horticulture differs in three ways from other kinds of farming. First, horticulturalists move their farm fields periodically to use locations with the best growing conditions. For this reason, horticulture is sometimes known as shifting cultivation. Second, horticultural societies use limited mechanical technologies to farm, relying on physical labor from people and animals, like oxen that may be used to pull a plow, instead of mechanical farm equipment. Finally, horticulture differs from other kinds of farming in its scale and purpose. Most farmers in the United States sell their crops as a source of income, but in horticultural societies crops are consumed by those who grow them or are exchanged with others in the community rather than sold for profit.

Horticultural societies are common around the world; this subsistence system feeds hundreds of thousands of people, primarily in tropical areas of south and central America, Southeast Asia, and Oceania. A vast array of horticultural crops may be grown by horticulturalists, and farmers use their specialized knowledge to select crops that have high yield compared to the amount of labor that must be invested to grow them. A good example is manioc, also known as cassava. Manioc can grow in a variety of tropical environments and has the distinct advantage of being able to remain in the ground for long periods without rotting. Compared to corn or wheat, which must be harvested within a particular window of time to avoid spoiling, manioc is flexible and easier to grow as well as to store or distribute to others. Bananas, plantains, rice, and yams are additional examples of popular horticultural crops. One thing all these plants have in common, though, is that they lack protein and other important nutrients. Horticultural societies must supplement their diets by raising animals such as pigs and chickens or by hunting and fishing.

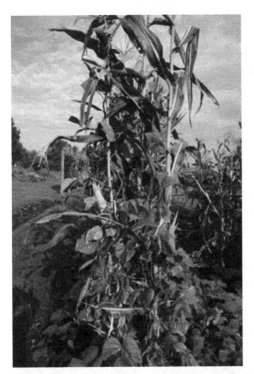

Figure 5: Bean plants grow up the stalk of a corn plant, while squash vines grow along the ground between corn stalks, inhibiting weed growth, an innovative technique developed by indigenous farmers in the Americas thousands of years ago.

Growing crops in the same location for several seasons leads to depletion of the nutrients in the soil as well as a concentration of insects and other pests and plant diseases. In agricultural systems like the one used in the United States, these problems are addressed through the use of fertilizers, pesticides, irrigation, and other technologies that can increase crop yields even in bad conditions. Horticulturalists respond to these problems by moving their farm fields to new locations. Often this means clearing a section of the forest to make room for a new garden, a task many horticulturalists accomplish by cutting down trees and setting controlled fires to burn away the undergrowth. This approach, sometimes referred to as "slash-and-burn," sounds destructive and has often been criticized, but the ecological impact is complex. Once abandoned, farm fields immediately begin to return to a forested state; over time, the quality of the soil is renewed. Farmers often return after several years to reuse a former field, and this recycling of farmland reduces the amount of forest that is disturbed. While they may relocate their farm fields with regularity, horticulturalists tend not to move their residences, so they rotate through gardens located within walking distance of their homes.

Horticulturalists practice multi-cropping, growing a variety of different plants in gardens that are biodiverse. Growing several different crops reduces the risk of relying on one kind of food and allows for intercropping, mixing plants in ways that are advantageous. A well-known and ingenious example of intercropping is the practice of growing beans, corns, and squash together. Native American farmers in the pre-colonial period knew that together these plants, sometimes called "the three sisters," were healthier than they were if grown separately. Rather than completely clearing farmland, horticulturalists often maintain some trees and even weeds around the garden as a habitat for predators that prey on garden pests. These practices, in addition to skillful rotation of the farmland itself, make horticultural gardens particularly resilient.

Food as Politics

Because daily life for horticulturalists revolves around care for crops, plants are not simply regarded as food but also become the basis for social relationships. In the Trobriand Islands, which are located in the Solomon Sea north of Papua New Guinea, yams are the staple crop. Just as a Maasai pastoralist gains respect by raising a large herd of animals, Trobriand Island farmers earn their reputations by having large numbers of yams. However, this is not as easy as it might seem. In Trobriand Island society every man maintains a yam garden, but he is not permitted to keep his entire crop. Women "own" the yams and men must share what they grow with their daughters, their sisters, and even with their wives' family members. Other yams must be given to the chief or saved to exchange on special occasions such as weddings, funerals, or festivals. With so many obligations, it is not surprising that the average man would have trouble building an impressive yam pile on his own. Fortunately, just as men have obligations to others, so too can they expect gifts from their sisters' husbands and their friends in the community.

A large pile of yams, displayed proudly in a man's specially constructed yam house, is an indication of how well he is respected by his family and friends. Maintaining these positive relationships requires constant work, and men must reciprocate gifts of yams received from others or risk losing those relationships. Men who are stingy or mean spirited will not receive many yams, and their lack of social approval will be obvious to everyone who glances at their empty yam houses. The chief has the largest yam house of all, but also the most obligations. To maintain the goodwill of the people, he is expected to sponsor feasts with his yam wealth and to support members of the community who may need yams throughout the year.

So central are yams to Trobriand Island life that yams have traditionally been regarded not as mere plants, but as living beings with minds of their own. Farmers talk to their yams, using a special tone and soft voice so as not to alarm the vegetables. Men who have been initiated into the secret practices of yam magic use incantations or magical charms to affect the growth of the plants, or alternatively to discourage the growth of a rival's crop. Yams are believed to have the ability to wander away from their fields at night unless magic is used to keep them in place. These practices show the close social and spiritual association between farmers and their crops.

Civilizing Beans

Beans are often associated with gastrointestinal problems, namely flatulence. It turns out that this is related to the history of the domestication of the bean. Beans, along with maize and squash, were one of the most important crops domesticated by Native Americans in the New World. The benefits of eating beans are best understood when viewed in relation to maize cultivation. From a purely nutritional point of view, beans are a good source of protein while corn is not. Corn is also deficient in the essential amino acids lysine and tryptophan. Eating maize and beans together provides more protein for hardworking farmers. In addition, maize and beans have a mutually beneficial relationship in the garden. Thanks to a symbiotic relationship with a bacteria known as Rhizobium, beans and almost all legumes fix usable nitrogen in the soil, increasing fertility for other plants grown nearby. When intercropped, maize benefits from this nitrogen fixing, and beans benefit from being able to attach their vines to the strong stalks of the maize. Squash, which grows large leaves that spread widely across the ground, are also beneficial to intercrop with maize and beans because the leaves reduce pest and weed invasion by providing ground cover.

Despite being nutritious and useful in the garden, beans were domesticated relatively late. In Mexico, there is evidence of bean domestication around 1000 BC, a thousand years later than the domestication of corn.[20] This is probably because of the gastrointestinal problems that come with eating beans. The flatulence is the result of certain chemicals found in the wild beans that were ancestral to today's domesticated species. The lack of digestibility surely made beans an unappetizing food in early human communities. However, soaking beans before cooking them and then boiling them over direct heat for several hours reduces these chemicals and makes beans much easier to stomach. The ability to boil water was the key to bringing beans to the table.

Archaeological studies in Central America have revealed that the invention of pottery was the technological breakthrough needed to boil beans. A particular type of pottery known as the "culinary shoe pot" was one of these technological innovations. The pots are used by placing the "foot" of the pot in the coals of a fire so heat can be transmitted through the vessel for long periods of time. Pots of this design have been found in the archaeological record throughout Central America in sites dating to the same period as the beginning of bean domestication and pots of similar design continue to be used throughout that region today. This example demonstrates the extent to which the expansion of the human diet has been linked to innovations in other areas of culture.

Figure 6: A Culinary Shoe Pot from Oaxaca, Mexico. Courtesy of the Burke Museum of Natural History and Culture, Catalog Number 2009–117/536

Figure 7: Clay Cooking Pots in the Republic of Suriname. Courtesy of Karina Noriega.

Agriculture

"The adoption of agriculture, supposedly our most decisive step toward a better life, was in many ways a catastrophe from which we have never recovered."
—Jared Diamond [21]

Agriculture is defined as the cultivation of domesticated plants and animals using technologies such as irrigation, draft animals, mechanization, and inputs such as fertilizers and pesticides that allow for intensive and continuous use of land resources. About 10,000 years ago, human societies entered a period of rapid innovation in subsistence technologies that paved the way for the emergence of agriculture. The transition from foraging to farming has been described as the **Neolithic Revolution**. Neolithic means "new stone age," a name referring to the very different looking stone tools produced during this time period. The Neolithic was characterized by an explosion of new technologies, not all of them made from stone, which were geared toward agricultural tasks, rather than hunting or processing gathered plant foods. These new tools included scythes for harvesting plants, and adzes or hoes for tilling the soil. These technological developments began to dramatically improve yields and allow human communities to support larger and larger numbers of people on food produced in less space. It is important to remember that the invention of agriculture was not necessarily an advance in efficiency, because more work had to go in to producing more food. Instead, it was an *intensification* of horticultural strategies. As a subsistence system, agriculture is quite different from other ways of making a living, and the invention of agriculture had far-ranging effects on the development of human communities. In analyzing agriculture and its impacts, anthropologists focus on four important characteristics shared by agricultural communities.

The first characteristic of agriculture is reliance on a few **staple crops**, foods that form the backbone of the subsistence system. An example of a staple crop would be rice in China, or potatoes in Ireland. In agricultural societies, farmers generally grow a surplus of these staple crops, more than they need for their own tables, which are then sold for profit. The reliance on a single plant species, or **mono-cropping**, can lead to decreased dietary diversity and carries the risk of malnutrition compared to a more diverse diet. Other risks include crop failure associated with bad weather conditions or blight, leading to famine and malnutrition, conditions that are common in agricultural communities.

A second hallmark of agriculture is the link between intensive farming and a rapid increase in human population density. The archaeological record shows that human communities grew quickly around the time agriculture was developing, but this raises an interesting question. Did the availability of more food lead to increases in human population? Or, did pressure to provide for a growing population spur humans to develop better farming techniques? This question has been debated for many years. Ester Boserup, who studied the emergence of agriculture, concluded that growth in human populations preceded the development of agriculture, forcing communities to develop innovations in technology. However, the improved productive capabilities of agriculture came at a cost. People were able to produce more food with agriculture, but only by working harder and investing more in the maintenance of the land. The life of a farmer involved more daily hours of work compared to the lifestyle of a forager, so agricultural communities had an incentive to have larger families so that children could help with farm labor. However, the presence of more children also meant more mouths to feed, increasing the pressure to further expand agricultural production. In this way, agriculture and population growth became a cycle.

A third characteristic of agriculture is the development of a division of labor, a system in which individuals in a society begin to specialize in certain roles or tasks. Building houses, for instance, becomes a full-time job separate from farming. The division of labor was possible because higher yields from agriculture meant that the quest for food no longer required everyone's participation. This feature of agriculture is what has allowed nonagricultural occupations such as scientists, religious specialists, politicians, lawyers, and academics to emerge and flourish.

The emergence of specialized occupations and an agricultural system geared toward producing surplus rather than subsistence changed the economics of human communities. The final characteristic of agriculture is its tendency to create wealth differences. For anthropologists, agriculture is a critical factor explaining the origins of social class and wealth inequality. The more complex an economic system becomes, the more opportunities individuals or factions within the society have to manipulate the economy for their own benefit. Who do you suppose provided the bulk of the labor power needed in early agricultural communities? Elites found ways to pass this burden to others. Agricultural societies were among the first to utilize enslaved and indentured labor.

Although the development of agriculture is generally regarded as a significant technological achievement that made our contemporary way of life possible, agriculture can also be viewed as a more ominous development that forced us to invest more time and labor in our food supply while yielding a lower quality of life.[22] Agriculture created conditions that led to the expansion of social inequality, violent conflict between communities, and environmental degradation. For these reasons, some scientists like Jared Diamond have argued that the invention of agriculture was humanity's worst mistake.

The Origins of Agriculture

Some of the most contested and exciting questions in anthropology center on the origins of agriculture. How did humans come to adopt an agricultural way of life? What came first, permanent settlements or agriculture? Did agriculture develop first in places with rich natural resources, or in places where making a living from the land was more difficult? Why did agriculture arise nearly simultaneously in so many world regions? These questions are primarily investigated by archaeologists, anthropologists who study cultures of the past by recovering the material remains of their settlements. Archaeological evidence suggests that the transition to agriculture occurred over a long period of time, across many generations.

Lewis Binford, an archaeologist who studied the origins of agriculture, observed that humans were living in permanent settlements before the end of the last ice age 10,000–12,000 years ago. He believed that as human populations grew, some communities were forced into marginal natural environments where it was difficult to get food from foraging, pastoralism, or horticulture. He argued that the pressure of living in these "tension zones" led to agricultural innovation.[23] Although inventing agriculture might seem like a challenge for humanity, the cultural anthropologist Leslie White pointed out that by this time in human history all communities had substantial practical knowledge of the natural world and the plant and animal species they depended on for survival. "The cultivation of plants required no new facts or knowledge. Agriculture was simply a new kind of relationship between man—or more properly, woman—and plants."[24] By moving plants into new environments and controlling their growth, people were able to ensure a better food supply.

This may explain why domestication arose, but why did it take so long for humans to develop agriculture? Why did many societies all over the world develop agriculture nearly simultaneously? One possible answer is found in the climate change that followed the end of the last ice age. Warming temperatures and shifting environmental zones led to the extinction of the megafauna human hunters had been relying upon such as musk ox, woolly mammoth and woolly rhinoceros, and giant deer. Many animals once preyed on these species, such as the cave lion and spotted hyena, but humans may have adapted culturally by reorienting their diets toward domesticated plant and animal species.

There are some other interesting theories about how and why agriculture developed. Brian Hayden, an archaeologist specializing in political ecology, the use of resources to achieve political goals, has suggested that agriculture arose as some members of society began to accumulate resources in order to sponsor feasts and give gifts designed to influence others. This "feasting theory" suggests that agriculture was not a response to the necessities of survival, but part of a quest for power among some members of society.[25] This model is intriguing because it explains why some of the earliest domesticates such as chili peppers and avocados are not staple foods and are not even particularly nutritious. In fact, many of the earliest plants cultivated were not intended to produce food for meals, but rather to produce ingredients for alcoholic beverages.

For example, the wild ancestor of corn, a plant called teosinte, has an edible "ear" so small that it would have cost more calories to chew than the nutrition it provided. This led some archaeologists to theorize that it was in fact the sweetness in the stalk of the plant that farmers wanted to utilize to ferment a corn-based alcoholic beverage still consumed in many parts of Central America called *chicha*. It might have been that only after years of cultivating the crop for its stalk that farmers found uses for the ear, which later was selectively bred to grow to the sizes we are familiar with today.

Teosinte   Modern Corn

Figure 8: Domestication involves the manipulation of plant and animal species to promote characteristics that are useful to the gardeners, such as the size. The evolution of the modern corn from the ancestral teosinte followed selective breeding practices of farmers in the Americas.

THE GLOBAL AGRICULTURE SYSTEM

"We can indeed eliminate the scourge of hunger in our lifetime. We must be the Zero Hunger generation."

—José Graziano da Silva, Director General of the Food and Agricultural Organization of the United Nations [26]

Despite agriculture's tremendous productivity, food shortages, malnutrition, and famines are common around the world. How can this be? Many people assume that the world's agricultural systems are not capable of producing enough food for everyone, but this is incorrect. Evidence from agricultural research demonstrates that there is enough worldwide agricultural capacity to feed everyone on the planet.[27] The problem is that this capacity is unevenly distributed. Some countries produce much more food than they need, and others much less. In addition, distribution systems are inefficient and much food is lost to waste or spoilage. It is also true that in an agricultural economy food costs money, and worldwide many people who are starving or undernourished lack food because they cannot pay for it, not because food itself is unavailable.

Let's return for a moment to the concept of meals and where our food actually comes from. Walking down the aisles of our local grocery store, we are surrounded by products that come from far away: apples from Chile, coffee from Guatemala, beans from India. This is evidence that our economy is organized around what anthropologists refer to as a **world system**, a complex web through which goods circulate around the globe. In the world system, complex chains of distribution separate the producers of goods from the consumers. Agricultural products travel long distances from their points of origin to reach consumers in the grocery store, passing through many hands along the way. The series of steps a food like apples or coffee takes from the field to the store is known as a **commodity chain**.

The commodity chain for agricultural products begins in the farms where plant and animal foods are produced. Farmers generally do not sell their produce directly to consumers, but instead sell to large food processors that refine the food into a more useable form. Coffee beans, for instance, must be roasted before they can be sold. Following processing, food moves to wholesalers who will package it for sale to retail establishments like grocery stores. As foods move through the commodity chain,

Figure 9: Links in the Commodity Chain for Coffee: As the coffee changes hands from the growers, to the exporters, to the importers, and then to the retail distributers, the value of the coffee increases. Consider the differences in wage between these workers.

they become more valuable. Coffee beans harvested fresh from the field are worth $1.40 per pound to the farmer, but sell for $10–$20 at Starbucks.[28]

The fact that food is more valuable at the end of the commodity chain than at the beginning has several consequences for human communities. The most obvious of these is the reality that farming is not a particularly lucrative occupation, particularly for small-scale farmers in developing countries. Though their labor makes profit for others, these farmers see the lowest financial returns. Another effect of global commodity chains is that food moves very far from its point of origin. For wealthy people, this means having access to a variety of foods in the grocery store, including things like strawberries or mangos in the middle of winter, but in order to serve markets in wealthy countries, food is diverted away from the locales where it is grown. When quinoa, a high-protein grain grown in Bolivia, became popular with health enthusiasts in wealthy countries, the price of this food more than tripled. Local populations began to export their quinoa crop rather than eating it, replacing this nutritious traditional food with white bread and Coca-Cola, which were much cheaper, but contributed to increased rates of obesity and diabetes.[29] The global travels of the food supply have also affected social relations that were once strengthened by participation in food growing and sharing. Distance and competition have replaced these communal experiences. Many people yearn for more connection with their food, a sentiment that fuels things like "foodie culture," farm-to-table restaurants, and farmer's markets.

CONCLUSION

This chapter began with a consideration of meals, but revealed that each individual meal is part of a diet generated through a particular subsistence system. Many of our daily experiences, including our attitudes, skills, and relationships with others, are influenced by our subsistence system. Knowing that the Earth has been transformed for thousands of years by human subsistence activities, we must also consider the ways in which our future will be shaped by the present. Are we managing our resources in a sustainable way? How will we continue to feed growing populations in the future? Think about it next time you sit down to eat a meal.

DISCUSSION QUESTIONS

1. A hallmark of agriculture is the separation of food production from food consumption; many people know almost nothing about where their food has come from. How does this lack of knowledge affect the food choices people make? How useful are efforts to change food labels to notify shoppers about the use of farming techniques such as genetic modification or organic growing for consumers? What other steps could be taken to make people more knowledgeable about the journey that food takes from farm to table?
2. The global commodity chains that bring food from many countries to grocery stores in the United States give wealthy consumers a great variety of food choices, but the farmers at the beginning of the commodity chain earn very little money. What kinds of solutions might help reduce the concentration of wealth at the end of the commodity chain?
3. Mono-cropping is a feature of industrial food production and has the benefit of producing staple foods like wheat and corn in vast quantities, but mono-cropping makes our diet less diverse. Are the effects of agricultural mono-cropping reflected in your own everyday diet? How many different plant foods do you eat on a regular basis? How difficult would it be for you to obtain a more diverse diet by shopping in the same places you shop now?

GLOSSARY

Agriculture: the cultivation of domesticated plants and animals using technologies that allow for intensive use of the land.

Broad spectrum diet: a diet based on a wide range of food resources.

Built environment: spaces that are human-made, including cultivated land as well as buildings.

Carrying capacity: a measurement of the number of calories that can be extracted from a particular unit of land in order to support a human population.

Commodity chain: the series of steps a food takes from location where it is produced to the store where it is sold to consumers.

Delayed return system: techniques for obtaining food that require an investment of work over a period of time before the food becomes available for consumption. Farming is a delayed return system due to the passage of time between planting and harvest. The opposite is an **immediate return system** in which the food acquired can be immediately consumed. Foraging is an immediate return system.

Domestic economy: the work associated with obtaining food for a family or household.

Foodways: the cultural norms and attitudes surrounding food and eating.

Foraging: a subsistence system that relies on wild plant and animal food resources. This system is sometimes called "hunting and gathering."

Historical ecology: the study of how human cultures have developed over time as a result of interactions with the environment.

Horticulture: a subsistence system based on the small-scale cultivation of crops intended primarily for the direct consumption of the household or immediate community.

Modes of subsistence: the techniques used by the members of a society to obtain food. Anthropologists classify subsistence into four broad categories: foraging, pastoralism, horticulture, and agriculture.

Mono-cropping: the reliance on a single plant species as a food source. Mono-cropping leads to decreased dietary diversity and carries the risk of malnutrition compared to a more diverse diet.

Neolithic Revolution: a period of rapid innovation in subsistence technologies that began 10,000 years ago and led to the emergence of agriculture. Neolithic means "new stone age," a name referring to the stone tools produced during this time period.

Pastoralism: a subsistence system in which people raise herds of domesticated livestock.

Staple crops: foods that form the backbone of the subsistence system by providing the majority of the calories a society consumes.

Subsistence system: the set of skills, practices, and technologies used by members of a society to acquire and distribute food.

World system: a complex economic system through which goods circulate around the globe. The world system for food is characterized by a separation of the producers of goods from the consumers.

ABOUT THE AUTHOR

Isaac Shearn earned his PhD in 2014 at the University of Florida and is an adjunct professor at the Community College of Baltimore County. His work focuses on the archaeology and ethnohistory of the Caribbean and South America, with a focus on public archaeology, developing inclusive and participatory methods. His ongoing research in Dominica allows him to pursue his second major passion in life besides archaeology: music. He has played drums for a Dominican reggae band since 2010.

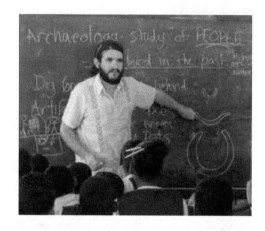

BIBLIOGRAPHY

Binford, Lewis. "Post-Pleistocene adaptations." In *New Perspectives in Archeology,* edited by Sally Binford and Lewis Binford, 313–41. New York: Aldine, 1968.

Boserup, Ester. *The Conditions of Agricultural Growth: The Economics of Agrarian Change Under Population Pressure.* Rutgers, NJ: Transaction Publishers, 2005.

Diamond, Jared. "The Worst Mistake in the History of the Human Race," *Discover,* May 1987, http://discovermagazine.com/1987/may/02-the-worst-mistake-in-the-history-of-the-human-race

Fiedel, Stuart J. "Man's Best Friend -- Mammoth's Worst Enemy? A Speculative Essay on the Role of Dogs in Paleoindian Colonization and Megafaunal Extinction." *World Archaeology* 37 (2005): 11–25.

Food and Agriculture Organization of the United Nations. *The State of Food Insecurity in the World.* Rome: The United Nations, 2015.

———. "World Hunger Falls to Under 800 Million, Eradication Possible." World Food Program, May 27, 2015, https://www.wfp.org/news/news-release/world-hunger-falls-under-800-million-eradication-next-goal-0

Fortune, R. F. *Sorcerers of Dobu: The Social Anthropology of the Dobu Islanders of the Western Pacific.* London: G. Routledge and Sons, 1963 [1932].

Hardin, Garrett. "Tragedy of the Commons." *Science* 162 no. 3859 (1968): 1243–1248.

Hawkes, Kristen and James F. O'Connell. "Affluent Hunters? Some Comments in Light of the Alyawara Case." *American Anthropologist* 83(1981): 622–626.

Hawkes, Kristen, Kim Hill and James F. O'Connell. "Why Hunters Gather: Optimal Foraging and the Aché of Eastern Paraguay." *American Ethnologist* 9 (1982):379–398.

Hayden, Brian. "The Proof is in the Pudding: Feasting and the Origins of Domestication." *Current Anthropology* 50 (2009):597–601, 708–9.

Lee, Richard B. *The !Kung San: Men, Women, and Work in a Foraging Society.* Cambridge: Cambridge University Press, 1979.

———. "What Hunters Do for a Living, or, How to Make Out on Scarce Resources." In *Man the Hunter,* edited by Richard Lee and Irven DeVore. Chicago: Aldine, 1968.

Lee, Richard B. and Irven DeVore, editors. *Man the Hunter.* New York: Aldine, 1968.

Llewellyn-Davies, Melissa. "Two Contexts of Solidarity." In *Women United, Women Divided: Comparative Studies of Ten Contemporary Cultures,* edited by Patricia Caplan and Janet M. Bujra. Bloomington, IN: Indiana University Press 1979.

Malthus, Thomas. *An Essay on the Principle of Population.* London: J. Johnson, 1798.

Nelson, Fred. "Natural Conservationists? Evaluating the Impact of Pastoralist Land Use Practices on Tanzania's Wildlife Economy." *Pastoralism: Research, Policy and Practice* 2012.

Paoletti, Maurizio G., E. Buscardo, D.J. Vanderjagt, A. Pastuszyn, L. Pizzoferrato, Y.S. Huang, L.T. Chuang, M. Millon, H. Cerda, F. Torres, and R.H. Glew. "Nutrient Content of Earthworms Consumed by Ye'Kuana Amerindians of the Alto Orinoco of Venezuela." *Proceedings of the Royal Society: Biological Sciences* 270 (2003): 249–257.

Politis, Gustavo. *Nukak: Ethnoarchaeology of an Amazonian People.* Walnut Creek, CA: Left Coast Press, 2007.

Rosenberg, Harriet G. "Complaint Discourse, Aging, and Caregiving Among the !Kung San of Botswana." In *The Cultural Context of Aging*, edited by Jay Sokolovsky, 19–41. New York: Bergin and Garvey, 1990.

Sahlins, Marshall. "The Original Affluent Society." In *Stone Age Economics*, edited by Marshall Sahlins, 1–39. London: Tavistock, 1972.

Wallace, Melanie and Sanford Low. *Maasai Women*, Film, Produced by Michael Ambrosino. Watertown: CT: Documentary Educational Resources, 1980.

White, Leslie. *The Evolution of Culture: The Development of Civilization to the Fall of Rome.* New York: McGraw Hill, 1959.

NOTES

1. Thomas Malthus, *An Essay on the Principle of Population* (London: J. Johnson, 1798), 4.

2. Ester Boserup, *The Conditions of Agricultural Growth: The Economics of Agrarian Change Under Population Pressure* (Rutgers, NJ: Transaction Publishers, 2005).

3. Richard B. Lee, "What Hunters Do for a Living, or, How to Make Out on Scarce Resources," in *Man the Hunter*, ed. Richard Lee and Irven DeVore (Chicago: Aldine, 1968), 33.

4. Maurizio G.Paoletti, E. Buscardo, DJ Vanderjagt, A Pastuszyn, L Pizzoferrato, YS Huang, et al., "Nutrient Content of Earthworms Consumed by Ye'Kuana Amerindians of the Alto Orinoco of Venezuela," *Proceedings of the Royal Society: Biological Sciences* 270 (2003): 249–257.

5. Kristen Hawkes, Kim Hill and James F. O'Connell, "Why Hunters Gather: Optimal Foraging and the Aché of Eastern Paraguay," *American Ethnologist* 9 (1982):379–398.

6. Richard Lee, *The !Kung San: Men, Women, and Work in a Foraging Society* (Cambridge: Cambridge University Press, 1979).

7. For more information about intergenerational dynamics among foragers see Kathryn Keith "Childhood Learning and the Distribution of Knowledge in Foraging Societies," *Archaeological Papers of the American Anthropological Association* 15 (2005): 27–40 and Harriet G. Rosenberg, "Complaint Discourse, Aging, and Caregiving among the !Kung San of Botswana," in *The Cultural Context of Aging*, ed. Jay Sokolovsky (New York: Bergin and Garvey, 1990)19–41. The quotation is from Rosenberg page 29.

8. For a discussion of generosity and sharing in foraging communities see Lorna Marshall, "Sharing, Talking, and Giving: Relief of Social Tensions among !Kung Bushmen," *Africa: Journal of the International African Institute* 31(1961):231–249 and Lester Hiatt, "Traditional Attitudes to Land Resources," in *Aboriginal Sites, Rites and Resource Development*, ed. R. M. Berndt (Perth: University of Western Australia Press. 1982) 13–26.

9. Richard B. Lee and Irven DeVore, eds. *Man the Hunter* (New York: Aldine, 1968).

10. Marshall Sahlins, "The Original Affluent Society," in *Stone Age Economics*, ed. Marshall Sahlins (London: Tavistock, 1972) 1–39.

11. Kristen Hawkes and James F. O'Connell, "Affluent Hunters? Some Comments in Light of the Alyawara Case," *American Anthropologist* 83(1981): 622–626.

12. See for example Robert J. Gordon, *The Bushman Myth: The Making of a Namibian Underclass* (Boulder, CO: Westview Press, 2000).

13. Gustavo Politis, *Nukak: Ethnoarchaeology of an Amazonian People* (Walnut Creek, CA: Left Coast Press, 2007).

14. Stuart J. Fiedel, "Man's Best Friend -- Mammoth's Worst Enemy? A Speculative Essay on the Role of Dogs in Paleoindian Colonization and Megafaunal Extinction," *World Archaeology* 37 (2005): 11–25.

15. Melanie Wallace and Sanford Low, *Maasai Women*, Film, Produced by Michael Ambrosino (1980, Watertown: CT: Documentary Educational Resources).

16. Melissa Llewellyn-Davies, "Two Contexts of Solidarity," in *Women United, Women Divided: Comparative Studies of Ten Contemporary Cultures*, ed. Patricia Caplan and Janet M. Bujra (Bloomington, IN: Indiana University Press 1979), 208.

17. Ibid., 234.

18. Fred Nelson, "Natural Conservationists? Evaluating the Impact of Pastoralist Land Use Practices on Tanzania's Wildlife Economy," *Pastoralism: Research, Policy and Practice* 2012.

19. R. F. Fortune, *Sorcerers of Dobu: The Social Anthropology of the Dobu Islanders of the Western Pacific* (London: G. Routledge and Sons, 1963 [1932]),107–109.

20. For more information about the archaeological evidence for the timing of bean domestication, see Michael Blake, John E. Clark, Barbara Voorhies, George Michaels, Michael W. Love, Mary E. Pye, Arthur A. Demarest, and Barbara Arroyo, "Radiocarbon Chronology for the Late Archaic and Formative Periods on the Pacific Coast of Southeastern Mesoamerica," Ancient Mesoamerica 6 (1995):161–183. Another useful source is Lawrence Kaplan and Thomas F. Lynch, "Phaseolus (Fabaceae) in Archaeology: AMS Radiocarbon Dates and their Significance for Pre-Columbian Agriculture," *Economic Botany* 53 no. 3(1999): 261–272. There is also interesting linguistic evidence that the word for bean entered the Mayan language around 3400 BC. For more information, see Cecil H Brown, "Prehistoric Chronology of the Common Bean in the New World: The Linguistic Evidence." *American Anthropologist* 108 no.3 (2006): 507–516

23. Lewis Binford, "Post-Pleistocene Adaptations," in New Perspectives in Archeology, ed. Sally and Lewis Binford, 313–41 (New York: Aldine, 1968).

24. Leslie White, The Evolution of Culture: *The Development of Civilization to the Fall of Rome* (New York: McGraw Hill, 1959), 284.

25. Brian Hayden, "The Proof is in the Pudding: Feasting and the Origins of Domestication," Current Anthropology 50 (2009):597–601, 708–9.

21. Jared Diamond, "The Worst Mistake in the History of the Human Race," *Discover*, May 1987, http://discover magazine.com/1987/may/02-the-worst-mistake-in-the-history-of-the-human-race

22. See for example Marshall Sahlins' argument in *Stone Age Economics* (Chicago: Aldine Atherton, 1972).

26. Food and Agriculture Organization of the United Nations, "World Hunger Falls to Under 800 Million, Eradication Possible," May 27, 2015, accessed May 10, 2015, https://www.wfp.org/news/news-release/world-hunger-falls-under-800-million-eradication-next-goal-0

27. Food and Agriculture Organization of the United Nations, *The State of Food Insecurity in the World* (Rome: FAO, 2015)

28. Information about the current prices paid to coffee farmers is available from the International Coffee Organization: http://www.ico.org/coffee_prices.asp

29. This phenomenon has been observed in many countries. For an ethnographic analysis of the health effects of the decline of traditional foods in Guatemala, see Emily Yates-Doerr, *The Weight of Obesity: Hunger and Global Health in Postwar Guatemala* (Berkeley: University of California Press, 2015).

ECONOMICS

Sarah Lyon, University of Kentucky
sarah.lyon@uky.edu
http://anthropology.as.uky.edu/users/smlyon3

LEARNING OBJECTIVES

- Define economic anthropology and identify ways in which economic anthropology differs from the field of Economics.

- Describe the characteristics of the three modes of production: domestic production, tributary production, and capitalist production.

- Compare reciprocity, redistribution, and market modes of exchange.

- Assess the significance of general purpose money for economic exchange.

- Evaluate the ways in which commodities become personally and socially meaningful.

- Use a political economy perspective to assess examples of global economic inequality and structural violence.

One of the hallmarks of the human species is our flexibility: culture enables humans to thrive in extreme artic and desert environments, to make our homes in cities and rural settings alike. Yet amidst this great diversity there are also universals. For example, all humans, like all organisms, must eat. We all must make our living in the world, whether we do so through foraging, farming, or factory work. At its heart, economic anthropology is a study of livelihoods: how humans work to obtain the material necessities such as food, clothing, and shelter that sustain our lives. Across time and space, different societies have organized their economic lives in radically different ways. Economic anthropologists explore this diversity, focusing on how people produce, exchange, and consume material objects and the role that immaterial things such as labor, services, and knowledge play in our efforts to secure our livelihood.[1] As humans, we all have the same basic needs, but understanding how and why we meet those needs—in often shared but sometimes unique ways—is what shapes the field of economic anthropology.

Economic anthropology is always in dialogue (whether implicitly or explicitly) with the discipline of economics.[2] However, there are several important differences between the two disciplines. Perhaps most importantly, economic anthropology encompasses the production, exchange, consumption, meaning, and uses of both material objects and immaterial services, whereas contemporary economics focuses primarily on market exchanges. In addition, economic anthropologists dispute the idea that all individual thoughts, choices, and behaviors can be understood through a narrow lens of rational, self-interested decision-making. When asking why people choose to buy a new shirt rather than shoes, anthropologists, and increasingly economists, look beyond the motives of ***Homo economicus*** to determine how social, cultural, political, and institutional forces shape humans' everyday decisions.[3]

As a discipline, economics studies the decisions made by people and businesses and how these decisions interact in the marketplace. Economists' models generally rest on several assumptions: that people know what they want, that their economic choices express these wants, and that their wants are defined by their culture. Economics is a normative theory because it specifies how people *should* act if they want to make efficient economic decisions. In contrast, anthropology is a largely descriptive social science; we analyze what people *actually do* and why they do it. Economic anthropologists do not necessarily assume that people know what they want (or *why* they want it) or that they are free to act on their own individual desires.

Rather than simply focusing on market exchanges and individual decision-making, anthropologists consider three distinct phases of economic activity: production, exchange, and consumption. Production involves transforming nature and raw materials into the material goods that are useful and/or necessary for humans. Exchange involves how these goods are distributed among people. Finally, consumption refers to how we use these material goods: for example, by eating food or constructing homes out of bricks. This chapter explores each of these dimensions of economic life in detail, concluding with an overview of how anthropologists understand and challenge the economic inequalities that structure everyday life in the twenty-first century.

MODES OF PRODUCTION

A key concept in anthropological studies of economic life is the **mode of production**, or the social relations through which human labor is used to transform energy from nature using tools, skills, organization, and knowledge. This concept originated with anthropologist Eric Wolf, who was strongly influenced by the social theorist Karl Marx. Marx argued that human consciousness is not determined by our cosmologies or beliefs but instead by our most basic human activity: work. Wolf identified three distinct modes of production in human history: domestic (kin-ordered), tributary, and capitalist.[4] Domestic or kin-ordered production organizes work on the basis of family relations and does not necessarily involve formal social domination, or the control of and power over other people. However, power and authority may be exerted over specific groups based on age and gender. In the tributary mode of production, the primary producer pays tribute in the form of material goods or labor to another individual or group of individuals who controls production through political, religious, or military force. The third mode, capitalism, is the one most familiar to us. The capitalist mode of production has three central features: (1) private property is owned by members of the capitalist class; (2) workers sell their labor power to the capitalists in order to survive; and (3) surpluses of wealth are produced, and these surpluses are either kept as profit or reinvested in production in order to generate further surplus. As we will see in the next section, Modes of Exchange, capitalism also links markets to trade and money in very unique ways. First, though, we will take a closer look at each of the three modes of production.

Domestic Production

The domestic, or kin-ordered, mode of production characterizes the lives of foragers and small-scale **subsistence farmers** with social structures that are more egalitarian than those characterizing the other modes of production (though these structures are still shaped by age- and gender-based forms of inequality). In the domestic mode of production, labor is organized on the basis of kinship relations (which is why this form of production is also known as kin-ordered). In southern Mexico and parts of Central America, many indigenous people primarily make their living through small-scale subsistence maize farming. Subsistence farmers produce food for their family's own consumption (rather than to sell). In this family production system, the men generally clear the fields and the whole family works together to plant the seeds. Until the plants sprout, the children spend their days in the fields protecting the newly planted crops. The men then weed the crops and harvest the corn cobs, and, finally, the women work to dry the corn and remove the kernels from the cobs for storage. Over the course of the year mothers and daughters typically grind the corn by hand using a *metate*, or grinding stone (or, if they are lucky, they might have access to a mechanical grinder). Ultimately, the corn is used to make the daily tortillas the family consumes at each meal. This example demonstrates how the domestic mode of production organizes labor and daily activities within families according to age and gender.

Figure 1: Woman grinding corn with a metate.

Foraging societies are also characterized by (1) the collective ownership of the primary **means of production**, (2) lower rates of social domination, and (3) sharing. For example, the Dobe Ju/'hoansi (also known as the !Kung), a society of approximately 45,000 people living in the Kalahari Desert of Botswana and Namibia, typically live in small groups consisting of siblings of both sexes, their spouses, and children. They all live in a single camp and move together for part of the year. Typically women collect plant foods and men hunt for meat. These resources are pooled within family groups and distributed within wider kin networks when necessary. However, women will also kill animals when the opportunity presents itself, and men spend time collecting plant foods, even when hunting.

As discussed in the Marriage and Family chapter, kinship relations are determined by culture, not biology. Interestingly, in addition to genealogical kinship, the Dobe Ju/'hoansi recognize kinship relations on the basis of gender-linked names; there are relatively few names, and in this society the possession of common names trumps genealogical ties. This means that an individual would call anyone with his father's name "father." The Dobe Ju/'hoansi have a third kinship system that is based on the principle that an older person determines the kinship terms that will be used in relation with another individual (so, for example, an elderly woman may refer to a young male as her nephew or grandson, thus creating a kin relationship). The effect of these three simultaneous kinship systems is that virtually everyone is kin in Ju/'hoansi society—those who are biologically related and those who are not. This successfully expands the range of individuals with whom products of labor, such as meat from a kill, must be shared.[5] These beliefs and the behaviors they inspire reinforce key elements of the domestic mode of production: collective ownership, low levels of social domination, and sharing.

Tributary Production

The tributary mode of production is found in social systems divided into classes of rulers and subjects. Subjects, typically farmers and/or herders, produce for themselves and their families, but they also give a proportion of their goods or labor to their rulers as tribute. The tributary mode of production characterizes a variety of precapitalist, state-level societies found in Europe, Asia, Africa, and the Americas. These societies share several common features: (1) the dominant units of production are communities organized around kinship relations; (2) the state's society depends on the local communities, and the tribute collected is used by the ruling class rather than exchanged or reinvested; (3) relationships between producers and rulers are often conflictual; and (4) production is controlled politically rather than through the direct control of the means of production. Some historic tributary systems, such as those found in feudal Europe and medieval Japan, were loosely organized, whereas others, such as the pre-contact Inca Empire and imperial China, were tightly managed.

In the Chinese imperial system, rulers not only demanded tribute in the form of material goods but also organized large-scale production and state-organized projects such as irrigation, roads, and flood control. In addition to accumulating agricultural surpluses, imperial officials also controlled large industrial and commercial enterprises, acquiring necessary products, such as salt, porcelain, or bricks, through nonmarket mechanisms. The rulers of most tributary systems were determined through descent and/or military and political service. However, the 1,000-year imperial Chinese system (CE 960–1911) was unique in that new members were accepted based on their performance in examinations that any male could take, even males of low status.[6] Despite this exception, the Chinese imperial system exhibits many hallmarks of the tributary mode of production, including the political control of production and the collection of tribute to support state projects and the ruling classes.

Capitalist Production

The capitalist mode of production is the most recent. While many of us may find it difficult to conceive of an alternative to capitalism, it has in fact only existed for a mere fraction of human history, first originating with the North American and western European industrial revolution during the seventeenth and eighteenth centuries. Capitalism is distinguished from the other two modes of production as an economic system based on private property owned by a capitalist class. In the domestic and tributary modes of production, workers typically own their means of production (for example, the land they farm). However, in the capitalist mode of production, workers typically do not own the factories they work in or the businesses they work for, and so they sell their labor power to other people, the capitalists, in order to survive. By keeping wages low, capitalists are able to sell the products of the workers' labor for more than it costs to produce the products. This enables capitalists, or those who own the means of production, to generate a surplus that is either kept as profit or reinvested in production with the goal of generating additional surplus. Therefore, an important distinguishing feature of the capitalist mode of production is that workers are separated from the means of production (for example, from the factories they work in or the businesses they work for), whereas in the domestic and tributary modes workers are not separated from the means of production (they own their own land or they have free access to hunting and foraging grounds). In the domestic and tributary modes of production, workers also retain control over the goods they produce (or a portion of them), and they control their own labor, deciding when and when not to work.[7] However, this is not true within capitalism. A factory worker does not own the widget that she helps build in a factory, and she cannot decide when she would like to show up at work each day.

Economic anthropologists stress that people and communities are differentially integrated into the capitalist mode of production. For example, some subsistence farmers may also produce a small crop of agricultural commodities in order to earn cash income to pay for necessities, such as machetes or farm tools, that they cannot make themselves. Many of us have had "informal" jobs tending a neighbor's children or mowing someone's lawn. Informal work such as this, where one does not work on a full-time, contracted basis, is especially important in developing countries around the world where informal employment comprises one-half to three-quarters of nonagricultural employment.[8]

Even in our own capitalist society, many of us regularly produce and exchange goods and services outside of the so-called formal marketplace: baking zucchini bread for a cousin who shares her vegetable garden's produce, for example, or buying fair-trade chocolate from a cooperative grocery store. We might spend Sundays volunteering in a church's nursery, or perhaps moonlighting as a server for a friend's catering business, working "under the table" for cash. Each of these examples highlights how even in advanced capitalist societies, we engage in diverse economic practices every day. If, as some suggest, economic anthropology is at its heart a search for alternatives to capitalism, it is useful to explore the many diverse economies that are thriving alongside capitalist modes of production and exchange.[9]

Fair-Trade Coffee Farmers: 21st Century Peasants

Small-scale, semi-subsistence farmers make up the largest single group of people on the planet today. Once known as peasants, these people pose an interesting conundrum to economic anthropologists because they live their lives both inside and outside of global capitalism and state societies. These farmers primarily use their own labor to grow the food their families eat. They might also produce some type of commodity for sale. For example, many of the indigenous corn farmers in southern Mexico and Central America discussed earlier also produce small amounts of coffee that they sell in order to earn money to buy school supplies for their children, building supplies for their homes, clothing, and other things that they cannot produce themselves.

There are between 20 and 25 million small farmers growing coffee in more than 50 countries around the world. A portion of these small coffee farmers are organized into cooperatives in order to collectively sell their coffee as fair-trade certified. Fair trade is a trading partnership, based on dialogue, transparency, and respect, that seeks greater equity in international trade. According to

Fairtrade International, fair trade supports farmers and workers to combat poverty and strengthen their livelihoods by establishing a minimum price for as many fair-trade products as possible; providing, on top of stable prices, a fair-trade premium; improving the terms of trade for farmers by providing access to information, clear contracts with pre-payments, access to markets and financing; and promoting better living wages and working conditions.[10] In order to certify their coffee, small farmers must belong to democratically run producers' associations in which participation is open to all eligible growers, regardless of ethnicity, gender, religion, or political affiliation.

To better understand how indigenous farmers practice kin-organized subsistence maize production while simultaneously producing an agricultural commodity for global markets, I conducted long-term research in a highland Guatemala community.[11] In 1977 a small number of Tz'utujil Maya coffee farmers formed a cooperative, *La Voz Que Clama en el Desierto* (A Voice Crying Out in the Wilderness), with the goal of securing higher prices for their agricultural products and escaping the severe poverty they struggled against on a daily basis. Since the early 1990s the group has produced high-quality organic and fair-trade certified coffee for the U.S. market.

The farmers work tirelessly to ensure that their families have sufficient corn to eat *and* that their coffee meets the cooperative's high standards of quality. The members of La Voz refer to their coffee trees as their "children" who they have lovingly tended for decades. High-quality, organic coffee production is time consuming and arduous—it requires almost daily attention. During the coffee harvest between December and March, wives, husbands, and children work together to pick the coffee cherries by hand as they ripen and carry them to the wet mill each afternoon.

Figure 2: Sorting coffee beans.

While these farmers are producing a product for the global market, it is not strictly a capitalist mode of production. They own their own land and they sell the fruits of their labor for guaranteed prices. They also work cooperatively with one another, pooling and exchanging their labor, in order to guarantee the smooth functioning of their organization. This cooperation, while essential, is hard work. Because the fair-trade system does not rely on anonymous market exchanges, members of La Voz must also dedicate time to nurturing their relationships with the coffee importers, roasters, advocates, and consumers who support all their hard work through promotion and purchases. This means attending receptions when buyers visit, dressing up in traditional clothing to pick coffee on film for marketing materials, and putting up with questions from nosy anthropologists.

Because the coffee farmers also produce much of the food their families consume, they enjoy a great deal of flexibility. In times of hardship, they can redirect their labor to other activities by intensifying corn production, migrating in search of wage labor, or planting other crops. Their ultimate goal is to maintain the family's economic autonomy, which is rooted in ownership of the means of production—in this case, their land. A close examination of these farmers' lives reveals that they are not relics of a precapitalist system. Instead, their economic activity is uniquely adapted to the contemporary global economy in order to ensure their long-term survival.

Salaula in Zambia: The Informal Economy

The informal economy includes a diverse range of activities that are unregulated (and untaxed) by the state: rickshaw pullers in Calcutta, street vendors in Mexico City, and scrap-metal recyclers in Lexington, Kentucky, are all considered informal workers. Informal economies include people who are informally self-employed *and* those working informally for other people's enterprises. In some parts of the world the informal economy is a significant source of income and revenue. In Sub-Saharan Africa, for example, the informal economy generates nearly 40 percent as much revenue as that included in the "official" gross domestic product.[12] Consequently, the informal economy is of great interest to economic anthropologists. However, the term "informal economy" is critiqued by some scholars since often what we refer to as informal economies are actually quite formal and organized, even though this organization is not regulated by the state and may be based on an internal logic that makes the most sense to those who participate in the exchanges.

Karen Hansen provides an in-depth look at the lives of vendors in the *salaula*, the secondhand clothing markets in Zambia in southern Africa.[13] Salaula, a term that literally means "to rummage through a pile," is an unusual industry that begins in many of our own homes. In today's era of fast fashion in which Americans buy more than 20 billion garments each year (that's 68 garments per person!), many of us regularly bag up our gently used, unfashionable clothing and drop it off at a nearby Goodwill shop.[14] Only about half of these donated clothes actually end up in charity thrift stores. The rest are sold to one of the nearly 300 firms that specialize in the global clothing recycling business. The textile recycling firms sort the clothing by grades; the higher-quality items are sent to Central America, and the lowest grades go to African and Asian countries. In Sub-Saharan Africa an estimated 50 percent of purchased clothing consists of these secondhand imports, referred to by some consumers as "dead man's clothes" because of the belief that they come from the deceased.[15] In Zambia the secondhand clothes are imported in bulk by 40 wholesale firms that, in turn, sell the clothes to salaula traders. The traders sell the clothes out of their homes and in large public markets.

Typically the people working as salaula traders have either never had formal-sector jobs or have lost their jobs in the public or private sector. Often they start selling in order to accumulate money for other activities or as a sideline business. Hansen found that there were slightly more female sellers and that women were more likely to be single heads of households. Successful salaula trading requires business acumen and practical skills. Flourishing traders cultivate their consumer knowledge, develop sales strategies, and experiment with display and pricing. While salaula trading has relatively low barriers to entry (one simply has to purchase a bale of clothing from a wholesale importer in order to get started), in this informal market scale is important: salaula moves best when traders have a lot of it on offer. Traders also have to understand the local cultural politics in order to successfully earn a living in this sector. For example, salaula is different from used clothing from people someone knows. In fact, secondhand clothing with folds and wrinkles from the bale is often the most desirable because it is easily identifiable as "genuine" salaula.[16]

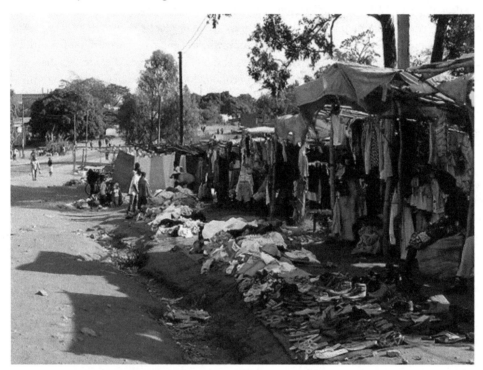

Figure 3: Roadside Salaula trader, Zambia

The global salaula commodity chain presents an interesting example of how material goods can flow in and out of capitalist modes of production and exchange. For example, I might buy a dress that was produced in a factory to give (not sell!) to my young niece. After wearing the dress for several months, Maddie will probably outgrow it, and her Mom will drop it off at the nearby Goodwill shop. There is a 50 percent chance that the dress will be sold by the charity to a clothing recycler who will export it to Zambia or a nearby country. From there the dress will end up in a bale of clothing that is purchased by a salaula trader in Lusaka. At this point the dress enters the informal economy as the salaula markets are unregulated and untaxed. A consumer might buy the dress and realize that it does not quite fit her own daughter. She might then take it to her neighbor, who works informally as a tailor, for alternations. Rather than paying her neighbor for the work on the dress, the consumer might instead arrange to reciprocate at a later date by cleaning the tailor's home. This single item of clothing that has traveled the globe and moved in and out of formal and informal markets highlights how diverse our economic lives really are, a theme that we will return to at the end of this chapter.

MODES OF EXCHANGE

There are three distinct ways to integrate economic and social relations and distribute material goods. Contemporary economics only studies the first, market exchange. Most economic models are unable to explain the second two, reciprocity and redistribution, because they have different underlying logics. Economic anthropology, on the other hand, provides rich and nuanced perspective into how diverse modes of exchange shape, and are shaped by, everyday life across space and time. Anthropologists understand market exchange to be a form of trade that today most commonly involves general purpose money, bargaining, and supply and demand price mechanisms. In contrast, reciprocity involves the exchange of goods and services and is rooted in a mutual sense of obligation and identity. Anthropologists have identified three distinct types of reciprocity, which we will explore shortly: generalized, balanced, and negative.[17] Finally, redistribution occurs when an authority of some type (a temple priest, a chief, or even an institution such as the Internal Revenue Service) collects economic contributions from all community members and then redistributes these back in the form of goods and services. Redistribution requires centralized social organization, even if at a small scale (for example, within the foraging societies discussed above). As we will see, various modes of exchange can and do coexist, even within capitalism.

Reciprocity

While early economic anthropology often seemed focused on detailed investigations of seemingly exotic economic practices, anthropologists such as Bronislaw Malinowski and Marcel Mauss used ethnographic research and findings to critique Western, capitalist economic systems. Today, many follow in this tradition and some would agree with Keith Hart's statement that economic anthropology "at its best has always been a search for an alternative to capitalism."[18] Mauss, a French anthropologist, was one of the first scholars to provide an in-depth exploration of reciprocity and the role that gifts play in cultural systems around the world.[19] Mauss asked why humans feel obliged to reciprocate when they receive a gift. His answer was that giving and reciprocating gifts, whether these are material objects or our time, creates links between the people involved.[20]

Over the past century, anthropologists have devoted considerable attention to the topic of reciprocity. It is an attractive one because of the seemingly moral nature of gifts: many of us hope that humans are not solely self-interested, antisocial economic actors. Gifts are about social relations, not just about the gifts themselves; as we will see, giving a gift that contains a bit of oneself builds a social relationship with the person who receives it.[21] Studying reciprocity gives anthropologists unique insights into the moral economy, or the processes through which customs, cultural values, beliefs, and social coercion influence our economic behavior. The economy can be understood as a symbolic reflection of the cultural order and the sense of right and wrong that people adhere to within that cultural order.[22] This means that economic behavior is a unique cultural practice, one that varies across time and space.

Generalized Reciprocity

Consider a young child. Friends and family members probably purchase numerous gifts for the child, small and large. People give freely of their time: changing diapers, cooking meals, driving the child to soccer practice, and tucking the child in at night. These myriad gifts of toys and time are not written down; we do not keep a running tally of everything we give our children. However, as children grow older they begin to reciprocate these gifts: mowing an elderly grandmother's yard, cooking dinner for a parent who has to work late, or buying an expensive gift for an older sibling. When we gift without reckoning the exact value of the gift or expecting a specific thing in return we are practicing **generalized reciprocity**. This form of reciprocity occurs within the closest social relationships where exchange happens so frequently that monitoring the value of each item or service given and received would be impossible, and to do so would lead to tension and quite possibly the eventual dissolution of the relationship.

However, generalized reciprocity is not necessarily limited to households. In my own suburban Kentucky neighborhood we engage in many forms of generalized reciprocity. For example, we regularly cook and deliver meals for our neighbors who have a new baby, a sick parent, or recently deceased relative. Similarly, at Halloween we give out handfuls of candy (sometimes spending $50 or more in the process). I do not keep a close tally of which kid received which candy bar, nor do my young daughters pay close attention to which houses gave more or less desirable candy this year. In other cultures, generalized reciprocity is the norm rather than the exception. Recall the Dobe Ju/'hoansi foragers who live in the Kalahari Desert: they have a flexible and overlapping kinship system which ensures that the products of their hunting and gathering are shared widely across the entire community. This generalized reciprocity reinforces the solidarity of the group; however, it also means that Dobe Ju/'hoansi have very few individual possessions and generosity is a prized personality trait.

Balanced Reciprocity

Unlike generalized reciprocity, **balanced reciprocity** is more of a direct exchange in which something is traded or given with the expectation that something of equal value will be returned within a specific time period. This form of reciprocity involves three distinct stages: the gift must be given, it has to be received, and a reciprocal gift has to be returned. A key aspect of balanced reciprocity is that without reciprocation within an appropriate time frame, the exchange system will falter and the social relationship might end. Balanced reciprocity generally occurs at a social level more distant than the family, but it usually occurs among people who know each other. In other words, complete strangers would be unlikely to engage in balanced reciprocity because they would not be able to trust the person to reciprocate within an acceptable period of time.

The Kula ring system of exchange found in the Trobriand Islands in the South Pacific is one example of balanced reciprocity. A Kula ring involves the ceremonial exchange of shell and bead necklaces *(soulava)* for shell arm bands *(mwali)* between trading partners living on different islands. The arm bands and necklaces constantly circulate and only have symbolic value, meaning they bring the temporary owner honor and prestige but cannot be bought or sold for money. Malinowski was the first anthropologist to study the Kula ring, and he found that although participants did not profit materially from the exchange, it served several important functions in Trobriand society.[23] Because participants formed relationships with trading participants on other islands, the Kula ring helped solidify alliances among tribes, and overseas partners became allies in a land of danger and insecurity.

Figure 4: Mwali from the Kula Exchange.

Along with arm bands and necklaces, Kula participants were also engaging in more mundane forms of trade, bartering from one island to another. Additionally, songs, customs, and cultural influences also traveled along the Kula route. Finally, although ownership of the arm bands and necklaces was always temporary (for eventually participants are expected to gift the items to other partners in the ring), Kula participants took great pride and pleasure in the items they received. The Kula ring exhibits all the hallmarks of balanced reciprocity: necklaces are traded for armbands with the expectation that objects of equal value will be returned within a specific time period.

The Work of Reciprocity at Christmas

How many of us give and receive gifts during the holiday season? Christmas is undeniably a religious celebration, yet while nine in ten Americans say they celebrate Christmas, about half view it to be more of a secular holiday. Perhaps this is why eight in ten non-Christians in the United States now celebrate Christmas.[24] How and why has this one date in the liturgical calendar come to be so central to U.S. culture and what does gift giving have to do with it? In 1865, Christmas was declared a national holiday; just 25 years later, *Ladies' Home Journal* was already complaining that the holiday had become overly commercialized.[25] A recent survey of U.S. citizens found that we continue to be frustrated with the commercialization of the season: one-third say they dislike the materialism of the holidays, one-fifth are unhappy with the expenses of the season, and one in ten dislikes holiday shopping in crowded malls and stores.[26]

When asked what they like most about the holiday season, 70 percent of U.S. residents say spending time with family and friends. This raises the question of how and why reciprocal gift giving has become so central to the social relationships we hope to nurture at Christmas. The anthropologist

James Carrier argues that the affectionate giving at the heart of modern Christmas is in fact a celebration of personal social relations. [27] Among our family members and closest friends this gift giving is *generalized* and more about the expression of sentiment. When we exchange gifts with those outside this small circle it tends to be more *balanced*, and we expect some form of equivalent reciprocation. If I spend $50 on a lavish gift for a friend, my feelings will undoubtedly be hurt when she reciprocates with a $5 gift card to Starbucks.

Christmas shopping is arduous—we probably all know someone who heads to the stores at midnight on Black Friday to get a jumpstart on their consumption. Throughout the month of December we complain about how crowded the stores are and how tired we are of wrapping presents. Let's face it: Christmas is a lot of work! Recall how the reciprocity of the Kula ring served many functions in addition to the simple exchange of symbolic arm bands and shell necklaces. Similarly, Christmas gift giving is about more than exchanging commodities. In order to cement our social relationships we buy and wrap gifts (even figuratively by placing a giant red bow on oversize items like a new bicycle) in order to symbolically transform the impersonal commodities that populate our everyday lives into meaningful gifts. The ritual of shopping, wrapping, giving, and receiving proves to us that we can create a sphere of love and intimacy alongside the world of anonymous, monetary exchange. The ritualistic exchange of gifts is accompanied by other traditions, such as the circulation of holiday cards that have no economic or practical value, but instead are used to reinforce social relationships. When we view Christmas through a moral economy lens, we come to understand how our economic behavior is shaped by our historical customs, cultural values, beliefs, and even our need to maintain appearances. Christmas is hard work, but with any luck we will reap the rewards of strong relational bonds. [28]

Negative Reciprocity

Unlike balanced and generalized reciprocity, **negative reciprocity** is an attempt to get something for nothing. It is the most impersonal of the three forms of reciprocity and it commonly exists among people who do not know each other well because close relationships are incompatible with attempts to take advantage of other people. Gambling is a good example of negative reciprocity, and some would argue that market exchange, in which one participant aims to buy low while the other aims to sell high, can also be a form of negative reciprocity.

The emails always begin with a friendly salutation: "Dear Beloved Friend, I know this message will come to you as surprised but permit me of my desire to go into business relationship with you." The introduction is often followed by a long involved story of deaths and unexpected inheritances: "I am Miss Naomi Surugaba, a daughter to late Al-badari Surugaba of Libya whom was murdered during the recent civil war in Libya in March 2011 . . . my late Father came to Cotonou Benin republic with USD 4,200,000.00 (US$4.2M) which he deposited in a Bank here . . . for safe keeping. I am here seeking for an avenue to transfer the fund to you . . . . Please I will offer you 20% of the total sum for your assistance . . . ."[29] The emails are crafted to invoke a sense of balanced reciprocity: the authors tell us how trustworthy and esteemed we are and offer to give us a percentage of the money in exchange for our assistance. However, most savvy recipients immediately recognize that these scams are in fact a form of negative reciprocity since they know they will never actually receive the promised money and, in fact, will probably lose money if they give their bank account information to their correspondent.

The anthropologist Daniel Smith studied the motives and practices of Nigerian email scammers who are responsible for approximately one-fifth of these types of emails that flood Western inboxes.[30]

He found that 419 scams, as they are known in Nigeria (after the section of the criminal code outlaw- ing fraud), emerged in the largest African state (Nigeria has more than 130 million residents, nearly 70 percent of whom live below the poverty line) in the late 1990s when there were few legitimate economic opportunities for the large number of educated young people who had the English skills and technological expertise necessary for successful scams. Smith spoke with some of the Nigerians sending these emails and found that they dreamed of a big payoff someday. They reportedly felt bad for people who were duped, but said that if Americans were greedy enough to fall for it they got what they deserved.

The typical email correspondence always emphasizes the urgency, confidentiality, and reciprocity of the proposed arrangement. Smith argues that the 419 scams mimic long-standing cultural prac- tices around kinship and patronage relations. While clearly 419 scammers are practicing negative reciprocity by trying to get something for nothing (unfortunately we will never receive the 20 percent of the $4.2 million that Miss Naomi Surugaba promised us), many in the United States continue to be lured in by the veneer of balanced reciprocity. The FBI receives an estimated 4,000 complaints about advance fee scams each year, and annual victim losses total over $55 million.[31]

Redistribution

Redistribution is the accumulation of goods or labor by a particular person or institution for the purpose of dispersal at a later date. Redistribution is found in all societies. For example, within households we pool our labor and resources, yet we rarely distribute these outside of our family. For redistribution to become a central economic process, a society must have a centralized political appa- ratus to coordinate and enforce the practice.

Redistribution can occur alongside other forms of exchange. For example, in the United States ev- eryone who works in the formal sector pays federal taxes to the Internal Revenue Service. During the 2015 fiscal year the IRS collected $3.3 trillion in federal revenue. It processed 243 million returns, and 119 million of these resulted in a tax refund. In total, $403.3 billion tax dollars were redistrib- uted by this central political apparatus.[32] Even if I did not receive a cash refund from the IRS, I still benefited from the redistribution in the form of federal services and infrastructure.

Sometimes economic practices that appear to be merely reciprocal gift exchanges are revealed to be forms of redistribution after closer inspection. The potlatch system of the Native American groups living in the United States and Canadian northwestern coastal area was long understood as an example of functional gift giving. Traditionally, two groups of clans would perform highly ritual- ized exchanges of food, blankets, and ritual objects. The system produced status and prestige among participants: by giving away more goods than another person, a chief could build his reputation and gain new respect within the community. After contact with settlers, the excessive gift giving during potlatches escalated to the point that early anthropologists described it as a "war of property."[33]

Later anthropological studies of the potlatch revealed that rather than wasting, burning, or giving away their property to display their wealth, the groups were actually giving away goods that other groups could use and then waiting for a later potlatch when they would receive things not available in their own region. This was important because the availability of food hunted, fished, and foraged by native communities could be highly variable. The anthropologist Stuart Piddocke found that the potlatch primarily served a livelihood function by ensuring the redistribution of goods between groups with surpluses and those with deficits.[34]

Markets

The third way that societies distribute goods and services is through market exchange. Markets are social institutions with prices or exchange equivalencies. Markets do not necessarily have to be localized in a geographic place (e.g., a marketplace), but they cannot exist without institutions to govern the exchanges. Market and reciprocal exchange appear to share similar features: one person gives something and the other receives something. A key distinction between the two is that market exchanges are regulated by supply and demand mechanisms. The forces of supply and demand can create risk for people living in societies that largely distribute goods through market exchange. If we lose our jobs, we may not be able to buy food for our families. In contrast, if a member of a Dobe Ju/'hoansi community is hurt and unable to gather foods today, she will continue to eat as a result of generalized reciprocal exchanges.

Market exchanges are based on transactions, or changes in the status of a good or service between people, such as a sale. While market exchange is generally less personal than reciprocal exchange, personalized transactions between people who have a relationship that endures beyond a single exchange do exist. Atomized transactions are impersonal ones between people who have no relationship with each other beyond the short term of the exchange. These are generally short-run, closed-ended transactions with few implications for the future. In contrast, personalized transactions occur between people who have a relationship that endures past the exchange and might include both social and economic elements. The transactors are embedded in networks of social relations and might even have knowledge of the other's personality, family, or personal circumstances that helps them trust that the exchange will be satisfactory. Economic exchanges within families, for example when a child begins to work for a family business, are extreme examples of personalized market exchange.

To better understand the differences between transactions between relative strangers and those that are more personalized, consider the different options one has for a haircut: a person can stop by a chain salon such as Great Clips and leave twenty minutes later after spending $15 to have his hair trimmed by someone he has never met before, or he can develop an ongoing relationship with a hair stylist or barber he regularly visits. These appointments may last an hour or even longer, and he and his stylist probably chat about each other's lives, the weather, or politics. At Christmas he may even bring a small gift or give an extra tip. He trusts his stylist to cut his hair the way he likes it because of their long history of personalized transactions.

Maine Lobster Markets

To better understand the nature of market transactions, anthropologist James Acheson studied the economic lives of Maine fishermen and lobster dealers.[35] The lobster market is highly sensitive to supply and demand: catch volumes and prices change radically over the course of the year. For example, during the winter months, lobster catches are typically low because the animals are inactive and fishermen are reluctant to go out into the cold and stormy seas for small catches. Beginning in April, lobsters become more active and, as the water warms, they migrate toward shore and catch volumes increase. In May prices fall dramatically; supply is high but there are relatively few tourists and demand is low. In June and July catch volume decreases again when lobsters molt and are difficult to catch, but demand increases due to the large influx of tourists, which, in turn, leads to higher prices. In the fall, after the tourists have left, catch volume increases again as a new class of recently molted lobsters become available to the fishermen. In other words, catch and price are inversely related: when the catch is lowest, the price is highest, and when the catch is highest, the price is lowest.

The fishermen generally sell their lobsters to wholesalers and have very little idea where the lobsters go, how many hands they pass through on their way to the consumer, how prices are set, or why they vary over the course of the year. In other words, from the fisherman's point of view the process is shrouded in fog, mystery, and rumor. Acheson found that in order to manage the inherent risk posed by this variable market, fishermen form long-term, personalized economic relationships with particular dealers. The dealers' goal is to ensure a large, steady supply of lobsters for as low a price as possible. In order to do so, they make contracts with fishermen to always buy all of the lobster they have to sell no matter how glutted the market might be. In exchange, the fishermen agree to sell their catches for the going rate and forfeit the right to bargain over price. The dealers provide added incentives to the fishermen: for example, they will allow fishermen to use their dock at no cost and supply them with gasoline, diesel fuel, paint, buoys, and gloves at cost or with only a small markup. They also often provide interest-free loans to their fishermen for boats, equipment, and traps. In sum, the Maine fishermen and the dealers have, over time, developed highly personalized exchange relations in order to manage the risky lobster market. While these market exchanges last over many seasons and rely on a certain degree of trust, neither the fishermen nor the dealers would characterize the relationship as reciprocal—they are buying and selling lobster, not exchanging gifts.

Money

While general purpose money is not a prerequisite for market exchanges, most commercial transactions today do involve the exchange of money. In our own society, and in most parts of the world, general purpose money can be exchanged for all manner of goods and services. General purpose money serves as a medium of exchange, a tool for storing wealth, and as a way to assign interchangeable values. It reflects our ideas about the generalized interchangeability of all things—it makes products and services from all over the world commensurable in terms of a single metric. In so doing, it increases opportunities for unequal exchange.[36] As we will see, different societies have attempted to challenge this notion of interchangeability and the inequalities it can foster in different ways.

Tiv Spheres of Exchange

Prior to colonialism, the Tiv people in Nigeria had an economic system governed by a moral hierarchy of values that challenged the idea that all objects can be made commensurable through general purpose money. The anthropologists Paul and Laura Bohannan developed the theory of spheres of exchange after recognizing that the Tiv had three distinct economic arenas and that each arena had its own form of money.[37] The subsistence sphere included locally produced foods (yams, grains, and vegetables), chickens, goats, and household utensils. The second sphere encompassed slaves, cattle, white cloth, and metal bars. Finally, the third, most prestigious sphere was limited to marriageable females. Excluded completely from the Tiv spheres of exchange were labor (because it was always reciprocally exchanged) and land (which was not owned per se, but rather communally held within families).

The Tiv were able to convert their wealth upwards through the spheres of exchange. For example, a Tiv man could trade a portion of his yam harvest for slaves that, in turn, could be given as bride-wealth for a marriageable female. However, it was considered immoral to convert wealth downwards: no honorable man would exchange slaves or brass rods for food.[38] The Bohannans found that this moral economy quickly collapsed when it was incorporated into the contemporary realm of general purpose money. When items in any of the three spheres could be exchanged for general purpose money, the Tiv could no longer maintain separate categories of exchangeable items. The Bohannans concluded that the moral meanings of money—in other words, how exchange is culturally conceived—can have very significant material implications for people's everyday lives.[39]

Local Currency Systems: Ithaca HOURS

While we may take our general purpose currency for granted, as the Tiv example demonstrates, money is profoundly symbolic and political. Money is not only the measure of value but also the purpose of much of our activity, and money shapes economic relations by creating inequalities and obliterating qualitative differences.[40] In other words, I might pay a babysitter $50 to watch my children for the evening, and I might spend $50 on a new sweater the next day. While these two expenses are commensurable through general purpose money, qualitatively they are in fact radically different in terms of the sentiment I attach to each (and I would not ever try to pay my babysitter in sweaters).

Some communities explicitly acknowledge the political and symbolic components of money and develop complementary currency systems with the goal of maximizing transactions in a geographically bounded area, such as within a single city. The goal is to encourage people to connect more directly with each other than they might do when shopping in corporate stores using general purpose money.[41] For example, the city of Ithaca, New York, promotes its local economy and community self-reliance through the use of Ithaca HOURS.[42] More than 900 participants accept Ithaca HOURS for goods and services, and some local employers and employees even pay or receive partial wages in the complementary currency. The currency has been in circulation since 1991, and the system was incorporated as a nonprofit organization in 1998. Today it is administered by a board of elected volunteers. Ithaca HOURS circulate in denominations of two, one, one-half, one-fourth, one-eighth, and one-tenth HOURS ($20, $10, $5, $2.50, $1.25, and $1, respectively). The HOURS are put into circulation through "disbursements" given to registered organization members, through small interest-free loans to local businesses, and through grants to community organizations. The name "HOURS" evokes the principle of labor exchange and the idea that a unit of time is equal for everyone.[43]

The anthropologist Faidra Papavasiliou studied the impact of the Ithaca HOURS currency system. She found that while the complementary currency does not necessarily create full economic equality, it does create deeper connections among community members and local businesses, helping to demystify and personalize exchange (much as we saw with the lobstermen and dealers).[44] The Ithaca HOURS system also

Figure 5: An Ithaca Hour note.

offers important networking opportunities for locally owned businesses and, because it provides zero interest business loans, it serves as a form of security against economic crisis.[45] Finally, the Ithaca HOURS complementary currency system encourages community members to shop at locally owned businesses. As we will see in the next section, where we choose to shop and what we choose to buy forms a large part of our lives and cultural identity. The HOURS system demonstrates a relatively successful approach to challenging the inequalities fostered by general purpose money.

CONSUMPTION AND GLOBAL CAPITALISM

Consumption refers to the process of buying, eating, or using a resource, food, commodity, or service. Anthropologists understand consumption more specifically as the forms of behavior that connect our economic activity with the cultural symbols that give our lives meaning.[46] People's consumption patterns are a large part of their lives, and economic anthropologists explore why, how, and when people consume what they do. The answers to these questions lie in people's ideologies and identities as members of a social group; each culture is different and each consumes in its own way. Consumption is always social even when it addresses physical needs. For example, all humans need to eat, but people around the world have radically different ideas of what foods and flavors are most desirable and appropriate.

We use our material possessions to meet our needs (for example, we wear clothing to protect us from the environment), regulate our social lives, and affirm the rightful order of things.[47] Anthropologists understand that the commodities we buy are not just good for eating or shelter, they are good for *thinking*: in acquiring and possessing particular goods, people make visible and stable the categories of culture.[48] For example, consumption helps us establish and defend differences among people and occasions: I might wear a specific t-shirt and cap to a baseball game with friends in order to distinguish myself as a fan of a particular team. In the process, I make myself easily identifiable within the larger fan community. However, I probably would not wear this same outfit to a job interview because it would be inappropriate for the occasion.

Economic anthropologists are also interested in why objects become status symbols and how these come to be experienced as an aspect of the self.[49] Objects have a "social life" during which they may pass through various statuses: a silver cake server begins its life as a commodity for sale in a store. [50] However, imagine that someone's great-grandmother used that server to cut the cake at her wedding, and it became a cherished family heirloom passed down from one generation to the next. Unfortunately, the server ended up in the hands of a cousin who did not feel a sentimental attachment to this object. She sold it to a gold and silver broker for currency and it was transformed into an anonymous commodity. That broker in turn sold it to a dealer who melted it down, turning the once cherished cake server back into a raw material.

Transforming Barbie Dolls

We have already learned about the hard work that Americans devote to converting impersonal commodities into sentimental gifts at Christmastime with the goal of nourishing their closest social bonds. Consumers in capitalist systems continuously attempt to reshape the meaning of the commodities that businesses brand, package, and market to us.[51] The anthropologist Elizabeth Chin conducted ethnographic research among young African American children in a poor neighborhood of New Haven, Connecticut, exploring the intersection of consumption, inequality, and cultural identity.

Chin specifically looked at "ethnically correct" Barbie dolls, arguing that while they may represent some progress in comparison to the past when only white Barbies were sold, they also reinforce outdated understandings of biological race and ethnicity. Rather than dismantling race and class boundaries, the "ethnic" dolls create segregated toy shelves that in fact mirror the segregation that young black children experience in their schools and neighborhoods.

The young black girls that Chin researched were unable to afford these $20 brand-name dolls and typically played with less expensive, generic Barbie dolls that were white.[52] The girls used their imaginations and worked to transform their dolls by giving them hairstyles like their own, braiding and curling the dolls' long straight hair in order to integrate the dolls into their own worlds.[53] A quick perusal of the Internet reveals numerous tutorials and blogs devoted to black Barbie hairstyling, demonstrating that the young New Haven girls are not the only ones working to transform these store-bought commodities in socially meaningful ways.[54]

Consumption in the Developing World

Consumption provides us with a window into globalization, which we will learn more about in the Globalization chapter. Over the past several decades, as global capitalism expanded its reach into developing countries around the world, many people fretted that the growing influx of Western products would lead to cultural homogeneity and even cultural imperialism. Some argued that with every McDonald's constructed, the values and beliefs of the West were being imposed on non-Western societies. However, anthropologists have systematically challenged this thesis by providing a more sophisticated understanding of local cultural contexts. They demonstrate that people do not become Westernized simply by buying Western commodities, any more than I become somehow more Japanese after eating at my favorite neighborhood hibachi restaurant. In fact, anthropological research shows that Western commodities can sometimes lead to a resurgence of local identities and an affirmation of local processes over global patterns.

The Children Cry for Bread

The anthropologist Mary Wesimantel researched how families adapt to changing economic circumstances, including the introduction of Western products into their indigenous community of Zumbagua, Ecuador. Once subsistence barley farmers, men from Zumbagua began to migrate to cities in search of work while the women stayed home to care for the children and continue to farm barley for home consumption. The men periodically returned home, bringing cash earnings and urban luxuries such as bread. The children associated this bread with modernity and city life, and they preferred to eat it rather than the traditional staple food of toasted ground barley, grown and cooked by their mothers. The children "cried" for the bread their fathers brought home. Yet, their mothers resisted their pleas and continued to feed them grains from their own fields because barley consumption was considered a core component of indigenous identity.[55] This example illustrates the complex negotiations that emerge within families and communities when they are increasingly integrated into a global economy and exposed to Western goods.

Consumption, Status, and Recognition among the Elite in China

In other parts of the world, the consumption of Western goods can be used to cement social and economic status within local networks. John Osburg studied the "new elite" in China, the class of entrepreneurs who have successfully navigated the recent transitions in the Chinese economy since the early 1990s when private businesses and foreign investment began to steadily expand their reach in this communist country.[56] Osburg found that the new elite do not constitute a coherent class defined by income level or occupation. Instead, they occupy an unstable and contested category and consequently rely on the consumption of Western-style goods and services in order to stabilize their identities.

Osburg argues that the whole point of elite consumption in Chengdu, China, is to make one's economic, social, and cultural capital as transparent and legible as possible to the widest audience in order to let everyone know one is wealthy and well connected. Consequently, the Chengdu elite favor easily recognizable and pricey brand names. However, consumption is not simply an arena of status display. Instead, Osburg shows how it is a form of social practice through which relationships with other elites are forged: the shared consumption of conventional luxury objects like liquor and tobacco solidifies relationships among the privileged.[57]

Commodities and Global Capitalism

In his 1967 speech "A Christmas Sermon on Peace," the Reverend Martin Luther King, Jr. reminded us that all life is interrelated:

> We are all caught in an inescapable network of mutuality, tied into a single garment of destiny. . . Did you ever stop to think that you can't leave for your job in the morning without being dependent on most of the world? You get up in the morning and reach over for the sponge, and that's handed to you by a Pacific Islander. You reach for a bar of soap, given to you at the hands of a Frenchman. And then you go into the kitchen to drink your coffee for the morning, and that's poured into your cup by a South American. . . And before you finish eating breakfast in the morning, you've depended on more than half the world.[58]

King's words are even truer today than they were in the late 1960s. Due to the intensification of global capitalism, the vast majority of the commodities we buy and the food we consume come to us from distant places; while such global supply chains are not new, they have become increasingly dense in an age of container shipping and overnight air deliveries.

Recall that a commodity is any good that is produced for sale or exchange for other goods. However, commodities are more than just a means to acquire general purpose money. They also embody social relations of production, the identities of businesses, and particular geographic locales. Many economic anthropologists today study global flows through the lens of a concrete substance that makes a circuit through various locales, exploring the social lives of agrifood commodities such as mutton, coffee, sushi, and sugar.[59] In following these commodities along their supply chains, anthropologists highlight not only relations of production but also the power of ideas, images, and noneconomic actors. These studies of specific commodities are a powerful method to show how capitalism has grown, spread, and penetrated agrarian societies around the world.[60]

Darjeeling Tea

The anthropologist Sarah Besky researched Darjeeling tea production in India to better understand how consumer desires are mapped onto distant locations.[61] In India, tea plantation owners are attempting to reinvent their product for 21st century markets through the use of fair-trade certification (discussed earlier in this chapter) and Geographical Indication Status (GI). GI is an international property-rights system, regulated by the World Trade Organization, that legally protects the rights of people in certain places to produce certain commodities. For example, bourbon must come

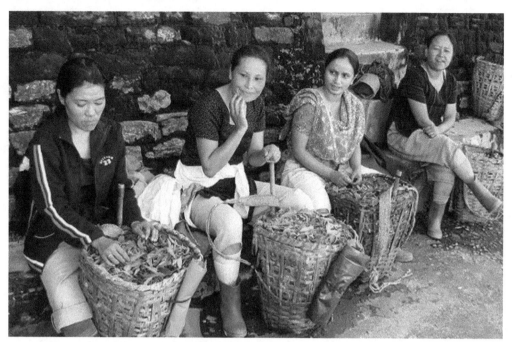

Figure 6: Tea Workers in Darjeeling, India.

from Kentucky, Mezcal can only be produced in certain parts of Mexico, and sparkling wine can only be called champagne if it originated in France. Similarly, in order to legally be sold as "Darjeeling tea," the tea leaves must come from the Darjeeling district of the Indian state of West Bengal.

Besky explores how the meaning of Darjeeling tea is created through three interrelated processes: (1) extensive marketing campaigns aimed at educating consumers about the unique Darjeeling taste, (2) the application of international law to define the geographic borders within which Darjeeling tea can be produced, and (3) the introduction of tea plantation-based tourism. What the Darjeeling label hides is the fact that tea plantations are highly unequal systems with economic relationships that date back to the colonial era: workers depend upon plantation owners not just for money but also for food, medical care, schools, and housing. Even when we pay more for Darjeeling tea, the premium price is not always returned to the workers in the form of higher wages. Besky's research shows how capitalism and market exchange shapes the daily lives of people around the world. The final section of this chapter explores the ways in which economic anthropologists understand and question structural inequalities in the world today.

POLITICAL ECONOMY: UNDERSTANDING INEQUALITY

Humans are fundamentally social, and our culture is always shared and patterned: we live our lives in groups. However, not all groups serve the needs of their members, and some people have more power than others, meaning they can make the weak consent through threats and coercion. Within all societies there are classes of people defined by the kinds of property they own and/or the kinds of work they engage in.[62] Beginning in the 1960s, an increasing number of anthropologists began to study the world around them through the lens of **political economy**. This approach recognizes that the economy is central to everyday life but contextualizes economic relations within state structures, political processes, social structures, and cultural values.[63] Some political economic anthropologists focus on how societies and markets have historically evolved while others ask how individuals deal with the forces that oppress them, focusing on historical legacies of social domination and marginalization. [64]

Karl Marx famously wrote, "Men make their own history, but they do not make it as they please; they do not make it under self-selected circumstances, but under circumstances existing already, given and transmitted from the past."[65] In other words, while humans are inherently creative, our possibilities are limited by the structural realities of our everyday lives.

Consider a typical college student. Is this student happy with the courses her department or college is offering? Are there courses that she needs to graduate that are not being offered yet? She is free to choose among the listed courses, but she cannot choose which courses are available. This depends on factors beyond her control as a student: who is available to teach which topics or what the administration has decided is important enough to offer. So, her agency and ability to choose is highly constrained by the structures in place. In the same way, political economies constrain people's choices and define the terms by which we must live. Importantly, it is not simply structures that determine our choices and actions; these are also shaped by our community.

Just as our college student may come to think of the requirements she has to fulfill for her degree as just the way it is (even if she does not want to take that theory course!), people come to think of their available choices in everyday life as simply the natural order of things. However, the degree of agency one has depends on the amount of power one has and the degree to which one understands the structural dimensions of one's life. This focus on power and structural relations parallels an anthropological understanding of culture as a holistic system: economic relations never exist by themselves, apart from social and political institutions.

Structural Violence and the Politics of Aid in Haiti

Anthropologists interested in understanding economic inequalities often research forms of structural violence present in the communities where they work.[66] **Structural violence** is a form of violence in which a social structure or institution harms people by preventing them from meeting their basic needs. In other words, how political and economic forces structure risk for various forms of suffering within a population. Structural violence can include things like infectious disease, hunger, and violence (torture, rape, crime, etc.).

In the United States we tend to focus on individuals and personal experiences. A popular narrative holds that if you work hard enough you can "pull yourself up by your bootstraps" in this country of immigrants and economic opportunity. The converse of this ideology is victim blaming: the logic is that if people are poor it is their own fault.[67] However, studying structural violence helps us understand that for some people there simply is no getting ahead and all one can hope for is survival.

The conditions of everyday life in Haiti, which only worsened after the 2010 earthquake, are a good example of how structural violence limits individual opportunities. Haiti is the most unequal country in Latin America and the Caribbean: the richest 20 percent of its population holds more than 64 percent of its total wealth, while the poorest 20 percent hold barely one percent. The starkest contrast is between the urban and rural areas: almost 70 percent of Haiti's rural households are chronically poor (vs. 20 percent in cities), meaning they survive on less than $2 a day and lack access to basic goods and services.[68] Haiti suffers from widespread unemployment and underemployment, and more than two-thirds of people in the labor force do not have formal jobs. The population is not well educated, and more than 40 percent of the population over the age of 15 is illiterate.[69] According to the World Food Programme, more than 100,000 Haitian children under the age of five suffer from acute malnutrition and one in three children is stunted (or irreversibly short for their age). Only 50 percent of households have access to safe water, and only 25 percent have adequate sanitation.[70]

On January 12, 2010, a devastating 7.0 magnitude earthquake struck this highly unequal and impoverished nation, killing more than 160,000 people and displacing close to 1.5 million more. Because the earthquake's epicenter was near the capital city, the National Palace and the majority of Haiti's governmental offices were almost completely destroyed. The government lost an estimated 17 percent of its workforce. Other vital infrastructure, such as hospitals, communication systems, and roads, was also damaged, making it harder to respond to immediate needs after the quake.[71]

The world responded with one of its most generous outpourings of aid in recent history. By March 1, 2010, half of all U.S. citizens had donated a combined total of $1 billion for the relief effort (worldwide $2.2 billion was raised), and on March 31, 2010 international agencies pledged $5.3 billion over the next 18 months.[72] The anthropologist Mark Schuller studied the aftermath of the earthquake and the politics of humanitarianism in Haiti. He found that little of this aid ever reached Haiti's most vulnerable people, the 1.5 million people living in the IDP (internally displaced persons) camps. Less than one percent of the aid actually was given to the Haitian government. The largest single recipient was the U.S. military (33 percent), and the majority of the aid was dispersed to foreign-run non-governmental organizations (NGOs) working in Haiti.

Because so little of this aid reached the people on the ground who needed it most, seven months following the disaster 40 percent of the IDP camps did not have access to water, and 30 percent did not have toilets of any kind. Only ten percent of families in the camps had a tent and the rest slept under tarps or bedsheets. Only 20 percent of the camps had education, health care, or mental health facilities on-site.[73] Schuller argues that this failure constitutes a violation of the Haitian IDP's human rights, and it is linked to a long history of exploitative relations between Haiti and the rest of the world.

Haiti is the second oldest republic in the Western Hemisphere (after the United States), having declared its independence from France in 1804. Years later, in order to earn diplomatic recognition from the French government, Haiti agreed to pay financial reparations to the powerful nation from 1825 to 1947. In order to do so, Haiti was forced to take out large loans from U.S. and European banks at high interest rates. During the twentieth century, the country suffered at the hands of brutal dictatorships, and its foreign debts continued to increase. Schuller argues that the world system continually applied pressure to Haiti, draining its resources and forcing it into the debt bondage that kept it from developing. In the process, this system contributed to the very surplus that allowed powerful Western nations to develop.[74]

When the earthquake struck, Haiti's economy already revolved around international aid and foreign remittances sent by migrants (which represented approximately 25 percent of the gross domestic product).[75] Haiti had become a republic of NGOs that attract the nation's most educated, talented workers (because they can pay significantly higher wages than the national government, for example). Schuller argues that the NGOs constitute a form of "trickle-down imperialism" as they reproduce the world system.[76] The relief money funneled through these organizations ended up supporting a new elite class rather than the impoverished multitudes that so desperately need the assistance.

CONCLUSION

Anthropologists have identified forms of structural inequality in countless places around the world. As we will learn in the Public Anthropology chapter, anthropology can be a powerful tool for addressing the pressing social issues of our times. When anthropological research is presented in an accessible and easily understood form, it can effectively encourage meaningful public conversations about questions such as how to best disperse relief aid after natural disasters.

One of economic anthropology's most important lessons is that multiple forms of economic production and exchange structure our daily lives and social relationships. As we have seen throughout this chapter, people simultaneously participate in both market and reciprocal exchanges on a regular basis. For example, I may buy lunch for a friend today with the idea that she will return the favor next week when she cooks me supper. Building on this anthropological idea of economic diversity, some scholars argue that in order to address the economic inequalities surrounding us we should collectively work to construct a community economy, or a space for economic decision-making that recognizes and negotiates our interdependence with other humans, other species, and our environment. J. K. Gibson-Graham, Jenny Cameron, and Stephen Healy argue that in the process of recognizing and negotiating this interdependence, we become a community.[77]

At the heart of the community economies framework is an understanding of economic diversity that parallels anthropological perspectives. The economic iceberg is a visual that nicely illustrates this diversity.[78] Above the waterline are economic activities that are visible in mainstream economic accounts, things like formal wage labor and shopping for groceries in a supermarket. Below the waterline we find the wide range of people, places, and activities that contribute to our well-being. This conceptual tool helps us to explore interrelationships that cannot be captured through mechanical market feedback loops.[79]

The most prevalent form of labor around the world is the unpaid work that is conducted within the household, the family, and the neighborhood or wider community. When we include these activities in our understanding of the diverse economy, we also reposition many people who may see themselves (or are labeled by others) as unemployed or economically inactive subjects.[80] When we highlight these different kinds of labor and forms of compensation we expand the scope of economic identities that fall outside the narrow range valued by market production and exchange (employer, employee, or entrepreneur).[81] Recognizing our mutual connections and the surplus possibilities in our own community is an important first step toward building an alternative economy, one that privileges community spheres rather than market spheres and supports equality over inequality. This also resonates with one of economic anthropology's central goals: searching for alternatives to the exploitative capitalist relations that structure the daily lives of so many people around the world today. [82]

DISCUSSION QUESTIONS

1. Why are the economic activities of people like the fair trade coffee farmers described in this chapter challenging to characterize? What benefits do the coffee farmers hope to achieve by participating in a fair trade cooperative? Why would participating in the global economy actually make these farming families more independent?

2. This chapter includes several examples of the ways in which economic production, consumption, and exchange link our lives to those of people in other parts of the world. Thinking about your own daily economic activities, how is your lifestyle dependent on people in other places? In what ways might your consumption choices be connected to global economic inequality?

3. General purpose money is used for most transactions in our society. How is the act of purchasing an object with money different from trading or gift-giving in terms of the social

and personal connections involved? Would an alternative like the Ithaca HOURS system be beneficial to your community?

4. The Barbie doll is a product that represents rigid cultural ideas about race, but Elizabeth Chin discovered in her research that girls who play with these dolls transform the dolls' appearance and racial identity. What are some other examples of products that people purchase and modify as a form of personal expression or social commentary?

GLOSSARY

Balanced reciprocity: the exchange of something with the expectation that something of equal value will be returned within a specific time period.

Consumption: the process of buying, eating, or using a resource, food, commodity, or service.

Generalized reciprocity: giving without expecting a specific thing in return.

General purpose money: a medium of exchange that can be used in all economic transactions.

Homo economicus: a term used to describe a person who would make rational decisions in ways predicted by economic theories.

Means of production: the resources used to produce goods in a society such as land for farming or factories.

Mode of production: the social relations through which human labor is used to transform energy from nature using tools, skills, organization, and knowledge.

Negative reciprocity: an attempt to get something for nothing; exchange in which both parties try to take advantage of the other.

Political economy: an approach in anthropology that investigates the historical evolution of economic relationships as well as the contemporary political processes and social structures that contribute to differences in income and wealth.

Redistribution: the accumulation of goods or labor by a particular person or institution for the purpose of dispersal at a later date.

Structural violence: a form of violence in which a social structure or institution harms people by preventing them from meeting their basic needs.

Subsistence farmers: people who raise plants and animals for their own consumption, but not for sale to others.

ABOUT THE AUTHOR

Sarah Lyon is an Associate Professor of Anthropology at the University of Kentucky. Her work is situated at the juncture of development studies, economic anthropology and food studies. She is particularly interested in how alternative food networks such as fair trade work to create and sustain diverse economies in the United States and Latin America.

BIBLIOGRAPHY

Acheson, James. *The Lobster Gangs of Maine.* Lebanon, NH: University Press of New England, 1988.

Besky, Sarah. *The Darjeeling Distinction: Labor and Justice on Fair-Trade Tea Plantations in India.* Berkeley: University of California Press, 2014.

Bohannan, Paul and Laura Bohannan. *Tiv Economy.* Evanston, IL: Northwestern University Press, 1968.

Carrier, James. *Gifts and Commodities: Exchange and Western Capitalism Since 1700.* New York: Routledge, 1995.

Chin, Elizabeth. *Purchasing Power: Black Kids and American Consumer Culture.* Minneapolis: University of Minnesota Press, 2001.

Gibson-Graham, J. K., Jenny Cameron, and Stephen Healy. *Take Back the Economy: An Ethical Guide for Transforming Our Communities.* Minneapolis: University of Minnesota Press, 2013.

Hansen, Karen. *Salaula: The World of Secondhand Clothing and Zambia.* Chicago: University of Chicago Press, 2000.

Hart, Keith. "Money in Twentieth Century Anthropology." In *A Handbook of Economic Anthropology*, edited by James Carrier. Northampton, MA: Edward Elgar, 2012.

King, Martin Luther Jr. "A Christmas Sermon on Peace, December 24, 1967," http://thekingcenter.org/archive/document/christmas-sermon.

Lyon, Sarah. *Coffee and Community: Maya Farmers and Fair Trade Markets.* Boulder: University Press of Colorado, 2011.

Marx, Karl. "The Eighteenth Brumaire of Louis Napoleon." In *The Marx-Engels Reader*, edited by Robert C. Tucker. New York: W. W. Norton, 1978[1852].

Mauss, Marcel. *The Gift: The Form and Reason for Exchange in Archaic Societies.* London: Routledge, 1990[1925].

Osburg, John. *Anxious Wealth: Money and Morality Among China's New Rich.* Stanford, CA: Stanford University Press, 2013.

Papavasiliou, Faidra. "Fair Money, Fair Trade: Tracing Alternative Consumption in a Local Currency Economy." In *Fair Trade and Social Justice: Global Ethnographies*, edited by Sarah Lyon and Mark Moberg. New York: New York University Press, 2010.

Piddocke, Stuart. "The Potlatch System of the Southern Kwakiutl: A New Perspective," *Southwestern Journal of Anthropology* 21 (1965).

Schuller, Mark. "Haiti's Disaster after the Disaster: the IDP Camps and Cholera," *Journal of Humanitarian Assistance*, December 10, 2013. https://sites.tufts.edu/jha/archives/869

————. *Killing with Kindness: Haiti, International Aid, and NGOs.* New Brunswick, NJ: Rutgers University Press, 2012.

Smith, Daniel. *A Culture of Corruption: Everyday Deception and Popular Discontent in Nigeria.* Princeton, NJ: Princeton University Press, 2007.

Wesimantel, Mary. *Food, Gender, and Poverty in the Ecuadorian Andes.* Philadelphia: University of Pennsylvania Press, 1988.

Wolf, Eric. *Europe and the People without History.* Berkeley: University of California Press, 1982.

NOTES

1. James Carrier, "Introduction," in *A Handbook of Economic Anthropology,* ed. James Carrier (Northampton, MA: Edward Elgar, 2012), 4.

2. Richard Wilk and Lisa Cliggett, *Economies and Cultures: Foundations of Economic Anthropology* (Boulder, CO: Westview Press, 2007), 37.

3. Carol Tarvis,"How Homo Economicus Went Extinct," *Wall Street Journal,* May 15, 2015, http://www.wsj.com/articles/how-homo-economicus-went-extinct-1431721255

4. Eric Wolf, *Europe and the People without History* (Berkeley: University of California Press, 1982).

5. Richard Lee, *The Dobe Ju/'hoansi* (Belmont, CA: Wadsworth Publishing, 2013). See also, Thomas Patterson, "Distribution and Redistribution," in *A Handbook of Economic Anthropology,* ed. James Carrier (Northampton, MA: Edward Elgar, 2012).

6. Hill Gates, *China's Motor: A Thousand Years of Petty Capitalism* (New York: Cornell University Press, 1996).

7. Thomas Patterson, "Distribution and Redistribution," in *A Handbook of Economic Anthropology,* ed. James Carrier (Northampton, MA: Edward Elgar, 2012), 204.

8. Martha Alter Chen, "The Informal Economy in Comparative Perspective," in *A Handbook of Economic Anthropology,* ed. James Carrier (Northampton, MA: Edward Elgar, 2012), 493.

9. Keith Hart, "Money in Twentieth Century Anthropology," in *A Handbook of Economic Anthropology,* ed. James Carrier (Northampton, MA: Edward Elgar, 2012).

10. See www.fairtrade.net for more information.

11. Sarah Lyon, *Coffee and Community: Maya Farmers and Fair Trade Markets* (Boulder: University Press of Colorado, 2011).

12. Friedrich Schneider, Andreas Buehn, and Claudio E. Montenegro, "Shadow Economies from All Over the World: New Estimates for 162 Countries from 1999 to 2007," *World Bank Policy Research Working Paper No. 5356,* July 2010. https://openknowledge.worldbank.org/bitstream/handle/10986/3928/WPS5356.pdf?sequence=1.

13. Karen Hansen, *Salaula: The World of Secondhand Clothing and Zambia* (Chicago: University of Chicago Press, 2000).

14. Elizabeth Cline, *Overdressed: The Shockingly High Cost of Cheap Fashion* (New York: Portfolio, 2013).

15. Robyn Curnow and Teo Kermeliotis, "Is Your Old T-Shirt Hurting African Economies?" *CNN,* April 12, 2013, http://www.cnn.com/2013/04/12/business/second-hand-clothes-africa/.

16. Karen Hansen, *Salaula.*

17. Marshall Sahlins, *Stone Age Economics* (Chicago: Aldine, 1972).

18. Keith Hart, "Money in Twentieth Century Anthropology," 179.

19. Marcel Mauss, *The Gift: The Form and Reason for Exchange in Archaic Societies* (London: Routledge, 1990[1925]).

20. Richard Wilk and Lisa Cliggett, *Economies and Cultures: Foundations of Economic Anthropology,* 158.

21. Ibid.,162.

22. Ibid.,120.

23. Bronislaw Malinowski, *Argonauts of the Western Pacific* (New York: Dutton, 1961[1922]).

24. Pew Research Center, "Celebrating Christmas and the Holidays Then and Now," December 18, 2013. http://www.pew-forum.org/2013/12/18/celebrating-christmas-and-the-holidays-then-and-now/.

25. James Carrier, *Gifts and Commodities: Exchange and Western Capitalism since 1700* (New York: Routledge, 1995), 189

26. Pew Research Center, "Celebrating Christmas and the Holidays Then and Now."

27. James Carrier, *Gifts and Commodities.*

28. Ibid., 178.

29. Erika Eichelberger, "What I Learned Hanging out with Nigerian Email Scammers," *Mother Jones,* March 20, 2014. http://www.motherjones.com/politics/2014/03/what-i-learned-from-nigerian-scammers.

30. Daniel Smith, *A Culture of Corruption: Everyday Deception and Popular Discontent in Nigeria* (Princeton, NJ: Princeton University Press, 2007).

31. Erika Eichelberger, "What I Learned Hanging out with Nigerian Email Scammers."

32. Internal Revenue Service, *2015 Data Book* (Washington D.C. Internal Revenue Service, 2016).

33. Richard Wilk and Lisa Cliggett, *Economies and Cultures,*156.

34. Stuart Piddocke, "The Potlatch System of the Southern Kwakiutl: A New Perspective," *Southwestern Journal of Anthropology* 21 (1965).

35. James Acheson, *The Lobster Gangs of Maine* (Lebanon, NH: University Press of New England, 1988).

36. Alf Hornborg, "Learning from the Tiv: Why a Sustainable Economy Would Have to Be 'Multicentric,'" *Culture and Agriculture* 29 (2007): 64.

37. Paul Bohannan and Laura Bohannan, *Tiv Economy* (Evanston, IL: Northwestern University Press, 1968).

38. Paul Bohannan, "Some Principles of Exchange and Investment among the Tiv," *American Anthropologist* 57 (1955): 65.

39. Ibid., 64.

40. Faidra Papavasiliou, "Fair Money, Fair Trade: Tracing Alternative Consumption in a Local Currency Economy," in *Fair Trade and Social Justice: Global Ethnographies,* ed. Sarah Lyon and Mark Moberg (New York: New York University Press, 2010).

41. J. K. Gibson-Graham, Jenny Cameron, and Stephen Healy, *Take Back the Economy: An Ethical Guide for Transforming Our Communities* (Minneapolis: University of Minnesota Press, 2013).

42. For more information, see http://ithacahours.info/

43. Faidra Papavasiliou, "Fair Money, Fair Trade: Tracing Alternative Consumption in a Local Currency Economy."

44. Ibid.

45. Ibid., 216.

46. Rudi Colloredo-Mansfeld, "Consumption: From Cultural Theory to the Ethnography of Capitalism," in *Handbook of Sociocultural Anthropology,* ed. James Carrier and Deborah Gewertz (New York: Berg Publishers, 2013), 319.

47. Ibid.

48. Mary Douglas and Baron Isherwood, *A World of Goods: Toward an Anthropology of Consumption* (New York: Basic Books, 1979).

49. Colloredo-Mansfeld, "Consumption: From Cultural Theory to the Ethnography of Capitalism."

50. Arjun Appadurai, *The Social Life of Things: Commodities in Cultural Perspective* (Cambridge: Cambridge University Press, 1986).

51. Colloredo-Mansfeld, "Consumption: From Cultural Theory to the Ethnography of Capitalism," 329.

52. See for instance, http://www.target.com/p/barbie-endless-curls-african-american-barbie-doll/-/A-15203859

53. Elizabeth Chin, *Purchasing Power: Black Kids and American Consumer Culture* (Minneapolis: University of Minnesota Press, 2001).

54. For example, https://playbarbies.wordpress.com/2011/06/02/custom-rotini-or-halo-hair/

55. Mary Wesimantel, *Food, Gender, and Poverty in the Ecuadorian Andes* (Philadelphia: University of Pennsylvania Press, 1988).

56. John Osburg, *Anxious Wealth: Money and Morality among China's New Rich* (Stanford, CA: Stanford University Press, 2013).

57. Ibid., 121.

58. Martin Luther King, Jr., *A Christmas Sermon on Peace,* December 24, 1967, http://thekingcenter.org/archive/document/christmas-sermon.

59. Some examples of this literature include Deborah Gewertz and Frederick Errington, *Cheap Meat: Flap Food Nations in the Pacific Islands* (Berkeley: University of California Press, 2010); Sarah Lyon, *Coffee and Community: Maya Farmers and Fair Trade Markets* (Boulder: University Press of Colorado, 2011); Theodore Bestor, *Tsukiji: The Fish Market at the Center of the World* (Berkeley: University of California Press, 2004) and Sidney Mintz, *Sweetness and Power: The Place of Sugar in Modern History* (New York: Penguin, 1985).

60. Colloredo-Mansfeld, "Consumption: From Cultural Theory to the Ethnography of Capitalism," 326.

61. Sarah Besky, *The Darjeeling Distinction: Labor and Justice on Fair-Trade Tea Plantations in India* (Berkeley: University of California Press, 2014).

62. Wilk and Cliggett, *Economies and Cultures: Foundations of Economic Anthropology*, 84, 95.

63. Josiah Heyman, "Political Economy," in *Handbook of Sociocultural Anthropology*, ed. James Carrier and Deborah Gewertz (New York: Berg Publishers, 2013), 89.

64. The historical evolution of societies and markets is explored by Eric Wolf in *Europe and the People without History* (Berkeley: University of California Press, 1982). The legacies of social domination and marginalization are discussed by Philippe Bourgois in *In Search of Respect: Selling Crack in El Barrio* (Cambridge: Cambridge University Press, 1995).

65. Karl Marx, *The Eighteenth Brumaire of Louis Napoleon,* in The Marx-Engels Reader, 2nd Edition, ed. Robert C. Tucker (New York: W. W. Norton, 1978[1852]).

66. Johan Galtung, "Violence, Peace, and Peace Research," *Journal of Peace Research* 6 no. 3(1969): 167–191.

67. See Max Weber's work *The Protestant Ethic and the Spirit of Capitalism* available at http://xroads.virginia.edu/~HYPER/WEBER/cover.html

68. "Living Conditions in Haiti's Capital Improve, but Rural Communities Remain Very Poor," World Bank, July 11, 2014. http://www.worldbank.org/en/news/feature/2014/07/11/while-living-conditions-in-port-au-prince-are-improving-haiti-countryside-remains-very-poor.

69. "CIA Factbook: Haiti," https://www.cia.gov/library/publications/the-world-factbook/geos/ha.html.

70. "Ten Facts about Hunger in Haiti," https://www.wfp.org/stories/10-facts-about-hunger-haiti.

71. Mark Schuller, "Haiti's Disaster after the Disaster: the IDP Camps and Cholera," *Journal of Humanitarian Assistance*, December 10, 2013. https://sites.tufts.edu/jha/archives/869

72. Ibid.

73. Ibid.

74. Mark Schuller, *Killing with Kindness: Haiti, International Aid, and NGOs* (New Brunswick, NJ: Rutgers University Press, 2012).

75. Terry Buss, *Haiti in the Balance: Why Foreign Aid has Failed and What We Can Do about It* (Washington D.C.: The Brookings Institute, 2008).

76. Mark Schuller, *Killing with Kindness*.

77. J. K. Gibson-Graham, Jenny Cameron, and Stephen Healy, *Take Back the Economy: An Ethical Guide for Transforming Our Communities* (Minneapolis: University of Minnesota Press, 2013), xix.

78. Byrne, Ken, "Iceberg Image," http://www.communityeconomies.org/Home/Key-Ideas.

79. Gibson-Graham, Cameron, and Healy, *Take Back the Economy,* 11.

80. J. K. Gibson-Graham, *A Postcapitalist Politics* (Minneapolis: University of Minnesota Press, 2006), 62–63.

81. Ibid., 65.

82. Keith Hart, "Money in Twentieth Century Anthropology."

POLITICAL ANTHROPOLOGY: A CROSS-CULTURAL COMPARISON

Paul McDowell, Santa Barbara City College
McDowell@sbcc.edu
paulanthropus@cox.net

LEARNING OBJECTIVES

- Identify the four levels of socio-cultural integration (band, tribe, chiefdom, and state) and describe their characteristics.

- Compare systems of leadership in egalitarian and non-egalitarian societies.

- Describe systems used in tribes and chiefdoms to achieve social integration and encourage connections between people.

- Assess the benefits and problems associated with state-level political organizations.

- Evaluate the extent to which the Islamic State meets the formal criteria for a state-level political organization.

All cultures have one element in common: they somehow exercise social control over their own members. Even small foraging societies such as the Ju/'hoansi or !Kung, the Inuit (or "Eskimo") of the Arctic north, and aboriginal Australians experience disputes that must be contained if inter-personal conflicts are to be reduced or eliminated. As societies become more complex, means of control increase accordingly. The study of these means of control are the subject of political anthropology.

BASIC CONCEPTS IN POLITICAL ANTHROPOLOGY

Like the "invisible hand" of the market to which Adam Smith refers in analyzing the workings of capitalism, two forces govern the workings of politics: power—the ability to induce behavior of others in specified ways by means of coercion or use or threat of physical force—and authority—the ability to induce behavior of others by persuasion.[1] Extreme examples of the exercise of power are the gulags (prison camps) in Stalinist Russia, the death camps in Nazi-ruled Germany and Eastern Europe, and so-called Supermax prisons such as Pelican Bay in California and the prison for "enemy combatants" in Guantanamo Bay, Cuba, by the United States. In all of these settings, prisoners comply or are punished or executed. At the other extreme are most forager societies, which typically exercise authority more often than power. Groups in those societies comply with the wishes of their most persuasive members.

In actuality, power and authority are points on a continuum and both are present in every society to some degree. Even Hitler, who exercised absolute power in many ways, had to hold the Nuremberg rallies to generate popular support for his regime and persuade the German population that his leadership was the way to national salvation. In the Soviet Union, leaders had a great deal of coercive and physical power but still felt the need to hold parades and mass rallies on May Day every year to persuade people to remain attached to their vision of a communal society. At the other end of the political spectrum, societies that tend to use persuasion through authority also have some forms of coercive power. Among the Inuit, for example, individuals who flagrantly violated group norms could be punished, including by homicide.[2]

A related concept in both politics and law is **legitimacy:** the perception that an individual has a valid right to leadership. Legitimacy is particularly applicable to complex societies that require centralized decision-making. Historically, the right to rule has been based on various principles. In agricultural states such as ancient Mesopotamia, the Aztec, and the Inca, justification for the rule of particular individuals was based on hereditary succession and typically granted to the eldest son of the ruler. Even this principle could be uncertain at times, as was the case when the Inca emperor Atahualpa had just defeated his rival and brother Huascar when the Spaniards arrived in Peru in 1533.[3]

In many cases, supernatural beliefs were invoked to establish legitimacy and justify rule by an elite. Incan emperors derived their right to rule from the Sun God and Aztec rulers from Huitzilopochtli (Hummingbird-to-the-Left). European monarchs invoked a divine right to rule that was reinforced by the Church of England in Britain and by the Roman Catholic Church in other countries prior to the Reformation. In India, the dominance of the Brahmin elite over the other **castes** is justified by karma, cumulative forces created by good and evil deeds in past lives. Secular equivalents also serve to justify rule by elites; examples include the promise of a worker's paradise in the former Soviet Union and racial purity of Aryans in Nazi Germany. In the United States and other democratic forms of government, legitimacy rests on the consent of the governed in periodic elections (though in the United States, the incoming president is sworn in using a Christian Bible despite alleged separation of church and state).

In some societies, dominance by an individual or group is viewed as unacceptable. Christopher Boehm (1999) developed the concept of **reverse dominance** to describe societies in which people rejected attempts by any individual to exercise power.[4] They achieved this aim using ridicule, criticism, disobedience, and strong disapproval and could banish extreme offenders. Richard Lee encountered this phenomenon when he presented the !Kung with whom he had worked over the preceding year with a fattened ox.[5] Rather than praising or thanking him, his hosts ridiculed the beast as scrawny, ill fed, and probably sick. This behavior is consistent with reverse dominance.

Even in societies that emphasize equality between people, decisions still have to be made. Sometimes particularly persuasive figures such as headmen make them, but persuasive figures who lack formal power are not free to make decisions without coming to a consensus with their fellows. To reach such consensus, there must be general agreement. Essentially, then, even if in a backhanded way, legitimacy characterizes societies that lack institutionalized leadership.

Another set of concepts refers to the reinforcements or consequences for compliance with the directive and laws of a society. **Positive reinforcements** are the rewards for compliance; examples include medals, financial incentives, and other forms of public recognition. **Negative reinforcements** punish noncompliance through fines, imprisonment, and death sentences. These reinforcements can be identified in every human society, even among foragers or others who have no written system of law. Reverse dominance is one form of negative reinforcement.

LEVELS OF SOCIO-CULTURAL INTEGRATION

If cultures of various sizes and configurations are to be compared, there must be some common basis for defining political organization. In many small communities, the family functions as a political unit. As Julian Steward wrote about the Shoshone, a Native American group in the Nevada basin, "all features of the relatively simple culture were integrated and functioned on a family level. The family was the reproductive, economic, educational, political, and religious unit."[6] In larger more complex societies, however, the functions of the family are taken over by larger social institutions. The resources of the economy, for example, are managed by authority figures outside the family who demand taxes or other tribute. The educational function of the family may be taken over by schools constituted under the authority of a government, and the authority structure in the family is likely to be subsumed under the greater power of the state. Therefore, anthropologists need methods for assessing political organizations that can be applied to many different kinds of communities. This concept is called levels of socio-cultural integration.

Elman Service (1975) developed an influential scheme for categorizing the political character of societies that recognized four levels of socio-cultural integration: **band**, **tribe**, **chiefdom**, and **state**.[7] A band is the smallest unit of political organization, consisting of only a few families and no formal leadership positions. Tribes have larger populations but are organized around family ties and have fluid or shifting systems of temporary leadership. Chiefdoms are large political units in which the chief, who usually is determined by heredity, holds a formal position of power. States are the most complex form of political organization and are characterized by a central government that has a monopoly over legitimate uses of physical force, a sizeable bureaucracy, a system of formal laws, and a standing military force.

Each type of political integration can be further categorized as **egalitarian**, **ranked**, or **stratified**. Band societies and tribal societies generally are considered egalitarian—there is no great difference in status or power between individuals and there are as many valued status positions in the societies as there are persons able to fill them. Chiefdoms are ranked societies; there are substantial differences in the wealth and social status of individuals based on how closely related they are to the chief. In ranked societies, there are a limited number of positions of power or status, and only a few can occupy them. State societies are stratified. There are large differences in the wealth, status, and power of individuals based on unequal access to resources and positions of power. Socio-economic classes, for instance, are forms of stratification in many state societies.[8]

EGALITARIAN SOCIETIES

We humans are not equal in all things. The status of women is low relative to the status of men in many, if not most, societies as we will see. There is also the matter of age. In some societies, the aged enjoy greater prestige than the young; in others, the aged are subjected to discrimination in employment and other areas. Even in Japan, which has traditionally been known for its respect for elders, the prestige of the aged is in decline. And we vary in terms of our abilities. Some are more eloquent or skilled technically than others; some are expert craft persons while others are not; some excel at conceptual thought, whereas for the rest of us, there is always the *For Dummies* book series to manage our computers, software, and other parts of our daily lives such as wine and sex.

In a complex society, it may seem that **social classes**—differences in wealth and status—are, like death and taxes, inevitable: that one is born into wealth, poverty, or somewhere in between and has no say in the matter, at least at the start of life, and that social class is an involuntary position in society. However, is social class universal? As they say, let's look at the record, in this case ethnographies. We find that among foragers, there is no advantage to hoarding food; in most climates, it will rot before one's eyes. Nor is there much personal property, and leadership, where it exists, is informal. In forager societies, the basic ingredients for social class do not exist. Foragers such as the !Kung, Inuit, and aboriginal Australians, are **egalitarian** societies in which there are few differences between members in wealth, status, and power. Highly skilled and less skilled hunters do not belong to different strata in the way that the captains of industry do from you and me. The less skilled hunters in egalitarian societies receive a share of the meat and have the right to be heard on important decisions. Egalitarian societies also lack a government or centralized leadership. Their leaders, known as headmen or big men, emerge by consensus of the group. Foraging societies are always egalitarian, but so are many societies that practice horticulture or pastoralism. In terms of political organization, egalitarian societies can be either bands or tribes.

BAND-LEVEL POLITICAL ORGANIZATION

Societies organized as a band typically comprise foragers who rely on hunting and gathering and are therefore nomadic, are few in number (rarely exceeding 100 persons), and form small groups consisting of a few families and a shifting population. Bands lack formal leadership. Richard Lee went so far as to say that the Dobe! Kung had no leaders. To quote one of his informants, "Of course we have headmen. Each one of us is headman over himself."[9] At most, a band's leader is *primus inter pares* or "first among equals" assuming anyone is first at all. Modesty is a valued trait; arrogance and competitiveness are not acceptable in societies characterized by reverse dominance. What leadership there is in band societies tends to be transient and subject to shifting circumstances. For example, among the Paiute in North America, "rabbit bosses" coordinated rabbit drives during the hunting season but played no leadership role otherwise. Some "leaders" are excellent mediators who are called on when individuals are involved in disputes while others are perceived as skilled shamans or future-seers who are consulted periodically. There are no formal offices or rules of succession.[10]

Bands were probably the first political unit to come into existence outside the family itself. There is some debate in anthropology about how the earliest bands were organized. Elman Service argued that patrilocal bands organized around groups of related men served as the prototype, reasoning that groups centered on male family relationships made sense because male cooperation was essential to hunting.[11] M. Kay Martin and Barbara Voorhies pointed out in rebuttal that gathering vegetable foods, which typically was viewed as women's work, actually contributed a greater number of calories in most cultures and thus that matrilocal bands organized around groups of related women would be closer to the norm.[12] Indeed, in societies in which hunting is the primary source of food, such as the Inuit, women tend to be subordinate to men while men and women tend to have roughly equal status in societies that mainly gather plants for food.

Law in Band Societies

Within bands of people, disputes are typically resolved informally. There are no formal mediators or any organizational equivalent of a court of law. A good mediator may emerge—or may not. In some cultures, duels are employed. Among the Inuit, for example, disputants engage in a duel using songs in which, drum in hand, they chant insults at each other before an audience. The audience selects the better chanter and thereby the winner in the dispute.[13] The Mbuti of the African Congo use ridicule; even children berate adults for laziness, quarreling, or selfishness. If ridicule fails, the Mbuti elders evaluate the dispute carefully, determine the cause, and, in extreme cases, walk to the center of the camp and criticize the individuals by name, using humor to soften their criticism—the group, after all, must get along.[14]

Warfare in Band Societies

Nevertheless, conflict does sometimes break out into war between bands and, sometimes, within them. Such warfare is usually sporadic and short-lived since bands do not have formal leadership structures or enough warriors to sustain conflict for long. Most of the conflict arises from interpersonal arguments. Among the Tiwi of Australia, for example, failure of one band to reciprocate another band's wife-giving with one of its own female relative led to abduction of women by the aggrieved band, precipitating a "war" that involved some spear-throwing (many did not shoot straight and even some of the onlookers were wounded) but mostly violent talk and verbal abuse.[15] For the Dobe !Kung, Lee found 22 cases of homicide by males and other periodic episodes of violence, mostly in disputes over women—not quite the gentle souls Elizabeth Marshall Thomas depicted in her *Harmless People* (1959).[16]

TRIBAL POLITICAL ORGANIZATION

Whereas bands involve small populations without structure, tribal societies involve at least two well-defined groups linked together in some way and range in population from about 100 to as many as 5,000 people. Though their social institutions can be fairly complex, there are no centralized political structures or offices in the strict sense of those terms. There may be headmen, but there are no rules of succession and sons do not necessarily succeed their fathers as is the case with chiefdoms. Tribal leadership roles are open to anyone—in practice, usually men, especially elder men who acquire leadership positions because of their personal abilities and qualities. Leaders in tribes do not have a means of coercing others or formal powers associated with their positions. Instead, they must persuade others to take actions they feel are needed. A Yanomami headsman, for instance, said that he would never issue an order unless he knew it would be obeyed. The headman Kaobawä exercised influence by example and by making suggestions and warning of consequences of taking or not taking an action.[17]

Like bands, tribes are egalitarian societies. Some individuals in a tribe do sometimes accumulate personal property but not to the extent that other tribe members are deprived. And every (almost always male) person has the opportunity to become a headman or leader and, like bands, one's leadership position can be situational. One man may be a good mediator, another an exemplary warrior, and a third capable of leading a hunt or finding a more ideal area for cultivation or grazing herds. An example illustrating this kind of leadership is the **big man** of New Guinea; the term is derived from the languages of New Guinean tribes (literally meaning "man of influence"). The big man is one who has acquired followers by doing favors they cannot possibly repay, such as settling their debts or providing bride-wealth. He might also acquire as many wives as possible to create alliances with his wives' families. His wives could work to care for as many pigs as possible, for example, and in due course, he could sponsor a pig feast that would serve to put more tribe members in his debt and shame his rivals. It is worth noting that the followers, incapable of repaying the Big Man's gifts, stand metaphorically as beggars to him.[18]

Still, a big man does not have the power of a monarch. His role is not hereditary. His son must demonstrate his worth and acquire his own following—he must become a big man in his own right.

Furthermore, there usually are other big men in the village who are his potential rivals. Another man who proves himself capable of acquiring a following can displace the existing big man. The big man also has no power to coerce—no army or police force. He cannot prevent a follower from joining another big man, nor can he force the follower to pay any debt owed. There is no New Guinean equivalent of a U.S. marshal. Therefore, he can have his way only by diplomacy and persuasion—which do not always work.[19]

Tribal Systems of Social Integration

Tribal societies have much larger populations than bands and thus must have mechanisms for creating and maintaining connections between tribe members. The family ties that unite members of a band are not sufficient to maintain solidarity and cohesion in the larger population of a tribe. Some of the systems that knit tribes together are based on family (kin) relationships, including various kinds of marriage and family lineage systems, but there are also ways to foster tribal solidarity outside of family arrangements through systems that unite members of a tribe by age or gender.

Integration through Age Grades and Age Sets

Tribes use various systems to encourage solidarity or feelings of connectedness between people who are not related by family ties. These systems, sometimes known as **sodalities**, unite people across family groups. In one sense, all societies are divided into age categories. In the U.S. educational system, for instance, children are matched to grades in school according to their age—six-year-olds in first grade and thirteen-year-olds in eighth grade. Other cultures, however, have established complex age-based social structures. Many pastoralists in East Africa, for example, have age grades and age sets. **Age sets** are named categories to which men of a certain age are assigned at birth. **Age grades** are groups of men who are close to one another in age and share similar duties or responsibilities. All men cycle through each age grade over the course of their lifetimes. As the age sets advance, the men assume the duties associated with each age grade.

An example of this kind of tribal society is the Tiriki of Kenya. From birth to about fifteen years of age, boys become members of one of seven named age sets. When the last boy is recruited, that age set closes and a new one opens. For example, young and adult males who belonged to the "Juma" age set in 1939 became warriors by 1954. The "Mayima" were already warriors in 1939 and became elder warriors during that period. In precolonial times, men of the warrior age grade defended the herds of the Tiriki and conducted raids on other tribes while the elder warriors acquired cattle and houses and took on wives. There were recurring reports of husbands who were much older than their wives, who had married early in life, often as young as fifteen or sixteen. As solid citizens of the Tiriki, the elder warriors also handled decision-making functions of the tribe as a whole; their legislation affected the entire village while also representing their own kin groups. The other age sets also moved up through age grades in the fifteen-year period. The elder warriors in 1939, "Nyonje," became the judicial elders by 1954. Their function was to resolve disputes that arose between individuals, families, and kin groups, of which some elders were a part. The "Jiminigayi," judicial elders in 1939, became ritual elders in 1954, handling supernatural functions that involved the entire Tiriki community. During this period, the open age set was "Kabalach." Its prior members had all grown old or died by 1939 and new boys joined it between 1939 and 1954. Thus, the Tiriki age sets moved in continuous 105-

year cycles. This age grade and age set system encourages bonds between men of similar ages. Their loyalty to their families is tempered by their responsibilities to their fellows of the same age.[20]

Traditional Duties of Age Grade	Age Sets 1939	Age Sets 1954	Age Sets 1979	Age Sets 1994
Retired or Deceased: 91-105	Kabalach	Golongolo	Jiminigayi	Nyonje
Ritual Elders: 76-90	Golongolo	Jiminigayi	Nyonje	Mayina
Judicial Elders: 61-750	Jiminigayi	Nyonje	Mayina	Juma
Elder Warriors : 46-60	Nyonje	Mayina	Juma	Sawe
Warriors: 31-45	Mayina	Juma	Sawe	Kabalach
Initiated and Uninitiated Youths: 16-30	Juma	Sawe	Kabalach	Golongolo
Small Boys: 0-15	Sawe	Kabalach	Golongolo	Jiminigayi

Figure 1: Grades and age sets among the Tiriki. Reprinted with permission of Kendall Hunt Publishing Company.

Integration through Bachelor Associations and Men's Houses

Among most, if not all, tribes of New Guinea, the existence of men's houses serves to cut across family lineage groups in a village. Perhaps the most fastidious case of male association in New Guinea is the bachelor association of the Mae-Enga, who live in the northern highlands. In their culture, a boy becomes conscious of the distance between males and females before he leaves home at age five to live in the men's house. Women are regarded as potentially unclean, and strict codes that minimize male-female relations are enforced. *Sanggai* festivals reinforce this division. During the festival, every youth of age 15 or 16 goes into seclusion in the forest and observes additional restrictions, such as avoiding pigs (which are cared for by women) and avoiding gazing at the ground lest he see female footprints or pig feces.[21] One can see, therefore, that every boy commits his loyalty to the men's house early in life even though he remains a member of his birth family. Men's houses are the center of male activities. There, they draw up strategies for warfare, conduct ritual activities involving magic and honoring of ancestral spirits, and plan and rehearse periodic pig feasts.

Integration through Gifts and Feasting

Exchanges and the informal obligations associated with them are primary devices by which bands and tribes maintain a degree of order and forestall armed conflict, which was viewed as the "state of nature" for tribal societies by Locke and Hobbes, in the absence of exercises of force by police or an army. Marcel Mauss, nephew and student of eminent French sociologist Emile Durkheim, attempted in 1925 to explain gift giving and its attendant obligations cross-culturally in his book, *The Gift: Forms and Functions of Exchange in Archaic Societies.* He started with the assumption that two groups have an imperative to establish a relationship of some kind. There are three options when they meet for the first time. They could pass each other by and never see each other again. They may resort to arms with an uncertain outcome. One could wipe the other out or, more likely, win at great cost of men and property or fight to a draw. The third option is to "come to terms" with each other by establishing a more or less permanent relationship.[22] Exchanging gifts is one way for groups to establish this relationship.

These gift exchanges are quite different from Western ideas about gifts. In societies that lack a central government, formal law enforcement powers, and collection agents, the gift exchanges are obligatory and have the force of law in the absence of law. Mauss referred to them as "total prestations."

Though no Dun and Bradstreet agents would come to collect, the potential for conflict that could break out at any time reinforced the obligations.[23] According to Mauss, the first obligation is to give; it must be met if a group is to extend social ties to others. The second obligation is to receive; refusal of a gift constitutes rejection of the offer of friendship as well. Conflicts can arise from the perceived insult of a rejected offer. The third obligation is to repay. One who fails to make a gift in return will be seen as in debt—in essence, a beggar. Mauss offered several ethnographic cases that illustrated these obligations. Every gift conferred power to the giver, expressed by the Polynesian terms *mana* (an intangible supernatural force) and *hau* (among the Maori, the "spirit of the gift," which must be returned to its owner).[24] Marriage and its associated obligations also can be viewed as a form of gift-giving as one family "gives" a bride or groom to the other.

Basics of Marriage, Family, and Kinship

Understanding social solidarity in tribal societies requires knowledge of family structures, which are also known as kinship systems. The romantic view of marriage in today's mass media is largely a product of Hollywood movies and romance novels from mass-market publishers such as Harlequin. In most cultures around the world, marriage is largely a device that links two families together; this is why arranged marriage is so common from a cross-cultural perspective. And, as Voltaire admonished, if we are to discuss anything, we need to define our terms.

Marriage is defined in numerous ways, usually (but not always) involving a tie between a woman and a man. Same-sex marriage is also common in many cultures. Nuclear families consist of parents and their children. Extended families consist of three generations or more of relatives connected by marriage and descent.

In the diagrams below, triangles represent males and circles represent females. Vertical lines represent a **generational link** connecting, say, a man with his father. Horizontal lines above two figures are **sibling links**; thus, a triangle connected to a circle represents a brother and sister. Equal signs connect husbands and wives. Sometimes a diagram may render use of an equal sign unrealistic; in those cases, a horizontal line drawn *below* the two figures shows a marriage link.

Most rules of descent generally fall into one of two categories. **Bilateral descent** (commonly used in the United States) recognizes both the mother's and the father's "sides" of the family while **unilineal descent** recognizes only one sex-based "side" of the family. Unilineal descent can be **patrilineal**, recognizing only relatives through a line of male ancestors, or **matrilineal**, recognizing only relatives through a line of female ancestors.

Groups made up of two or more extended families can be connected as larger groups linked by kinship ties. A **lineage** consists of individuals who can trace or demonstrate their descent through a line of males or females to the founding ancestor.

For further discussion of this topic, consult the Family and Marriage chapter.

Integration through Marriage

Most tribal societies' political organizations involve marriage, which is a logical vehicle for creating alliances between groups. One of the most well-documented types of marriage alliance is bilateral cross-cousin marriage in which a man marries his cross-cousin—one he is related to through two links, his father's sister and his mother's brother. These marriages have been documented among the

Yanomami, an indigenous group living in Venezuela and Brazil. Yanomami villages are typically populated by two or more extended family groups also known as lineages. Disputes and disagreements are bound to occur, and these tensions can potentially escalate to open conflict or even physical violence. Bilateral cross-cousin marriage provides a means of linking lineage groups together over time through the exchange of brides. Because cross-cousin marriage links people together by both marriage and blood ties (kinship), these unions can reduce tension between the groups or at least provide an incentive for members of rival lineages to work together.

To get a more detailed picture of how marriages integrate family groups, consider the following family diagrams. In these diagrams, triangles represent males and circles represent females. Vertical lines represent a generational link connecting, say, a man to his father. Horizontal lines above two figures are sibling links; thus, a triangle connected to a circle by a horizontal line represents a brother and sister. Equal signs connect husbands and wives. In some diagrams in which use of an equal sign is not realistic, a horizontal line drawn *below* the two figures shows their marriage link.

Figure 2 depicts the alliance created by the bilateral cross-cousin marriage system. In this figure, uppercase letters represent males and lowercase letters represent females, Thus, X refers to all of the males of Lineage X and Y refers to all of the males of Lineage Y; likewise, x refers to all of the females of Lineage X and y refers to all of the females of Lineage Y.

Consider the third generation in the diagram. X_3 has married y_3 (the horizontal line below the figures), creating an **affinal** link. Trace the relationship between

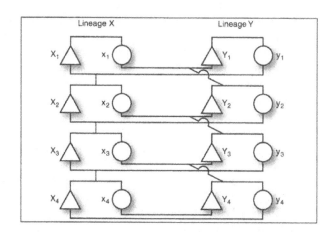

Figure 2: Bilateral cross-cousin marriage. Reprinted with permission of Kendall Hunt Publishing Company.

X_3 and y_3 through their matrilateral links—the links between a mother and her brother. You can see from the diagram that X_3's mother is x_2 and her brother is Y_2 and his daughter is y_3. Therefore, y_3 is X_3's mother's brother's daughter.

Now trace the patrilateral links of this couple—the links between a father and his sister. X_3's father is X_2 and X_2's sister is x_2, who married Y_2, which makes her daughter y_3—his father's sister's daughter. Work your way through the description and diagram until you are comfortable understanding the connections.

Now do the same thing with Y_3 by tracing his matrilateral ties with his wife x_3. His mother is x_2 and her brother is X_2, which makes his mother's brother's daughter x_3. On the patrilateral, his father is Y_2, and Y_2's sister is y_2, who is married to X_2 Therefore, their daughter is x3.

This example represents the ideal **bilateral cross-cousin marriage**: a man marries a woman who is *both* his mother's brother's daughter and his father's sister's daughter. The man's matrilateral cross-cousin and patrilateral cross-cousin are the same woman! Thus, the two lineages have discharged their obligations to one another in the same generation. Lineage X provides a daughter to lineage Y and lineage Y reciprocates with a daughter. Each of the lineages therefore retains its potential to reproduce in the next generation. The obligation incurred by lineage Y from taking lineage X's daughter in marriage has been repaid by giving a daughter in marriage to lineage X.

This type of marriage is what Robin Fox, following Claude Levi-Strauss, called **restricted exchange**.[25] Notice that only two extended families can engage in this exchange. Society remains relatively simple because it can expand only by splitting off. And, as we will see later, when daughter villages split off, the two lineages move together.

Not all marriages can conform to this type of exchange. Often, the patrilateral cross-cousin is not the same person; there may be two or more persons. Furthermore, in some situations, a man can marry either a matrilateral or a patrilateral cross-cousin but not both. The example of the ideal type of cross-cousin marriage is used to demonstrate the logical outcome of such unions.

Integration through a Segmentary Lineage

Another type of kin-based integrative mechanism is a segmentary lineage. As previously noted, a lineage is a group of people who can trace or demonstrate their descent from a founding ancestor through a line of males or a line of females. A **segmentary lineage** is a hierarchy of lineages that contains both close and relatively distant family members. At the base are several minimal lineages whose members trace their descent from their founder back two or three generations. At the top is the founder of all of the lineages, and two or more maximal lineages can derive from the founder's lineage. Between the maximal and the minimal lineages are several intermediate lineages. For purposes of simplicity, we will discuss only the maximal and minimal lineages.

One characteristic of segmentary lineages is complementary opposition. To illustrate, consider the chart in Figure 3, which presents two maximal lineages, A and B, each having two minimal lineages: A1 and A2 for A and B1 and B2 for B.

Suppose A1 starts a feud with A2 over cattle theft. Since A1 and A2 are of the same maximal lineage, their feud is likely to be contained within that lineage, and B1 and B2 are likely to ignore the conflict since it is no concern of theirs. Now suppose A2 attacks B1 for cattle theft. In that case, A1 might unite with A2 to feud with B1, who B2 join in to defend. Thus, the feud would involve everyone in maximal lineage A against everyone in maximal lineage B. Finally, consider an attack by an outside tribe against A1. In response, both maximal lineages might rise up and defend A1.

The classic examples of segmentary lineages were described by E. E. Evans-Pritchard (1940) in his discussion of the Nuer, pastoralists who lived in southern Sudan.[26] Paul Bohannan (1989) also described this system among the Tiv, who were West African pastoralists, and Robert Murphy and Leonard Kasdan (1959) analyzed the importance of these lineages among the Bedouin of the Middle East.[27] Segmentary lineages often develop in environments in which a tribal society is surrounded by several other tribal societies. Hostility between the tribes induces their members to retain ties with their kin and to mobilize them when external conflicts arise. An example of this is ties maintained between the Nuer and the Dinka. Once a conflict is over, segmentary lineages typically dissolve into their constituent units. Another attribute of segmentary lineages is local genealogical segmentation, meaning close lineages dwell near each other, providing a physical reminder of their genealogy.[28] A Bedouin proverb summarizes the philosophy behind segmentary lineages:

> I against my brother
> I and my brother against my cousin
> I, my brother, and my cousin against the world

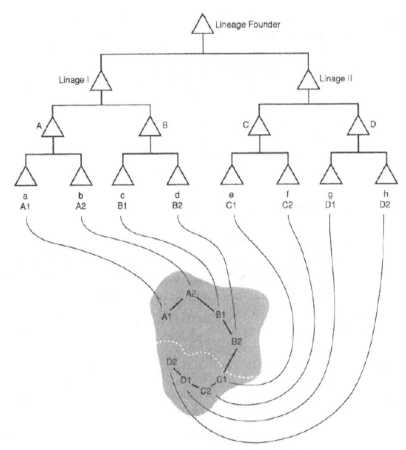

Figure 3: Segmentary lineage model. Note connection of each lineage, regardless of relative size, to its territory. Reprinted with permission of Kendall Hunt Publishing Company.

Segmentary lineages regulate both warfare and inheritance and property rights. As noted by Sahlins (1961) in studies of the Nuer, tribes in which such lineages occur typically have relatively large populations of close to 100,000 persons.[29]

Law in Tribal Societies

Tribal societies generally lack systems of **codified law** whereby damages, crimes, remedies, and punishments are specified. Only state-level political systems can determine, usually by writing formal laws, which behaviors are permissible and which are not (discussed later in this chapter). In tribes, there are no systems of law enforcement whereby an agency such as the police, the sheriff, or an army can enforce laws enacted by an appropriate authority. And, as already noted, headman and big men cannot force their will on others.

In tribal societies, as in all societies, conflicts arise between individuals. Sometimes the issues are equivalent to crimes—taking of property or commitment of violence—that are not considered legitimate in a given society. Other issues are civil disagreements—questions of ownership, damage to property, an accidental death. In tribal societies, the aim is not so much to determine guilt or innocence or to assign criminal or civil responsibility as it is to resolve conflict, which can be accomplished in various ways. The parties might choose to avoid each other. Bands, tribes, and kin groups often move away from each other geographically, which is much easier for them to do than for people living in complex societies.

One issue in tribal societies, as in all societies, is guilt or innocence. When no one witnesses an offense or an account is deemed unreliable, tribal societies sometimes rely on the supernatural. **Oaths**, for example, involve calling on a deity to bear witness to the truth of what one says; the oath given in court is a holdover from this practice. An **ordeal** is used to determine guilt or innocence by submitting the accused to dangerous, painful, or risky tests believed to be controlled by supernatural forces. The poison oracle used by the Azande of the Sudan and the Congo is an ordeal based on their belief that most misfortunes are induced by witchcraft (in this case, witchcraft refers to ill feeling of one person toward another). A chicken is force fed a strychnine concoction known as *benge* just as the name of the suspect is called out. If the chicken dies, the suspect is deemed guilty and is punished or goes through reconciliation.[30]

A more commonly exercised option is to find ways to resolve the dispute. In small groups, an unresolved question can quickly escalate to violence and disrupt the group. The first step is often negotiation; the parties attempt to resolve the conflict by direct discussion in hope of arriving at an agreement. Offenders sometimes make a ritual apology, particularly if they are sensitive to community opinion. In Fiji, for example, offenders make ceremonial apologies called *i soro,* one of the meanings of which is "I surrender." An intermediary speaks, offers a token gift to the offended party, and asks for forgiveness, and the request is rarely rejected.[31]

When negotiation or a ritual apology fails, often the next step is to recruit a third party to mediate a settlement as there is no official who has the power to enforce a settlement. A classic example in the anthropological literature is the Leopard Skin Chief among the Nuer, who is identified by a leopard skin wrap around his shoulders. He is not a chief but is a mediator. The position is hereditary, has religious overtones, and is responsible for the social well-being of the tribal segment. He typically is called on for serious matters such as murder. The culprit immediately goes to the residence of the Leopard Skin Chief, who cuts the culprit's arm until blood flows. If the culprit fears vengeance by the dead man's family, he remains at the residence, which is considered a sanctuary, and the Leopard Skin Chief then acts as a go-between for the families of the perpetrator and the dead man.

The Leopard Skin Chief cannot force the parties to settle and cannot enforce any settlement they reach. The source of his influence is the desire for the parties to avoid a feud that could escalate into an ever-widening conflict involving kin descended from different ancestors. He urges the aggrieved family to accept compensation, usually in the form of cattle. When such an agreement is reached, the chief collects the 40 to 50 head of cattle and takes them to the dead man's home, where he performs various sacrifices of cleansing and atonement.[32]

This discussion demonstrates the preference most tribal societies have for mediation given the potentially serious consequences of a long-term feud. Even in societies organized as states, mediation is often preferred. In the agrarian town of Talea, Mexico, for example, even serious crimes are mediated in the interest of preserving a degree of local harmony. The national authorities often tolerate local settlements if they maintain the peace.[33]

Warfare in Tribal Societies

What happens if mediation fails and the Leopard Skin Chief cannot convince the aggrieved clan to accept cattle in place of their loved one? War. In tribal societies, wars vary in cause, intensity, and duration, but they tend to be less deadly than those run by states because of tribes' relatively small populations and limited technologies.

Tribes engage in warfare more often than bands, both internally and externally. Among pastoralists, both successful and attempted thefts of cattle frequently spark conflict. Among pre-state societies, pastoralists have a reputation for being the most prone to warfare. However, horticulturalists also engage in warfare, as the film *Dead Birds*, which describes warfare among the highland Dani of west New Guinea (Irian Jaya), attests. Among anthropologists, there is a "protein debate" regarding causes of warfare. Marvin Harris in a 1974 study of the Yanomami claimed that warfare arose there because of a protein deficiency associated with a scarcity of game, and Kenneth Good supported that thesis in finding that the game a Yanomami villager brought in barely supported the village.[34] He could not link this variable to warfare, however. In rebuttal, Napoleon Chagnon linked warfare among the Yanomami with abduction of women rather than disagreements over hunting territory, and findings from other cultures have tended to agree with Chagnon's theory.[35]

Tribal wars vary in duration. **Raids** are short-term uses of physical force that are organized and planned to achieve a limited objective such as acquisition of cattle (pastoralists) or other forms of wealth and, often, abduction of women, usually from neighboring communities.[36] **Feuds** are longer in duration and represent a state of recurring hostilities between families, lineages, or other kin groups. In a feud, the responsibility to avenge rests with the entire group, and the murder of any kin member is considered appropriate because the kin group as a whole is considered responsible for the transgression. Among the Dani, for example, vengeance is an obligation; spirits are said to dog the victim's clan until its members murder someone from the perpetrator's clan.[37]

RANKED SOCIETIES AND CHIEFDOMS

Unlike egalitarian societies, **ranked societies** (sometimes called "rank societies") involve greater differentiation between individuals and the kin groups to which they belong. These differences can be, and often are, inherited, but there are no significant restrictions in these societies on access to basic resources. All individuals can meet their basic needs. The most important differences between people of different ranks are based on **sumptuary rules**—norms that permit persons of higher rank to enjoy greater social status by wearing distinctive clothing, jewelry, and/or decorations denied those of lower rank. Every family group or lineage in the community is ranked in a hierarchy of prestige and power. Furthermore, within families, siblings are ranked by birth order and villages can also be ranked.

The concept of a ranked society leads us directly to the characteristics of **chiefdoms**. Unlike the position of headman in a band, the position of **chief** is an *office*—a permanent political status that demands a successor when the current chief dies. There are, therefore, two concepts of **chief:** the man (women rarely, if ever, occupy these posts) and the office. Thus the expression "The king is dead, long live the king." With the New Guinean big man, there is no formal succession. Other big men will be recognized and eventually take the place of one who dies, but there is no rule stipulating that his eldest son or any son must succeed him. For chiefs, there *must* be a successor and there are rules of succession.

Political chiefdoms usually are accompanied by an economic exchange system known as redistribution in which goods and services flow from the population at large to the central authority represented by the chief. It then becomes the task of the chief to return the flow of goods in another form. The chapter on economics provides additional information about redistribution economies.

These political and economic principles are exemplified by the potlatch custom of the Kwakwaka'wakw and other indigenous groups who lived in chiefdom societies along the northwest coast of North America from the extreme northwest tip of California through the coasts of Oregon, Washington, British Columbia, and southern Alaska. Potlatch ceremonies observed major events such as births, deaths, marriages of important persons, and installment of a new chief. Families prepared for the event by collecting food and other valuables such as fish, berries, blankets, animal skins, carved boxes, and copper. At the potlatch, several ceremonies were held, dances were performed by their "owners," and speeches delivered. The new chief was watched very carefully. Members of the society noted the eloquence of his speech, the grace of his presence, and any mistakes he made, however egregious or trivial. Next came the distribution of gifts, and again the chief was observed. Was he generous with his gifts? Was the value of his gifts appropriate to the rank of the recipient or did he give valuable presents to individuals of relatively low rank? Did his wealth allow him to offer valuable objects?

The next phase of the potlatch was critical to the chief's validation of his position. Visitor after visitor would arise and give long speeches evaluating the worthiness of this successor to the chieftainship of his father. If his performance had so far met their expectations, if his gifts were appropriate, the guests' speeches praised him accordingly. They were less than adulatory if the chief had not performed to their expectations and they deemed the formal eligibility of the successor insufficient. He had to perform. If he did, then the guests' praise not only legitimized the new chief in his role, but also it ensured some measure of peace between villages. Thus, in addition to being a festive event, the potlatch determined the successor's legitimacy and served as a form of diplomacy between groups.[38]

Much has been made among anthropologists of rivalry potlatches in which competitive gifts were given by rival pretenders to the chieftainship. Philip Drucker argued that competitive potlatches were a product of sudden demographic changes among the indigenous groups on the northwest coast.[39] When smallpox and other diseases decimated hundreds, many potential successors to the chieftainship died, leading to situations in which several potential successors might be eligible for the chieftainship. Thus, competition in potlatch ceremonies became extreme with blankets or copper repaid with ever-larger piles and competitors who destroyed their own valuables to demonstrate their wealth. The events became so raucous that the Canadian government outlawed the displays in the early part of the twentieth century.[40] Prior to that time, it had been sufficient for a successor who was chosen beforehand to present appropriate gifts.[41]

Kin-Based Integrative Mechanisms: Conical Clans

With the centralization of society, kinship is most likely to continue playing a role, albeit a new one. Among Northwest Coast Indians, for example, the ranking model has every lineage ranked, one above the other, siblings ranked in order of birth, and even villages in a ranking scale. Drucker points out that the further north one goes, the more rigid the ranking scheme is. The most northerly of these coastal peoples trace their descent matrilineally; indeed, the Haida consist of four clans. Those further south tend to be patrilineal, and some show characteristics of an ambilineal descent group. It is still unclear, for example, whether the Kwakiutl *numaym* are patrilineal clans or ambilineal descent groups.

In the accompanying diagram (Figure 4), assuming patrilineal descent, the eldest male within a given lineage becomes the chief of his district , that is, Chief a in the area of Local Lineage A, which is the older intermediate lineage (Intermediate Lineage I) relative to the founding clan ancestor. Chief b is the oldest male in Local Lineage B, which, in turn, is the oldest intermediate lineage (again Intermediate Lineage I) relative to the founding clan ancestor. Chief c is the oldest male of local Lineage C descended from the second oldest intermediate lineage (Intermediate Lineage II) relative to the founding clan ancestor, and Chief d is the oldest male of Local Lineage D, descended from the second oldest intermediate Lineage (Intermediate Lineage II) relative to the founding clan ancestor.

Figure 4: Conical clan design of a chiefdom. Scheme is based on relative siblings age and patrilineal descent. Eldest sons appear to the left. Reprinted with permission of Kendall Hunt Publishing Company.

Nor does this end the process. Chief a, as head of Local Lineage A, also heads the district of Intermediate Lineage I while Chief c heads Local Lineage C in the district of Intermediate lineage II. Finally, the entire chiefdom is headed by the eldest male (Chief a) of the entire district governed by the descendants of the clan ancestor.

Integration through Marriage

Because chiefdoms cannot enforce their power by controlling resources or by having a monopoly on the use of force, they rely on integrative mechanisms that cut across kinship groups. As with tribal societies, marriage provides chiefdoms with a framework for encouraging social cohesion. However, since chiefdoms have more-elaborate status hierarchies than tribes, marriages tend to reinforce ranks.

A particular kind of marriage known as **matrilateral cross-cousin** demonstrates this effect and is illustrated by the diagram in Figure 4. The figure shows three **patrilineages** (family lineage groups based on descent from a common male ancestor) that are labeled A, B, and C. Consider the marriage between man B_2 and woman a_2. As you can see, they are linked by B_1 (ego's father) and his sister (a_2), who is married to A_1 and bears daughter a_2. If you look at other partners, you will notice that all of the women move to the right: a_2 and B_2's daughter, b_3, will marry C_3 and bear a daughter, c_4.

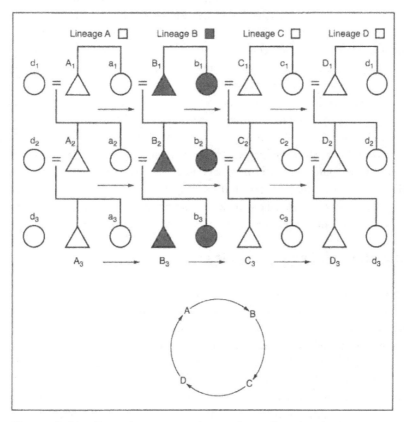

Figure 5: Matrilateral cross-cousin marriage. Reprinted with permission of Kendall Hunt Publishing Company.

Viewed from the top of a flow diagram, the three lineages marry in a circle and at least three lineages are needed for this arrangement to work. The Purum of India, for example, practiced matrilateral cross-cousin marriage among seven lineages. Notice that lineage B cannot return the gift of A's daughter with one of its own. If A_2 married b_2, he would be marrying his patrilateral cross-cousin who is linked to him through A_1, his sister a_1, and her daughter b_2. Therefore, b_2 must marry C_2 and lineage B can never repay lineage A for the loss of their daughters—trace their links to find out why. Since lineage B cannot meet the third of Mauss' obligations. B is a beggar relative to A. And lineage C is a beggar relative to lineage B. Paradoxically, lineage A (which gives its daughters to B) owes lineage C because it obtains its brides from lineage C. In this system, there appears to be an equality of inequality.

The patrilineal cross-cousin marriage system also operates in a complex society in highland Burma known as the Kachin. In that system, the wife-giving lineage is known as *mayu* and the wife-receiving lineage as *dama* to the lineage that gave it a wife. Thus, in addition to other mechanisms of dominance, higher-ranked lineages maintain their superiority by giving daughters to lower-ranked lineages and reinforce the relations between social classes through the *mayu-dama* relationship.[42]

The Kachin are not alone in using interclass marriage to reinforce dominance. The Natchez peoples, a matrilineal society of the Mississippi region of North America, were divided into four classes: Great Sun chiefs, noble lineages, honored lineages, and inferior "stinkards." Unlike the Kachin, however, their marriage system was a way to upward mobility. The child of a woman who married a man of lower status assumed his/her mother's status. Thus, if a Great Sun woman married a stinkard, the child would become a Great Sun. If a stinkard man were to marry a Great Sun woman, the child would become a stinkard. The same relationship obtained between women of noble lineage and honored lineage and men of lower status. Only two stinkard partners would maintain that stratum, which was continuously replenished with people in warfare.[43]

Other societies maintained status in different ways. Brother-sister marriages, for example, were common in the royal lineages of the Inca, the Ancient Egyptians, and the Hawaiians, which sought to keep their lineages "pure." Another, more-common type was **patrilateral parallel-cousin marriage** in which men married their fathers' brothers' daughters. This marriage system, which operated among many Middle Eastern nomadic societies, including the Rwala Bedouin chiefdoms, consolidated their herds, an important consideration for lineages wishing to maintain their wealth.[44]

Integration through Secret Societies

Poro and *sande* secret societies for men and women, respectively, are found in the Mande-speaking peoples of West Africa, particularly in Liberia, Sierra Leone, the Ivory Coast, and Guinea. The societies are illegal under Guinea's national laws. Elsewhere, they are legal and membership is universally mandatory under local laws. They function in both political and religious sectors of society. So how can such societies be secret if all men and women must join? According to Beryl Bellman, who is a member of a *poro* association, the standard among the Kpelle of Liberia is an *ability* to keep secrets. Members of the community are entrusted with the political and religious responsibilities associated with the society only after they learn to keep secrets.[45] There are two political structures in *poros* and *sandes*: the "secular" and the "sacred." The secular structure consists of the town chief, neighborhood and kin group headmen, and elders. The sacred structure (the *zo*) is composed of a hierarchy of "priests" of the *poro* and the *sande* in the neighborhood, and among the Kpelle the *poro* and *sande* *zo* take turns dealing with in-town fighting, rapes, homicides, incest, and land disputes. They, like leopard skin chiefs, play an important role in mediation. The *zo* of both the *poro* and *sande* are held in great respect and even feared. Some authors have suggested that sacred structure strengthens the secular political authority because chiefs and landowners occupy the most powerful positions in the *zo*.[46] Consequently, these chiefdoms seem to have developed formative elements of a stratified society and a state, as we see in the next section.

STRATIFIED SOCIETIES

Opposite from egalitarian societies in the spectrum of social classes is the stratified society, which is defined as one in which elites who are a numerical minority control the strategic resources that sustain life. Strategic resources include water for states that depend on irrigation agriculture, land in agricultural societies, and oil in industrial societies. Capital and products and resources used for further production are modes of production that rely on oil and other fossil fuels such as natural gas in industrial societies. (Current political movements call for the substitution of solar and wind power for fossil fuels.)

Operationally, **stratification** is, as the term implies, a social structure that involves two or more largely mutually exclusive populations. An extreme example is the caste system of traditional Indian society, which draws its legitimacy from Hinduism. In **caste systems**, membership is determined by birth and remains fixed for life, and social mobility—moving from one social class to another—is not an option. Nor can persons of different castes marry; that is, they are endogamous. Although efforts have been made to abolish castes since India achieved independence in 1947, they still predominate in rural areas.

India's caste system consists of four *varna*, pure castes, and one collectively known as *Dalit* and sometimes as *Harijan*—in English, "untouchables," reflecting the notion that for any *varna* caste member to touch or even see a *Dalit* pollutes them. The topmost *varna* caste is the *Brahmin* or priestly caste. It is composed of priests, governmental officials and bureaucrats at all levels, and other professionals. The next highest is the *Kshatriya*, the warrior caste, which includes soldiers and other military personnel and the police and their equivalents. Next are the *Vaishyas*, who are craftsmen and merchants, followed by the *Sudras* (pronounced "shudra"), who are peasants and menial workers. Metaphorically, they represent the parts of *Manu*, who is said to have given rise to the human race through dismemberment. The head corresponds to *Brahmin*, the arms to *Kshatriya*, the thighs to *Vaishya*, and the feet to the *Sudra*.

There are also a variety of subcastes in India. The most important are the hundreds, if not thousands, of occupational subcastes known as *jatis*. Wheelwrights, ironworkers, landed peasants, landless farmworkers, tailors of various types, and barbers all belong to different *jatis*. Like the broader castes, *jatis* are endogamous and one is born into them. They form the basis of the *jajmani* relationship, which involves the provider of a particular service, the *jajman*, and the recipient of the service, the *kamin*. Training is involved in these occupations but one cannot change vocations. Furthermore, the relationship between the *jajman* and the *kamin* is determined by previous generations. If I were to provide you, my *kamin,* with haircutting services, it would be because my father cut your father's hair. In other words, you would be stuck with me regardless of how poor a barber I might be. This system represents another example of an economy as an instituted process, an economy embedded in society.[47]

Similar restrictions apply to those excluded from the *varna* castes, the "untouchables" or *Dalit*. Under the worst restrictions, *Dalits* were thought to pollute other castes. If the shadow of a *Dalit* fell on a *Brahmin*, the *Brahmin* immediately went home to bathe. Thus, at various times and locations, the untouchables were also unseeable, able to come out only at night.[48] *Dalits* were born into jobs considered polluting to other castes, particularly work involving dead animals, such as butchering (Hinduism discourages consumption of meat so the clients were Muslims, Christians, and believers of other religions), skinning, tanning, and shoemaking with leather. Contact between an upper caste person and a person of any lower caste, even if "pure," was also considered polluting and was strictly forbidden.

The theological basis of caste relations is *karma*—the belief that one's caste in this life is the cumulative product of one's acts in past lives, which extends to all beings, from minerals to animals to gods. Therefore, though soul class mobility is nonexistent during a lifetime, it is possible between lifetimes. *Brahmins* justified their station by claiming that they must have done good in their past lives. However, there are indications that the untouchable *Dalits* and other lower castes are not convinced of their legitimation.[49]

Although India's system is the most extreme, it not the only caste system. In Japan, a caste known as *Burakumin* is similar in status to *Dalits*. Though they are no different in physical appearance from other Japanese people, the *Burakumin* people have been forced to live in ghettos for centuries. They descend from people who worked in the leather tanning industry, a low-status occupation, and still work in leather industries such as shoemaking. Marriage between *Burakumin* and other Japanese people is restricted, and their children are excluded from public schools.[50]

Some degree of social mobility characterizes all societies, but even so-called open-class societies are not as mobile as one might think. In the United States, for example, actual movement up the social latter is rare despite Horatio Alger and rags-to-riches myths. Stories of individuals "making it" through hard work ignore the majority of individuals whose hard work does not pay off or who actually experience downward mobility. Indeed, the Occupy Movement, which began in 2011, recognizes a dichotomy in American society of the 1 percent (millionaires and billionaires) versus the 99 percent (everyone else), and self-styled socialist Bernie Sanders made this the catch phrase of his campaign for the Democratic Party's presidential nomination. In India (a closed-class society), on the other hand, there are exceptions to the caste system. In Rajasthan, for example, those who own or control most of the land are not of the warrior caste as one might expect; they are of the lowest caste and their tenants and laborers are *Brahmins*.[51]

STATE LEVEL OF POLITICAL ORGANIZATION

The state is the most formal of the four levels of political organization under study here. In states, political power is centralized in a government that exercises a monopoly over the legitimate use of force.[52] It is important to understand that the exercise of force constitutes a last resort; one hallmark of a weak state is frequent use of physical force to maintain order. States develop in societies with large, often ethnically diverse populations—hundreds of thousands or more—and are characterized by complex economies that can be driven by command or by the market, social stratification, and an intensive agricultural or industrial base.

Several characteristics accompany a monopoly over use of legitimate force in a state. First, like tribes and chiefdoms, states occupy a more or less clearly defined territory or land defined by boundaries that separate it from other political entities that may or not be states (exceptions are associated with the Islamic State and are addressed later). Ancient Egypt was a state bounded on the west by desert and possibly forager or tribal nomadic peoples. Mesopotamia was a series of city-states competing for territory with other city-states.

Heads of state can be individuals designated as kings, emperors, or monarchs under other names or can be democratically elected, in fact or in name—military dictators, for example, are often called presidents. Usually, states establish some board or group of councilors (e.g., the cabinet in the United States and the politburo in the former Soviet Union.) Often, such councils are supplemented with one or two legislative assemblies. The Roman Empire had a senate (which originated as a body of councilors) and as many as four assemblies that combined patrician (elite) and plebian (general population) influences. Today, nearly all of the world's countries have some sort of an assembly, but many rubber-stamp the executive's decisions (or play an obstructionist role, as in the U.S. Congress during the Obama administration).

States also have an administrative bureaucracy that handles public functions provided for by executive orders and/or legislation. Formally, the administrative offices are typically arranged in a hierarchy and the top offices delegate specific functions to lower ones. Similar hierarchies are established for the personnel in a branch. In general, agricultural societies tend to rely on inter-personal relations in the administrative structure while industrial states rely on rational hierarchical structures.[53]

An additional state power is taxation—a system of redistribution in which all citizens are required to participate. This power is exercised in various ways. Examples include the *mitá* or labor tax of the Inca, the tributary systems of Mesopotamia, and monetary taxes familiar to us today and to numerous subjects throughout the history of the state. Control over others' resources is an influential mechanism undergirding the power of the state.

A less tangible but no less powerful characteristic of states is their **ideologies**, which are designed to reinforce the right of powerholders to rule. Ideologies can manifest in philosophical forms, such as the divine right of kings in pre-industrial Europe, karma and the caste system in India, consent of the governed in the United States, and the metaphorical family in Imperial China. More often, ideologies are less indirect and less perceptible as propaganda. We might watch the Super Bowl or follow the latest antics of the Kardashians, oblivious to the notion that both are diversions from the reality of power in this society. Young Americans, for example, may be drawn to military service to fight in Iraq by patriotic ideologies just as their parents or grandparents were drawn to service during the Vietnam War. In a multitude of ways across many cultures, Plato's parable of the shadows in the cave—that watchers misperceive shadows as reality—has served to reinforce political ideologies.

Finally, there is delegation of the state's coercive power. The state's need to use coercive power betrays an important weakness—subjects and citizens often refuse to recognize the powerholders' right to rule. Even when the legitimacy of power is not questioned, the use and/or threat of force serves to maintain the state, and that function is delegated to agencies such as the police to maintain internal order and to the military to defend the state against real and perceived enemies and, in many cases, to expand the state's territory. Current examples include a lack of accountability for the killing of black men and women by police officers; the killing of Michael Brown by Darren Wilson in Ferguson, Missouri, is a defining example.

State and Nation

Though **state** and **nation** are often used interchangeably, they are not the same thing. A state is a coercive political institution; a nation is an ethnic population. There currently are about 200 states in the world, and many of them did not exist before World War II. Meanwhile, there are around 5,000 nations identified by their language, territorial base, history, and political organization.[54] Few states are conterminous with a nation (a nation that wholly comprises the state). Even in Japan, where millions of the country's people are of a single ethnicity, there is a significant indigenous minority known as the Ainu who at one time were a distinct biological population as well as an ethnic group. Only recently has Japanese society opened its doors to immigrants, mostly from Korea and Taiwan. The vast majority of states in the world, including the United States, are multi-national.

Some ethnicities/nations have no state of their own. The Kurds, who reside in adjacent areas of Turkey, Syria, Iraq, and Iran, are one such nation. In the colonial era, the Mande-speaking peoples ranged across at least four West African countries, and borders between the countries were drawn without respect to the tribal identities of the people living there. Diasporas, the scattering of a people of one ethnicity across the globe, are another classic example. The diaspora of Ashkenazi and Sephardic Jews is well-known. Many others, such as the Chinese, have more recently been forced to flee their homelands. The current ongoing mass migration of Syrians induced by formation of the Islamic State and the war in Syria is but the most recent example.

Formation of States

How do states form? One precondition is the presence of a **stratified society** in which an elite minority controls life-sustaining strategic resources. Another is increased agricultural productivity that provides support for a larger population. Neither, however, is a sufficient cause for development of a state. A group of people who are dissatisfied with conditions in their home region has a motive to move elsewhere—unless there is nowhere else to go and they are circumscribed. **Circumscription** can arise when a region is hemmed in by a geographic feature such as mountain ranges or desert and when migrants would have to change their subsistence strategies, perhaps having to move from agriculture back to foraging, herding, or horticulture or to adapt to an urban industrialized environment. The Inca Empire did not colonize on a massive scale beyond northern Chile to the south or into the Amazon because indigenous people there could simply pick up and move elsewhere. Still, the majority of the Inca population did not have that option. Circumscription also results when a desirable adjacent region is taken by other states or chiefdoms.[55]

Who, then, were the original subjects of these states? One short answer is **peasants**, a term derived from the French *paysan*, which means "countryman." Peasantry entered the anthropological literature relatively late. In his 800-page tome *Anthropology* published in 1948, Alfred L. Kroeber defined peasantry in less than a sentence: "part societies with part cultures."[56] Robert Redfield defined peasantry as a "little tradition" set against a "great tradition" of national state society.[57] Louis Fallers argued in 1961 against calling African cultivators "peasants" because they had not lived in the context of a state-based civilization long enough.[58]

Thus, peasants had been defined in reference to some larger society, usually an empire, a state, or a civilization. In light of this, Wolf sought to place the definition of peasant on a structural footing.[59] Using a funding metaphor, he compared peasants with what he called "primitive cultivators." Both primitive cultivators and peasants have to provide for a "caloric fund" by growing food and, by extension, provide for clothing, shelter, and all other necessities of life. Second, both must provide for a "replacement fund"—not only reserving seeds for next year's crop but also repairing their houses, replacing broken pots, and rebuilding fences. And both primitive cultivators and peasants must provide a "ceremonial fund" for rites of passage and fiestas. They differ in that peasants live in states and primitive cultivators do not. The state exercises domain over peasants' resources, requiring peasants to provide a "fund of rent." That fund appears in many guises, including tribute in kind, monetary taxes, and forced labor to an empire or lord. In Wolf's conception, primitive cultivators are free of these obligations to the state.[60]

Subjects of states are not necessarily landed; there is a long history of landless populations. Slavery has long coexisted with the state, and forced labor without compensation goes back to chiefdoms such as Kwakwaka'wakw. Long before Portuguese, Spanish, and English seafarers began trading slaves from the west coast of Africa, Arab groups enslaved people from Africa and Europe.[61]

For peasants, **proletarianization**— loss of land—has been a continuous process. One example is landed gentry in eighteenth century England who found that sheepherding was more profitable than tribute from peasants and removed the peasants from the land.[62] A similar process occurred when Guatemala's liberal president privatized the land of Mayan peasants that, until 1877, had been held communally.[63]

Law and Order in States

At the level of the state, the law becomes an increasingly formal process. Procedures are more and more regularly defined, and categories of breaches in civil and criminal law emerge, together with remedies for those breaches. Early agricultural states formalized legal rules and punishments through codes, formal courts, police forces, and legal specialists such as lawyers and judges. Mediation could still be practiced, but it often was supplanted by adjudication in which a judge's decision was binding on all parties. Decisions could be appealed to a higher authority, but any final decision must be accepted by all concerned.

The first known system of codified law was enacted under the warrior king Hammurabi in Babylon (present day Iraq). This law was based on standardized procedures for dealing with civil and criminal offenses, and subsequent decisions were based on precedents (previous decisions). Crimes became offenses not only against other parties but also against the state. Other states developed similar codes of law, including China, Southeast Asia, and state-level Aztec and Inca societies. Two interpretations, which are not necessarily mutually exclusive, have arisen about the political function of codified systems of law. Fried (1978) argued, based on his analysis of the Hammurabi codes, that such laws reinforced a system of inequality by protecting the rights of an elite class and keeping peasants subordinates.[64] This is consistent with the theory of a stratified society as already defined. Another interpretation is that maintenance of social and political order is crucial for agricultural states since any disruption in the state would lead to neglect of agricultural production that would be deleterious to all members of the state regardless of their social status. Civil laws ensure, at least in theory, that all disputing parties receive a hearing—so long as high legal expenses and bureaucratic logjams do not cancel out the process. Criminal laws, again in theory, ensure the protection of all citizens from offenses ranging from theft to homicide.

Inevitably, laws fail to achieve their aims. The United States, for example, has one of the highest crime rates in the industrial world despite having an extensive criminal legal system. The number of homicides in New York City in 1990 exceeded the number of deaths from colon and breast cancer and all accidents combined.[65] Although the rate of violent crime in the United States declined during the mid-1990s, it occurred thanks more to the construction of more prisons per capita (in California) than of schools. Nationwide, there currently are more than one million prisoners in state and federal correctional institutions, one of the highest national rates in the industrial world.[66] Since the 1990s, little has changed in terms of imprisonment in the United States. Funds continue to go to prisons rather than schools, affecting the education of minority communities and expanding "slave labor" in prisons, according to Michelle Alexander who, in 2012, called the current system the school-to-prison pipeline.[67]

Warfare in States

Warfare occurs in all human societies but at no other level of political organization is it as widespread as in states. Indeed, warfare was integral to the formation of the agricultural state. As governing elites accumulated more resources, warfare became a major means of increasing their surpluses.[68] And as the wealth of states became a target of nomadic pastoralists, the primary motivation for warfare shifted from control of resources to control of neighboring populations.[69]

A further shift came with the advent of industrial society when industrial technologies driven by fossil fuels allowed states to invade distant countries. A primary motivation for these wars was to establish economic and political hegemony over foreign populations. World War I, World War II, and lesser wars of the past century have driven various countries to develop ever more sophisticated and deadly technologies, including wireless communication devices for remote warfare, tanks, stealth aircraft, nuclear weapons, and unmanned aircraft called drones, which have been used in conflicts in the Middle East and Afghanistan. Competition among nations has led to the emergence of the United States as the most militarily powerful nation in the world.

The expansion of warfare by societies organized as states has not come without cost. Every nation-state has involved civilians in its military adventures, and almost everyone has been involved in those wars in some way—if not as militarily, then as member of the civilian workforce in military industries. World War II created an unprecedented armament industry in the United States, Britain, Germany, and Japan, among others, and the aerospace industry underwent expansion in the so-called Cold War that followed. Today, one can scarcely overlook the role of the process of globalization to explain how the United States, for now an empire, has influenced the peoples of other countries in the world.

Stability and Duration of States

It should be noted that states have a clear tendency toward instability despite trappings designed to induce awe in the wider population. Few states have lasted a thousand years. The American state is more than 240 years old but increases in extreme wealth and poverty, escalating budget and trade deficits, a war initiated under false pretenses, escalating social problems, and a highly controversial presidential election suggest growing instability. Jared Diamond's book *Collapse* (2004) compared the decline and fall of Easter Island, Chaco Canyon, and the Maya with contemporary societies such as the United States, and he found that overtaxing the environment caused the collapse of those three societies.[70] Chalmers Johnson (2004) similarly argued that a state of perpetual war, loss of democratic institutions, systematic deception by the state, and financial overextension contributed to the decline of the Roman Empire and will likely contribute to the demise of the United States "with the speed of FedEx."[71]

Why states decline is not difficult to fathom. Extreme disparities in wealth, use of force to keep populations in line, the stripping of people's resources (such as the enclosures in England that removed peasants from their land), and the harshness of many laws all should create a general animosity toward the elite in a state.

Yet, until recently (following the election of Donald Trump), no one in the United States was taking to the streets calling for the president to resign or decrying the government as illegitimate. In something of a paradox, widespread animosity does not necessarily lead to dissolution of a state or to an overthrow of the elite. Thomas Frank addressed this issue in *What's the Matter with Kansas?* (2004). Despite the fact that jobs have been shipped abroad, that once-vibrant cities like Wichita are virtual ghost towns, and that both congress and the state legislature have voted against social programs time and again, Kansans continue to vote the Republicans whose policies are responsible for these conditions into office.

Nor is this confined to Kansas or the United States. That slaves tolerated slavery for hundreds of years (despite periodic revolts such as the one under Nat Turner in 1831), that workers tolerated extreme conditions in factories and mines long before unionization, that there was no peasant revolt strong enough to reverse the enclosures in England—all demand an explanation. Frank discusses reinforcing variables, such as propaganda by televangelists and Rush Limbaugh but offers little explanation beside them.[72] However, recent works have provided new explanations. Days before Donald Trump won the presidential election on November 8, 2016, sociologist Arlie Russell Hochschild released a book that partially explains how Trump appealed to the most marginalized populations of the United States, residents around Lake Charles in southwestern Louisiana. In the book, *Strangers in Their Own Land* (2016), Hochschild contends that the predominantly white residents there saw the federal government providing preferential treatment for blacks, women, and other marginalized populations under affirmative action programs while putting white working-class individuals further back in line for governmental assistance. The people Hochschild interviewed were fully aware that a corporate petroleum company had polluted Lake Charles and hired nonlocal technicians and Filipino workers to staff local positions, but they nonetheless expressed their intent to vote for a billionaire for president based on his promise to bring outsourced jobs back to "America" and to make the country "great again." Other books, including Thomas Frank's *Listen Liberal* (2016), Nancy Isenberg's *White Trash* (2016), and Matt Wray's *Not Quite White: White Trash and the Boundaries of Whiteness* (2006), address the decline of the United States' political power domestically and worldwide. These books all link Trump's successful election to marginalization of lower-class whites and raise questions about how dissatisfaction with the state finds expression in political processes.

Stratification and the State: Recent Developments

States elsewhere and the stratified societies that sustain them have undergone significant changes and, in some instances, dramatic transformations in recent years. Consider ISIS, formed in reaction to the ill-advised U.S. intervention in Iraq in 2003, which will be discussed in greater detail below. Other states have failed; Somalia has all but dissolved and is beset by piracy, Yemen is highly unstable due in part to the Saudi invasion, and Syria is being decimated by conflict between the Bashar Assad government and a variety of rebel groups from moderate reform movements to extremist jihadi groups, al-Nusra and ISIS. Despite Myanmar's (formerly Burma) partial transition from a militarized government to an elective one, the Muslim minority there, known as Rohingya, has been subjected to discrimination and many have been forced to flee to neighboring Bangladesh. Meanwhile, Bangladesh has been unable to enforce safety regulations to foreign investors as witnessed by the collapse of a clothing factory in 2013 that took the lives of more than 1,100 workers.

ISIS OR THE ISLAMIC STATE: A STATE IN FORMATION?

Around the beginning of 2014, a new state arguably began to form as the Islamic State of Iraq (ISI) metamorphosed into the Islamic State of Iraq and Syria (ISIS) and then to simply the Islamic State (IS) (In the following discussion, I use the terms ISIS and Islamic State interchangeably.). Though it may be controversial to claim that ISIS has achieved formal political organization as a state, many of the elements that characterize a state-level organization apply. ISIS has an armed force that has initially proven successful in one battle after another, resources and revenue (however ill-gotten its money and assets such as oil may be), an administrative structure, a body of law, and its own banking system and currency. Despite recent losses of territory, its operations have been extended well beyond the boundaries of Iraq and Syria, and territorial control is not the only measure of its influence. From this perspective, the Islamic State is of value for testing our definitions of a state and assessing the extent to which the characteristics of a state described here apply to this new political formation.

Though few people worldwide approve ISIS's activities or ideology, the damage the group has unleashed is not necessarily inconsistent with a new state in formation. Few, if any, states were conceived without violence in one form or another. The United States was formed by theft of land from indigenous people, a revolutionary war, and the kidnapping and sale of entire populations from the region we now know as West Africa into slavery. Most of the founders were slave owners and many, such as George Washington, obtained their wealth from speculating on stolen land. This history was replicated in Canada and Australia and, earlier, in the Near East and China. All states, at some point, have perpetrated what today are defined as crimes. We should think carefully when considering the Islamic State as an exception to the historical pattern.

The Islamic State, if it is indeed a state, came into being following the American invasion of Iraq. The process began with the Gulf War in 1991 in which Iraq invaded Kuwait and was expelled by an alliance led by the United States. Then, in March 2003, the George W. Bush administration chose to invade Iraq, deposing the regime of Saddam Hussein the following month and occupying the country; U.S. troops finally withdrew in 2011. Some consider the outcome of the decision to invade and occupy Iraq a worst-case blowback to a military action—the unintended negative consequence of waging war against a Third World country creating a Frankenstein's monster known as ISIS, the Islamic State, the Islamic Caliphate, and a host of other names.

ISIS is a theocracy organized as a self-styled caliphate that formally came into being on June 29, 2014, the first day of the holy month of Ramadan. Kidnapped journalists were beheaded, the so-called apostates were crucified, and the second city of Iraq, Mosul, fell to a rag-tag group of fighters numbering fewer than 1,500. The Caliphate of Ibrahim in the person of Abu Bakr al-Baghdadi came to be known around the world.[73]

What is the Islamic State? Loretta Napoleoni (2014) offers a concise definition differentiating it from other terrorist and Al Qaeda inspired movements:

> Where IS [the Islamic State] does outmatch past armed organizations is in military prowess, media manipulation, social programs, and, above all, nation building . . . These enhancements spring from the ability of the Islamic State to adapt to a fast-changing, post-Cold-War environment.[74]

In short, the Islamic State began not with advanced weaponry—it has no navy, no air force, no nuclear missiles—but with the latest communication technology along with the techniques of persuasion via the internet it attempts to create a nation-state based on the Salafist model of the four caliphs who succeeded the prophet Muhammad in the late seventh century, which is based on strict interpretation of the Qu'ran.[75]

So, is ISIS a state in formation?[76] First of all, as Abdel Bari Atwan and Malcolm Nance both point out, ISIS is well organized and staffed by numerous experienced military officials. Many, if not most, are former Iraqi Ba'athist administrators who were fired after Saddam Hussein was toppled in late April 2003.[77] Second, ISIS has established a banking system based in Mosul with its own currency of gold, silver, and copper coins. Third, it is well-financed; its assets range from oil to purloined currency, though it has been strapped for cash recently. Fourth, it has a long-term strategy of ethnic cleansing in the hope of creating a unitary population of Sunni believers steeped in the Salafist ideological tradition akin to the Saudis' Wahabi tradition. Fifth, it has a solid strategy for expanding its forces by recruiting foreign fighters from around the world and educating its young people in the ways of Salafist Islam. Based on those facts, I argue that the Islamic State is a state in formation.[78]

Citing the Montevideo Convention of Rights and Duties of States held in 1933, Atwan contends that there are two types of states: declaratory and constitutive. A declaratory entity has a clearly defined territory, a permanent population, and a government capable of controlling the population, its territory, and its resources, and it is recognized by other states. A constitutive state has the same attributes but is not necessarily recognized by other states. ISIS is more like a constitutive state since it is not recognized by any other states.[79] Napoleoni added the concept of a shell state, which she defined as an "armed organization [that] assembles the socio-economic infrastructure" such as taxation and employment services among others of a state "without the political one. i.e., no territory, no self-determination."[80]

Administrative Apparatus and Functions

The best way to understand ISIS as a formative state is to analyze its administrative apparatus and the functions of its subdivisions. As Atwan and Nance point out, ISIS is highly centralized with the caliph—Abu Bakr al-Baghdadi, also known as Ibrahim—as representative and, arguably, a descendant of the prophet Muhammad and so constitutes the ultimate authority of the state.[81] However, ISIS's organization is such that if he or any other authority is killed in war, other trained individuals can readily take his place. There are two deputies in each of two senior positions, and they make the final decisions concerning the affairs of ISIS. Reports of the killing of ISIS senior staff members have tended to overlook this arrangement.[82] Decisions are carried out by lower-level deputies in the administration who are allowed discretion in how those orders are implemented, allowing officials to use local knowledge to best execute the directives. These attributes—ready replacement of staff and local decision-making power—provide flexibility to the centralized administrative structure associated with ISIS.[83]

Baghdadi and his deputies rely on various councils and department committees that form their "cabinet." The top level of administration also has a powerful Shura (consultative) council that endorses the Sharia (religious legal) council's choice of caliph and then provides advice to him. The Shura council oversees the affairs of state, manages communication, and issues orders to the chain of command and ensures that they are implemented. The twelve-member Shura council is made up members selected by Baghdadi and is headed by one of the senior deputies.[84]

The Sharia council is charged with formulating regulations and administrative routines consistent with law as spelled out in the Qu'ran and with selecting the caliphs, who are endorsed by the Shura council. It also oversees all matters related to the administration as a whole and manages the judicial affairs of the body politic. Although the Western press has emphasized the more draconian penalties categorized as *hudd* such as amputations for theft and capital punishment by beheadings and crucifixion, ISIS's legal system also allows judges to impose less-severe *tazeer* punishments designed to publicly shame a miscreant with the aim of reform and rehabilitation. How frequently these two types of enforcement are used is a statistical question that would require a survey that simply cannot be conducted at this time.[85]

What is the relationship of the top administrators and their councils to the regional and local administrative bodies? The story begins with incorporation of those bodies into the state. When a city, town, or administrative unit is first occupied by ISIS forces, the first order of business in addition to maintaining the existing police force is to establish a Sharia police force that aims to work toward the "purity" of the Islamic State. Thus, women are enjoined to wear black robes and to veil and men are likewise ordered to wear modest clothing. The "moral police" are dispatched to ensure acceptable behavior and dress, and both the regular and the moral police (the *hisbah*) are outfitted with black uniforms bearing a white Islamic State insignia.[86]

Several councils handle the main issues of Islamic State polity and society. The innumerable challenges to the Islamic State's authority are dealt with by the security and intelligence council. Its functions include growing networks throughout the Islamic State and beyond, maintaining border controls, imposing punishments on dissidents, and eliminating borders set by treaties such as the Sykes-Picot agreement of 1916. The military council is charged with defending ISIS's existing borders, expanding into new areas, and incorporating foreign fighters into the ranks.[87] It is also charged with ethnic cleansing of non-Sunni Muslims, Yazidis, Jews, and Christians to ensure a single ethnic group to facilitate effective control even though the Qu'ran explicitly accommodates all "people of the book," which includes all Christians, Jews, and Muslims.[88] Writes Napoleoni:

> In particular, cleansing its territory of Shia from its territory offers many advantages for nation-building, gaining support of local Sunni populations, producing a more homogeneous population with fewer opportunities for sectarianism, and freeing up resources to offer fighters the spoils of war.[89]

Coordinating with the military council is the Islamic State Institution for Public Information, which is the main source of ISIS information, covering everything from current events to announcements of ISIS polities. Detractors have dubbed it the ministry of propaganda. The public information institute conducts outreach via the media and internet to contact potential recruits from abroad as foreign fighters and women as wives of fighters.

ISIS also has an economic council that oversees the wealth it has obtained by taking over oil fields in the region, assimilating local governments and nongovernment banks in regions it has overrun, demanding ransom for captured foreign supporters from allies such as Saudi Arabia (its formal connection has been questioned), and collecting Islamic taxes: *jieya* from non-Muslim residents and *zakat*, taxes that are part of obligatory alms provided for in the Qu'ran, from Muslims who can afford it. The economic council's accounting system consists of an annual budget and monthly reports. Analysts concur that, in Atwan's words, "this level of bureaucratic process and accountability is indicative of a large, well-organized, state-like entity."[90]

Finally, to sustain ISIS, the Education Council oversees the provision of education and the curriculum, which promote strict Salafist interpretation of the Qu'ran. Several topics are banned from the curriculum, including the evolutionary model of biology and philosophy. The curriculum includes training in warfare for boys at sixteen years of age and training in domestic skills for girls.[91]

The final significant institution under ISIS, the Islamic Service Council, oversees public services such as maintenance of infrastructures—roads, bridges, electricity lines. In towns and cities under its control, the council operates a rationing system for consumer goods and discourages traders from selling to people who do not carry the card with the group's logo on it. Napoleoni argues that filling potholes, restoring electricity and phone lines, and providing other public services are important components in securing the loyalty of residents of territories overrun by ISIS.

Decline or a Change in Strategy?

Over the past two years, there has been a massive emigration of Syrians and Iraqis out of the region. Why is this occurring? Is the Islamic State in a period of decline or is it adapting its guerilla strategy and tactics. During this period, ISIS lost territory in Iraq and Syria. The city of Sinjar, Syria, fell to the Kurdish Peshmerga army in late 2015, followed by the fall of Tikrit, Anbar, and Fallujah to the Iraqi army early in 2016. The battle for Mosul in Iraq started October 17, 2016, and ISIS has been pursuing a scorched-earth defense, including using residents as human shields. As this chapter was being written, ISIS had been ejected from East Mosul but only after massive property destruction and massacres of its residents by ISIS. Reports from Syria noted that the de facto capital of ISIS, Raqqa in Syria has been subjected to attacks; one of ISIS's supply routes passed through Sinjar. In addition, Aleppo in Syria was destroyed as ISIS competed with other rebel groups and with the Syrian army under Bashar Assad. Aleppo was eventually reclaimed by the Syrian government, but tens of thousands of the city's residents were killed or displaced.

Despite recent setbacks, ISIS has so far retained significant territories in Syria and Iraq and gained control of areas in northern Libya (which it later lost), the Sinai region in Egypt, Afghanistan, Chechnya, Indonesia, and the Philippines. It has established alliances with Boko Haram in West Africa and with other groups in Gaza, Lebanon, and Algeria, and ISIS units have been identified in places as far away as Brazil and Norway. ISIS attacks have occurred in France—twice in Paris and once in Nice—and in Brussels, Belgium, and future attacks against the United Kingdom, Germany, and Italy have been threatened. ISIS also claimed responsibility for attacks in the United States on a nightclub in Orlando, Florida, a staff party in San Bernardino, California, on students and staff at Ohio State University, and threatened to attack the Macy's Thanksgiving parade, leading to exceptionally tight security there. What ISIS lacks in territory, it makes up for with alliances and operations abroad.

Atwan has noted that ISIS strategists took these potential defeats into account long before they occurred. The military council has generally avoided defending sites ISIS could not hold and concentrated on theatres they could win or defend. These incidents and countless others appear to be part of the so-called Snake in the Rocks strategy cited by Napoleoni, which is similar to the strategy used by China's Mao Zedong, who concentrated his Communist forces in the countryside rather than in cities. Ho Chi Minh used a similar strategy in the Vietnam War against France and the United States.

A cardinal rule of the guerrilla strategy, painfully established by drawn-out conflicts in China, Vietnam, and Cuba, is that one must elicit the support of the people. In this regard, ISIS's imposition of the Salafist/Wahabi model of Islam is proving problematic. Cockburn provides a laundry list of constraints associated with strict Salafist Islam, including prohibitions against wearing jeans and makeup, smoking cigarettes or hubble-bubbles (hookahs), and keeping stores open during times of prayer. Women are required to wear the abaya (black robe) and veil and are not permitted to gather in public places, including stores. Men must wear beards, and barbers who agree to shave their beards off are punished. The punishments for violating these rules are whipping, amputation of limbs, and beheading.[92]

Life under ISIS

A cardinal rule of the guerrilla strategy, painfully established by drawn-out conflicts in China, Vietnam, and Cuba, is that one must elicit the support of the people. In this regard, ISIS's imposition of the Salafist/Wahabi model of Islam is proving problematic. Cockburn provides a laundry list of constraints associated with strict Salafist Islam, including prohibitions against wearing jeans and makeup, smoking cigarettes or hubble-bubbles (hookahs), and keeping stores open during times of prayer. Women are required to wear the abaya (black robe) and veil and are not permitted, unless accompanied by a man, to gather in public places, including stores. Men must wear beards, and barbers who agree to shave their beards off are punished. The punishments for violating these rules are whipping, amputation of limbs, and beheading.[93]

Recent accounts on the retaking of Mosul, first in the eastern district and (as of this writing), parts of the western district, report both on the fleeing of hundreds of residents from the city and the discovery of mass graves in and around Mosul. Two recent case studies are provided here.

According to Patrick Cockburn, author of *Chaos and Caliphate*, Hamza is a 33-year-old man from Fallujah, Iraq, who joined ISIS fighters when they took over the city. He was initially attracted to ISIS because of his religious beliefs. Two months before he was interviewed by Cockburn, however, he defected because he was repulsed by initiation rites in which ISIS fighters killed prisoners, some of whom were people he knew, and the raping of Yazidi women who were forced into sex slavery as what ISIS called "pagans." When he balked at executing a Sunni prisoner who had worked with the Shia Iraqi government (also called "pagans"), he was not punished; instead, he was also offered sexual services by a Yazidi woman who, as a pagan, was a suitable target for ISIS fighters. The rapes and executions finally compelled him to leave, and after five days (with help from reliable friends), he arrived safely to his destination outside ISIS-controlled territory. Hamza recalled that "At the beginning, I thought they were fighting for Allah, but later I discovered they were far from the principles of Islam…The justice they were calling for when they first arrived in Fallujah turned out to be only words."[94]

New literature has also surfaced that contradicts in part the claims by Napoleoni and Atwan about life in the ISIS-controlled areas of Iraq and Raqqa. The *Raqqa Diaries*, authored by "Samer" and edited by the BBC's Mike Thomson, shows how daily life is closely monitored in a running diary. Samer himself was sentenced to forty lashes for speaking out against the beheadings, his father was killed in an airstrike of a house next door, and his mother, wounded in the same air raid, was hospitalized. He notes the spiraling high costs of food, the restrictions on purchasing a television set, lest the viewer sees what is going on in the West, and the frequent executions for minor offenses. He reports the stoning to death of a woman. Even the length of a man's pants is monitored. In the end, Samer escaped to northern Syria and contacted the BBC to provide his account.[95]

Recent Updates

As of late March 2017, the Iraqi invasion of Mosul has resulted in its control of the eastern district and an attack on western parts of the city. Mass graves have been discovered in and near Mosul, and there is a massive emigration of its residents. Indeed, this emigration of Syrians and Iraqis that has occupied the headlines for the past year is in part the product of the ISIS conflict. Raqqa is under siege and has been bombed for several months, according to recent reports, but remains under ISIS control. In the meantime, In addition to battles in Syria and Iraq, in which ISIS has lost substantial ground—Fallujah, Anbar province, Tikrit—ISIS has resorted to terror attacks, not only in Paris, Nice, Brussels, Orlando, and San Bernardino, but also in other parts of the globe, from Brazil and Norway to Chechnya in Russia, Mindanao in the Philippines, and even in China. In the past two days of this writing, ISIS attacks have elicited Afghanistan's request for U.S. military intervention against not only the Taliban but also the Islamic State. Finally, a stolen minivan driven by Khalid Masood ran over a group of pedestrians in front of the British Parliament on March 22, 2017, the day this text was edited. The ISIS press agency Aamaq claimed the Islamic State's responsibility for the attack on March 23; its claim is yet to be verified.

Based on all of this evidence, it is reasonable to conclude that ISIS is well-organized and has at least some of the attributes of a state. Though there have been setbacks, some quite extensive, the organization has extended its operations and alliances in territories well outside Syria and Iraq. However, it is also evident that the attempt to impose strict Islamic order is alienating many people despite various incentives for loyalty in ISIS-captured territory. The desire to impose a strict Wahabi-Salafist model of Islam on the populations it conquers could thwart its efforts as those societies are not accustomed to living according to such rules.

CONCLUSION

Citing both state and stateless societies, this chapter has examined levels of socio-cultural integration, types of social class (from none to stratified), and mechanisms of social control exercised in various forms of political organization from foragers to large, fully developed states. The chapter offers explanations for these patterns, and additional theories are provided by the works in the bibliography. Still, there are many more questions than answers. Why does socio-economic inequality arise in the first place? How do states reinforce (or generate) inequality? Societies that have not developed a state have lasted far longer—about 100,000 to 150,000 years longer—than societies that became states. Will states persist despite the demonstrable disadvantages they present for the majority of their citizens?

A Chinese curse wishes that you may "live in interesting times."
These are interesting times indeed.

DISCUSSION QUESTIONS

1. In large communities, it can be difficult for people to feel a sense of connection or loyalty to people outside their immediate families. Choose one of the social-integration techniques used in tribes and chiefdoms and explain why it can successfully encourage solidarity between people. Can you identify similar systems for encouraging social integration in your own community?
2. Although state societies are efficient in organizing people and resources, they also are associated with many disadvantages, such as extreme disparities in wealth, use of force to keep people in line, and harsh laws. Given these difficulties, why do you think the state has survived? Do you think human populations can develop alternative political organizations in the future?
3. McDowell presents detailed information about the organization of the Islamic State. Does the Islamic State meet the seven criteria for a state-level society? Why is it important to understand whether ISIS is or is not likely to become a state?

GLOSSARY

Affinal: family relationships created through marriage.

Age grades: groups of men who are close to one another in age and share similar duties or responsibilities.

Age sets: named categories to which men of a certain age are assigned at birth.

Band: the smallest unit of political organization, consisting of only a few families and no formal leadership positions.

Big man: a form of temporary or situational leadership; influence results from acquiring followers.

Bilateral cross-cousin marriage: a man marries a woman who is *both* his mother's brother's daughter and his father's sister's daughter.

Bilateral descent: kinship (family) systems that recognize both the mother's and the father's "sides" of the family.

Caste system: the division of society into hierarchical levels; one's position is determined by birth and remains fixed for life.

Chiefdom: large political units in which the chief, who usually is determined by heredity, holds a formal position of power.

Circumscription: the enclosure of an area by a geographic feature such as mountain ranges or desert or by the boundaries of a state.

Codified law: formal legal systems in which damages, crimes, remedies, and punishments are specified.

Egalitarian: societies in which there is no great difference in status or power between individuals and there are as many valued status positions in the societies as there are persons able to fill them.

Feuds: disputes of long duration characterized by a state of recurring hostilities between families, lineages, or other kin groups.

Ideologies: ideas designed to reinforce the right of powerholders to rule.

Legitimacy: the perception that an individual has a valid right to leadership.

Lineage: individuals who can trace or demonstrate their descent through a line of males or females back to a founding ancestor.

Matrilateral cross-cousin marriage: a man marries a woman who is his mother's brother's daughter.

Matrilineal: kinship (family) systems that recognize only relatives through a line of female ancestors.

Nation: an ethnic population.

Negative reinforcements: punishments for noncompliance through fines, imprisonment, and death sentences.

Oaths: the practice of calling on a deity to bear witness to the truth of what one says.

Ordeal: a test used to determine guilt or innocence by submitting the accused to dangerous, painful, or risky tests believed to be controlled by supernatural forces.

Patrilineal: kinship (family) systems that recognize only relatives through a line of male ancestors.

Peasants: residents of a state who earn a living through farming.

Poro and sande: secret societies for men and women, respectively, found in the Mande-speaking peoples of West Africa, particularly in Liberia, Sierra Leone, the Ivory Coast, and Guinea.

Positive reinforcements: rewards for compliance; examples include medals, financial incentives, and other forms of public recognition.

Proletarianization: a process through which farmers are removed from the land and forced to take wage labor employment.

Raids: short-term uses of physical force organized and planned to achieve a limited objective.

Ranked: societies in which there are substantial differences in the wealth and social status of individuals; there are a limited number of positions of power or status, and only a few can occupy them.

Restricted exchange: a marriage system in which only two extended families can engage in this exchange.

Reverse dominance: societies in which people reject attempts by any individual to exercise power.

Segmentary lineage: a hierarchy of lineages that contains both close and relatively distant family members.

Social classes: the division of society into groups based on wealth and status.

Sodality: a system used to encourage solidarity or feelings of connectedness between people who are not related by family ties.

State: the most complex form of political organization characterized by a central government that has a monopoly over legitimate uses of physical force, a sizeable bureaucracy, a system of formal laws, and a standing military force.

Stratified: societies in which there are large differences in the wealth, status, and power of individuals based on unequal access to resources and positions of power.

Sumptuary rules: norms that permit persons of higher rank to enjoy greater social status by wearing distinctive clothing, jewelry, and/or decorations denied those of lower rank.

Tribe: political units organized around family ties that have fluid or shifting systems of temporary leadership.

Unilineal descent: kinship (family) systems that recognize only one sex-based "side" of the family.

ABOUT THE AUTHOR

Paul McDowell (Ph.D. University of British Columbia, 1974) examined the transition of the civil-religious hierarchy in a factory and peasant community in Guatemala to a secular town government and church organization called Accion Catolica. He is the author of *Cultural Anthropology: A Concise Introduction* and *Cultures Around the World: An Ethnographic Reader*; he has also read several papers on the political globalization of Guatemala.

BIBLIOGRAPHY

Alexander, Michelle. *The New Jim Crow: Mass Incarceration in the Age of Color Blindness*. New York: The New Press, 2010.

Atwan, Abdel Bari. *Islamic State: The Digital Caliphate*. London: Saqi Books, 2015.

Befu, Harumi. *Japan: An Anthropological Introduction*. San Francisco: Chandler, 1971.

Bellman, Beryl. *The Language of Secrecy: Symbols and Metaphors in Poro Ritual*. New Brunswick, NJ: Rutgers University Press, 1984.

Bledsoe, Caroline H. *Women and Marriage in Kpelle Society*. Stanford, CA: Stanford University Press, 1980.

Boehm, Christopher. *Hierarchy in the Forest: The Evolution of Egalitarian Behavior*. Cambridge, MA: Harvard University Press, 1999.

Bohannan, Paul. *Justice and Judgment among the Tiv*. Prospect Heights, IL: Waveland Press, 1989.

Butterfield, Fox. 1996. "Study Finds Disparity of Justice for Blacks." *New York Times*, February 13: 8A.

Carneiro, Robert. "On the Relationship between Size of Population and Complexity of Social Organization." *Southwest Journal of Anthropology* 23 (1967): 234–243.

————. "A Theory of the Origin of the State." *Science* 169 no. 3947 (1970):733–738.

————. "Chiefdom: Precursor to the State." In *The Transition to Statehood in the New World,* edited by Grant Jones and Grant, and Robert Kautz, 37–75. New York: Cambridge University Press, 1981.

Chagnon, Napoleon. *Yanomamo.* New York: Holt, Rinehart and Winston, 1997.

Childe, V. Gordon. "The Urban Revolution." *Town Planning Review* 21 (1950):3–17.

Clay, J.W. "What's a Nation?" In *Talking about People,* edited by William Haviland and R.J. Gordon. Mountain View, CA: Mayfield, 1996.

Cockburn, Patrick. *The Age of Jihad.* London: Verso, 2016.

————. *Chaos and Caliphate: Jihadis and the West in the Struggle for the Middle East.* New York: OR Books, 2016.

Diamond, Jared. *Collapse: How Societies Choose to Fail or Succeed.* New York: Viking, 2004.

Drucker, Philip. *Indians of the Northwest Coast.* New York: Natural History Press, 1955.

Ember, Melvin, and Carol Ember. *Cultural Anthropology.* Upper Saddle River, NJ: Prentice-Hall, 2002.

Evans-Pritchard, Edward E. *The Nuer.* Oxford, UK: Oxford University Press, 1940.

————. *Witchcraft, Oracles and Magic among the Azande.* Oxford: Oxford University Press, 1976.

Fallers, Louis. "Are African Cultivators to Be Called Peasants?" *Current Anthropology* 2 no. 2 (1961): 108–110.

Fox, Robin. *Kinship and Marriage.* Harmondsworth, UK: Penguin, 1967.

Frank, Thomas. *What's the Matter with Kansas? How Conservatives Won the Heart of America.* New York: Metropolitan Books, 2004.

————. *Listen Liberal: Or, Whatever Happened To the Party of the People?* New York: Metropolitan Books, 2016.

Fried, Morton. *The Evolution of Political Society: An Essay in Political Anthropology.* New York: McGraw-Hill, 1967.

————. "The State, the Chicken, and the Egg or What Came First?" In *Origins of the State,* edited by Ronald Cohen and Elman Service. Philadelphia: Institute for the Study of Human Issues, 1978.

Good, Kenneth. *Into The Heart: One Man's Pursuit of Love and Knowledge among the Yanomami.* Upper Saddle River, NJ: Prentice-Hall, 1997.

Harris, Marvin. *Cows, Pigs, Wars, and Witches.* New York: Vintage, 1974.

Harris, Marvin, and Orna Johnson. *Cultural Anthropology.* Boston: Allyn and Bacon, 2003.

Hart, C.W.M, Arnold R. Pilling, and Jane Goodale. *The Tiwi of North Australia.* New York: Holt, Rinehart and Winston, 1988.

Haviland, William. *Cultural Anthropology: The Human Challenge.* Belmont, CA: Wadsworth, 2005.

Heider, Karl. *The Dugum Dani: A Papuan Culture in the Highlands of West New Guinea.* Chicago: Aldine, 1970.

Hochschild, Arlie Russell. *Strangers in Their Own Land: Anger and Mourning of Our Political Divide.* New York: New Press, 2016.

Hoebel, E. Adamson. *The Law of Primitive Man.* New York: Atheneum, 1968 [1954].

Isenberg, Nancy. *White Trash: The 400 Year Untold History of Class in America.* New York: Viking, 2016.

Johnson, Chalmers. *The Sorrows of Empire: Militarism, Secrecy, and the End of the Republic.* New York: Metropolitan Books, 2004.

Khare, Ravindra. *The Untouchable as Himself: Identity and Pragmatism among the Lucknow Chamars.* New York: Cambridge University Press, 1984.

Koch, Klaus-Friedrich, Soraya Altorki, Andrew Arno and Letitia Hickson. "Ritual Reconciliation and the Obviation of Grievances: A Comparative Study in the Ethnography of Law." *Ethnology* 16 (1977): 269–284.

Kroeber, Alfred L. *Anthropology.* New York: Harcourt, Brace, and World, 1948.

Lancaster, William. *The Rwala Bedouin Today.* Prospect Heights, IL: Waveland Press, 1997.

Lee, Richard. *The Dobe Jul'hoansi.* New York: Thomson, 2003.

Little, Kenneth. "The Political Function of the Poro, Part 1." *Africa* 35 (1965): 349–365.

Long, Bruce. "Reincarnation." *Encyclopedia of Religion,* Vol. 12, 265–269. New York: Macmillan, 1987.

Maloney, William. "Dharma." *Encyclopedia of Religion,* Vol. 4, 239–332. New York: Macmillan, 1987.

————. "Karma." *Encyclopedia of Religion,* Vol. 8, 261–266. New York: Macmillan, 1987.

Martin, M. Kay, and Barbara Voorhies. *Female of the Species*. New York: Columbia University Press, 1975.

Mauss, Marcel. *The Gift: The Form and Reason for Exchange in Archaic Societies*. London: Routledge, 2001 [1925].

McCants, William. *The Isis Apocalypse: The History, Strategy, and Doomsday Vision of the Islamic State*. New York: St. Martins, 2015.

McDowell, Paul V. "Political and Religious Change in a Guatemalan Factory Community." Ph.D. Diss., University of British Columbia, 1974.

———. "The Decline of the Civil-Religious Hierarchy: The Case of Cantel." *NorthSouth: Canadian Journal of Latin American Studies* 35 no. 10 (1980): 17–35.

Meggitt, Mervyn. *Blood is their Argument: Warfare among the Mae-Enga*. Palo Alto, CA: Mayfield, 1977.

Murphy, Robert F, and Leonard Kasdan. "The Structure of Parallel Cousin Marriage." *American Anthropologist* 61 no. 1 (1959.):17–29.

Nader, Laura. *Harmony Ideology: Justice and Control in a Zapotec Mountain Village*. Stanford: Stanford University Press, 1991.

Nance, Malcolm. *Defeating ISIS: Who They Are, What They Want, What They Believe*. New York: Skyhorse Press, 2016.

Napoleoni, Loretta. *The Islamic Phoenix: The Islamic State and the Redrawing of the Middle East*. New York: Seven Stories Press, 2014.

Oliver, Douglas. *A Solomon Island Society: Kinship and Leadership among the Siuai of Bougainville*. Cambridge, MA: Harvard University Press, 1955.

Otterbein, Keith. "The Anthropology of War." In *Handbook of Social and Cultural Anthropology*, edited by John Huntington. Chicago: Rand McNally, 1974.

———. *The Evolution of War: A Cross-cultural Study*. New Haven, CT: Human Relation Area Files, 1989.

Perelman, Michael. *The Invention of Capitalism: Classical Political Economy and the Secret History of Primitive Accumulation*. Durham, NC: Duke University Press, 2000.

Polanyi, Karl. *The Great Transformation*. New York: Beacon Press, 1944.

Redfield, Robert. *The Little Community and Peasant Society and Culture*. Chicago: University of Chicago Press, 1989.

Roberts, Sam. "Fighting the Tide of Bloodshed on Streets Resembling a War Zone." *New York Times*, November 15, 1993: B12.

Sahlins, Marshall. "The Segmentary Lineage: An Organization of Predatory Expansion." *American Anthropologist* 63 (1961):322–343.

Sangree, Walter. "The Bantu Tiriki of Western Kenya." In *Peoples of Africa,* edited by James Gibbs. New York: Holt, Rinehart and Winston, 1965.

Scupin, Raymond. *Cultural Anthropology: A Global Perspective*. Upper Saddle River, NJ: Pearson, 2012.

Service, Elman. *Primitive Social Organization: An Evolutionary Perspective*. New York: Random House, 1962.

———. *Origins of the State and Civilization: The Process of Cultural Evolution*. New York: W.W. Norton, 1975.

———. *Profiles of Ethnology*. New York: Harper Collins, 1978.

Stavrianos, Leften S. *Global Rift*. New York: Quill, 1974.

Steward, Julian. *The Theory of Culture Change: The Methodology of Multilinear Evolution*. Urbana: University of Illinois Press, 1955.

Strathern, Andrew, and Pamela J. Stewart. *Collaborations and Conflict: A Leader through Time*. Belmont, CA: Wadsworth, 1999.

Thomas, Elizabeth Marshall. *The Harmless People*. New York: Knopf, 1959.

Turnbull, Colin. 1963. *The Forest People: A Study of the Pygmies of the Congo*. New York: Simon and Schuster.

———. "The Mbuti Pygmies in the Congo." In *Peoples of Africa*, edited by James Gibbs, 279–318. New York: Holt, Rinehart and Winston, 1965.

———. *The Mbuti Pygmies: Change and Adaptation*. New York: Holt, Rinehart and Winston, 1983.

Weber, Max. *The Theory of Social and Economic Organization*. New York: Free Press, 1997 [1947].

White, Douglas. "Rethinking Polygyny, Co-wives, Codes, and Cultural Systems." *Current Anthropology* 29 no. 4 (1988): 529–533.

Wray, Matt. *Not Quite White: White Trash and the Boundaries of Whiteness.* Durham, NC: Duke University Press, 2006.

Wolf, Eric R. "Closed Corporate Communities in Mesoamerica and Central Java." *Southwestern Journal of Anthropology* 13 no. 1 (1957):1–18.

———. *Peasants.* Englewood Cliffs, NJ: Prentice-Hall, 1966.

NOTES

Portions of this chapter were first published in *Cultural Anthropology: A Concise Introduction* by Paul McDowell and are reproduced here with permission of Kendall Hunt Publishing company.

1. Morton Fried, *The Evolution of Political Society: An Essay in Political Anthropology* (New York: McGraw-Hill, 1967).

2. E. Adamson Hoebel, *The Law of Primitive Man* (New York: Atheneum, 1968 [1954]). For a critique of Hoebel see John Steckley, *White Lies about the Inuit* (Toronto: University of Toronto Press, 2007).

3. Elman Service, *Origins of the State and Civilization: The Process of Cultural Evolution* (New York: W.W. Norton, 1975).

4. Christopher Boehm. *Hierarchy in the Forest: The Evolution of Egalitarian Behavior.* Cambridge, MA: Harvard University Press, 1999.

5. Richard Lee, *The Dobe Ju/'hoansi* (New York: Thomson, 2003).

6. Julian Steward, *The Theory of Culture Change: The Methodology of Multilinear Evolution* (Urbana: University of Illinois Press, 1955), 54.

7. Elman Service, *Origins of the State and Civilization.*

8. Morton Fried, *The Evolution of Political Society.*

9. Richard Lee, *The Dobe Ju/'hoansi*, 109–111.

10. Julian Steward, *The Theory of Culture Change.*

11. Elman Service, *Primitive Social Organization: An Evolutionary Perspective* (New York: Random House, 1962).

12. M. Kay Martin and Barbara Voorhies, *Female of the Species* (New York: Columbia University Press, 1975).

13. E. Adamson Hoebel, *The Law of Primitive Man*, 168.

14. See Colin Turnbull, *The Forest People: A Study of the Pygmies of the Congo* (New York: Simon and Schuster, 1963) and Colin Turnbull, *The Mbuti Pygmies: Change and Adaptation* (New York: Holt, Rinehart and Winston, 1983).

15. C.W. Merton Hart, Arnold R. Pilling, and Jane Goodale. *The Tiwi of North Australia* (New York: Holt, Rinehart and Winston, 1988).

16. Richard Lee, *The Dobe Ju/'hoansi*, 112–118.

17. Napoleon Chagnon, *Yanomamo* (New York: Holt, Rinehart and Winston, 1997), 133–137.

18. Marcel Mauss, *The Gift: The Form and Reason for Exchange in Archaic Societies* (London: Routledge, 2001 [1925]).

19. Douglas Oliver, *A Solomon Island Society: Kinship and Leadership among the Siuai of Bougainville* (Cambridge, MA: Harvard University Press, 1955). For an account of Ongka, the big man in a Kawelka village, see Andrew Strathern and Pamela J. Stewart, *Collaborations and Conflict: A Leader through Time* (Belmont, CA: Wadsworth, 1999).

20. Walter Sangree, "The Bantu Tiriki of Western Kenya," in *Peoples of Africa*, James Gibbs, ed. (New York: Holt, Rinehart and Winston, 1965), 71. The reader will notice the discrepancies between Sangree's description of age grades and sets—15 year for each, totaling a cycle of 105 years—and his chart from which the one shown here is extrapolated to 1994. First, the age grade "small boys," is 10 years, not 15. Second, the age grade "ritual elders" is 20 years, not 15. Why this discrepancy exists, Sangree does not answer. This discrepancy demonstrates the questions raised when ideal types do not match all the ethnographic information. For example, if the Jiminigayi ranged 15 years in 1939, why did they suddenly expand to a range of 20 years in 1954? By the same token, why did the Sawe age set cover 10 years in 1939 and expand to 15 years in 1954? It is discrepancies such as this that raise questions and drive further research

21. Mervyn Meggitt, *Blood Is Their Argument: Warfare among the Mae-Enga* (Palo Alto, CA: Mayfield, 1977) 202–224.

22. Marcel Mauss, *The Gift.*

23. Ibid.

24. Ibid.

25. Claude Levi-Strauss' concept is further described in Robin Fox, *Kinship and Marriage* (Harmondsworth, UK: Penguin, 1967), 182–187.

26. Evans-Pritchard, Edward E. *The Nuer.* Oxford, UK: Oxford University Press, 1940.

27. Paul Bohannan, *Justice and Judgment among the Tiv.* Prospect Heights, IL: Waveland Press, 1989. And Murphy, Robert F, and Leonard Kasdan. "The Structure of Parallel Cousin Marriage." *American Anthropologist* 61 no. 1 (1959.):17–29.

28. Marshall Sahlins, "The Segmentary Lineage: An Organization of Predatory Expansion." *American Anthropologist* 63 (1961):322–343.

29. Ibid.

30. E.E. Evans-Pritchard, *Witchcraft, Oracles, and Magic among the Azande* (Oxford: Oxford University Press,1976).

31. Klaus-Friedrich Koch et al., "Ritual Reconciliation and the Obviation of Grievances: A Comparative Study in the Ethnography of Law." *Ethnology* 16 (1977):269–270.

32. E.E. Evans-Pritchard, *The Nuer* (Oxford, UK: Oxford University Press, 1940), 291.

33. Laura Nader, *Harmony Ideology: Justice and Control in a Zapotec Mountain Village.* (Stanford: Stanford University Press, 1991).

34. Marvin Harris, *Cows, Pigs, Wars, and Witches.* New York: Vintage, 1974. Good, Kenneth. *Into The Heart: One Man's Pursuit of Love and Knowledge among the Yanomami.* Upper Saddle River, NJ: Prentice-Hall, 1997.

35. Napoleon Chagnon, *Yanomamo*, 91–97.

36. Douglas White, "Rethinking Polygyny, Co-wives, Codes, and Cultural Systems," *Current Anthropology* 29 no. 4 (1988): 529–533.

37. Karl Heider, *The Dugum Dani: A Papuan Culture in the Highlands of West New Guinea* (Chicago: Aldine, 1970).

38. Philip Drucker, *Indians of the Northwest Coast* (New York: Natural History Press, 1955).

39. Ibid.

40. For more information about the reasons for the potlatch ban, see Douglas Cole and Ira Chaiken, *An Iron Hand upon the People: The Law against the Potlatch on the Northwest Coast* (Seattle: University of Washington Press, 1990). The website of the U'Mista Cultural Society in Alert Bay, British Columbia, Canada offers more information about potlatch traditions and the impact of the ban: www.umista.ca.

41. Philip Drucker, *Indians of the Northwest Coast.*

42. Edmund Leach, cited in Robin Fox, *Kinship and Marriage*, 215–216.

43. Raymond Scupin, *Cultural Anthropology: A Global Perspective* (Upper Saddle River, NJ: Pearson, 2012).

44. The information comes from William Lancaster, *The Rwala Bedouin Today* (Prospect Heights, IL: Waveland Press, 1997) and Elman Service, *Profiles of Ethnology* (New York: Harper Collins, 1978).

45. Beryl Bellman, *The Language of Secrecy: Symbols and Metaphors in Poro Ritual* (New Brunswick, NJ: Rutgers University Press, 1984).

46. Kenneth Little, "The Political Function of the Poro, Part 1." *Africa* 35 (1965):349–365. See also Caroline Bledsoe, *Women and Marriage in Kpelle Society* (Stanford: Stanford University Press, 1980).

47. Karl Polanyi, *The Great Transformation* (New York: Beacon Press, 1944).

48. Bruce Long, "Reincarnation," *Encyclopedia of Religion* (New York: Macmillan, 1987) and William Maloney, "Dharma," *Encyclopedia of Religion*, Vol. 4 (New York: Macmillan, 1987).

49. Ravindra Khare, *The Untouchable as Himself: Identity and Pragmatism among the Lucknow Chamars* (New York: Cambridge University Press, 1984).

50. Harumi Befu, *Japan: An Anthropological Introduction* (San Francisco: Chandler, 1971).

51. William Haviland, *Cultural Anthropology: The Human Challenge.*

52. Morton Fried, *The Evolution of Political Society: An Essay in Political Anthropology* (New York: McGraw-Hill, 1967) and Max Weber, *The Theory of Social and Economic Organization* (New York: Free Press, 1997 [1947]).

53. For instance, Max Weber, *The Theory of Social and Economic Organization.*

54. J.W. Clay, "What's a Nation?" in *Talking about People*, William Haviland and R.J. Gordon, eds. (Mountain View, CA: Mayfield), 1996.

55. Robert Carneiro, "A Theory of the Origin of the State." *Science* 169 no. 3947 (1970): 733–738 and Robert Carneiro, "Chiefdom: Precursor to the State," in *The Transition to Statehood in the New World*, Grant Jones and Robert Kautz, eds. 37–75. New York: Cambridge University Press.

56. Alfred L. Kroeber, *Anthropology* (New York: Harcourt, Brace, and World, 1948), 284.

57. Robert Redfield, *The Little Community and Peasant Society and Culture* (Chicago: University of Chicago Press, 1989).

58. Louis Fallers, "Are African Cultivators to Be Called Peasants?" *Current Anthropology* 2 no. 2 (1961): 108–110.

59. Eric Wolf, *Peasants.* Englewood Cliffs, NJ: Prentice-Hall, 1966.

60. Ibid.

61. Leften S. Stavrianos, *Global Rift* (New York: Quill, 1974).

62. Michael Perelman, *The Invention of Capitalism: Classical Political Economy and the Secret History of Primitive Accumulation* (Durham, NC: Duke University Press, 2000), 38–59.

63. For more information about land privatization, see Paul V. McDowell, "Political and Religious Change in a Guatemalan Factory Community." Ph.D. Diss., University of British Columbia, 1974 and Paul V. McDowell, "The Decline of the Civil-Religious Hierarchy: The Case of Cantel." *NorthSouth: Canadian Journal of Latin American Studies* 35 no. 10 (1980):17–35.

64. Morton Fried "The State, the Chicken, and the Egg or What Came First?" In *Origins of the State*, edited by Ronald Cohen and Elman Service. Philadelphia: Institute for the Study of Human Issues, 1978.

65. Sam Roberts, "Fighting the Tide of Bloodshed on Streets Resembling a War Zone." *New York Times*, November 15, 1993: B12.

66. Fox Butterfield, "Study Finds Disparity of Justice for Blacks." *New York Times*, Feb. 13, 1996 8A.

67. Michelle Alexander, *The New Jim Crow: Mass Incarceration in the Age of Color Blindness*. New York: The New Press, 2010.

68. V. Gordon Childe, "The Urban Revolution." *Town Planning Review* 21 (1950): 3–17.

69. Keith Otterbein "The Anthropology of War," in *Handbook of Social and Cultural Anthropology*, John Huntington, ed. (Chicago: Rand McNally, 1974) and *The Evolution of War: A Cross-cultural Study* (New Haven, CT: Human Relation Area Files, 1989).

70. Jared Diamond, *Collapse: How Societies Choose to Fail or Succeed* (New York: Viking, 2004).

71. Chalmers Johnson, *The Sorrows of Empires: Militarism, Secrecy, and the End of the Republic* (New York: Metropolitan Books, 2005), 285.

72. Thomas Frank, *What's the Matter with Kansas? How Conservatives Won the Heart of America* (New York: Metropolitan Books, 2004).

73. See, for instance, an end-times interpretation of ISIS by William McCants, *The ISIS Apocalypse: The History, Strategy, and Doomsday Vision of the Islamic State* (New York: St. Martins, 2015); a backgrounder on the crises by Patrick Cockburn, *Jihadis and the West in the Struggle for the Middle East* (New York: OR Books, 2016); an update by Patrick Cockburn that details ISIS's role in the crisis, *Age of Jihad: The Islamic State and the Great War for the Middle East* (London: Verso, 2016); and a comprehensive text on ISIS by Malcolm Nance, *Defeating Isis: Who They Are, How They Fight, What They Believe* (New York: Skyhorse Press, 2016).

74. Loretta Napoleoni, *The Islamic Phoenix: The Islamic State and the Redrawing of the Middle East*. (New York: Seven Stories Press, 2014), 3.

75. Ibid.

76. For this initial analysis, the ethnographic present is the time period from July 2014 to February 2015.

77. Malcolm Nance, *Defeating Isis: Who They Are, How They Fight, What They Believe* (New York: Skyhorse Press, 2016). Abdel Bari Atwan, *Islamic State: The Digital Caliphate* (London: Saqi Books, 2015), 132–136 and Malcolm Nance, *Defeating ISIS: Who They Are, How They Fight, What They Believe* (New York: Skyhorse Press, 2016), 28.

78. The information comes from Abdel Bari Atwan, *Islamic State: The Digital Caliphate* (London: Saqi Books, 2015), 132–136 and Malcolm Nance, *Defeating ISIS: Who They Are, How They Fight, What They Believe* (New York: Skyhorse Press, 2016), 28.

79. Abdel Bari Atwan, *Islamic State*, 3–4.

80. Loretta Napoleoni, *The Islamic Phoenix*, 124.

81. Malcolm Nance, *Defeating Isis: Who They Are, How They Fight, What They Believe* (New York: Skyhorse Press, 2016).

82. Abdel Bari Atwan, *Islamic State*, 131–137; Nance, *Defeating Isis,* 50–67.

83. Ibid., 132.

84. Ibid., 132.

85. Ibid., 134.

86. Ibid., 133.

87. Ibid., 134–135

88. Ibid., and Patrick Cockburn, *Chaos and Caliphate: Jihadis and the West in the Struggle for the Middle East.*

89. Loretta Napoleoni, *The Islamic Phoenix*, 96.

90. Abdel Bari Atwan, *Islamic State*, 135.

91. Ibid.

92. Patrick Cockburn, *Chaos and Caliphate*, 397.

93. Ibid.

94. Ibid., 382–386.

95. Samer, *The Raqqa Diaries* (London: Interlink Publishing Group, 2017).

FAMILY AND MARRIAGE

Mary Kay Gilliland, Central Arizona College
maryk.gilliland@centralaz.edu

LEARNING OBJECTIVES

- Describe the variety of human families cross-culturally with examples.

- Discuss variation in parental rights and responsibilities.

- Distinguish between matrilineal, patrilineal, and bilateral kinship systems.

- Identify the differences between kinship establish by blood and kinship established by marriage.

- Evaluate the differences between dowry and bridewealth as well as between different types of post-marital residence.

- Recognize patterns of family and marriage and explain why these patterns represent rational decisions within the cultural contexts.

Family and marriage may at first seem to be familiar topics. Families exist in all societies and they are part of what makes us human. However, societies around the world demonstrate tremendous variation in cultural understandings of family and marriage. Ideas about how people are related to each other, what kind of marriage would be ideal, when people should have children, who should care for children, and many other family related matters differ cross-culturally. While the function of families is to fulfill basic human needs such as providing for children, defining parental roles, regulating sexuality, and passing property and knowledge between generations, there are many variations or patterns of family life that can meet these needs. This chapter introduces some of the more common patterns of family life found around the world. It is important to remember that within any cultural framework variation does occur. Some variations on the standard pattern fall within what would be culturally considered the "range of acceptable alternatives." Other family forms are not entirely accepted, but would still be recognized by most members of the community as reasonable.

RIGHTS, RESPONSIBILITIES, STATUSES, AND ROLES IN FAMILIES

Some of the earliest research in cultural anthropology explored differences in ideas about family. Lewis Henry Morgan, a lawyer who also conducted early anthropological studies of Native American cultures, documented the words used to describe family members in the Iroquois language.[1] In the book *Systems of Consanguinity and Affinity of the Human Family* (1871), he explained that words used to describe family members, such as "mother" or "cousin," were important because they indicated the rights and responsibilities associated with particular family members both within households and the larger community. This can be seen in the labels we have for family members—titles like father or aunt—that describe how a person fits into a family as well as the obligations he or she has to others.

The concepts of status and role are useful for thinking about the behaviors that are expected of individuals who occupy various positions in the family. The terms were first used by anthropologist Ralph Linton and they have since been widely incorporated into social science terminology.[2] For anthropologists, a **status** is any culturally-designated position a person occupies in a particular setting. Within the setting of a family, many statuses can exist such as "father," "mother," "maternal grandparent," and "younger brother." Of course, cultures may define the statuses involved in a family differently. **Role** is the set of behaviors expected of an individual who occupies a particular status. A person who has the status of "mother," for instance, would generally have the role of caring for her children.

Roles, like statuses, are cultural ideals or expectations and there will be variation in how individuals meet these expectations. Statuses and roles also change within cultures over time. In the not-so-distant past in the United States, the roles associated with the status of "mother" in a typical Euro-American middle-income family included caring for children and keeping a house; they probably did not include working for wages outside the home. It was rare for fathers to engage in regular, day-to-day housekeeping or childcare roles, though they sometimes "helped out," to use the jargon of the time. Today, it is much more common for a father to be an equal partner in caring for children or a house or to sometimes take a primary role in child and house care as a "stay at home father" or as a "single father." The concepts of status and role help us think about cultural ideals and what the majority within a cultural group tends to do. They also help us describe and document culture change. With respect to family and marriage, these concepts help us compare family systems across cultures.

KINSHIP AND DESCENT

Kinship is the word used to describe culturally recognized ties between members of a family. Kinship includes the terms, or social statuses, used to define family members and the roles or expected behaviors associated with these statuses. Kinship encompasses relationships formed through blood connections (consanguineal), such as those created between parents and children, as well as relationships created through marriage ties (affinal), such as in-laws (see Figure 1). Kinship can also include "chosen kin," who have no formal blood or marriage ties, but consider themselves to be family. Adoptive parents, for instance, are culturally recognized as parents to the children they raise even though they are not related by blood.

Figure 1: These young Maasai women from Western Tanzania are affinal kin, who share responsibilities for childcare. Maasai men often have multiple wives who share domestic responsibilities. Photo used with permission of Laura Tubelle de González.

While there is quite a bit of variation in families cross-culturally, it is also true that many families can be categorized into broad types based on what anthropologists call a kinship system. The **kinship system** refers to the pattern of culturally recognized relationships between family members. Some cultures create kinship through only a single parental line or "side" of the family. For instance, families in many parts of the world are defined by **patrilineal descent**: the paternal line of the family, or fathers and their children. In other societies, **matrilineal descent** defines membership in the kinship group through the maternal line of relationships between mothers and their children. Both kinds of kinship are considered **unilineal** because they involve descent through only one line or side of the family. It is important to keep in mind that systems of descent define culturally recognized "kin," but these rules do not restrict relationships or emotional bonds between people. Mothers in patrilineal societies have close and loving relationships with their children even though they are not members of the same patrilineage.[3] In the United States, for instance, last names traditionally follow a pattern of patrilineal descent: children receive last names from their fathers. This does not mean that the bonds between mothers and children are reduced. **Bilateral descent** is another way of creating kinship. Bilateral descent means that families are defined by descent from both the father and the mother's sides of the family. In bilateral descent, which is common in the United States, children recognize both their mother's and father's family members as relatives.

As we will see below, the **descent groups** that are created by these kinship systems provide members with a sense of identity and social support. Kinship groups may also control economic resources and dictate decisions about where people can live, who they can marry, and what happens to their property after death. Anthropologists use **kinship diagrams** to help visualize descent groups and kinship. Figure 2 is a simple example of a kinship diagram. This diagram has been designed to help you see the difference between the kinship groups created by a bilateral descent system and a unilineal system.

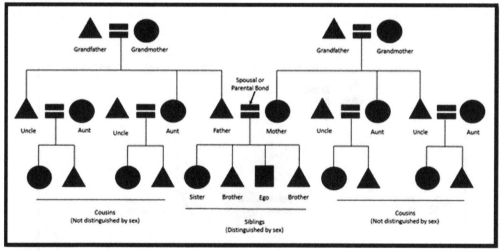

Figure 2: This kinship chart illustrates bilateral descent.

Kinship diagrams use a specific person, who by convention is called Ego, as a starting point. The people shown on the chart are Ego's relatives. In Figure 2, Ego is in the middle of the bottom row. Most kinship diagrams use a triangle to represent males and a circle to represent females. Conventionally, an "equals sign" placed between two individuals indicates a marriage. A single line, or a hyphen, can be used to indicate a recognized union without marriage such as a couple living together or engaged and living together, sometimes with children.

Children are linked to their parents by a vertical line that extends down from the equals sign. A sibling group is represented by a horizontal line that encompasses the group. Usually children are represented from left to right—oldest to youngest. Other conventions for these charts include darkening the symbol or drawing a diagonal line through the symbol to indicate that a person is deceased. A diagonal line may be drawn through the equals sign if a marriage has ended.

Figure 2 shows a diagram of three generations of a typical **bilateral** (two sides) kinship group, focused on parents and children, with aunts, uncles, cousins, grandparents and grandchildren. Note that everyone in the diagram is related to everyone else in the diagram, even though they may not interact on a regular basis. The group could potentially be very large, and everyone related through blood, marriage, or adoption is included.

The next two kinship diagram show how the descent group changes in unilineal kinship systems like a patrilineal system (father's line) or a matrilineal system (mother's line). The roles of the family members in relationship to one another are also likely to be different because descent is based on **lineage**: descent from a common ancestor. In a patrilineal system, children are always members of their father's lineage group (Figure 3). In a matrilineal system, children are always members of their mother's lineage group (Figure 4). In both cases, individuals remain a part of their birth lineage throughout their lives, even after marriage. Typically, people must marry someone outside their own lineage. In figures 3 and 4, the shaded symbols represent people who are in the same lineage. The unshaded symbols represent people who have married into the lineage.

In general, **bilateral** kinship is more focused on individuals rather than a single lineage of ancestors as seen in **unlineal** descent. Each person in a bilateral system has a slightly different group of relatives. For example, my brother's relatives through marriage (his in-laws) are included in his kinship group, but are not included in mine. His wife's siblings and children are also included in his group, but not in mine. If we were in a patrilineal or matrilineal system, my brother and I would largely share the same group of relatives.

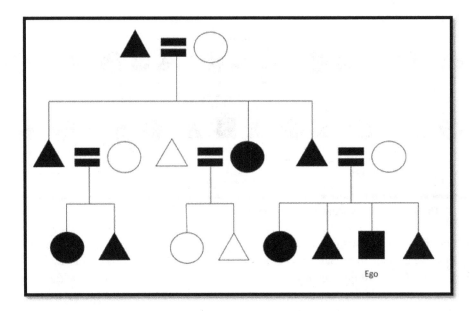

Figure 3: This kinship chart shows a patrilineal household with Ego in father's lineage.

Matrilineages and patrilineages are not just mirror images of each other. They create groups that behave somewhat differently. Contrary to some popular ideas, matrilineages are not **matriarchal**. The terms "matriarchy" and "patriarchy" refer to the power structure in a society. In a patriarchal society, men have more authority and the ability to make more decisions than do women. A father may have the right to make certain decisions for his wife or wives, and for his children, or any other dependents. In matrilineal societies, men usually still have greater power, but women may be subject more to the power of their brothers or uncles (relatives through their mother's side of the family) rather than their fathers.

Among the matrilineal Hopi, for example, a mothers' brother is more likely to be a figure of authority than a father. The mother's brothers have important roles in the lives of their sisters' children. These roles include ceremonial obligations and the responsibility to teach the skills that are associated with men and men's activities. Men are the keepers of important ritual knowledge so while women are respected, men are still likely to hold more authority.

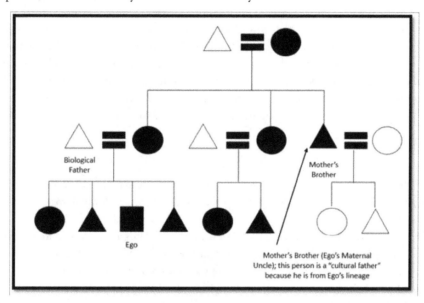

Figure 4: This kinship chart shows a matrilineal household with Ego in mother's lineage.

The Nayar of southern India offer an interesting example of gender roles in a matrilineal society. In the seventeenth and eighteenth centuries, men and women did not live together after marriage because the husbands, who were not part of the matrilineage, were not considered relatives. Women lived for their entire lives in extended family homes with their mothers and siblings. The male siblings in the household had the social role of father and were important father figures in the lives of their sisters' children. The biological fathers of the children had only a limited role in their lives. Instead, these men were busy raising their own sisters' children. Despite the matrilineal focus of the household, Nayar communities were not matriarchies. The position of power in the household was held by an elder male, often the oldest male sibling.

The consequences of this kind of system are intriguing. Men did not have strong ties to their biological offspring. Marriages were fluid and men and women could have more than one spouse, but the children always remained with their mothers.[4] Cross-culturally it does seem to be the case that in matrilineal societies women tend to have more freedom to make decisions about sex and marriage. Children are members of their mother's kinship group, whether the mother is married or not, so there is often less concern about the social legitimacy of children or fatherhood.

Some anthropologists have suggested that marriages are less stable in matrilineal societies than in patrilineal ones, but this varies as well. Among the matrilineal Iroquois, for example, women owned the longhouses. Men moved into their wives' family houses at marriage. If a woman wanted to divorce her husband, she could simply put his belongings outside. In that society, however, men and women also spent significant time apart. Men were hunters and warriors, often away from the home. Women were the farmers and tended to the home. This, as much as matrilineality, could have contributed to less formality or disapproval of divorce. There was no concern about the division of property. The longhouse belonged to the mother's family, and children belonged to their mother's clan. Men would always have a home with their sisters and mother, in their own matrilineal longhouse.[5]

Kinship charts can be useful when doing field research and particularly helpful when documenting changes in families over time. In my own field research, it was easy to document changes that occurred in a relatively short time, likely linked to urbanization, such as changes in family size, in prevalence of divorce, and in increased numbers of unmarried adults. These patterns had emerged in the surveys and interviews I conducted, but they jumped off the pages when I reviewed the kinship charts. Creating kinship charts was a very helpful technique in my field research. I also used them as small gifts for the people who helped with my research and they were very much appreciated.

KINSHIP TERMS

Another way to compare ideas about family across cultures is to categorize them based on **kinship terminology**: the terms used in a language to describe relatives. George Murdock was one of the first anthropologists to undertake this kind of comparison and he suggested that the kinship systems of the world could be placed in six categories based on the kinds of words a society used to describe relatives.[6] In some kinship systems, brothers, sisters, and all first cousins call each other brother and sister. In such a system, not only one's biological father, but all one's father's brothers would be called "father," and all of one's mother's sisters, along with one's biological mother, would be called "mother." Murdock and subsequent anthropologists refer to this as the Hawaiian system because it was found historically in Hawaii. In Hawaiian kinship terminology there are a smaller number of kinship terms and they tend to reflect generation and gender while merging nuclear families into a larger grouping. In other words, you, your brothers and sisters, and cousins would all be called "child" by your parents and your aunts and uncles.

Other systems are more complicated with different terms for father's elder brother, younger brother, grandparents on either side and so on. Each pattern was named for a cultural group in which this pattern was found. The system that most Americans follow is referred to as the Eskimo system, a name that comes from the old way of referring to the Inuit, an indigenous people of the Arctic (Figure 1). Placing cultures into categories based on kinship terminology is no longer a primary focus of anthropological studies of kinship. Differences in kinship terminology do provide insight into differences in the way people think about families and the roles people play within them.

Sometimes the differences in categorizing relatives and in terminology reflect patrilineal and matrilineal systems of descent. For example, in a patrilineal system, your father's brothers are members of your lineage or clan; your mother's brothers do not belong to the same lineage or clan and may or may not be counted as relatives. If they are counted, they likely are called something different from what you would call your father's brother. Similar differences would be present in a matrilineal society.

An Example from Croatia

In many U.S. families, any brother of your mother or father is called "uncle." In other kinship systems, however, some uncles and aunts count as members of the family and others do not. In Croatia, which was historically a patrilineal society, all uncles are recognized by their nephews and nieces regardless of whether they are brothers of the mother or the father. But, the uncle is called by a specific name that depends on which side of the family he is on; different roles are associated with different types of uncles.

A child born into a traditional Croatian family will call his aunts and uncles *stric* and *strina* if they are his father's brothers and their wives. He will call his mother's brothers and their wives *ujak* and *ujna*. The words *tetka* or *tetak* can be used to refer to anyone who is a sister of either of his parents or a husband of any of his parents' sisters. The third category, *tetka* or *tetak*, has no reference to "side" of the family; all are either *tetka* or *tetak*.

These terms are not simply words. They reflect ideas about belonging and include expectations of behavior. Because of the patrilineage, individuals are more likely to live with their father's extended family and more likely to inherit from their father's family, but mothers and children are very close. Fathers are perceived as authority figures and are owed deference and respect. A father's brother is also an authority figure. Mothers, however, are supposed to be nurturing and a mother's brother is regarded as having a mother-like role. This is someone who spoils his sister's children in ways he may not spoil his own. A young person may turn to a maternal uncle, or mother's brother in a difficult situation and expects that a maternal uncle will help him and maintain confidentiality. These concepts are so much a part of the culture that one may refer to a more distant relative or an adult friend as a "mother's brother" if that person plays this kind of nurturing role in one's life. These terms harken back to an earlier agricultural society in which a typical family, household, and economic unit was a joint patrilineal and extended family. Children saw their maternal uncles less frequently, usually only on special occasions. Because brothers are also supposed to be very fond of sisters and protective of them, those additional associations are attached to the roles of maternal uncles. Both father's sisters and mother's sisters move to their own husbands' houses at marriage and are seen even less often. This probably reflects the more generic, blended term for aunts and uncles in both these categories.[7]

Similar differences are found in Croatian names for other relatives. Side of the family is important, at least for close relatives. Married couples have different names for in-laws if the in-law is a husband's parent or a wife's parent. Becoming the mother of a married son is higher in social status than becoming the mother of a married daughter. A man's mother gains authority over a new daughter-in-law, who usually leaves her own family to live with her husband's family and work side by side with her mother-in-law in a house.

An Example from China

In traditional Chinese society, families distinguished terminologically between mother's side and father's side with different names for grandparents as well as aunts, uncles, and in-laws. Siblings used terms that distinguished between siblings by gender, as we do in English with "brother" and "sister," but also had terms to distinguish between older and younger siblings. Intriguingly, however, the Chinese word for "he/she/it" is a single term, *ta* with no reference to gender or age. The traditional Chinese family was an extended patrilineal family, with women moving into the husband's family household. In most regions, typically brothers stayed together in adulthood. Children grew up knowing their fathers' families, but not their mothers' families. Some Chinese families still live this way, but urbanization and changes in housing and economic livelihood have made large extended families increasingly less practical.

A Navajo Example

In Navajo (or *Diné*) society, children are "born for" their father's families but "born to" their mother's families, the clan to which they belong primarily. The term **clan** refers to a group of people who have a general notion of common descent that is not attached to a specific ancestor. Some clans trace their common ancestry to a common mythological ancestor. Because clan membership is so important to identity and to social expectations in Navajo culture, when people meet they exchange clan information first to find out how they stand in relationship to each other. People are expected to marry outside the clans of their mothers or fathers. Individuals have responsibilities to both sides of the family, but especially to the matrilineal clan. Clans are so large that people may not know every individual member, and may not even live in the same vicinity as all clan members, but rights and obligations to any clan members remain strong in people's thinking and in practical behavior. I recently had the experience at the community college where I work in Central Arizona of hearing a young Navajo woman introduce herself in a public setting. She began her address in Navajo, and then translated. Her introduction included reference to her clan memberships, and she concluded by saying that these clan ties are part of what makes her a Navajo woman.

An Example from the United States

In many cases, cultures assign "ownership" of a child, or responsibilities for that child anyway, to some person or group other than the mother. In the United States, if one were to question people about who is in their families, they would probably start by naming both their parents, though increasingly single parent families are the norm. Typically, however, children consider themselves equally related to a mother and a father even if one or both are absent from their life. This makes sense because most American families organize themselves according to the principles of bilateral descent, as discussed above, and do not show a preference for one side of their family or the other. So, on further inquiry, we might discover that there are siblings (distinguished with different words by gender, but not birth order), and grandparents on either side of the family who count as family or extended family. Aunts, uncles, and cousins, along with in-laws, round out the typical list of U.S. family members. It is not uncommon for individuals to know more about one side of the family than the other, but given the nature of bilateral descent the idea that people on each side of the family are equally "related" is generally accepted. The notion of bilateral descent is built into legal understandings of family rights and responsibilities in the United States. In a divorce in most states, for example, parents are likely to share time somewhat equally with a minor child and to have joint decision-making and financial responsibility for that child's needs as part of a parental agreement, unless one parent is unable or unwilling to participate as an equal.

MARRIAGE AND FAMILY

In a basic biological sense, women give birth and the minimal family unit in most, though not all societies, is mother and child. Cultures elaborate that basic relationship and build on it to create units that are culturally considered central to social life. Families grow through the birth or adoption of children and through new adult relationships often recognized as marriage. In our own society, it is only culturally acceptable to be married to one spouse at a time though we may practice what is sometimes called **serial monogamy**, or marriage to a succession of spouses one after the other. This is reinforced by religious systems, and more importantly in U.S. society, by law. Plural marriages are not allowed; they are illegal although they do exist because they are encouraged under some religions or ideologies. In the United States, couples are legally allowed to divorce and remarry, but not all religions cultural groups support this practice.

When anthropologists talk of family structures, we distinguish among several standard family types any of which can be the typical or preferred family unit in a culture. First is the **nuclear family**: parents who are in a culturally-recognized relationship, such as marriage, along with their minor or dependent children. This family type is also known as a conjugal family. A non-conjugal nuclear family might be a single parent with dependent children, because of the death of one spouse or divorce or because a marriage never occurred. Next is the **extended family**: a family of at least three-generations sharing a household. A **stem family** is a version of an extended family that includes an older couple and one of their adult children with a spouse (or spouses) and children. In situations where one child in a family is designated to inherit, it is more likely that only the inheriting child will remain with the parents when he or she becomes an adult and marries. While this is often an oldest male, it is sometimes a different child. In Burma or Myanmar for example, the youngest daughter was considered the ideal caretaker of elderly parents, and was generally designated to inherit.[8] The other children will "marry out" or find other means to support themselves.

A **joint family** is a very large extended family that includes multiple generations. Adult children of one gender, often the males, remain in the household with their spouses and children and they have collective rights to family property. Unmarried adult children of both genders may also remain in the family group. For example, a household could include a set of grandparents, all of their adult sons with their wives and children, and unmarried adult daughters. A joint family in rare cases could have dozens of people, such as the traditional *zadruga* of Croatia, discussed in greater detail below.

Polygamous families are based on plural marriages in which there are multiple wives or, in rarer cases, multiple husbands. These families may live in nuclear or extended family households and they may or may not be close to each other spatially (see discussion of households below). The terms step family or blended family are used to describe families that develop when adults who have been widowed or divorced marry again and bring children from previous partnerships together. These families are common in many countries with high divorce rates. A wonderful fictional example was *The Brady Bunch* of 1970s television.

Who Can You Marry?

Cultural expectations define appropriate potential marriage partners. Cultural rules emphasizing the need to marry within a cultural group are known as **endogamy**. People are sometimes expected to marry within religious communities, to marry someone who is ethnically or racially similar or who comes from a similar economic or educational background. These are endogamous marriages: marriages within a group. Cultural expectations for marriage outside a particular group are called **exogamy**. Many cultures require that individuals marry only outside their own kinship groups, for instance. In the United States laws prevent marriage between close relatives such as first cousins. There was a time in the not so distant past, however, when it was culturally preferred for Europeans, and Euro-Americans to marry first cousins. Royalty and aristocrats were known to betroth their children to relatives, often cousins. Charles Darwin, who was British, married his first cousin Emma. This was often done to keep property and wealth in the family.

In some societies, however, a cousin might be a preferred marriage partner. In some Middle Eastern societies, **patrilateral cousin marriage**—marrying a male or female cousin on your father's side—is preferred. Some cultures prohibit marriage with a cousin who is in your lineage but, prefer that you marry a cousin who is not in your lineage. For example, if you live in a society that traces kinship patrilineally, cousins from your father's brothers or sisters would be forbidden as marriage partners, but cousins from your mother's brothers or sisters might be considered excellent marriage partners.

Arranged marriages were typical in many cultures around the world in the past including in the United States. Marriages are arranged by families for many reasons: because the families have something in common, for financial reasons, to match people with others from the "correct" social, economic or religious group, and for many other reasons. In India today, some people practice a kind of modified arranged marriage practice that allows the potential spouses to meet and spend time together before agreeing to a match. The meeting may take place through a mutual friend, a family member, community matchmaker, or even a Marriage Meet even in which members of the same community (caste) are invited to gather (see Figure 5). Although arranged marriages still exist in urban cities such as Mumbai, love matches are increasingly common. In general, as long as the social requirements are met, love matches may be accepted by the families involved.

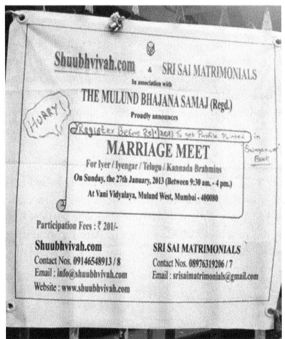

Figure 5: This advertisement for "Marriage Meet" in Mumbai, India welcomes "boys" and "girls" from the community to participate in a Marriage Meet, in which young people can mingle with and get to know potential spouses in a fun atmosphere. Photo used with permission of Laura Tubelle de González.

Polygamy refers to any marriage in which there are multiple partners. There are two kinds of polygamy: polygyny and polyandry. **Polygyny** refers to marriages in which there is one husband and multiple wives. In some societies that practice polygyny, the preference is for **sororal polygyny**, or the marriage of one man to several sisters. In such cases, it is sometimes believed that sisters will get along better as co-wives. **Polyandry** describes marriages with one wife and multiple husbands. As with polygyny, **fraternal polyandry** is common and involves the marriage of a woman to a group of brothers.

In some cultures, if a man's wife dies, especially if he has no children, or has young children, it is thought to be best for him to marry one of his deceased wife's sisters. A sister, it is believed, is a reasonable substitution for the lost wife and likely a more loving mother to any children left behind. This practice might also prevent the need to return property exchanged at marriage, such as **dowry** (payments made to the groom's family before marriage), or **bridewealth** (payments made to the bride's family before marriage). The practice of a man marrying the sister of his deceased wife is called **sororate** marriage. In the case of a husband's death, some societies prefer that a woman marry one of her husband's brothers, and in some cases this might be preferred even if he already has a wife. This practice is called **levirate** marriage. This latter practice is described in the Old Testament.[9]

Family Size

Cultural rules generally define not only who makes up a family but also how many people should be in it. In some cultures, larger families are considered ideal. In others, smaller families are preferred. These ideas are often linked to both practical and ideological considerations. Practical considerations might include the availability of housing, work patterns, childcare, the economic contribution children make to a family, or the cost of raising children. Ideological considerations include religious values related to families. In the 1990s, I carried out field research in Croatia, investigating ideas about families. An overwhelming majority of the people I interviewed believed that the ideal family would include three children. Most of these families commented that in their own living memories people preferred as many children as possible so that there would be assistance for farm work. When I was there, however, large families were no longer regarded as practical. Within the same general region, families in urban settings overwhelmingly said that one child was ideal. A shortage of housing was the single most important factor for limiting family size to one child in cities. In both the rural and urban settings in Croatia, most people were Roman Catholic and may have been ideologically predisposed to larger families, but practical considerations were more important to both groups when it came to matters of family size.

During the same period in the 1990s, it was common for families in the United States to say that the ideal family included two children and preferably one of each gender (anecdotal). This of course varies based on factors which include, but are not limited to the ethnicity and religion of the family. In another example, the People's Republic of China, where I lived and worked, had an official one-child policy.[10] A family that included only one child was not a widespread cultural ideal. Most families wished for more children, but had to settle for less.

Families, Households and Domestic Groups

A **family** can be defined as the smallest group of individuals who see themselves as connected to one another. They are usually part of larger kinship groups, but with whom they may not interact on a daily basis. Families tend to reside together and share economic opportunities and other rights and responsibilities. Family rights and responsibilities are a significant part of understanding families and how they work. In the United States, for example, minor children have a right to be supported materially by their parents or other legal guardians. Parents have a responsibility to support and nurture their children. Spouses have a right to mutual support from each other and property acquired during a marriage is considered "common property" in many U.S. states unless specified otherwise by a pre-nuptial agreement. Some family responsibilities are cultural and not legal. Many such responsibilities are reinforced by religious or other ideological notions.

Family members who reside together are called **households**. A household may include larger kinship groups who think of themselves as separate but related families. Households may also include non-family or kin members, or could even consist exclusively of non-related people who think of themselves as family. Many studies of families cross-culturally have focused on household groups because it is households that are the location for many of the day-to-day activities of a society. Households are important social units in any community

Sometimes families or households are spread across several residential units but think of themselves as a single group for many purposes. In Croatia, because of urban housing constraints, some extended family households operate across one or more residential spaces. An older couple and their married children might live in apartments near each other and cooperate on childcare and cooking as a single household unit. **Domestic group** is another term that can be used to describe a household. Domestic groups can describe any group of people who reside together and share activities pertaining to domestic life including but not limited to childcare, elder care, cooking and economic support, even if they might not describe themselves as "family."

Households may include nuclear families, extended families, joint extended families, or even combinations of families that share a residence and other property as well as rights and responsibilities. In certain regions of Croatia large agricultural households were incredibly numerous. I carried out research in a region known as Slavonia, which from the seventeenth through the nineteenth centuries was was near the border of the Austro-Hungarian and Ottoman Empires. Families in portions of this region were referred to as *zadruzi* (plural) or a *zadruga* (singular). They sometimes numbered up to 100 members, all related through blood and marriage. But these households were much more than a nuclear or even a joint extended family. They were more like small towns with specialists within the household group who did things such as shoe horses or sew. These very large households supported a military culture where men between sixteen and sixty years old had to be ready for military service.[11] A Croatian anthropologist in the 1800s reported that one family was so large that an elderly woman died and this was not noticed for three days! The local government in this case forced the family to divide, separating their property and residing in smaller numbers.[12]

Creating Families: Patterns of Marriage

As described above, families can be created in many different ways. A marriage is a cultural, social, and legal process that brings two or more individuals together to create a new family unit. Most cultures have ideas about how marriages should be arranged (whether by families or by the individuals involved), at what age this should occur, what the married partners should have in common (including economic status, religion, ethnicity and so on), and what cultural, religious and legal processes make a marriage valid. In the United States, strong cultural norms suggest that individuals should marry for love and not for other reasons. It is not unusual, however, for communities to teach children to follow certain group norms in choosing a marriage partner. Some religious communities, for example, will not recognize marriages contracted across religious lines. Some families strongly prefer that their children marry individuals with similar economic, cultural, or ethnic backgrounds. Because families tend to socialize with other families similar to themselves, young people are more likely to meet others similar to themselves.

Marriage Exchanges: Dowry and Bridewealth

In many societies, marriages are affirmed with an exchange of property. This is usually the case in places where families have a hand in arranging a marriage. A property exchange recognizes the challenges faced by a family that loses a member and by a family that takes on a new member. These practices also reflect different notions about the value of the new family member.

Dowry payments are known from U.S. and Western European history. A **dowry** is a gift given by a bride's family to either the bride or to the groom's family at the time of the marriage. In societies that practice dowry, families often spend many years accumulating the gift. In some villages in the former Yugoslavia, the dowry was meant to provide for a woman if she became a widow. The dowry was her share of her family's property and reflected the tradition that land was usually inherited by a woman's brothers. The dowry might include coins, often woven together in a kind of apron and worn on her wedding day. This form of dowry also represented a statement of wealth, prestige or high status for both families; her family's ability to give this kind of wealth, and the prestige of the family who was acquiring a desirable new bride. Her dowry also could include linens and other useful items to be used during her years as a wife. In more recent times, dowries have become extravagant, including things like refrigerators, cars, and houses.

A dowry can also represent the higher status of the groom's family and its ability to demand a payment for taking on the economic responsibility of a young wife. This was of thinking about dowry is more typical of societies in which women are less valued than men. A good dowry enables a woman's family to marry into a better family. In parts of India, a dowry could sometimes be so large that it would be paid in installments. Bride burnings, killing a bride, could happen if her family did not continue to make the agreed upon payments (though there may be other reasons for this awful crime in individual cases). This of course is illegal, but does sometimes occur.[13]

Historically, dowry was most common in agricultural societies. Land was the most valuable commodity and usually land stayed in the hands of men. Women who did not marry were sometimes seen as a burden on their own families because they were not perceived as making an economic contribution and they represented another mouth to feed. A dowry was important for a woman to take with her into a marriage because the groom's family had the upper economic hand. It helped ease the tension of her arrival in the household, especially if the dowry was substantial.

Bridewealth, by contrast, often represents a higher value placed on women and their ability to work and produce children. Bridewealth is an exchange of valuables given from a man's family to the family of his new wife. Bridewealth is common in pastoralist societies in which people make their living by raising domesticated animals. The Masaai are example of one such group. A cattle-herding culture located in Kenya and Tanzania, the Maasai pay bridewealth based on the desirability of the woman. Culturally defined attributes such as her age, beauty, virginity, and her ability to work contribute to a woman's value. The economic value placed on women does not mean that women in such societies necessarily have much freedom, but it does sometimes give them some leverage in their new domestic situations. In rare cases, there might be simultaneous exchanges of dowry and bridewealth. In such cases, often the bridewealth gift was more of a token than a substantial economic contribution.

Post-Marital Residence

Every culture has ideas about where a newly married couple should live. In the United States and in Western Europe, it is usually expected that a new couple create a new domestic unit or household. Ideally they should live together in a place separate from either of their **families of orientation**: the families in which they were raised. They are expected to create a new **family of procreation**: a new household for raising children. The goal of most couples is to eventually live separately from their original families so that they can focus on their new relationship and be independent. This kind of residence after marriage is called **neolocal residence** (new location). Increasingly, many couples establish a residence together before marriage or may skip the formal marriage altogether.

Another common pattern around the world is **patrilocal residence** (father's location). This means that a couple generally resides with the husband's father's family after marriage. This is a multi-generational practice. The new husband's own mother likely moved into the household when she married his father. Patrilocal residence is common around the world. It creates larger households that can be useful in farming economies. Today, with increasing urbanization and with the very different kinds of jobs associated with industrial capitalism, patrilocal residence has become less common.

A less common pattern worldwide is matrilocal residence. In matrilocal residence societies, men leave their matrilineal families at marriage and move in with their wives' mothers' families. Quite a few Native American groups practiced matrilocal residence, including the Hopi and the Navajo (or *Diné*) in the Southwest, and the Haudenosaunee (or Iroquois) tribes in the Great Lakes region. A very interesting residence pattern found within matrilineal societies is **avunculocal residence** (uncle's location). It means that a couple will live with the wife's mother's brother. In matrilineal societies, in which important property, knowledge, or social position are linked with men, the preference is to keep wealth within the matrilineal household. Property and other cultural items are passed not from biological fathers to sons, but from maternal uncles to nephews. In doing so, property is kept within the matriline (see Figure 3).

An excellent example of avunculocal residence is found in the Trobriand Islands in Papua New Guinea. In families where there was position of authority or significant wealth it was common for a young man to go live with or near his mother's brother at the time of his marriage. Trobriand Islanders passed important magical knowledge and political positions through the mother's lineage. The son of a chief would not become a chief. Instead, the chief's maternal nephew would inherit the position. Trobriand kinship and family life is rich and complicated. Anthropologist Annette Weiner describes men and women as carrying out complementary roles and both men and women are valued culturally. This is not a matriarchy, nor is it a true patriarchy.

The avunculocal arrangement is so important that a man or woman without a cross-gender sibling will adopt one. A woman must have a brother to plant yam gardens for her husband when she marries. A man must have a sister to participate in exchanges of women's wealth on his behalf to enhance his position, and also to ensure that his soul is eventually reborn, after death, into the matrilineage. Family life and the passing of knowledge was changing rapidly in the Trobriand Islands at the end of Weiner's work; more people were converting to Christianity, and while belief in magic was not yet disappearing, Christians could not inherit their uncles' magic. This is an example of a culture in transition. At the same time, however, Trobriand Islanders valued their traditions, culture, and language, and were loathe to lose them altogether.[14]

Patrilocal residence is usually associated with patrilineal descent. Property, knowledge, and positions are inherited through the father's family or the husband's father's family. In the case of patrilocal residence, it was sometimes difficult for a woman to return to her original family if her marriage ended due to death or divorce. The latter was often considered socially shaming and in patrilineal societies women were often blamed for ending the marriage regardless of the actual circumstances. **Matrilocal residence** is usually associated with matrilineal descent. Property, knowledge, and positions are inherited through the mother's family, or the wife's mother's family. Matrilineal and matrilocal societies tended to be less concerned with divorce. Men always had a home with their mothers, aunts, and sisters and might even come and go during a marriage, carrying out responsibilities to their maternal relatives and staying with them from time to time. Explaining the differences between patrilocal and matrilocal residences risks stereotyping. That said, it is likely that those cultures in which women marry "out" are less likely to value women while those in which men leave their families at marriage are more inclusive of women. This may have something to do with economics and ideologies, but must be examined in each cultural context.

Bilocal residence (two locations) or ambilocal residence (either location) represent two additional and related residential patterns. They are essentially the same and mean that a couple may live with or near either the husband's or wife's family after marriage. A striking example comes from the island of Dobu, a place that is not far from the Trobriand Islands in Papua New Guinea. In Dobu society, which was traditionally matrilineal and practiced village exogamy, a married couple would alternate years living in the husband's village and in the wife's village.[15] In cases of bilocal or ambilocal residence while a couple has the choice to live with either the husband's or wife's family, a choice is made based on which location is best able to accommodate new members or which location needs the additional labor that comes from new members. Once the choice of residence is made, the married couple usually remains in one place.

Inheritance

The inheritance of family property is often a part of cultural values and roles for families. In 1991, when Croatia was on the verge of war, I remember a woman speaking about her house going to her eldest son. Her young daughter was sitting with us at the time, and said to her mother in surprise, "Mama, why not me?" Her mother stroked her head and smiled at her, but was firm when she said "Because you are female." It is typical worldwide, particularly in agricultural societies, for men to inherit family property. The best-known pattern is inheritance by the oldest male. Joint inheritance by brothers, with the oldest brother nominally in charge of the family, is also fairly widespread in joint and extended families. As mentioned above, however, other patterns are found, including property that passes from maternal uncle to maternal nephew in the Trobriand Islands, and inheritance of the family house and corresponding responsibility to care for the older generation by the youngest daughter in Burmese families. This is a further reminder that family organization and expectations are linked to economic systems and to the resources available to the family. Pattern of family life and marriage do not exist apart from the physical and economic environment, and other cultural practices.

Same-Sex Marriage

In the United States, Canada as well as other countries, two individuals of the same sex may be legally married, but in these countries as well as other places, same-sex couples have been creating households and families for centuries, long before legal recognition. Same-sex marriages are documented, for instance, in the history of Native American groups from the Great Plains. On the Plains, men who preferred to dress and take on the roles of women were allowed to marry other men. It was assumed that if one partner gathered plant food and prepared food, the other partner should have a complementary role like hunting. Androgynous individuals, males who preferred female roles or dress, and females who took on male roles, were not condemned but regarded as "two-spirits," a label that had positive connotations.

Two-spirits were considered to embody a third gender combining elements of both male and female. The key to the two-spirit gender identity was behavior: what individuals did in their communities.[16] If a person who was born with a male biological sex felt his identity and chosen lifestyle best matched the social role recognized as female, he could move into a third gender two-spirit category. Today, Native American groups set their own laws regarding same-sex marriage. Many recognize two-spirit individuals, and accept marriage of a two-spirit person to a person of the same biological sex. Although some nations still do not permit same-sex marriage between tribal members, one of the largest tribal nations, the Cherokee legalized same-sex marriages in 2016.

Adoption

Adoption is another way that people form family ties. In the United States, usually it is infants or minor children who are adopted by a non-parental family member like a grandparent, an aunt or uncle, or an older sibling, or by a non-family member. This is usually done when a biological parent is unable or unwilling to raise a child. The decision to give up a child through adoption is a complicated one, and one that parents do not make easily.

In other societies, adoption is viewed differently. In some Pacific Island societies, children who are adopted are considered fortunate because they have two sets of parents; children are not given for adoption because a parent is unwilling or unable to care for them, but rather to honor the adoptive parents. Martha Ward described a young woman in Pohnpei, Micronesia, who had a child for her grandmother, to keep her company in her older years. In another case she described a child who went to dinner at a relative's house and stayed for a number of years in a kind of adoptive situation. In such cases, children retain relationships with biological and adoptive family members, and may even move fluidly between them.[17]

One of the more unusual forms of adoption is adopted-daughter marriage, or *sim pua* marriage. It is found in Taiwan and described by anthropologist Margery Wolf. Wolf worked in Taiwan in the mid-1900s. At that time, Taiwanese families strongly preferred sons over daughters. Sons stayed with their families in adulthood, produced the next generation, cared for parents in old age, and carried on the tradition of ancestor veneration so that one would not become a "wandering ghost" after death. Daughters were regarded as expensive. People believed that they raised daughters for someone else. Dowries and weddings for grown daughters were expensive. Families worried that they would not be able to find suitable husbands for their grown daughters, who would remain a burden on their natal families in their later years, not producers of children or contributors in any other way.[18]

As a result a custom developed of giving up daughters to other families as future daughters-in-law. Mothers would give up their own daughters as infants, only to take in very quickly an adopted daughter from someone else. Sometimes the future wife was adopted before the family had a son. It was said that an adopted daughter/daughter-in-law would "lead in a son." Adopted daughters were reportedly not treated well. They had to do housework, help with childcare, and were not given any privileges such as education. They were often older than their eventual husbands, and had a lower status in the family than their adoptive brothers. There were reports of an adopted daughter being treated badly by adopted siblings, and then being expected to later marry one of them. Wolf reports a very low birth rate among couples who were raised as siblings. Pressure to engage in these kinds of adoptions usually came from a mother-in-law, or the husband's mother, or a grandmother of the infant girl who had decision-making power in the family because she was the mother of an adult son. Grandmothers saw this kind of arrangement as advantageous to the family, according to Wolf, because birth mothers were more likely to beunhappy about losing a baby daughter, and because caring for another child brought in a future daughter-in-law.[19]

FAMILIES AND CULTURE CHANGE

Families are adaptive groups that help address common societal concerns related to child-rearing, sexual relationships between adults, and gender roles within the household. While there are norms and ideals, expectations and understandings regarding families in all cultures, there are also always situations that represent variations on that norm. Sometimes these are areas where we begin to see culture change. In the United States in the 1960s, young people began to live together openly outside of marriage as couples. Those relationships were often socially disapproved, but today it is much more socially acceptable and common for people to live together prior to marriage or even instead of marriage. Often the couple will also have children before they decide to marry. An ideological variation that began nearly sixty years ago has led to a widespread culture change in attitudes toward marriage.

In the Croatian Republic of Yugoslavia in the 1980s, shortly after the death of long-time leader Josip Broz "Tito," it was still expected that a young couple would live with a husband's family at marriage. At that time, I was engaged in fieldwork that focused on social change. The socialist government had implemented legislation and social programs to support women moving out of traditional roles, becoming educated and productive members of the workforce, and participating in the professional class. There was state-funded daycare and liberal legislation regarding birth control and abortion among other efforts to improve or change the traditional roles of women.

In reality, however, marriage and parenthood were still highly valued. Couples often married at a young age and women tended to still be responsible for all housework. Women themselves valued keeping a clean house, cooking homemade food from scratch without using prepared foods, and caring for their families. Most young wives and mothers lived with their husbands' families. Traditionally, mothers of sons gained power and respect in the family from their married son and daughter-in-law. In the past this relationship was sometimes described as a difficult one, with a daughter-in-law having little say in family and household life. Some of that seemed to persist in the 1980s. Women living with mothers-in-law did not have a great deal of freedom of choice and had to prove themselves at home, leaving less time to think about progressing in education or work.[20]

In an urban environment, however, housing was in short supply. If a family had two sons and one was already married and still living with his natal family, the second son might live with the wife's family at marriage if that family had the space. In these situations, which were not considered ideal but still were in the range of acceptable alternatives, young married women found themselves living with their own mothers rather than a mother-in-law. A mother tended to make life easier for her own daughter rather than insisting that she do quite so much household work. Mothers and daughters were more often easy partners in a household. The mother-in-law of a young man tended not to make his life difficult, but rather to regard him fondly. Women who lived with their own families after marriage were more likely to be able to continue their education, take promotions at work, make more of the opportunities that were provided under socialism.

In Croatia, government engineered policies alone did not produce changes in family patterns or gender roles. It was a variety of factors, including economic pressures and housing shortages, which combined to create an environment in which families changed. It became increasingly common for couples to live with the wife's family and eventually to live on their own. Today in Croatia, women have a great deal of freedom of choice, are likely to live alone with their husbands or, like in the United States, Canada, and European countries, to live with a partner outside of marriage. Change occurs in family life when social and cultural conditions also change.

CONCLUSION

The institutions of the family and marriage are found in all societies and are part of cultural understandings of the way the world should work. In all cultures there are variations that are acceptable as well as situations in which people cannot quite meet the ideal. How people construct families varies greatly from one society to another, but there are patterns across cultures that are linked to economics, religion, and other cultural and environmental factors. The study of families and marriage is an important part of anthropology because family and household groups play a central role in defining relationships between people and making society function. While there is nothing in biology that dictates that a family group be organized in a particular way, our cultural expectations leads to ideas about families that seem "natural" to us. As cultures change over time, ideas about family also adapt to new circumstances.

DISCUSSION QUESTIONS

1. Why is it important for anthropologists to understand the kinship, descent, and family relationships that exist in the cultures they study? In what ways can family relationships structure the lives of individuals?

2. Status and role define the position of people within the family as well as the behaviors they are expected to perform. What are some of the statuses and roles found in families in your community? How have these changed over time?

3. In this chapter, Gilliland describes several different patterns of family organization including nuclear families, extended families, and joint families. While small nuclear families are common in the United States, larger families are common in many other societies. What do you think are some of the practical effects of both small and large families on everyday life?

GLOSSARY

Avunculocal: married individuals live with or near an uncle.

Bilateral descent: descent is recognized through both the father and the mother's sides of the family.

Bridewealth: payments made to the bride's family by the groom's family before marriage.

Clan: a group of people who have a general notion of common descent that is not attached to a specific biological ancestor.

Descent groups: relationships that provide members with a sense of identity and social support based on ties of shared ancestry.

Domestic group: a term that can be used to describe a group of people who live together even if members do not consider themselves to be family.

Dowry: payments made to the groom's family by the bride's family before marriage.

Endogamy: a term describing expectations that individuals must marry within a particular group.

Exogamy: a term describing expectations that individuals must marry outside a particular group.

Extended family: a family of at least three-generations sharing a household.

Family: the smallest group of individuals who see themselves as connected to one another. Family of orientation: the family in which an individual is raised.

Family of procreation: a new household formed for the purpose of conceiving and raising children.

Household: family members who reside together.

Joint family: a very large extended family that includes multiple generations.

Kinship: term used to describe culturally recognized ties between members of a family, the social statuses used to define family members, and the expected behaviors associated with these statuses.

Kinship diagrams: charts used by anthropologists to visually represent relationships between members of a kinship group.

Kinship system: the pattern of culturally recognized relationships between family members.

Kinship terminology: the terms used in a language to describe relatives.

Levirate: the practice of a woman marrying one of her deceased husband's brothers.

Lineage: term used to describe any form of descent from a common ancestor.

Matriarchal: a society in which women have authority to make decisions.

Matrilineal descent: a kinship group created through the maternal line (mothers and their children).

Matrilocal residence: married individuals live with or near the wife's mother's family.

Neolocal residence: newly married individuals establish a household separate from other family members.

Nuclear family: a parent or parents who are in a culturally-recognized relationship, such as marriage, along with minor or dependent children.

Patrilateral cousin marriage: the practice of marrying a male or female cousin on the father's side of the family.

Patrilineal descent: a kinship group created through the paternal line (fathers and their children).

Patrilocal residence: married individuals live with or near the husband's father's family.

Polygamous: families based on plural marriages in which there are multiple wives or, in rarer cases, multiple husbands.

Polyandry: marriages with one wife and multiple husbands.

Polygyny: marriages in which there is one husband and multiple wives.

Role: the set of behaviors expected of an individual who occupies a particular status.

Serial monogamy: marriage to a succession of spouses one after the other.

Sororate marriage: the practice of a man marrying the sister of his deceased wife.

Status: any culturally-designated position a person occupies in a particular setting.

Stem family: a version of an extended family that includes an older couple and one of their adult children with a spouse (or spouses) and children.

Unilineal: descent is recognized through only one line or side of the family.

ABOUT THE AUTHOR

Mary K. Gilliland, Ph.D. (also published as Mary K. Gilliland Olsen) earned a B.A. from Bryn Mawr College, with Honors in Anthropology; and M.A. and Ph.D. degrees in anthropology from the University of California, San Diego. Her primary research took place in the former Yugoslavia (1982–4, 1990–1), Croatia (1993, 1995, 1996–7) and with displaced Bosnians, Croats and Serbs in the United States (2001–3). In Croatia, Mary Kay was affiliated with the *Filozofski Fakultet* in Zagreb, the Ethnographic Museum in Slavonski Brod (Croatia/ Yugoslavia), and with the Institute for Anthropological Research (Zagreb, Croatia both pre- and post-independence).
She has a continuing affiliation as a member of the editorial board for the *Collegium Antropologicum: The Journal of the Institute for Anthropological Research*, and was named a Lifetime Member of the Croatian Anthropological Society. Mary Kay has also collaborated in projects in Asia, including People's Republic of China (primarily Xinjiang, Western China), Mongolia and Vietnam. Her areas of research interest and publication include culture and social change, gender and ethnic identity, family, marriage and intergenerational relationships. Primarily a "teaching anthropologist," Mary Kay was full-time faculty and Department Chair at Pima Community College in Tucson, Arizona from 1989–2006. She maintains an ongoing relationship as Associate Adjunct Professor of Anthropology at the University of Arizona. She has taught at San Diego Mesa College, University of California, San Diego and the University of Zagreb. Since 2006 she has held a variety of administrative positions including Academic Dean, Vice President of Instruction and is currently Vice President of Academic Affairs at Central Arizona College.

NOTES

1. Lewis Henry Morgan, *Systems of Consanguinity and Affinity of the Human Family* (Washington D.C.: Smithsonian Institution, 1871).

2. Ralph Linton, *The Study of Man* (New York: D. Appleton-Century Company,1936).

3. In a patrilineal society, children are members of their father's patrilineage. A mother belongs to her own father's patrilineage, while the children belong to their father's patrilineage.

4. Kathleen Gough, "Variation in Matrilineal Systems," in D. Schneider and K. Gough, eds., *Matrilineal Kinship, Part 2* (Berkeley: University of California Press, 1961). See also Kathleen Gough, *The Traditional Kinship System of the Nayars of Malabar (Cambridge, MA: Harvard University Press, 1954).*

5. See for example Merlin Myers, *Households and Families of the Longhouse Iroquois at Six Nations Reserve* (Lincoln, NE: University of Nebraska Press, 2006).

6. George P. Murdock, *Social Structure* (New York: MacMillan, 1949).

7. Vera St. Ehrlich, Family in Transition: A Study of 300 Yugoslav Villages. Princeton: Princeton University Press, 1966. See also Gilliland, M. 1986. The Maintenance of Family Values in a Yugoslav Town. Ann Arbor, Michigan: UMI International.

8. Melford Spiro, *Kinship and Marriage in Burma: A Cultural and Psychodynamic Analysis* (Berkeley, CA: University of California Press, 1977).

9. Laura Tubelle de González, "Modern Arranged Marriage in Mumbai" *Teaching Anthropology: SACC Notes* 19 (2015). http://sacc-dev.americananthro.org/wp-content/uploads/TASN-191-192-spring-fall-20131.pdf.

10. The one-child policy was introduced in 1979. It was phased out beginning in 2015 and was replaced by a two-child policy.

11. See Vera St. Ehrlich, Family in Transition: A Study of 300 Yugoslav Villages. Princeton: Princeton University Press, 1966.

12. Luka Lukic, Varos: Zbornik za narodi zivot i obicaje juznih slavena. Jugoslavenska akademija znanosti i umjetnosti. Zagreb. god. 24, str. 32.238, 1919.

13. There are many news reports about this practice. See for instance Subodh Varnal, "Dowry Death: One Bride Burnt Every Hour," *The Times of India*, January 27, 2012 http://timesofindia.indiatimes.com/india/Dowry-death-One-bride-burnt-every-hour/articleshow/11644691.cms

14. Annette B. Weiner, *The Trobrianders of Papua New Guinea* (New York: Holt, Rinehart and Winston, 1988).

15. Reo Fortune, *Sorcerers of Dobu* (New York: E.P. Dutton and Co., 1932).

16. See for instance Will Roscoe, *Changing Ones: Third and Fourth Genders in Native North America* (New York: Palgrave Macmillan, 1998).

17. Martha Ward, *Nest in the Wind: Adventures in Anthropology on a Tropical Island* (Long Grove, IL: Waveland Press, 2005).

18. Margery Wolf, *Women and the Family in Rural Taiwan* (Palo Alto, CA: Stanford University Press, 1972).

19. Ibid.

20. Olsen, M. K. G., "Authority and Conflict in Slavonian Households: The Effects of Social Environment on Intra-Household Processes" in The Household Economy: Reconsidering the Domestic Mode of Production, Richard Wilk, ed., 149-170 (Colorado: Westview Press, 1989).

RACE AND ETHNICITY

Justin D. García, Millersville University of Pennsylvania
jgarcia@millersville.edu
http://www.millersville.edu/socanth/faculty/GARCIA,%20Dr.%20Justin.php

LEARNING OBJECTIVES

- Define the term reification and explain how the concept of race has been reified throughout history.

- Explain why a biological basis for human race categories does not exist.

- Discuss what anthropologists mean when they say that race is a socially constructed concept and explain how race has been socially constructed in the United States and Brazil.

- Identify what is meant by racial formation, hypodescent, and the one-drop rule.

- Describe how ethnicity is different from race, how ethnic groups are different from racial groups, and what is meant by symbolic ethnicity and pan-ethnicity.

- Summarize the history of immigration to the United States, explaining how different waves of immigrant groups have been perceived as racially different and have shifted popular understandings of "race."

- Analyze ways in which the racial and ethnic compositions of professional sports have shifted over time and how those shifts resulted from changing social and cultural circumstances that drew new groups into sports.

Suppose someone asked you the following open-ended questions: How would you define the word **race** as it applies to groups of human beings? How many human races are there and what are they? For each of the races you identify, what are the important or key criteria that distinguish each group (what characteristics or features are unique to each group that differentiate it from the others)? Discussions about race and racism are often highly emotional and encompass a wide range of emotions, including discomfort, fear, defensiveness, anger, and insecurity—why is this such an emotional topic in society and why do you think it is so difficult for individuals to discuss race dispassionately?

How would you respond to these questions? I pose these thought-provoking questions to students enrolled in my Introduction to Cultural Anthropology course just before we begin the unit on race and ethnicity in a worksheet and ask them to answer each question fully to the best of their ability without doing any outside research. At the next class, I assign the students to small groups of five to eight depending on the size of the class and give them a few minutes to share their responses to the questions with one another. We then collectively discuss their responses as a class. Their responses are often very interesting and quite revealing and generate memorable classroom dialogues.

"DUDE, WHAT ARE YOU?!"

Ordinarily, students select a college major or minor by carefully considering their personal interests, particular subjects that pique their curiosity, and fields they feel would be a good basis for future professional careers. Technically, my decision to major in anthropology and later earn a master's degree and doctorate in anthropology was mine alone, but I tell my friends and students, only partly as a joke, that my choice of major was made for me to some degree by people I encountered as a child, teenager, and young adult. Since middle school, I had noticed that many people—complete strangers, classmates, coworkers, and friends—seemed to find my physical appearance confusing or abnormal, often leading them to ask me questions like "What are you?" and

"What's your race?" Others simply assumed my heritage as if it was self-evident and easily defined and then interacted with me according to their conclusions.

Figure 1: The Common Threads mural at Broad and Spring Garden Streets in Philadelphia, PA highlights the cultural diversity of the city.

These subjective determinations varied wildly from person to person and from situation to situation. I distinctly recall, for example, an incident in a souvenir shop at the beach in Ocean City, Maryland, shortly after I graduated from high school. A middle-aged merchant attempted to persuade me to purchase a T-shirt that boldly declared "100% Italian . . . and Proud of It!" with bubbled letters that spelled "Italian" shaded green, white, and red. Despite my repeated efforts to convince the merchant that I was not of Italian ethnic heritage, he refused to believe me. On another occasion during my mid-twenties while I was studying for my doctoral degree at Temple University, I was walking down Diamond Street in North Philadelphia, Pennsylvania, passing through a predominantly African American neighborhood. As I passed a group of six male teenagers socializing on the steps of a row house, one of them shouted "Hey, honky! What are you doing in this neighborhood?" Somewhat startled at being labeled a "honky," (something I had never been called before), I looked at the group and erupted in laughter, which produced looks of surprise and disbelief in return. As I proceeded to walk a few more blocks and reached the predominantly Puerto Rican neighborhood of Lower Kensington, three young women flirtatiously addressed me as *papí* (an affectionate Spanish slang term for man). My transformation from "honky" to "*papí*" in a span of ten minutes spoke volumes about my life history and social experiences—and sparked my interest in cultural and physical anthropology.

Throughout my life, my physical appearance has provided me with countless unique and memorable experiences that have emphasized the significance of race and ethnicity as **socially constructed** concepts in America and other societies. My fascination with this subject is therefore both personal and professional; a lifetime of questions and assumptions from others regarding my racial and ethnic background have cultivated my interest in these topics. I noticed that my perceived race or ethnicity, much like beauty, rested in the eye of the beholder as individuals in different regions of the country (and outside of the United States) often perceived me as having different specific heritages. For example, as a teenager living in York County, Pennsylvania, senior citizens and middle-aged individuals usually assumed I was "white," while younger residents often saw me as "Puerto Rican" or generically "Hispanic" or "Latino." When I lived in Philadelphia, locals mostly assumed I was "Italian American," but many Puerto Ricans, Mexicans, and Dominicans, in the City of Brotherly Love often took me for either "Puerto Rican" or "Cuban."

My experiences in the southwest were a different matter altogether. During my time in Texas, New Mexico, and Colorado, local residents—regardless of their respective heritages—commonly assumed I was of Mexican descent. At times, local Mexican Americans addressed me as *carnal* (pronounced CAR-nahl), a term often used to imply a strong sense of community among Mexican American men that is somewhat akin to frequent use of the label "brother" among African American men. On more occasions than I can count, people assumed that I spoke Spanish. Once, in Los Angeles, someone from the Spanish-language television network Univisión attempted to interview me about my thoughts on an immigration bill pending in the California legislature. My West Coast friends and professional colleagues were surprised to hear that I was usually assumed to be Puerto Rican, Italian, or simply "white" on the East Coast, and one of my closest friends from graduate school—a Mexican American woman from northern California—once memorably stated that she would not "even assume" that I was "half white."

I have a rather ambiguous physical appearance—a shaved head, brown eyes, and a black mustache and goatee. Depending on who one asks, I have either a "pasty white" or "somewhat olive" complexion, and my last name is often the single biggest factor that leads people on the East Coast to conclude that I am Puerto Rican. My experiences are examples of what sociologists Michael Omi and Howard Winant (1986) referred to as "racial commonsense"—a deeply entrenched social belief that another person's racial or ethnic background is obvious and easily determined from brief glances and can be used to predict a person's culture, behavior, and personality. Reality, of course, is far more complex. One's racial or ethnic background cannot necessarily be accurately determined based on physical appearance alone, and an individual's "race" does not necessarily determine his or her "culture," which in turn does not determine "personality." Yet, these perceptions remain.

IS ANTHROPOLOGY THE "SCIENCE OF RACE?"

Anthropology was sometimes referred to as the "science of race" during the eighteenth and nineteenth centuries when physical anthropologists sought a biological basis for categorizing humans into racial types.[1] Since World War II, important research by anthropologists has revealed that racial categories are socially and culturally defined concepts and that racial labels and their definitions vary widely around the world. In other words, different countries have different racial categories, and different ways of classifying their citizens into these categories.[2] At the same time, significant genetic studies conducted by physical anthropologists since the 1970s have revealed that biologically distinct human races do not exist. Certainly, humans vary in terms of physical and genetic characteristics such as skin color, hair texture, and eye shape, but those variations cannot be used as criteria to biologically classify racial groups with scientific accuracy. Let us turn our attention to understanding why humans cannot be scientifically divided into biologically distinct races.

Race: A Discredited Concept in Human Biology

At some point in your life, you have probably been asked to identify your race on a college form, job application, government or military form, or some other official document. And most likely, you were required to select from a list of choices rather than given the ability to respond freely. The frequency with which we are exposed to four or five common racial labels—"white," "black," "Caucasian," and "Asian," for example—tends to promote the illusion that racial categories are natural, objective, and evident divisions. After all, if Justin Timberlake, Jay-Z, and Jackie Chan stood side by side, those common racial labels might seem to make sense. What could be more objective, more conclusive, than this evidence before our very eyes? By this point, you might be thinking that anthropologists have gone completely insane in denying biological human races!

Physical anthropologists have identified several important concepts regarding the true nature of humans' physical, genetic, and biological variation that have discredited race as a biological concept. Many of the issues presented in this section are discussed in further detail in Race: Are We So Different, a website created by the American Anthropological Association. The American Anthropological Association (AAA) launched the website to educate the public about the true nature of human biological and cultural variation and challenge common misperceptions about race. This is an important endeavor because race is a complicated, often emotionally charged topic, leading many people to rely on their personal opinions and hearsay when drawing conclusions about people who are different from them. The website is highly interactive, featuring multimedia illustrations and online quizzes designed to increase visitors' knowledge of human variation. I encourage you to explore the website as you will likely find answers to several of the questions you may still be asking after reading this chapter.[3]

Before explaining why distinct biological races do not exist among humans, I must point out that one of the biggest reasons so many people continue to believe in the existence of biological human races is that the idea has been intensively **reified** in literature, the media, and culture for more than three hundred years. Reification refers to the process in which an inaccurate concept or idea is so heavily promoted and circulated among people that it begins to take on a life of its own. Over centuries, the notion of biological human races became engrained—unquestioned, accepted, and regarded as a concrete "truth." Studies of human physical and cultural variation from a scientific and anthropological perspective have allowed us to move beyond reified thinking and toward an improved understanding of the true complexity of human diversity.

The reification of race has a long history. Especially during the eighteenth and nineteenth centuries, philosophers and scholars attempted to identify various human races. They perceived "races" as specific divisions of humans who shared certain physical and biological features that distinguished them from other groups of humans. This historic notion of race may seem clear-cut and innocent enough, but it quickly led to problems as social theorists attempted to classify people by race. One of the most basic difficulties was the actual number of human races: how many were there, who were they, and what grounds distinguished them? Despite more than three centuries of such effort, no clear-cut scientific consensus was established for a precise number of human races.

One of the earliest and most influential attempts at producing a racial classification system came from Swedish botanist Carolus Linnaeus, who argued in *Systema Naturae* (1735) for the existence of four human races: *Americanus* (Native American / American Indian), *Europaeus* (European), *Asiaticus* (East Asian), and *Africanus* (African). These categories correspond with common racial labels used in the United States for census and demographic purposes today. However, in 1795, German physician and anthropologist Johann Blumenbach suggested that there were five races, which he labeled as *Caucasian* (white), *Mongolian* (yellow or East Asian), *Ethiopian* (black or African), *American* (red or American Indian), *Malayan* (brown or Pacific Islander). Importantly, Blumenbach listed the races in this exact order, which he believed reflected their natural historical descent from the "primeval" Caucasian original to "extreme varieties."[4] Although he was a committed abolitionist, Blumenbach nevertheless felt that his "Caucasian" race (named after the Caucasus Mountains of Central Asia, where he believed humans had originated) represented the original variety of humankind from which the other races had degenerated.

By the early twentieth century, many social philosophers and scholars had accepted the idea of three human races: the so-called *Caucasoid*, *Negroid*, and *Mongoloid* groups that corresponded with regions of Europe, sub-Saharan Africa, and East Asia, respectively. However, the three-race theory faced serious criticism given that numerous peoples from several geographic regions were omitted from the classification, including Australian Aborigines, Asian Indians, American Indians, and inhabitants of the South Pacific Islands. Those groups could not be easily pigeonholed into racial categories regardless of how loosely the categories were defined. Australian Aborigines, for example, often have dark complexions (a trait they appeared to share with Africans) but reddish or blondish hair (a trait shared with northern Europeans). Likewise, many Indians living on the Asian subcontinent have complexions that are as dark or darker than those of many Africans and African Americans. Because of these seeming contradictions, some academics began to argue in favor of larger numbers of human races—five, nine, twenty, sixty, and more.[5]

During the 1920s and 1930s, some scholars asserted that Europeans were comprised of more than one "white" or "Caucasian" race: *Nordic*, *Alpine*, and *Mediterranean* (named for the geographic regions of Europe from

Figure 2: In *Systema Naturae*, Carolus Linnaeus attempted to create a taxonomy for all living things, including people.

which they descended). These European races, they alleged, exhibited obvious physical traits that distinguished them from one another and thus served as racial boundaries. For example, "Nordics" were said to consist of peoples of Northern Europe—Scandinavia, the British Isles, and Northern Germany—while "Alpines" came from the Alps Mountains of Central Europe and included French, Swiss, Northern Italians, and Southern Germans. People from southern Europe—including Portuguese, Spanish, Southern Italians, Sicilians, Greeks, and Albanians—comprised the "Mediterranean" race. Most Americans today would find this racial classification system bizarre, but its proponents argued for it on the basis that one would observe striking physical differences between a Swede or Norwegian and a Sicilian. Similar efforts were made to "carve up" the populations of Africa and Asia into geographically local, specific races.[6]

The fundamental point here is that any effort to classify human populations into racial categories is inherently arbitrary and subjective rather than scientific and objective. These racial classification schemes simply reflected their proponents' desires to "slice the pie" of human physical variation according to the particular trait(s) they preferred to establish as the major, defining criteria of their classification system. Two major types of "race classifiers" have emerged over the past 300 years: *lumpers* and *splitters*. Lumpers have classified races by large geographic tracts (often continents) and produced a small number of broad, general racial categories, as reflected in Linnaeus's original classification scheme and later three-race theories. Splitters have subdivided continent-wide racial categories into specific, more localized regional races and attempted to devise more "precise" racial labels for these specific groups, such as the three European races described earlier. Consequently, splitters have tried to identify many more human races than lumpers.

Racial labels, whether from a lumper or a splitter model, clearly attempt to identify and describe *something*. So why do these racial labels not accurately describe human physical and biological variation? To understand why, we must keep in mind that racial labels are distinct, discrete categories while human physical and biological variations (such as skin color, hair color and texture, eye color, height, nose shape, and distribution of blood types) are *continuous* rather than discrete.

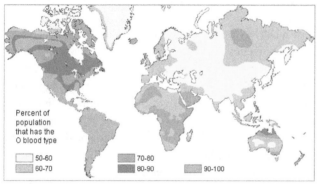

Figure 3: The global distribution of Type O blood reflects a clinal pattern.

Physical anthropologists use the term **cline** to refer to differences in the traits that occur in populations across a geographical area. In a cline, a trait may be more common in one geographical area than another, but the variation is gradual and continuous with no sharp breaks. A prominent example of clinal variation among humans is skin color. Think of it this way: Do all "white" persons who you know actually share the same skin complexion? Likewise, do all "black" persons who you know share an identical skin complexion? The answer, obviously, is no, since human skin color does not occur in just 3, 5, or even 50 shades. The reality is that human skin color, as a continuous trait, exists as a spectrum from very light to very dark with every possible hue, shade, and tone in between.

Imagine two people—one from Sweden and one from Nigeria—standing side by side. If we looked only at those two individuals and ignored people who inhabit the regions between Sweden and Nigeria, it would be easy to reach the faulty conclusion that they represented two distinct human racial groups, one light ("white") and one dark ("black"). [7] However, if we walked from Nigeria to Sweden, we would gain a fuller understanding of human skin color because we would see that skin color generally became gradually lighter the further north we traveled from the equator. At no point during this imaginary walk would we reach a point at which the people abruptly changed skin color. As physical anthropologists such as John Relethford (2004) and C. Loring Brace (2005) have noted, the average range of skin color gradually changes over geographic space. North Africans are generally lighter-skinned than Central Africans, and southern Europeans are generally lighter-skinned than North Africans. In turn, northern Italians are generally lighter-skinned than Sicilians, and the Irish, Danes, and Swedes are generally lighter-skinned than northern Italians and Hungarians. Thus, human skin color cannot be used as a definitive marker of racial boundaries.

There are a few notable exceptions to this general rule of lighter-complexioned people inhabiting northern latitudes. The Chukchi of Eastern Siberia and Inuits of Alaska, Canada, and Greenland have darker skin than other Eurasian people living at similar latitudes, such as Scandinavians. Physical anthropologists have explained this exception in terms of the distinct dietary customs of indigenous Arctic groups, which have traditionally been based on certain native meats and fish that are rich in Vitamin D (polar bears, whales, seals, and trout).

What does Vitamin D have to do with skin color? The answer is intriguing! Dark skin blocks most of the sun's dangerous ultraviolet rays, which is advantageous in tropical environments where sunlight is most intense. Exposure to high levels of ultraviolent radiation can damage skin cells, causing cancer, and also destroy the body's supply of folate, a nutrient essential for reproduction. Folate deficiency in women can cause severe birth defects in their babies. Melanin, the pigment produced in skin cells, acts as a natural sunblock, protecting skin cells from damage, and preventing the breakdown of folate. However, exposure to sunlight has an important positive health effect: stimulating the production of vitamin D. Vitamin D is essential for the health of bones and the immune system. In areas where ultraviolent radiation is strong, there is no problem producing enough Vitamin D, even as darker skin filters ultraviolet radiation.[8]

In environments where the sun's rays are much less intense, a different problem occurs: not enough sunlight penetrates the skin to enable the production of Vitamin D. Over the course of human evolution, natural selection favored the evolution of lighter skin as humans migrated and settled farther from the equator to ensure that weaker rays of sunlight could adequately penetrate our skin. The diet of indigenous populations of the Arctic region provided sufficient amounts of Vitamin D to ensure their health. This reduced the selective pressure toward the evolution of lighter skin among the Inuit and the Chukchi. Physical anthropologist Nina Jablonski (2012) has also noted that natural selection could have favored darker skin in Arctic regions because high levels of ultraviolet radiation from the sun are reflected from snow and ice during the summer months.

Still, many people in the United States remain convinced that biologically distinct human races exist and are easy to identify, declaring that they can walk down any street in the United States and easily determine who is "white" and who is "black." The United States was populated historically by immigrants from a small number of world regions who did not reflect the full spectrum of human physical variation. The earliest settlers in the North American colonies overwhelmingly came from Northern Europe (particularly, Britain, France, Germany, and Ireland), regions where skin colors tend to be among the lightest in the world. Slaves brought to the United States during the colonial period came largely from the western coast of Central Africa, a region where skin color tends to be among the darkest in the world. Consequently, when we look at today's descendants of these groups, we are not looking at accurate, proportional representations of the total range of human skin color; instead, we are looking, in effect, at opposite ends of a spectrum, where striking differences are inevitable. More recent waves of immigrants who have come to the United States from other world regions have brought a wider range of skin colors, shaping a continuum of skin color that defies classification into a few simple categories.

Physical anthropologists have also found that there are no specific genetic traits that are exclusive to a "racial" group. For the concept of human races to have biological significance, an analysis of multiple genetic traits would have to consistently produce the same racial classifications. In other words, a racial classification scheme for skin color would also have to reflect classifications by blood type, hair texture, eye shape, lactose intolerance, and other traits often mistakenly assumed to be "racial" characteristics. An analysis based on any one of those characteristics individually would produce a unique set of racial categories because variations in human physical and genetic are **nonconcordant**. Each trait is inherited independently, not "bundled together" with other traits and inherited as a package. There is no correlation between skin color and other characteristics such as blood type and lactose intolerance.

A prominent example of nonconcordance is sickle-cell anemia, which people often mistakenly think of as a disease that only affects Africans, African Americans, and "black" persons. In fact, the sickle-cell allele (the version of the gene that causes sickle-cell anemia when a person inherits two copies) is relatively common among people whose ancestors are from regions where a certain strain of malaria, *Plasmodium falciparum*, is prevalent, namely Central and Western Africa and parts of Mediterranean Europe, the Arabian peninsula, and India. The sickle-cell trait thus is not exclusively African or "black." The erroneous perceptions are relately primarily to the fact that the ancestors of U.S. African Americans came predominantly from Western Africa, where the sickle-cell gene is prevalent, and are therefore more recognizable than populations of other ancestries and regions where the sickle-cell gene is common, such as southern Europe and Arabia.[9]

Another trait commonly mistaken as defining race is the epicanthic eye fold typically associated with people of East Asian ancestry. The epicanthic eye fold at the outer corner of the eyelid produces the eye shape that people in the United States typically associate with people from China and Japan, but is also common in people from Central Asia, parts of Eastern Europe and Scandinavia, some American Indian groups, and the Khoi San of southern Africa.

Figure 4: The ability to digest the lactose found in dairy products is more common in some populations than others.

In college, I took a course titled "Nutrition" because I thought it would be an easy way to boost my grade point average. The professor of the class, an authoritarian man in his late 60s or early 70s, routinely declared that "Asians can't drink milk!" When this assertion was challenged by various students, including a woman who claimed that her best friend was Korean and drank milk and ate ice cream all the time, the professor only became more strident, doubling down on his dairy diatribe and defiantly vowing that he would not "ignore the facts" for "purposes of political correctness." However, it is scientific accuracy, not political correctness, we should be concerned about, and lactose tolerance is a complex topic. Lactose is a sugar that is naturally present in milk and dairy products, and an enzyme, lactase, breaks it down into two simpler sugars that can be digested by the body. Ordinarily, humans (and other mammals) stop producing lactase after infancy, and approximately 75 percent of humans are thus lactose intolerant and cannot naturally digest milk. Lactose intolerance is a natural, normal condition. However, some people continue to produce lactase into adulthood and can naturally digest milk and dairy products. This lactose persistence developed through natural selection, primarily among people in regions that had long histories of dairy farming (including the Middle East, Northern Europe, Eastern Europe, East Africa, and Northern India). In other areas and for some groups of people, dairy products were introduced relatively recently (such as East Asia, Southern Europe, and Western and Southern Africa and among Australian Aborigines and American Indians) and lactose persistence has not developed yet.[10]

The idea of biological human races emphasizes differences, both real and perceived, *between* groups and ignores or overlooks differences *within* groups. The biological differences between "whites" and "blacks" and between "blacks" and "Asians" are assumed to be greater than the biological differences among "whites" and among "blacks." The opposite is actually true; the overwhelming majority of genetic diversity in humans (88–92 percent) is found within people who live on the same continent.[11] Also, keep in mind that human beings are one of the most genetically similar of all species. There is nearly six times more genetic variation among white-tailed deer in the southern United States than in all humans! Consider our closest living relative, the chimpanzee. Chimpanzees' natural habitat is confined to central Africa and parts of western Africa, yet four genetically distinct groups occupy those regions and they are far more genetically distinct than humans who live on different continents. That humans exhibit such a low level of genetic variation compared to other species reflects the fact that we are a relatively recent species; modern humans (*Homo sapiens*) first appeared in East Africa just under 200,000 years ago.[12]

Physical anthropologists today analyze human biological variation by examining specific genetic traits to understand how those traits originated and evolved over time and why some genetic traits are more common in certain populations. Since much of our biological diversity occurs mostly within (rather than between) continental regions once believed to be the homelands of distinct races, the concept of race is meaningless in any study of human biology. Franz Boas, considered the father of modern U.S. anthropology, was the first prominent anthropologist to challenge racial thinking directly during the early twentieth century. A professor of anthropology at Columbia University in New York City and a Jewish immigrant from Germany, Boas established anthropology in the United States as a four-field academic discipline consisting of archaeology, physical/biological anthropology, cultural anthropology, and linguistics. His approach challenged conventional thinking at the time that humans could be separated into biological races endowed with unique intellectual, moral, and physical abilities.

In one of his most famous studies, Boas challenged craniometrics, in which the size and shape of skulls of various groups were measured as a way of assigning relative intelligence and moral behavior. Boas noted that the size and shape of the skull were not fixed characteristics within groups and were instead influenced by the environment. Children born in the United States to parents of various immigrant groups, for example, had slightly different average skull shapes than children born and raised in the homelands of those immigrant groups. The differences reflected relative access to nutrition and other socio-economic dimensions. In his famous 1909 essay "Race Problems in America," Boas challenged the commonly held idea that immigrants to the United States from Italy, Poland, Russia, Greece, the Austro-Hungarian Empire, and other southern and eastern European nations were a threat to America's "racial purity." He pointed out that the British, Germans, and Scandinavians (popularly believed at the time to be the "true white" heritages that gave the United States its superior qualities) were not themselves "racially pure." Instead, many different tribal and cultural groups had intermixed over the centuries.[13] In fact, Boas asserted, the notion of "racial purity" was utter nonsense. As present-day anthropologist Jonathan Marks (1994) noted, "You may group humans into a small number of races if you want to, but you are denied biology as a support for it."[14]

Race as a Social Concept

Just because the idea of distinct biological human races is not a valid scientific concept does not mean, and should not be interpreted as implying, that "there is no such thing as race" or that "race isn't real." Race is indeed real but it is a concept based on arbitrary social and cultural definitions rather than biology or science. Thus, racial categories such as "white" and "black" are as real as categories of "American" and "African." Many things in the world are real but are not biological. So, while race does not reflect biological characteristics, it reflects socially constructed concepts defined subjectively by societies to reflect notions of division that are perceived to be significant. Some sociologists and anthropologists now use the term *social races* instead, seeking to emphasize their cultural and arbitrary roots.

Race is most accurately thought of as a socio-historical concept. Michael Omi and Howard Winant noted that "Racial categories and the meaning of race are given concrete expression by the specific social relations and historical context in which they are embedded."[15] In other words, racial labels ultimately reflect a society's social attitudes and cultural beliefs regarding notions of group differences. And since racial categories are culturally defined, they can vary from one society to another as well as change over time within a society. Omi and Winant referred to this as **racial formation**—"the process by which social, economic, and political forces determine the content and importance of racial categories."[16]

The process of racial formation is vividly illustrated by the idea of "whiteness" in the United States. Over the course of U.S. history, the concept of "whiteness" expanded to include various immigrant groups that once were targets of racist beliefs and discrimination. In the mid 1800s, for example, Irish Catholic immigrants faced intense hostility from America's Anglo-Protestant mainstream society, and anti-Irish politicians and journalists depicted the Irish as racially different and inferior. Newspaper cartoons frequently portrayed Irish Catholics in apelike fashion: overweight, knuckle dragging, and brutish. In the early twentieth century, Italian and Jewish immigrants were typically perceived as racially distinct from America's Anglo-Protestant "white" majority as well. They were said to belong to the inferior "Mediterranean" and "Jewish" races. Today, Irish, Italian, and Jewish Americans are fully considered "white," and many people find it hard to believe that they once were perceived otherwise. Racial categories as an aspect of culture are typically learned, internalized, and accepted without question or critical thought in a process not so different from children learning their native language as they grow up.

A primary contributor to expansion of the definition of "whiteness" in the United States was the rise of many members of those immigrant groups in social status after World War II.[17] Hundreds of suburban housing developments were constructed on the edge of the nation's major cities during the 1940s and 1950s to accommodate returning soldiers, the Serviceman's Readjustment Act of 1944 offered a series of benefits for military veterans, including free college education or technical training and cost-of-living stipends funded by the federal government for veterans pursuing higher education. In addition, veterans could obtain guaranteed low-interest loans for homes and for starting their own farms or businesses. The act was in effect from 1944 through 1956 and was *theoretically* available to all military veterans who served at least four months in uniform and were honorably discharged, but the legislation did not contain anti-discrimination provisions and most African American veterans were denied benefits because private banks refused to provide the loans and restrictive language by homeowners' associations prohibited sales of homes to nonwhites. The male children and grandchildren of European immigrant groups benefited tremendously from the act. They were able to obtain college educations, formerly available only to the affluent, at no cost, leading to professional white-collar careers, and to purchase low-cost suburban homes that increased substantially in value over time. The act has been credited, more than anything else, with creating the modern middle class of U.S. society and transforming the majority of "white" Americans from renters into homeowners.[18] As the children of Irish, Jewish, Italian, Greek, Anglo-Saxon, and Eastern

European parents grew up together in the suburbs, formed friendships, and dated and married one another, the old social boundaries that defined "whiteness" were redefined.[19]

Race is a socially constructed concept but it is not a trivial matter. On the contrary, one's race often has a dramatic impact on everyday life. In the United States, for example, people often use race—their personal understanding of race—to predict "who" a person is and "what" a person is like in terms of personality, behavior, and other qualities. Because of this tendency to characterize others and make assumptions about them, people can be uncomfortable or defensive when they mistake someone's background or cannot easily determine "what" someone is, as revealed in statements such as "You don't *look* black!" or "You *talk* like a white person. Such statements reveal fixed notions about "blackness" and "whiteness" and what members of each race will be like, reflecting their socially constructed and seemingly "common sense" understanding of the world.

Since the 1990s, scholars and anti-racism activists have discussed "white privilege" as a basic feature of race as a lived experience in the United States. Peggy McIntosh coined the term in a famous 1988 essay, "White Privilege: Unpacking the Invisible Knapsack," in which she identified more than two dozen accumulated unearned benefits and advantages associated with being a "white" person in the United States. The benefits ranged from relatively minor things, such as knowing that "flesh color" Band-Aids would match her skin, to major determinants of life experiences and opportunities, such as being assured that she would never be asked to speak on behalf of her entire race, being able to curse and get angry in public without others assuming she was acting that way because of her race, and not having to teach her children that police officers and the general public would view them as suspicious or criminal because of their race. In 2015, MTV aired a documentary on white privilege, simply titled *White People*, to raise awareness of this issue among Millennials. In the documentary, young "white" Americans from various geographic, social, and class backgrounds discussed their experiences with race.

White privilege has gained significant attention and is an important tool for understanding how race is often connected to everyday experiences and opportunities, but we must remember that no group is homogenous or monolithic. "White" persons receive varying degrees of privilege and social advantage, and other important characteristics, such as social class, gender, sexual orientation, and (dis)ability, shape individuals' overall lives and how they experience society. John Hartigan, an urban anthropologist, has written extensively about these characteristics. His *Racial Situations: Class Predicaments of Whiteness in Detroit* (1999) discusses the lives of "white" residents in three neighborhoods in Detroit, Michigan, that vary significantly socio-economically—one impoverished, one working class, and one upper middle class. Hartigan reveals that social class has played a major role in shaping strikingly different identities among these "white" residents and how, accordingly, social relations between "whites" and "blacks" in the neighborhoods vary from camaraderie and companionship to conflict.

RACE IN THREE NATIONS: THE UNITED STATES, BRAZIL, AND JAPAN

To better understand how race is constructed around the world, consider how the United States, Brazil, and Japan define racial categories. In the United States, race has traditionally been rigidly constructed, and Americans have long perceived racial categories as discrete and mutually exclusive: a person who had one "black" parent and one "white" parent was seen simply as "black." The institution of slavery played a major role in defining how the United States has classified people by race through the *one-drop rule*, which required that any trace of known or recorded non-European ("non-white") ancestry was used to automatically exclude a person from being classified as "white." Someone with one "black" grandparent and three "white" grandparents or one "black" great-grand-parent and seven "white" great-grandparents was classified under the one-drop rule simply as "black." The original purpose of the one-drop rule was to ensure that children born from sexual unions (some consensual but many forced) between slave-owner fathers and enslaved women would be born into slave status.[20]

Consider President Barack Obama. Obama is of biracial heritage; his mother was "white" of Euro-American descent and his father was a "black" man from Kenya. The media often refer to Obama simply as "black" or "African American," such as when he is referred to as the nation's "first black President," and never refer to him as "white."[21] Whiteness in the United States has long been understood and legally defined as implying "racial purity" despite the biological absurdity of the notion, and to be considered "white," one could have no known ancestors of black, American Indian, Asian, or other "non-white" backgrounds. Cultural anthropologists also refer to the one-drop rule as **hypodescent**, a term coined by anthropologist Marvin Harris in the 1960s to refer to a socially constructed racial classification system in which a person of mixed racial heritage is automatically categorized as a member of the less (or least) privileged group.[22]

Another example is birth certificates issued by U.S. hospitals, which, until relatively recently, used a precise formula to determine the appropriate racial classification for a newborn. If one parent was "white" and the other was "non-white," the child was classified as the race of the "non-white" parent; if neither parent was "white," the child was classified as the race of the father.

Not until very recently have the United States government, the media, and pop culture begun to officially acknowledge and embrace biracial and multiracial individuals. The 2000 census was the first to allow respondents to identify as more than one race. Currently, a grassroots movement that is expanding across the United States, led by organizations such as Project RACE (Reclassify All Children Equally) and Swirl, seeks to raise public awareness of biracial and multiracial people who sometimes still experience social prejudice for being of mixed race and/or resentment from peers who disapprove of their decision to identify with all of their backgrounds instead of just one. Prominent biracial and multiracial celebrities such as Tiger Woods, Alicia Keys, Mariah Carey, Beyoncé Knowles, Bruno Mars, and Dwayne "The Rock" Johnson and the election of Barack Obama have also prompted people in the United States to reconsider the problematic nature of rigid, discrete racial categories.

In 1977, the U.S. government established five official racial categories under Office of Management and Budget (OMB) Directive 15 that provided a basis for recordkeeping and compiling of statistical information to facilitate collection of demographic information by the Census Bureau and to ensure compliance with federal civil rights legislation and work-place anti-discrimination policies. Those categories and their definitions, which are still used today, are (a) "*White*: a person having origins in any of the original peoples of Europe, North Africa, or the Middle East;" (b) "*Black or African American*: a person having origins in any of the black racial groups of Africa;" (c) "*American Indian or Alaskan Native*: a person having origins in any of the original peoples of North and South America (including Central America), and who maintains tribal affiliation or community attachment;" (d) "*Asian*: a person having origins in any of the original peoples of the Far East, Southeast Asia, or the Indian subcontinent;" and (e) "*Native Hawaiian or Other Pacific Islander*: a person having origins in any of the original peoples of Hawaii, Guam, Samoa, or the Pacific Islands." In addition, OMB Directive 15 established *Hispanic or Latino* as a separate *ethnic* (not racial) category; on official documents, individuals are asked to identify their racial background and whether they are of Hispanic/Latino ethnic heritage. The official definition of Hispanic or Latino is "a person of Mexican, Puerto Rican, Cuban, South or Central American, or other Spanish culture or origin, regardless of race."

OMB Directive 15's terminology and definitions have generated considerable criticism and controversy. The complex fundamental question is whether such categories are practical and actually reflect how individuals choose to self-identify. Terms such as "non-Hispanic white" and "Black Hispanic," both a result of the directive, are baffling to many people in the United States who perceive Hispanics/Latinos as a separate group from whites and blacks. Others oppose any governmental attempt to classify people by race, on both liberal and conservative political grounds. In 1997, the American Anthropological Association unsuccessfully advocated for a cessation of federal efforts to coercively classify Americans by race, arguing instead that individuals should be given the opportunity to identify their ethnic and/or national heritages (such as their country or countries of ancestry).

Brazil's concept of race is much more fluid, flexible, and multifaceted. The differences between Brazil and the United States are particularly striking because the countries have similar histories. Both nations were born of European colonialism in the New World, established major plantation economies that relied on large numbers of African slaves, and subsequently experienced large waves of immigration from around the world (particularly Europe) following the abolition of slavery. Despite those similarities, significant contrasts in how race is perceived in these two societies persist, which is sometimes summarized in the expression "The United States has a color line, while Brazil has a color continuum."[23] In Brazil, races are typically viewed as points on a continuum in which one gradually blends into another; "white" and "black" are opposite ends of a continuum that incorporates many intermediate color-based racial labels that have no equivalent in the United States.

The Brazilian term for these categories, which correspond to the concept of race in the United States, is *tipos*, which directly translates into Portuguese as "types."[24] Rather than describing what is believed to be a person's biological or genetic ancestry, *tipos* describe slight but noticeable differences in physical appearance. Examples include *loura*, a person with a very fair complexion, straight blonde hair, and blue or green eyes; *sarará*, a light-complexioned person with tightly curled blondish or reddish hair, blue or green eyes, a wide nose, and thick lips; and *cabo verde*, an individual with dark skin, brown eyes, straight black hair, a narrow nose, and thin lips. Sociologists and anthropologists have identified more than 125 *tipos* in Brazil, and small villages of only 500 people may feature 40 or more depending on how residents describe one another. Some of the labels vary from region to region, reflecting local cultural differences.

Since Brazilians perceive race based on phenotypes or outward physical appearance rather than as an extension of geographically based biological and genetic descent, individual members of a family can be seen as different *tipos*. This may seem bewildering to those who think of race as a fixed identity inherited from one's parents even though it is generally acknowledged that family members often have different physical features, such as sisters who have strikingly different eye colors, hair colors, and/or complexions. In Brazil, those differences are frequently viewed as significant enough to assign different *tipos*. Cultural anthropologist Conrad Phillip Kottak, who conducted ethnographic fieldwork in Brazil, noted that something as minor as a suntan or sunburn could lead to a person temporarily being described as a different *tipo* until the effects of the tanning or burning wore off.[25]

Another major difference in the construction of race in the United States and Brazil is the more fluid and flexible nature of race in Brazil, which is reflected in a popular Brazilian saying: "Money whitens." As darker-complexioned individuals increase their social class status (by, for example, graduating from college and obtaining high-salaried, professional positions), they generally come to be seen as a somewhat lighter *tipo* and light-complexioned individuals who become poorer may be viewed as a slightly darker *tipo*. In the United States, social class has no bearing on one's racial designation; a non-white person who achieves upward social mobility and accrues greater education and wealth may be seen by some as more "socially desirable" because of social class but does not change racial classification.

Brazil's Institute of Geography and Statistics established five official racial categories in 1940 to facilitate collection of demographic information that are still in use today: *branco* (white), *prêto* (black), *pardo* (brown), *amarelo* (yellow), and indígena (indigenous). These racial categories are similar to the ones established in the United States under OMB Directive 15 and to Linnaeus' proposed **taxonomy** in the 18th century. *Pardo* is unique to Brazil and denotes a person of both *branco* and *prêto* heritage. Many Brazilians object to these government categories and prefer *tipos*.

The more fluid construction of race in Brazil is accompanied by generally less hostile, more benign social interactions between people of different colors and complexions, which has contributed to Brazil being seen as a "racial paradise" and a "racial democracy" rainbow nation free of the harsh prejudices and societal discrimination that has characterized other multiracial nations such as the United States and South Africa.[26] The "racial democracy" image has long been embraced by the government and elites in Brazil as a way to provide the country with a distinct identity in the international community. However, scholars in Brazil and the United States have questioned the extent to which racial equality exists in Brazil despite the appearance of interracial congeniality on the surface. Many light-complexioned Brazilians reject the idea that racial discrimination and inequalities persist and regard such claims as divisive while Afro-Brazilians have drawn attention to these inequalities in recent years.

Figure 5: A scene from the Black Women's March against Racism and Violence in Brasilia, Brazil, 2015.

Though Afro-Brazilians comprise approximately half of the country's population, they have historically accounted for less than 2 percent of all university students, and severe economic disparities between *tipos* remain prominent in Brazil to this day.[27] The majority of the country's Afro-Brazilians lives in the less-affluent northern region, site of the original sugar cane plantations while the majority of Brazilians of European descent live in the industrial and considerably wealthier southern region.[28] The *favelas* (slums) located on the edge of major cities such as Rio de Janeiro and São Paolo, which often lack electricity or running water, are inhabited largely by Afro-Brazilians, who are half as likely to have a working toilet in their homes as the overall Brazilian population.

There are significant economic differences between Brazilians according to their official racial designation. According to government statistics, *prêtos* have higher unemployment and poverty rates than other groups in Brazil and *brancos* earn 57 percent more than *prêtos* for the same occupation. Furthermore, the vast majority of Brazilians in leadership positions in politics, the military, the media, and education are *branco* or *pardo*. Inter-racial marriage occurs more frequently in Brazil than in the United States, but most of the marriages are between *prêtos* and *pardos* and not between *brancos* and either *prêtos* or *pardos*. Another significant area of concern centers on brutality and mistreatment of darker-complexioned Brazilians. As a result, some scholars of race and racism describe Brazil as a prominent example of a **pigmentocracy**: a society characterized by a strong correlation between a person's skin color and their social class.

Afro-Brazilian activism has grown substantially since the 1980s, inspired in part by the successes of the Civil Rights movement in the United States and by actions taken by the Brazilian government since the early 2000s. One of the Brazilian government's strategies has been to implement U.S.-style affirmative action policies in education and employment to increase the number of Afro-Brazilians in the nation's professional ranks and decrease the degree of economic disparity. Those efforts sparked an intense backlash among lighter-complexioned Brazilians and created a complex social and political dilemma: who, exactly, should be considered "dark/black enough" for inclusion in affirmative action, who makes that decision, and on what grounds will the decision be based? Many Brazilian families include relatives whose complexions are quite different and the country has clear racial categories only in terms of its demographic statistics. Nevertheless, Luiz Inacio Lula da Silva, Brazil's president from 2003 through 2011, made promotion of greater racial equality a prominent objective of his administration. In addition to supporting affirmative action policies, Lula appointed four Afro-Brazilians to his cabinet, appointed the first Afro-Brazilian justice to the nation's supreme court, and established a government office for promotion of racial equality. These recent developments have led many in Brazil and elsewhere to reconsider the accuracy of Brazil's designation as a racial democracy, which has been as a central component of its national identity for decades.

Scholars mostly agree that race relations are more relaxed and genteel in Brazil than in the United States. They tend to disagree about why that is the case. Some have suggested that the differences in racial constructions stem from important colonial-era distinctions that set the tone for years to come. A common expression describing the situation is: "the United States had two British parents while Brazil had a Portuguese father and an African mother." British settlers who colonized North America thoroughly subjugated their slaves, intermarriage was rare, and African cultural influences on mainstream U.S. society were marginalized compared to British cultural traditions and customs. In Brazil, on the other hand, sexual and marital unions between the Portuguese settlers, who were overwhelmingly male, and female Africans were common, creating individuals who exhibit a wide range of physical appearances. Sexual unions certainly occurred in the United States between male European slave masters and female African slaves, but the one-drop rule ensured that any children born of such unions would be classified as "black" and as slaves. In Brazil in the late nineteenth and early twentieth centuries, the government and the Roman Catholic Church strongly encouraged European descended men to marry the African and indigenous women they impregnated in order to "whiten" the nation.[29] The United States government did not advocate for interracial families and most states had anti-miscegenation laws. The United States also implemented an official, government-sanctioned system of **Jim Crow** racial segregation laws in that had no equivalent in Brazil.

Japan represents an example of a third way of constructing race that is not associated with Western society or African slavery. Japanese society is more diverse than many people realize; the number of Korean, Chinese, Indian, and Brazilian immigrants began to increase in the 1980s, and the number of children who had one Japanese and one non-Japanese parent has increased substantially since the 1950s, driven in part by children fathered by American military men stationed in Japan. Yet, one segment of Japan's population known as the *burakumin* (formerly called the *eta*, a word meaning "pure

Figure 6: Jiichirō Matsumoto, a leader of the Buraku Liberation League.

filth") vividly illustrates the arbitrary nature of racial categories. Though physically and genetically indistinguishable from other Japanese people, the burakumin are a socially stigmatized and outcast group. They are descendants of people who worked dirty, low-prestige jobs that involved handling dead and slaughtered animals during the feudal era of Japan in the 1600s, 1700s, and 1800s. In feudal times, they were forced to live in communities separated from the rest of society, had to wear a patch of leather on their clothing to symbolize their burakumin status, and were not permitted to marry non-burakumins.[30]

Japan no longer legally prohibits marriage between burakumin and non-burakumin (today, approximately 75 percent of burakumins are married to non-burakumins), but prejudices and discrimination persist, particularly among older generations, and the marriages remain socially stigmatized. Employment for the burakumin remains concentrated in low-paying occupations involving physical labor despite the relative affluence and advanced education in Japanese society overall. Burakumin earn only about 60 percent of the national average household income.[31] Stereotypes of the burakumin as unintelligent, lazy, and violent still exist, but burakumin men account for a significant portion of Japan's professional athletes in popular sports such as baseball and sumo wrestling, an interesting pattern that reflects events in the United States, where racially stigmatized groups have long found relatively abundant opportunities for upward mobility in professional sports.

ETHNICITY AND ETHNIC GROUPS

The terms race and ethnicity are similar and there is a degree of overlap between them. The average person frequently uses the terms "race" and "ethnicity" interchangeably as synonyms and anthropologists also recognize that race and ethnicity are overlapping concepts. Both race and ethnic identity draw on an identification with others based on common ancestry and shared cultural traits.[32] As discussed earlier, a *race* is a social construction that defines groups of humans based on arbitrary physical and/or biological traits that are believed to distinguish them from other humans. An **ethnic group**, on the other hand, claims a distinct identity based on cultural characteristics and a shared ancestry that are believed to give its members a unique sense of peoplehood or heritage.

The cultural characteristics used to define ethnic groups vary; they include specific languages spoken, religions practiced, and distinct patterns of dress, diet, customs, holidays, and other markers of distinction. In some societies, ethnic groups are geographically concentrated in particular regions, as with the Kurds in Turkey and Iraq and the Basques in northern Spain.

Ethnicity refers to the degree to which a person identifies with and feels an attachment to a particular ethnic group. As a component of a person's identity, ethnicity is a fluid, complex phenomenon that is highly variable. Many individuals view their ethnicity as an important element of their personal and social identity. Numerous psychological, social, and familial factors play a role in ethnicity, and ethnic identity is most accurately understood as a range or continuum populated by people at every point. One's sense of ethnicity can also fluctuate across time. Children of Korean immigrants living in an overwhelmingly white town, for example, may choose to self-identify simply as "American" during their middle school and high school years to fit in with their classmates and then choose to self-identify as "Korean," "Korean American," or "Asian American" in college or later in life as their social settings change or from a desire to connect more strongly with their family history and heritage. Do you consider your ethnicity an important part of your identity? Why do you feel the way you do?

In the United States, ethnic identity can sometimes be primarily or purely symbolic in nature. Sociologists and anthropologists use the term **symbolic ethnicity** to describe limited or occasional displays of ethnic pride and identity that are primarily *expressive*—for public display—rather than *instrumental* as a major component of their daily social lives. Symbolic ethnicity is pervasive in U.S. society; consider customs such as "Kiss Me, I'm Irish!" buttons and bumper stickers, Puerto Rican flag necklaces, decals of the Virgin of Guadalupe, replicas of the Aztec stone calendar, and tattoos of Celtic crosses or of the map of Italy in green, white, and red stripes. When I was a teenager in the early to mid-1990s, medallions shaped like the African continent became popular among young African Americans after the release of Spike Lee's film *Malcolm X* in 1992 and in response to clothing worn by socially conscious rappers and rap groups of the era, such as Public Enemy. During that same time, I surprised workers in a pizzeria in suburban Philadelphia when I asked them, in Spanish, what part of Mexico they came from. They wanted to know how I knew they were Mexican as they said they usually were presumed to be Italian or Puerto Rican. I replied, "The Virgin of Guadalupe gave it away!" while pointing to the miniature figurine of the iconic national symbol of Mexico on the counter near the register.

In the United States, ethnic identity can sometimes be largely symbolic particularly for descendants of the various European immigrant groups who settled in the United States during the nineteenth and early twentieth centuries. Regardless of whether their grandparents and great-grandparents migrated from Italy, Ireland, Germany, Poland, Russia, the Austro-Hungarian Empire, Greece, Scandinavia, or elsewhere, these third and fourth generation Americans likely do not speak their ancestors' languages and have lost most or all of the cultural customs and traditions their ancestors brought to the United States. A

Figure 7: Many people in the United States cherish their ethnic identities and cultural traditions. This Hindu altar is from a home in San Diego, California.

few traditions, such as favorite family recipes or distinct customs associated with the celebration of a holiday, that originated in their homelands may be retained by family members across generations, reinforcing a sense of ethnic heritage and identity today. More recent immigrants are likely to retain more of the language and cultural traditions of their countries of origin. Non-European immigrants groups from Asia, Africa, the Middle East, Latin America, and the Caribbean also experience significant linguistic and cultural losses over generations, but may also continue to self-identify with their ethnic backgrounds if they do not feel fully incorporated into U.S. society because they "stick out" physically from Euro-American society and experience prejudice and discrimination. Psychological, sociological, and anthropological studies have indicated that retaining a strong sense of ethnic pride and identification is common among ethnic minorities in the United States and other nations as a means of coping with and overcoming societal bigotry.

While there have been periods of inter-ethnic tension between various European immigrant and ethnic groups in the United States, such as English-German and Irish-Italian conflicts, the descendants of these groups today have been assimilated, to a very large degree, into the general racial category of "white."

Ethnic groups and ethnicity, like race, are socially constructed identities created at particular moments in history under particular social conditions. The earliest views of ethnicity assumed that people had innate, unchanging ethnic identities and loyalties. In actuality, ethnic identities shift and are recreated over time and across societies. Anthropologists call this process **ethnogenesis**— gradual emergence of a new, distinct ethnic identity in response to changing social circumstances. For example, people whose ancestors came from what we know as Ireland may identify themselves as Irish Americans and generations of their ancestors as Irish, but at one time, people living in that part of the world identified themselves as Celtic.

In the United States, ethnogenesis has led to a number of new ethnic identities, including African American, Native American, American Indian, and Italian American. Slaves brought to America in the colonial period came primarily from Central and Western Africa and represented dozens of ethnic heritages, including Yoruba, Igbo, Akan, and Chamba, that had unique languages, religions, and cultures that were quickly lost because slaves were not permitted to speak their own languages or practice their customs and religions. Over time, a new unified identity emerged among their descendants. But that identity continues to evolve, as reflected by the transitions in the label used to identify it: from "colored" (early 1900s) to "Negro" (1930s–1960s) to "Black" (late 1960s to the present) and "African American" (1980s to the present).

A MELTING POT OR A SALAD BOWL?

There is tremendous ethnic, linguistic, and cultural diversity throughout the United States, largely resulting from a long history and ongoing identification as a "nation of immigrants" that attracted millions of newcomers from every continent. Still, elected officials and residents ardently disagree about how the United States should approach this diversity and incorporate immigrant, ethnic, and cultural minority groups into the larger framework of American society. The fundamental question is whether cultural minority groups should be encouraged to forego their ethnic and cultural identities and **acculturate** to the values, traditions, and customs of mainstream culture or should be allowed and encouraged to retain key elements of their identities and heritages. This is a highly emotional question. Matters of cultural identity are often deeply personal and associated with strongly held beliefs about the defining features of their countries' national identities. Over the past 400 years, three distinct social philosophies have developed from efforts to promote national unity and tranquility in societies that have experienced large-scale immigration: assimilation, multiculturalism, and amalgamation.

Assimilation encourages and may even demand that members of ethnic and immigrant minority groups abandon their native customs, traditions, languages, and identities as quickly as possible and adopt those of mainstream society—"When in Rome, do as the Romans do." Advocates of assimilation generally view a strong sense of national unity based on a shared linguistic and cultural heritage as the best way to promote a strong national identity and avoid ethnic conflict. They point, for example, to ethnic warfare and genocide in Rwanda and the former Yugoslavia during the 1990s and to recent independence movements by French Canadians in Quebec and in Scotland as evidence of negative consequences of groups retaining a strong sense of loyalty and identification with their ethnic or linguistic communities. The "English as the Official Language" movement in the United States is another example. People are concerned that U.S. unity is weakened by immigrants who do not learn to speak English. In recent years, the U.S. Census Bureau has identified more than 300 languages spoken in the United States. In 2010, more than 60 million people representing 21 percent of the total U.S. population spoke a language other than English at home and 38 million of those people spoke Spanish.

Multiculturalism takes a different view of assimilation, arguing that ethnic and cultural diversity is a positive quality that enriches a society and encouraging respect for cultural differences. The basic belief behind multiculturalism is that group differences, in and of themselves, do not spark tension, and society should promote tolerance for differences rather than urging members of immigrant, ethnic, and cultural minority groups to shed their customs and identities. Vivid examples of multiculturalism can be seen in major cities across the United States, such as New York, where ethnic neighborhoods such as Chinatown and Little Italy border one another, and Los Angeles, which features many diverse neighborhoods, including Little Tokyo, Koreatown, Filipinotown, Little Armenia, and Little Ethiopia. The ultimate objective of multiculturalism is to promote peaceful coexistence while allowing each ethnic community to preserve its unique heritage and identity. Multiculturalism is the official governmental policy of Canada; it was codified in 1988 under the Canadian Multiculturalism Act, which declares that "multiculturalism reflects the cultural and racial diversity of Canadian society and acknowledges the freedom of all members of Canadian society to preserve, enhance, and share their cultural heritage."[33]

Amalgamation promotes hybridization of diverse cultural groups in a multiethnic society. Members of distinct ethnic and cultural groups freely intermingle, interact, and live among one another with cultural exchanges and, ultimately, inter-ethnic dating and intermarriage occurring as the social and cultural barriers between groups fade over time. Amalgamation is similar to assimilation in that a strong, unified national culture is viewed as the desired end result but differs because it represents a more thorough "melting pot" that blends the various groups in a society (the dominant/mainstream group and minority groups) into a new hybridized cultural identity rather than expecting minority groups to conform to the majority's standards.

Debate is ongoing among sociologists, anthropologists, historians, and political pundits regarding the relative merits of each approach and which, if any, most accurately describes the United States. It is a complex and often contentious question because people may confuse their personal ideologies (what they think the United States should strive for) with social reality (what actually occurs). Furthermore, the United States is a large, complex country geographically that is comprised of large urban centers with millions of residents, moderately populated areas characterized by small towns, and mostly rural communities with only several hundred or a few thousand inhabitants. The nature of social and cultural life varies significantly with the setting in which it occurs.

ANTHROPOLOGY MEETS POPULAR CULTURE: SPORTS, RACE/ETHNICITY AND DIVERSITY

Throughout this chapter, I have stated that the concept of race is a socially constructed idea and explained why biologically distinct human races do not exist. Still, many in the United States cling to a belief in the existence of biological racial groups (regardless of their racial and ethnic backgrounds). Historically, the nature of popular sports in the United States has been offered as "proof" of biological differences between races in terms of natural athletic skills and abilities. In this regard, the world of sports has served as an important social institution in which notions of biological racial differences become reified—mistakenly assumed as objective, real, and factual. Specifically, many Americans have noted the large numbers of African Americans in Olympic sprinting, the National Football League (NFL), and the National Basketball Association (NBA) and interpreted their disproportionate number as perceived "evidence" or "proof" that "blacks" have unique genes, muscles, bone structures, and/or other biological qualities that make them superior athletes relative to people from other racial backgrounds—that they are "naturally gifted" runners and jumpers and thus predominate in sports.

This topic sparked intense media attention in 2012 during the lead-up to that year's Olympics in London. Michael Johnson, a retired African American track star who won gold medals at the 1992, 1996, and 2000 Summer Olympic Games, declared that "black" Americans and West Indians (of Jamaican, Trinidadian, Barbadian, and other Caribbean descent) dominated international sprinting competitions because they possessed a "superior athletic gene" that resulted from slavery: "All my life, I believed I became an athlete through my own determination, but it's impossible to think that being descended from slaves hasn't left an imprint through the generations . . . slavery has benefitted descendants like me. I believe there is a superior athletic gene in us."[34] Others have previously expressed similar ideas, such as writer John Entine, who suggested in his book, *Taboo: Why Black Athletes Dominate Sports and Why We're Afraid to Talk About It* (2000), that the brutal nature of the trans-Atlantic slave trade and harsh conditions of slavery in the Americas produced slaves who could move faster and who had stronger, more durable bodies than the general population and that those supposedly hardier bodies persisted in today's African Americans and Afro-Caribbeans, giving them important athletic advantages over others. In a similar vein, former CBS sportscaster Jimmy "The Greek" Snyder claimed, on the eve of Super Bowl XXII in 1988, that African Americans comprised the majority of NFL players because they were "bred that way" during slavery as a form of selective breeding between bigger and stronger slaves much like had been done with racehorses. Snyder was fired from CBS shortly after amid a tidal wave of controversy and furor. Racial stereotypes regarding perceptions of innate differences in athletic ability were a major theme in the 1992 comedy film *White Men Can't Jump*, which starred Wesley Snipes and Woody Harrelson as an inter-racial pair of basketball street hustlers.

Despite such beliefs, even among people who otherwise do not harbor racist sentiments, the notion of innate "black" athletic supremacy is obviously misguided, fallacious, and self-contradictory when we examine the demographic composition of the full range of sports in the United States rather than focusing solely on a few extremely popular sports that pay high salaries and have long served as inspiration for upward mobility and fame in a society in which educational and employment opportunities for lower-income and impoverished minority groups (often concentrated in inner-city communities) have rarely been equivalent to those of middle-class and affluent "whites" living in small towns and suburban communities. Take the myth that "blacks" have an innately superior jumping ability. The idea that "white men can't jump" stems from the relatively small number of white American players in the NBA and has been reified by the fact that only one "white" player (Brent Barry of the Los Angeles Clippers in 1996) has ever won the NBA's annual slam-dunk contest. However, the stereotype would be completely inverted if we look at the demographic composition and results of high jump competitions. The high jump is arguably a better gauge of leaping ability than a slam-dunk contest since it requires raising the entire body over a horizontal bar and prohibits extension of the arms overhead, thus diminishing any potential advantage from height. For decades, both the men's and the women's international high jump competitions have been dominated by white athletes from the United States and Europe. Yet no one attributes their success to "white racial genes." American society does not have a generational history of viewing people who are socially identified as "white" in terms of body type and physical prowess as it does with African Americans.

The same dynamic is at play if we compare basketball with volleyball. Both sports require similar sets of skills, namely, jumping, speed, agility, endurance, and outstanding hand-eye coordination. Nevertheless, beach volleyball has tended to be dominated by "white" athletes from the United States, Canada, Australia, and Europe while indoor volleyball is more "racially balanced" (if we assume that biological human races actually exist) since the powerhouse indoor volleyball nations are the United States, China, Japan, Brazil, Cuba, and Russia.

Thus, a variety of factors, including cultural affinities and preferences, social access and opportunities, existence of a societal infrastructure that supports youth participation and development in particular sports, and the degree of prestige assigned to various sports by nations, cultures, and ethnic communities, all play significant roles in influencing the concentration of social and/or ethnic groups in particular sports. It is not a matter of individual or group skills or talents; important socio-economic dimensions shape who participates in a sport and who excels. Think about a sport in which you have participated or have followed closely. What social dynamics do you associate with that sport in terms of the gender, race/ethnicity, and social class of the athletes who predominate in it?

For additional insight into the important role that social dynamics play in shaping the racial/ethnic, social class, and cultural dimensions of athletes, let us briefly consider three sports: basketball, boxing, and football. While basketball is a national sport played throughout the United States, it also has long been associated with urban/inner-city environments, and many professional American basketball players have come from working class and lower-income backgrounds. This trend dates to the 1930s, when Jewish players and teams dominated professional basketball in the United States. That dominance was commonly explained by the media in terms of the alleged "scheming," "flashiness," and "artful dodging" nature of the "Jewish culture." In other words, Jews were believed to have a fundamental talent for hoops that explained their over-representation in the sport. In reality, most Jewish immigrants in the early twentieth century lived in working class, urban neighborhoods such as New York City, Philadelphia, and Chicago where basketball was a popular sport in the local social fabric of working-class communities.[35]

By 1992, approximately 90 percent of NBA players were African American, and the league's demographics once again fueled rumors that a racial/ethnic group was "naturally gifted" in basketball. However, within ten short years, foreign-born players largely from Eastern European nations such as Lithuania, Germany, Poland, Latvia, Serbia, Croatia, Russia, Ukraine, and Turkey accounted for nearly 20 percent of the starting line-ups of NBA teams. The first player selected in the 2002 NBA draft was seven-foot six-inch center Yao Ming, a native of Shanghai, China, and by the early 2000s, the United States had lost some of its traditional dominance of international basketball as several nations began to catch up because of the tremendous globalization of basketball's popularity.

Like basketball, boxing has been an urban sport popular among working-class ethnic groups. During the early twentieth century, both amateur and professional boxing in the United States were dominated by European immigrant groups, particularly the Irish, Italians, and Jewish Americans. As with basketball, which inspired the "hoop dreams" of inner-city youths to escape poverty by reaching the professional ranks, boxing provided sons of lower-income European immigrants with dreams of upward mobility, fame, and fortune. In fact, it was one of the few American sports that thrived during the Great Depression, attracting a wave of impoverished young people who saw pugilism as a ticket to financial security. Throughout the first half of the twentieth century, intra-European ethnic rivalries (Irish vs. Italian, Italian vs. Jewish) were common in U.S. boxing; fighters were seen as quasi-ambassadors of their respective neighborhoods and ethnic communities.

The demographic composition of boxers began to change in the latter half of the twentieth century when formerly stigmatized and racialized Eastern European immigrant groups began to be perceived simply as "white" and mainstream. They attained middle-class status and relocated to the newly established suburbs, and boxing underwent a profound racial and ethnic transition. New urban minority groups—African Americans, Puerto Ricans, and Mexican Americans who moved into inner-city neighborhoods vacated by Europeans began to dominate boxing.

Finally, consider football, which has surpassed baseball as the most popular spectator sport in the United States and is popular with all social classes, races/ethnicities, and regions. Collegiate and professional football rosters are also undergoing a demographic change; a growing number of current National College Athletic Association and NFL players were born outside the mainland United States. Since the 1980s, many athletes from American Samoa, a U.S. territory in the South Pacific, have joined U.S. football teams. A boy in American Samoa is an astounding 56 times more likely to make the NFL than a boy born and raised on the U.S. mainland![36] American Samoa's rapid transformation into a gridiron powerhouse is the result of several inter-related factors that dramatically increased the appeal of the sport across the tiny island, including the cultural influence of American missionaries who introduced football. Expanding migration of Samoans to Hawaii and California in recent decades has also fostered their interest in football, which has trickled back to the South Pacific, and the NFL is working to expand the popularity of football in American Samoa.[37] Similarly, Major League Baseball has been promoting baseball in the Dominican Republic, Korea, and Japan in recent years.

CONCLUSION

Issues of race, racism, and ethnic relations remain among the most contentious social and political topics in the United States and throughout the world. Anthropology offers valuable information to the public regarding these issues, as anthropological knowledge encourages individuals to "think outside the box" about race and ethnicity. This "thinking outside the box" includes understanding that racial and ethnic categories are socially constructed rather than natural, biological divisions of humankind and realizing that the current racial and ethnic categories that exist in the United States today do not necessarily reflect categories used in other countries. Physical anthropologists, who study human evolution, epidemiology, and genetics, are uniquely qualified to explain why distinct biological human races do not exist. Nevertheless, race and ethnicity—as social constructs—continue to be used as criteria for prejudice, discrimination, exclusion, and stereotypes well into the twenty-first century. Cultural anthropologists play a crucial role in informing the public how the concept of race originated, how racial categories have shifted over time, how race and ethnicity are constructed differently within various nations across the world, and how the current racial and ethnic categories utilized in the United States were arbitrarily labeled and defined by the federal government under OMB Directive 15 in 1977. Understanding the complex nature of clines and continuous biological human variation, along with an awareness of the distinct ways in which race and ethnicity have been constructed in different nations, enables us to recognize racial and ethnic labels not as self-evident biological divisions of humans, but instead as socially created categories that vary cross-culturally.

DISCUSSION QUESTIONS

1. García describes the reasons that race is considered a "discredited concept in human biology." Despite this scientific fact, most people continue to believe that race is "real." Why do you think race has continued to be an important social reality even after it has been discredited scientifically?
2. The process of racial formation is different in every society. In the United States, the "one-drop rule" and hypodescent have historically affected the way people with multiracial backgrounds have been racialized. How have ideas about multiracial identity been changing in the past few decades? As the number of people who identify as "multiracial" increases, do you think there will be changes in the way we think about other racial categories?
3. Members of some ethnic groups are able to practice symbolic ethnicity, limited or occasional displays of ethnic pride and identity. Why can ethnicity be displayed in an optional way while race cannot?
4. There is no scientific evidence supporting the idea that racial or ethnic background provides a biological advantage in sports. Instead, a variety of social dynamics, including cultural affinities and preferences as well as access and opportunities influence who will become involved in particular sports. Think about a sport in which you have participated or have followed closely. What social dynamics do you think are most responsible for affecting the racial, ethnic, gender, or social class composition of the athletes who participate?

GLOSSARY

Acculturation: loss of a minority group's cultural distinctiveness in relation to the dominant culture.

Amalgamation: interactions between members of distinct ethnic and cultural groups that reduce barriers between the groups over time.

Assimilation: pressure placed on minority groups to adopt the customs and traditions of the dominant culture.

Cline: differences in the traits that occur in populations across a geographical area. In a cline, a trait may be more common in one geographical area than another, but the variation is gradual and continuous, with no sharp breaks.

Ethnic group: people in a society who claim a distinct identity for themselves based on shared cultural characteristics and ancestry.

Ethnicity: the degree to which a person identifies with and feels an attachment to a particular ethnic group.

Ethnogenesis: gradual emergence of new ethnicities in response to changing social circumstances.

Hypodescent: a racial classification system that assigns a person with mixed racial heritage to the racial category that is considered least privileged.

Jim Crow: a term used to describe laws passed by state and local governments in the United States during the early twentieth century to enforce racial segregation of public and private places.

Multiculturalism: maintenance of multiple cultural traditions in a single society.

Nonconcordant: genetic traits that are inherited independently rather than as a package.

One-drop rule: the practice of excluding a person with any non-white ancestry from the white racial category.

Pigmentocracy: a society characterized by strong correlation between a person's skin color and his or her social class.

Race: an attempt to categorize humans based on observed physical differences.

Racial formation: the process of defining and redefining racial categories in a society.

Reified: the process by which an inaccurate concept or idea is accepted as "truth."

Socially constructed: a concept developed by society that is maintained over time through social interactions that make the idea seem "real."

Symbolic ethnicity: limited or occasional displays of ethnic pride and identity that are primarily for public display.

Taxonomy: a system of classification.

ABOUT THE AUTHOR

I am an Assistant Professor of Anthropology at Millersville University of Pennsylvania, a public state-owned university located approximately 70 miles west of Philadelphia. I earned my Ph.D. in Anthropology from Temple University in 2011, with a specific focus in urban anthropology. I currently live in Chester County, Pennsylvania in suburban Philadelphia. My research interests include U.S. immigration, social constructs of race and ethnicity, urban social/cultural life, U.S. popular culture, human evolution/the hominid lineage, and anthropological theory. Aside from anthropology, my hobbies include lifting weights, watching sports (particularly boxing, football, and basketball) and movies, traveling, and playing video games (the Grand Theft Auto series is my personal favorite).

BIBLIOGRAPHY

Boas, Franz. "Race Problems in America." *Science* 29 no. 752 (1909): 839–849.
Brace, C. Loring. *'Race' is a Four-Letter Word: The Genesis of the Concept*. New York: Oxford University Press, 2005.

Entine, John. *Taboo: Why Black Athletes Dominate Sports and Why We're Afraid to Talk About It.* New York: Public Affairs Publishing, 2000.

Hartigan, John. *Racial Situations: Class Predicaments of Whiteness in Detroit.* Princeton, NJ: Princeton University Press, 1999.

Jablonski, Nina. *Living Color: The Biological and Social Meaning of Skin Color.* Berkeley, CA: University of California Press, 2012.

Marks, Jonathan. "Black, White, Other." *Natural History* December, 1994: 32–35.

McIntosh, Peggy. "White Privilege and Male Privilege: A Personal Account of Coming to See Correspondences through Work in Women's Studies." Working Paper 189. Wellesley, MA: Wellesley College Center for Research on Women, 1988.

Omi, Michael and Howard Winant. *Racial Formation in the United States.* New York: Routledge, 2014[1986].

Relethford, John H. *Reflections Of Our Past: How Human History Is Revealed In Our Genes.* Boulder, CO: Westview Press, 2004.

NOTES

1. For more information about efforts to establish a "scientific" basis for race in the 18th and 19th centuries, see the "History" section of the *Race: Are We So Different* website: http://www.understandingrace.org. Stephen Jay Gould's book, *The Mismeasure of Man* (New York: W.W. Norton, 1996), has a detailed discussion of the "scientific" methods used by Morton and others.

2. More information about the social construction of racial categories in the United States can be found in Audrey Smedley, *Race in North America: Origin and Evolution of a Worldview* (Boulder, CO: Westview Press, 2007) and Nell Irvin Painter, *The History of White People* (New York: W.W. Norton, 2010).

3. More discussion of the material in this section can be found in Carol Mukhopadhyay, Rosemary Henze, and Yolanda Moses, *How Real Is Race? A Sourcebook on Race, Culture, and Biology* (Lanham, MD: Rowman & Littlefield, 2013). Chapters 5 and 6 discuss the cultural construction of racial categories as a form of classification. The *Race: Are We So Different* website and its companion resources for teachers and researchers also explore the ideas described here.

4. Johann Friedrich Blumenbach, *On the Natural Varieties of Mankind: De Generis Humani Varietate Nativa* (New York: Bergman Publishers, 1775).

5. For details about how these categories were established, see Stephen Jay Gould, *The Mismeasure of Man.*

6. For a discussion of the efforts to subdivide racial groups in the nineteenth century and its connection to eugenics, see Carol Mukhopadhyay, Rosemary Henze, and Yolanda Moses, *How Real Is Race? A Sourcebook on Race, Culture, and Biology.*

7. For more information about the genetic variation between human groups that puts this example in context see Sheldon Krimsky and Kathleen Sloan, *Race and the Genetic Revolution: Science, Myth, and Culture* (New York: Columbia University Press, 2011), 174-180.

8. Carol Mukhopadhyay et. al *How Real Is Race? A Sourcebook on Race, Culture, and Biology*, 43-48.

9. Ibid., 50-52.

10. Ibid., 50-51.

11. Ibid., 62.

12. Alan R. Templeton, "Human Races: A Genetic and Evolutionary Perspective" *American Anthropologist* 100 no. 3 (1998): 632-650.

13. For more information about the efforts of Franz Boas to refute the race concept in science, see Franz Boas, "Changes in the Bodily Form of Descendants of Immigrants" *American Anthropologist* 14 (1912): 530-562.

14. Jonathan Marks, "Black, White, Other," 35.

15. Michael Omi and Howard Winant, *Racial Formation in the United States*, 64.

16. Ibid., 61

17. For more information about the social construction of whiteness in U.S. History see Nell Irvin Painter, *The History of White People*; Noel Ignatiev, *How the Irish Became White* (New York: Routledge, 1995). For more information about the economic aspects of the construction of whiteness both before and after World War II, see David Roediger, *The Wages of Whiteness: Race and the Making of the American Working Class* (Chicago, IL: Haymarket, 2007) and George Lipsitz, *The Possessive Investment in Whiteness* (Philadelphia: Temple University Press, 1998).

18. For a detailed discussion of this process see Douglas S. Massey and Nancy Denton, *American Apartheid: Segregation and the Making of the Underclass* (Cambridge, MA: Harvard University Press, 1993) and Ira Katznelson, *When Affirmative Action was White: An Untold History of Racial Inequality in Twentieth Century America* (New York: W.W. Norton and Company, 2005).

19. For more information on these historical developments and their social ramifications, see Karen Brodkin, *How Jews Became White Folks and What That Says About Race in America* (New Brunswick, NJ: Rutgers University Press, 1998) or David

Roediger, *Working Toward Whiteness: How America's Immigrants Became White—The Strange Journey From Ellis Island to the Suburbs* (New York: Basic Books, 2005).

20. While the one-drop rule was intended to protect the institution of slavery, a more nuanced view of racial identity has existed throughout U.S. History. For a history of the racial categories used historically in the United States census, including several mixed-race categories, see the Pew Research Center's "What Census Calls Us: Historical Timeline." http://www.pew-socialtrends.org/interactives/multiracial-timeline/

21. It is important to note that President Obama has also stated that he self-identifies as black. See for instance, Sam Roberts and Peter Baker. 2010. "Asked to Declare His Race, Obama Checks 'Black.'" *The New York Times*, April 2. http://www.ny-times.com/2010/04/03/us/politics/03census.html

22. This concept is discussed in more detail in chapter 9 of Carol Mukhopadhyay et. al *How Real Is Race: A Sourebook on Race, Culture, and Biology*.

23. Edward Telles originated this expression in his book *Race in Another America: The Significance of Skin Color in Brazil* (Princeton, NJ: Princeton University Press, 2004).

24. More information about the Brazilian concepts of race described in this section is available in Jefferson M. Fish, "Mixed Blood: An Analytical Method of Classifying Race." *Psychology Today*, November 1, 1995. https://www.psychologytoday.com/articles/199511/mixed-blood

25. Conrad Kottak, *Anthropology: Appreciating Cultural Diversity* (New York: McGraw-Hill, 2013).

26. See for instance the PBS documentary *Brazil: A Racial Paradise*, written and presented by Henry Louis Gates, Jr.. For a detailed critique of the idea of Brazil as a "racial democracy," see Michael Hanchard (ed), *Racial Politics in Contemporary Brazil* (Durham, NC: Duke University Press, 1999).

27. Robert J. Cottrol, *The Long Lingering Shadow: Slavery, Race, and Law in the American Hemisphere* (Athens, GA: University of Georgia Press, 2013), 246.

28. Ibid., 145

29. For more information about Brazil's official policy toward mixed-race children during this era see Thomas E. Skidmore, *Black Into White: Race and Nationality in Brazilian Thought* (Durham, NC: Duke University Press, 1992).

30. For a detailed discussion of stratification without race, see chapter 8 of Carol Mukhopadyay et. al *How Real is Race? A Sourcebook on Race, Culture, and Biology*.

31. For more information about the status of Burakumin in Japan see Emily A. Su-lan Reber, "Buraku Mondai in Japan: Historical and Modern Perspectives and Directions for the Future." *Harvard Human Rights Journal* 12 (1999): 298

32. The distinction between race and ethnicity is a complex and controversial one within anthropology. Some anthropologists combine these concepts in acknowledgement of the overlap between them. See for instance Karen Brodkin. *How Jews Became White and What This Says About Race in America*.

33. Canadian Multicultural Act, 1985. http://laws-lois.justice.gc.ca/eng/acts/C-18.7/FullText.html

34. Rene Lynch, "Michael Johnson Says Slave Descendants Make Better Athletes" *Los Angeles Times*, July 5, 2012.

35. The 2010 documentary *The First Basket* by David Vyorst describes the experiences of Jewish basketball players in the mid-twentieth century U.S.

36. Scott Pelley, America Samoa: Football Island. *CBS News*, September 17, 2010 http://www.cbsnews.com/news/american-samoa-football-island-17-09-2010/

37. Ibid.

GENDER AND SEXUALITY

Carol C. Mukhopadhyay, San Jose State University
carol.mukhopadhyay@sjsu.edu
http://www.sjsu.edu/people/carol.mukhopadhyay

Tami Blumenfield, Furman University
tami.blumenfield@furman.edu
http://www.furman.edu/academics/asianstudies/meet-our-faculty/Pages/Tami-Blumenfield.aspx
https://twitter.com/TBlumenfield

with Susan Harper, Texas Woman's University
susanharperteaches@gmail.com

and

with Abby Gondek
abbygondek@outlook.com
http://fiu.academia.edu/AbbyGondek
https://www.facebook.com/abby.gondek

LEARNING OBJECTIVES

- Identify ways in which culture shapes sex/gender and sexuality.

- Describe ways in which gender and sexuality organize and structure the societies in which we live.

- Assess the range of possible ways of constructing gender and sexuality by sharing examples from different cultures, including small-scale societies.

- Analyze how anthropology as a discipline is affected by gender ideology and gender norms.

- Evaluate cultural "origin" stories that are not supported by anthropological data.

INTRODUCTION: SEX AND GENDER ACCORDING TO ANTHROPOLOGISTS[1]

Anthropologists are fond of pointing out that much of what we take for granted as "natural" in our lives is actually cultural—it is not grounded in the natural world or in biology but invented by humans.[2] Because culture is invented, it takes different forms in different places and changes over time in those places. Living in the twenty-first century, we have witnessed how rapidly and dramatically culture can change, from ways of communicating to the emergence of same-sex marriage. Similarly, many of us live in culturally diverse settings and experience how varied human cultural inventions can be.

We readily accept that clothing, language, and music are cultural—invented, created, and alterable—but often find it difficult to accept that gender and sexuality are not natural but deeply embedded in and shaped by culture. We struggle with the idea that the division of humans into two and only two categories, "male" and "female," is not universal, that "male" and "female" are cultural concepts that take different forms and have different meanings cross-culturally. Similarly, human sexuality, rather than being simply natural is one of the most culturally significant, shaped, regulated, and symbolic of all human capacities. The concept of humans as either "heterosexual" or "homosexual" is a culturally and historically specific invention that is increasingly being challenged in the United States and elsewhere.

Part of the problem is that gender has a biological component, unlike other types of cultural inventions such as a sewing machine, cell phone, or poem. We do have bodies and there are some male-female differences, including in reproductive capacities and roles, albeit far fewer than we have been taught. Similarly, sexuality, sexual desires and responses, are partially rooted in human natural capacities. However, in many ways, sexuality and gender are like food. We have a biologically rooted need to eat to survive and we have the capacity to enjoy eating. What constitutes "food," what is "delicious" or "repulsive," the contexts and meanings that surround food and human eating—those are cultural. Many potentially edible items are not "food" (rats, bumblebees, and cats in the United States, for example), and the concept of "food" itself is embedded in elaborate conventions about eating: how, when, with whom, where, "utensils," for what purposes? A "romantic dinner" at a "gourmet restaurant" is a complex cultural invention.

In short, gender and sexuality, like eating, have biological components. But cultures, over time, have erected complex and elaborate edifices around them, creating systems of meaning that often barely resemble what is natural and innate. We experience gender and sexuality largely through the prism of the culture or cultures to which we have been exposed and in which we have been raised.

In this chapter, we are asking you to reflect deeply on the ways in which what we have been taught to think of as natural, that is, our sex, gender, and our sexuality, is, in fact, deeply embedded in and shaped by our culture. We challenge you to explore exactly which, if any, aspects of our gender and our sexuality are totally natural.

One powerful aspect of culture, and a reason cultural norms feel so natural, is that we learn culture the way we learn our native language: without formal instruction, in social contexts, picking it up from others around us, without thinking. Soon, it becomes deeply embedded in our brains. We no longer think consciously about what the sounds we hear when someone says "hello" mean unless we do not speak English. Nor is it difficult to "tell the time" on a "clock" even though "time" and "clocks" are complex cultural inventions.

The same principles apply to gender and sexuality. We learn very early (by at least age three) about the categories of gender in our culture—that individuals are either "male" or "female" and that elaborate beliefs, behaviors, and meanings are associated with each gender. We can think of this complex set of ideas as a **gender ideology** or a **cultural model of gender.** All societies have gender ideologies, just as they have belief systems about other significant areas of life, such as health and disease, the natural world, and social relationships, including family. For an activity related to this section, see Activity 1.

FOUNDATIONS OF THE ANTHROPOLOGY OF GENDER

Gender Ideologies, Biology, and Culture

Gender vs. Sex

Words can reveal cultural beliefs. A good example is the term "sex." In the past, sex referred both to sexuality and to someone's biologic sex: male or female. Today, although sex still refers to sexuality, "gender" now means the categories male, female, or increasingly, other gender possibilities. Why has this occurred?

The change in terminology reflects profound alterations in gender ideology in the United States (and elsewhere). In the past, influenced by Judeo-Christian religion and nineteenth and twentieth century scientific beliefs, biology (and reproductive capacity) was literally considered to be destiny. Males and females, at least "normal" males and females, were thought to be born with different intellectual, physical, and moral capacities, preferences, tastes, personalities, and predispositions for violence and suffering.[3]

Ironically, many cultures, including European Christianity in the Middle Ages, viewed women as having a strong, often "insatiable" sexual "drive" and capacity. But by the nineteenth century, women and their sexuality were largely defined in reproductive terms, as in their capacity to "carry a man's child." Even late-twentieth-century human sexuality texts often referred only to "reproductive systems," to genitals as "reproductive" organs, and excluded the "clitoris" and other female organs of sexual pleasure that had no reproductive function. For women, the primary, if not sole, legitimate purpose of sexuality was reproduction.[4]

Nineteenth and mid-twentieth century European and U.S. gender ideologies linked sexuality and gender in other ways.[5] Sexual preference—the sex to whom one was attracted—was "naturally" heterosexual, at least among "normal" humans, and "normal," according to mid-twentieth century Freudian-influenced psychology, was defined largely by whether one adhered to conventional gender roles for males and females. So, appropriately, "masculine" men were "naturally" attracted to "feminine" women and vice versa. Homosexuality, too, was depicted not just as a sexual preference but as gender-inappropriate role behavior, down to gestures and color of clothing.[6] This is apparent in old stereotypes of gay men as "effeminate" (acting like a female, wearing "female" fabrics such as silk or colors such as pink, and participating in "feminine" professions like ballet) and of lesbian women as "butch" (cropped hair, riding motorcycles, wearing leather—prototypical masculinity). Once again, separate phenomena—sexual preference and gender role performance—were conflated because of beliefs that rooted both in biology. "Abnormality" in one sphere (sexual preference) was linked to "abnormality" in the other sphere (gendered capacities and preferences).

In short, the gender and sexual ideologies were based on **biological determinism.** According to this theory, males and females were supposedly born fundamentally different reproductively and in other major capacities and preferences and were "naturally" (biologically) sexually attracted to each other, although women's sexual "drive" was not very well developed relative to men's and was reproductively oriented.

Rejecting Biological Determinism

Decades of research on gender and sexuality, including by feminist anthropologists, has challenged these old theories, particularly biological determinism. We now understand that cultures, not nature, create the gender ideologies that go along with being born male or female and the ideologies vary widely, cross-culturally. What is considered "man's work" in some societies, such as carrying heavy loads, or farming, can be "woman's work" in others. What is "masculine" and "feminine" varies: pink and blue, for example, are culturally invented gender-color linkages, and skirts and "make-up" can be worn by men, indeed by "warriors." Hindu deities, male and female, are highly decorated and difficult to distinguish, at least by conventional masculinist U.S. stereotypes (see examples and Figures 1 and 2).

Women can be thought of as stronger ("tougher," more "rational") than men. Phyllis Kaberry, an anthropologist who studied the Nsaw of Cameroon in the 1940s, said males in that culture argued that land preparation for the rizga crop was "a woman's job, which is too strenuous for the men" and that "women could carry heavy loads because they had stronger foreheads."[7] Among the Aka who live

Figure 1: Hindu deities: Vishnu and his many "avatars" or forms (all male).

Figure 2: Hindu Deities: Vishnu and Goddess Shiva plus avatars.

in the present-day Central African Republic, fathers have close, intimate, relationships with infants, play major roles in all aspects of infant-care, and can sometimes produce breast milk.[8] As for sexual desires, research on the human sexual response by William H. Masters and Virginia E. Johnson established that men and women have equal biological capacities for sexual pleasure and orgasm and that, because males generally ejaculate simultaneously with orgasm, it is easier for women than men to have multiple orgasms.[9]

Gender: A Cultural Invention and a Social Role

One's **biologic sex** is a different phenomenon than one's **gender**, which is socially and historically constructed.[10] Gender is a set of culturally invented expectations and therefore constitutes a role one assumes, learns, and performs, more or less consciously. It is an "identity" one can in theory choose, at least in some societies, although there is tremendous pressure, as in the United States, to conform to the gender role and identity linked to your biologic sex.

This is a profound transformation in how we think about both gender and sexuality. The reality of human biology is that males and females are shockingly similar.[11] There is arguably more variability **within** than **between** each gender, especially taking into account the enormous variability in human physical traits among human populations globally.[12] Notice, for example, the variability in height in the two photos of U.S. college students shown in Figures 3 and 4. Which gender is "taller"? Much of what has been defined as "biological" is actually cultural, so the possibilities for transformation and change are nearly endless! That can be liberating, especially when we are young and want to create identities that fit our particular configuration of abilities and preferences. It can also be upsetting to people who have deeply internalized and who want to maintain the old gender ideology.

The Gender Binary and Beyond

We anthropologists, as noted earlier, love to shake up notions of what is "natural" and "normal." One common assumption is that all cultures divide human beings into two and only two genders,

Figure 3: Gender variability: students in a Human Sexuality Class at San Jose State University with Dr. Carol Mukhopadhyay, 2010.

Figure 4: Gender variability: students in Kalamazoo at Michigan State University, with Dr. Carol Mukhopadhyay, 2010.

a **binary** or dualistic model of gender. However, in some cultures gender is more fluid and flexible, allowing individuals born as one biologic sex to assume another gender or creating more than two genders from which individuals can select. Examples of non-binary cultures come from pre-contact Native America. Anthropologists such as Ruth Benedict long ago identified a fairly widespread phenomenon of so-called "two-spirit" people, individuals who did not comfortably conform to the gender roles and gender ideology normally associated with their biologic sex. Among the pre-contact Zuni Pueblo in New Mexico, which was a relatively gender-egalitarian horticultural society, for example, individuals could choose an alternative role of "not-men" or "not-women." A two-spirited Zuni man would do the work and wear clothing normally associated with females, having shown a preference for female-identified activities and symbols at an early age. In some, but not all cases, he would eventually marry a man. Early European ethnocentric reports often described it as a form of homosexuality. Anthropologists suggested more-complex motivations, including dreams of selection by spirits, individual psychologies, biological characteristics, and negative aspects of male roles (e.g., warfare). Most significantly, these alternative gender roles were acceptable, publicly recognized, and sometimes venerated.[13]

Less is known about additional gender roles available to biological women, although stories of "manly hearted women" suggest a parallel among some Native American groups. For example, a Kutenai woman known to have lived in 1811 was originally married to a French-Canadian man but then returned to the Kutenai and assumed a male gender role, changing her name to Kauxuma nupika (Gone-to-the-Spirits), becoming a spiritual prophet, and eventually marrying a woman.[14]

A well-known example of a non-binary gender system is found among the Hijra in India. Often called a **third gender**, these individuals are usually biologically male but adopt female clothing, gestures, and names; eschew sexual desire and sexual activity; and go through religious rituals that give them certain divine powers, including blessing or cursing couples' fertility and performing at weddings and births. Hijra may undergo voluntary surgical removal of genitals through a "nirvan" or rebirth operation. Some hijra are males born with ambiguous external genitals, such as a particularly small penis or testicles that did not fully descend.[15]

Research has shown that individuals with ambiguous genitals, sometimes called "intersex," are surprisingly common. Martha Ward and Monica Edelstein estimate that such intersex individuals constitute five percent of human births.[16] So what are cultures to do when faced with an infant or child who cannot easily be "sexed?" Some cultures, including the United States, used to force children into one of the two binary categories, even if it required surgery or hormone therapy. But in other places, such as India and among the Isthmus Zapotec in southern Oaxaca, Mexico, they have instead created a third gender category that has an institutional identity and role to perform in society.[17]

These cross-cultural examples demonstrate that the traditional rigid binary gender model in the United States is neither universal nor necessary. While all cultures recognize at least two biological sexes, usually based on genitals visible at birth, and have created at least two gender roles, many cultures go beyond the binary model, offering a third or fourth gender category. Other cultures allow individuals to adopt, without sanctions, a gender role that is not congruent with their biological sex. In short, biology need not be destiny when it comes to gender roles, as we are increasingly discovering in the United States.

Variability among Binary Cultures

Even societies with a binary gender system exhibit enormous variability in the meanings and practices associated with being male or female. Sometimes male-female distinctions pervade virtually all aspects of life, structuring space, work, social life, communication, body decoration, and expressive forms such as music. For instance, both genders may farm, but may have separate fields for "male" and "female" crops and gender-specific crop rituals. Or, the village public space may be spatially segregated with a "men's house" (a special dwelling only for men, like a "men's club") and a "women's house." In some societies, such as the Sambia of New Guinea, even when married couples occupy the same house, the space within the house is divided into male and female areas.[18]

Women and men can also have gender-specific religious rituals and deities and use gender-identified tools. There are cases of "male" and "female" foods, rains, and even "languages" (including words, verb forms, pronouns, inflections, and writing systems; one example is the Nu Shu writing system used by some women in parts of China in the twentieth century).[19] Gender ideologies can emphasize differences in character, capacities, and morality, sometimes portraying males and females as "opposites" on a continuum.

In societies that are highly segregated by gender, gender relationships sometimes are seen as hostile or oppositional with one of the genders (usually female) viewed as potentially threatening. Female bodily fluids, such as menstrual blood and vaginal secretions, can be dangerous, damaging to men, "impure," and "polluting," especially in ritual contexts. In other cases, however, menstrual blood is associated with positive power. A girl's first menstruation may be celebrated publicly with elaborate community rituals, as among the Bemba in southern Africa, and subsequent monthly flows bring special privileges.[20] Men in some small-scale societies go through ritualized nose-bleeding, sometimes called "male menstruation," though the meanings are quite complex.[21]

Gender Relations: Separate and Unequal

Of course, gender-differentiation is not unique to small-scale societies like the Sambia. Virtually all major world religions have traditionally segregated males and females spatially and "marked" them in other ways. Look at eighteenth- and nineteenth- century churches, which had gender-specific seating; at contemporary Saudi Arabia, Iranian, and conservative Malaysian mosques; and at Orthodox Jewish temples today in Israel and the United States.

Ambivalence and even fear of female sexuality, or negative associations with female bodily fluids, such as menstrual blood, are widespread in the world's major religions. Orthodox Jewish women are not supposed to sleep in the same bed as their husbands when menstruating. In Kypseli, Greece, people believe that menstruating women can cause wine to go bad.[22] In some Catholic Portuguese villages, menstruating women are restricted from preparing fresh pork sausages and from being in the room where the sausages are made as their presence is believed to cause the pork to spoil. Contact with these women also supposedly wilts plants and causes inexplicable movements of objects.[23] Orthodox forms of Hinduism prohibit menstruating women from activities such as cooking and attending temple.

These traditions are being challenged. A 2016 British Broadcasting Company (BBC) television program, for example, described "Happy to Bleed," a movement in India to change negative attitudes about menstruation and eliminate the ban on menstruating-age women entering the famous Sabriamala Temple in Kerala.[24]

Emergence of Public (Male) vs. Domestic (Female) Spheres

In large stratified and centralized societies—that is, the powerful empires (so-called "civilizations") that have dominated much of the world for the past several thousand years—a "public" vs. "private" or "domestic" distinction appears. The public, extra-family sphere of life is a relatively recent development in human history even though most of us have grown up in or around cities and towns with their obvious public spaces, physical manifestations of the political, economic, and other extra-family institutions that characterize large-scale societies. In such settings, it is easy to identify the domestic or private spaces families occupy, but a similar public-domestic distinction exists in villages. The public sphere is associated with, and often dominated by, males. The domestic sphere, in contrast, is primarily associated with women—though it, too, can be divided into male and female spheres. In India, for example, where households frequently consist of multi-generational groups of male siblings and their families, there often are "lounging" spaces where men congregate, smoke pipes, chat, and meet visitors. Women's spaces typically focus around the kitchen or cooking hearth (if outside) or at other sites of women's activities.[25] In some cases, an inner court is the women's area while the outer porch and roads that connect the houses are male spaces. In some Middle Eastern villages, women create over-the-roof paths for visiting each other without going "outside" into male spaces.[26]

The gender division between public and private/domestic, however, is as symbolic as it is spatial, often emphasizing a gender ideology of social separation between males and females (except young children), social regulation of sexuality and marriage, and male rights and control over females (wives, daughters, sisters, and mothers). It manifests as separate spaces in mosques, sex-segregated schools, and separate "ladies compartments" on trains, as in India (Figure 5).

Of course, it is impossible to separate the genders completely. Rural women pass through the more-public spaces of a village to fetch water and firewood and to work in agricultural fields. Women shop in public markets, though that can be a "man's job." As girls more often attend school, as in India, they take public transportation and thus travel through public "male" spaces even if they travel to all-girl schools (Figure 6). At college, they can be immersed in and even live on campuses where men predominate, especially if they are studying engineering, computer science, or other technical subjects (Figure 7).

Figure 5: A women only train car in India. Photograph by Ajay Tallam, 2007.

Figure 6: All-girls' school in Bangalore, India. Photograph by Carol Mukhopadhyay, 1989.

Figure 7: Management studies graduate students at CUSAT-Cochin University of Science and Technology, Kerala, India. Photograph by Carol Mukhopadhyay, 1989.

This can severely limit Indian girls' educational and occupational choices, particularly for girls who come from relatively conservative families or regions.[27]

One way in which women navigate "male" spaces is by adopting routes, behavior (avoiding eye contact), and/or clothing that create separation.[28] The term "purdah," the separation or segregation of women from men, literally means "veiling," although other devices can be used. In nineteenth century Jaipur, Rajasthan, royal Rajput women inhabited the inner courtyard spaces of the palace. But an elaborate false building front, the hawa mahal, allowed them to view the comings and goings on the street without being exposed to the public male gaze.

As demand for educating girls has grown in traditionally sexually segregated societies, all-girl schools have been constructed (see Figure 6), paralleling processes in the late nineteenth and early twentieth century in the United States. At the university level, however, prestigious schools that offer high-demand subjects such as engineering often have historically been all-male, excluding women as Harvard once did.[29] In other cases, there are no female faculty members teaching traditionally male subjects like engineering at all-women colleges. In Saudi Arabia, women's universities have taught courses using closed-circuit television to avoid violating norms of sexual segregation, particularly for young, unmarried women.[30] In countries such as India, gynecologists and obstetricians have been predominantly female, in part because families object to male doctors examining and treating women. Thus, in places that do not have female physicians, women's health can suffer.

Sanctions, Sexuality, Honor, and Shame

Penalties for deviating from the rules of social separation vary across and within cultures. In small communities, neighbors and extended family kin can simply report inappropriate behavior, especially between unmarried young adults, to other family members. More severe and sometimes violent responses by family members can occur, especially if the family's "honor" is involved—that is, if the young adults, especially girls, engage in activities that would "shame" or dishonor the family. Honor and shame are complex concepts that are often linked to sexuality, especially female sexuality, and to behavior by family members that involves or hints at sexual impropriety. The Turkish film *Mustang*, nominated for the 2016 best foreign film Academy Award, offers a good illustration of how concepts of sexualized honor and shame operate.

We hear in the news of "honor killings" carried out by conservative Muslims in countries such as Pakistan and powerfully portrayed in documentaries such as *A Girl in the River: The Price of Forgiveness* (2015).[31] But it is not just Islam. Some orthodox sectors of major religions, including Christianity, Judaism, and Hinduism, may hold similar views about "honor" and "shame" and impose sometimes violent sanctions against those who violate sexuality-related codes. The brutal 2012 gang rape-murder of a young woman on a bus in Delhi, though perpetrated by strangers, was rationalized by the men who committed the crime (and their defense attorney) as a legitimate response to the woman's "shameful" behavior—traveling on a bus at night with a male friend, implying sexual impropriety.[32]

Social separation, sex-segregated schools, and penalties for inappropriate sexual behavior have also existed in the United States and Europe, especially among upper-strata women for whom female "purity" was traditionally emphasized. Chastity belts in Europe, whether or not actually used, symbolized the idea that a woman's sexuality belonged solely to her husband, thus precluding her from engaging not only in premarital and extra-marital sex but also in masturbation (Figure 8).[33] In Nathaniel Hawthorne's *The Scarlet Letter*, set in mid-sixteenth century Massachusetts, Hester was forced to wear a scarlet A on her dress and to stand on a public scaffold for three hours a day, a relatively nonviolent but powerful form of shaming and punishment. Stoning women to death for sexually inappropriate behavior, especially adultery, and other violent sanctions may have occurred in some European Christian and Jewish communities.

Rape, so frequent in warfare past and present, also can bring shame to the victim and her family, particularly in sexually conservative societies. During the 1971 Bangladesh war of independence against Pakistan, East Bengali women who were raped by soldiers were ostracized by their families because of the "shame" their rape had brought. During the partition of India into India and Pakistan in 1947, some Sikh families reportedly forced daughters to jump into wells to drown rather than risk being raped by strangers.[34]

Figure 8: A sketch of a chastity belt, c. 1405.

Alternative Models of Gender: Complementary and Fluid

Not all binary cultures are gender-segregated; nor does gender hostility necessarily accompany gender separation. Nor are all binary cultures deeply concerned with, some might say obsessed with, regulating female sexuality and marriage. Premarital and extra-marital sex can even be common and acceptable, as among the !Kung San and Trobriand Islanders.[35] And men are not always clearly ranked over women as they typically are in stratified large-scale centralized societies with "patriarchal" systems. Instead, the two genders can be seen as complementary, equally valued and both recognized as necessary to society. Different need not mean unequal. The Lahu of southwest China and Thailand exemplify a complementary gender system in which men and women have distinct expected roles but a male-female pair is necessary to accomplish most daily tasks (Figure 9). A male-female pair historically took responsibility for local leadership. Male-female **dyads** completed daily household tasks in tandem and worked together in the fields. The title of anthropologist Shanshan Du's book, *Chopsticks Only Work in Pairs* (1999), encapsulates how complementary gender roles defined Lahu

Figure 9: Lahu farmers in Chiangmai, Thailand.

society. A single chopstick is not very useful; neither is a single person, man or woman, in a dual-focused society.[36]

Like the Lahu, the nearby Na believe men and women both play crucial roles in a family and household. Women are associated with birth and life while men take on tasks such as butchering animals and preparing for funerals (Figures 10 and 11). Every Na house has two large pillars in the central hearth room, one representing male identity and one representing female identity. Both are crucial, and the house might well topple symbolically without both pillars. As sociologist Zhou Huashan explained in his 2002 book about the Na, this is a society that "values women without diminishing men."[37]

Anthropologists have also encountered relatively androgynous gender-binary cultures. In these cultures, some gender differentiation exists but "gender bending" and role-crossing are frequent, accepted, and reflect circumstances and individual capacities and preferences. Examples are the !Kung San mentioned earlier, Native American Washoe in the United States, and some segments of European societies in countries such as Sweden and Finland and, increasingly, in the United States.[38] Contemporary twenty-first century gender ideologies tend to emphasize commonality, not difference: shared human traits, flexibility, fluidity, and individual expression.

Even cultures with fairly well-defined gender roles do not necessarily view them as fixed, biologically rooted, permanent, "essentialist," or "naturalized" as occurred in the traditional gender ideology in the United States.[39] Gender may not even be an "identity" in a psychological sense but, rather, a

Figure 10: A Na woman, Sigih Lamu, weeds rice seedlings outside her family's home in southwest China's Yunnan Province. Photograph by Tami Blumenfield, 2002.

Figure 11: Na men carry a wooden structure to be used at a funeral. Photograph by Tami Blumenfield, 2002.

social role one assumes in a particular social context just as one moves between being a student, a daughter, an employee, a wife or husband, president of the bicycle club, and a musician.

Cultures also change over time through internal and external forces such as trade, conquest, colonialism, globalization, immigration, mass media, and, especially, films. Within every culture, there is tremendous diversity in class, ethnicity, religion, region, education level, and generation, as well as diversity related to more-individual family circumstances, predilections, and experiences. Gender expectations also vary with one's age and stage in life as well as one's social role, even within the family (e.g., "wife" vs. "sister" vs. "mother" vs. "mother-in-law" and "father" vs. "son" vs. "brother" vs "father-in-law"). Finally, people can appear to conform to cultural norms but find ways of working around or ignoring them.

Even in highly male-dominated, sexually segregated societies, women find ways to pursue their own goals, to be actors, and to push the boundaries of the gender system. Among Egyptian Awlad 'Ali Bedouin families, for example, women rarely socialized outside their home compounds or with unrelated men. But within their spheres, they freely interacted with other women, could influence their husbands, and wrote and sang poetic couplets as expressive outlets.[40] In some of the poorest and least-developed areas of central India, where **patrilocal** extended-family male-controlled households reign, activist Sampat Pal has organized local rural women to combat violence based on dishonor and gender.[41] Her so-called "Gulabi Gang," the subject of two films, illustrates both the possibilities of resistance and the difficulties of changing a deeply embedded system based on gender, caste, and class system (Figure 12).[42] For a related activity, see Activity 2: Understanding Gender from a Martian Perspective.

Figure 12: Gulabi Gang in India.

Unraveling Our Gender Myths: Primate Roots, "Man the Hunter," and Other "Origin Stories" of Gender and Male Dominance

Even unencumbered by pregnancy or infants, a female hunter would be less fleet, generally less strong, possibly more prone to changes in emotional *tonus* as a consequence of the estrus cycle, and less able to adapt to changes in temperature than males.[43]
—U.S. anthropologist, 1969

Women don't ride motorcycles because they can't; they can't because they are not strong enough to put their legs down to stop it.[44]
—Five-year-old boy, Los Angeles, 1980

Men hunted because women were not allowed to come out of their houses and roam about in forests.[45]
—Pre-college student in India, 1990

All cultures have "creation" stories. Many have elaborate gender-related creation stories that describe the origins of males and females, their gender-specific traits, their relationships and sexual proclivities, and, sometimes, how one gender came to "dominate" the other. Our culture is no different. The Judeo-Christian Bible, like the Koran and other religious texts, addresses origins and gender (think of Adam and Eve), and traditional folk tales, songs, dances, and epic stories, such as the Ramayana in Hinduism and Shakespeare's *The Taming of the Shrew*, treat similar themes.

Science, too, has sought to understand gender differences. In the late nineteenth and early twentieth centuries, a number of scientists, immersed in Darwinian theories, began to explore the evolutionary roots of what they assumed to be universal: male dominance. Of course, scientists, like the rest of us, view the world partially through their own cultural lenses and through a gendered version. Prior to the 1970s, women and gender relations were largely invisible in the research literature and most researchers were male so it is not surprising that 1960s theories reflected prevailing male-oriented folk beliefs about gender.[46]

The Hunting Way of Life "Molds Man" (and Woman)

The most popular and persistent theories argued that male dominance is universal, rooted in species-wide gendered biological traits that we acquired, first as part of our primate heritage, and further developed as we evolved from apes into humans. Emergence of "the hunting way of life" plays a major role in this story. Crucial components include: a diet consisting primarily of meat, obtained through planned, cooperative hunts, by all-male groups, that lasted several days and covered a wide territory. Such hunts would require persistence, skill, and physical stamina; tool kits to kill, butcher, transport, preserve, and share the meat; and a social organization consisting of a stable home base and a monogamous nuclear family. Several biological changes were attributed to adopting this way of life: a larger and more complex brain, human language, an upright posture (and humans' unique foot and stride), loss of body hair, a long period of infant dependency, and the absence of "estrus" (ovulation-related female sexual arousal) (Figure 13), which made females sexually "receptive" throughout the monthly cycle. Other human characteristics purportedly made sex more enjoyable: frontal sex and fleshier breasts, buttocks, and genitals, especially the human penis. Making sex "sexier," some speculated, cemented the pair-bond, helping to keep the man "around" and the family unit stable.[47]

Hunting was also linked to a "world view" in which the flight of animals from humans seemed natural and (male) aggression became normal, frequent, easy to learn,

Figure 13: Female baboon in estrus. Photograph by Carol Mukhopadhyay, Tanzania, 2010.

Figure 14: Baboon pair in tree: male-female voluntary relations. Photograph by Carol Mukhopadhyay, Tanzania, 2010.

rewarded, and enjoyable. War, some have suggested, might psychologically be simply a form of hunting and pleasurable for male participants.[48] The Hunting Way of Life, in short, "molded man," giving our species its distinctive characteristics. And as a result, we contemporary humans cannot erase the effects of our hunting past even though we live in cities, stalk nothing but a parking place, and can omit meat from our diets.

> The biology, psychology, and customs that separate us from the apes—all these we owe to the hunters of time past. And, although the record is incomplete and speculation looms larger than fact, for those who would understand the origin and nature of human behavior there is no choice but to try to understand "Man the Hunter."
> —Washburn and Lancaster (1974)[49]

Gender roles and male dominance were supposed to be part of our evolutionary heritage. Males evolved to be food-providers—stronger, more aggressive, more effective leaders with cooperative and bonding capacities, planning skills, and technological inventiveness (tool-making). In this creation story, females never acquired those capacities because they were burdened by their reproductive roles—pregnancy, giving birth, lactation, and child care—and thus became dependent on males for food and protection. The gender gap widened over time. As males initiated, explored, invented, women stayed at home, nurtured, immersed themselves in domestic life. The result: men are active, women are passive; men are leaders, women are followers; men are dominant, women are subordinate.

Many of us have heard pieces of this Hunting Way of Life story. Some of the men Mukhopadhyay interviewed in Los Angeles in the late 1970s invoked "our hunting past" to explain why they—and men generally—operated barbeques rather than their wives. Women's qualifications to be president were questioned on biological grounds such as "stamina" and "toughness." Her women informants, all hospital nurses, doubted their navigational abilities, courage, and strength despite working in intensive care and regularly lifting heavy male patients. Mukhopadhyay encountered serious scholars who cited women's menstrual cycle and "emotional instability" during ovulation to explain why women "can't" hunt.

Similar stories are invoked today for everything from some men's love of hunting to why men dominate "technical" fields, accumulate tools, have extra-marital affairs or commit the vast majority of homicides. Strength and toughness remain defining characteristics of masculinity in the United States, and these themes often permeate national political debates.[50] One element in the complex debate over gun control is the male-masculine strength-through-guns and man-the-hunter association, and it is still difficult for some males in the United States to feel comfortable with their soft, nurturant, emotional, and artistic sides.[51]

What is most striking about man-the-hunter scenarios is how closely they resemble 1950s U.S. models of family and gender, which were rooted in the late nineteenth century "cult of domesticity" and "true womanhood." Father is "head" of the family and the final authority, whether in household decisions or in disciplining children. As "provider," Father goes "outside" into the cold, cruel world, hunting for work. Mother, as "chief mom," remains "inside" at the home base, creating a domestic refuge against the "survival of the fittest" "jungle." American anthropologists seemed to have subconsciously projected their own folk models onto our early human ancestors.

Altering this supposedly "fundamental" gender system, according to widely read authors in the 1970s, would go against our basic "human nature." This belief was applied to the political arena, then a virtually all-male domain, especially at state and national levels. The following quote from 1971 is particularly relevant and worthy of critical evaluation since, for the first time, a major U.S. political party selected a woman as its 2016 presidential candidate (See Text Box 3, Gender and the Presidential Election).

> To make women equal participants in the political process, we will have to change the very process itself, which means changing a pattern bred into our behavior over the millennia.
> —Lionel Tiger and Robin Fox[52]

Replacing Stories with Reality

Decades of research, much of it by a new generation of women scholars, have altered our view of the hunting way of life in our evolutionary past.[53] For example, the old stereotype of primates as living in male-centered, male-dominated groups does not accurately describe our closest primate relatives, gorillas, chimpanzees, and bonobos. The stereotypes came from 1960s research on savannah, ground-dwelling baboons that suggested they were organized socially by a stable male-dominance hierarchy, the "core" of the group, that was established through force, regulated sexual access to females, and provided internal and external defense of the "troop" in a supposedly hostile savannah environ-

Figure 15: Rhesus monkeys at the Periyar Reserve in Kerala, India. Photograph by Carol Mukhopadhyay, Tanzania, 2010.

Figure 16: Baboon group with infants being carried by male. Photograph by Carol Mukhopadhyay, Tanzania, 2010.

ment.[54] Females lacked hierarchies or coalitions, were passive, and were part of dominant male "harems."

Critics first argued that baboons, as monkeys rather than apes, were too far removed from humans evolutionarily to tell us much about early human social organization. Then, further research on baboons living in other environments by primatologists such as Thelma Rowell discovered that those baboons were neither male-focused nor male-dominated. Instead, the stable group core was **matrifocal**—a mother and her offspring constituted the central and enduring ties. Nor did males control female sexuality. Quite the contrary in fact. Females mated freely and frequently, choosing males of all ages, sometimes establishing special relationships—- "friends with favors." Dominance, while infrequent, was not based simply on size or strength; it was learned, situational, and often stress-induced. And like other primates, both male and female baboons used sophisticated strategies, dubbed "primate politics," to predict and manipulate the intricate social networks in which they lived.[55]

Rowell also restudied the savannah baboons. Even they did not fit the baboon "stereotype." She found that their groups were loosely structured with no specialized stable male-leadership coalitions and were sociable, matrifocal, and infant-centered much like the Rhesus monkeys pictured below (see Figure 15). Females actively initiated sexual encounters with a variety of male partners. When attacked by predators or frightened by some other major threat, males, rather than "defending the troop," typically would flee, running away first and leaving the females carrying infants to follow behind (Figures 16).[56]

Man the Hunter, the Meat-Eater?

The second, more important challenge was to key assumptions about the hunting way of life. Archaeological and paleontological fossil evidence and ethnographic data from contemporary foragers revealed that hunting and meat it provided were not the primary subsistence mode. Instead, gathered foods such as plants, nuts, fruits, roots and small fish found in rivers and ponds constituted the bulk of such diets and provided the most stable food source in all but a few settings (northerly climates, herd migration routes, and specific geographical and historical settings). When meat was important, it was more often "scavenged" or "caught" than hunted.

A major symposium on human evolution concluded that "opportunistic" "scavenging" was probably the best description of early human hunting activities. Often, tools found in pre-modern human sites such as caves would have been more appropriate for "smashing" scavenged bones than hunting live animals.[57] Hunting, when carried out, generally did not involve large-scale, all-male, cooperative expeditions involving extensive planning and lengthy expeditions over a wide territorial range. Instead, as among the Hadza of Tanzania, hunting was likely typically conducted by a single male, or perhaps two males, for a couple of hours, often without success. When hunting collectively, as occurs among the Mbuti in the Central African rainforest, groups of families likely participated with women and men driving animals into nets. Among the Agta of the Philippines, women rather than men hunt collectively using dogs to herd animals to a place where they can be killed.[58] And !Kung San men, despite what was shown in the 1957 ethnographic film *The Hunters*, do not normally hunt giraffe; they usually pursue small animals such as hares, rats, and gophers.

Discrediting the Hunting Hypothesis

Once the "hunting-meat" hypothesis was discredited, other parts of the theory began to unravel, especially the link between male dominance and female economic dependency. We now know that for most of human history—99 percent of it prior to the invention of agriculture some 10,000 or so years ago—women have "worked," often providing the stable sources of food for their family. Richard Lee, Marjorie Shostak, and others have detailed, with caloric counts and time-work estimates, the significance of women's gathering contributions even in societies such as the !Kung San, in which hunting occurs regularly.[59] In foraging societies that rely primarily on fish, women also play a major role, "collecting" fish from rivers, lakes, and ponds. The exceptions are atypical environments such as the Arctic.

Of course, "meat-getting" is a narrow definition of "food getting" or "subsistence" work. Many food processing activities are time-consuming. Collecting water and firewood is crucial, heavy work and is often done by women (Figure 17). Making and maintaining clothing, housing, and tools also occupy a significant amount of time. Early humans, both male and female, invented an array of items for carrying things (babies, wood, water), dug tubers, processed nuts, and cooked food. The invention of string some 24,000 years ago, a discovery so essential that it produced what some have called the "String Revolution," is attributed to women.[60] There is the "work of kinship," of "healing,"

Figure 17: Collecting firewood in Bansankusu, Democratic Republic of Congo.

of "ritual," of "teaching" the next generation, and emotional "work. All are part of the work of living and of the "invisible" work that women do.

Nor is it just hunting that requires intelligence, planning, cooperation, and detailed knowledge. Foragers have lived in a wide variety of environments across the globe, some more challenging than others (such as Alaska). In all of these groups, both males and females have needed and have developed intensive detailed knowledge of local flora and fauna and strategies for using those resources. Human social interactions also require sophisticated mental and communication skills, both verbal and nonverbal. In short, humans' complex brains and other modern traits developed as an adaptation to complex social life, a lengthy period of child-dependency and child-rearing that required cooperative nurturing, and many different kinds of "work" that even the simplest human societies performed.

Refuting Pregnancy and Motherhood as Debilitating

Finally, cross-cultural data refutes another central man-the-hunter stereotype: the "burden" of pregnancy and child care. Women's reproductive roles do not generally prevent them from food-getting, including hunting; among the Agta, women hunt when pregnant. Foraging societies accommodate the work-reproduction "conflict" by spacing out their pregnancies using indigenous methods of "family planning" such as prolonged breast feeding, long post-pregnancy periods of sexual inactivity, and native herbs and medicinal plants. Child care, even for infants, is rarely solely the responsibility of the birth mother. Instead, multiple caretakers are the norm: spouses, children, other relatives, and neighbors.[61] Reciprocity is the key to human social life and to survival in small-scale societies, and reciprocal child care is but one example of such reciprocity. Children and infants accompany their mothers (or fathers) on gathering trips, as among the !Kung San, and on Aka collective net-hunting expeditions. Agta women carry nursing infants with them when gathering-hunting, leaving older children at home in the care of spouses or other relatives.[62]

In pre-industrial horticultural and agricultural societies, having children and "working" are not incompatible—quite the opposite! Anthropologists long ago identified "female farming systems," especially in parts of Africa and Southeast Asia, in which farming is predominantly a woman's job and men "help out" as needed.[63]

In most agricultural societies, women who do not come from high-status or wealthy families perform a significant amount of agricultural labor, though it often goes unrecognized in the dominant gender ideology. Wet-rice agriculture, common in south and southeast Asia, is labor-intensive, particularly weeding and transplanting rice seedlings, which are often done by women (Figure 10). Harvesting rice, wheat, and other grains also entails essential input by women. Yet the Indian Census traditionally records only male family members as "farmers." In the United States, women's work on family-owned farms is often invisible.[64]

Women may accommodate their reproductive and child-rearing roles by engaging in work that is more compatible with child care, such as cooking, and in activities that occur closer to home and are interruptible and perhaps less dangerous, though cooking fires, stoves, and implements such as knives certainly can cause harm![65] More often, women adjust their food-getting "work" in response to the demands of pregnancy, breast-feeding, and other child care activities. They gather or process nuts while their children are napping; they take their children with them to the fields to weed or harvest and, in more recent times, to urban construction sites in places such as India, where women often do the heaviest (and lowest-paid) work.

In the United States, despite a long-standing cultural model of the stay-at-home mom, some mothers have always worked outside the home, mainly out of economic necessity. This shifting group includes single-divorced-widowed mothers and married African-Americans (pre- and post-slavery), immigrants, and Euro-American women with limited financial resources. But workplace policies (except during World War II) have historically made it harder rather than easier for women (and men) to carry out family responsibilities, including requiring married women and pregnant women to quit their jobs.[66] Circumstances have not improved much. While pregnant women in the United States are no longer automatically dismissed from their jobs—at least not legally—the United States lags far behind most European countries in providing affordable child care and paid parental leave.

Family and Marriage: A Cultural Construct and a Social Invention

Unraveling the theory of the hunting-way-of-life scenario, especially female dependence on males, undermines the "naturalness" of the nuclear family with its male-provider-protector and female-domestic-child-care division of labor. More than one hundred years of cross-cultural research has revealed the varied forms humans have invented for "partnering"—living in households, raising children, establishing long-term relationships, transmitting valuables to offspring, and other social behaviors associated with "family." Once again, the universality and evolutionary origins of the U.S. form of the human family is more fiction than fact, a projection of our cultural model of family and gender roles onto the past and onto the entire human species.

Family: Biology and Culture

What **is** natural about the family? Like gender and sexuality, there is a biological component. There is a biological mother and a biological father, although the mother plays a significantly larger and longer role from the time of conception through the end of infant's dependence. In the past, conception usually required sexual intercourse, but that is no longer the case thanks to sperm banks, which have made the embodied male potentially obsolete, biologically speaking. There is also a biological relationship between parents and offspring—again, more obvious in the case of the mother since the baby develops in and emerges from her body. Nevertheless, DNA and genes are real and influence the traits and potentialities of the next generation.

Beyond those biological "realities," culture and society seem to take over, building on—or ignoring—biology. We all know there are biological fathers who may be unaware of or not concerned about their biological offspring and not involved in their care and biological mothers who, after giving birth, give up their children through adoption or to other family members. In recent decades, technology has allowed women to act as "surrogate mothers," using their bodies as carriers for implanted fertilized eggs of couples who wish to have a child. On the other hand, we all probably know of excellent parents who are not the children's biological mothers and fathers, and "legal" parenthood through adoption can have more-profound parenting consequences for children than biological parenthood.

When we think of good (or bad) parents, or of someone as a really "good mother," as an "excellent father," as two "wonderful mothers," we are not talking biology. We usually are thinking of a set of cultural and behavioral expectations, and being an adoptive rather than a biological parent isn't really the issue. Clearly, then, parenthood, mother-father relationships, and other kinship relationships (with siblings, grandparents, and uncles-aunts) are not simply rooted in biology but are also social roles, legal relationships, meanings and expectations constructed by human cultures in specific social and historical contexts. This is not to deny the importance of kinship; it is fundamental, especially in small-scale pre-industrial societies. But kinship is as much about culture as it is about biology. Biology, in a sense, is only the beginning—and may not be necessary.

Marriage also is not "natural." It is a cultural invention that involves various meanings and functions in different cultural contexts. We all know that it is not necessary to be married to have sex or to have children. Indeed, in the United States, a growing number of women who give birth are not married, and the percent of unmarried women giving birth is higher in many northwestern European countries such as Sweden.[67] Cross-culturally, marriage seems to be primarily about **societal regulation of relationships**—a social contract between two individuals and, often, their families, that specifies rights and obligations of married individuals and of the offspring that married women produce. Some anthropologists have argued that marriage IS primarily about children and "descent"—who will "own" children.[68] To whom will they belong? With what rights, obligations, social statuses, access to resources, group identities, and all the other assets—and liabilities—that exist within a society? Children have historically been essential for family survival—for literal reproduction and for social reproduction.

Think, for a moment, about our taken-for-granted assumptions about to whom children belong.[69] Clearly, children emerge from a woman's body and, indeed, after approximately nine months, it is her body that has nurtured and "grown" this child. But who "owns" that child legally—to whom it "belongs" and the beliefs associated with how it was conceived and about who played a role in its conception—is not a biological given. Not in human societies. One fascinating puzzle in human evolution is how females lost control over their sexuality and their offspring! Why do so many, though not all, cultural theories of procreation consider women's role as minor, if not irrelevant—not as the "seed," for example, but merely as a "carrier" of the male seed she will eventually "deliver" to its "owner"? Thus, having a child biologically is not equivalent to social "ownership." Marriage, cross-culturally, deals with social ownership of offspring. What conditions must be met? What exchanges must occur, particularly between families or kinship groups, for that offspring to be theirs, his, hers—for it to be a legitimate "heir"?

Marriage is, then, a "contract," usually between families, even if unwritten. Throughout most of human history, kinship groups and, later, religious institutions have regulated marriage. Most major religions today have formal laws and marriage "contracts," even in societies with "civil" marriage codes. In some countries, like India, there is a separate marriage code for each major religion in addition to a secular, civil marriage code. Who children "belong to" is rarely solely about biology, and when biology is involved, it is biology shaped by society and culture. The notion of an "illegitimate" child in the United States has not been about biology but about "legitimacy," that is, whether the child was the result of a legally recognized relationship that entitled offspring to certain rights, including inheritance.

From this perspective, what we think of as a "normal" or "natural" family in the United States is actually a culturally and historically specific, legally codified set of relationships between two individuals and, to some extent, their families. Cross-culturally, the U.S. (and "traditional" British-Euro-American) nuclear family is quite unusual and atypical. Married couples in the United States "ideally" establish a separate household, a nuclear-family-based household, rather than living with one spouse's parents and forming a larger multi-generational household, often referred to as an "extended" family, which is the most common form of family structure. In addition, U.S. marriages are monogamous—legally, one may have only one husband or wife at a time. But a majority of societies that have been studied by anthropologists have allowed polygamy (multiple spouses). Polygyny (one husband, multiple wives) is most common but polyandry (one wife, multiple husbands) also occurs; occasionally marriages involve multiple husbands and multiple wives. Separate spouses, particularly wives, often have their own dwelling space, commonly shared with their children, but usually live in one compound, with their husbands' parents and his relatives. Across cultures, then, most households tend to be versions of extended-family-based groups.

These two contrasts alone lead to families in the United States that are smaller and focused more on the husband-wife (or spousal) and parent-child relationships; other relatives are more distant, literally and often conceptually. They are also more "independent"—or, some would say, more dependent on a smaller set of relationships to fulfill family responsibilities for work, child care, finances, emotional companionship, and even sexual obligations. Other things being equal, the death or loss of a spouse in a "traditional" U.S. family has a bigger impact than such a loss in an extended family household (see Text Box 1). On the other hand, nuclear families own and control their incomes and other assets, unlike many extended families in which those are jointly held. This ownership and control of resources can give couples and wives in nuclear families greater freedom.

There are other cross-cultural variations in family, marriage and kinship: in expectations for spouses and children, exchanges between families, inheritance rules, marriage rituals, ideal ages and characteristics of spouses, conditions for dissolving a marriage and remarriage after a spouse's death, attitudes about premarital, extra-marital, and marital sexuality, and so forth. How "descent" is calculated is a social-cultural process that carves out a smaller "group" of "kin" from all of the potential relatives in which individuals have rights (e.g., to property, assistance, political representation) and obligations (economic, social). Often there are explicit norms about who one should and should not marry, including which relatives. Marriage between people we call "cousins" is common cross-culturally. These variations in the definition of marriage and family reflect what human cultures do with the biological "facts of life," creating many different kinds of marriage, family, and kinship systems.

Another major contrast between the U.S. and many other cultures is that our husband-wife relationship is based on free choice and "romantic love." Marriages are arranged by the couple and reflect their desires rather than the desires of larger societal groups. Of course, even in the United States, that has never been entirely the case. Informal prohibitions, often imposed by families, have shaped (and continue to shape) individual choices, such as marrying outside one's religion, racial/ethnic group, and socio-economic class or within one's gender. Some religions explicitly forbid marrying someone from another religion. But U.S. formal government prohibitions have also existed, such as laws against inter-racial marriage, which were only declared unconstitutional in 1967 (Loving v. Virginia).

These so-called anti-miscegenation laws, directed mainly at European-American and African-Americans, were designed to preserve the race-based system of social stratification in the United States.[70] They did not affect both genders equally but reflected the intersection of gender with class and racial inequality. During slavery, most inter-racial sexual activity was initiated by Euro-American males. It was not uncommon for male slave owners to have illicit, often forced sexual relations with female slaves. The laws were created so that children of slave women inherited their mother's racial and slave status, thereby also adding to the slave property of the "father."

Euro-American women's relationships with African-American men, though far less frequent and usually voluntary, posed special problems. Offspring would inherit the mother's "free" status and increase the free African-American population or possibly end up "passing" as "White." Social and legal weapons were used to prevent such relationships. Euro-American women, especially poorer women, who were involved sexually with African-American men were stereotyped as prostitutes, sexually depraved, and outcasts. Laws were passed that fined them for such behavior or required them to work as indentured servants for the child's father's slave owner; other laws prohibited cohabitation between a "White" and someone of African descent.

Post-slavery anti-miscegenation laws tried to preserve the "color line" biologically by outlawing mating and to maintain the legal "purity" and status of Euro-American lineages by outlawing inter-racial marriage. In reality, of course, inter-racial mating continued, but inter-racial offspring did not have the rights of "legitimate" children. By the 1920s, some states, like Virginia, had outlawed "Whites" from marrying anyone who had a "single drop" of African blood. By 1924, 38 states had outlawed Black-White marriages, and as late as the 1950s, inter-racial marriage bans existed in almost half of the states and had been extended to Native Americans, Mexicans, "East Indians," Malays, and other groups designated "not White."[71]

Overall, stratified inegalitarian societies tend to have the strictest controls over marriage. Such control is especially common when some groups are considered inherently superior to others, be it racially, castes, or "royal" blood. Patriarchal societies closely regulate and restrict premarital sexual contacts of women, especially higher-status women. One function of marriage in these societies is to reproduce the existing social structure, partially by insuring that marriages and any offspring resulting from them will maintain and potentially increase the social standing of the families involved. Elite, dominant groups have the most to lose in terms of status and wealth, including inheritances. "Royalty" in Britain, for example, traditionally are not supposed to marry "commoners" so as to ensure that the royal "blood," titles, and other privileges remain in the "royal" family.

Cross-culturally, even in small-scale societies that are relatively egalitarian such as the San and the Trobriand Islanders studied by Annette Weiner, marriage is rarely a purely individual choice left to the wishes—and whims of, or "electricity" between—the two spouses.[72] This is not to say that spouses never have input or prior contact; they may know each other and even have grown up together. In most societies, however, a marriage usually has profound social consequences and is far too important to be "simply" an individual choice. Since marriages affect families and kin economically, socially, and politically, family members (especially elders) play a major role in arranging marriages along lines consistent with their own goals and using their own criteria. Families sometimes arrange their children's marriages when the children are quite young. In Nuosu communities of southwest China, some families held formal engagement ceremonies for babies to, ideally, cement a good cross-cousin partnership, though no marital relationship would occur until much later.[73] There also can be conventional categories of relatives who are supposed to marry each other so young girls might know that their future husbands will be particular cousins, and the girls might play or interact with them at family functions as children.[74]

This does not mean that romantic love is purely a recent or U.S. and European phenomenon. Romantic love is widespread even in cultures that have strong views on arranging marriages. Traditional cultures in India, both Hindu and Muslim, are filled with "love stories" expressed in songs, paintings, and famous temple sculptures. One of the most beautiful buildings in the world, the Taj Mahal, is a monument to Shah Jahan's love for his wife. Where young girls' marriages are arranged, often to older men (as among the Maasai), we know that those girls, once married, sometimes take "lovers" about whom they sing "love songs" and with whom they engage in sexual relations.[75] Truly, romantic love, sex, and marriage can exist independently.

Nevertheless, cross-culturally and historically, marriages based on free choice and romantic love are relatively unusual and recent. Clearly, young people all over the world are attracted to the idea, which is "romanticized" in Bollywood films, popular music, poetry, and other forms of contemporary popular culture. No wonder so many families—and conservative social and religious groups—are concerned, if not terrified, of losing control over young people's mating and marriage behavior (see, for example, the excellent PBS documentary *The World before Her*).[76] A social revolution is truly underway and we haven't even gotten to same-sex sex and same-sex marriage.

Text Box 1: What Can We Learn from the Na? Shattering Ideas about Family and Relationships
By Tami Blumenfield

We have certain expectations about the trajectories of relationships and family life in the United States—young people meet, fall in love, purchase a diamond, and then marry. To some extent, this specific view of family is changing as same-sex relationships and no-longer-new reproductive technologies expand our views of what family can and cannot be. Still, quite often, we think about family in a rigid, heteronormative context, assuming that everyone wants the same thing.

What if we think about family in an entirely different way? In fact, many people already do. In 2014, 10 percent of American adults lived in cohabiting relationships. Meanwhile, 51 percent were married in state-endorsed relationships, and that percentage has been dropping fast.[77] Those numbers may sound familiar as part of politicians' "focus on the family," decrying the number of children born to unmarried parents and bemoaning the weakening of an institution they hold dear (even though their colleagues are frequently exposed in the news for sexual indiscretions).

It is true that adults with limited resources face challenges raising children when they have limited access to affordable, high-quality child care. They struggle when living wage jobs migrate to other countries or other states where workers earn less. In an economic system that encourages concentration of resources in a tiny fraction of the population, it is no wonder that they struggle. But is the institution of marriage really to blame? The number of cohabiting unmarried individuals is high in many parts of Europe as well, but with better support structures in place, parents fare much better. They enjoy parental leave policies that mandate their jobs be held for them upon return from leave. They also benefit from strong educational systems and state-subsidized child care, and their children enjoy better outcomes than ours.

Critics see the "focus on the family" by U.S. politicians as a convenient political trick that turns attention away from crucial policy issues and refocuses it on the plight of the institution of marriage and the fate of the nation's children. Few people can easily dismiss these concerns, even if they do not reflect their own lived realities. And besides, the family model trumpeted by politicians as lost is but one form of family that is not universal even in the United States, much less among all human groups, as sociologist Stephanie Coontz convincingly argued in books including *The Way We Never Were* (1992) and *The Way We Really Are* (1997). In fact, the "focus on family" ignores the diverse ways peoples on this continent have organized their relationships. For Hopi, a Native American group living in what is today the southwestern United States, for example, it is their mother's kin rather than their husbands' from whom they draw support. The Navajo, Kiowa, and Iroquois Native American cultures all organize their family units and arrange their relationships differently.

Na people living in the foothills of the Himalayas have many ways to structure family relationships. One relationship structure looks like what we might expect in a place where people make their living from the land and raise livestock to sustain themselves. Young adults marry, and brides sometimes moves into the husband's childhood home and live with his parents. They have children, who live with them, and they work together. A second Na family structure looks much less familiar: young adults live in large, extended family households with several generations and form romantic relationships with someone from another household. When they are ready, the young man seeks permission to spend the night in the young woman's room. If both parties desire, their relationship can evolve into a long-term one, but they do not marry and do not live together in the same household. When a child is conceived, or before if the couple chooses, their relationship moves from a secretive one to one about which others know. Even so, the young man rarely spends daylight hours with his partner. Instead, he returns to his own family's home to help with farming and other work there. The state is not involved in their relationship, and their money is not pooled either, though presents change hands. If either partner becomes disenchanted with the other, the relationship need not persist. Their children remain in the mother's home, nurtured by adults who love them deeply—not just by their mothers but also by their grandmothers, maternal aunts, maternal uncles, and often older cousins as well. They enjoy everyday life with an extended family (Figure 18). The third Na family structure mixes the preceding two systems. Someone joins a larger household as a spouse. Perhaps the family lacked enough women or men to manage the household and farming tasks adequately or the couple faced pressure from the government to marry.

As an anthropologist who has done fieldwork in Na communities since 2001, I can attest to the loving and nurturing families their system encourages. It protects adults as well as children. Women who are suffering in a relationship can end it with limited consequences for their children, who do not need to relocate to a new house and adjust to a new lifestyle. Lawyers need not get involved, as they often must in divorce cases elsewhere in the world. A man who cannot afford to build a new house for his family—a significant pressure for people in many areas of China that prevents young men from marrying or delays their marriages—can still enjoy a relationship or can choose, instead, to

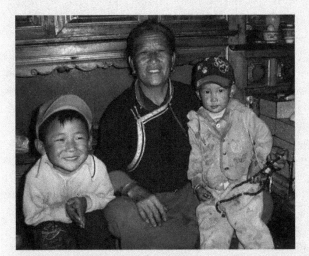

Figure 18: Na grandmother with her maternal grandchildren. They live in the same household, along with the grandmother's adult sons and her daughter, the children's mother. Photograph by Tami Blumenfeld, 2002.

devote himself to his role as an uncle. Women and men who do not feel the urge to pursue romantic lives are protected in this system as well; they can contribute to their natal families without having to worry that no one will look out for them as they age.

Like any system composed of real people, Na systems are not perfect, and neither are the people who represent them. In the last few decades, people have flocked to Lugu Lake hoping to catch a glimpse of this unusual society, and many tourists and tour guides have mistakenly taken Na flexibility in relationships as signifying a land of casual sex with no recognition of paternity. These are highly problematic assumptions that offend my Na acquaintances deeply. Na people have fathers and know who they are, and they often enjoy close relationships despite living apart. In fact, fathers are deeply involved in children's lives and often participate in everyday child-rearing activities. Of course, as in other parts of the world, some fathers participate more than others. Fathers and their birth families also take responsibility for contributing to school expenses and make other financial contributions as circumstances permit. Clearly, this is not a community in which men do not fulfill responsibilities as fathers. It is one in which the responsibilities and how they are fulfilled varies markedly from those of fathers living in other places and cultures.

Though problems exist in Na communities and their relationship patterns are already changing and transforming them, it is encouraging that so many people can live satisfied lives in this flexible system. The Na shatter our expectations about how families and relationships should be organized. They also inspire us to ask whether we can, and should, adapt part of their ethos into our own society.[78]

For more information, see the TEDx FurmanU presentation by Tami Blumenfield.

Male Dominance: Universal and Biologically Rooted?

Unraveling the myth of the hunting way of life and women's dependence on male hunting undermined the logic behind the argument for biologically rooted male dominance. Still, for feminist scholars, the question of male dominance remained important. Was it universal, "natural," inevitable, and unalterable? Were some societies gender-egalitarian? Was gender inequality a cultural phenomenon, a product of culturally and historically specific conditions?

Research in the 1970s and 1980s addressed these questions.[79] Some argued that "sexual asymmetry" was universal and resulted from complex cultural processes related to women's reproductive roles.[80] Others presented evidence of gender equality in small-scale societies (such as the !Kung San and Native American Iroquois) but argued that it had disappeared with the rise of private property and "the state."[81] Still others focused on evaluating the "status of women" using multiple "variables" or identifying "key determinants" (e.g., economic, political, ecological, social, and cultural) of women's status.[82] By the late 1980s, scholars realized how difficult it was to define, much less measure, male dominance across cultures and even the "status of women" in one culture.

Think of our own society or the area in which you live. How would you go about assessing the "status of women" to determine whether it is male-dominated? What would you examine? What information would you gather and from whom? What difficulties might you encounter when making a judgment? Might men and women have different views? Then imagine trying to compare the status of women in your region to the status of women in, let's say, the Philippines, Japan, or China or in a kin-based, small society like that of the Minangkabau living in Indonesia and the !Kung San in Botswana. Next, how might Martians, upon arriving in your city, decide whether you live in a "male dominated" culture? What would they notice? What would they have difficulty deciphering? This experiment gives you an idea of what anthropologists confronted—except they were trying to include all societies that ever existed. Many were accessible only through archaeological and paleontological evidence or through historical records, often made by travelers, sailors, or missionaries. Surviving small-scale cultures were surrounded by more-powerful societies that often imposed their cultures and gender ideologies on those under their control.

For example, the !Kung San of Southern Africa when studied by anthropologists, had already been pushed by European colonial rulers into marginal areas. Most were living on "reserves" similar to Indian reservations in the United States. Others lived in market towns and were sometimes involved in the tourist industry and in films such as the ethnographically flawed and ethnocentric film *The Gods Must Be Crazy* (1980). !Kung San women at the time were learning European Christian ideas about sexuality, clothing, and covering their breasts, and children were attending missionary-established schools, which taught the church's and European views of gender and spousal roles along with the Bible, Jesus, and the Virgin Mary. During the struggle against apartheid in South Africa, the South African military tried to recruit San to fight against the South West Africa People's Organization (SWAPO), taunting reluctant !Kung San men by calling them "chicken" and assuming, erroneously, that the !Kung San shared their "tough guys / tough guise" version of masculinity.[83]

Given the complexity of evaluating "universal male dominance," scholars abandoned the search for simple "global" answers, for key "determinants" of women's status that would apply to all societies. A 1988 *Annual Review of Anthropology* article by Mukhopadhyay and Higgins concluded that "One of the profound realizations of the past ten years is that the original questions, still unanswerable, may be both naive and inappropriate."[84] Among other things, the concept of "status" contains at least five separate, potentially independent components: economics, power/authority, prestige, autonomy, and gender ideologies/beliefs. One's life-cycle stage, kinship role, class, and other socio-economic and social-identity variables affect one's gender status. Thus, even within a single culture, women's lives are not uniform.[85]

New Directions in the Anthropology of Gender

More-recent research has been focused on improving the ethnographic and archaeological record and re-examining old material. Some have turned from cause-effect relations to better understanding how gender systems work and focusing on a single culture or cultural region. Others have explored a single topic, such as menstrual blood and cultural concepts of masculinity and infertility across cultures.[86]

Many American anthropologists "returned home," looking with fresh eyes at the diversity of women's lives in their own society: working-class women, immigrant women, women of various ethnic and racial groups, and women in different geographic regions and occupations.[87] Some ethnographers, for example, immersed themselves in the abortion debates, conducting fieldwork to understand the perspective and logic behind pro-choice and anti-choice activists in North Dakota. Others headed to college campuses, studying the "culture of romance" or fraternity gang rape.[88] Peggy Sanday's work on sexual coercion, including her cross-cultural study of rape-prone societies, was followed by other studies of power-coercion-gender relationships, such as using new reproductive technologies for selecting the sex of children.[89]

Many previously unexplored areas such as the discourse around reproduction, representations of women in medical professions, images in popular culture, and international development policies (which had virtually ignored gender) came under critical scrutiny.[90] Others worked on identifying complex local factors and processes that produce particular configurations of gender and gender relations, such as the **patrifocal** (male-focused) cultural model of family in many parts of India.[91] Sexuality studies expanded, challenging existing binary paradigms, making visible the lives of lesbian mothers and other traditionally marginalized sexualities and identities.[92]

The past virtual invisibility of women in archaeology disappeared as a host of new studies was published, often by feminist anthropologists, including a pioneering volume by Joan Gero and Margaret Conkey, *Engendering Archaeology: Women and Prehistory*. That book gave rise to a multi-volume series specifically on gender and archaeology edited by Sarah Nelson. Everything from divisions of labor to power relations to sexuality could be scrutinized in the archaeological record.[93]

Some anthropologists argued that there are recurring patterns despite the complexity and variability of human gender systems. One is the impact of women's economic contributions on their power, prestige, and autonomy.[94] Women's work, alone, does not necessarily give them control or ownership of what they produce. It is not always valued and does not necessarily lead to political power. Women in many cultures engage in agricultural labor, but the fields are often owned and controlled by their husbands' families or by a landlord, as in many parts of India and Iran.[95] The women have little authority, prestige, or autonomy.[96] Many foraging and some horticultural societies, on the other hand, recognize women's economic and reproductive contributions, and that recognition may reflect relative equality in other spheres as well, including sexuality. Gender relations seem more egalitarian, overall, in small-scale societies such as the San, Trobrianders, and Na, in part because they are kinship-based, often with relatively few valuable resources that can be accumulated; those that exist are communally owned, usually by kinship groups in which both women and men have rights.

Another factor in gender equality is the social environment. Positive social relations—an absence of constant hostility or warfare with neighbors—seems to be correlated with relatively egalitarian gender relations. In contrast, militarized societies—whether small-scale horticultural groups like the Sambia who perceive their neighbors as potential enemies or large-scale stratified societies with formal military organizations and vast empires—seem to benefit men more than women overall.[97] Warrior societies culturally value men's roles, and warfare gives men access to economic and political resources.

As to old stereotypes about why men are warriors, there may be another explanation. From a reproductive standpoint, men are far more expendable than women, especially women of reproductive age.[98] While this theme has not yet been taken up by many anthropologists, male roles in warfare could be more about expendability than supposed greater male strength, aggressiveness, or courage. One can ask why it has taken so long for women in the United States to be allowed to fly combat missions? Certainly it is not about women not being strong enough to carry the plane.[99]

Patriarchy . . . But What about Matriarchy?

The rise of stratified agriculture-intensive centralized "states" has tended to produce transformations in gender relations and gender ideologies that some have called **patriarchy**, a male-dominated political and authority structure and an ideology that privileges males over females overall and in every strata of society. Gender intersects with class and, often, with religion, caste, and ethnicity. So, while there could be powerful queens, males took precedence over females within royal families, and while upper-class Brahmin women in India could have male servants, they had far fewer formal assets, power, and rights than their brothers and husbands. Also, as noted earlier, families strictly controlled their movements, interactions with males, "social reputations," and marriages. Similarly, while twentieth-century British colonial women in British-controlled India had power over some Indian men, they still could not vote, hold high political office, control their own fertility or sexuality, or exercise other rights available to their male counterparts.[100] Of course, poor lower-class lower-caste Indian women were (and still are) the most vulnerable and mistreated in India, more so overall than their brothers, husbands, fathers, or sons.

On the other hand, we have yet to find any "matriarchies," that is, female-dominated societies in which the extent and range of women's power, authority, status, and privilege parallels men's in patriarchal societies. In the twentieth century, some anthropologists at first confused "matriarchy" with **matrilineal**. In matrilineal societies, descent or membership in a kinship group is transmitted from mothers to their children (male and female) and then, through daughters, to their children, and so forth (as in many Na families). Matrilineal societies create woman-centered kinship groups in which having daughters is often more important to "continuing the line" than having sons, and living arrangements after marriage often center around related women in a **matrilocal** extended family household (See Text Box 1, What Can We Learn from the Na?). Female sexuality may become less regulated since it is the mother who carries the "seed" of the lineage. In this sense, it is the reverse of the kinds of patrilineal, patrilocal, patrifocal male-oriented kinship groups and households one finds in many patriarchal societies. Peggy Sanday suggested, on these and other grounds, that the Minangkabau, a major ethnic group in Indonesia, is a matriarchy.[101]

Ethnographic data have shown that males, especially as members of matrilineages, can be powerful in matrilineal societies. Warfare, as previously mentioned, along with political and social stratification can alter gender dynamics. The Nayar (in Kerala, India), the Minangkabau, and the Na are matrilineal societies embedded in, or influenced by, dominant cultures and patriarchal religions such as Islam and Hinduism. The society of the Na in China is also **matrifocal** in some ways. Thus, the larger context, including contemporary global processes, can undermine women's power and status.[102] At the same time, though, many societies are clearly matrifocal, are relatively female-centered, and do not have the kinds of gender ideologies and systems found in most patriarchal societies.[103] Text Boxes 1 and 2 provide examples of such systems.

Text Box 2: Does Black Matriarchy Exist in Brazil? Histories of Slavery and African Cultural Survivals in Afro-Brazilian Religion
By Abby Gondek

Candomblé is an Afro-Brazilian spirit possession religion in which Yoruba (West African) deities called *orixás* are honored at religious sites called *terreiros* where the Candomblé priestesses (*mães do santo*) and their "daughters" (*filhas do santo*) live. One of the central "hubs" of Candomblé worship in Brazil is the northeastern state of Bahia, where Afro-Brazilns make up more than 80 percent of the population in the capital city, Salvador. Brazil's geography is perceived through the lenses of race and class since Bahia, a majority Afro-Brazilian state, is viewed as underdeveloped, backward, and poor relative to the whiter and wealthier Southern region.[104]

In the 1930s, a Jewish female anthropologist Ruth Landes provided a different perspective about Bahia, one that emphasized black women's communal power. During the time in which Landes conducted her research, the Brazilian police persecuted Candomblé communities for "harboring communists." The Brazilian government was linked with Nazism, torture, rape, and racism, and Afro-Brazilians resisted this oppression.[105] Also during this period, debate began among social scientists about whether Candomblé was a matriarchal religion in which women were the primary spiritual leaders. The debate was rooted in the question of where "black matriarchy" came from. Was it a result of the history of slavery or was it an African "cultural survival"? The debate was simultaneously about the power and importance of Afro-Brazilian women in spiritual and cultural life.

On one side of the debate was E. Franklin Frazier, an African-American sociologist trained at University of Chicago, who maintained that Candomblé and the lack of legal marriage gave women their important position in Bahia. He believed that black women had been matriarchal authorities since the slavery period and described them as defiant and self-reliant. On the other side of the debate was anthropologist Melville Herskovits, who was trained by German immigrant Franz Boas at Columbia University. Herskovits believed that black women's economic roles demonstrated African cultural survivals, but downplayed the priestesses' importance in Candomblé.[106] Herskovits portrayed patriarchy rather than matriarchy as the central organizing principle in Bahia. He argued that African cultural survivals in Brazil came from the patrilineal practices of Dahomey and Yoruba in West Africa and portrayed Bahian communities as male-centered with wives and "concubines" catering to men and battling each other for male attention.

Ruth Landes and her work triggered the debate about "black matriarchy" in Bahia. Landes had studied with anthropologists Franz Boas and Ruth Benedict at Columbia University. She began her studies of Candomblé in 1938 in Salvador, Bahia, working with her research partner, guide, and significant other, Edison Carneiro, a scholar of Afro-Brazilian studies and journalist, resulting in publication in 1947 of *The City of Women*.[107] Landes contended that Afro-Brazilian women were the powerful matriarchal leaders of *terreiros* de Candomblé. She called them matriarchal because she argued that their leadership was "made up almost exclusively of women and, in any case controlled by women."[108] Landes claimed that the women provided spiritual advice and sexual relationships in exchange for financial support from male patrons of the *terreiros*. She also explained that newer *caboclo* houses (in which indigenous spirits were worshipped in addition to Yoruba spirits) had less-stringent guidelines and allowed men to become priests and dance for the gods, actions considered taboo in the Yoruba tradition. Landes elaborated that these men were primarily "passive" homosexuals. She looked down on this "modern" development, which she viewed as detracting from the supposedly "pure" woman-centered Yoruba (West African) practices.[109]

Even Landes' (controversial) argument about homosexuality was part of her claim about matriarchy; she contended that the homosexual men who became *pais do santo* ("fathers of the saint," or Candomblé priests) had previously been "outcasts"—prostitutes and vagrants who were hounded by the police. By becoming like the "mothers" and acting as women, they could gain status and respect. Landes was strongly influenced by both Edison Carneiro's opinion and the convictions of Martiniano Eliseu do Bonfim (a revered *babalaô* or "father of the secrets") and the women priestesses of the traditional houses (*Gantois*, *Casa Branca*, and *Ilê Axé Opô Afonjá*) with whom she spent the majority of her time. Thus, her writings likely represent the views of her primary informants, making her work unique; at that time, anthropologists (ethnocentrically) considered themselves more knowledgeable about the cultures they studied than the people in those cultures.

Landes incorporated ideas from the pre-Brazil research of E. Franklin Frazier and Melville Herskovits to contend that the existence of the matriarchy in Bahia rested on women's economic positions, sexuality, and capacities, which were influenced by (1) white slave owners' preference for black women as heads of families and the inculcation of leadership traits in black women and not black men and (2) the history of women's roles as property owners, market sellers, priestesses, and warriors in West Africa.[110]

Landes' findings continue to be critiqued in contemporary academic contexts because some scholars disagree with her matriarchy thesis and her views about homosexual *pais* and *filhos do santo*. J. Lorand Matory, director of African and African-American research at Duke University, has taken one of the strongest positions against Landes, arguing that she altered the evidence to argue for the existence of the "*cult matriarchate*." Matory believes that her division between "new" and "traditional" houses is a false one and that men traditionally were the leaders in Candomblé. In fact, Matory contends that, at the time of Landes' research, more men than women were acting as priests.[111] In contrast, Cheryl Sterling sees Landes' *The City of Women* as "still relevant today as the first feminist account of Candomblé" and maintains that Candomblé is a space in which Afro-Brazilian women are the "supreme authority" and that the *terreiro* is an enclave of "female power." The Brazilian state stereotypes black women as socially pathological with "unstable" family structures, making them "sub-citizens," but Sterling argues that Candomblé is a space in which female blackness prevails.[112]

Has Civilization "Advanced" Women's Position?

Ironically, some nineteenth- and twentieth-century writers and social scientists, such as Herbert Spencer, have argued that women's positions "advanced" with civilization, especially under European influence, at least relative to so-called "primitive" societies. The picture is complicated, but the opposite may actually be true. Most anthropological studies have suggested that "civilization," "colonialism," "development," and "globalization" have been mixed blessings for women.[113] Their traditional workloads tend to increase while they are simultaneously excluded from new opportunities in agricultural cash crops, trading, and technology. Sometimes they lose traditional rights (e.g., to property) within extended family kinship groups or experience increased pressure from men to be the upholders of cultural traditions, whether in clothing or marriage practices. On the other hand, new political, economic, and educational opportunities can open up for women, allowing them not only to contribute to their families but to delay marriage, pursue alternatives to marriage, and, if they marry, to have a more powerful voice in their marriages.[114]

Deeply embedded cultural-origin stories are extremely powerful, difficult to unravel, and can persist despite contradictory evidence, in part because of their familiarity. They resemble what people have seen and experienced throughout their lifetimes, even in the twenty-first century, despite all the changes. Yet, nineteenth and twentieth century cultural models are also continuously reinforced and reproduced in every generation through powerful devices: children's stories; rituals like Valentine's Day; fashion, advertisements, music, video games, and popular culture generally; and in financial, political, legal, and military institutions and leaders. But profound transformations can produce a "backlash," as in U.S. movements to restore "traditional" family forms, "traditional" male and female roles, sexual abstinence-virginity, and the "sanctity" of heterosexual marriage.[115] Some would argue that backlash elements were at work in the 2016 Presidential and Congressional elections (see Text Box 3).

Cultural origin stories also persist because they are **legitimizing ideologies**—complex belief systems often developed by those in power to rationalize, explain, and perpetuate systems of inequality. The hunting-way-of-life theory of human evolution, for example, both naturalizes and essentializes male dominance and other gender-related traits and provides an origin story and a legitimizing ideology for the "traditional" U.S. nuclear family as "fundamental to human social organization and life." It also can be used to justify "spousal rape" and domestic violence, treating both as private family matters and, in the past, as male "rights." Not surprisingly, elements of the traditional nuclear family model appear in the 2015 U.S. Supreme Court case that legalized same-sex marriage, especially in the dissenting views. And cultural models of gender and family played a role in the 2016 U.S. Presidential election. For a related activity, see Activity 3 below.

Text Box 3: Gender and the 2016 U.S. Presidential Election
By Carol C. Mukhopadhyay

The 2016 presidential election was gender precedent-setting in ways that will take decades to analyze (see for example Gail Collins). For the first time, a major U.S. political party chose a woman as its presidential candidate. And while Hillary Rodham Clinton did not win the electoral college, she won the popular vote, the first woman to do so, and by nearly three million votes. As a cultural anthropologist who has long studied women and politics, I offer a few preliminary observations on the role of gender in the 2016 presidential election.[116]

Women on the Political Leadership Stage

From a positive perspective, for the first time, two women (Republican Carly Fiorina and Democrat Hillary Clinton) participated in televised presidential primary debates and one went on to the "finals." Millions of people, including children, saw articulate, accomplished, powerful women competing with men to be "Commander-in-Chief." During the 2016 Democratic National Convention, the country watched a major political party and key male leaders celebrate the life and professional and leadership-relevant achievements of a woman, its presidential nominee. The role-modeling impacts are enormous—and, one hopes, long-lasting.

The Gendered White House Family

The 2016 presidential campaign challenged, at least momentarily, the traditional, taken-for-granted, gendered institution of the White House first "family." What if the president's spouse were male? This would wreck havoc with the conventional "first lady" role! Traditionally, the spouse, even if highly educated, becomes the "help mate" and "listener," handles "domestic affairs," organizes and attends important social occasions, and works on gender-appropriate projects such as children's health. Hillary Clinton was roundly criticized, as first lady, for venturing beyond the "domestic sphere" and pursuing health care reform in Bill Clinton's administration even though she had indisputably relevant professional expertise. Michelle Obama, with her Harvard law degree and prior career as a lawyer, became best known as "First Mom" and a "fashion-setter" whose clothing was discussed and emulated. While she was a very positive role model, especially for African-Americans, and developed major initiatives to combat childhood obesity and promote fresh food, she did not challenge gender conventions. How many girls remember her professional credentials and achievements?

Had Hillary Clinton won, the need to confront gendered elements of the conventional White House family would have come to the forefront as the "first gentleman" role gradually evolved. Certainly, no one would have expected Bill Clinton to choose china patterns, redecorate the living quarters, or become a "fashion trend-setter."

Consensual Sexual Interactions: Which Century Are We In?

The 2016 presidential campaign stimulated discussion of other often-ignored gender-related topics. Despite some progress, sexual harassment and sexual assault, including rape, remain widespread in the workplace and on college campuses (cf. Stanford case, The Hunting Ground). Yet there has been enormous pressure on women—and institutions—to remain silent.

In October 2016, after a video was released of Donald Trump bragging about his ability to sexually grope women he did not know, the presidential candidate said it was only "locker room talk"...not anything he had ever done. Hearing these denials, several women, some well-known, came forth with convincing claims that Trump had groped them or in other ways engaged in inappropriate, non-consensual sexual behavior. Trump responded by denying the charges, insulting the accusers, and threatening lawsuits against the claimants and news media organizations that published the reports.[117] For many women, the video aroused memories of their own recurring experiences with sexual harassment and assault. After the video was released, Kelly Oxford started a tidal wave of women unburdening long-kept secrets with her tweet: "Women: tweet me your first assaults." Others went on record denouncing Trumps' talk and behavior, and the hashtag #NotOkay surged on Twitter.

In a normal U.S. presidential election, the video and repeated accusations of sexual assault would have forced the candidate to withdraw (as happened with Gary Hart in a previous election). Instead, accusers experienced a backlash not only from Trump but from some media organizations and Trump supporters, illustrating why women are reluctant to come forth or press sexual charges, especially against powerful men (see the 1991 Anita Hill-Clarence Thomas case). These voters' reactions and the continued willingness of so many others to vote for the candidate suggest that "locker room banter" and unwanted sexual advances are still considered normal and acceptable among significant segments of our population. After all, "boys will be boys," at least in the old (false) baboon stereotype of male behavior! Clearly, we need more public conversations about what constitutes appropriate and consensual sexually related behavior.

Sexism: Alive and Well

The 2016 presidential campaign revealed that sexism is alive and well, though not always recognized, explicit, or acknowledged even when obvious (see article by Lynn Sherr). The media, both before and after the election, generally underplayed the impact of sexism despite research showing that sexist attitudes, not political party, were more likely to predict voters preference for Donald Trump over Hillary Clinton.[118]

The campaign also reflected a persistent double standard. Despite widespread agreement that Hillary Clinton was highly qualified to be president, her judgment, competence, "stamina," and even her proven accomplishments were subjected to scrutiny and criticism not normally applied to similarly experienced male candidates. Additional gender-specific criteria were imposed: "likeability," "smiling enough," "warmth," and appearance. She did not "look" "presidential"—an image of leadership that evoked the stereotype baboon model! But being six feet tall with large biceps and acting "tough" and "aggressive" probably would have disqualified her, as a woman, from the start! Other traits that are acceptable in men—ambitious, goal-focused, strategic, "wanting" the presidency—were treated as liabilities in Clinton, part of a "power-hungry" critique, as though women are not legitimately supposed to pursue or hold power.

Patriarchal Stereotypes of Women

Hillary Clinton's candidacy seems to have activated long-standing patriarchal stereotypes and images of women. One is the "good vs. bad" woman opposition. The "good" woman is chaste, obedient, nurturing, self-sacrificing, gentle—the Virgin Mary/Mother figure. The "bad" woman is greedy, selfish, independent, aggressive, and often, sexually active—importantly, she lies, deceives, is totally untrustworthy. Bad ("nasty") women in myths and reality must be punished for their transgressions; they are dangerous to men and threaten the social order.

As a researcher and someone who had many conversations with voters during this election, I was shocked by the intensity and level of animosity directed at Hillary Clinton. It was palpable, and it went far beyond a normal critique of a normal candidate. At Republican rallies, mass shouts of "lock her up" and T-shirts and bumper stickers bearing slogans like "Trump that Bitch" (and worse) bore a frightening resemblance to violence-inciting hate-speech historically directed at African-Americans and at Jews, gays, and socialists in Nazi Germany, as well as to hate-filled speech that fueled Medieval European witch-burnings in which thousands (if not millions), mainly women, were burned at the stake ["burn the witch"].[119] Clinton was indeed challenging "traditional" gender roles in U.S. politics, the workplace, and at home. Patriarchy was being threatened, and many, though not all, voters found that profoundly disturbing even though they did not necessarily recognize it or admit it.[120]

Beyond that, there is a long tradition of blaming women for personal and societal disasters—for convincing Adam to eat the forbidden fruit, for the breakup of joint family households in places like India. Women often become the repository for people's frustrations when things "go wrong" (Remember the spoiled sausage in Portuguese culture discussed earlier in this chapter?). Women—like minorities, immigrants, and "evil empires"—are culturally familiar, available targets to which one can legitimately assign blame, frustration, and even rage, as we saw in the 2016 election.[121]

Hillary Clinton as a Symbol of Change

Ironically, Hillary Clinton was depicted and criticized during the campaign as a symbol of the "establishment" while her key opponents stood for "change." I think it is just the opposite. Hillary Clinton and her campaign and coalition symbolized (and embraced) the major transformations—indeed, upheavals—that have occurred in the United States since the 1960s. It is not just feminism and a new definition of masculinity that rejects the old baboon male-dominance tough-guy model, although that is one change.[122] While economic anxiety and "white nationalism" both played roles, the election was also about an "America" that is changing demographically, socially, religiously, sexually, linguistically, technologically, and ideologically—changing what constitutes "truth" and reality. For many in rural areas, outside forces—especially the government, run by liberal, urban elites—are seen as trying to control one's way of life with gun control, environmental regulations, ending coal mining, banning school (Christian) prayer, requiring schools to teach evolution and comprehensive sex education (vs. abstinence only). Hillary Clinton, her coalition, and her alignment with the Obama White House, not just with its policies but with an African-American "first family," symbolized the intersection of all these social, demographic, and cultural transformations. She truly represented "change."

Ironically, Clinton's opponents, even in the Democratic Party, were more "establishment" candidates culturally, demographically, and in their gender relationships. Bernie Sanders attracted an enormous, enthusiastic following and came close to winning the Democratic presidential primary. Yet his rhetoric and policy proposals, while unusual in twenty-first century mainstream politics, resembled the economic inequality, anti-Wall Street, "it's only about economics" focus of early twentieth century democratic socialists such as Eugene Debs and Norman Thomas and of progressive Henry Wallace. And, not surprisingly, Sanders appealed largely to Euro-American demographic groups rather than to the broader spectrum of twenty-first century voters.

In short, the election and the candidacy of Hillary Rodham Clinton symbolized more than half a century of enormous change—and a choice between continuing that change or selecting a candidate who symbolized what was traditional, familiar, and, to many, more comfortable. Whether the transformations of the past fifty years will be reversed remains to be seen.[123]

Discussion

From a global perspective, the United States lags behind many countries in women's political leadership and representation. For national legislative bodies, U.S. women constitute only 19 percent of Congress, **below** the world average of 23 percent, below the average in the Americas, 28 percent, and far below Nordic countries, 41 percent. The U.S. ranks 104th of 193 countries in the world (see http://www.ipu.org/wmn-e/classif.htm). When it comes to political leadership, over 65 nations have elected at least one woman as their head of state, including countries with predominantly Muslim, Christian, Jewish, Hindu, and/or Buddhist populations. (see https://www.theglobalist.com/women-on-top-of-the-political-world/.) Yet the U.S. still has never elected a woman President (or even Vice-President). Are you surprised by these data or by some of the countries that rank higher than the United States? Why? What do you think are some of the reasons the US lags behind so many other countries?

Additional Resources and Links
Center for American Women and Politics
Presidential Gender Watch: http://presidentialgenderwatch.org/
Institute for Women's Policy Research
Pew Research Institute (U.S. and international data)
United Nations, UN Women

CONTEMPORARY ANTHROPOLOGICAL APPROACHES TO STUDYING SEXUALITY AND GENDER

Contemporary anthropology now recognizes the crucial role played by gender in human society. Anthropologists in the post-2000 era have focused on exploring fluidity within and beyond sexuality, incorporating a gendered lens in all anthropological research, and applying feminist science frameworks, discourse-narrative analyses, political theory, critical studies of race, and queer theory to better understand and theorize gendered dynamics and power. Pleasure, desire, trauma, mobility, boundaries, reproduction, violence, coercion, bio-politics, globalization, neoliberal "development" policies and discourses, immigration, and other areas of anthropological inquiry have also informed gender and sexuality studies. We next discuss some of those trends.[124]

Heteronormativity and Sexuality in the United States

In the long history of human sexual relationships, we see that most involve people from different biological sexes, but some societies recognize and even celebrate partnerships between members of the same biological sex.[125] In some places, religious institutions formalize unions while in others unions are recognized only once they result in a pregnancy or live birth. Thus, what many people in the United States consider "normal," such as the partnership of one man and one woman in a sexually exclusive relationship legitimized by the state and federal government and often sanctioned by a religious institution, is actually **heteronormative**. **Heteronormativity** is a term coined by French philosopher Michel Foucault to refer to the often-unnoticed system of rights and privileges that accompany normative sexual choices and family formation. For example, a "biologically female" woman attracted to a "biologically male" man who pursued that attraction and formed a relationship with that man would be following a heteronormative pattern in the United States. If she married him, she would be continuing to follow societal expectations related to gender and sexuality and would be agreeing to state involvement in her love life as she formalizes her relationship.

Despite pervasive messages reinforcing heteronormative social relations, people find other ways to satisfy their sexual desires and organize their families. Many people continue to choose partners from the so-called "opposite" sex, a phrase that reflects the old U.S. bipolar view of males and females as being at opposite ends of a range of characteristics (strong-weak, active-passive, hard-soft, outside-inside, Mars-Venus).[126] Others select partners from the same biological sex. Increasingly, people are choosing partners who attract them—perhaps female, perhaps male, and perhaps someone with ambiguous physical sexual characteristics.

Labels have changed rapidly in the United States during the twenty-first century as a wider range of sexual orientations has been openly acknowledged, accompanied by a shift in our binary view of sexuality. Rather than thinking of individuals as either heterosexual OR homosexual, scholars and activists now recognize a *spectrum* of sexual orientations. Given the U.S. focus on identity, it is not surprising that a range of new personhood categories, such as bisexual, queer, questioning, lesbian, and gay have emerged to reflect a more-fluid, shifting, expansive, and ambiguous conception of sexuality and sexual identity.

Transgender, meanwhile, is a category for people who transition from one sex to another, male to female or female to male, using a number of methods. Anthropologist David Valentine explored how the concept of "transgender" became established in the United States and found that many people who were identified by others as transgender did not embrace the label themselves. This label, too, has undergone a profound shift in usage, and the high-profile transition by Caitlyn Jenner in the mid-2010s has further shifted how people think about those who identify as transgender.[127]

By 2011, an estimated 8.7 million people in the United States identified as lesbian, gay, bisexual, and/or transgender.[128] These communities represent a vibrant, growing, and increasingly politically and economically powerful segment of the population. While people who identify as gay, lesbian, bisexual, and transgender—or any of a number of other sexual and gender minorities—have existed throughout the United States' history, it is only since the Stonewall uprisings of 1969 that the modern LGBT movement has been a key force in U.S. society.[129] Some activists, community members, and scholars argue that LGBT (lesbian, gay, bisexual, and/or transgender) is a better choice of labels than GLBT since it puts lesbian identity in the foreground—a key issue because the term "gay" is often used as an umbrella term and can erase recognition of individuals who are not gay males. Recently, the acronym has been expanded to include LGBTQ (queer or questioning), LGBTQQ (both queer and questioning), LGBTQIA (queer/questioning, intersex, and/or asexual), and LGBTQAIA (adding allies as well).

Like the U.S. population overall, the LGBTQ community is extremely diverse. Some African-Americans prefer the term "same-gender loving" because the other terms are seen as developed by and for "white people." Emphasizing the importance and power of words, Jafari Sinclaire Allen explains that "same-gender loving" was "coined by the black queer activist Cleo Manago [around 1995] to mark a distinction between 'gay' and 'lesbian' culture and identification, and black men and women who have sex with members of the same sex."[130] While scholars continue to use gay, lesbian, and queer and the U.S. Centers for Disease Control uses MSM (men who have sex with men), "same-gender loving" resonates in some urban communities.

Not everyone who might fit one of the LGBTQQIA designations consciously identifies with a group defined by sexual orientation. Some people highlight their other identities, as Minnesotans, for example, or their ethnicity, religion, profession, or hobby—whatever they consider central and important in their lives. Some scholars argue that heteronormativity allows people who self-identify as heterosexual the luxury of not being defined by their sexual orientation. They suggest that those who identify with the sex and gender they were assigned at birth be referred to as **cisgender**.[131] Only when labels are universal rather than used only for non-normative groups, they argue, will people become aware of discrimination based on differences in sexual preference.

Though people are urging adoption of sexual identity labels, not everyone is embracing the move to self-identify in a specific category. Thus, a man who is attracted to both men and women might self-identify as bisexual and join activist communities while another might prefer not to be incorporated into any sexual-preference-based politics. Some people prefer to eliminate acronyms altogether, instead embracing terms such as *genderfluid* and *genderqueer* that recognize a spectrum instead of a static identity. This freedom to self-identify or avoid categories altogether is important. Most of all, these shifts and debates demonstrate that, like the terms themselves, LGBTQ communities in the United States are diverse and dynamic with often-changing priorities and makeup.

Changing Attitudes toward LGBTQ People in the United States

In the last two decades, attitudes toward LGBTQ—particularly lesbian, gay and bisexual—people have changed dramatically. The most sweeping change is the extension of marriage rights to lesbian, gay, and bisexual people. The first state to extend marriage rights was Massachusetts in 2003. By 2014, more than half of U.S. Americans said they believed same-sex couples should have the right to marry, and on June 26, 2015, in *Obergefell v. Hodges*, the U.S. supreme court declared that same-sex couples had the legal right to marry.[132] Few civil rights movements have seen such progress in such a short period of time. While many factors have influenced the shift in attitudes, sociologists and anthropologists have identified increased awareness of and exposure to LGBTQ people through the media and personal interactions as playing key roles.[133]

Legalization of same-sex marriage also helped normalize same-sex parenting. Sarah, whose three young children—including a set of twins—are mothered by Sarah and her partner, was active in campaigns for marriage equality in Minnesota and ecstatic when the campaign succeeded in 2013 (see Text Box 4).

However, legalization of same-sex marriage has not been welcomed everywhere in the United States. Anthropologist Jessica Johnson's ethnographic work profiling a Seattle-based megachurch from 2006 through 2008 initially explored their efforts to oppose same-sex marriage. Later, she shifted her focus to the rhetoric of gender, masculinity, and cisgender sexuality used by the church and its pastor.[134] Official church communications dismissed homosexuality as aberrant and mobilized members to advocate against same-sex marriage. The church's efforts were not successful.

Interestingly, activists and gender studies scholars express concern over incorporating marriage—a heteronormative institution some consider oppressive—into queer spaces not previously governed by state authority. These concerns may be overshadowed by a desire for normative lives and legal protections, but as sociologist Tamara Metz and others have argued, legally intertwining passion, romance, sexual intimacy, and economic rights and responsibilities is not necessarily a move in the right direction.[135] As Miriam Smith has written, "We must move beyond thinking of same-sex marriage and relationship recognition as struggles that pit allegedly normalized or assimilated same-sex couples against queer politics and sensibilities and, rather, recognize the increasingly complex gender politics of same-sex marriage and relationship recognition, a politics that implicates groups beyond the LGBT community."[136]

While U.S. culture on the whole has become more supportive and accepting of LGBTQ people, they still face challenges. Sexual orientation and gender identity are not federally protected statuses. Thus, in 32 states (as of 2016), employers can legally refuse to hire and can fire someone simply for being LGBTQ.[137] Even in states where queer people have legal protection, transgender and other gender-diverse people do not. LGBTQ people can be legally denied housing and other important resources heterosexual people take for granted. LGBTQ youth made up 40 percent of homeless young people in the United States in 2012 and are often thrust into homelessness by family rejection.[138] Transgender people are the most vulnerable and experience high levels of violence, including homicide. See Activity 4: Bathroom Transgression.

Text Box 4: Moving Toward Marriage Equality in Minnesota: Sarah's Letter

In 2013, the Minnesota state legislature voted on whether to approve same-sex marriage. Before the vote, a woman named Sarah made the difficult decision to advocate publicly for the bill's approval. In the process, she wrote the following letter.

Dear Minnesota Senator,

This is an open letter to you in support of the marriage equality bill. I may not be your constituent, and you may already know how you are planning to vote, but I ask you to read this letter with an open mind and heart nonetheless.

I want same-sex marriage for the same reasons as many others. My partner Abby and I met in the first days of 2004 and have created a loving home together with our three kids and two cats. We had a commitment ceremony in 2007 in Minneapolis and were legally married in Vancouver during our "honeymoon." We want our marriage to be recognized because our kids deserve to have married parents, and because we constantly face increased stress as a result of having our relationship not recognized. But that's not why I'm writing. I'm writing because there is one conversation I have over and over again with my son that puts a pit in my stomach each time, and I'm ready for that pit to go away.

Abby and I both wear wedding bands. We designed them prior to our ceremony and spent more time on that decision than we did on the flowers, dresses, and music combined. Our son is now three and a half and, like other kids his age, he asks about everything. All the time. When I get him dressed, change his diaper (please let him be potty-trained soon), or wipe his nose, he sees my ring. And he always asks:

"Mama, what's that ring on your finger?"

"It's my wedding band."

"Why you wear a wedding band?"

"Because when Ima and I got married, we picked out wedding bands and now we wear them every day. It shows that we love each other."

"I want wear wedding band."

"Someday when you're all grown up, you'll fall in love and get married. And you'll get to wear a wedding band, too."

"I'll grow up and get married? And then I get a wedding band?"

"Yep."

"Okay."

And then he goes about his day. This conversation may seem silly and harmless to you, but read it again. Look at how many times the issue of marriage comes up. We call it a wedding band, but every time we say that, we know it's not completely true because we were not legally wed in Minnesota. When I tell my son about our marriage or our wedding, I know I'm hiding a secret from him, but am I really supposed to explain that it was a "commitment ceremony" and we are "committed, but not "married"? He's too young to be saddled with the pain that comes from being left out. He looks at our pictures and sees that his parents made a commitment to each other because of love. He doesn't understand his grandfather's speech recognizing how bittersweet the day was because the state we call home refused to bless our union as it blesses the unions of our friends. And he doesn't understand that, when I tell him he will grow up and get married, his marriage will (most likely) be part of a tradition from which his parents are excluded.

I am grateful that he is blissfully unaware right now. Imagine having the conversation with your children. Imagine the pain you would feel if innocent conversations with your child reminded you constantly that your love is not valued by your community. Don't get me wrong; our friends and family treated our ceremony as they would a legal wedding. We had a phenomenal time with good food, music, laughter, and joy. If our ceremony in Minneapolis had been enough, though, we wouldn't have bothered to get legally married in Vancouver. There is something so powerful and intangible about walking into a government office and walking out with a marriage license. We are grateful we had the opportunity there, and simply wish our state would recognize our commitment as the marriage that it is.

Take a look at the picture of my family. It's outdated, primarily because we can't get our kids to sit still long enough for a photo. I'm on the right, Abby on the left. Our son is now 3.5 and our girls (twins) are almost 2. We can appreciate that this is a difficult vote for many of you and we would be honored if you think of our family and the im-

Figure 19: Sarah's family photo.

pact this vote will have on us. We know many people outside of the Twin Cities never have a chance to meet families like ours. Tell them about us, if it helps. We are happy to answer any questions you may have. Thank you for reading.

Sincerely,

Sarah

Minneapolis, Minnesota

April 2013

Note: Minnesota legalized same-sex marriage in 2013.

Sexuality outside the United States

Same-sex sexual and romantic relationships probably exist in every society, but concepts like "gay," "lesbian," and "bisexual" are cultural products that, in many ways, reflect a culturally specific gender ideology and a set of beliefs about how sexual preferences develop. In many cultures (such as the Sambia discussed above), same-sex sex is a behavior, not an identity. Some individuals in India identify as practicing "female-female sexuality" or "male-male sexuality." The film *Fire* by Mira Nair aroused tremendous controversy in India partly because it depicted a same-sex relationship between two married women somewhat graphically and because it suggested alternatives available to women stuck in unhappy and abusive patriarchal marriages.[139] Whether one is "homosexual" or "heterosexual" may not be linked simply to engaging in same-sex sexual behavior. Instead, as among some Brazilian males, your status in the sexual relationship, literally and symbolically, depends on (or determines!) whether you are the inserter or the penetrated.[140] Which would you expect involves higher status?

Even anthropologists who are sensitive to cross-cultural variations in the terms and understandings that accompany same-sex sexual and romantic relationships can still unconsciously project their own meanings onto other cultures. Evelyn Blackwood, an American, described how surprised she was to realize that her Sumatran lover, who called herself a "Tombois," had a different conception of what constituted a "lesbian" identity and lesbian relationship than she did.[141] We must be careful not to assume that other cultures share LGBTQ identities as they are understood in the United States and many European countries.

Furthermore, each country has its own approach to sexuality and marriage, and reproduction often plays a central role. In Israel, an embrace of pro-natalist policies for Jewish Israelis has meant that expensive reproductive technologies such as in vitro fertilization are provided to women at no cost or are heavily subsidized. An Israeli gay activist described how surprised queer activists from other countries were when they found that nearly all Israeli female same-sex couples were raising children. (This embrace of same-sex parenting did not extend to male couples, for whom the state did not provide assisted reproductive support.) The pro-natalist policies can be traced in part to Israel's emergence as a state: founded in the aftermath of persecution and systematic genocide of Jewish residents of Europe from 1937 through 1945, Israel initially promoted policies that encouraged births at least in part as resistance to Nazi attempts to destroy the Jewish people. The contexts may be less dramatic elsewhere, but local and national histories often inform policies and practices.

In Thailand, Ara Wilson has explored how biological women embrace identities as *toms* and *dees*. Although these terms seem to be derived from English-language concepts (*dees* is etymologically related to "ladies"), suggesting international influences, the ubiquity and acceptance of *toms* and *dees* in Thailand does diverge from patterns in the United States.[142]

In China (as elsewhere), the experiences of those involved in male-male sexuality and those involved in female-female sexuality can differ. In her book *Shanghai Lalas: Female Tongzhi Communities and Politics in Urban China*, Lucetta Yip Lo Kam discusses how lesbians in China note their lack of public social spaces compared with gay men.[143] Even the words *lala* and *tongzhi* index different categories from the English terms: *lala* encompasses lesbian, bisexual, and transgendered people while *tongzhi* is a gloss term that usually refers to gay men but has been expanded in the last two decades to other uses. (*Tongzhi* is a cooptation of the Chinese-language socialist-era term for *comrade*.)

Language makes a difference in how individuals and communities articulate their identities. Anthropologists such as Kam have commented on how sharing their own backgrounds with those with whom they work can be instrumental in gaining trust and building rapport. Her identity as a Chinese-speaking queer anthropologist and activist from Hong Kong helped women in Shanghai feel comfortable speaking with her and willing to include her in their networks.[144]

From these examples, we see that approaches to sexuality in different parts of the world are evolving, just as gender norms in the United States are undergoing tremendous shifts. Anthropologists often cross boundaries to research these changes, and their contributions will continue to shape understandings of the broad range of approaches to sexuality.

Anthropology of the Body

Another important topic for anthropologists interested in gender and sexuality is the anthropology of the body, sometimes referred to as embodied anthropology. Viewing the human body as an analytic category offers exciting new theoretical possibilities.[145] Topics that have attracted particular attention include popular and scientific representations of the body; (dis)ability; the anthropology of obesity; the politics of reproduction; coercion; complex issues associated with genital modifications such as female circumcision; and the relationship between bodies and borders.[146] Who can cross which lines physically (think about national borders), emotionally, psychologically, and socially? Embodied anthropology foregrounds these questions.

Anthropologists increasingly write about their own experiences using an auto-ethnographic mode. For example, Pamela Runestad examined how her time as a patient in a Japanese maternity ward influenced her understanding of the importance of carefully crafted meals and nutrition for HIV/AIDS patients.[147] In subsequent research on HIV/AIDS in Japan, she probed more deeply into how patients' nourishment inside and outside clinical settings affected their perceptions of health.

Anthropology of the body overlaps with work on gender and sexuality, including the discourse surrounding women's bodies and reproductive functions. Emily Martin's pioneering book, *The Woman in the Body*, critically examined lay women and medical descriptions of menstruation, child-bearing, and menopause in the United States. She identified a scientific ideology of reproduction that is infused with traditional U.S. binary gender stereotypes similar to those in man-the-hunter origin stories. In her classic essay about what she calls a "scientific fairy tale," Martin describes how U.S. biology texts represented the egg and sperm as romantic partners whose actions are described with passive or active verbs according to gendered assumptions.[148]

I realized that the picture of egg and sperm drawn in popular as well as scientific accounts of reproductive biology relies on stereotypes central to our cultural definitions of male and female. The stereotypes imply not only that female biological processes are less worthy than their male counterparts but also that women are less worthy than men. Part of my goal in writing this article is to shine a bright light on the gender stereotypes hidden within the scientific language of biology.[149]

Subsequent work has challenged the "sperm penetrates egg" model of fertilization, noting that it is medically inaccurate and reinforces male-active-dominant, female-passive (penetrated) gender models. In reality, the egg and sperm fuse, but the egg activates the sperm by releasing molecules that are crucial for it to find and adhere to the egg.[150] Old videos like *The Miracle of Life* offer, in their narration and background music, striking examples of the cultural ideology of reproduction in the United States that Martin and others have described.[151]

In another classic essay, Corinne Hayden explored interactions between biology, family, and gender among lesbian couples. Even though both members of the lesbian couples she studied did not necessarily contribute biologically to their offspring, the women and their families found ways to embrace these biological differences and develop a new formulation of family that involved biological connection but was not limited to it.[152]

Some research analyzes the body, especially the female body, as a site of coercion and expression of power relations by individuals (e.g., partner rape and domestic violence), but state-sanctioned collective acts also occur, such as using women as "sex slaves" (Japan's so-called "Comfort Women" during World War II) and using civilian rape as a form of psychological warfare. Anthropologists document other ways in which states exert power over bodies—through family planning policies (China's planned birth policy), legislation that bans (or permits) artificial forms of contraception and abortion, and government programs to promote fertility, including subsidized infertility treatments.[153] For example, Turkish anthropologists have described how state policies in Turkey have appropriated, for state purposes, sexual issues of concern to Turkish families, such as assisted reproduction for disabled war veterans and treatment of vaginismus, a condition that prevents women from engaging in sexual intercourse. Power relationships are also associated with new reproductive technologies. For example, the availability of amniocentesis often contributes to shifts in the ratio of male and female babies born. Unequal power relations are also in play between surrogate mothers (often poor women) and wealthier surrogate families desiring children.[154]

Women in Anthropology

As seen earlier in this chapter, female anthropologists have always played a key role in anthropology. In sex-segregated societies, they have had unique access to women's worlds. Recently, they have analyzed how gender might affect styles of authorship and authority in ethnographies. Social characteristics, including gender, race, class, sexuality, and religion, also influence how an anthropologist engages in fieldwork and how she and her colleagues relate to one another.[155] Sometimes the identity of an anthropologist creates new opportunities for deeper understanding and connection, but at other times one's personal identity can create professional challenges.

Fieldwork

Women face particular challenges when conducting fieldwork regardless of the culture but particularly in sex-segregated and patriarchal societies. Sometimes women are perceived as more vulnerable than men to sexual harassment, and their romantic choices in fieldwork situations are subject to greater scrutiny than choices made by men in similar situations.[156] Women may be more likely to juggle family responsibilities and professional projects and bring children with them for fieldwork. At first glance, this practice may raise eyebrows because of the risks it brings to accompanying children and because of potential negative impacts on the anthropologist's planned work, but many female anthropologists have found fieldwork undertaken with their families to be a transformative experience both professionally and personally. Whereas appearing as a decontextualized single fieldworker can arouse suspicion, arriving at a field site with the recognizable identities of parent, daughter, or spouse can help people conceptualize the anthropologist as someone with a role beyond camera-toting interviewer and observer. At the same time, arriving as a multi-person group also complicates what Jocelyn Linnekin called "impression management." One's child is often less aware of delicate matters and less sensitive in communicating preferences to hosts, causing potentially embarrassing situations but also creating levity that might otherwise be slow to develop. Fieldwork as a family unit also allows for a different rhythm to the elusive work-life balance; many families have reported cherishing time spent together during fieldwork since they rarely had so much time together in their activity-filled home settings.[157]

More anthropologists now conduct fieldwork in their home communities. Some wish to explore theoretical and empirical questions best examined in local field sites. Others are reluctant or unable to relocate their families or partners temporarily. Conducting fieldwork close to home can also be a less expensive option than going abroad! But the boundaries of field and home can become quite porous. In their writings, women anthropologists reveal how the realms of public and private and political and personal are connected in the field/home. Innovative, activist, and self-reflective studies address intersections that other scholars treat separately.[158]

Academic Anthropology in the United States

Though the representation of women in U.S. academic anthropology is now proportional to their numbers in the Ph.D. pool, discrepancies remain between male and female anthropology professors in rank and publication rates. A 2008 report on the status of women in anthropology, for example, found evidence of continuity of the "old boys' network"—the tendency for men in positions of power to develop relationships with other men, which creates pooled resources, positive performance evaluations, and promotions for those men but not for women. Furthermore, since women in the United States are usually socialized to avoid making demands, they often accept lower salary offers than could have been negotiated, which can have significant long-term financial consequences.[159]

Women are also over-represented among non-tenure-track anthropology faculty members who are often paid relatively small per-course stipends and whose teaching leaves little time for research and publishing. Some married women prioritize their partners' careers, limiting their own geographic flexibility and job (and fieldwork) opportunities. Left with few academic job options in a given area, they may leave academia altogether.[160]

On a positive note, women have an increasingly prominent place in the highest ranks of anthropology, including as president of the American Anthropological Association. Nonetheless, systemic gender inequality continues to affect the careers of female anthropologists. Given what we know about gender systems, we should not be surprised.

Masculinity Studies

Students in gender studies and anthropology courses on gender are often surprised to find that they will be learning about men as well as women. Early women's studies initially employed what has been called an "add women and stir" approach, which led to examinations of gender as a social construct and of women's issues in contemporary society. In the 1990s, women's studies expanded to become gender studies, incorporating the study of other genders, sexuality, and issues of gender and social justice.[161] Gender was recognized as being fundamentally relational: femaleness is linked to maleness, femininity to masculinity. One outgrowth of that work is the field of "masculinity studies."[162]

Masculinity studies goes beyond men and their roles to explore the relational aspects of gender. One focus is the enculturation processes through which boys learn about and learn to perform "manhood." Many U.S. studies (and several excellent videos, such as *Tough Guise* by Jackson Katz), have examined the role of popular culture in teaching boys our culture's key concepts of masculinity, such as being "tough" and "strong," and shown how this "tough guise" stance affects men's relationships with women, with other men, and with societal institutions, reinforcing a culture of violent masculinity. Sociologist Michael Kimmel has further suggested that boys are taught that they live in a "perilous world" he terms "Guyland."[163]

Anthropologists began exploring concepts of masculinity cross-culturally as early as the 1970s, resulting in several key publications in 1981, including Herdt's first book on the Sambia of New Guinea and Ortner and Whitehead's volume, *Sexual Meanings*. In 1990, Gilmore analyzed cross-cultural ethnographic data in his *Manhood in the Making: Cultural Concepts in Masculinity*.[164] Other work followed, including a provocative video on the Sambia, *Guardians of the Flutes*. But the growth of studies of men and masculinity in the United States also stimulated new research approaches, such as "performative" aspects of masculinity and how gender functions in wealthier, post-industrial societies and communities with access to new technologies and mass media.[165]

Anthropologists sometimes turn to unconventional information sources as they explore gendered culture, including popular television commercials. Interestingly, the 2015 Super Bowl commercials produced for the Always feminine product brand also focused on gender themes in its #Likeagirl campaign, which probed the damaging connotations of the phrases "throw like a girl" and "run like a girl" by first asking boys and girls to act out running and throwing, and then asking them to act out a *girl* running and throwing. A companion clip further explored the negative impacts of anti-girl messages, provoking dialogue among Super Bowl viewers and in social media spaces (though, ironically, that dialogue was intended to promote consumption of feminine products). As the clips remind us, while boys and men play major roles in perceptions related to gender, so do the women who raise them, often reinforcing gendered expectations for play and aspiration. Of course, women, like men, are enculturated into their culture's gender ideology.[166] Both girls and boys—and adults—are profoundly influenced by popular culture.

Though scholars from many disciplines publish important work on masculinity, anthropologists, with their cross-cultural research and perspectives, have significantly deepened and enriched interdisciplinary understandings. Anthropologists have made strong contributions not only by providing nuanced portrayals (of, for example, men in prison, heroin users, migrant laborers, college students, and athletes in the United States) but also through offering vivid accounts of expectations of men in other societies, including the relationship between those expectations and warfare. This can include differences in expectations based on a person's age, other role-based variations, and transformation of traditional roles as a result of globalization.[167]

Not all societies expect men to be "tough guys/guise," and those that do go about it in different ways and result in different impacts on men and women.[168] For example, in Sichuan Province in China, young Nuosu men must prove their maturity through risky behavior such as theft. In recent years, theft has been supplanted for many by heroin use, particularly as young men have left their home communities for urban areas (where they are often feared by city residents and attract suspicion).[169] Meanwhile, in the Middle East, technologies such as assisted reproduction are challenging and reshaping ideas about masculinity among some Arab men, particularly men who acknowledge and struggle with infertility. There and elsewhere, conceptions of fatherhood are considered crucial components of masculinity. In Japan, for example, a man who has not fathered a child is not considered to be fully adult.[170]

Elsewhere, as we saw in the first part of this chapter, men are expected to be gentle nurturers of young children and to behave in ways that do not fit typical U.S. stereotypes. In Na communities, men dote on babies and small children, often rushing to pick them up when they enter a room. In South Korea, men in wildly popular singing groups wear eyeliner and elaborate clothing that would be unusual for U.S. groups, and throughout China and India, as in many other parts of the world, heterosexual men walk down the street holding hands or arm-in-arm without causing raised eyebrows. Physical contact between men, especially in sex-segregated societies, is probably far more common than contact between men and women! Touch is a human form of intimacy that need not have sexual implications. So if male-male relations are the most intimate in a society, physical expressions of those relations are "normal" overall unless there is a cultural fear of male physical intimacy. There is much more nuance in actual behavior than initial appearances lead people to believe.

Anthropologists are also applying approaches taken in American studies to other cultures. They are engaging in more-intimate discussions of males' self-perceptions, dilemmas, and challenges and have not hesitated to intercede, carefully, in the communities in which they work. Visual anthropologist Harjant Gill, conducting research in the Punjab region of India, began asking men about pressures they faced and found that the conversations prompted unexpected reflection. Gill titled his film *Mardistan (Macholand)* and shepherded the film through television broadcasts and smaller-scale viewings to encourage wide discussion in India of the issues he explored.[171] For a related activity, see Activity 5: Analyzing Gendered Stereotypes and Masculinity in Music Videos.

CONCLUSION

In 1968, a cigarette company in the United States decided to target women as tobacco consumers and used a clever marketing campaign to entice them to take up smoking. "You've come a long way, baby!" billboards proclaimed. Women, according to the carefully constructed rhetoric, had moved away from their historic oppressed status and could—and should—now enjoy the full complement of twentieth-century consumer pleasures. Like men, they deserved to enjoy themselves and relax with a cigarette. The campaigns were extremely successful; within several years, smoking rates among women had increased dramatically. But had women really come a long way? We now know that tobacco (including in vaporized form) is a highly addictive substance and that its use is correlated with a host of serious health conditions. In responding to the marketing rhetoric, women moved into a new sphere of bodily pleasure and possibly enjoyed increased independence, but they did so at a huge cost to their health. They also succumbed to a long-term financial relationship with tobacco companies who relied on addicting individuals in order to profit. Knowing about the structures at work behind the scenes and the risks they took, few people today would agree that women's embrace of tobacco represented a huge step forward.

Perhaps saying "You've come a long way, baby!" with the cynical interpretation with which we read it today can serve as an analogy for our contemporary explorations of gender and culture. Certainly, many women in the United States today enjoy heightened freedoms. We can travel to previously forbidden spaces, study disciplines long considered the domain of men, shape our families to meet our own needs, work in whatever field we choose, and, we believe, live according to our own wishes. But we would be naive to ignore how gender continues to shape, constrain, and inform our lives. The research and methods of anthropology can help us become more aware of the ongoing consequences of our gendered heritage and the ways in which we are all complicit in maintaining gender ideologies that limit and restrict people's possibilities.

By committing to speak out against subtle, gender-based discrimination and to support those struggling along difficult paths, today's anthropologists can emulate pioneers such as Franz Boas and Margaret Mead, who sought to fuse research and action. May we all be kinder to those who differ from the norm, whatever that norm may be. Only then will we all—women, men and those who identify with neither category—have truly come a long way. (But we will leave the infantilizing "baby" to those tobacco companies!)

DISCUSSION QUESTIONS

1. What is "natural" about how you experience gender and human sexuality? What aspects are at least partially shaped by culture? How do other cultures' beliefs and practices regarding gender and sexuality differ from those commonly found in the United States? Are there any parallels? Does it depend on which U.S. community we are talking about? What about your own beliefs and practices?
2. Reflect on the various ways you have "learned" about gender and sexuality throughout your life. Which influences do you think had the biggest impact?
3. How important is your gender to how you think about yourself, to your "identity" or self-definition, to your everyday life? Reflect on what it would be like to be a different gender.
4. How important is your "sexuality" and "sexual orientation" to how you think about yourself, to your identity or self-definition? Reflect on what it would be like if you altered your sexual identity or practices.
5. In what ways have your school settings been shaped by and around gender norms?
6. How are anthropologists influenced by gender norms? How has this affected the discipline of anthropology?

GLOSSARY

Androgyny: cultural definitions of gender that recognize some gender differentiation, but also accept "gender bending" and role-crossing according to individual capacities and preferences.

Binary model of gender: cultural definitions of gender that include only two identities--male and female.

Biologic sex: refers to male and female identity based on internal and external sex organs and chromosomes. While male and female are the most common biologic sexes, a percentage of the human population is intersex with ambiguous or mixed biological sex characteristics.

Biological determinism: a theory that biological differences between males and females leads to fundamentally different capacities, preferences, and gendered behaviors. This scientifically unsupported view suggests that gender roles are rooted in biology, not culture.

Cisgender: a term used to describe those who identify with the sex and gender they were assigned at birth.

Dyads: two people in a socially approved pairing. One example is a married couple.

Gender: the set of culturally and historically invented beliefs and expectations about gender that one learns and performs. Gender is an "identity" one can choose in some societies, but there is pressure in all societies to conform to expected gender roles and identities.

Gender ideology: a complex set of beliefs about gender and gendered capacities, propensities, preferences, identities and socially expected behaviors and interactions that apply to males, females, and other gender categories. Gender ideology can differ among cultures and is acquired through enculturation. Also known as a cultural model of gender.

Heteronormativity: a term coined by French philosopher Michel Foucault to refer to the often-unnoticed system of rights and privileges that accompany normative sexual choices and family formation.

Legitimizing ideologies: a set of complex belief systems, often developed by those in power, to rationalize, explain, and perpetuate systems of inequality.

Matrifocal: groups of related females (e.g. mother-her sisters-their offspring) form the core of the family and constitute the family's most central and enduring social and emotional ties.

Matrilineal: societies where descent or kinship group membership is transmitted through women, from mothers to their children (male and female), and then through daughters, to their children, and so forth.

Matrilocal: a woman-centered kinship group where living arrangements after marriage often center around households containing related women.

Patriarchy: describes a society with a male-dominated political and authority structure and an ideology that privileges males over females in domestic and public spheres.

Patrifocal: groups of related males (e.g. a father-his brothers) and their male offspring form the core of the family and constitute the family's most central and enduring social and emotional ties.

Patrilineal: societies where descent or kinship group membership is transmitted through men, from men to their children (male and female), and then through sons, to their children, and so forth.

Patrilocal: a male-centered kinship group where living arrangements after marriage often center around households containing related men.

Third gender: a gender identity that exists in non-binary gender systems offering one or more gender roles separate from male or female.

Transgender: a category for people who transition from one sex to another, either male-to-female or female-to-male.

ACTIVITIES

Activity 1: How Does Gender Shape Your Life?

Think about everything, and we do mean **everything**, you did since waking up this morning. Include micro-behaviors, tiny behavioral acts that take minutes or even seconds, as well as objects, substances, and language, spoken and written. Think about all the "cultural" (i.e. not found "in nature") artifacts associated with these behaviors. For example, while urinating is natural, your "toilet" is a cultural invention. Now, which activities and behaviors were in some way "gendered"? That is, which had an element associated with "female" or "male" in some way?

As you think about how gender has shaped your life today, consider:

- What did you sleep in?
- How did you handle bodily functions?
- How did you clean yourself?
- How did you modify your body? (e.g. "shaving", "makeup," "deodorant")
- What do the names for products, like deodorants, perfumes or aftershave, convey?

List all these gendered (and gender-neutral) aspects of your day thus far. Also consider: how typical is today? Would a weekend involve more or less "gendered" dimensions?

Activity 2. Understanding Gender from a Martian Perspective.

If you were a Martian, what would you have to "know" or "learn" in order to follow gender rules on a college campus? As you consider your response, think about the following questions.

- In what ways are we a gender "binary" culture? An "opposite sex" culture? An "androgynous" culture?
- Are areas of U.S. life informally sexually segregated? Are there, informally, "male" and "female" spheres? Are there male spheres where women are not supposed to go? Or spheres where if they go, they incur certain risks? Are there any parallels for men who enter female spheres?
- Are there any elements of an "honor" and "shame" culture in the U.S. that a Martian should be aware of? What about in your own social circle?

Activity 3. Ethnographic Interview: How has Gender Changed Over Time?

Interview someone at least age 65 (if you are close to 65, find someone a generation older or younger than you). Ask that person: What kind of changes in gender roles, gender relations, gender restrictions or privileges have occurred within your lifetime? After you conclude your interview, compare notes with others to find common threads. Then ask someone closer to your age what changes they anticipate may happen their lifetime?

Activity 4. Bathroom Transgression.

Transgender people often face dilemmas when needing to use public restrooms. As a way to experience what it's like to be an ally, some people have started intentionally using bathrooms designated for others—an issue that took on a heightened relevance in 2016, when North Carolina banned transgender people from using sex-segregated bathrooms that did not correspond to the sex registered on their birth certificates. As part of this activity, consider whether you dare enter the bathroom you don't normally use. If you do, then try it! What happens when you enter the men's room, or the women's room? How are these boundaries patrolled and enforced? Many European countries offer unisex facilities; do you think the U.S. should do so as well? Or do you agree with some politicians in North Carolina who cited safety concerns for public restroom use by transgender individuals?

Note: keep safety in mind if you choose this activity, and beware of settings where people may be hostile to an experiment like this.

Activity 5. Analyzing Gendered Stereotypes and Masculinity in Music Videos.

Popular culture plays an enormous role in shaping our ideas about gender, about femininity and masculinity, and about sexuality. Watch several of the videos below, paying careful attention to how these concepts are visible in current music videos. Do they draw on gendered stereotypes or push boundaries of expected gendered norms? Specify which videos you watched in your response, and also look for examples of other videos that could stimulate fruitful conversations about masculinity, femininity and other gender dynamics.

- Watch Maddi & Tae, "Girl in a Country Song." This song is partly a response to Blake Shelton—"Boys 'Round Here," and Florida Georgia Line—"Get your Shine On." What do you think of Maddi & Tae's portrayal of men in their video? How does it compare with portrayals of women in videos by Blake Shelton and Florida Georgia Line?
- Compare "Bitch in Business" (created by MBA students), to "Girl in a Country Song." Pay particular attention to the third and fourth verses of "Bitch in Business." Would you change any lyrics, or do you think they are justified? What about the word "Bitch" itself? Is it problematic? In what ways? Do words matter? Can you really change the historically negative associations of a word, like "bitch" or "slut"? Are there parallels to ethnic slurs?
- Compare Niki Minaj and Lady Gaga: how do they deploy gender in their songs, lyrics and videos? How do their strategies compare to a male artist from a similar genre?
- Compare Sir Mix-A-Lot, "Baby Got Back" and Niki Minaj, "Anaconda." How do they deploy gender in their songs, lyrics, and videos? Is there any significant difference between what Minaj does in her video and what Sir Mix-a-Lot does in his? How is race used in these videos?
- Should the music video industry be regulated and if so, in what ways and why? Does it make a difference if the videos are frequently consumed by (and marketed to) young people, pre-teens and teens, rather than adults who have a more fully-developed personal sense of identity? What concerns might you as a parent have?

For further exploration and analysis, view the video, *Hip-Hop: Beyond Beats and Rhymes* (http://www.mediaed.org/). Do you think the analysis provided by filmmaker Byron Hurt can be applied to these music videos?

Also view *Dreamworlds 3* (http://www.mediaed.org/), which analyzes the stories told in popular culture about gender and sexuality. How well does this analysis apply to contemporary videos, including the ones that you've just viewed?

RESOURCES FOR FURTHER EXPLORATION

Educational Media Companies and Distributors:

- Documentary Education Resources. http://www.der.org. One of the earliest distributors of anthropology-ethnographic films. Includes older, but still very useful, ethnographic films. Such films document ways of life that are rapidly disappearing.
- Media Education Foundation. http://www.mediaed.org/ Focuses on contemporary USA culture, with a wide range of videos analyzing mass media, popular culture, and advertising. . Videos often include teaching guides.
- Women Make Movies. www.wmm.com. Wide range of films/videos by women filmmakers on diverse topics, social groups, both within the US and throughout the world. One of the earliest distributors of films on gender.
- Women's Media Center. www.womensmediacenter.com/ More U.S.-centered resources, especially contemporary issues of women's representation in the media.

Some Key Accessible Readings by Anthropologists:

Brettell, Carolyn and Brettell, Carolyn B. and Carolyn F. Sargent, eds. *Gender in Cross-Cultural Perspective.* 6th edition (New York: Routledge, 2012). Excellent collection of articles, with overviews. Also includes a Film Bibliography for each topical section of the book.

Geller, Pamela L. and Miranda K. Stockett, eds., *Feminist Anthropology: Past, Present, and Future* (Philadelphia: University of Pennsylvania Press, 2006). Many articles by biological and archeological anthropologists.

Hodgson, Dorothy L., ed. *The Gender, Culture, and Power Reader.* (New York: Oxford University Press, 2016). Useful reader for students and non-specialist readers. Includes a wide range of articles, often adapted from longer academic articles.

Ellen Lewin, ed., *Feminist Anthropology: A Reader* (Malden, MA: Blackwell Publishing, 2006). Excellent collection with introductory essay by editor, a pioneer in feminist and Lesbian-Gay studies.

Strum, Shirley and Fedigan, Linda, eds., *Primate Encounters: Models of Science, Gender and Society* (Chicago: University of Chicago Press, 2000).

Ward, Martha and Monica Edelstein, *A World full of Women.* 6th edition (New York: Routledge/Taylor Francis, 2014). Readable overview of the field.

Some Useful Organizational Websites

American Men's Studies Association
Association for Feminist Anthropology, American Anthropological Association
VOICES: Journal of the Association for Feminist Anthropology
Book reviews from the Association for Feminist Anthropology
Association for Queer Anthropology
Center for American Women and Politics, Rutgers University
Feminist Majority Foundation
Guttmacher Center (Research on reproductive health)
National Women's Studies Association
Planned Parenthood

ABOUT THE AUTHORS

Dr. Mukhopadhyay specializes in gender, sexuality, race/ethnicity, and culture-cognition, with research in the USA and India on gendered families, politics, and science-engineering. In graduate school she co-created one of the earliest gender-culture courses. She has developed numerous gender classes and taught, for 20 years, a popular anthropology and gender-oriented, multi-section Human Sexuality course. Gender-related publications include: *Cognitive Anthropology Through a Gendered Lens* (2011). *How Exportable are Western Theories of Gendered Science?* (2009), *A Feminist Cognitive Anthropology: The Case of Women and Mathematics* (2004), *Women, Education and Family Structure in India* (1994, with S. Seymour). She co-authored an early *Annual Review of Anthropology* article on gender (1988) and is in the Association for Feminist Anthropology. In other work, she served as a Key Advisor for the AAA RACE project; co-authored *How Real is Race: A Sourcebook on Race, Culture and Biology*, (2nd Edition, 2014) and promotes active learning approaches to teaching about culture (cf.2007).

Tami Blumenfield is Assistant Professor of Asian Studies at Furman University and was a 2016 Fulbright Scholar affiliated with Yunnan University. Since 2001, she has been engaged in a long-term ethnographic fieldwork project in northwest Yunnan Province, studying changes in education, social life, and ecology in Na communities. Blumenfield is the co-editor of *Cultural Heritage Politics in China*, with Helaine Silverman (2013), and of *Doing Fieldwork in China...With Kids!* with Candice Cornet (2016). Blumenfield also produced *Some Na Ceremonies*, a Berkeley Media film by Onci Archei and Ruheng Duoji. Blumenfield holds a PhD in Sociocultural Anthropology from the University of Washington.

Susan Harper, Ph.D., is an educator, activist, and advocate in Dallas, Texas. She holds a Ph.D. in Cultural Anthropology from Southern Methodist University and a Graduate Certificate in Women's Studies from Texas Woman's University. Her ethnographic research focuses on New Religious Movements, primarily NeoPaganism, in the American South; the intersection of gender, sexuality, and religious identity; and ses, sexuality, and sex education. Her work has been published in the *Journal of Bisexuality*. Susan is passionate about a variety of social justice causes, including domestic and intimate partner violence prevention and recovery, sexual assault prevention and recovery, LGBTQ equality and inclusion, and educational justice. She has given presentations on LGBTQ+ equality and inclusion to a variety of audiences, including the North Texas Society of Human Resource Managers, The Turning Point Rape Crisis Center, and various religious organizations. She teaches courses in anthropology, sociology, and Women's and Gender Studies at various universities and colleges in the DFW area. She also serves as Graduate Reader/Editor for Texas Woman's

University. She is currently working on an autoethnography about burlesque and visual anthropology project exploring the use of Pinterest by practitioners of NeoPaganism.

Abby Gondek is a PhD candidate in Global and Socio-cultural Studies (majoring in Anthropology/Sociology) at Florida International University in Miami, Florida. She defended her dissertation proposal in April 2016. Her project, "Jewish Women's Transracial, Transdisciplinary and Transnational Social Science Networks, 1920–1970" uses social network analysis and grounded theory methodology to understand the relationships between the anti-racist and pro-political/economic justice stance taken by Jewish female social scientists and their Jewish gendered-racialized subjectivities. Further information about her work is available from http://transform-art-gender.webs.com and http://abbygondek.blogspot.com as well as https://www.instagram.com/abbygondek/.

ACKNOWLEDGMENTS

The authors wish to thank the many people who supported this writing project. We especially appreciate the editorial guidance of Nina Brown and the constructive feedback from two anonymous reviewers. We are grateful to our students as well, particularly those in Blumenfield's Gender in East Asia at Furman University who read a draft version of this chapter in 2016 and shared feedback that helped us improve the chapter, and to Mukhopadhyay's students at California State University Chico and at San Jose State University. We also thank the many individuals who shared their lives with us and with other anthropologists, enabling us to understand and appreciate the breadth, depth, and richness of human cultural diversity. Finally, Carol Mukhopadhyay extends her thanks to Nina Brown and Tami Blumenfield, and to Susan Seymour, on many levels, for help on the 2016 Gender and the Presidential Election text box.

NOTES

1. The Introduction and much of the material in the Foundations segment draws upon and synthesizes Mukhopadhyay's decades of research, writing, and teaching courses on culture, gender, and human sexuality. Some of it has been published. Other material comes from lecture notes. See http://www.sjsu.edu/people/carol.mukhopadhyay.

2. We use quotation marks here and elsewhere in the chapter to alert readers to a culturally specific, culturally invented concept in the United States. We need to approach U.S. cultural inventions the same way we would a concept we encountered in a foreign, so-called "exotic" culture.

3. See Carolyn B. Brettell and Carolyn F. Sargent, *Gender in Cross-Cultural Perspective* (New York: Routledge, 2005). Also, Anne Fausto-Sterling, *Myths of Gender. Biological Theories About Women and Men* (New York: Basic Books, 1991). For some web-based examples of these nineteenth century views, see article at http://www.bl.uk/romantics-and-victorians/articles/gender-roles-in-the-19th-century. For a list of descriptive terms, see http://www2.ivcc.edu/gen2002/Women_in_the_Nineteenth_Century.htm.

4. For an example of a textbook, see Herant A. Katchadurian, *Fundamentals of Human Sexuality* (Fort Worth, TX: Holt, Rinehart and Winston, 1989). See also Linda Stone, *Kinship and Gender: An Introduction* (Boulder, CO: Westview Press, 2013).

5. Material in the following paragraphs comes from Mukhopadhyay, unpublished Human Sexuality lecture notes.

6. Herant A. Katchadurian, *Fundamentals of Human Sexuality*, 365.

7. Phyllis Kaberry, *Women of the Grassfields. A Study of the Economic Position of Women in Bamenda, British Cameroons* (Colonial Research publication 14. London: Her Majesty's Stationery Office.1952) The image comes from the cover of her book, which is also available online: http://www.era.anthropology.ac.uk/Kaberry/Kaberry_text/.

8. See Barry S. Hewlett, *Intimate Fathers: The Nature and Context of Aka Pygmy Paternal Infant Care* (Ann Arbor: University of Michigan Press, 1991); and personal communication with Mukhopadhyay.

9. W.H. Masters and V.E. Johnson, *Human Sexual Response (New York: Bantam Books, 1966).*

10. Some feminist scholars have also questioned the "naturalness" of the biological categories male and female. See for example, Judith Butler, *Gender Trouble: Feminism and the Subversion of Identity* (New York: Routledge, 1999 [1990]).

11. For genital similarities, see Janet S. Hyde and John D. DeLamater, *Understanding Human Sexuality* (McGraw Hill, 2014), 94–101. For more parallels, see Mukhopadhyay's online Human Sexuality course materials, at www.sjsu.edu/people/carol.mukhopadhyay.

12. For some idea of the enormous variability in human physical characteristics, see Chapter 1 and Chapter 2 in C. Mukhopadhyay, R. Henze, and Y. Moses, *How Real is Race: Race, Culture and Biology* (Lanham, MD: Rowman and Littlefield, 2014).

13. Information about alternative gender roles in pre-contact Native American communities can be found in Martha Ward and Monica Edelstein, *A World Full of Women* (Boston: Pearson, 2013). Also, see the 2011 PBS Independent Lens film *Two Spirits* for an account of the role of two-spirit ideology in Navajo communities, including the story of a Navajo teenager who was the victim of a hate crime because of his two-spirit identity.

14. Martha Ward and Monica Edelstein, *A World Full of Women.*

15. Serena Nanda, *Neither Man nor Woman: the Hijras of India* (Boston, MA: Cengage, 1999); Serena Nanda, *Gender Diversity: Cross-cultural Variations* (Prospect Heights, IL: Waveland 2000); and Gayatri Reddy and Serena Nanda, "Hijras: An "Alternative" Sex/Gender in India," in *Gender in Cross-Cultural Perspective*, ed. C. Brettell and C. Sargent, 278–285 (Upper Saddle River New Jersey: Pearson, 2005).

16. Janet S. Hyde and John D. DeLamater, *Understanding Human Sexuality*, 99; Martha Ward and Monica Edelstein, *A World Full of Women.*

17. Beverly Chinas, personal communication with Mukhopadhyay. See also her writings on Isthmus Zapotec women such as: Beverly Chinas, *The Isthmus Zapotecs: A Matrifocal Culture of Mexico* (New York: Harcourt Brace College Publishers 1997). For a film on this culture, see Maureen Gosling and Ellen Osborne, *Blossoms of Fire, Film* (San Francisco: Film Arts Foundation, 2001).

18. Gilbert Herdt, *The Sambia* (New York: Holt Rinehart and Winston, 2006). For an excellent film see Gilbert Herdt, *Guardians of the Flutes* (London UK: BBC, 1994).

19. More information about the Nu shu writing system can be found in the film by Yue-Qing Yang, *Nu Shu: A Hidden Language of Women in China* (New York: Women Make Movies, 1999).

20. Ernestine Friedl, *Women and Men: An Anthropologist's View* (New York: Holt, Rinehart and Winston, 1975). See Audrey Richards, *Chisungu: A Girl's Initiation Ceremony among the Bemba of Zambia* (London: Faber, 1956) and A. Richards, *Land, Labour and Diet in Northern Rhodesia, An Economic Study of the Bemba Tribe* (London: Oxford, 1939).

21. See for example, Ian Hogbin, *The Island of Menstruating Men: Religion in Wogeo, New Guinea* (Scranton, PA: Chandler Publishing Company, 1970).

22. Susannah M Hoffman, Richard A Cowan and Paul Aratow, *Kypseli: Men and Women Apart A Divided Reality* (Berkeley CA: Berkeley Media, 1976).

23. Denise Lawrence, Menstrual Politics: Women and Pigs in Rural Portugal, in *Blood Magic: The Anthropology of Menstruation*, ed. Thomas Buckley and Alma Gottlieb, 117–136 (Berkeley: University of California Press. 1988.), 122–123.

24. See http://www.bbc.co.uk/programmes/p03k6k0h. Some women are posing with photos of menstrual pads and hashtags #happytobleed: http://www.independent.co.uk/news/world/asia/indian-women-launch-happy-to-bleed-campaign-to-protest-against-sexist-religious-rule-a6748396.html.

25. See the film by Michael Camerini and Rina Gill, *Dadi's Family* (Watertown, MA: DER, 1981).

26. Cynthia Nelson, "Public and Private Politics: Women in the Middle Eastern World" *American Ethnologist* 1 no. 3 (1974): 551–56.

27. Carol C. Mukhopadhyay, "Family Structure and Indian Women's Participation in Science and Engineering," in *Women, Education and Family Structure in India*, ed. Carol C. Mukhopadhyay and Susan Seymour, 103–133 (Boulder: Westview Press, 1994).

28. Elizabeth Fernea, *Guests of the Sheik.an Ethnography of an Iraqi Village* (New York: Anchor Books, 1965).

29. Susan Seymour, *Cora Du Bois: Anthropologist, Diplomat, Agent* (Lincoln, NE: University of Nebraska Press, 2015).

30. Carol C. Mukhopadhyay, "Women in Science: Is the Glass Ceiling Disappearing?" Proceedings of conference organized by the National Institute of Science and Technology Development Studies, the Department of Science and Technology, Government of India; Indian Council of Social Science Research; and the Indo-U.S. Science and Technology Forum. March 8–10, 2004. New Delhi, India.

31. See for instance, http://www.newyorker.com/culture/culture-desk/a-powerful-documentary-about-pakistans-honor-killings and http://www.latimes.com/world/afghanistan-pakistan/la-fg-pakistan-oscar-20160229-story.html.

32. For more details, see the film by Leslee Udwin, *India's Daughter* (Firenze, Italy: Berta Film). The Wikipedia article about the film notes the reluctance of the Indian government to air the film in India, https://en.wikipedia.org/wiki/India's_Daughter.

33. For a critique of the "myth" of the medieval chastity belt, see http://www.telegraph.co.uk/women/sex/chastity-belts-the-odd-truth-about-locking-up-womens-genitalia.

34. See for example, the film by Sabiha Sumar, *Silent Waters* (Mumbai, India: Shringar Film). While this is not a documentary, the film reflects the tumultuous history of the partition into two countries.

35. For the !Kung San, see Marjorie Shostak, *Nisa: Life and Words of a Kung Woman* (New York: Vintage, 1983). For Trobrianders, see Annette B. Weiner, *The Trobrianders of Papua New Guinea* (New York: Holt Rinehart and Winston, 1987).

36. Shanshan Du, *Chopsticks Only Work in Pairs: Gender Unity and Gender Equality Among the Lahu of Southwest China* (New York: Columbia University Press, 1999).

37. Zhou Huashan, *Zhong nu bu qingnan de muxi mosuo: Wufu de guodu?* [Matrilineal Mosuo, *Valuing Women without Devaluing Men: A Society without Fathers or Husbands?*] (Beijing: Guangming Ribao Chubanshe, 2009 [2001]).

38. Ernestine Friedl, *Women and Men: An Anthropologist's View* (Holt, Rinehart and Winston, 1975).

39. Carol C. Mukhopadhyay, "Sati or Shakti: Women, Culture and Politics in India," in *Perspectives on Power: Women in Asia, Africa and Latin America*, ed. Jean O'Barr, 11–26 (Durham: Center for International Studies, Duke University 1982).

40. Lila Abu-Lughod, *Writing Women's Worlds: Bedouin Stories* (Berkeley: University of California Press, 2008).

41. Mukhopadhyay and Seymour use the term "patrifocal" to describe households that consist of related males, usually brothers, and their sons, and the spouses and children of those males. See C. Mukhopadhyay and S. Seymour, "Introduction" in *Women, Family, and Education in India* (Boulder: Westview Press, 1994).

42. For powerful documentaries see, the film by Nishta Jain, *Gulabi Gang* (Stavanger, Norway: Kudos Family Distribution, 2012); and the film by Kim Longinotto, *Pink Saris* (New York: Women Make Movies, 2011).

43. Lionel Tiger, *Men in Groups* (New Brunswick, NJ: Transaction Publishers, 2005[1969]), 45.

44. Carol C. Mukhopadhyay, *The Sexual Division of Labor in the Family*, PhD Dissertation, University of California, Riverside, 1980, 192.

45. Carol C. Mukhopadhyay, fieldnotes, India; and Mukhopadhyay, *The Cultural Context of Gendered Science: The Case of India*, 2001, www.sjsu.edu/people/carol.mukhopadhyay/papers.

46. For example, the major symposium on Man the Hunter sponsored by Wenner-Gren Foundation for Anthropological Research included only four women among more than sixty listed participants. See Richard B. Lee and Irven DeVore, *Man the Hunter* (Chicago: Aldine Atherton, 1972[1968]), xiv–xvi.

47. Mukhopadhyay, Lecture Notes, Human Sexuality, Gender and Culture.

48. S.Washburn and C.S. Lancaster, "The Evolution of Hunting." in *Man the Hunter*, 299.

49. Ibid., 303.

50. Jackson Katz, *Tough Guise 2: Violence, Manhood and American Culture* (Northampton, MA: Media Education Foundation, 2013).

51. Abigail Disney and Kathleen Hughes, *The Armor of Light* (New York: Fork Films, 2015).

52. Lionel Tiger and Robin Fox, *The Imperial Animal* (New York: Transaction Publishers, 1997 [1971]), 101.

53. Some useful reviews include the following: Linda M. Fedigan, "The Changing Role of Women in Models of Human Evolution" *Annual Review of Anthropology* 16 (1986): 25–66; Linda Fedigan, *Primate Paradigms: Sex Roles and Social Bonds* (Chicago: University of Chicago Press, 1992); Pamela L. Geller and Miranda K. Stockett. *Feminist Anthropology: Past, Present, and Future (*Philadelphia: University of Pennsylvania Press 2006); Joan M. Gero and Margaret W. Conkey, *Engendering Archeology: Women and Prehistory* (Malden, MA: Blackwell Publishers, 1991); Shirley Strum and Linda Fedigan *Primate Encounters: Models of Science, Gender and Society.* (Chicago: University of Chicago Press, 2000); Meredith F. Small, *What's Love Got to Do with It? The Evolution of Human Mating* (New York: Doubleday, 1995); Nancy Makepeace Tanner, *On Becoming Human* (Cambridge: Cambridge University Press, 1981). For a readable short article, see Meredith Small, "What's Love Got to Do with It," *Discover Magazine*, June 1991, 46–51.

54. Irven DeVore, ed. *Primate Behavior* (New York: Holt, Rinehart and Winston, 1965).

55. Ibid. Also, for primate politics in particular, see Sarah B. Hrdy, *The Woman That Never Evolved* (Cambridge, MA: Harvard University Press, 1999 [1981]). See also Hrdy's website http://www.citrona.com/hrdy.html.

56. Thelma Rowell. *Social Behaviour of Monkeys* (New York: Penguin Books, 1972). For an excellent online article on Rowell's work with additional references, read Vinciane Despret, "Culture and Gender Do Not Dissolve into How Scientists 'Read' Nature: Thelma Rowell's Heterodoxy." In *Rebels of Life. Iconoclastic Biologists in the Twentieth Century, edited by* O. Hartman and M. Friedrich (New Haven: Yale University Press, 2008), 340–355. http://www.vincianedespret.be/2010/04/culture-and-gender-do-not-dissolve-into-how-scientists-read-nature-thelma-rowells-heterodoxy/.

57. See Richard B. Lee and Irven DeVore, eds. *Man the Hunter* (Chicago: Aldine Atherton, 1972[1968]).

58. See Estioko-Griffin, Agnes A. Daughters of the Forest. *Natural History* 95(5):36–43 (May 1986).

59. Richard B. Lee, *The !Kung San. Men, Women and Work in a Foraging Society* (Cambridge, UK: Cambridge University Press, 1979).

60. Martha Ward and Monica Edelstein, *A World Full of Women*, 26.

61. Susan Seymour, "Multiple Caretaking of Infants and Young Children: An Area in Critical Need of a Feminist Psychological Anthropology," *Ethos* 32 no. (2004): 538–556.

62. Serena Nanda and Richard L. Warms, *Cultural Anthropology* (Belmont, CA: Wadsworth, 2006), 274.

63. Ester Boserup, *Women's Role in Economic Development* (New York: St. Martin's Press, 1970); Barbara D. Miller, *Cultural Anthropology* (Pearson/Allyn and Bacon, 2012).

64. Mauma Downie and Christina Gladwin, *Florida Farm Wives: They Help the Family Farm Survive* (Gainesville: Food and Resource Economics Department, University of Florida, 1981).

65. Judith K. Brown, "A Note on the Division of Labor by Sex," *American Anthropologist* 72 (1970):1073–78.

66. See www.momsrising.org for some contemporary examples of the challenges and obstacles workplaces pose for working mothers, as well as efforts to advocate for improved accommodation of parenting and working.

67. Conrad Kottak, *Cultural Anthropology. Appreciating Cultural Diversity* (New York: McGraw Hill, 2013).

68. See C. Mukhopadhyay, Human Sexuality Lecture notes, for the following analysis, available from http://www.sjsu.edu/people/carol.mukhopadhyay/courses/AnthBioHS140/. See also Mukhopadhyay, Part II, "Culture Creates Race," especially chapter 7 and 9, in Carol Mukhopahdyay, R. Henze and Y. Moses *How Real is Race? A Sourcebook on Race, Culture and Biology* (Lanham, MD: Rowman & Littlefield, 2014).

69. Ibid.

70. This and subsequent material comes from C. Mukhopadhyay, Part 2, especially chapter 9, and p. 182–185, in Carol Mukhopahdyay, R. Henze and Y. Moses. *How Real is Race? A Sourcebook on Race, Culture and Biology, 2nd edition* (Lanham, MD: Rowman & Littlefield, 2014).

71. Carol C. Mukhopadhyay, Yolanda Moses and Rosemary Henze, *How Real is Race?*, Chapter 9.

72. Annette B. Weiner, *The Trobrianders of Papua New Guinea* (New York: Holt Rinehart and Winston, 1987).

73. Lu Hui, "Preferential Bilateral-Cross-Cousin Marriage among the Nuosu in Liangshan," in *Perspectives on the Yi of Southwest China*, Stevan Harrell, ed. (Berkeley, CA: University of California Press, 2001).

74. Elizabeth Fernea, *Guests of the Sheik*.

75. See the film *Maasai Women*, 1980.

76. An excellent documentary on two alternative paths some women take in contemporary India: the Miss India path and the fundamentalist Hindu path. Filmed in India, *The World Before Her*, http://www.pbs.org/pov/worldbeforeher/.

77. See https://contemporaryfamilies.org/the-way-we-still-never-were-brief-report/ and https://www.pri.org/stories/2014-09-14/singles-now-outnumber-married-people-america-and-thats-good-thing for background and links to detailed information.

78. Material in this text box was adapted from "What Can We Learn from the Na? Shattering Ideas about Family and Relationships," a TEDx FurmanU presentation by Tami Blumenfield. See also Tami Blumenfield, "Chinese Tour Groups in Europe, Chinese Tour Groups in Yunnan: Narrating a Nation in the World" *The China Beat* June 2, 2011. http://www.thechinabeat.org/?p=3494; Siobhan M. Mattison, Brooke Scelza, and Tami Blumenfield, "Paternal Investment and the Positive Effects of Fathers among the Matrilineal Mosuo (Na) of Southwest China" *American Anthropologist* 116 no. 3 (2014): 591–610; Tami Blumenfield, "Resilience in Mountainous Southwest China: Adopting a Socio-Ecological Approach to Community Change," in *Worlds in the Making: Interethnicity and the Processes of Generating Meaning in Southwestern China, Cahiers d'Extrême Asie* 23 (2014).

79. See reviews in Naomi Quinn, "Anthropological Studies of Women's Status," *Annual Review of Anthropology* 6 (1977): 181–225; Carol Mukhopadhyay and Patricia Higgins, "Anthropological Studies of the Status of Women Revisited: l977-l987" *Annual Review of Anthropology* 17 (1988):461–95.

80. Michelle Rosaldo and Louise Lamphere, ed. *Woman, Culture and Society* (Stanford: Stanford University Press, 1974).

81. Rayna Rapp Reiter, ed. *Toward an Anthropology of Women* (New York: Monthly Review Press, 1975); Karen Sacks, *Sisters and Wives. The Past and Future of Sexual Equality* (Westport, CT: Greenwood, 1979).

82. Peggy Sanday, *Female Power and Male Dominance: On the Origins of Sexual Inequality* (Cambridge: Cambridge University Press, 1981).

83. For an alternative ethnographic, research based video see *N!ai: The Story of a !Kung Woman*. 1980.

84. Carol Mukhopadhyay and Patricia Higgins, "Anthropological Studies of the Status of Women Revisited: l977-l987," *Annual Review of Anthropology* 17 (1988), 462.

85. Ibid.

86. See for example, Evelyn Blackwood. *Webs of Power. Women, Kin, and Community in a Sumatran Village* (Lanham, MD: Rowman and Littlefield. 2000); Marcia Inhorn, *Infertility and Patriarchy: The Cultural Politics of Gender and Family Life in Egypt* (Philadelphia: University of Pennsylvania Press, 1996); Thomas Buckley and Alma Gottlieb, ed. Blood Magic. *The Anthropology of Menstruation.* (Berkeley: University of California Press, 1988); Marcia Inhorn, and Frank Van Balen, eds. *Infertility around the Globe: New Thinking on Childlessness, Gender and Reproductive Technologies* (Berkeley: University of California Press, 2002).

87. Johnnetta Cole, ed. *All American Women: Lines That Divide, Ties That Bind* (New York:Free Press, 1986). Louise Lamphere, Helena Ragone and Patricia Zavella, eds. *Situated Lives: Gender and Culture in Everyday Life.* (New York: Routledge, 1997).

88. See for example, Faye Ginsburg. *Contested Lives: The Abortion Debate in an American Community* (Berkeley: University of California Press, 1989); Dorothy Holland and Margaret Eisenhart. *Educated in Romance.* (Chicago: University of Chicago, 1990); Peggy Sanday, *Fraternity Gang Rape: Sex, Brotherhood, and Privilege on Campus.* (New York: New York University Press, 2007).

89. Peggy Sanday, "The Socio-cultural Context of Rape: A Cross-cultural Study" *Journal of Social Issues* 37 no. 5 (1981): 5–27. See also Conrad Kottak, *Cultural Anthropology. Appreciating Cultural Diversity* (New York: McGraw Hill, 2013); Veena Das,

Violence, Gender and Subjectivity, *Annual Reviews of Anthropology* 37 (2008):283–299; Tulsi Patel, ed. *Sex-Selective Abortion in India. Gender, Society and New Reproductive Technologies* (New Delhi, India: Sage Publications, 2007).

90. Eleanor Leacock and Helen I. Safa, eds., *Women's Work: Development and the Division of Labor by Gender* (South Hadley, MA: Bergin & Garvey, 1986); Nandini Gunewardena and Ann Kingsolver, eds. *The Gender of Globalization: Women Navigating Cultural and Economic Marginalities* (Santa Fe, NM: School for Advanced Research Press, 2008); Kay B. Warren and Susan C. Bourque, "Women, Technology, and Development Ideologies. Frameworks and Findings," in Sandra Morgen, ed. *Critical Reviews for Research and Teaching* (Washington, DC: American Anthropological Association Publication, 1989), 382–410.

91. Carol C. Mukhopadhyay and Susan Seymour, ed. *Women, Education and Family Structure in India* (Boulder: Westview Press, 1994).

92. Ellen Lewin, *Lesbian Mothers: Accounts of Gender in American Culture* (Ithaca, NY: Cornell University Press. 1993).

93. See Joan Gero and Margaret Conkey, ed. *Engendering Archeology. Women and Prehistory* (Oxford: Oxford University Press, 1991); Sarah M. Nelson, *Worlds of Gender. The Archeology of Women's Lives Around the Globe.* (Lanham, MD: Altamira, 2007). See also earlier volumes. Rosemary A. Joyce, *Ancient Bodies, Ancient Lives: Sex, Gender and Archeology* (New York: Thames and Hudson, 2008); Barbara Voss, "Sexuality Studies in Archeology," *Annual Review of Anthropology* 37 (2008): 317–336.

94. The following analysis was developed by Mukhopadhyay in scholarly papers and in lecture notes.

95. Mary E. Hegland, *Days of Revolution: Political Unrest in an Iranian Village* (Stanford, CA: Stanford University Press, 2015).

96. This analysis was developed by Mukhopadhyay in scholarly papers and in lecture notes. An example of this pattern from Iran is Mary E. Hegland, *Days of Revolution*.

97. Conrad Kottak, *Cultural Anthropology. Appreciating Cultural Diversity.15th ed.* (McGraw Hill, 2013).

98. E. Friedl, *Women and Men: An Anthropologist's View;* C. Mukhopadhyay and Patricia Higgins, "Anthropological Studies of the Status of Women Revisited: 1977–1987." *Annual Review of Anthropology* 17 (1988): 461–495.

99. One 1970s male pilot, when asked about why there were no women pilots, said, without thinking, "Because women aren't strong enough to fly the plane!" He then realized what he'd said and laughed. From Mukhopadhyay, field notes, 1980.

100. Ann Stoler, "Making Empire Respectable. The Politics of Race and Sexual Morality in Twentieth-century Colonial Cultures," in *Situated Lives. Gender and Culture in Everyday Life*, ed. Louise Lamphere, H. Ragone, and P. Zavella, 373–399 (New York: Routledge, 1997).

101. Peggy Sanday, *Women at the Center: Life in a Modern Matriarchy* (Cornell: Cornell University Press, 2002).

102. Mukhopadhyay, lecture notes, Gender and Culture.

103. See for instance Annette B. Weiner, *The Trobrianders of Papua New Guinea*; Martha Ward and Monica Edelstein, *A World Full of Women;* Carolyn B. Brettell and Carolyn F. Sargent, eds. *Gender in Cross-Cultural Perspective.*

104. Kirsten Marie Ernst, *"Rios, Pontes E Overdrives:" Northeastern Regionalism in a Globalized Brazil* (Berkeley: University of California Press, 2007); John Collins, "'BUT WHAT IF I SHOULD NEED TO DEFECATE IN YOUR NEIGHBOR-HOOD, MADAME?': Empire, Redemption, and the 'Tradition of the Oppressed' in a Brazilian World Heritage Site," *Cultural Anthropology* 23 no. 2 (2012): 279–328; Jan Rocha, "Analysis: Brazil's 'Racial Democracy'" *BBC News*, April 19, 2000; Allan Charles Dawson, "Food and Spirits: Religion, Gender, and Identity in the 'African' Cuisine of Northeast Brazil," *African and Black Diaspora* 5 (2012): 243–263; Alan P Marcus "Sex, Color and Geography: Racialized Relations in Brazil and Its Predicaments" *Annals of the Association of American Geographers* 103(5): 1282–1299.

105. Ruth Landes, *The City of Women* (New York: The MacMillan Company, 1947), 2, 6–13, 61–64, 92, 106.

106. E. Franklin Frazier, "The Negro Family in Bahia, Brazil" *American Sociological Review* 7 no. 4 (1942): 476–477; E. Franklin Frazier, *The Negro Family in the United States* (Chicago: University of Chicago, 1939), 125. For the opposing view, see Mark Alan Healey, "'The Sweet Matriarchy of Bahia': Ruth Landes' Ethnography of Race and Gender." *Disposition: The Cultural Practice of Latinamericanism II* 23 no. 50 (1998)·101.

107. See Melville J. Herskovits, "The Negro in Bahia, Brazil: A Problem in Method" *American Sociological Review* 8 no. 4 (1943): 395–396; Edison Carneiro, "Letters from Edison Carneiro to Ruth Landes: Dating from September 28, 1938 to March 14, 1946" (Washington, DC: Box 2 Ruth Landes Papers, National Anthropological Archives, Smithsonian Institution, 1938); Ruth Landes, *The City of Women* (New York: MacMillan Company, 1947).

108. Ruth Landes, "Fetish Worship in Brazil" *The Journal of American Folklore* 53 no. 210(1940): 261.

109. Ruth Landes, *The City of Women* (New York: MacMillan Company, 1947), 31–32, 37.

110. Ruth Landes, "Negro Slavery and Female Status" *African Affairs* 52 no. 206 (1953): 55. Also, Ruth Landes, "A Cult Matriarchate and Male Homosexuality" *The Journal of Abnormal and Social Psychology* 35 no. 3 (1940): 386–387, 393–394; Ruth Landes, "Negro Slavery and Female Status," *African Affairs* 52 no. 206 (1953): 55–57.

111. J. Lorand Matory, "Gendered Agendas: The Secrets Scholars Keep about Yorùbá-Atlantic Religion," *Gender & History* 15 no. 3 (2003): 413.

112. Cheryl Sterling, "Women-Space, Power, and the Sacred in Afro-Brazilian Culture," *The Global South* 4 no. 1 (2010): 71–93.

113. Nandini Gunewardena and Ann Kingsolver, *The Gender of Globalization: Women Navigating Cultural and Economic Marginalities* (Santa Fe, NM: School for Advanced Research Press, 2008).

114. Women's political power, when exerted, may go unnoticed by the global media. For an example, see the documentary *Pray the Devil to Hell* on women's role in forcing Liberian President Charles Taylor from office and leading to the election of

Ellen Johnson Sirleaf as President. For an excellent documentary on some of the alternative paths contemporary women in India are taking, see *The World before Her*. For more on changes in women's education in India, see Carol C. Mukhopadhyay. 2001. "The Cultural Context of Gendered Science: The Case of India." Available at http://www.sjsu.edu/people/carol.mukhopadhyay/papers/

115. See the excellent film *The Purity Myth: The Virginity Movement's War Against Women*. Available through Media Education Foundation.

116. Carol C. Mukhopadhyay. 1982. "Sati or Shakti: Women, Culture and Politics in India." In *Perspectives on Power: Women in Asia, Africa and Latin America,* edited by Jean O'Barr, 11–26. Durham, NC: Center for International Studies, Duke University; Carol C. Mukhopadhyay. 2008. "Sati or Shakti: An Update in Light of Contemporary U.S. Presidential Politics." Paper presented at *Gender and Politics from a Feminist Anthropological Perspective*. November 2008, San Francisco. On the 2016 Election, see: Carol Mukhopadhyay.. "Gender and Trump," *Social Justice* blog, January 19, 2017, http://www.socialjusticejournal.org/gender-and-trump/.

117. For more information on the initial Trump video, see http://time.com/4523755/donald-trump-leaked-tape-impact. For coverage of the women accusing Trump and his response, see http://www.cnn.com/2016/10/14/politics/trump-women-accusers/index.html. For coverage of Trumps' response to the allegations, see http://time.com/4531872/donald-trump-sexual-assault-accusers-attack.

118. Carly Wayne, Nicholas Valentino and Marzia Oceno. 2016. "How Sexism Drives Support for Donald Trump." *Washington Post*, October 23. https://www.washingtonpost.com/news/monkey-cage/wp/2016/10/23/how-sexism-drives-support-for-donald-trump. Also see Libby Nelson. 2016. "Hostility toward Women Is One of the Strongest Predictors of Trump Support." *Vox*. November 1. http://www.vox.com/2016/11/1/13480416/trump-supporters-sexism. For an article that also covers research by psychologists, see Emily Crockett. 2016. "Why Misogyny Won." *Vox*. November 15. http://www.vox.com/identities/2016/11/15/13571478/trump-president-sexual-assault-sexism-misogyny-won.

119. For examples of anti-Clinton rhetoric, see article and associated video at http://www.huffingtonpost.com/entry/deplorable-anti-clinton-merch-at-trump-rallies_us_572836e1e4b016f378936c22. Figures for numbers of witches killed range from thousands to millions, with most suggesting at least 60,000–80,000 and probably far more. Regardless, it is estimated that 75–80 percent were women. See for example Douglas Linder. 2005. "A Brief History of Witchcraft Persecutions before Salem" http://law2.umkc.edu/faculty/projects/ftrials/salem/witchhistory.html and http://womenshistory.about.com/od/witcheseurope/a/Witch-Hunts-In-Europe-Timeline.htm.

120. Mark DiCamillo of the Field Poll suggested one reason polls were wrong is that female Trump voters hid their actual voting preferences from pollsters. DiCamillo is quoted in Debra J. Saunders. 2016. "How Herd Mentality Blinded Pollsters to Trump Potential." *San Francisco Chronicle*. November 13, E3.

121. For a critique of those who "blame" Euro-American ("white") women for Hillary Clinton's defeat, see the article by Kelly Dittmar. 2016. "No, Women Didn't Abandon Clinton, Nor Did She Fail to Win Their Support." *Ms. Magazine*. November 14. http://msmagazine.com/blog/2016/11/14/women-didnt-abandon-clinton/.

122. See Women in the World. 2016. "Donald Trump's Victory Threatens to Upend Progressive Notions of Masculinity." November 20. http://nytlive.nytimes.com/womenintheworld/2016/11/20/donald-trumps-victory-threatens-to-upend-progressive-notions-of-masculinity/.

123. For a powerful video reaction and interpretation of this election, see https://vimeo.com/191751334.

124. There is a huge body of research on these (and other) topics that we simply have not been able to cover in one chapter of a book. We hope the material and references we have provided will give readers a starting point for further investigation!

125. Many gender studies scholars have moved away from labeling people "biologically female" or "biologically male," shifting instead to terms like "assigned female at birth" and "assigned male at birth." Terms that foreground assignment help recognize the fluidity of gender identity and the existence of intersex people who do not fit neatly into those categories.

126. Carol C. Mukhopadhyay, "A Feminist Cognitive Anthropology: The Case of Women and Mathematics" *Ethos* 32 no. 4 (2004): 458–492.

127. David Valentine, *Imagining Transgender: An Ethnography of a Category* (Durham, NC: Duke University Press, 2007). See also Jessi Hempel, "My Brother's Pregnancy and the Making of a New American Family" *TIME* September 2016. http://time.com/4475634/trans-man-pregnancy-evan./

128. Gary G. Gates, "How Many People are Lesbian, Gay, Bisexual and Transgender?" University of California, Los Angeles: Williams Institute, 2011. http://williamsinstitute.law.ucla.edu/research/census-lgbt-demographics-studies/how-many-people-are-lesbian-gay-bisexual-and-transgender./

129. David Carter, *Stonewall: The Riots that Sparked a Gay Revolution* (St. Martin's Griffin, 2010); Eric Marcus, *Making Gay History: The Half-Century Fight for Lesbian and Gay Equal Rights* (New York: Harper Collins, 2002).

130. Jafari Sinclaire Allen, "'In the Life' In Diaspora: Autonomy / Desire / Community," in *Routledge Handbook of Sexuality, Health and Rights*, ed. Peter Aggleton and Richard Parker (New York: Routledge, 2010), 459.

131. Kristen Schilt and Laurel Westbrook, "Doing Gender, Doing Heteronormativity: 'Gender Normals,' Transgender People, and the Social Maintenance of Heterosexuality" *Gender and Society* 23 no. 4 (2009): 440–464.

132. Justin McCarthy, "Same-Sex Marriage Support Reaches New High at 55%." Gallup. http://www.gallup.com/poll/169640/sex-marriage-support-reaches-new-high.aspx.

133. Ellen Lewin and William Leap, *Out in Theory: The Emergence of Lesbian and Gay Anthropology* (Urbana: University of Illinois Press, 2002); William Leap and Ellen Lewin, *Out in the Field: Reflections of Lesbian and Gay Anthropologist* (Urbana: University of Illinois Press, 1996).

134. Jessica Johnson, "The Citizen-Soldier: Masculinity, War, and Sacrifice at an Emerging Church in Seattle, Washington." *Political and Legal Anthropology Review* 33 no. 2 (2010): 326–351.

135. Tamara Metz, *Untying the Knot: Marriage, the State, and the Case for Their Divorce* (Princeton: Princeton University Press, 2010).

136. Miriam Smith, "Gender Politics and the Same-Sex Marriage Debate in the United States," Social Politics 17 no. 1 (2010): 1–28. Quote is on p.1

137. Luke Malone, "Here Are The 32 States Where You Can Be Fired For Being LGBT," Vocativ.com, February 12, 2015. http://www.vocativ.com/culture/lgbt/lgbt-rights-kansas/.

138. The Williams Institute. 2012. "America's Shame: 40% of Homeless Youth are LGBT Kids." San Diego Gay and Lesbian News, 13 July. http://williamsinstitute.law.ucla.edu/press/americas-shame-40-of-homeless-youth-are-lgbt-kids/.

139. *Fire*, film by Mira Nair. 1996. https://www.youtube.com/watch?v=i2yW8BtM8sw.

140. Don Kulick, "The Gender of Brazilian Transgendered Prostitutes" *American Anthropologist* 99 no. 3 (1997): 574–585.

141. Evelyn Blackwood, "Tombois in West Sumatra: Constructing Masculinity and Erotic Desire," in *Feminist Anthropology: A Reader*, ed. Ellen Lewin, 411–434 (Malden, MA: Blackwell Publishing, 2006).

142. Ara Wilson, *The Intimate Economies of Bangkok: Tomboys, Tycoons, and Avon Ladies in the Global City* (Berkeley: University of California Press, 2004).

143. Lucetta Yip Lo Kam, *Shanghai Lalas: Female Tongzhi Communities and Politics in Urban China*. Hong Kong: Hong Kong University Press, 2012).

144. Ibid.

145. Frances E. Mascia-Lees, ed., *A Companion to the Anthropology of the Body and Embodiment* (Malden, MA: Wiley-Blackwell, 2011).

146. Don Kulick and Jens Rydström, *Loneliness and Its Opposite: Sex, Disability, and the Ethics of Engagement* (Durham, NC: Duke University Press, 2015); Susan Greenhalgh, *Fat-Talk Nation: The Human Costs of America's War on Fat* (Ithaca, NY: Cornell University Press, 2015); Ellen *Gruenbaum, The Female Circumcision Controversy: An Anthropological Perspective (Philadelphia: University of Pennsylvania Press, 2001);* Seth M. Holmes, *Fresh Fruit, Broken Bodies: Migrant Farmworkers in the United States* (Berkeley: University of California Press, 2013); Eithne Luibhéid, *Entry Denied: Controlling Sexuality at the Border* (Minneapolis: University of Minnesota Press, 2002).

147. Pamela Runestad, "The Medical Anthropologist as the Patient: Developing Research Questions on Hospital Food in Japan through Auto-Ethnography,"*ASIANetwork Exchange* 23 no. 1 (2016):66–82.

148. Emily Martin, *The Woman in the Body* (New York: St. Martin's Press, 1987); Emily Martin, "The Egg and the Sperm: How Science Has Constructed a Romance Based on Stereotypical Male-Female Roles" *Signs* 16 no. 3 (1991): 485–501.

149. Emily Martin, "The Egg and the Sperm," 485.

150. David H. Freedman, "The Aggressive Egg," *Discover,* June, 1992, 61–65.

151. *The Miracle of Life*, 1983. There was a sequel in 2001: http://www.pbs.org/wgbh/nova/body/life-greatest-miracle.html.

152. Corinne P. Hayden, "Gender, Genetics and Generation: Reformulating Biology in Lesbian Kinship," *Cultural Anthropology* 10 no. 1 (1995): 41–63.

153. For some of the positive results for women, see Vanessa Fong, "China's One-Child Policy and the Empowerment of Urban Daughters," *American Anthropologist* 104 no. 4 (2002): 1098–1109.

154. The examples from Turkey come from: "The Biopolitics of the Family in Turkey: neoconservatism, sexuality and reproduction." Session at 2015 American Anthropological Association meetings, Denver; and from a paper given by Sen Gupta in session 4–0615, "Development, Gender, and the neoliberal Social Imaginary," at the 2015 American Anthropological Association meetings, Denver. There is a huge body of research on these topics (and others) that we simply could not cover in one chapter. We hope the references we have provided will give readers a starting point for further investigation!

155. Ruth Behar, "Introduction: Out of Exile," in *Women Writing Culture*, ed. Ruth Behar and Deborah Gordon (Berkeley: University of California Press, 1995); Peggy Golde, *Women in the Field: Anthropological Experiences* (Chicago, IL: Aldine Publishing Company, 1970); Nancy J. Parezo, *Hidden Scholars: Women Anthropologists and the Native American Southwest* (Albuquerque: University of New Mexico Press, 1993), 5–9.

156. Helen Brannagh, "Sex 'Suggested' and Power Play: Notes on Harassment in the Field," in *China: New Faces of Ethnography*, ed. Bettina Gransow, Pal Nyiri, and Shiaw-Chian Fong (Piscataway, NJ: Verlag, 2005); Fran Markowitz and Michael Ashkenaziand, *Sex, Sexuality, and the Anthropologist* (Chicago: University of Chicago Press, 1999).

157. See Candice Cornet and Tami Blumenfield, "Anthropological Fieldwork and Families in China and Beyond," in *Doing Fieldwork in China...with Kids! The Dynamics of Accompanied Fieldwork in the People's Republic*, ed. Candice Cornet and Tami Blumenfield (Copenhagen: NIAS Press, 2006); Tami Blumenfield, "Blurred Boundaries of Learning and Ethnography in an Era of Constant Connectedness: Lessons from Fieldwork with Children in Southwest China," ibid, 69–85. Additional perspectives from a father-son duo and a mother-daughter pair in the same volume are those by Eriberto P. Lozada Jr. and E. Patrick Lozada III, "Opening the Door (开门): Doing Fieldwork with Children in Rural China," and by Jeanne L. Shea,

"Clean Your Plate and Don't Be Polite: An American Mother's Education in Early Childhood Parenting and Family Life in Shanghai, China." For another discussion of how children influence perceptions of a fieldworking parent, see Jocelyn Linnekin, "Family and Other Uncontrollables: Impression Management in Accompanied Fieldwork," in *Fieldwork and Families: Constructing New Models for Ethnographic Research*, ed. Juliana Flinn, Leslie Marshall, and Jocelyn Armstrong (Honolulu: Hawaii University Press, 1998), 71–83.

158. Lynn Bolles, "Telling the Story Straight: Black Feminist Intellectual Thought in Anthropology" *Transforming Anthropology: Journal of the Association of Black Anthropologists* 21 no. 1 (2013): 63–64.

159. See Christina Wasson et al., *We've Come a Long Way, Maybe: Academic Climate Report of the Committee on the Status of Women in Anthropology*, 2008, 5, 8. Available from https://web.csulb.edu/~lemaster/Publications%20(PDFs)/2008-coswa-academic-climate-report.pdf and Elizabeth Rudd, E. Morrison, J. Picciano, and Maresi Nerad, "Social Science PhDs—Five+ Years Out: Anthropology Report. CIRGE Report 2008-01," 2008. http://www.education.uw.edu/cirge/social-science-phds-five-years-out-anthropology-report-2/.

160. Ibid.

161. See Agatha M. Beins and Judith L. Kennedy, *Women's Studies for the Future: Foundations, Interrogations, Politics* (Rutgers, NJ: Rutgers University Press, 2005); Florence Howe and Mari Jo Buhl, *The Politics of Women's Studies: Testimony from the 30 Founding Mothers* (New York: The Feminist Press, 2000); Marilyn J. Boxer and Caroline Stimpson, *When Women Ask the Questions: Creating Women's Studies in America* (Baltimore: Johns Hopkins University Press, 2001); Susan Shaw and Janet Lee, *Women's Voices, Feminist Visions* (New York: McGraw Hill, 2014).

162. Rachel Adams and Michael Savan, *The Masculinity Studies Reader* (New York: Wiley-Blackwell, 2002); Judith Keagan Gardiner, *Masculinity Studies and Feminist Theory* (New York: Columbia University Press, 2002); Matthew C. Gutmann, "Trafficking in Men: The Anthropology of Masculinity," *Annual Review of Anthropology* 26 no. 1 (2007): 385–409. There were a number of earlier explorations of masculinity, several focused on African-American males. See for example Michelle Wallace, *Black Macho and the Myth of the Superwoman* (New York: Warner Books, 1980).

163. See especially numerous films available through Media Education Foundation and Women Make Movies. See also Susan Bordo, *The Male Body: A New Look at Men in Public and in Private* (New York: Farrar Straus and Giroux, 1999); Rebecca Solnit, *Men Explain Things to Me* (Chicago: Haymarket Books, 2014). Also, Jackson Katz' film *Tough Guise 2: Violence, Media, and the Crisis in Masculinity* (2013) and the website www.jacksonkatz.com/ have other books, articles, and workshops on gender violence prevention. See also Michael Kimmel, *Guyland: The Perilous World Where Boys Become Men* (New York: Harper Perennial, 2009).

164. Thomas Grego, *Mehinaku: The Drama of Daily Life in a Brazilian Indian Village* (Chicago: University of Chicago Press, 1977). See also Paula Brown and Georgeda Buchbinder, *Man and Woman in the New Guinea Highlands* (Washington DC: American Anthropological Association, 1976); Gilbert Herdt, *Guardians of the Flutes* (film); Stanley Brandeis, *Metaphors of Masculinity: Sex and Status in Andalusian Folklore* (Philadelphia: University of Pennsylvania Press, 1980); Sherry B. Ortner and Harriet Whitehead, *Sexual Meanings* (Cambridge: Cambridge University Press, 1981); David Gilmore, *Manhood in the Making: Cultural Concepts of Masculinity* (New Haven: Yale University Press, 1990).

165. See article by Matthew C. Guttman, "Trafficking in Men: The Anthropology of Masculinity," *Annual Review of Anthropology* 26 (2007): 385–409.

166. See several excellent videos through Media Education Foundation including *Dreamworlds 3, Killing Us Softly 4, The Purity Myth* as well as those addressing masculinity such as *Tough Guise 2, Joystick Warriors, and Hip Hop: Beyond Beats and Rhymes*.

167. Philippe Bourgois and Jeffrey Schonberg, *Righteous Dopefiend* (Berkeley: University of California Press, 2009); Seth M. Holmes, *Fresh Fruit, Broken Bodies: Migrant Farmworkers in the United States* (Berkeley: University of California Press, 2013); Mary H. Moran, "Warriors or Soldiers? Masculinity and Ritual Transvestism in the Liberian Civil War," in *Situated Lives*, ed. Louise Lamphere, Helena Ragone, and Patricia Zavella, 440–450. New York: Routledge, 1997); Kimberly Theidon, "Reconstructing Masculinities: The Disarmament, Demobilization, and Reintegration of Former Combatants in Colombia," in *The Gender, Culture, and Power Reader*, ed. Dorothy Hodgson, 420–429 (New York: Oxford University Press, 2016); Casey High, "Warriors, Hunters, and Bruce Lee: Gendered Agency and the Transformation of Amazonian Masculinity" *American Ethnologist* 37 no. 4 (2010): 753–770.

168. James W. Messerschmidt, *Masculinities in the Making: From the Local to the Global* (Lanham, MD: Rowman Littlefield, 2015).

169. Liu Shao-hua, *Passage to Manhood: Youth, Masculinity, and Migration in Southwest China* (Stanford, CA: Stanford University Press, 2010).

170. See Marcia C. Inhorn, *The New Arab Man: Emergent Masculinities, Technologies, and Islam in the Middle East* (Princeton, NJ: Princeton University Press, 2012); Marcia C. Inhorn, Wendy Chavkin, and Jose-Alberto Navarro, *Globalized Fatherhood*. New York: Berghahn. For discussion of Japan, see Mark J. McLelland. 2005. "Salarymen Doing Queer: Gay Men and the Heterosexual Public Sphere in Japan," in *Genders, Transgenders and Sexualities in Japan*, edited by M. J. McLelland and R. Dasgupta, 96–110 (New York: Routledge, 2014).

171. Dipanita Nath, "Mardistan: Four Men Talk about Masculinity in Harjant Gill's Film," *The Indian Express*, August 25, 2014. http://indianexpress.com/article/cities/delhi/be-a-super-man./ The film is available online: https://www.youtube.com/watch?v=tSrGuXTEHsk.

RELIGION

Sashur Henninger-Rener, University of LaVerne and the Los Angeles Community College District
sashur.henninger@gmail.com

LEARNING OBJECTIVES

- Define religion and explain its significance in human cultures.
- Summarize theories developed by anthropologists to explain the importance of supernatural beliefs in human communities.
- Identify the four elements of religion (cosmology, belief in the supernatural, rules of behavior, and rituals) and explain how each element contributes to religious practices.
- Define rites of passage, rites of intensification, and rites of revitalization and explain the purpose of each type of ritual.

Humans have always wondered about the meaning of the life, the nature of the universe, and the forces that shape our lives. While it is impossible to know for sure how the people who lived thousands of years ago answered these kinds of questions, there are some clues. Fifty thousand years ago, human communities buried the dead with stone tools, shells, animal bones, and other objects, a practice that suggests they were preparing the deceased for an afterlife, or a world beyond this one. Thirty thousand years ago, artists entered the Chauvet cave in France and painted dramatic scenes of animals on the cave walls along with abstract symbols that suggest the images were part of a supernatural belief system, possibly one focused on ensuring safety or success in hunting (Figure 1).[1] A few thousand years later, collections of small clay sculptures, known as Venus figurines, began appearing across Eurasia. They seem to express ideas about fertility or motherhood and may have been viewed as magical (Figure 2).[2]

Because ideas about the supernatural are part of every human culture, understanding these beliefs is important to anthropologists. However, studying supernatural beliefs is challenging for several reasons. The first difficulty arises

Figure 1: An image from the Chauvet cave painted about 32,000 years ago. The paintings may have been part of religious ceremonies intended to ensure success in hunting.

Figure 2: The Venus of Willendorf figurine was made between 28,000 and 25,000 BC and may have been associated with spiritual beliefs about motherhood or fertility.

from the challenge of defining the topic itself. The word "religion," which is commonly used in the United States to refer to participation in a distinct form of faith such as Christianity, Islam, or Judaism, is not a universally recognized idea. Many cultures have no word for "religion" at all and many societies do not make a clear distinction between beliefs or practices that are "religious," or "spiritual" and other habits that are an ordinary part of daily life. For instance, leaving an incense offering in a household shrine dedicated to the spirits of the ancestors may be viewed as a simple part of the daily routine rather than a "religious" practice. There are societies that believe in supernatural beings, but do not call them "gods." Some societies do not see a distinction between the natural and the supernatural observing, instead, that the spirits share the same physical world as humans. Concepts like "heaven," "hell," or even "prayer" do not exist in many societies. The divide between "religion" and related ideas like "spirituality" or even "magic" is also murky in some cultural contexts.

To study supernatural beliefs, anthropologists must cultivate a perspective of cultural relativism and strive to understand beliefs from an emic or insider's perspective. Imposing the definitions or assumptions from one culture on another is likely to lead to misunderstandings. One example of this problem can be found in the early anthropological research of Sir James Frazer who attempted to compose the first comprehensive study of the world's major magical and religious belief systems. Frazer was part of early generation of anthropologists whose work was based on reading and questionnaires mailed to missionaries and colonial officials rather than travel and participant-observation. As a result, he had only minimal information about the beliefs he wrote about and he was quick to apply his own opinions. In *The Golden Bough* (1890) he dismissed many of the spiritual beliefs he documented: "I look upon [them] not merely as false but as preposterous and absurd."[3] His contemporary, Sir E.B. Tylor, was less dismissive of unfamiliar belief systems, but he defined religion minimally and, for some, in overly narrow terms as "the belief in supernatural beings." This definition excludes much of what people around the world actually believe.[4] As researchers gained more information about other cultures, their ideas about religion became more complex. The sociologist Emile Durkheim recognized that religion was not simply a belief in "supernatural beings," but a set of practices and social institutions that brought members of a community together. Religion, he said, was "a unified system of beliefs and practices relative to sacred things, that is to say, things set aside and forbidden—beliefs and practices which unite into one single moral community called a Church, all those who adhere to them."[5]

Durkheim's analysis of religion emphasized the significance of spiritual beliefs for relationships between people. Subsequent anthropological research in communities around the world has confirmed that rituals associated with beliefs in the supernatural play a significant role in structuring community life, providing rules or guidelines for behavior, and bonding members of a community to one another. Interestingly, religious "beings," such as gods or spirits, also demonstrate social qualities.

Most of the time, these beings are imagined in familiar terms as entities with personalities, desires, and "agency," an ability to make decisions and take action. Supernatural beings, in other words, are not so different from people.[6] In keeping with this idea, **religion** can be defined as "the means by which human society and culture is extended to include the nonhuman."[7] This definition is deliberately broad and can be used to encompass many different kinds of belief systems.

Many religions involve ideas or rituals that could be described as "magical" and the relationship between religion and magic is complex. In his book *A General Theory of Magic* (1902), Marcel Mauss suggested that religion and magic were two opposite poles on a spectrum of spiritual beliefs. Magic was at one end of the spectrum; it was private, secret, and individual. Religion was at the opposite end of the spectrum; it was public and oriented toward bringing the community together.[8] Although Mauss' formulation presented religion and magic as part of the same general way of thinking, many contemporary anthropologists are convinced that making a distinction between religion and magic is artificial and usually not particularly useful. With this caution in mind, **magic** can be defined as practices intended to bring supernatural forces under one's personal control. **Sorcerers** are individuals who seek to use magic for their own purposes. It is important to remember that both magic and sorcery are labels that have historically been used by outsiders, including anthropologists, to describe spiritual beliefs with which they are unfamiliar. Words from the local language are almost always preferable for representing how people think about themselves.

THEORIES OF RELIGION

Sir James Frazer's effort to interpret religious mythology was the first of many attempts to understand the reasons why cultures develop various kinds of spiritual beliefs. In the early twentieth century, many anthropologists applied a functional approach to this problem by focusing on the ways religion addressed human needs. Bronislaw Malinowski (1931), who conducted research in the Trobriand Islands located near Papua New Guinea, believed that religious beliefs met psychological needs. He observed that religion "is not born out of speculation or reflection, still less out of illusion or apprehension, but rather, out of the real tragedies of human life, out of the conflict between human plans and realities."[9]

At the time of Malinowski's research, the Trobriand Islanders participated in an event called the kula ring, a tradition that required men to build canoes and sail on long and dangerous journeys between neighboring islands to exchange ritual items. Malinowski noticed that before these dangerous trips several complex rituals had to be performed, but ordinary sailing for fishing trips required no special preparations. What was the difference? Malinowski concluded that the longer trips were not only more dangerous, but also provoked more anxiety because the men felt they had less control over what might happen. On long voyages, there were many things that could go wrong, few of which could be planned for or avoided. He argued that religious rituals provided a way to reduce or control anxiety when anticipating these conditions.[10] The use of rituals to reduce anxiety has been documented in many other settings. George Gmelch (1971) documented forms of "baseball magic" among professional athletes. Baseball players, for instance, have rituals related to how they eat, dress, and even drive to the ballpark, rituals they believe contribute to good luck.[11]

As a functionalist, Malinowski believed that religion provided shared values and behavioral norms that created solidarity between people. The sociologist Emile Durkheim also believed that religion played an important role in building connections between people by creating shared definitions of the sacred and profane. **Sacred** objects or ideas are set apart from the ordinary and treated with great respect or care while **profane** objects or ideas are ordinary and can be treated with disregard or contempt. Sacred things could include a God or gods, a natural phenomenon, an animal or many other things. Religion, Durkheim concluded, was "a unified system of beliefs and practices relative to sacred things, that is to say, things set apart and forbidden—beliefs and practices that unite, into one single moral community called a Church, all those who adhere to them."[12] Once a person or a thing was designated as sacred, Durkheim believed that celebrating it through ritual was a powerful way to unite communities around shared values.[13] In addition, celebrating the sacred can create an intense emotional experience Durkheim referred to as **collective effervescence**, a passion or energy that arises when groups of people share the same thoughts and emotions. The experience of collective effervescence magnifies the emotional impact of an event and can create a sense of awe or wonder.[14]

Following Durkheim, many anthropologists, including Dame Mary Douglas, have found it useful to explore the ways in which definitions of sacred and profane structure religious beliefs. In her book *Purity and Danger* (1966), Douglas analyzed the way in which cultural ideas about things that were "dirty" or "impure" influenced religious beliefs. The kosher dietary rules observed by Jews were one prominent example of the application of this kind of thinking.[15]

The philosopher and historian Karl Marx famously called religion "the opium of the people."[16] He viewed religion as an ideology, a way of thinking that attempts to justify inequalities in power and status. In his view, religion created an illusion of happiness that helped people cope with the economic difficulties of life under capitalism. As an institution, Marx believed that the Christian church helped to legitimize and support the political and economic inequality of the working class by encouraging ordinary people to orient themselves toward the afterlife, where they could expect to receive comfort and happiness. He argued that the obedience and conformity advocated by religious leaders as a means of reaching heaven also persuaded people not to fight for better economic or social conditions in their current lives. Numerous examples of the use of religion to legitimize or justify power differences have been documented cross-culturally including the existence of divine rulers, who were believed to be empowered by the Gods themselves, in ancient Egyptian and Incan societies. A glimpse of the legitimizing role of religion is also seen in the U.S. practice of having elected officials take an oath of office using the Bible or another holy book.

The psychologist Sigmund Freud believed that religion is the institution that prevents us from acting upon our deepest and most awful desires. One of his most famous examples is the Oedipal complex, the story of Oedipus who (unknowingly) had a sexual relationship with his mother and, once he discovered this, ripped out his own eyes in a violent and gory death. One possible interpretation of this story is that there is an unconscious sexual desire among males for their mothers and among females their fathers. These desires can never be acknowledged, let alone acted on, because of the damage they would cause to society.[17] In one of his most well-known works, *Totem and Taboo,* Freud proposes that religious beliefs provide rules or restrictions that keep the worst anti-social instincts, like the Oedipal complex, suppressed. He developed the idea of "totemic religions," belief systems based on the worship of a particular animal or object, and suggested that the purpose of these religions was to regulate interactions with socially significant and potentially disruptive objects and relationships.[18]

One interesting interpretation of religious beliefs that builds on the work of Durkheim, Marx, and Freud is Marvin Harris' analysis of the Hindu prohibition against killing cows. In Hinduism, the cow is honored and treated with respect because of its fertility, gentle nature, and association with some Hindu deities. In his book *Cow, Pigs, Wars, and Witches* (1974), Harris suggested that these religious ideas about the cow were actually based in an economic reality. In India, cows are more valuable alive as a source of milk or for doing work in the fields than they are dead as meat. For this reason, he argued, cows were defined as sacred and set apart from other kinds of animals that could be killed and eaten. The subsequent development of religious explanations for cows' specialness reinforced and legitimated the special treatment.[19]

A symbolic approach to the study of religion developed in the mid-twentieth century and presented new ways of analyzing supernatural beliefs. Clifford Geertz, one of the anthropologists responsible for creating the symbolic approach, defined religion as "a system of symbols which acts to establish powerful, persuasive, and long-lasting moods and motivations.... by formulating conceptions of a general order of existence and clothing these conceptions with such an aura of factuality that the moods and motivations seem uniquely realistic."[20] Geertz suggested that religious practices were a way to enact or make visible important cultural ideas. The symbols used in any religion, such as a cross or even a cow, can be interpreted or "read" by anthropologists to discern important cultural values. At the same time, religious symbols reinforce values or aspirations in members of the religious community. The Christian cross, which is associated with both death and resurrection, demonstrates ideas about sacrifice and putting the needs of others in the community first. The cross also symbolizes deeper ideas about the nature of life itself: that suffering can have positive outcomes and that there is something beyond the current reality.

A symbolic approach to religion treats religious beliefs as a kind of "text" or "performance" that can be interpreted by outsiders. Like the other theories described in this section, symbolic approaches present some risk of misinterpretation. Religious beliefs involve complex combinations of personal and social values as well as embodied or visceral feelings that cannot always be appreciated or even recognized by outsiders. The persistently large gap between emic (insider) and etic (outsider) explanations for religious beliefs and practices makes the study of religion one of the most challenging topics in cultural anthropology.

ELEMENTS OF RELIGION

Despite the wide variety of supernatural beliefs found in cultures around the world, most belief systems do share some common elements. The first of these characteristic is **cosmology**, an explanation for the origin or history of the world. Religious cosmologies provide "big picture" explanations for how human life was created and provide a perspective on the forces or powers at work in the world. A second characteristic of religion is a belief in the **supernatural**, a realm beyond direct human experience. This belief could include a God or gods, but this is not a requirement. Quite a few religious beliefs, as discussed below, involve more abstract ideas about supernatural forces. Most religions also share a third characteristic: **rules governing behavior**. These rules define proper conduct for individuals and for society as a whole and are oriented toward bringing individual actions into harmony with spiritual beliefs. A fourth element is **ritual**, practices or ceremonies that serve a religious purpose and are usually supervised by religious specialists. Rituals may be oriented toward the supernatural, such as rituals designed to please the gods, but at the same time they address the needs of individuals or the community as a whole. Funeral rituals, for instance, may be designed to ensure the passage of a deceased person to the afterlife, but also simultaneously provide emotional comfort to those who are grieving and provide an outlet for the community to express care and support.

Religious Cosmologies

Religious cosmologies are ways of explaining the origin of the universe and the principles or "order" that governs reality. In its simplest form, a cosmology can be an origin story, an explanation for the history, present state, and possible futures of the world and the origins of the people, spirits, divinities, and forces that populate it. The ancient Greeks had an origin story that began with an act of creation from Chaos, the first thing to exist. The deities Erebus, representing darkness, and Nyx, representing night, were born from Chaos. Nyx gave birth to Aether (light) and Hemera (day). Hemera and Nyx took turns exiting the underworld, creating the phenomenon of day and night. Aether and Hemera next created Gaia (Earth), the mother of all life, who gave birth to the sky, the mountains, the sea, and eventually to a pantheon of gods. One of these gods, Prometheus, shaped humans out of mud and gave them the gift of fire. This origin story reflects many significant cultural ideas. One of these is the depiction of a world organized into a hierarchy with gods at the top and humans obligated to honor them.

Traditional Navajo origin stories provide a different view of the organization of the universe. These stories suggested that the world is a set of fourteen stacked "plates" or "platters." Creation began at the lowest levels and gradually spread to the top. The lower levels contained animals like insects as well as animal-people and bird-people who lived in their own fully-formed worlds with distinct cultures and societies. At the top level, First Man and First Woman eventually emerged and began making preparations for other humans, creating a sweat lodge, hoghan (traditional house), and preparing sacred medicine bundles. During a special ceremony, the first human men and women were formed and they created those who followed.[21] Like the Greek origin story, the Navajo cosmology explains human identity and emphasizes the debt humans owe to their supernatural ancestors.

The first two chapters of the Biblical Book of Genesis, which is the foundation for both Judaism and Christianity, describe the creation of the world and all living creatures. The exact words vary in different translations, but describe a God responsible for creating the world and everything in it: "In the beginning God created the heavens and the earth." The six-day process began with the division of light from darkness, land from water, and heaven from earth. On the fifth day, "God created the great sea monsters and every living creature that moves, with which the waters swarmed after their kind, and every winged bird after its kind; and God saw that it was good."[22] On the sixth day, "God created man in His own image, in the image of God He created him; male and female He created them."[23] This cosmology differs from the others in describing an act of creation by a single deity, God, but shares with the Greek and Navajo versions a description of creation that emphasizes the relationship between people and their creator.

Reading these cosmologies also raises the question of how they should be interpreted. Are these origin stories regarded as literal truth in the cultures in which they originated? Or, are the stories metaphorical and symbolic? There is no simple answer to this question. Within any culture, individuals may disagree about the nature of their own religious traditions. Christians, for instance, differ in the extent to which they view the contents of the Bible as fact. Cultural relativism requires that anthropologists avoid making judgments about whether any cultural idea, including religious beliefs, is "correct" or "true." Instead, a more useful approach is to try to understand the multiple ways people interpret or make sense of their religious beliefs. In addition it is important to consider the function a religious cosmology has in the wider society. As Bronislaw Malinowski observed, a myth or origin story is not an "idle tale, but a hard-worked active force."[24]

Belief in the Supernatural

Another characteristic shared by most religions is a concept of the supernatural, spirits, divinities, or forces not governed by natural laws. The supernatural can take many forms. Some supernatural entities are **anthropomorphic**, having human characteristics. Other supernatural forces are more generalized, seen in phenomena like the power of the wind. The amount of involvement that supernatural forces or entities have in the lives of humans varies cross-culturally.

Abstract Forces

Many cultures are organized around belief in an impersonal supernatural force, a type of religion known as **animatism**. The idea of *mana* is one example. The word itself comes from Oceania and may originally have meant "powerful wind," "lightning" or "storm." Today, it still refers to power, but in a more general sense. Aram Oroi, a pastor from the Solomon Islands, has compared mana to turning on a flashlight: "You sense something powerful but unseen, and then—*click*—its power is made manifest in the world."[25] Traditionally, the ability to accumulate mana in certain locations, or in one's own body, was to become potent or successful.[26] Certain locations such as mountains or ancient sites (*marae*) have particularly strong mana. Likewise, individual behaviors, including sexual or violent acts, were traditionally viewed as ways to accumulate mana for oneself.

Interestingly, the idea of *mana* has spread far beyond its original cultural context. In 1993, Richard Garfield incorporated the idea in the card game Magic: The Gathering. Players of the game, which has sold millions of copies since its introduction, use mana as a source of power to battle wizards and magical creatures. Mana is also a source of power in the immensely popular computer game World of Warcraft.[27] These examples do show **cultural appropriation**, the act of copying an idea from another culture and in the process distorting its meaning. However, they also demonstrate how compelling animist ideas about abstract supernatural power are across cultures. Another well-known example of animism in popular culture is "the Force" depicted in the George Lucas *Star Wars* films. The Force is depicted as flowing through everything and is used by Luke Skywalker as a source of potency and insight when he destroys the Death Star.

Spirits

The line between the natural and the supernatural can be blurry. Many people believe that humans have a supernatural or spiritual element that coexists within their natural bodies. In Christianity, this element is called the soul. In Hinduism, it is the *atman*.[28] The Tausūg, a group who live in the Philippines, believe that the soul has four parts: a transcendent soul that stays in the spiritual realm even when a person is alive; a life-soul that is attached to the body, but can move through dreams; the breath, which is always attached to the body, and the spirit-soul, which is like a person's shadow.[29]

Many people believe that the spirit survives after an individual dies, sometimes remaining on Earth and sometimes departing for a supernatural realm. Spirits, or "ghosts," who remain on Earth may continue to play an active role in the lives of their families and communities. Some will be well-intentioned and others will be malevolent. Almost universally, spirits of the deceased are assumed to be needy and to make demands on the living. For this reason, many cultures have traditions for the veneration of the dead, rituals intended to honor the deceased, or to win their favor or cooperation. When treated properly, ancestor spirits can be messengers to gods, and can act on behalf of the living

Figure 3: A spirit house in Thailand. The houses provide shelter for local spirits that could trouble humans if they become displeased.

after receiving prayers or requests. If they are displeased, ancestor spirits can become aggravated and wreak havoc on the living through illness and suffering. To avoid these problems, offerings in the form of favorite foods, drinks, and gifts are made to appease the spirits. In China, as well as in many other countries, **filial piety** requires that the living continue to care for the ancestors. [30] In Madagascar, where bad luck and misfortune can be attributed to spirits of the dead who believe they have been neglected, a body may be repeatedly exhumed and shown respect by cleaning the bones. [31]

If humans contain a supernatural spirit, essence, or soul, it is logical to think that non-human entities may have their own sparks of the divine. Religions based on the idea that plants, animals, inanimate objects, and even natural phenomena like weather have a spiritual or supernatural element are called **animism**. The first anthropological description of animism came from Sir Edward Burnett Tylor, who believed it was the earliest type of religious practice to develop in human societies. [32] Tylor suggested that ordinary parts of the human experience, such as dreaming, formed the basis for spiritual beliefs. When people dream, they may perceive that they have traveled to another place, or may be able to communicate with deceased members of their families. This sense of altered consciousness gives rise to ideas that the world is more than it seems. Tylor suggested that these experiences, combined with a pressing need to answer questions about the meaning of life, were the basis for all religious systems. [33] He also assumed that animist religions evolved into what he viewed as more sophisticated religious systems involving a God or gods.

Figure 4: The first torii at the entrance to Nikkō Tōshō-gū, Tochigi Prefecture, Japan.

Today, Tylor's views about the evolution of religion are considered misguided. No belief system is inherently more sophisticated than another. Several animist religions exist today and have millions of adherents. One of the most well-known is Shintoism, the traditional religion of Japan. Shintoism recognizes spirits known as *kami* that exist in plants, animals, rocks, places and sometimes people. Certain locations have particularly strong connections to the kami, including mountains, forests, waterfalls, and shrines. Shinto shrines in Japan are marked by *torii* gates that mark the separation between ordinary reality and sacred space (Figure 4).

Gods

The most powerful non-human spirits are gods, though in practice there is no universal definition of a "god" that would be recognized by all people. In general, gods are extremely powerful and not part of nature—not human, or animal. Despite their unnaturalness, many gods have personalities or qualities that are recognizable and relatable to humans. They are often anthropomorphic, imagined in human form, or **zoomorphic**, imagined in animal form. In some religions, gods interact directly with humans while in others they are more remote.

Anthropologists categorize belief systems organized around a God or gods using the terms monotheism and polytheism. **Monotheistic** religions recognize a single supreme God. The largest monotheistic religions in the world today are Christianity, Islam, and Judaism. Together these religions have more than 3.8 billion adherents worldwide.[34] **Polytheistic** religions include several gods. Hinduism, one of the world's largest polytheistic religions with more than 1 billion practitioners, has a pantheon of deities each with different capabilities and concerns.[35]

Rules of Behavior

Religious beliefs are an important element of social control because these beliefs help to define acceptable behaviors as well as punishments, including supernatural consequences, for misbehavior. One well-known example are the ideas expressed in the Ten Commandments, which are incorporated in the teachings of Christianity, Islam, and Judaism and prohibit behaviors such as theft, murder, adultery, dishonesty, and jealousy while also emphasizing the need for honor and respect between people. Behavior that violates the commandments brings both social disapproval from other members of the religious community and potential punishment from God.

Buddhism, the world's fourth largest religion, demonstrates the strong connection between spiritual beliefs and rules for everyday behavior. Buddhists follow the teachings of Buddha, who was an ordinary human who achieved wisdom through study and discipline. There is no God or gods in Buddhism. Instead, individuals who practice Buddhism use techniques like meditation to achieve the insight necessary to lead a meaningful life and ultimately, after many lifetimes, to achieve the goal of *nirvana*, release from suffering.

Although Buddhism defies easy categorization into any anthropological category, there is an element of animatism represented by *karma*, a moral force in the universe. Individual actions have effects on one's karma. Kindness toward others, for instance, yields positive karma while acts that are disapproved in Buddhist teachings, such as killing an animal, create negative karma. The amount of positive karma a person builds-up in a lifetime is important because it will determine how the individual will be reborn. **Reincarnation,** the idea that a living being can begin another life in a new body after death, is a feature of several religions. In Buddhism, the form of a human's reincarnation depends on the quality of the karma developed during life. Rebirth in a human form is considered good fortune because humans have the ability to control their own thoughts and behaviors. They can follow the Noble Eightfold Path, rules based on the teachings of Buddha that emphasize the need for discipline, restraint, humility, and kindness in every aspect of life. [36]

Rituals and Religious Practitioners

The most easily observed elements of any religious belief system are rituals. Victor Turner (1972) defined ritual as "a stereotyped sequence of activities ... performed in a sequestered place, and designed to influence preternatural entities or forces on behalf of the actors' goals and interests."[37] Rituals have a concrete purpose or goal, such as a wedding ritual that results in a religiously sanctioned union between people, but rituals are also symbolic. The objects and activities involved in rituals "stand in for" or mean more than what they actually are. In a wedding ceremony in the United States, the white color of the wedding dress is a traditional symbol of purity.

A large amount of anthropological research has focused on identifying and interpreting religious rituals in a wide variety of communities. Although the details of these practices differ in various cultural settings, it is possible to categorize them into types based on their goals. One type of ritual is a **rite of passage**, a ceremony designed to transition individuals between life stages.[38] A second type of ritual is a **rite of intensification**, actions designed to bring a community together, often following a period of crisis.[39] **Revitalization rituals**, which also often follow periods of crisis in a community, are ambitious attempts to resolve serious problems, such as war, famine, or poverty through a spiritual or supernatural intervention.[40]

Rites of Passage

In his original description of rites of passage, Arnold Van Gennep (1909) noted that these rituals were carried out in three distinct stages: separation, liminality, and incorporation. During the first stage, individuals are removed from their current social identity and begin preparations to enter the next stage of life. The liminal period that follows is a time in which individuals often undergo tests, trials, or activities designed to prepare them for their new social roles. In the final stage of incorporation, individuals return to the community with a new socially recognized status.[41]

Rites of passage that transition children into a new status as adults are common around the world. In Xhosa communities in South Africa, teenage boys were traditionally transitioned to manhood using a series of acts that moved them through each of the three ritual stages. In the separation stage, the boys leave their homes and are circumcised; they cannot express distress or signs of pain during the procedure. Following the circumcision, they live in isolation while their wounds heal, a liminal phase during which they do not talk to anyone other than boys who are also undergoing the rite of passage. This stressful time helps to build bonds between the boys that will follow them through their lives as adult men. Before their journey home, the isolated living quarters are burned to the ground, symbolizing the loss of childhood. When the participants return to their community, the incorporation phase, they are recognized as men and allowed to learn the secret stories of the community.[42]

Rites of Intensification

Rites of intensification are also extremely common in communities worldwide. These rituals are used to bind members of the community together, to create a sense of **communitas** or unity that encourages people to see themselves as members of community. One particularly dramatic example of this ritual is the Nagol land diving ceremony held each spring on the island of Pentecost in Vanuatu in the South Pacific. Like many rituals, land diving has several goals. One of these is to help ensure a good harvest by impressing the spirits with a dramatic display of bravery. To accomplish this, men from the community construct wooden towers sixty to eighty feet high, tie ropes made from tree vines around their ankles, and jump head-first toward the ground (Figure 5). Preparations for the land diving involve almost every member of the community. Men spend a month or more working together to build the tower and collect the vines. The women of the community prepare special costumes and dances for the occasion and ev-

Figure 5: Land Diving on Pentecost Island, Vanuatu.

eryone takes care of land divers who may be injured during the dive. Both the preparations for the land diving and the festivities that follow are a powerful rite of intensification. Interestingly, the ritual is simultaneously a rite of passage; boys can be recognized as men by jumping from high portions of the tower witnessed by elders of the community.[43]

Rites of Revitalization

All rites of revitalization originate in difficult or even catastrophic circumstances. One notable example is a ritual that developed on the island of Tanna in the South Pacific. During World War II, many islands in the South Pacific were used by the U.S. military as temporary bases. Tanna was one of these locations and this formerly isolated community experienced an extremely rapid transformation as the U.S. military introduced modern conveniences such as electricity and automobiles. In an attempt to make sense of these developments, the island's residents developed a variety of theories about the reason for these changes. One possible explanation was that the foreign materials had been given to the islanders by a powerful deity or ancestral spirit, an entity who eventually acquired the name John Frum. The name may be based on a common name the islanders would have encountered while the military base was in operation: "John from America."

When the war ended and the U.S. military departed, the residents of Tanna experienced a kind of trauma as the material goods they had enjoyed disappeared and the John Frum ritual began. Each year on February fifteenth, many of the island's residents construct copies of U.S. airplanes, runways, or towers and march in military formation with replicas of military rifles and American blue jeans. The ritual is intended to attract John Frum, and the material wealth he controls, back to the island. Although the ritual has not yet had its intended transformative effect, the participants continue the ritual. When asked to explain his continued faith, one village elder explained: "You Christians have been waiting 2,000 years for Jesus to return to Earth, and you haven't given up hope."[44] This John Frum custom is sometimes called a **cargo cult**, a term used to describe rituals that seek to attract material prosperity. Although the John Frum ritual is focused on commodities, or "cargo," the term cargo cult is generally not preferred by anthropologists because it oversimplifies the complex motivations involved in the ritual. The word "cult" also has connotations with fringe or dangerous beliefs and this association also distorts understanding of the practice.

Religious Practitioners

Since rituals can be extremely complicated and the outcome is of vital importance to the community, specialist practitioners are often charged with responsibility for supervising the details. In many settings, religious specialists have a high social status and are treated with great respect. Some may become relatively wealthy by charging for their services while others may be impoverished, sometimes deliberately as a rejection of the material world. There is no universal terminology for religious practitioners, but there are three important categories: priests, prophets, and shamans.

Priests, who may be of any gender, are full-time religious practitioners. The position of priest emerges only in societies with substantial occupational specialization. Priests are the intermediaries between God (or the gods) and humans. Religious traditions vary in terms of the qualifications required for individuals entering the priesthood. In Christian traditions, it is common for priests to complete a program of formal higher education. Hindu priests, known as *pujari*, must learn the sacred language Sanskrit and spend many years becoming proficient in Hindu ceremonies. They must also follow strict lifestyle restrictions such as a vegetarian diet. Traditionally, only men from the Brahmin caste were eligible to become pujari, but this is changing. Today, people from other castes, as well as women, are joining the priesthood. One notable feature of societies that utilize full-time spiritual practitioners is a separation between ordinary believers and the God or gods. As intermediaries, priests have substantial authority to set the rules associated with worship practice and to control access to religious rites.[45]

The term **shaman** has been used for hundreds of years to refer to a part time religious practitioner. Shamans carry out religious rituals when needed, but also participate in the normal work of the community. A shaman's religious practice depends on an ability to engage in direct communication with the spirits, gods, or supernatural realm. An important quality of a shaman is the ability to transcend normal reality in order to communicate with and perhaps even manipulate supernatural forces in an alternate world. This ability can be inherited or learned.[46] Transcending from the ordinary to the spiritual realm gives shamans the ability to do many things such as locate lost people or animals or heal the sick by identifying the spiritual cause of illness.

Among the Chukchi, who live in northern Russia, the role of the shaman is thought to be a special calling, one that may be especially appropriate for people whose personality traits seem abnormal in the context of the community. Young people who suffer from nervousness, anxiety, or moodiness, for example may feel a call to take up shamanistic practice.[47] There has been some research suggesting that shamanism may be a culturally accepted way to deal with conditions like schizophrenia.[48] If true, this might be because achieving an altered state of consciousness is essential for shamanic work. Entering an altered state, which can be achieved through dreams, hallucinogenic drugs, rhythmic music, exhaustion through dance, or other means, makes it possible for shamans to directly engage with the supernatural realm.

Shamans of the upper Amazon in South America have been using *ayahuasca*, a drink made from plants that have hallucinogenic effects, for centuries. The effects of ayahuasca start with the nervous system:

One under the control of the narcotic sees unroll before him quite a spectacle: most lovely landscapes, monstrous animals, vipers which approach and wind down his body or are entwined like rolls of thick cable, at a few centimeters distance; as well, one sees who are true friends and those who betray him or who have done him ill; he observes the cause of the illness which he sustains, at the same time being presented with the most advantageous remedy; he takes part in fantastic hunts; the things which he most dearly loves or abhors acquire in these moments extraordinary vividness and color, and the scenes in which his life normally develop adopt the most beautiful and emotional expression.[49]

Among the Shipibo people of Peru, ayahuasca is thought to be the substance that allows the soul of a shaman to leave his body in order to retrieve a soul that has been lost or stolen. In many cultures, soul loss is the predominant explanation for illness. The Shipibo believe that the soul is a separate entity from the body, one that is capable of leaving and returning at will. Shamans can also steal souls. The community shaman, under the influence of ayahuasca, is able to find and retrieve a soul, perhaps even killing the enemy as revenge.[50]

Anthropologist Scott Hutson (2000) has described similarities between the altered state of consciousness achieved by shamans and the mental states induced during a rave, a large dance party characterized by loud music with repetitive patterns. In a rave, bright lights, exhausting dance, and sometimes the use of hallucinogenic drugs, induce similar psychological effects to shamanic trancing. Hutson argues that through the rave individuals are able to enter altered states of consciousness characterized by a "self-forgetfulness" and an ability to transcend the ordinary self. The DJ at these events is often called a "techno-shaman," an interesting allusion to the guiding role traditional shamans play in their cultures.[51]

A **prophet** is a person who claims to have direct communication with the supernatural realm and who can communicate divine messages to others. Many religious communities originated with prophecies, including Islam which is based on teachings revealed to the prophet Muhammad by God. In Christianity and Judaism, Moses is an example of a prophet who received direct revelations from God. Another example of a historically significant prophet is Joseph Smith who founded the Church of Latter Day Saints, after receiving a prophecy from an angel named Moroni who guided him to the location of a buried set of golden plates. The information from the golden plates became the basis for the Book of Mormon.

The major distinction between a priest and the prophet is the source of their authority. A priest gets his or her authority from the scripture and occupational position in a formally organized religious institution. A prophet derives authority from his or her direct connection to the divine and ability to convince others of his or her legitimacy through charisma. The kind of insight and guidance prophets offer can be extremely compelling, particularly in times of social upheaval or suffering.

One prophet who had enormous influence was David Koresh, the leader of the Branch Davidians, a schism of the Seventh Day Adventist Church. The Branch Davidians were **millenarians,** people who believe that major transformations of the world are imminent. David Koresh was extremely charismatic; he was handsome and an eloquent speaker. He offered refuge and solace to people in need and in the process he preached about the coming of an apocalypse, which he believed would be caused by the intrusion of the United States government on the Branch Davidian's lifestyle. Koresh was so influential that when the United States government did eventually try to enter the Branch Davidian compound in Waco, Texas in 1993 to search for illegal weapons, members of the group resisted and exchanged gunfire with federal agents. Eventually, under circumstances that are still disputed, a fire erupted in the compound and eighty-six people, including Koresh, were killed.[52] Ultimately, the U.S. government helped to fulfill the apocalyptic vision of the group and David Koresh became a martyr. The Branch Davidians evolved into a new group, "Branch, Lord our Righteousness," and today many await Koresh's return.[53]

CONCLUSION

Religion is of central importance to the lives of people in the majority of the world's cultures; more than eight-in-ten people worldwide identify with a religious group.[54] However, it is also true that the number of people who say that they have no religious affiliation is growing. There are now about as many people in the world who consider themselves religiously "unaffiliated" as there are Roman Catholics.[55] This is an important reminder that religions, like culture itself, are highly dynamic and subject to constant changes in interpretation and allegiance. Anthropology offers a unique perspective for the study of religious beliefs, the way people think about the supernatural, and how the values and behaviors these beliefs inspire contribute to the lives of individuals and communities. No single set of theories or vocabulary can completely capture the richness of the religious diversity that exists in the world today, but cultural anthropology provides a toolkit for understanding the emotional, social, and spiritual contributions that religion makes to the human experience.

DISCUSSION QUESTIONS

1. This chapter describes theories about religion developed by Durkheim, Marx, and Freud. What are the strengths and weaknesses of each theory? Which theory would be the most useful if you were attempting to learn about the religious beliefs of another culture?
2. Rites of passage and rites of intensification are an important part of many religious traditions, but these same rituals also exist in secular (non-religious) contexts. What are some examples of these rituals in your own community? What role do these rituals play in bringing people together?
3. Durkheim argued that a distinction between the sacred and the profane was a key characteristic of religion. Thinking about your own culture, what are some examples of ideas or objects that are considered "sacred"? What are the rules concerning how these objects or ideas should be treated? What are the penalties for people who do not follow these rules?

GLOSSARY

Animatism: a religious system organized around a belief in an impersonal supernatural force.

Animism: a religious system organized around a belief that plants, animals, inanimate objects, or natural phenomena have a spiritual or supernatural element.

Anthropomorphic: an object or being that has human characteristics.

Cargo cult: a term sometimes used to describe rituals that seek to attract material prosperity. The term is generally not preferred by anthropologists.

Collective effervescence: the passion or energy that arises when groups of people share the same thoughts and emotions.

Cosmology: an explanation for the origin or history of the world.

Cultural appropriation: the act of copying an idea from another culture and in the process distorting its meaning.

Filial piety: a tradition requiring that the young provide care for the elderly and in some cases ancestral spirits.

Magic: practices intended to bring supernatural forces under one's personal control.

Millenarians: people who believe that major transformations of the world are imminent.

Monotheistic: religious systems that recognize a single supreme God.

Polytheistic: religious systems that recognize several gods.

Priests: full-time religious practitioners.

Profane: objects or ideas are ordinary and can be treated with disregard or contempt.

Prophet: a person who claims to have direct communication with the supernatural realm and who can communicate divine messages to others.

Reincarnation: the idea that a living being can begin another life in a new body after death.

Religion: the extension of human society and culture to include the supernatural.

Revitalization rituals: attempts to resolve serious problems, such as war, famine or poverty through a spiritual or supernatural intervention.

Rite of intensification: actions designed to bring a community together, often following a period of crisis.

Rite of passage: a ceremony designed to transition individuals between life stages.

Sacred: objects or ideas are set apart from the ordinary and treated with great respect or care.

Shaman: a part time religious practitioner who carries out religious rituals when needed, but also participates in the normal work of the community.

Sorcerer: an individual who seeks to use magic for his or her own purposes.

Supernatural: describes entities or forces not governed by natural laws.

Zoomorphic: an object or being that has animal characteristics.

ABOUT THE AUTHOR

Sashur Henninger-Rener is an anthropologist with research in the fields of comparative religion and psychological anthropology. She received a Master of Arts from Columbia University in the City of New York in Anthropology and has since been researching and teaching. Currently, Sashur is teaching with The University of LaVerne and the Los Angeles Community College District in the fields of Cultural and Biological Anthropology. In her free time, Sashur enjoys traveling the world, visiting archaeological and cultural sites along the way. She and her husband are actively involved in animal rescuing, hoping to eventually found their own animal rescue for animals that are waiting to find homes.

NOTES

1. See Jean Clottes, *Cave Art* (London: Phaidon, 2010)
2. O. Soffer, J. M. Adovasio, and D. C. Hyland "The 'Venus' Figurines: Textiles, Basketry, Gender, and Status in the Upper Paleolithic" *Current Anthropology* 41 n. 4 (2000):511-537.
3. James Frazer, *The Golden Bough* (New York: Macmillan and Company, 1958[1890]),vii.
4. Edward B. Tylor, *Primitive Culture* (London: John Murray, 1871).
5. Emile Durkheim, *The Elementary Forms of Religious Life*, tr. Joseph R. Swain (London: George Allen and Unwin, 1965[1915]), 62.
6. Jack David Eller, Introducing Anthropology of Religion (New York: Rouledge, 2007), 9.
7. Ibid.

8. Marcel Mauss, *A General Theory of Magic* (London, Routledge, 1972[1902]), 24.

9. Bronislaw Malinowski, *Culture* (New York: MacMillan Publishing, 1931).

10. Bronislaw Malinowski, "Rational Mastery by Man of his Surroundings," in *Magic, Science, & Religion* (New York: McGraw Hill, 1955).

11. George Gmelch, "Baseball Magic" *Transaction* 8(1971): 39-41.

12. Emile Durkheim, *Elementary Forms of Religious Life* (New York: The Free Press, 1912).

13. Ibid.

14. Kenneth D. Allan, *Explorations in Classic Sociological Theory: Seeing the Social World,* (Thousand Oaks, CA: Pine Forge Press, 2005).

15. Mary Douglas, *Purity and Danger* (London: Routledge, 1966).

16. Karl Marx, *Critique of Hegel's Philosophy of Right* (Oxford: Oxford University Press, 1970[1844]).

17. Charles Rycroft, *A Critical Dictionary of Psychoanalysis* (London: Puffin Press, 1995).

18. Sigmund Freud, *Totem and Taboo* (New York: W.W. Norton & Company, 1950).

19. Marvin Harris, *Cows, Pigs, Wars and Witches: The Riddles of Culture* (New York: Random House, 1974).

20. Clifford Geertz, "Religion as a Cultural System," in *The Interpretation of Cultures: Selected Essays,* ed. Clifford Geertz, 87-125 (London: Fontana Press, 1993), 90-91.

21. Sam D. Gill, *Sacred Words: A Study of Navajo Religion and Prayer* (Westport, CT: Greenwood Publishing, 1981), 52.

22. Gen. 1:21 NASB

23. Gen. 1:27 NASB

24. Bronislaw Malinowski, *Magic, Science and Religion and Other Essays* (Westport, CT Greenwood Press, 1984[1926]), 199

25. The quote comes from Aram Oroi, "Press the button, mama!:"Mana and Christianity on Makira in the Solomon Islands" (paper presented at the Australia and New Zealand Association of Theological Schools Conference held in Auckland, June/July 2013). His work is cited in Alex Golub, "The History of Mana: How an Austronesian Concept Became a Video Game Mechanic" *The Appendix* 2 no. 2 (2014) http://theappendix.net/issues/2014/4/the-history-of-mana-how-an-austronesian-concept-became-a-video-game-mechanic

26. Roger M. Keesing, "Rethinking 'Mana'" *Journal of Anthropological Research* 40 no. 1 (1984):137-156.

27. Alex Golub, "The History of Mana."

28. Jack David Eller, I*ntroducing Anthropology of Religion.*

29. Thomas M. Kiefer, *The Tausũg: Violence and Law in a Philippine Moslem Society* (New York: Holt Rinehart, 1972).

30. Charles Ikels, *Filial Piety: Practice and Discourse in Contemporary East Asia* (Stanford: Stanford University Press, 2004.)

31. "Madagascar's Dance with the Dead," *BBC,* http://news.bbc.co.uk/2/hi/programmes/from_our_own_correspondent/7562898.stm.

32. Edward B. Tylor, *Primitive Culture.*

33. Edward B. Tylor, "The Limits of Savage Religion" *Journal of the Royal Anthropological Institute* 21(1892): 283–301.

34. Pew Research Center, "The Future of World Religions: Population Growth Projections, 2010-2050," April 2, 2015 http://www.pewforum.org/2015/04/02/religious-projections-2010-2050/

35. The characterization of Hinduism as polytheistic is contested. The deities in Hinduism can be viewed as a manifestation of Brahman, the most significant supernatural force.

36. Andrew Skilton, *A Concise History of Buddhism* (New York: Barnes and Noble Publishing, 2000).

37. Victor Turner, "Symbols in African Ritual" *Science* 179 (1972): 1100-05.

38. Arnold *Van Gennep, The Rites of Passage (Hove, UK: Psychology Press, 1960).*

39. Eliot Dismore Chapple and Carleton Stevens Coon, *Principles of Anthropology* (New York: Henry Holt and Company, 1953).

40. Anthony F.C. Wallace, "Revitalization Movements" *American Anthropologist* 58 (1956): 264-281.

41. Victor W. Turner, "Betwixt and Between: The Liminal Period in Rites de Passage," *The Proceedings of the New American Ethnological Society,* 1964.

42. Casey Golomski, "Rites of Passage: 1900's to Present: Africa," in *Cultural Sociology of the Middle East, Asia, & Africa: An Encyclopedia* (Thousand Oaks: Sage Publications, 2012).

43. For more information see Marc Tabani, "The Carnival of Custom: Land Dives, Millenarian Parades and Other Spectacular Ritualizations in Vanuatu" *Oceania* 80 no. 3 (2010): 309–329.

44. Paul Raffaele, "In John They Trust," *Smithsonian Magazine,* http://www.smithsonianmag.com/people-places/in-john-they-trust-109294882/?no-ist=&page=1.

45. Victor W. Turner, "Religious Specialists," *International Encyclopedia of the Social Sciences,* 13(1972): 437-444.

46. Piers Vitebsky, "Shamanism," *Indigenous Religions: A Companion,* ed. Graham Harvey(New York: Bloomsbury Academic, 2000).

47. Waldemar G. Bogoras, The Chukchi of Northeastern Asia American Anthropologist 3 no. 1(1901):80-108.

48. Rick Strassman, *DMT: The Spirit Molecule* (South Paris, ME: Park Street Press, 2000).

49. Avencio Villarejo, *Asi es la selva* (Lima, Peru: Centro de Estudios Teologicos de la Amazonia, 1988).

50. Robert L. Carneiro, "The Amahuaca and the Spirit World" *Ethnology* 3(1964): 6-11.

51. Scott R. Hutson, "The Rave: Spiritual Healing in Modern Western Subcultures," *Anthropological Quarterly* 73(2000): 35-49.

52. Kenneth G.C. Newport, *The Branch Davidians of Waco: The History and Beliefs of an Apocalyptic Movement* (London: Oxford University Press, 2006).

53. John Burnett, "Two Decades Later: Some Branch Davidians Still Believe," National Public Radio http://www.npr.org/2013/04/20/178063471/two-decades-later-some-branch-davidians-still-believe.

54. Pew Research Center, "The Global Religious Landscape," December 18, 2012. http://www.pewforum.org/2012/12/18/global-religious-landscape-exec/

55. Ibid.

GLOBALIZATION

Lauren Miller Griffith, Texas Tech University
lauren.griffith@ttu.edu
https://www.depts.ttu.edu/sasw/People/Griffith.php

Jonathan S. Marion, University of Arkansas
marion@uark.edu
https://fulbright.uark.edu/departments/anthropology/directory/profile.php?uId=marion

LEARNING OBJECTIVES

- Define globalization and the 5 "scapes" that can be used to characterize global flows or exchanges.
- Explain the relationship between globalization and the creation of new "glocal" lifestyles and forms of consumption.
- Describe some of the ways people use agency to respond to globalization including syncretism and participation in alternative markets.
- Assess the relationship between globalization, neoliberalism, and neocolonialism.
- Evaluate the advantages and disadvantages of the intensification of globalization.
- Discuss the implications of globalization for anthropology.

It is Tuesday on campus as you enter the dining hall. The day's hot lunch entrées include Caribbean jerk pork with mango salsa and a side of collard greens. The next station is offering made-to-order Asian stir-fry. At the sandwich counter, tuna salad, an all-American classic, is being served in a pita. Now, are these dishes authentic? That, of course, depends on how you define authenticity.[1] A similar question was asked at Oberlin College in December 2015 when a group of students claimed that adapting foreign cuisines constituted a form of social injustice.[2] Their claim, which raised a great deal of controversy, was that the cafeteria's appropriation and poor execution of ethnic dishes was disrespectful to the cultures from which those recipes were taken. Many people dismissed the students' concerns as either an overreaction or as an attempt to rephrase a perennial complaint (bad cafeteria food) in a politically loaded language of social justice likely to garner a response from the administration. Regardless of what one thinks about this case, it *is* revealing of how college campuses—as well as the larger societies in which they are situated—have changed over time. The fact that dishes like sushi and banh mi sandwiches are even available in an Ohio college cafeteria suggests that globalization has intensified. The fact that the students would be reflexive enough to question the ethical implications of appropriating foreign cuisine suggests that we are truly in a new era. But what, in fact, is globalization?

OVERVIEW AND EARLY GLOBALIZATION

Globalization is a word commonly used in public discourse, but it is often loosely defined in today's society (much like the word "culture" itself). First appearing in the English language in the 1940s, the term "globalization" is now commonplace and is used to discuss the circulation of goods, the fast and furious exchange of ideas, and the movement of people.[3] Despite its common use, it seems that the many people using the term are often not defining it in the same way. Some treat globalization as simply an economic issue while others focus more on the social and political aspects. What is clear, however, is that globalization has influenced many different facets of contemporary social life. This actually makes globalization an ideal topic of study for anthropologists, who pride themselves on taking a holistic approach to culture (see the Development of Anthropological Ideas chapter). For our purposes, we adopt political scientist Manfred Steger's definition of globalization: "the intensification of worldwide social relations which link distant localities in such a way that local happenings are shaped by events occurring many miles away and vice versa."[4]

It is challenging to determine precisely when globalization began. Although some people discuss globalization as if it was an entirely new process without historical antecedents, in truth its precursors have been going on for a very long time. In this chapter, we argue that the distinguishing feature of globalization in the contemporary era is the speed, rather than the scope, of global interactions. Early modern technological innovations hastened globalization.[5] For instance, the invention of the wheel created a need for permanent roads that would facilitate transport of animal drawn carts. These wheeled vehicles increased people's mobility, which in turn facilitated the sharing of both goods and ideas. Even before the invention of the wheel, the creation of written communication systems allowed ideas to be shared between people in distant locations.

Certainly extensive empires have existed at various times throughout human history, including Chinese dynasties (the Han dynasty, 206 BCE-220 CE, for instance, reached the same size the Roman Empire achieved much later); the Ottoman Empire, and the Roman Empire. Most recently in world history, European colonial expansion into Africa, Asia and the Americas marked another landmark of globalization. As discussed in the Development of Anthropological Ideas chapter, *colonialism* refers to the political, social, economic, and cultural domination of a territory and its people by a foreign power for an extended period of time. Technically, colonialism can be practiced by any group that is powerful enough to subdue other groups—and this certainly would be an accurate term for Ottoman and Roman imperial expansion—but as a term, colonialism is typically associated with the actions of European countries starting in the 1500s and lasting through the 1900s. During this period, European colonial powers divvied up "unclaimed" land with little regard for ethnic groups who already lived in those places, their political structures, belief systems, or lifeways. By 1914, European nations ruled more than 85 percent of the world, and it is not by accident that the image of the world most often seen on conventional maps continues to be very Eurocentric in its orientation (see map).

Colonialism in the Americas was the result of European conquest of newly "discovered" territories during the Age of Exploration. Columbus was likely not the first explorer to reach the Americas, but his "discovery" intensified Europeans' desires to colonize this "new" territory. European leaders began expanding their spheres of influence in Europe before turning their attention to lands further afield; the successes they had in colonizing nearby lands, amplified by a growing demand for trade items found in "the Orient," fueled their enthusiasm for exploration outside the region. The Catholic Church also supported this economically motivated mission, as it coincided with a weakening of their religious-stronghold in places like England, Germany, and France.

One of the most devastating features of the colonial period was the forced labor of both indigenous Americans and Africans who were enslaved and shipped off as chattel. Between 1525 and 1866, 12.5 million slaves were sent to the New World from Africa. Treated as chattel, only 10.7 million Africans survived until arriving in the Americas. The U.S. imported approximately 450,000 of these slaves. It is not by coincidence that the ethically irredeemable shipment of slaves to the Americas corresponded to massive shipments of goods to Europe and down the west coast of Africa. As far as the total scope of international flows, however, European colonialism pales in comparison to the scope of globalization that has transpired since the 1990s.

Contemporary globalization, at least in terms of economics, is perhaps best pinpointed as coinciding with the conclusion of World War II and the Bretton Woods Conference.[6] The agreements made at the Bretton Woods Conference led to the creation of the International Monetary Fund (IMF) as well as the International Bank for Reconstruction and Development, which later became the World Bank (WB). It also laid the groundwork for the World Trade Organization (WTO). Taken together, these three organizations have had a tremendous role in accelerating globalization and in shaping the lives of people in the developing world. The very idea of governing bodies like the United Nations, or regulatory institutions like the IMF and WB, that exist outside the confines of a specific nation-state—now widely referenced as Non-Governmental Organizations (NGOs)—contributes to undermining local sovereignty.[7] Although local, regional, and national identities and affiliations retain salience in the global era, their importance has shifted relative to the growing sense many people have of being citizens of the world.

THE ACCELERATION OF GLOBALIZATION

The 5 "Scapes" of Globalization

As we have already established, globalization refers to the increasing pace and scope of interconnections crisscrossing the globe. Anthropologist Arjun Appadurai has discussed this in terms of five specific "scapes" or flows: ethnoscapes, technoscapes, ideoscapes, financescapes, and mediascapes. Thinking of globalization in terms of the people, things, and ideas that flow across national boundaries is a productive framework for understanding the shifting social landscapes in which contemporary people are often embedded in their daily lives. Questions about where people migrate, their reasons for migration, the pace at which they travel, the ways their lives change as a result of their travels, and how their original communities change can all be addressed within this framework. Questions about goods and ideas that travel without the accompaniment of human agents can also be answered using Appadurai's notion of scapes.

Ethnoscape refers to the flow of people across boundaries. While people such as labor migrants or refugees (see case study below) travel out of necessity or in search of better opportunities for themselves and their families, leisure travelers are also part of this scape. The World Tourism Organization, a specialized branch of the United Nations, argues that tourism is one of the fastest growing commercial sectors and that approximately one in eleven jobs is related to tourism in some way.[8] Tourism typically puts people from developed parts of the world in contact with people in the developing world, which creates both opportunities and challenges for all involved. While there is the potential for tourists to be positively affected by their experiences with "the Other" while travelling, the tourism industry has also received its share of criticisms. Individuals from wealthier countries like the U.S., even if they are not wealthy themselves by the standards of the United States, are able to indulge in luxuries while traveling abroad in poorer nations like those found in the Caribbean. There is a fine line between a) tourists expecting service while on vacation and b) tourists treating local people like *servants*. This latter scenario exemplifies the unequal power relationships that develop in these kinds of situations, and such power relationships concern responsible social scientists.[9]

Technoscape refers to flows of technology. Apple's iPhone is just one example of how the movement of technologies across boundaries can radically affect day-to-day life for people all along the commodity chain. Sales records are surpassed with each release of a new iPhone, with lines of customers spilling out of Apple stores and snaking around the block. Demand for this new product drives a fast and furious pace of production. Workers who are struggling to keep up with demand are subjected to labor conditions most iPhone users would find abhorrent; some even commit suicide as a result. The revenue associated with the production and export of technological goods is drastically altering the international distribution of wealth. As the pace of technological innovation increases, so does the flow of technology. This is not, of course, an entirely new phenomenon; earlier technologies have also drastically and irrevocably changed the human experience. For example, the large-scale production and distribution of the printing press throughout Europe (and beyond) dramatically changed the ways in which people thought of themselves—as members not only of local communities, but of national communities as well.[10]

Ideoscape refers to the flow of ideas. This can be small-scale, such as an individual posting her or his personal views on Facebook for public consumption, or it can be larger and more systematic. Missionaries provide a key example. Christian missionaries to the Amazon region made it their explicit goal to spread their religious doctrines. As the experiences of missionary-turned-anthropologist Daniel Everett show, however, local people do not necessarily interpret the ideas they are brought in the way missionaries expect.[11] In addition to the fact that all people have agency to accept, reject, or adapt the ideologies that are introduced to or imposed on them (see syncretism below). The structure of the language spoken by the Pirahã makes it difficult to provide direct translations of the gospel.[12]

Financescape refers to the flow of money across political borders. Like the other flows discussed by Appadurai, this phenomenon has been occurring for centuries. The Spanish, for example, conscripted indigenous laborers to mine the silver veins of the Potosí mines of Bolivia. The vast riches extracted from this region were used to pay Spain's debts in northern Europe. The pace of the global transfer of money has only accelerated and today transactions in the New York Stock Exchange, the Nikkei index, and other such finance hubs have nearly immediate effects on economies around the world.

Mediascape refers to the flow of media across borders. In earlier historic periods, it could take weeks or even months for entertainment and education content to travel from one location to another. From the telegraph to the telephone, and now the Internet (and myriad other digital communication technologies), media are far more easily and rapidly shared regardless of geographic borders. For example, Brazilian telenovelas may provide entertainment on long-distance African bus trips, Bollywood films are shown in Canadian cinemas, and people from around the world regularly watch mega-events such as the World Cup and the Olympics from wherever they may live.

While the five scapes defined by Appadurai provide useful tools for thinking about these various forms of circulation, disentangling them in this way can also be misleading. Ultimately, the phenomena studied by most anthropologists will involve more than one of these scapes. Take clothing for instance. Kelsey Timmerman, an author whose undergraduate concentration was in anthropology, was inspired to find out more about the lives of the people who made his clothing.[13] In a single day, he found, the average American might be wearing clothes made in Honduras, Bangladesh, Cambodia, and China. Something as seemingly simple as a T-shirt can actually involve all five of Appadurai's scapes. The transnational corporations responsible for the production of these shirts themselves are part of capitalism, an idea which has become part of the international ideoscape. The financescape is altered by a company in the U.S. contracting a production facility in another country where labor costs are cheaper. The equipment needed to create these T-shirts is purchased and delivered to the production facility, thus altering the technoscape. The ethnoscape is affected by individuals migrating from their homes in rural villages to city centers, often disrupting traditional residence patterns in the process. Finally, the mediascape is involved in the marketing of these T-shirts.

SELECTIVE IMPORTATION AND ADAPTATION

Glocalization

Globalization most certainly changes the landscape of contemporary social life (see our discussion of Appadurai above). Yet it would be a mistake to think of globalization as a state that emerges without human agency. In most cases, people make decisions regarding whether or not they want to adopt a new product or idea that has been made available to them via globalization. They also have the ability to determine the ways in which that product or idea will be used, including many far different from what was originally intended. A cast-off Boy Scout uniform, for example, may be adopted by a Maasai village leader as a symbol of his authority when dealing with Tanzanian government officials.[14]

First emerging in the late 1980s, the term **glocalization** refers to the adaptation of global ideas into locally palatable forms.[15] In some instances, this may be done as a profit-generating scheme by transnational corporations. For example, McDonald's offers vastly different menu items in different countries. While a Big Mac may be the American favorite, when in India you might try a McAloo Tikki™ (a breadcrumb-coated potato and pea patty), in Hong Kong mixed veggies and egg mini twisty pasta in a chicken broth for breakfast, in Thailand corn pies or pineapple pies, or a Steak Mince 'N' Cheese pie in New Zealand. In other cases, people rather than corporations find innovative ways to adopt and adapt foreign ideas. The Zapotec of Oaxaca, Mexico, for example, have found a way to adapt globally available consumer goods to fit their longstanding cultural traditions. Traditionally, when a member of the community dies, that individual's relatives have an obligation to ease his or her passing to the afterlife. One part of this obligation is making an extraordinary number of tamales for the mourners who come to pay their respects at the home altar that has been erected for the deceased. These tamales are intended to be taken home and were once shared in traditional earthen containers. Rather than disrupting this tradition, the introduction of modern consumer goods like Tupperware has made the old tradition of sharing food easier.[16] In this case, Zapotec culture is not threatened by the introduction of foreign goods and ideas because the community incorporates new things into their pre-existing practices without completely trading old ideas for new ones. Practices like these provide evidence that fears about globalization leading to nothing but cultural homogenization may be exaggerations. Yet, other communities refuse these products precisely because they equate modernization and globalization with culture loss. For example, Nobel Peace Prize recipient Dr. Rigoberta Menchu recounts how adamantly the Maya elders where she was raised warned the youth away from consuming Coca-Cola or even using modern corn mills rather than the traditional mano and metate.[17]

Case Study: Both Global *and* Local –Salsa Dancing Around the World

While there are a variety of texts regarding the histories of salsa music and dancing, as it exists today the salsa scene is inseparable from the five flows of globalization described above.[18] Take for instance the vast number of salsa "congresses" and festivals held worldwide throughout the year. People from near and far travel to these events as dance students, social participants, performers, and instructors (the *ethnoscape*). Travel to and from these events, often internationally, depends on modern transportation (the *technoscape*). What is being taught, shared, and communicated at these events is, primarily ideas about different dancing style and techniques (the *ideoscape*). In addition to the costs of gas/park-ing/airfare or the like, registration, hotel rooms, lessons, DJs/bands, and other services are all available because they are being paid for (the *financescape*). Finally, these events could not exist as they do today without online advertising (see Figure 1 for an example), work-shop and performance schedules, and event registration, let alone video-clips of the fea-

tured teachers and performers (the *mediascape*). Indeed, the very fact that dancers can come from disparate locations and all successfully dance with each other—even in the absence of a com-mon spoken language—testifies to the globaliza-tion involved in such dance forms today.[19]

The widely shared patterning of movement to music in this dance genre does not, however, ne-gate the very real differences between local iter-ations. Featured in the very title of ethnomusicol-ogist Sydney Hutchinson's recent edited volume, *Salsa World: A Global Dance in Local Contexts*, real differences between local contexts, practic-es, and meanings are shown in chapters dedicat-ed to the salsa scenes in New York, New Jersey, Los Angeles, rural America, Cuba, Puerto Rico, Colombia (Cali), Dominican Republic (Santo Do-mingo), France, Spain (Barcelona), and Japan.[20] Learning to dance at family gatherings is differ-ent from learning in a studio. Learning to dance to music that plays in every building on the street is different from learning in a setting with entirely different local instruments. Learning to dance is different when everyone comes from the same general socioeconomic and ethnic background compared to learning in extremely heteroge-neous urban settings. This set of comparisons could continue for quite some time. The point is that even global forms take on local shapes.[21]

Figure 1: Advertisement for the New Zealand Salsa Congress, 2012.

Lifestyle, Taste, and Conspicuous Consumption

While some aspects of globalization are best studied at the societal level, others are best examined at smaller scales such as the trends visible within specific socio-economic strata or even at the level of individual decision-making. The concept of "lifestyle" refers to the creative, reflexive, and sometimes even ironic ways in which individuals perform various social identities (see the Performance chap-ter in this volume). Sociologist David Chaney describes lifestyles as "characteristic modes of social engagement, or narratives of identity, in which the actions concerned can embed the metaphors at hand."[22] The lifestyles we live and portray, then, can be seen as reflexive projects (see the Fieldwork chapter for more information about reflexivity) in the sense that they display both to ourselves and to our audiences who we think we are, who we want to be, and who we want to be seen to be.

Chaney argues that people only feel the need to differentiate themselves when confronted with an array of available styles of living.[23] Societies organized via organic solidarity (versus mechanical) are predicated on different goods, skills, and tasks. Within this framework, the rise of a consumerist economy enables individuals to exhibit their identities through the purchase and conspicuous use of various goods.[24] Globalization has increased the variety of goods available for individuals to purchase—as well as people's awareness of these products—thus expanding the range of identities that can be performed through their consumption habits (see the Gender and Sexuality chapter for more on performance of identity). In some situations, identity is an individual project, with conspicuous consumption used to display one's sense of self. For example, a student who feels alienated by the conservative, "preppy," students at her East Coast school can cultivate an alternative identity by growing dreadlocks, wearing Bob Marley T-shirts, and practicing djembe drumming, all of which are associated with the African diaspora outside the United States.

Critics have argued that a consequence of globalization is the homogenization of culture. Along similar lines, some have worried that the rapid expansion of the leisure market would decrease the diversity of cultural products (e.g. books, movies) consumed by the populace. The disappearance of small-scale shops and restaurants has certainly been an outcome of the rise of global conglomerates, but the homogenization of culture is not a foregone conclusion.[25] Globalization enables individuals in far-flung corners of the world to encounter new ideas, commodities, belief systems, and voluntary groups to which they might choose to belong. At times these are at the expense of existing options, but it is also important to acknowledge that people make choices and can select the options or opportunities that most resonate with them. The concept of lifestyle thus highlights the degree of decision-making available to individual actors who can pick and choose from global commodities, ideas, and activities. At the same time as individual choices are involved, the decisions made and the assemblages selected are far from random. Participating in a lifestyle implies knowledge about consumption; knowing how to distinguish between goods is a form of symbolic capital that further enhances the standing of the individual.[26]

How much free will, freedom of choice, or autonomy an individual actually has is an age-old question far beyond the scope of this chapter, but in many cases a person's consumption patterns are actually a reflection of the social class in which she or he was raised—even when an individual thinks he or she is selectively adopting elements from global flows that fit with his or her unique identity. In other words, an individual's "taste" is actually an outgrowth of his or her **habitus**, the embodied dispositions that arise from one's enculturation in a specific social setting.[27] Habitus results in a feeling of ease within specific settings. For example, children who have been raised in upper-class homes are able to more seamlessly integrate into elite boarding schools than classmates on scholarships who might find norms of dining, dress, and overall comportment to be unfamiliar.[28] Habitus, the generative grammar for social action, generates tastes and, by extension, lifestyles.[29]

Recall the vignette that opened this chapter. The fact that the students of this prestigious liberal arts college are in the position to critique the ethical implications of specific recipes suggests that their life experiences are far different from the roughly one in seven households (totaling 17.5 million households) in the United States with low or very low food security.[30] Inevitably then, what people choose to consume from global offerings—and the discourses they generate around those consumption choices—are often indicative of their social status. Once a commodity becomes part of these global flows, it is theoretically available to all people regardless of where they live. In actual practice, however, there are additional gatekeeping devices that ensure continued differentiation between social classes. Price will prevent many people from enjoying globally traded goods. While a Coca-Cola may seem commonplace to the average college student in the U.S., it is considered a luxury good in other parts of the world. Likewise, although Kobe steaks (which come from the Japanese *wagyu* cattle) are available in the U.S., it is a relatively small subgroup of Americans who would be able and willing to spend hundreds of dollars for a serving of meat. Having the knowledge necessary to discern between different goods and then utilize them according to socially prescribed norms is another mark of distinction between social classes, as anthropologist Pierre Bourdieu's work on taste made clear.[31]

GLOBALIZATION IN EVERYDAY LIFE

Although some within the discipline argue that anthropologists should report objectively on the cultures and social phenomena they study, given the structure of the discourse surrounding globalization, it is increasingly difficult to avoid being pigeonholed as "pro" or "anti" globalization. In truth though, globalization has had both positive and negative impacts.

Advantages of the Intensification of Globalization

As optimists, we will start with the "glass-half-full" interpretation of globalization. Political Scientist Manfred Steger has argued that "humane forms of globalization" have the potential to help us deal with some of the most pressing issues of our time, like rectifying the staggering inequalities between rich and poor or promoting conservation.[32] The mediascape has made people in the **Global North** increasingly aware of the social injustices happening in other parts of the world. In his book on the global garment industry, Kelsey Timmerman highlights the efforts undertaken by activists in the U.S., ranging from public demonstrations decrying the fur industry to boycotts of products produced in socially unsustainable ways.[33] While many of these efforts fall short of their intended outcome—and typically overlook the complexities of labor situations in the **Global South** where families often rely upon the labor of their children to make ends meet—such examples nonetheless underscore the connections people in one location now feel with others (who they will likely never meet) through the commodity chains that link them.

Globalization has also facilitated the rise of solidarity movements that would not have been likely in an earlier era. To take a recent example, within hours of the 2015 terrorist attacks in Paris, individuals from different nations and walks of life had changed their Facebook profile pictures to include the image of the French flag. This movement was criticized because of its Eurocentrism; the victims of a bombing in Beirut just the day before received far less international support than did the French victims. Shortcomings aside, it still stands as a testament to how quickly solidarity movements can gain momentum thanks to technological innovations like social media.

Micro-loan programs and crowd-source fundraising are yet more ways in which individuals from disparate circumstances are becoming linked in the global era. Kiva, for example, is a microfinance organization that enables anyone with an Internet connection to make a small ($25) donation to an individual or cooperative in various parts of the developing world. The projects for which individuals/groups are seeking funding are described on the Kiva website and donors choose one or more specific projects to support. The recipient must then repay the loan to Kiva with interest.

Crowd-source fundraising follows a similar principle, though without the requirement that money be paid back to the donors. One small-scale example involves funds gathered in this way for a faculty led applied visual research class in Dangriga, Belize in 2014. By generating a small pool of additional funding, 100 percent of the students' project fees could be dedicated to producing materials for local community partners (compared to other groups, who used some of these fees for student lunches or other items). As a result, the team was able to over-deliver on what had been promised to the community. The Sabal Cassava Farm (Belize's sole commercial cassava farm) had requested a new road sign as well as full-color marketing flyers. The Austin Rodriguez Drum Shop—a cultural resource center, and producer of traditional Garifuna drums—had wanted help updating their educational poster (see Figure 2a and 2b). For both groups the team was able to a) provide digital frames with all the research images (so that the local community partners had something "in hand" and could use as they wanted; b) use higher grade production materials, and c) start work on large-format, coffee-table style documents to be provided to each family *and* also copies to be donated to the local Gulisi Garifuna Museum.

Figure 2a: Original educational "poster" composed of photos, many water-damaged, attached to cardboard with layers of clear tape. Photograph by Jonathan S. Marion. All rights reserved.

Advances in transportation technologies, combined with an increased awareness of humanitarian crises abroad (an awareness that is largely facilitated by advances in communication technologies) also create new ethnoscapes. Programs like the Peace Corps have a relatively long history of sending Westerners into foreign nations to assist with humanitarian efforts on a regular basis. Other volunteers are mobilized in times of crisis. Medical professionals may volunteer their services during a disease epidemic, flocking to the regions others are trying to flee. Engineers may volunteer their time to help rebuild cities in the wake of natural disasters. And even lay people without a specialized skill set may lend their energy to helping others in the aftermath of a disaster, or by collecting

Figure 2b: Updated 3'x4' poster, documenting the entire drum-making process, with matte lamination to protect from water damage. Photograph by Jonathan S. Marion. All rights reserved.

and/or donating goods to be used in various relief efforts. In 2010, a devastating, 7.0 magnitude earthquake struck Haiti, affecting an estimated three million people. Thanks to widespread coverage of the crisis, the international response was immediate and intense with more than twenty countries contributing resources and personnel to assist in the recovery efforts. Clearly, then, there are also benefits facilitated by globalization.

Disadvantages of the Intensification of Globalization

In the previous section, we concluded by noting how the intensification of globalization can bring benefits to people in times of crisis. Yet it bears remembering and reiterating that sometimes such crises are themselves brought about by globalization. The decimation of indigenous tribes in the Americas, who had little to no resistance to the diseases carried by European explorers and settlers, is but one early example of this. Such changes to the world's ethnoscapes may also be accompanied by changes to local health. As epidemic after epidemic wreaked havoc on the indigenous peoples of the Americas, death rates in some tribes reached as high as 95 percent. Addressing a current instance, the research program on Climate Change, Agriculture and Food Security (CCAFS) coordinated by the University of Copenhagen in Denmark, has called attention to the role of human-caused climate change in creating the current Syrian refugee crisis (see case study by Laurie King below).[34]

Similarly, a current example of how globalization can spell disaster from a public health standpoint would be the concern in 2014 about infected airplane passengers bringing the Ebola virus from Africa to the U.S. In March 2014, the country of Guinea experienced an outbreak of the Ebola virus. From there, it spread into many countries in the western part of Africa. Medical professionals from the U.S. traveled to West Africa to assist with patient care. In October 2014, the Centers for Disease Control and Prevention (CDC) confirmed that a man who traveled from Liberia to the U.S. while asymptomatic became ill several days after reaching the U.S. and eventually succumbed to the disease. Several health workers in the U.S. also became ill with the virus, but were successfully treated. In response to this outbreak, the CDC increased screening efforts at the major ports of entry to the U.S.[35] However, these precautions did not quell the fears of many Americans who heatedly debated the possibility of instituting travel bans to and from countries with confirmed cases of Ebola.

The debates about travel bans to and from West Africa were a reminder of the xenophobic attitudes held by many Americans even in this age of globalization. There are many reasons for this. Racial prejudice is still very much a reality in today's world (see the Race and Ethnicity chapter) as is prejudice against other religions, non-normative gender identity, the differently abled, and others. In some ways, these fears have been heightened by globalization rather than diminished. Especially after the global recession of 2008, some nation-states have become fearful for their economic security and have found it easy to use marginalized populations as scapegoats. While advances in communication technology have enabled social justice focused solidarity movements (as discussed above), unfortunately the same media have been used as a platform for hate-mongering by others. Social media enables those who had previously only been schoolyard bullies to broadcast their taunts further than ever before. Terrorists post videos of unspeakable violence online and individuals whose hateful attitudes might have been curbed through the informal sanctions of gossip and marginalization in a smaller-scale society can now find communities of like-minded bigots in online chat rooms. By foregrounding the importance of the hypothetical "average" person, populist politics has engaged in scapegoating of minority ethnic and religious groups. This has been most apparent in the successful campaigns for the British Brexit vote on June 23, 2016 and the election of Donald Trump as President in the United States.

A portmanteau of "British" and "exit," Brexit refers to the vote to leave the European Union. (Headquartered in Brussels, Belgium, the European Union is an economic and political union of 28 nation-states founded on November 1, 1993 in Maastricht, Netherlands.) Both this and the election of Donald Trump as the 45th president of the U.S. represent backlash against some of the inequities generated by globalization. At the world scale, the Global North continues to extract wealth from the

Global South. More tellingly though is the widening wealth-gap even in "rich" countries. Without sufficient social protection, capitalism—a system wherein profit motivates political and economic decision making—has led to a situation in which the world's eight richest men (note the gendering) now control as much wealth as the bottom 50 percent of the entire world's population. In other words, eight men now have just as much money as 3.75 *billion* people combined and no nation in the world has a larger wealth-gap (the difference between those with the most and the least in a society) than the United States. So, while globalization has facilitated advantages for some, more and more people are being left behind. Social scientists often use the term "re-entrenchment" to describe efforts people make to reassert their traditional values and ways of life. While this impulse is understandable, many of these people are susceptible to the rhetoric of scapegoating: being told some other group is at fault for the problems they are facing. This is the double-edged sword of globalization. Additionally, in some cases globalization is forced on already marginal populations in peripheral nations through institutions like the IMF and World Bank. In these instances, globalization facilitates and amplifies the reach and impact of **neoliberalism**, a multi-faceted political and economic philosophy that emphasizes privatization and unregulated markets (see below).

GLOBALIZATION AND NEOLIBERALISM

Latin America provides a good example of how the shift from colonialism to neoliberalism has been disseminated through and exacerbated by globalization. By the beginning of the twentieth century, the Latin American colonies' independence from Spain and Portugal was secure, but the relations of power that prevailed during the colonial period had largely been replicated with local elites controlling the means of production. During this period, citizens individually and collectively endeavored to establish a new national identity. Despite nominal commitments to democracy throughout the region, patron/client relationships functioned as the primary political mechanism. Internal divisions ran deep in many Latin American countries, with the supporters (or clients) of rival elites periodically drawn into violent contests for rule on behalf of their patrons. In the last decade of the 1800s and the first decade of the 1900s, people in Latin America began to question the right of the elites to rule, as well as the hidden costs of modernization. Peasant uprisings, like the one that took place at Canudus in Brazil in 1896, were evidence of the shifting political framework. People also saw the imperialistic tendencies of the U.S. as a negative force of modernization which they hoped to avoid. Together, this led to a situation in which people in Latin America sought a national identity that resonated with their sense of self.

During this same period there was a slight but significant change in the economic structure of the region. The economy was still based on exports of agriculture and natural resources like minerals, and the profits remained in the hands of the elite. What was new, however, was the introduction and modest growth of manufacturing in the cities, which created new job opportunities. Economic diversification led to a more complex class structure and an emerging middle class. Unfortunately, this period of relative prosperity and stability soon ended. Because of the plentiful natural resources and the captive labor source "available" for exploitation in Latin America, wealthy landowners were able to undersell their European competitors on agricultural products and provide "exotic" minerals. The privileged position of Latin American landowner compared to European farmers led to widespread poverty among farmers in Europe, which led to out-migration and political instability in Europe. As locally born Latin American peasants migrated from the countryside to the cities *and* the cities filled with European immigrants, the landowning elite began to lose control, or at least the kind of power they used to hold over the farmers who worked their land and had no other work options.

While city living provided certain opportunities, it also introduced new challenges. In the city, for instance, people rarely had access to land for subsistence agriculture. This made them far more vulnerable to economic fluctuations, and the vulnerability of city living necessitated the adoption of new political philosophies. Urban poverty and desperation created a climate in which many people found socialist philosophies appealing, starting as early as the 1920s in some places like Brazil. Initially, union leaders and European immigrants who spread socialist ideas among the urban poor were punished by the state and often deported. Eventually such repressive tactics proved insufficient to curtail the swelling disruptions caused by strikes and related actions by the unions. Faced with a new political reality, the elite co-opted the public rhetoric of the urban masses. Realizing the need to cast themselves as allies to the urban workforce, the elites ushered in a period of modest reform with more protection for workers.

During this period, and as an extension of their work-related activism, the middle class also clamored for expansions of the social services provided by the state. Pressure from the middle class for more social services for citizens unfortunately played into growing xenophobia (fear of foreigners) resulting from the immigration of so many foreigners *and* faulty ideas about racial superiority communicated through a growing discourse of nationalism. In some places, the elites aligned with the middle classes if they saw it as politically advantageous. In other places, however, elites resisted incorporating the middle classes into the ruling structure and the elites' power ultimately was wrested away though military coups. While emerging leaders from the middle class continued relying on the export economic model, they directed a greater percentage of the profits back into social programs. Only after the stock market crash of the 1930s—and the resulting global recession—did those in power start to question the export model.

In the early part of the 1900s, Latin American countries largely supported free trade because they believed they had a competitive advantage. They believed that by producing the products their country/region was best suited to produce they would prosper on the world market. However, changing world circumstances meant that Latin American countries soon lost their advantage; average family size in industrialized countries began to decrease, lowering demand for Latin American commodities. When other countries with similar climates and topography began to grow the same crops, a global oversupply of agricultural products led to lower prices and worsened the decline of Latin America's financial status in the world market.

This economic downturn was amplified by the loss of British hegemony after World War II. Before the war, Great Britain and Latin America had enjoyed a stable exchange relationship with Latin America sending agricultural goods to Great Britain and the British sending manufactured goods to Latin America. As the U.S. rose in global power, Americans looked to Latin America as a new market for U.S. manufactured goods. In contrast to Great Britain though, the U.S. did not need to import Latin American agricultural goods because the U.S. produced enough of its own, production that was further protected by high import tariffs. Even if a consumer wanted to buy Latin American commodities, the commodities would be more expensive than domestic ones—even if actual costs were lower. Overall, Latin America sold its agricultural goods to Europe, including Great Britain, but Latin American exporters had to accept lower prices than ever before.

The United States' economic strategy toward Latin America was different than Great Britain's had been. For those commodities that could not be produced in the U.S., like bananas, U.S. companies went to Latin America so they could directly control the means of production. Although these commodities were grown and/or produced *in* Latin America, the profits were taken by foreign companies rather than local ones. This same process also happened with mining interests like tin and copper; U.S. companies purchased the mines in order to extract as much profit as possible. American companies were in a position to exploit the natural resources of these countries because the U.S. had the financial capital local communities lacked *and* the technological expertise needed to sustain these industries. This pattern curtailed the rate of economic growth throughout Latin America as well as in other regions where similar patterns developed.

The late 1920s through the 1950s saw many Latin American countries turning to nationalism—often through force—as both a cultural movement and an economic strategy. The middle classes were in a favor of curtailing the export economy that had been preferred by the elites, but did not have the political clout to win elections. Indeed, their agenda was regularly blocked by the elites who used their influence (i.e. with their clients) to press their interests, especially in the rural areas. With time, however, middle class men increasingly came to occupy military officer positions and used their newfound authority to put nationalist leaders in the presidencies. Nationalists argued that an over-dependence on agriculture had led to Latin America's vulnerable position in the international economy and called for a build-up of industry. They hoped to start producing the goods that they had been importing from the U.S. and Europe. Their goal: industrial self-sufficiency.

The state was instrumental in this economic reorganization, both helping people buy local goods and discouraging them from buying foreign goods. Doing this was far from as easy as it may sound. The state imposed high duties on goods destined for the export market in order to entice producers to sell their goods at home. At the same time, the state imposed high tariffs on the imports they wanted to replace with local products. With time (and struggle) these measures had their intended effects, making the locally produced goods comparatively more affordable—and therefore appealing—to local consumers.

As already noted, developing factories required capital and technological expertise from abroad, which in turn made the goods produced much more expensive. To help people afford such expensive goods, the state printed more money, generating massive inflation. (In some places this inflation would eventually reach 2,000 percent!) The combination of chronic inflation with high foreign debt emerged as an enduring problem in Latin America and other parts of the Global South. Countries crippled by high inflation and debt have turned to international institutions like the IMF and WB for relief and while the intentions may be good, borrowing money from these global institutions always comes with strings attached. When a country accepts a loan from the IMF or the WB, for instance, they must agree to a number of conditions such as privatizing state enterprises (see the case study on Bolivia's water crisis, below) and cutting spending on social services like healthcare and education. Borrowing countries are also required to adopt a number of policies intended to encourage free trade, such as the reduction or elimination of tariffs on imported goods and subsidies for domestically produced goods. Policies are put into place to encourage foreign investment. Transnational corporations have now reached the point that many of them rival nations in terms of revenue. In fact, as of 2009, "forty-four of the world's hundred largest economies are corporations."[36] It is an understatement to note that the policies forced on countries by lenders are often disruptive—if not entirely destructive—of locally preferred lifeways and preferences. Although the IMF and WB measures are intended to spark economic growth, the populace often winds up suffering in the wake of these changes. Colonialism has given way to a neocolonialism in which economic force achieves what used to require military force with transnational corporations benefiting from the exploitation of poorer nations.

Case Study: Privatization and Bolivia's Water Crisis

In 2000, Bolivians in the city of Cochambamba took to the streets to protest the exploitative practices of a transnational company that had won the right to provide water services in the city.[37] Anti-globalization activists celebrated this victory of mostly poor mestizo and indigenous people over capitalist giants, but the situation on the ground today is more complicated.

Water is one of the most essential elements on this planet. So how is it that a foreign company was given the right to determine who would have access to Bolivian water supplies and what the water would cost? The answer serves to highlight the fact that many former colonies like Bolivia have existed in a perpetual state of subordination to global superpowers. When Bolivia was a colony, Spain claimed the silver and other precious commodities that could be extracted from Bolivia's landscape, but after Bolivia became independent structural adjustment policies mandated by the International Monetary Fund and World Bank paved the way for foreign companies to plunder the country's natural resources. In other words, colonial style relationships have been replicated in a global system that forces impoverished countries to sell resources to satisfy creditors; "resource extraction is facilitated by debt relations."[38]

Like many countries in the Global South, Bolivia is deep in debt. A failed program of social reforms, coupled with government corruption, was worsened by a severe drought affecting Bolivian agriculture. In order to pay its debts in the 1980s, Bolivia agreed to structural adjustments mandated by the conditions of the country's World Bank and International Monetary Fund loans. One of the mandates of these loans was privatization of state-run enterprises like the water system. Proponents of privatizing such resources argue that the efficiency associated with for-profit businesses will also serve to conserve precious natural resources. Some have gone so far as to suggest that increases in water prices would help customers better grasp the preciousness of water and thereby encourage conservation. Of course, if customers conserve water too much the company managing water delivery will fail to make a profit, thus initiating a dangerous cycle. When companies anticipate that they will not see a return on their investment in infrastructure, they simply refuse to extend services to certain areas of the community.

What made the privatization of water in Bolivia so disastrous for the people of urban areas like Cochabamba was the rapid population growth they experienced starting in the latter half of the twentieth century (growth that continues in the present). Population pressures layered on top of the scarcity of water in the Bolivian natural environment makes access to potable water a perennial concern. Migration to urban areas was hastened by many different factors including land reform, privatization of mines and resultant layoffs, and severe droughts. This influx of migrants put pressure on urban infrastructure. To make matters worse, climate change led to a decline in the amount of surface water available. In 2015, Lake Poopó, the second largest lake in Bolivia, went dry and researchers are doubtful it will ever fully recover (see Figure 3).[39]

Figure 3: A fishing boat is stranded on the shrinking Lake Poopó, 2006.

In Cochabamba, organizing began in late 1999. Community members formed an organization called Coordinator for the Defense of Water and for Life, which was run using a direct form of democracy wherein everyone had an equal voice. This was empowering for peasants who were accustomed to being silenced and ignored in a centuries-old social hierarchy. This organization, in contrast, coordinated actions that cut across ethnic and class lines. As the situation came to a head, activists blockaded the roads in and out of the city and riot police were brought in from the capital. After several days of confrontations between the people and the military, local activists ousted the transnational company and reclaimed their water source.

Despite local's reclaiming control, however, they still lacked the infrastructure needed to effectively deliver what was once again "their" water. This forced them to look to international donors for assistance, which could recreate the very situation against which they so recently fought. Access to increasingly scarce water supplies is a growing problem. For example, plans to seize surface water from lakes creates conflicts with rural peasants who depend on these water sources for agricultural purposes. Unfortunately, such problems have emerged in many other places as well (such as throughout Africa and the Middle East), and are increasing in prevalence and severity amidst ongoing climate change. The question of whether or not water is a human right remains one that is heatedly debated by activists, CEOs, and others. (See a discussion of the position taken by Nestlé Chairman Peter Brabeck, who argues for the privatization of water, a position clearly at odds with the position taken by the United Nations General Assembly which, in 2010, recognized water and sanitation as human rights.)

RESPONSES TO GLOBALIZATION

Cultures are dynamic and respond to changes in both the social and physical environments in which they are embedded. While culture provides a template for action, people are also active agents who respond to challenges and opportunities in a variety of ways, some of which may be quite creative and novel. As such, it would be inaccurate to only see globalization as an impersonal force dictating the lives of people in their various localities. Rather, people regularly use a variety of strategies in responding to global forces. While a comprehensive catalog of these strategies is beyond the scope of this chapter, here we outline two key responses.

Syncretism

Syncretism refers to the combination of different beliefs—even those that are seemingly contradictory—into a new, harmonious whole. Though syncretism arises for a variety of reasons, in many cases it is as a response to globalization. In this section, we use the example of *Candomblé* as a way of demonstrating that syncretism is a form of agency used by people living under oppression.

Most often, anthropologists discuss syncretism within the context of religion. Anthropologists define religion as the cultural knowledge of the spiritual realm that humans use to cope with the ultimate problems of human existence (see the Religion chapter). *Candomblé* is an Afro-Brazilian spirit-possession religion, in which initiates serve as conduits between the human and supernatural realm. It is also an excellent example of a syncretic religion. The many gods in Candomblé, known as *orixás*, are personified: they all have personalities; experience the full range of human emotions like love, hatred, jealousy, and anger; and have individual histories that are known to practitioners. Each orixá is associated with a particular color, and practitioners of the religion often wear bead necklaces that correspond to the specific deity with whom they feel a connection (see Figure 4). Unlike Christianity (a monotheistic religion), Candomblé does not stress the duality of good and evil (or heaven and hell). Although on the surface these two religious traditions may seem very different, in actual practice, many adherents of Candomblé also identify as Christians, specifically Catholics. So how can this be?

Figure 4: Candomblé practitioners, Embu das Artes, Brazil, 2012.

Much like the orixás, Catholic saints are personified and have unique roles within the Catholic tradition. This feature of Catholicism—more so than any other major Christian denomination—facilitated a fairly seamless overlay with orixá worship. For example, *Iemanja*, the orixá who rules over the seas and is associated with fertility, is syncretized with Our Lady of Conception. *Ogum*, whose domain is war and whose ritual implements are the sword and shield, is syncretized with Saint Anthony.

Just to be clear, syncretism is in no way unique to Brazil or the African Diaspora; it frequently occurs when one group is confronted with and influenced by another (and typically one with more power). The reason syncretism is particularly common within Latin American religious systems is due to 1) the tenacity with which African slaves clung to their traditional beliefs; 2) the fervor of the Spanish and Portuguese belief that slaves *should* receive instruction in Catholicism, and 3) the realities of colonial life in which religious instruction for slaves was haphazard at best. This created the perfect climate within which African slaves could hide their traditional religious practices in plain sight.

Syncretism serves as a response to globalization insofar as it mediates overlapping frameworks. It would be unnecessary if people lived in a world where boundaries were clearly defined with no ideological exchanges taking place across those boundaries (if such a world ever existed). Since that is far from the lived reality for most people though, syncretism often serves as what James C. Scott categorizes as a "weapon of the weak"—a concept referring to the ways in which marginalized peoples can resist without directly challenging their oppressors (which could incite retaliation).[40] Examples might include mocking the elite behind their backs, subtle subversion, sabotage, or participation in alternative economies that bypass the elite. In the classroom, it can be rolling one's eyes behind the professor's back, or thinking that you are "getting away with something" when texting in class. So too in the case of Candomblé. Syncretism allowed the slaves and their descendants, who continue the tradition today, to create a façade of compliance with mandated worship within the Catholic tradition, while still continuing to pay homage to their own beliefs—and thus perpetuate their own ethnic identity—behind closed doors.

Participation in Alternative Markets

As discussed earlier, structural adjustments mandated by international bodies like the IMF and WB have left farmers in developing nations particularly vulnerable to the whims of global markets. Within this framework, "fair trade" has emerged as a way for socially-conscious consumers to support small farmers and artisans who have been affected by these policies. To be certified as fair trade, vendors must agree to a "fair" price, which will be adjusted upwards if the world market price rises above the fair trade threshold. If the world market price drops, fair trade farmers still make a decent living, which allows them to continue farming rather than abandon their fields for wage labor. While admirable in its intent, and unassailably beneficial to many, anthropological research reminds us that every situation is complex and that there is never a "one size fits all" perfect solution.

As you read about in the Fieldwork chapter, and have seen demonstrated throughout this text, anthropologists focus on the lived experience of people closest to the phenomenon they are studying. In the case of fair trade, then, anthropologists focus primarily on the farmers or artisans (although an anthropologist could also study the consumers or people who import fair trade goods or facilitate their sale). Looked at from farmers' perspectives, setting and maintaining fair wages for commodities like coffee or bananas ensures that farmers will not abandon farming when the world market prices drop. On the plus side, this helps ensure at least some stability for producers and consumers alike. One of the key features of fair trade is the social premium generated by fair trade contracts: the commitment that a certain percentage of the profit goes back into beneficial community projects such as education, infrastructure development, and healthcare. But, in order for this to be successful, it is the local community and not an outside entity (however well intentioned) that must get to decide how these premiums are used.

Although fair trade is very appealing, it bears remembering that not everyone benefits from fair trade in the same way. Individuals in leadership positions within fair trade cooperatives tend to have stronger relationships with the vendors than do average members, leading them to have more positive associations with the whole business of fair trade.[41] Similarly, people with more cultural and social capital will have more access to the benefits of fair trade. A cacao farmer with whom Lauren works in Belize, for example, pointed out that farmers with less education will always be taken advantage of by predatory traders, which is why they need the assistance of a well-structured growers' association when entering the free trade market. Also of concern is that in some communities fair trade disrupts traditional roles and relationships. For example in a Maya village in Guatemala, traditional gender roles were compromised, with men becoming even more dominant because their commodity (coffee) had a fair trade market whereas the women's main commodity (weaving) did not.[42]

In addition to the challenge of finding a market for one's goods, there are additional barriers to becoming involved in fair trade. For example, it used to be that farmers could sell relatively low quality coffee to fair trade organizations interested in social justice. Now, however, fair trade coffee must be of exceptional quality to compete with specialty coffees.[43] In and of itself this is not a bad thing, but remember that some of the elite coffee producers of today were once the low quality producers of old. In other words, the first generation of fair trade coffee farmers benefited from the many ways in which fair trade companies invested in their farms, their processing equipment, and their education in a way that newer participants cannot replicate. Indeed, once these initial farmers achieved a high quality coffee bean, there was less incentive for fair trade vendors to invest in new farms. Now that the bar has been set so high, it is much more difficult for new farmers to break into the fair trade market because they lack the equipment, experience, knowledge, and networks of farmers who have more longstanding relationships with fair trade companies.

Also worth noting are the many situations in which global standards conflict with local norms of decision making. To be labeled as fair trade within the European Union banana market, for example, bananas must be of an exceptionally high quality. Banana farms must conform to a number of other guidelines such as avoiding pesticides and creating a buffer zone between the banana trees and water sources. While this all may make sense in theory, it can be problematic in practice, such as in parts of the Caribbean where land is customarily passed from one generation to the next without being subdivide into individual parcels. In these cases, decisions about land use have to be made collectively. If some of the landowners want to farm according to fair trade guidelines but other individuals refuse to meet these globally mandated standards, the whole family is blocked from entering the fair trade market.[44]

IMPLICATIONS FOR ANTHROPOLOGY

As has been argued throughout this text, culture is dynamic. So too is anthropology as the field of study dedicated to culture. Although many students of anthropology (let alone the public at large) may have romantic visions of the lone ethnographer immersing her or himself in the rich community life of a rural village in a remote land, this is not the reality for most anthropologists today. An increasing number of anthropologists find themselves working in applied settings (see the Seeing Like an Anthropologist chapter), but even many of the more strictly identified "academic" anthropologists—those employed at colleges and universities—have begun working in settings that might well be familiar to the average person. Now that anthropologists understand the importance of global flows of money, people, and ideas the importance of doing research everywhere that these issues play out—at home (wherever that may be) as much as abroad—is clear.

Urban Anthropology

Globalization has become a powerful buzzword in contemporary society and it would be difficult to find anyone who has not been affected by it in at least some small way. The widespread influence of globalization on daily life around the world—whether directly (such as through multinational businesses) or indirectly (such as via climate change)—raises a number of questions that anthropologists have begun to ask. For example, an anthropologist might investigate the effects of global policies on people in different regions of the world. Why is it that the monetary policies of the International Monetary Fund and World Bank typically result in rich countries getting richer and the poor countries getting poorer? In her book *Beautiful Flowers of the Maquiladora* (1997), for example, Norma Iglesias Prieto gives an up-close portrait of the lives of Mexican women working in factories in the infamous border zone of Tijuana.[45] Although the working conditions in these factories are dangerous and the women are subjected to invasive scrutiny by male supervisors, many of the women profiled in the book nonetheless appreciate the little luxuries afforded by their work. Others value the opportunity to support their household or gain a small degree of financial independence from the male figures in their life. Unable to offer any artificially flat answer concerning whether globalization has been "good" or "bad" for such individuals, anthropologists focus on the lived experience of the people most affected by these global forces. What is it like to live in such environments? How has it changed over time? What have been the costs and benefits?

Especially amidst the overlapping flows of people and ideas, questions concerning mobility, transnationalism, and identity have all become increasingly important to the field of anthropology. Although some exceptions exist (see quinoa case study below), the general trend is for globalization to result in urbanization. With neoliberalism comes the loss of state-funded programs and jobs, the unsustainability of small farms, and the need for economic alternatives that are most commonly found in urban areas. While anthropologists have long studied cities and urban life, the concentration of populations in urban centers has added increasing importance to anthropologies of the city/metropolis in recent years.[46] Indeed, the term urban anthropology came into use to describe experiences of living in cities and the relationships of city life to broader social, political, and economic contexts including issues of globalization, poverty, and neoliberalism.[47] The heightened focus on the city in global context has also heightened awareness of and attention to issues of transnationalism: the understanding that people's lives may be lived and/or significantly influenced by events that cross the geopolitical borders of nation states.[48]

Case Study: Global Demand for Quinoa

When a group of people is afforded little status in a society, their food is often likewise denigrated.[49] Until recently, this held true for quinoa in Bolivian society, which was associated with indigenous peasants.[50] Mirroring "first world" patterns from the U.S. and Europe, city dwellers preferred foods like pasta and wheat-based products. Conspicuous consumption of these products provided them with an opportunity to showcase their "sophisticated" choices and tastes. Not surprisingly, there was little local demand for quinoa in Bolivian markets. Further undercutting the appeal of producing quinoa, the Bolivian government's adoption of neoliberal policies eliminated the meager financial protections available to peasant farmers. If that was not bad enough, a significant drought in the early 1980s spelled disaster for many small farmers in the southern Altiplano region of Bolivia. As a result of these overlapping and amplifying obstacles, many people moved to 1) cities, like La Paz; 2) nearby countries, like Chile, and even 3) to Europe.

The situation faced by Bolivian peasants is not unique. More than half of the world's people currently live in cities. This is the result of widespread urbanization that began at the end of World War II and stretched into the 1990s. As a result, many peasants lost access to their traditional modes of subsistence. Although migration to the city can provide benefits like access to education, infrastructure, and wage-labor, it can also result in a loss of identity and many peasants who migrate into cities are forced to subsist on the margins in substandard conditions, especially as they most often arrive without the social and cultural capital necessary to succeed in this new environment.

Fortuitously for indigenous Bolivians, the structural adjustments adopted by their government coincided with foreigners' growing interest in organic and health foods. Although it is often assumed that rural peasants only produce food for their own subsistence and for very local markets, this is not always the case. In some situations, peasants may bypass local markets entirely and export their commodities to places where they have more cultural capital, and hence financial value (see discussion of taste above). In the 1970s, the introduction of tractors to the region enabled farmers to cultivate quinoa in the lowlands in addition to the hillside terraces they had previously favored. In the 1980s, cooperative groups of farmers were able to find buyers in the Global North who were willing to import quinoa (see Figure 5). These cooperatives researched the best ways to expand production and invested in machines to make the process more efficient. Now, quinoa is such a valuable commodity that many of those individuals who had previously abandoned the region are now returning to the Altiplano. Yet this is not a simple success story, especially because there are serious issues associated with the re-peasantization of the Bolivian countryside and with the fact that a healthy local crop has been removed from many people's regular diets since it can be sold to the Global North.

Another serious issue raised by the reverse migration from the cities back to the Altiplano concerns environmental sustainability. It is easier to grow large quantities of quinoa in the flat lowlands than it is on the steep hillsides, but the lowland soil is much less conducive to its growth. The use of machinery has helped a great deal, but has also led to a decline in the use of llamas, which have a symbiotic relationship with quinoa. Farmers must now invest in fertilizer rather than using manure provided by their own animals. The global quinoa boom also raises questions about identity and communal decision-making. Conflict has arisen between families that stayed in the region and those that are returning from the cities. Pedro, a farmer who stayed in the region, says of the others "those people have returned – but as strangers."[51] The two groups often clash in terms of what it means to respect the land and how money from this new cash crop should be used.

So has the international demand for quinoa been a good thing for rural Bolivian peasants? In some ways yes, but in other ways no.; on the whole, it may be too soon to know for sure.

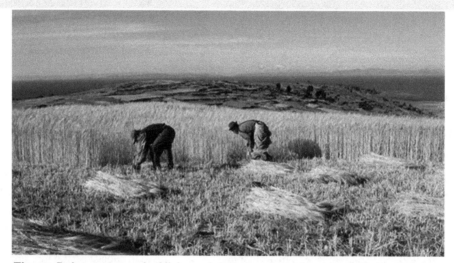

Figure 5: Aymara couple Alicia and Julio harvest wheat on their land above Lake Titicaca in Southern Peru. Other subsistence crops they raised included quinoa, barley, and potatoes, but the global market pressures such subsistence farmers to grow more quinoa as a "cash" crop to capitalize on the world demand. Juli, Peru, 2005. Photo by Jerome W. Corder. All rights reserved.

Changes in How—and "Where"—We Conduct Research

Globalization has changed not only what anthropologists research, but also how they approach those topics. Foregrounding the links between global processes and local settings, multi-sited ethnography examines specific topics and issues across different geographic field sites.[52] Multi-sited ethnography may be conducted when the subject of one's study involve and/or impact multiple locations and can be best understood by accounting for those multiple geographic contexts. For example, in her study of yoga, *Positioning Yoga: Balancing Acts Across Cultures*, Sarah Strauss (2005) found that her study would be incomplete if she focused only on Indians studying yoga. To understand this transnational phenomenon, she recognized the importance of also focusing on non-Indian practitioners of yoga who had gone to study yoga in its homeland.[53] Work such as that of Swedish anthropologist Ulf Hannerz, who studies news media correspondents, highlights the ways that people can be on the move, creating a community of study that is both multi-sited and multilocal.[54] Further work has expanded on these models, highlighting various *translocal* fieldsites: "locations" that cannot be geographically defined. Such models include calls for an activity-based anthropology (where it is the activity itself that is the "site" of the culture and/or the basis of the community)[55] and digital anthropology (where the field site exists online).[56]

Globalization in Application: The Syrian Situation Today (courtesy of Laurie King)

Syria today presents us with an apocalyptic landscape: major cities such as Homs have been reduced to rubble and anyone remaining there is starving. Since 2011, over 250,000 civilians have been killed by barrel bombs, shelling, internecine terrorist attacks, drone strikes, the use of chemical weapons, and Russian aerial assaults. Well-armed and well-funded Islamist militias control large swathes of the country and have, for all intents and purposes, erased the border between Syria and Iraq, thereby undoing the 1916 Sykes-Picot agreement that established the new nation-states of the modern Middle East after the fall of the Ottoman Empire.

The so-called Islamic State (IS/Da`esh) has destroyed world heritage sites such as Palmyra (Tadmur), ethnically cleansed non-Muslim towns, enslaved women, and flooded the global media with horrific images of beheadings, immolations, and mass executions. Aleppo, a city of stunning architectural beauty with a rich multi-cultural heritage, is now damaged beyond repair and largely uninhabitable as the result of fighting between IS, Syrian regime forces, and a diverse but largely Islamist Syrian opposition.

Farming in the Syrian countryside has come to a virtual halt. Since 2003, Syrian agriculture had been suffering from a prolonged drought, pushing many rural families into urban centers such as Damascus and Aleppo.[57] In 2015, the Svalbard Global Seed Vault (the "Doomsday Seed Vault") in Norway was accessed for the first time to obtain seeds needed for crops to feed the Syrian population.[58] Meanwhile, as any glance at the evening news demonstrates, millions of refugees continue to flow out of the country, mostly through the Syrian-Turkish border, before making dangerous trips in unsafe boats to Greece, hoping to get their families to Europe and away from the hell-scape that their country has become.

Five years ago, no scholar of Syrian society and politics could have predicted the dire conditions Syria now faces. Given the Assad regime's iron grip on all aspects of Syrian society since 1970, the dramatic transformations of the last five years were inconceivable at the beginning of 2011. The scapes and flows of globalization enumerated by Appadurai were largely absent from Syria over the last 40 years. The hardline Baathist regime of Hafez al-Assad, who came to power in 1970 through a bloodless coup, was profoundly insular and not open to the world—whether regionally or internationally—in the realms of finance and commerce. Never a major petroleum power, and not blessed with vast tracts of fertile land for farming, Syria's economy centered largely on industry and commerce.

Up until the mid-1980s, Syria had a highly centralized economy that eschewed private ownership of industry or services. With the end of the Cold War (during which Syria had been a client state of the USSR), and the ensuing dramatic shifts in regional power dynamics—most notably the 1991 Iraq war, which saw the rout of Saddam Hussein's forces from Kuwait and the diminution of the Iraqi Baathist regime's power—Syria emerged as a key regional player capable of leveraging concessions from other Arab states as well as the West. In exchange for joining the US-led coalition against Iraq, the United States and the international community raised no objections to Syria asserting direct and indirect control over its neighbor (and former mandatory province) Lebanon, where a series of interconnected civil, regional, and global wars had raged for fifteen years.

Syrian political and military control effectively put the Lebanese wars into a deep freeze between 1992 and 2005. While freedom of speech in Lebanon declined significantly under Syria's tutelage, an unregulated market economy flourished, centering on the massive post-war reconstruction boom. The Syrian economic elite—largely co-terminous with the regime—benefited significantly from business deals in Lebanon, while thousands of Syrian workers flooded into Lebanon to do construction work on the new city center and infra-structural repairs. The influx of money from Lebanon strengthened and entrenched the patron-client ties between the Syrian regime (whose members were also relatives by blood or marriage) and a growing class of wealthy businessmen, who owed their wealth to the regime. As Bassam Haddad notes, the insularity of and corruption within the regime and big business blurred the line between private and public domains, while sharpening class divisions within Syria.[59] Any attempts to foster political reform, economic transparency, and international commerce were viewed suspiciously by Syria's political, commercial, and military/intelligence elite.

In June 2000, Hafez Al-Assad died. His son Bashar, an ophthalmologist who had lived in London for many years, succeeded him. Local and international observers wondered if the new, foreign-educated young president would launch an era of economic reform and political decentralization. Bashar seemed keen to bring Syria into the Internet era, and his first years in power witnessed relatively free discussion of the need for economic and political reforms, heralded by the closing of the infamous Mezzeh prison, where many po-litical prisoners had been tortured and killed. But power remained in the hands of the few in the upper reaches of the Baath party, some of whom did not know whether or not to trust Bashar, who lacked the steely reserve and unquestioned authority of his father.

Although Syria lacked the sort of material and financial capital enjoyed by its neighbors, such as the oil-rich Gulf states, it enjoyed the benefits of symbolic capital as the sole, front-line Arab nationalist state opposing Israel and resisting any normalization of ties with the Jewish state in the post-Cold war era, even as the Palestinian Liberation organization and Jordan joined Egypt in establishing peace treaties with Israel. In the hope that Syria would come into the fold, the United States did not make harsh demands on Syria for internal reforms or regional economic integration.

In February 2005, in the wake of growing Lebanese dissatisfaction with Syria's control of the country, Prime Minister Rafiq Al-Hariri and over a dozen of his colleagues were killed in a massive suicide bomb while traveling in a motorcade through downtown Beirut. (To this day, no one knows decisively who was behind the car bomb, though many suspect Syrian involvement.) Massive, largely peaceful, demonstrations erupted in Beirut imme-diately, and within a matter of weeks, Syria was forced to end its occupation of Lebanon and retreat.

While Syria had not experienced a significant flow of people and wealth in and out of its borders for years, media and technology flows were growing in the first decade of the twenty-first century. The flow of ideas and images from Tunisia and Egypt in the wake of the Arab Spring uprisings of 2010-11 heralded Syria's first sustained experience with the dynamics of globalization, described in this text by political scientist Manfred Steger as: "the intensification of worldwide social relations which link distant localities in such a way that local happenings are shaped by events occurring many miles away, and vice versa."[60]

In February 2011, the regime lifted the ban on Facebook and You Tube following unprec-edented street protests on January 26, the day after the Egyptian protests began. (Before this, Syrians contravened the ban through proxy servers.) Soon, Facebook groups were organizing and even calling for a "Day of Rage" and encouraging people to come out to the streets to protest against the regime. Nothing came of this, though. Despite garnering thousands of "likes," no one seemed to be following the directives of the new Facebook pages.[61]

The Internet's impact in the Arab world has built upon the phenomenon of satellite television, particularly that of Al-Jazeera, which opened up new spaces of discourse and debate about political and human rights issues in the Arab world, thereby undermining the legitimacy and validity of state-owned news programs and the power structures underpinning them. While Al Jazeera instilled a powerful reformist spirit, blogs were particularly crucial in advancing and fortifying Arab activism efforts.

Before blogs, there were chat rooms, listservs, and email communication, all of which enhanced and expanded a cyber world of public discourse in some Arab states, but not in Syria. Some Egyptian bloggers called the Internet and social media "our lungs. If they cut them off, we will suffocate." As a result of Internet communications technology (ICT), social isolation in the Arab world began to give way to the formation of communities of conversation and debate, which ultimately evolved into social movements that took to the streets and made history in the real world. Our "networked society," to use Manuel Castell's phrase, connects us horizontally and allows us not only to communicate, but to self-communicate and self-create.[62] We not only consume the news, we now evaluate, filter, and respond to the news. We not only read headlines, our networked actions and reactions to breaking news can ripple out across countries and continents and make headlines.

While Western media paid considerable attention to Egypt's uprising, the Syrian uprisings were not as well covered. Perhaps this is because Egypt is part of the West's cultural imaginary. (Hollywood movies such as *Raiders of the Lost Ark* and popular culture depictions of pyramids, pharaohs, and the Valley of the Kings are all evidence of this.) Syria, a tightly controlled authoritarian state, had not been a destination for Western tourists, scholars, film producers, or even journalists for decades, so its street protests and popular struggles did not loom large in Western media coverage. While every major American news agency covered the uprising in Tahrir Square in Cairo in real time, news of protests and civil society activism in Syria did not always reach the rest of the world.

It seems that the Syrian regime underestimated its ability to channel or harness public opinion by lifting the ban on social media. Vigils, protests, and marches, all initially peaceful, began to appear on Syria's streets, drawing larger and larger crowds. The response of the regime, unaccustomed to public political expression, was quick and brutally repressive. Rather than scaring people into silence, the regime now confronted an armed opposition. Within just one year, social media protests had become street protests, which became street battles between pro- and anti-regime forces. Globalization, as experienced in Syria, has revealed the limits of an authoritarian regime's ability to control and constrain social action in the age of social media.

Syria is now experiencing flows of people across borders. Syrians are escaping to Turkey, Europe, Jordan, Lebanon and Iraq by the millions, creating the world's worst refugee crisis. Meanwhile, drawn to the message of the Islamic State (IS), young men and women from across the Middle East and as far afield as Europe and North America are traveling to the IS controlled territories of eastern Syria and Western Iraq to join in a "global jihad."

As the high-quality and gory video productions of IS demonstrate, technological and media resources, skills, and knowledge are flowing in and out of Syria's borders. Financial flows in oil wealth are now in the hands of IS, and food resources are flowing into the country when possible from international non-governmental organizations such as Mercy Corps. Syria is an example of the disadvantages of globalization, as well as an illustration of how quickly one country's crises can become global crises.

CONCLUSION

The term "globalization" is not simply a verbal shortcut for talking about contact, transmission, and transportation on the global scale. This chapter has shown that contact has existed across disparate locations throughout much of human history. As it is used and understood today, however, globalization is about much more than the total scope of contact; it references the speed and scale of such contact. Understood in this way, globalization *is* a modern phenomenon; it is not just how many places are connected, but in how many ways and with what frequency.

Where people once had to rely on horses or sail-driven ships to bring them to new locations, mass transportation (especially air travel) makes such commutes a part of many people's daily lives, and someone who had never seen a TV one week might end up visiting Jakarta, Cairo, or Toronto the next. News, which might have raced ahead via carrier pigeons can now be transmitted in a virtual instant, and information once confined to physical libraries can now be accessed on the smart phones carried by peoples around the world. Neither "good" nor "bad," globalization is a fact of life today. Whether a business woman flies between international hubs on a weekly basis or a man tends his garden on a remote plateau, both of their lives may be equally influenced by how a specific crop is received on the world market. Providing both opportunities and constraints, globalization now serves as the background—if not the stage—for how life gets lived, on the ground, by us all.

DISCUSSION QUESTIONS

1. In his research, Kelsey Timmerman discovered that the average American is wearing clothes made in many different countries. This demonstrates how everyday items can involve all five of Arjun Appadurai's scapes. Choose another product that is part of your everyday life. How many scapes can you connect it to?

2. Globalization makes new forms of consumption possible, but the effects of globalization on an individual's lifestyle vary based on many factors including socioeconomic status. In what ways is globalization experienced differently by people from wealthy countries compared to people in developing countries? How are producers of commodities like clothing or food affected differently by globalization than consumers?

3. In Latin America, globalization and neoliberalism have led to the development of policies, such as the privatization of the water supply, that reduce local control over important resources. In what ways is globalization a "double-edged" sword that brings both benefits and problems to developing countries?

4. Globalization presents the possibility of engaging in activity-based anthropology, where it is the activity itself that is the "'site'" studied, or digital anthropology, where the field site exists online. What kinds of activities or digital environments do you think would be interesting to study using this approach?

GLOSSARY

Commodity chain: the series of steps a food takes from location where it is produced to the store where it is sold to consumers.

Ethnoscape: the flow of people across boundaries.

Financescape: the flow of money across political borders.

Glocalization: the adaptation of global ideas into locally palatable forms

Habitus: the dispositions, attitudes, or preferences that are the learned basis for personal "taste" and lifestyles.

Ideoscape: the global flow of ideas.

Mediascape: the flow of media across borders.

Neoliberalism: the ideology of free-market capitalism emphasizing privatization and unregulated markets.

Syncretism: the combination of different beliefs, even those that are seemingly contradictory, into a new, harmonious whole.

Technoscape: the global flows of technology.

Global North: refers to the wealthier countries of the world. The definition includes countries that are sometimes called "First World" or "Highly Developed Economies."

Global South: refers to the poorest countries of the world. The definition includes countries that are sometimes called "Third World" or "Least Developed Economies."

ABOUT THE AUTHORS

Dr. Lauren Miller Griffith is an assistant professor of anthropology at Texas Tech University. Her research agenda focuses on the intersections of performance, tourism, and education in Brazil, Belize, and the USA. Specifically, she focuses on the Afro-Brazilian martial art *capoeira* and how non-Brazilian practitioners use travel to Brazil, the art's homeland, to increase their legitimacy within this genre. Dr. Griffith's current interests include the links between tourism, cultural heritage, and sustainability in Belize. She is particularly interested in how indigenous communities decide whether or not to participate in the growing tourism industry and the long-term effects of these decisions.

Dr. Jonathan S. Marion is an associate professor in the Department of Anthropology and a member of the Gender Studies Steering Committee at the University of Arkansas, and the author of *Ballroom: Culture and Costume in Competitive Dance* (2008), *Visual Research: A Concise Introduction to Thinking Visually* (2013, with Jerome Crowder), and *Ballroom Dance and Glamour* (2014). Currently the President of the Society for Humanistic Anthropology, and a Past-president of the Society of Visual Anthropology, Dr. Marion's ongoing research explores the interrelationships between performance, embodiment, gender, and identity, as well as issues of visual research ethics, theory, and methodology.

NOTES

1. See Charles Lindholm, *Culture and Authenticity* (New York: Wiley, 2007).
2. Robby Soave, "Oberlin College Students: Cafeteria Food is Racist," The Daily Beast, December 20, 2015 http://www.thedailybeast.com/articles/2015/12/20/oberlin-students-cafeteria-food-is-racist.html

3. Manfred Steger, *Globalization: A Very Short Introduction* (Oxford: Oxford University Press, 2013).

4. Steger, *Globalization*, 13.

5. Steger, *Globalization*.

6. Ibid.

7. Ibid.

8. United Nations World Tourism Organization, "Why Tourism," http://www2.unwto.org/content/why-tourism

9. To be fair, responsible policy makers and businesses, local communities, and travelers themselves may also be concerned with these issues.

10. See Benedict R. Anderson, *Imagined Communities: Reflections on the Origin and Spread of Nationalism* (London: Verso, 1983).

11. Daniel L. Everett, *Don't Sleep, There Are Snakes: Life and Language in the Amazonian Jungle* (New York: Vintage Books, 2009).

12. Daniel L. Everett, "What Does Pirahã Grammar Have to Teach Us About Human Language and the Mind?" *Wiley Interdisciplinary Reviews: Cognitive Science* 3 no. 6 (2012): 555-63.

13. Kelsey Timmerman, *Where Am I Wearing?* (Hoboken, New Jersey: John Wiley & Sons, Inc., 2012).

14. Robin Schmidt and Morten Vest, *Maasai on the Move*, Film, directed by Robin Schmidt and Morten Vest (2010, Danish Broadcasting Corporation).

15. See Chanchal Kumar Sharma, "Emerging Dimensions of Decentralisation Debate in the Age of Globalisation" *Indian Journal of Federal Studies* 19 no. 1 (2009): 47–65.

16. Anya Peterson Royce, *Becoming an Ancestor: The Isthmus Zapotec Way of Death* (Albany: State University of New York Press, 2011).

17. Rigoberta. I Menchu, *Rigoberta Menchu: An Indian Woman in Guatemala*, trans. Ann Wright (London: Verso, 1984).

18. See, for instance, Peter Wade, *Music, Race and Nation: Musica Tropical in Colombia* (Chicago: University of Chicago Press, 2000). Or, Lise Waxer, *The City of Musical Memory: Salsa, Record Grooves, and Popular Culture in Cali, Columbia* (Middletown, CT: Wesleyan University Press, 2002).

19. For more on traveling to train at such congresses and festivals—whether salsa, or any other embodied practice—see Griffith and Marion, *Apprenticeship Pilgrimage: Developing Expertise through Travel and Training* (Lexington: forthcoming).

20. Sydney Hutchinson, *Salsa World: A Global Dance in Local Contexts* (Philadelphia: Temple University Press, 2013).

21. Also see Lise Waxer, *Situating Salsa: Global Markets and Local Meanings in Latin Popular Culture* (New York: Routledge, 2002).

22. David Chaney, *Lifestyles* (London: Routledge, 1996), 92.

23. Chaney, *Lifestyles*.

24. Ibid.

25. Ibid., 24.

26. Ibid., 57.

27. Pierre Bourdieu, *Distinction: A Social Critique of the Judgment of Taste,* trans. Richard Nice (Cambridge, MA: Harvard University Press, 1984).

28. Shamus Rahman Khan, *Privilege: The Making of an Adolescent Elite at St. Paul's School* (Princeton, NJ: Princeton University Press, 2012).

29. Chaney, *Lifestyles,* 60.

30. Economic Research Service, United States Department of Agriculture, "Food Security Status of U.S. Households in 2014" http://www.ers.usda.gov/topics/food-nutrition-assistance/food-security-in-the-us/key-statistics-graphics.aspx

31. Pierre Bourdieu, *Distinction*.

32. Manfred Steger, *Globalization*, xiii.

33. Kelsey Timmerman, *Where Am I Wearing?*.

34. Bruce Campbell and Lisa Goddard, "Climate Change, Food Security and the Refugee Crisis: Connecting the Dots to Avoid Future Tragedy." https://ccafs.cgiar.org/blog/climate-change-food-security-and-refugee-crisis-connecting-dots-avoid-future-tragedy#.Vt1JXJMrLu4

35. Centers for Disease Control and Prevention, "2014 Ebola Outbreak in West Africa." http://www.cdc.gov/vhf/ebola/outbreaks/2014-west-africa/index.html.

36. Steger, *Globalization*, 54.

37. This case study is based on the work of Nicole Fabricant and Kathryn Hicks, "Bolivia's Next Water War: Historicizing the Struggles over Access to Water Resources in the Twenty-First Century" *Radical History Review* 116 (2013): 130-45.

38. Ibid., 131.

39. Thomson Reuters, "Lake Poopo, Bolivia's 2nd-Largest Lake, Dries Up" December 18, 2015, http://www.cbc.ca/news/technology/lake-poopo-bolivia-dries-up-1.3371359.

40. James C. Scott, *Weapons of the Weak: Everyday Forms of Peasant Resistance* (New Haven: Yale University Press, 1985).

41. Sarah Lyon and and Mark Moberg, eds. *Fair Trade and Social Justice* (New York: New York University Press, 2010).

42. Sarah Lyon, "A Market of Our Own: Women's Livelihoods and Fair Trade Markets," in *Fair Trade and Social Justice*, ed. Sarah Lyon and Mark Moberg (New York: New York University Press, 2010).

43. Julia Smith, "Fair Trade and the Specialty Coffee Market: Growing Alliances, Shifting Rivalries," in *Fair Trade and Social Justice*.

44. Mark Moberg, "A New World? Neoliberalism and Fair Trade Farming in the Eastern Caribbean," in *Fair Trade and Social Justice*.

45. Norma Iglesias Prieto, *Beautiful Flowers of the Maquiladora: Life Histories of Women Workers in Tijuana*, trans. Michael Stone and Gabrielle Winkler (Austin: University of Texas Press, 1985).

46. See, especially, Setha M. Low, "The Anthropology of Cities: Imagining and Theorizing the City" *Annual Review of Anthropology* 25 (1996):383-409 and Ulf Hannerz, *Exploring the City: Inquiries toward an Urban Anthropology* (New York: Columbia University Press, 1980).

47. For the Oxford Bibliography of "Urban Anthropology," see http://www.oxfordbibliographies.com/view/document/obo-9780199766567/obo-9780199766567-0026.xml. For a brief online overview, please see http://www.indiana.edu/~wanthro/URBAN.htm (prepared by Layla Al-Zubaidi).

48. See Andrew Irving, "Cities: An Anthropological Perspective" *Anthropology Matters* 6 no. 1 (2004):1-4. http://www.anthropologymatters.com/index.php/anth_matters/article/viewFile/105/207

49. This case study is based on the work of Tanya M. Kerssen, "Food Sovereignty and the Quinoa Boom: Challenges to Sustainable Re-Peasantisation in the Southern Altiplano of Bolivia" *Third World Quarterly* 36, no. 3 (2015): 489-507.

50. See Richard Wilk, "'Real Belizean Food': Building Local Identity in the Transnational Caribbean" *American Anthropologist* 101 no. 2 (1999): 244-55.

51. Quoted in Tanya M. Kerssen, "Food Sovereignty and the Quinoa Boom."

52. George E. Marcus, "Ethnography in/of the World System: The Emergence of Multi-Sited Ethnography." *Annual Review of Anthropology*, 24 (1995): 95-117. http://www.dourish.com/classes/readings/Marcus-MultiSitedEthnography-ARA.pdf. For a more recent perspective, see M.A. Falzon, *Multi-Sited Ethnography: Theory, Praxis and Locality in Contemporary Research* (Farnham, UK: Ashgate Publishing Limited, 2012).

53. Sarah Strauss, *Positioning Yoga: Balancing Acts across Cultures* (Oxford, UK: Berg, 2005).

54. Ulf Hannerz, "Being there… and there… and there! Reflections on Multi-Site Ethnography" *Ethnography* 4 no. 2 (2003): 201-216.

55. Jonathan S. Marion, "Beyond Ballroom: Activity as Performance, Embodiment, and Identity" *Human Mosaic* 36 no. 2 (2006): 7-16, 2006. Also see Jonathan S. Marion, *Ballroom: Culture and Costume in Competitive Dance* (Oxford, UK: Berg Publishing, 2008) and Jonathan S. Marion, "Circulation as Destination: Considerations from the Translocal Culture of Competitive Ballroom Dance" *Journal for the Anthropological Study of Human Movement* 17 no. (2012).

56. See Tom Boellstorff, *Coming of Age in Second Life: An Anthropologist Explores the Virtually Human* (Princeton University Press, 2009). For more on theory and method see Tom Boellstorff, Bonnie Nardi, Celia Pearce, and T. L. Taylor, *Ethnography and Virtual Worlds: A Handbook of Method* (Princeton University Press, 2012); Heather A. Horst and Daniel Miller, eds. *Digital* Anthropology (London, UK: Bloomsbury, 2012); and Sarah Pink, Heather Horst, John Postill, Larissa Hjorth, Tania Lewis, and Jo Tacchi, *Digital Ethnography: Principles and Practice.* (Thousand Oaks, CA: Sage, 2015).

57. Bassam Haddad, "The Syrian Regime's Business Backbone," *Middle East Report*, 262 no. 42 (2012). http://www.merip.org/mer/mer262/syrian-regimes-business-backbone

58. Alister Doyle, "Syrian War Spurs First Withdrawal from Doomsday Arctic Seed Vault" Reuters September 21, 2015. http://www.reuters.com/article/us-mideast-crisis-seeds-idUSKCN0RL1KA20150921 The report states: "Grethe Evjen, an expert at the Norwegian Agriculture Ministry, said the seeds had been requested by the International Center for Agricultural Research in Dry Areas (ICARDA). ICARDA moved its headquarters to Beirut from Aleppo in 2012 because of the war. 'ICARDA wants almost 130 boxes out of 325 it had deposited in the vault.'"

59. Haddad, "The Syrian Regime's Business Backbone."

60. Manfred Steger, *Globalization: A Very Short Introduction* (Oxford: Oxford University Press, 2013).

61. Joshka Wessels, "Syria Lifts Ban on Facebook and Youtube, Reflections on the 'Egypt Effect' in Syria" Sapiens Productions February 11, 2011, https://sapiensproductions.wordpress.com/2011/02/11/syria-lifts-ban-on-facebook-and-youtube-reflections-on-the-"egypt-effect"-in-syria-by-joshka-wessels/

62. Manuel Castells, "Communication, Power and Counter-power in the Network Society" *International Journal of Communications* 1 (2007): 238-266.

Culture and Sustainability: Environmental Anthropology in the Anthropocene

Christian T. Palmer, Windward Community College
ctpalmer@hawaii.edu

LEARNING OBJECTIVES

- Identify the methods and theories anthropologists use to examine human interactions with the environment.

- Define political ecology and explain its relationship to anthropology.

- Describe the Anthropocene and discuss how anthropology contributes to understanding the human role in environmental destruction.

- Explain how anthropology contributes to public discussions and the creation of public policy with lawmakers, activists, corporations, and others regarding major environmental challenges.

LIVING IN THE ANTHROPOCENE

We live on a planet where the climate—winds, precipitation, weather, temperatures—is being modified by the collective impact of the human species. I arrived at anthropology through an interest in understanding human impacts on the environment. I began by studying ethnobotany as an undergraduate and received a master's degree in environmental science. As I researched human-environmental dynamics, I realized that scientists had largely identified what needed to be done to address many of the world's pressing environmental problems, but few of the recommended changes had been adopted, thwarted by political, cultural, and economic forces. Anthropologists' approach is holistic; they seek to simultaneously understand all of the interactions of political, cultural, and economic factors to fully explore the complexity of human-environmental interactions. Thus, I felt that anthropology provided a good place to start to understand and begin to address some of the most important questions facing our species. For example, how can we provide for basic human needs while not sacrificing the welfare of other species? Why do many people say that they care about protecting the environment but then do nothing about it? What political, economic, and cultural factors are prohibiting world leaders from agreeing on solutions to global environmental challenges? To answer such questions, we must understand how humans think and act as groups, our socially and culturally mediated ways of interacting with each other, other species, and the world around us.

Arriving at Environmental Anthropology

In many ways, anthropology as a discipline is only now starting to address these questions. In December 2014, Bruno Latour, a French anthropologist, spoke to a standing-room-only audience at the American Anthropological

Association annual meeting in Washington, D.C., to discuss the relationship between the **Anthropo-cene** and anthropology.[1] Anthropocene is a term used to describe the period (or epoch) in geological time in which the effects of human activities have altered the fundamental geochemical cycles of the earth as a result of converting forests into fields and pastures and burning oil, gas, and coal on a large scale. Because human activities have changed the earth's atmosphere, anthropologists can make important contributions to studies of geology, chemistry, and meteorology by considering the effects of humans and their cultural systems. As Latour noted, the discipline of anthropology is uniquely qualified to provide insight into key components of current environmental crises by determining the reasons behind choices various groups of humans make, bridging the social and natural sciences, and studying contradictions between cultural universals (traits all humans have in common) and partic-ularities (interesting cultural differences).

This chapter summarizes how anthropologists have contributed to analysis and resolution of envi-ronmental concerns. I begin with a brief overview of anthropological analysis of human interactions with the environment and then explore how anthropological perspectives toward human-environ-mental interactions have changed over time. I end the chapter with a call to action—an invitation for students to use lessons they have learned from anthropology to challenge the kinds of thinking that have produced current environmental crises and see where those anthropological approaches take them. Environmental anthropology is an exciting subfield that will grow in importance as questions of environmental sustainability become increasingly central to scientific and popular conversations about the future of our species and the planet.

Humans and the Environment

If we think about anthropology from the classic four-field approach, which includes both physical anthropology and archaeology, many of the questions with which those disciplines have historically wrestled were related to our species' long-term relationship with the environment. Around two mil-lion years ago, climate changes decreased the amount of forest and expanded grasslands in Africa, which led to the early **Hominin** radiation (the geographic expansion of multiple Hominin species). It also led hominin species to walk upright, which freed their hands to make and use tools. Subse-quent climate changes, particularly expansions and contractions of glaciers associated with ice ages, also contributed to *Homo sapiens* expanding to new parts of the globe.

Fast-forwarding to the beginning of human agriculture roughly 10,000 years ago, we can see how the global expansion of *Homo sapiens* and their first permanent settlements and urban centers led to the development of agriculture, a profound new way of interacting with the environment. The ability of early humans to shape the landscape, first by simply encouraging wild plants to grow and later by planting and irrigating crops and domesticating plants and animals, set humans on the path toward our current problematic relationship with the planet. Archaeologists' questions about human diets, tools, and architecture inevitably explore how ancient civilizations interacted with their envi-ronments. For example, archaeologists examine the relative frequency of different kinds of pollen and tree rings over thousands of years to understand how landscapes changed over time through both human and natural processes.

Many archaeologists credit increased productivity that came with agriculture as the foundation of civilization, allowing humans to live in larger settlements, specialize in craft production, and develop social hierarchies and eventually math, writing, and science. From this perspective, the seeds of social complexity were contained within the first grains domesticated in the hills surrounding the Fertile

Crescent. Others have questioned the idea that the effects of agriculture were purely beneficial. For example, Marshall Sahlins called foraging (hunter-gatherer) societies "the original affluent societies" and noted that hunter-gatherers had more leisure time, healthier diets, more time to socialize, and greater social equality than agricultural or even industrial societies.[2] He also noted that they were affluent not because they had everything, but because they could easily meet their basic needs of food, shelter, and sociality. Others have looked at the advances in science, medicine, and communication technology and disagreed with Sahlins, arguing that we are better off with the developments brought by agriculture. Sahlins' critique of agriculture (and subsequently of civilization) should not be seen as a suggestion to deindustrialize; rather, it is a challenge to assumptions that Western civilization and its technological developments necessarily represent improvements for human societies. Perhaps the strongest argument against capitalism and industrialization is the real possibility of environmental collapse that those systems have brought.

Sahlins' analysis calls into question the idea that humans as a species are necessarily progressing through history and encourages us to think about how "necessities" are culturally constructed. Do we really need cars or cell phones to be happy? How about books and vaccines? Because many of our innovations in technology, agriculture, and transportation have come at the expense of the natural systems that support us, we need to think about human "progress" in relationship to its impact on the environment. The impacts of climate change from our dependence on fossil fuel, toxic byproducts from expanding chemical industries, and pollution of land, soil, and water from industrialized agriculture are a significant challenge to a vision of human history in which we expect things to get better and better.

Archaeological evidence of collapses of earlier societies—Harappan cities in the Indus River Valley, the Maya in Central America, and the Rapa Nui of Easter Island, for example—provides a sobering

Figure 1: The ball courts at Copan show the complexity and development of early Maya society. Research suggests that deforestation was one of the causes of the collapse of the city-state.

warning as many pre-historic cultures' practices were, at some level, environmentally unsustainable, leading to deforestation, soil salinization, or erosion.

For example, archaeologists have explored the collapse of a number of Maya cities from an environmental perspective.[3] After examining samples of pollen from nearby lakebeds, they determined the relative abundance of various ecosystems, such as cornfields and pine forests, over time. They found that deforestation in the uplands associated with an expanding population around the Maya city of Copan was one of the factors that led to the city's decline. Land was cleared to increase agricultural production and to harvest wood for the construction of houses, fueling cooking fires, and producing lime, which was used to make plaster for large-scale construction projects. The study suggests that prehistoric groups' lack of adequate environmental management systems could have affected their ability to maintain their complex urban societies—a warning for society today.

Another fascinating story of the complex relationships between culture, plants, and the economy relates to development of sugar cane plantations in the Caribbean. Anthropologist Sidney Mintz documented how our sweet tooth led to development of the slave trade, industrialization, capitalism, and colonization in the Americas.[4] He examined how sugar went from being a luxury good associated with the upper class as a spice and medicine to a regular staple for factory workers. The increased consumption of sugar associated with industrialization provided financial incentives for continuing slavery and colonization projects in the Americas. Mintz's work is not usually described as environmental anthropology, but his careful documentation of the relationship between people and sugar cane clearly demonstrates the importance of certain species of plants in shaping human history.

The question of how humans interact with their environment through hunting and gathering, agriculture, and deforestation is central to understanding how human groups meet their basic needs and continue to survive and develop. By examining these past and present cultural configurations critically and carefully, anthropology provides a valuable perspective from which to understand such environmental questions.

Sustainability and Public Anthropology

Environmental anthropology provides an opportunity for anthropologists to engage in larger public debates. The American Anthropological Association, for example, recently issued a Statement on Humanity and Climate Change meant to "to recognize anthropological contributions to global climate change-related issues, articulate new research directions, and provide the American Anthropological Association with actions and recommendations to support and promote anthropological investigation of these issues including the development of course curricula and application of anthropological theory and methods to the issues."[5] Such statements emphasize the importance of anthropological contributions to current scientific and political debates.

Anthropologists have become involved in environmental causes around the world. In Brazil, for example, they have worked with indigenous groups to maintain land claims, prevent deforestation, and organize against construction of large hydropower projects that threaten the river ecosystems.[6] Others have challenged development of parks throughout the world as a major conservation strategy for biodiversity and explored the impacts of those parks on local communities.[7] Studies of these diverse topics benefit from incorporation of an ethnographic perspective that emphasizes the importance of identity politics, connection to place, and cultural beliefs for understanding how groups of people interact with their environment. This work also reminds us that environmentalism and conservation are grounded in sets of beliefs, assumptions, and world views developed in Western Europe and North America and must be translated as environmentalists work in other cultures.

Environmental anthropology naturally lends itself to use of anthropological perspectives to inform and engage in public policy decisions, land-use management, and advocacy for indigenous communities, urban minorities, and other groups that are often under-represented in places of power and in traditional environmental movements. In that sense, environmental anthropology is a way to inform and connect with a variety of other disciplines that address similar questions of sustainability. Regardless of whether you decide to study anthropology, understanding the value of anthropological insights for environmental questions will allow you to better appreciate and understand the complexity of environmental questions in modern society and potential solutions. The next section examines the diverse ways that anthropologists have historically looked at the human-environmental dynamic, highlighting some of the key theories, methods, and approaches and how they have developed over time.

CULTURAL ECOLOGY

Early Cultural Ecologists

One of the earliest anthropologists to think systematically about the environment was Leslie White. His work built on earlier anthropological concepts of cultural evolution—the idea that cultures, like organisms, evolve over time and progress from simple to more complex. White described how cultures evolved through their ability to use energy as they domesticated plants and animals, captured the energy stored in fossil fuels, and developed nuclear power.[8] From this perspective, "human cultural evolution was best understood as a process of increasing control over the natural environment" through technological progress.[9] White's conclusions are at odds with Franz Boas' historical particularism, which rejected theories based on evolution that labeled cultures as more advanced or less advanced than others and instead looked at each society as a unique entity that had developed based on its particular history. Like earlier anthropologists, White viewed anthropology as a natural science in which one could generate scientific laws to understand cultural differences. His model is useful, however, when exploring the nature of change as our society increasingly harnessed new sources of energy to meet our wants and needs. He was writing at a time when the U.S. economy was booming and our technological future seemed promising, before the environmental movement raised awareness about harm caused by those technologies.

How the Future Looked 50 Years Ago

This National Public Radio Planet Money episode captures the enthusiasm for technological progress at the 1964 World's Fair, when little was known about the environmental damage such technologies would cause. How did people see the future in 1964? How is their idea of the future different from ours today?

Anthropologist Julian Steward first used the term **cultural ecology** to describe how cultures use and understand their environments. His fieldwork among the Shoshone emphasized the complex ways they had adapted to the dry terrain of the Great Basin between the Sierra Nevada and Rocky Mountain ranges. He described how a hunting and gathering subsistence economy that relied on pine nuts, grass seeds, berries, deer, elk, sheep, antelope, and rabbits shaped Shoshone culture. Their detailed knowledge of various microclimates and seasonal variations in resource availability structured their migration patterns, social interactions, and cultural belief systems.[10] Rather than looking for single evolutionary trajectories for cultures as White had done, Steward looked for multiple evolutionary pathways that led to different outcomes and stressed the variety of ways in which cultures could adapt to ecological conditions.

Both White and Steward were influenced by **materialism**, a Marxist concept that emphasized the ways in which human social and cultural practices were influenced by basic subsistence (economic) needs. Both were trained as scientists, which shaped how they looked at cultural variation. Steward was also influenced by **processual archaeology**, a scientific approach developed in the 1960s that focused primarily on relationships between past societies and the ecological systems they inhabited. The shift in anthropology represented by White and Steward's work led to increased use of scientific methods when analyzing and interpreting data. In subsequent decades, movements in both anthropology and archaeology criticized those scientific perspectives, challenging their objectivity, a process I examine in greater detail later in this chapter.

Pigs and Protein

Subsequent anthropologists built on the work of White and Steward, looking for ecological explanations for cultural beliefs and practices. They also drew on newly developed computer science to think about dynamic feedback systems in which cultural and ecological systems self-regulate to promote social stability—**homeostasis**. Some fascinating examples of this work include Roy Rappaport's work in Papua New Guinea and Marvin Harris' work in India.

Figure 2: Honoring the cow is a part of Hindu religious tradition.

Marvin Harris examined Hindu religious beliefs about sacred cattle from functional and materialist perspectives. Among Hindus in India, eating beef is forbidden and cows are seen as sacred animals associated with certain deities. From the perspective of a Western beef-loving country, such beliefs may seem irrational. Why would anyone not want to eat a juicy steak or hamburger? Rejecting earlier academics who regarded the Hindu practice as illogical, Harris argued that the practice makes perfect sense within the Hindu ecological and economic system. He argued that cows were sacred not because of cultural beliefs; instead, the cultural beliefs existed because of the economic and ecological importance of cows in India. Thus, Hindu restrictions regarding cows were an "adaptive" response to the local ecological system rather than the result of Hindu theology.[11] Harris explored the importance of cattle for milk production, dung for fuel and fertilizer, labor for plowing, and provision of meat and hides to the lowest caste, untouchables, who were able to slaughter and eat cows and tan their hides because they were already seen as ritually impure.

Roy Rappaport examined subsistence practices of the Tsembaga in Highland New Guinea, a group that planted taro, yams, sweet potatoes, and sugar cane and raised pigs. Rappaport used scientific terms and concepts such as caloric intake, carrying capacity, and mutualism to explain methods used by the Tsembaga to manage their resources. A population of pigs below a certain threshold provided a number of benefits, such as keeping villages clean by eating refuse and eating weeds in established gardens that had relatively large fruit trees that would not be damaged by the pigs. Once the population reached the threshold, the pigs ate more than weeds and garbage and began to create problems in gardens. In response, the people used periodic ritual feasts to trim the population back, returning the ecological system to equilibrium. Rappaport, like Harris, used ecological concepts to understand the Tsembaga subsistence practices, thus downplaying the role of cultural beliefs and emphasizing ecological constraints.

These early cultural ecologists viewed cultures as trying to reach and maintain social and ecological equilibrium. This idea aligned with ecological thinking at the time that emphasized the balance of nature and the importance of the various components of an ecosystem in maintaining that balance. However, environments and cultures were rapidly changing as colonization, globalization, and industrialization spread throughout the world. In many of those early cases, anthropologists had ignored these larger processes.

As ecologists began to develop more-complex models of how ecosystems change through long-term dynamic processes of **succession** and disturbances (such as storms, droughts, and El Niño events), anthropological approaches to the environment also changed. The next sections examine those shifts in anthropology as environmental movements developed in response to increasing degradation of natural environments.

Early anthropologists were notable for their attempts to understand how different groups of people interacted with their environments over time. Their work paved the way for future environmental anthropologists even though they generally were not directly concerned with environmental problems associated with modernity, such as pollution, tropical deforestation, species extinctions, erosion, and global warming. As people around the world became more familiar with such issues, environmental anthropologists took note and began to analyze those problems and accompanying conservation movements, especially in the developing world, which was still the primary focus of most anthropological research.

ETHNOECOLOGY

Slash-and-Burn versus Swidden Cultivation

Traditionally, anthropologists studied small communities in remote locations rather than urban societies. While much of that work examined rituals, political organizations, and kinship structures, some anthropologists focused on **ethnoecology**: use and knowledge of plants, animals, and ecosystems by traditional societies. Because those societies depended heavily on the natural world for food, medicine, and building materials, such knowledge was often essential to their survival.

As anthropologists, Harris and Rappaport worked to make the strange familiar by taking seemingly bizarre practices such as ritual slaughtering of pigs and sacredness of cows in India and explaining the practices within the context of the people's culture and environment. This work explains not only how and why people do what they do, but also the advantages of their systems in the environments in which they live. An indigenous practice long demonized by the media, environmental activists, and scientists is slash-and-burn agriculture in which small-scale farmers, mostly in tropical developing countries, cut down a forest, let the wood dry for a few weeks, and then burn it, clearing the land for cultivation. Initially, the farmers plant mostly perennial crops such as rice, beans, corn, taro, and manioc. Later, they gradually introduce tree crops, and the plot is left to regrow trees while they open new fields for crops. Every year, as the soil's fertility declines and insects become a problem in the original plot, new land is cleared to replace it. Environmentalists and developers have decried slash-and-burn cultivation as a major cause of deforestation, and governments in many tropical countries have prohibited farmers from cutting and burning forests.

Anthropologists have challenged these depictions and have documented that slash-and-burn cultivators possess detailed knowledge of their environment; their agricultural processes are sustainable indefinitely under the right conditions.[12] When there is a low population density and an adequate supply of land, slash-and-burn cultivation is a highly sustainable type of elongated crop rotation in which annuals are planted for a few years, followed first by tree crops and then by forest, rebuilding soil nutrients and mimicking natural processes of forest disturbance in which tree falls and storms periodically open up small patches of the forest. They used the term **swidden** cultivation instead of slash and burn to challenge the idea of the practice as inherently destructive. The surrounding forest allows the fields to quickly revert to forest thanks to seeds planted in the cleared area as birds roost in the trees and defecate into the clearing and as small rodents carry and bury the seeds. Furthermore, by mimicking natural processes, the small patches can enhance biodiversity by creating a greater variety of microclimates in a given area of forest.

The system breaks down when cleared forests are not allowed to regrow and instead are replaced with industrial agriculture, cattle raising, or logging operations that transform the open fields into pasture or permanent agricultural plots.[13] The system can also break down when small-holders are

Figure 3: Beans and bananas planted in a swidden field in Acre, Brazil. Note the fallen and burnt logs and the proximity of the forest. Photo by Christian Palmer.

forced to become more sedentary because the amount of land they control is reduced by arrival of new migrants or government land seizures. In that case, local farmers must replant areas more frequently and soil fertility declines. A desire to plant cash crops for external markets can also exacerbate these changes because food is no longer grown solely for local consumption and more land is put into agriculture. Anthropologists' studies uncovered the sustainability of these traditional practices, which were destructive only when outside forces pressured local farmers to modify their traditional farming systems.

Plants, People, and Culture

One branch of ethnoecology is ethnobotany, which studies traditional uses of plants for food, construction, dyes, crafts, and medicine. Scientists have estimated that 60 percent of all of the current medicinal drugs in use worldwide were originally derived from plant materials (many are now chemically manufactured). For example, aspirin came from the bark of willow trees and an important muscle relaxant used in open-heart surgery was developed from *curare*, the poison used on arrows and darts by indigenous groups throughout Central and South America. In light of such discoveries, ethnobotanists traveled to remote corners of the world to document the knowledge of shamans, healers, and traditional medical experts. They have also looked at psychoactive plants and their uses across cultures.

What The People of the Amazon Know That You Don't

This TED talk by ethnobotanist Mark Plotkin describes some important cases of knowledge of medicinal plants learned from indigenous people in the Amazon.

Ethnobotanical work is interdisciplinary, and while some ethnobotanists are anthropologists, many are botanists or come from other disciplines. Anthropologists who study ethnobotany must have a working knowledge of scientific methods for collecting plant specimens and of botanical classification systems and basic ecology. Similarly, archaeologists and paleobotanists study prehistoric people's relationships and use of plants, especially in terms of domestication of plants and animals.

The Kayapó project is a famous ethnobotanical study organized by Darrell Posey and a group of twenty natural and social scientists who examined how the Kayapó people of Brazil understood, managed, and interacted with the various ecosystems they encountered as the region was transformed from a dry savanna-like *Cerrado* to Amazonian rainforest.[14] By documenting Kayapó names for different ecosystems and methods they used to drop seeds and care for certain plants to expand islands of forest in the savanna, the project illustrated the complex ways in which indigenous groups shape the environments in which they live by documenting how the Kayapó cared for, managed, and enhanced forests to make them more productive.

Posey was also an activist who contributed to drafting of the Declaration of Belem, which called for governments and corporations to respect and justly compensate the intellectual property rights of indigenous groups, especially regarding medicinal plants. He accompanied Kayapó leaders to Washington, D.C., to protest construction of a large dam using funds from the World Bank. Pressure from numerous international groups led to a halt in the dam's construction (plans for the dam have recently been resurrected). Posey's identification of the Kayapó as guardians of the rainforest provided a powerful symbol that resonated with Western ideas of indigeneity and the moral high ground of environmental conservation.

In recent years, some anthropologists have questioned whether the idea of indigenous people having an innate positive connection to the environment—what some call the myth of the ecologically noble savage—is accurate.

The Myth of the Ecologically Noble Savage

The image of the noble savage developed many centuries ago in Western culture. From the beginning of European exploration and colonialism, Europeans described the "natives" they encountered primarily in negative terms, associating them with sexual promiscuity, indolence, cannibalism, and violence. The depictions changed as Romantic artists and writers rejected modernity and industrialization and called for people to return to an idealized, simpler past. That reactionary movement also celebrated indigenous societies as simple people living in an Eden-like state of innocence. French painter Paul Gauguin's works depicting scenes from his travels to the South Pacific are typical of this approach in their celebration of the colorful, easygoing, and natural existence of the natives. The continuing influence of these stories is evident in Disney's portrayal of Pocahontas and James Cameron's 2009 film *Avatar* in which the primitive Na`vi are closely connected to and defenders of an exotic and vibrant natural world. Cameron's depiction, which includes a sympathetic anthropologist, criticizes Western capitalism as willing to destroy nature for profit.

Disney's Pocahontas: Colors of the Wind Song

Disney's Pocahontas presents many of the stereotypes of the ecologically noble savage. What are these stereotypes? Where else do we see these kinds of depictions?

Despite its positive portrayals of indigenous groups, the idea of the ecologically noble savage tends to treat indigenous peoples as an imagined "other" constructed as the opposite of Western culture rather than endeavoring to understand the world views and complexities of indigenous cultures. Similarly, a naive interpretation of indigenous environmentalism may merely project an imaginary Western ideal onto another culture rather than make a legitimate observation about that culture on its own terms.

The Kayapó in the Amazon and another group known as the Penan, who live in the Indonesian rainforest, were both confronted in the past by plans to open logging roads in their traditional territories and build dams that would flood vast amounts of their land. These indigenous communities organized, sometimes with the aid of anthropologists who had connections to media and environmental organizations, to protect the forest. The combination of two causes—rainforest conservation and indigenous rights—was powerful, successfully grabbing media attention and raising money for conservation. Their success led to later instances of indigenous groups joining efforts to halt large-scale development projects. These movements were especially powerful symbolically because they articulated the longstanding Western idea of the environmentally noble savage as well as growing environmental concerns in Europe and North America.[15]

Some anthropologists have noted that these alliances were often fragile and rested on an imagined ideal of indigenous groups that was not always accurate. The Western media, they argue, imagined indigenous groups as ecologically noble savages, and the danger in that perspective is that the indigenous communities would be particularly vulnerable if they lost that symbolic purity and the power that came with it. The image of ecologically noble savages could break down if they were seen as promoting any kind of non-environmental practices or became too involved in messy national politics. Furthermore, indigenous groups' alliances with international activists tended to cast doubt on their patriotism and weaken their position in their own countries. Though these indigenous groups achieved visibility and some important victories, they remained vulnerable to negative press and needed to carefully manage their images.

It is important to note that depictions such as the ecologically noble savage rely on an overly simplistic portrayal of the indigenous "other." For example, some indigenous groups have been portrayed as inherently environmentalist even when they hunt animals that Western environmentalists want to preserve. Often, the more important questions for indigenous groups revolve around land rights and political sovereignty. Environmental concerns are associated with those issues rather than existing separately. The ramifications of these differences are explained in the next section, which discusses the people-versus-parks debate.

Land Claims and Mapping

One way that anthropologists have successfully used traditional ecological knowledge to advance indigenous rights is through advocacy on behalf of indigenous groups seeking to establish legal ownership or control over their traditional lands. This was first done in Alaska and Canada in the 1960s and 1970s. Indigenous groups wanted to map their seasonal movements for hunting, gathering, and other subsistence practices. The maps would demonstrate that they used the land in question and that it was important for their continued physical and cultural survival.

Since then, communities throughout the developing world have adopted similar strategies with the help of geographers and anthropologists to demarcate their lands. Often, lands used by indigenous groups are seen as empty because their population densities are quite low, and developers imagine the land as unused and open for taking. The production of maps by indigenous communities challenges those notions by inscribing the landscape with their names, relationships, and the human histories that mark their claim to the land. The maps become important symbols and tools for organizing local resistance against large development projects.

The non-governmental organization (NGO) Native Lands, for example, assisted in mapping the Mosquitia region of Honduras. Although the area, which consisted of 20,000 square kilometers, included 170 communities, most government maps showed it as practically empty. Earlier, in a backroom deal, the entire area had been granted as a logging concession to Stone Container Corporation, a Chicago-based company that made cardboard boxes and paper bags.[16] When Native Lands became involved in the early 1990s, mapping was used to bring the diverse communities in the region together to communicate their presence and advocate for an end to the logging concession. The power of maps to communicate the presence of indigenous people on the land is critical, especially when the indigenous groups lack legal ownership.

POLITICAL ECOLOGY

Questioning Science

In the 1960s, theoretical movements in the social sciences and humanities began to challenge the presumed benefits of modernity and science. These movements were led in part by feminist and post-colonial theorists who saw science as part of a patriarchal system that was complicit in the subjugation of women and colonized people throughout the world. In environmental sciences, this move to question the objectivity of science can be seen in political ecology, a diverse field that includes many anthropologists along with geographers, political scientists, sociologists, and other social scientists. Political ecology's primary message is the importance of examining environmental questions that seem, at first glance, to be strictly scientific (i.e., apolitical). Questions of cause and effect, for instance, are comprised of political and economic agendas that can be masked by a seemingly neutral language of scientific objectivity. By focusing our attention on the power dynamic in political dimensions of conservation, principally in the developing world, political ecologists illustrate why conservation efforts so often fail to achieve the desired goals.

In an early an influential study of political ecology, Piers Blaikie and others argued that soil erosion was not caused by many of the factors blamed by state governments, including overpopulation, bad farming practices, and environmental stresses. Instead, they found that state policies such as taxes forced farmers into capitalist economic systems that encouraged unsustainable farming practices.[17] From this perspective, soil erosion, which seemed to be primarily a local problem, was actually connected to national politics and needed to be addressed in that larger context. Once attention had been drawn to the relationship between state policies and soil erosion, the solution to the problem could no longer come from simply teaching small-scale farmers better soil conservation techniques. It required eliminating government practices and economic conditions that provided an incentive to use unsustainable farming practices.

Political ecology often focuses on the impacts of governments and corporations in establishing political and economic systems that constrain local behavior and challenges standard narratives regarding environmental destruction and conservation. Learning about political ecology can be difficult for environmentally minded people because it requires them to rethink many of their own positions and the science that supports them.

Revisionist Environmental History

Some of my favorite work in political ecology challenges the causes and effects of tropical deforestation. James Fairhead and Melissa Leach, for example, looked at tropical deforestation in the West African country of Guinea.[18] The state's forestry department and later conservation organizations described the savanna as containing only small fragments of a once extensive tropical forest. Administrators, foresters, and botanists had created forest policies based on the idea that this degradation was caused by local villagers as they cleared and burned forests to create fields for agriculture. Through careful study of historical archives, oral histories, and historical aerial photographs, Fairhead and Leach challenged these narratives. Instead, they argued that the remaining fragments of forest had been planted by local villagers who had gradually planted useful species around their villages, improving the soil for planting and generating other positive ecological changes. Rather than being the cause of the deforestation in areas that was previously forest, the villagers were creating the forest in an area that had previously been savanna through generations of hard work, turning the colonial narrative on its head.

Another fascinating tale comes from William Balee's work in the Amazon. Balee was a friend of Darrell Posey, and their work together got Balee thinking about the extent to which the Amazon rainforest is a product of human productive activities and not entirely natural processes. Balee disagreed with earlier anthropologists who had described how primitive groups were forced to adapt to the constraints imposed by fragile tropical ecosystems, such as declining soil fertility, a lack of plants and animals that provided protein, and other limiting factors that constrained their behavior. Balee examined a wide variety of ecosystems in the Amazon that seemed to have been created or significantly modified by human activity, including the forest islands of the Kayapó discussed by Posey, babassu palm forests, bamboo forests, Brazil nut forests near Maraba, and liana forests. His conservative estimated was that at least 12 percent of the Amazon, the largest rainforest on the planet, was a product of indigenous intervention. This conclusion challenged two major assumptions made about the rainforest and the people who lived there. First is the notion that indigenous groups were forced to adapt to the harsh environment of the rainforest. Instead, Balee found that they were resource managers who had developed ecosystems to better provide for their needs. Second is the notion that the Amazon was primeval, untouched, and pristine.[19] If we extend this analysis to other regions and ecosystems, it challenges the entire notion of "untouched nature." If the wildest, least populated, and largest rainforest in the world is already highly **anthropogenic,** or shaped by humans, what can we say about supposed ideas of wilderness in other places?

Environmental historian William Cronon tackled this question directly in his essay, "The Trouble with Wilderness, or Getting Back to the Wrong Nature."[20] Cronon argued that, by celebrating a nature supposedly untouched by human hands, we tend to forget about preserving the nature with which we come in contact every day. If we focus exclusively on a concept of **wilderness**, which excludes humans and human activities by definition, we may ignore ways to help humans better interact with nature, leading to conservation policies that try to create parks without anyone inside of them and do not fully consider agricultural and urban areas. It means that one must leave civilization behind to be in contact with nature. Cronon ended his essay with a plea:

> If wildness can stop being (just) out there and start being (also) in here, if it can start being as humane as it is natural, then perhaps we can get on with the unending task of struggling to live rightly in the world, not just in the garden, not just in the wilderness, but in the home that encompasses them both.[21]

Cronon's call to action is for humans to consider themselves fully part of nature and to look for ways to behave responsibly in that relationship. In a way, his message is similar to Bruno Latour's about the Anthropocene. By recognizing that nature does not exist outside of human activities, we must come to terms with the impacts of our lifestyles on the environment. Some may believe that this cheapens nature, making it less sacred and significant, but understanding the diverse ways in which humans have affected the environment should make us better able to appreciate and evaluate our interactions with it. Instead of seeing nature as outside of human activities, we need to consider how our food production, transportation, and habitation systems affect the environment.

People versus Parks

Generally, when we think of nature, we tend to think of national parks and other kinds of **protected areas** set aside for conservation under various categories. In the United States, these include national and state parks, forests, wilderness areas, recreation areas, and wildlife conservation areas. In most cases, people are allowed to visit these areas for recreational or scientific purposes but cannot live directly in them, and regulations control the kinds of activities allowed. Protected areas developed from the Western vision of nature that separates it from culture and assumes that one must exclude humans to conserve nature. This model of setting aside protected areas has been exported to the rest of the world and persists as the most common strategy for numerous environmental goals, including protection of watersheds, endangered plants and animals, and providing space for people to interact with nature.

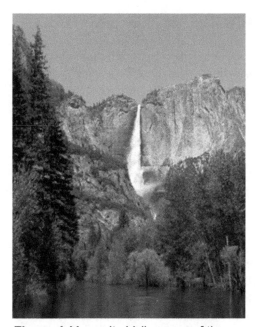

Figure 4: Yosemite Valley, one of the first national parks in the United States, established a precedent of setting aside natural areas for their scenic beauty, recreation, and conservation. Photo by Christian Palmer.

The most common example of a protected area is a national park. In the United States, national parks are so popular that they have been called "America's Best Idea." While I am an enthusiastic fan of national parks, I also recognize problems associated with the concept. We often forget, for example, that the "natural" state of such parks is mostly a recent phenomenon. Many Native American groups were systematically removed from parks (and rarely compensated) to make the parks "natural," and some parks, such as Mt. Rushmore in the Black Hills of South Dakota and Devil's Tower in Wyoming, are directly on top of sacred sites for Native Americans. In other areas of the world, especially in developing countries, most protected areas are occupied by groups of people who have lived there for decades or centuries and have legitimate claims to the land. Some may not be aware that their land is being transformed into a park and, once informed, are shocked by all of the new regulations they are expected to obey. In worst-case scenarios, they are evicted without compensation, becoming environmental refugees. From the perspective of such groups, the government seems to value elephants, tigers, or scenic vistas more than the people living on the land.

The conflicts that have developed between local communities in and around protected areas and state conservation officials and international conservation NGOs that advocate for the parks is referred to as the "people-versus-parks debate."[22] Communities, rather than seeing parks as preserving a public good that benefits everyone, view creation of a park as an effort by government officials to extend their power to remote rural areas. And those negative views can thwart conservation efforts when locals resent preferential treatment of animals and choose to poach or simply ignore the new regulations.

Conservation groups have begun to recognize that they must support economic development of local communities to get them on board with conservation efforts. When local residents benefit from jobs as park guards, tour guides, and research assistants, they recognize the positive economic benefits of conservation and support the initiatives. This approach aims to combine conservation and development, bringing together typically different objectives. Initially, this approach was a response to development policies associated with building infrastructure such as roads and dams that had huge environmental impacts and created negative press for the World Bank, the U.S. Agency for International Development (USAID), and other institutions that funded the projects. Now, most conservation projects incorporate development objectives, and the environmental impacts of development projects usually must be assessed. In addition, the failure of many of these projects has inspired governments and NGOs to include local communities in planning and operating conservation and development schemes.

Conservation and Sustainable Development

Since the early 1990s, environmental conservation organizations such as the Nature Conservancy and Conservation International and development organizations such as the World Bank and USAID have been working to bring conservation and development together. The structures and success of these approaches vary widely. Some aim to help local communities develop industries that depended on rainforests in nondestructive ways, such as non-timber forest products like rattan, rubber, medicines, and fruit. By assisting local communities in developing and marketing such products, the programs have provided them with economic alternatives that encourage people to preserve rainforests instead of chopping them down, a form of **sustainable development**.

The conservation and development project with which I am most familiar is related to **extractive reserves** in the Brazilian Amazon. I spent a summer doing research for my master's thesis on extractive reserves established by Brazilian rubber tappers in Acre, which is in the northwestern corner of the Brazilian Amazon. These rubber tappers live in the rainforest and tap natural rubber by scraping a long thin cut into the bark of the tree and returning later in the day to collect the sap that had dripped into a small container hung on the tree. Rubber trees do not grow together; they are spread out throughout the forest, requiring rubber tappers to walk several trails each day. Many also collect and sell Brazil nuts, which fall from ancient trees that live for centuries. Brazil nuts cannot be commercially grown so they must be collected from rainforests. Both of these economic activities require a healthy, mature forest. And although rubber can be produced synthetically, natural rubber is stronger, longer lasting, more flexible, and more resistant to heat than synthetic alternatives, making it ideal for use in medical and aeronautic industries where high-quality material is essential.

As cattle ranching expanded in the Amazon, rubber tappers were being evicted because they did not have formal title to the land on which they lived and worked. Led by local activist Chico Mendes, the rubber tappers organized and petitioned the government for the right to remain on the land. Mendes was eventually assassinated by owners of some of the cattle ranches who were unhappy about his activism, but ultimately, the movement was successful. Environmentalists who were worried about Amazonian deforestation joined forces with the rubber tappers, who were worried about their livelihoods, and together they created **extractive reserves**—protected areas owned by the federal government but managed by local communities of rubber tappers who could stay on the land indefinitely as long as they followed the environmental regulations they established. The model was successful and has since been expanded to include millions of hectares throughout the Amazon.

As with many conservation and development projects, the economic benefits of the extractive reserves were slow to accrue. When rubber prices

Figure 5: Rubber being tapped from a tree in the Brazilian Amazon. Photo by Christian Palmer.

fell in response to international commodity markets, many families stopped tapping rubber and focused on subsistence agriculture. In fact, some turned to cattle ranching, mimicking on a smaller scale many of the destructive processes they had originally protested. Because the regulations were poorly enforced, a number of families gradually turned old swidden fields into pastures instead of letting the fields revert to rainforest.

Despite these challenges, development of the land was significantly reduced relative to the original plan of allowing owners of large tracts to move in and convert large areas to pasture and soy plantations. Likewise, the rubber tappers, though still poor, had access to greater resources than they would if they have been evicted and forced to move to urban slums. Extractive reserves succeeded because they were implemented across vast areas of the Brazilian Amazon and provided rights to thousands of small landholders.

Significant challenges remain for organizations working to improve the standard of living of rubber tappers in Brazil and conserve biodiversity, and this case study illustrates many of the problems associated with conservation and development models. Often, the economic gains are limited and require compromises in terms of conservation benefits. Usually, neither local communities nor environmentalists are completely happy with the models and their results but also agree that compromise is better than the rampant destruction averted by a reserve. Research on political ecology from such case studies forces us to recognize that the debates are not solely about environmental ethics; they also involve control over valuable resources such as land, timber, and oil. Political ecology invites us to think about the local political and cultural processes that shape the outcomes of conservation projects and determine who benefits from such projects.

First World Political Ecology

A significant challenge for political ecologists is that most of the research so far has been done in the developing world; relatively few studies have been conducted in the United States and Europe. Some newer studies are aiming to showcase what political ecology might look like when applied to similar questions in the developed world. One such study came from the Sierra Nevada foothills in California. There, a participatory conservation project was being developed that would have included local conservation organizations, government offices, and other groups. Their goal was to create an environmental management plan for the region that would limit development and urban growth. They tried to bring together a variety of environmental and pro-development groups to dialogue but were met with an intense political backlash. Pro-development forces, rather than participating, mobilized politically to remove supporters of the plan from county government seats and derail the process. In first world countries, local groups can mobilize significant political and economic resources to influence the fate of a project. This is an unlikely scenario in the developing world where conservation organizations are generally more powerful than local communities.[23]

Clashes between environmentalists, who are often **exurban** migrants who moved from urban to rural areas for outdoor activities and scenic nature, and longtime residents who are involved in extractive industries such as mining, ranching, and agriculture are common in the western United States. In many cases, communities are bitterly divided over the importance of nearby public lands and the role of the federal government in managing those lands. In developing countries, political ecologists as a group tend to side with local communities and against government intervention. In the United States, left-leaning and environmental sympathies can push them to side with government intervention at the expense of local communities. Some political ecologists have noted this contradiction and called for local movements and their pushes against extension of states power to be taken more seriously, including in the United States.[24]

Another fascinating political ecology associated with the first world is a study by Paul Robbins and Julie Sharp that looked at the American lawn, noting that 23 percent of urban land in the United States is dedicated to lawns and that urban areas are growing at a rate of 675,000 hectares a year.[25] In addition, the vast majority of those lawns are sprayed with fertilizers, herbicides, and pesticides. Because these chemicals wash into waterways, lawns have an enormous collective environmental impact. Robbins and Sharp analyzed advertisements for lawn care products and interviewed and surveyed households across the country, leading to some startling discoveries. One of the strongest indicators of intensive and toxic lawn care was not a lack of knowledge about the environmental impacts of the products, but how well they knew the names of their neighbors. They describe the moral economy of a turf grass commons in which maintaining a healthy lawn signified important values of being connected to the community, your family, and nature. The aesthetics and family values associated with lawns outweighed concerns about environmental impacts, suggesting that water conservation activists must understand and address underlying cultural ideas about lawns in the United States.

Where's the Ecology?

Political ecologists Andrew Vayda and Bradley Walters have noted that the field of political ecology seems to be increasingly political, overemphasizing how different groups use environmental issues to gain control over land and resources and ignoring important ecological considerations.[26] They argue that political ecologists need to take the limits, constraints, and challenges associated with natural systems more seriously and research those systems in addition to local cultural and political systems. In a study of the destruction of mangrove forests in the Philippines, they examined both the role of local communities in the destruction and management of mangrove ecosystems and the natural limits that impede replanting in the area. The next section presents examples of anthropologists who thought creatively about how to integrate theories from the natural sciences back into anthropology while simultaneously questioning whether science provides unbiased objective results. This requires a careful balancing act but is necessary to generate an approach that respects the contributions of scientific and anthropological knowledge.

ADDITIONAL APPROACHES TO ENVIRONMENTAL ANTHROPOLOGY

Eco-justice: Race, Gender, and Environmental Destruction

Many environmental justice advocates are anthropologists and political ecologists. They examine environmental questions from the perspective of social equality, identifying impacts and risks associated with environmental damage that have disproportionately affected socially marginalized groups. For example, on the Hawaiian island of Oahu the trash incinerator and landfill are on the west side of the island where many native Hawaiians and other low-income groups live.[27] Locating landfills, incinerators, chemical plants, industrial factories, nuclear waste storage, and other environmentally hazardous facilities near communities of color, Native American reservations, and relatively poor communities is not accidental. A lack of economic and political power prevents residents of such communities from influencing the large industries and government agencies that determine where such facilities are placed.

The same process is at work when environmentally toxic jobs and waste storage facilities are out-sourced. For example, many computers and other electronic appliances that contain toxic components made from heavy metals are shipped to West Africa for disassembly and recycling.[28] This arrangement makes economic sense for consumers in relatively rich countries in North America and Europe, but the workers in Africa are out of sight and out of mind, often working without proper protection from the toxic metals or even training on their dangers. And as global supply chains have expanded, consumers in the United States rarely know where the clothes, electronics, and toys they purchase are made, the impacts of that production, or what happens to them after they dispose of them. By looking at these long complex commodity or supply chains, which cover products from their cradle to grave, social scientists interested in **eco-justice** can create awareness of these issues.

Anthropologists also work to connect **ecocide** (environmental destruction) with **ethnocide** (cultural destruction). In many indigenous communities worldwide, cultural activities and beliefs are connected to specific landscapes and ecologies. Consequently, as a logging or mining company moves in, it destroys both the environment and culture. Eco-justice studies call attention to these connections and seek to protect both culture and the environment and the relationship between them. Barbara Rose Johnston's work with Marshallese Islanders in Micronesia documented the impact of U.S. atomic bomb testing on the atolls and supported their claims for compensation from the United States for damage by carefully documenting the relationship between their culture and the contaminated landscapes ruined by nuclear testing.[29]

Anthropologists are often involved in these kinds of research projects because they are on the ground in remote locations around the world and share a disciplinary interest in raising awareness of cultural differences and inequality. They are also trained to examine categories of race, class, nationality, and other social factors that differentiate groups of people and are the basis for unequal treatment. While valuing cultural diversity, anthropologists also argue for a holistic perspective that universally values human life regardless of such differences.

Science and Technology Studies

The study of science and technology is a diverse field that uses social science methods to analyze the culture of science in industrialized and modern societies. Like political ecology and ethnoecology, science and technology studies question the objectivity of modern science to some extent and view science as a product of specific cultural understandings. These studies often look to the history of a science to understand its development in a specific cultural, political, and economic context.

An early developer of the discipline is Bruno Latour, who introduced the idea of the Anthropocene discussed at the beginning of this chapter. Latour's earlier work included a study, *Laboratory Life: The Social Construction of Scientific Facts* (1979), written with Steve Woolgar, that used the ethnographic technique of participant observation in a laboratory at the Salk Institute for Biological Sciences to determine how scientific knowledge is produced and challenged dominant narratives about the scientific method.[30] Other studies have examined concepts of race and indigeneity in the Human Genome Project and how remote sensing technologies shape how anthropologists interact with ecosystems in the Guatemalan rainforest.[31] As science and technology become increasingly important parts of our lived experiences and our understanding of the environment around us, anthropologists naturally analyze those connections.

Many anthropologists who study science and technology endeavor to make sure they do not throw the baby out with the bath water. They do not deny the important contributions of science and the scientific method. However, they also pay attention to the limitations and biases inherent in those methods.

Multispecies Ethnographies

Multispecies ethnographies challenge the centrality of humans in the world. Most of the stories we tell about ourselves and our place in the world and especially stories told by anthropologists revolve around *Homo sapiens*. Increasingly, though, some anthropologists have begun to think about how other species make decisions and exercise a degree of agency that can influence history. For example, Donna Haraway writes about dogs and how the relationship between dogs and humans has evolved over time. She criticizes people who anthropomorphize dogs and challenges her readers to understand dogs on their own terms.[32]

We can also think about the role of bacteria in human evolution and cultural development and remind ourselves that diseases, parasites, and symbiotic gut bacteria that allow us to eat certain kinds of foods have been very influential in shaping human history and cultural development over time. Other works have, for example, re-examined plant and animal domestication from non-human perspectives and explored how forests "think."[33] By carefully considering other species and ecological processes, we decenter our increasingly human-centered focus. Much of the work on multispecies ethnography has been done by feminist anthropologists who have already been at work for decades on similarly decentering male-focused histories of our species.

APPLYING ANTHROPOLOGY IN CONSERVATION

Reforestation

Anthropological analyses of the environment may seem overly theoretical and abstract, far removed from actual practices and the work of learning to live with and within our environment. Anthropologists may be seen as hidden in ivory towers of academia, disconnected from real world issues and problems. However, applied and activist anthropology offer avenues for anthropologists to tackle problems on the ground and make a direct difference. Applied anthropologists often work with conservation and development organizations to implement projects that depend on an accurate understanding of local cultures and practices to succeed.

Anthropologist Gerald Murray's doctoral dissertation examined land tenure among small-holders in Haiti. After finishing his dissertation work, Murray delivered a presentation to USAID on a Haitian reforestation project. He joked that if they gave him "a jeep and carte blanche access to a $50,000 checking account" he could prove his "anthropological assertions about peasant economic behavior and produce more trees on the ground than their multi-million-dollar Ministry of Agriculture charade."[34] USAID program officers accepted his challenge, inviting him to head a $4 million project to reforest Haiti. Using his understanding of Haitian small-holders, he drastically changed the USAID's approach. Instead of trying to convince small-holders that trees were valuable for their environmental services, he emphasized fast-growing species that could be sold for firewood, charcoal, and lumber. By giving the trees to the small-holders and allowing them to harvest and sell them whenever they wanted, he motivated them to plant and care for the seedlings like any other valuable cash crop. In prior projects, tree-cutting was prohibited and the trees belonged to the government. Consequently, no one took care of the trees and they were eventually destroyed by livestock or neglect and rarely reached maturity. Treating the trees as a cash crop motivated farmers to plant trees on their own land, thus meeting USAID's goals of stabilizing the soil and reducing illegal tree cutting (since farmers had access to stands of their own) and providing a direct economic benefit from selling wood. The project was a stunning success—20 million trees were planted in the first four years. By understanding local farmers' perspectives, Murray was able to work with Haitian small-holders instead of seeing them as an impediment to reforestation efforts.

A number of anthropologists are working with conservation and development organizations to assist them in understanding local cultures and implementing conservation and develop projects. This work is often done in teams in which anthropologists join with foresters, conservation biologists, agronomists, and others to implement projects. Because they often speak the local language, understand the peoples' perspectives, and are interested in close, on-the-ground observations, anthropologists make valuable contributions in support of conservation and economic development.

Climate Change

In 2014, the American Anthropological Association's Global Climate Change Task Force submitted a report on climate change that summarized anthropology's engagement with the issue. Currently, climate change is perhaps the single most important environmental issue worldwide, and our responses to it will shape the future of our species on the planet. The report identified the human causes and contributions to climate change and emphasized that climate change is already having an impact as rising sea levels are forcing residents of places such as Kiribati to flee their island homes and melting ice shelves threaten the subsistence practices and the lifestyle of Inuit groups in Alaska. These examples illustrate how the impacts of climate change will disproportionately affect groups who have contributed the least to the accumulation of greenhouses gases, highlighting the social inequality of impacts of climate change around the world.

The report analyzed drivers of climate change, focusing on consumption, land use, energy, and population growth. An anthropological analysis of consumption reminds us that the categories of "necessities" and "luxuries" are cultural constructs. For example, Western societies now accept cell phones as necessities despite the fact that humans survived perfectly well for thousands of years without them. As the global middle class expands and places new demands on ecosystems, a cultural understanding of social classes and related consumption practices will be increasingly important to analyses the causes of climate change and potential solutions.

The report also criticized much of the language of climate change and its focus on concepts of adaptation, vulnerability, and resilience that elided the differential impacts of climate change on different groups of people. The task force noted that proposed global solutions focused on top-down management strategies that did not take existing social issues of "poverty, marginalization, lack of education and information, and loss of control over resources" that structure vulnerability of different populations to the impacts of a warming planet into account. [35] The report also illustrates the power of language to shape certain debates and potential solutions to problems, an important piece of anthropological analysis.

At the end of the report, the task force recommended actions anthropologists could take to contribute to efforts to address global climate change, including reducing the carbon footprint of anthropological meetings, working with interdisciplinary research teams to continue research, and maintaining a research agenda that stresses the importance of anthropological contributions to discussions of climate change. Perhaps most interesting is their conclusion that many of the most innovative and creative approaches to addressing and mitigating the effects of climate change were occurring at local and regional levels, recognizing communities' innovative efforts to bypass national and international gridlock and develop approaches that reflect local realities and address local problems. The anthropological focus on local communities is a welcome change of perspective when, by definition, the scale of global climate change seems to preclude local involvement and solutions.

Anthropologists at Work in Conservation Organizations

Anthropologists work for international conservation organizations like Conservation International, The Nature Conservancy, and the World Wildlife Fund and with government agencies like the National Park Service, the Peace Corps, and USAID. They also work for smaller conservation organizations, urban planning initiatives, environmental education groups, environmental activist networks, and other initiatives aimed at reducing our negative impact on the planet.

Cultural Resources Management

Management of cultural resources is a growing field of anthropology that catalogs and preserves archaeological sites and historic places threatened by development, bringing together various principles developed in anthropology over the years. First, it recognizes the need to preserve both "natural" ecosystems and ecosystems shaped by past human activities. By connecting natural and human diversity, anthropologists recognize humans' interdependence with the environment over time. Second, cultural resource managers recognize the need for continuing involvement of indigenous communities with archaeological sites and seek their input to inform management plans and practices. As cultural resource management has become standard operating procedure, archaeologists have begun to meet with members of the local community and others who have a stake in their research. These interactions improve archaeological research and create the kind of cross-cultural bridges that strengthen the discipline. Finally, destruction of historical places and archaeological sites is a form of environmental destruction that, like climate change and species extinctions, requires us to critically examine the cultural values underlying that destruction.

CONCLUSION

The discipline of anthropology provides a unique perspective on human-environmental interactions and thus generates valuable insights into the social, political, and cultural complexity of modern environmental problems. Anthropologists are hard at work with governments, conservation organizations, and community groups to understand and solve complex environmental problems. I hope this discussion has challenged you to think about the environment and conservation in a new way, allowing you to help reframe these debates and develop innovative solutions to the complex problems that confront us.

DISCUSSION QUESTIONS

1. In what ways have anthropologists examined human interactions with the environment over time?
2. What is the myth of the ecologically noble savage? What are some recent examples of this myth? What is the impact of this idea on indigenous people?
3. How has research in political ecology challenged traditional conservation efforts? What are some of the problems with promoting parks or ecological reserves as solutions to environmental problems?
4. What is the Anthropocene? How has research in anthropology contributed to an improved understanding of how humans interact with the "natural" world?
5. What insights from anthropology do you think would be most useful to the public, environmental activists, and government officials when considering policies related to current environmental challenges?

GLOSSARY

Anthropocene: a term proposed to describe the current moment (or epoch) in geological time in which the effects of human activities have altered the fundamental geochemical cycles of the earth. There is some disagreement about when the Anthropocene period began—most likely, it began with industrialization.

Anthropogenic: environments and pollutants produced by human activities.

Cultural ecology: a subfield of cultural anthropology that explores the relationship between human cultural beliefs and practice and the ecosystems in which those beliefs and practices occur.

Cultural evolutionism: a theory popular in nineteenth and early twentieth century anthropology suggesting that societies evolved through stages from simple to advanced. This theory was later shown to be incorrect.

Ecocide: destruction of an environment, especially when done intentionally by humans.

Eco-justice: a movement to recognize and remedy the adverse relationship between social inequality and the harms and risks that come from environmental destruction and pollutants.

Ethnocide: destruction of a culture, often intentionally, through destruction of or removal from their territory, forced assimilation, or acculturation.

Ethnoecology: the relationships between cultural beliefs and practices and the local environment. Components include ethnobiology, ethnobotany, and ethnozoology.

Extractive reserves: community-managed protected areas designed to allow for sustainable extraction of certain natural resources (such as fish, rubber, Brazil nuts, and rattan) while maintaining key ecosystems in place.

Exurban: a term that describes the migration of generally affluent people from urban areas to rural areas for the amenities of nature, recreation, and scenic beauty associated with rural areas.

Historical particularism: the theory that every culture develops in a unique way due to its history, including the interaction of people with the natural environment.

Homeostasis: the movement of a particular system (a human body, an ecosystem) towards equilibrium. In ecology this is associated with the idea that ecosystems should remain at the climax (stable) ecosystem associated with an area.

Hominin: Humans (*Homo sapiens*) and their close relatives and immediate ancestors.

Materialism: a Marxist theory emphasizing the ways in which human social and cultural practices are influenced by basic subsistence (economic) needs.

Multispecies ethnographies: an ethnographic approach in which anthropologists include non-human species as active participants in a society or culture and study their influence and actions.

Political ecology: an interdisciplinary field of research that emphasizes the political and economic dimensions of environmental concerns.

Processual archaeology: a shift in archaeological studies toward scientific methods, testing of hypotheses, quantitative analysis, and theory-driven approaches and away from an earlier emphasis on typologies and descriptive analysis.

Protected areas: lands set aside for conservation of the environment for their scenic beauty, biodiversity, recreational value, and other reasons.

Succession: changes in types of species in an area over time. For example, it would describe the different ecosystems that gradually replace one other after a forest fire.

Sustainable development: development that can meet present needs without damaging the environment or limiting the potential for future generations.

Swidden: an agricultural practice, also called shifting cultivation and slash-and-burn, in which fields are cleared, burned, and planted for several seasons before being returned to fallow for an extended period.

Wilderness: a natural area that is untouched or unchanged by human activities and often seen as a cultural construct of the American West.

ABOUT THE AUTHOR

I grew up hiking and surfing in Hawaii and became interested in the environment and conservation. I studied Biology and International Cultural Studies at Brigham Young University-Hawaii as an undergraduate, including research on how traditional Hawaiian healers adapted to introduced plant species and diseases. My master's degree is in Environmental Science from the Yale School of Forestry and Environmental Studies where I researched extractive reserves in the Brazilian Amazon. My Ph.D. in Cultural Anthropology at the University of California, Santa Cruz focused on tourism, urban development, and conservation in a small fishing town in Northeastern Brazil that was transitioning to a tourist economy.

BIBLIOGRAPHY

Balee, William. *Cultural Forests of the Amazon: A Historical Ecology of People and Their Landscapes.* Tuscaloosa, AL: University of Alabama Press, 2013.

Cronon, William. "The Trouble with Wilderness: Or, Getting Back to the Wrong Nature." *Environmental History* (1996): 7–28.

Fiske, Shirley J., Susan A. Crate, Carole L. Crumley, Kathleen Galvin, Heather Lazrus, George Luber, Lisa Lucero, Anthony Oliver-Smith, Ben Orlove, Sarah Strauss, and Richard R. Wilk. "Changing the Atmosphere: Anthropology and Climate Change." *Final Report for the AAA Global Climate Change Task Force*. Arlington, VA: American Anthropological Association, 2014.

Murray, Gerald F. "The Domestication of Wood in Haiti: A Case Study in Applied Evolution." *Anthropological Praxis* (1987): 218.

Sahlins, Marshall. "The Original Affluent Society." In *The Politics of Egalitarianism: Theory and Practice*, edited by Jacqueline Solway, 79-98. New York: Berghahn Books, 2006.

White, Leslie. "Energy and the Evolution of Culture." In *Anthropological Theory: An Introductory History*, edited by R. Jon McGee and Richard L. Warms. Mountain View, CA: Mayfield Publishing Company, 2000.

NOTES

1. Bruno Latour, "Anthropology at the Time of the Anthropocene: A Personal View of What Is to be Studied," (paper presented at the annual meeting of the American Anthropological Association, Washington, D.C., December 2014) http://www.bruno-latour.fr/sites/default/files/139-AAA-Washington.pdf

2. Marshall Sahlins, "The Original Affluent Society," in *The Politics of Egalitarianism: Theory and Practice*, ed. Jacqueline Solway (New York: Berghahn Books, 2006), 79-98.

3. Elliot M. Abrams and David J. Rue, "The Cause and Consequences of Deforestation among the Prehistoric Maya," *Human Ecology* 16 no. 4 (1988): 377–395.

4. Sidney Mintz, *Sweetness and Power: The Place of Sugar in Modern History* (New York: Viking and Penguin, 1985).

5. S.J. Fiske, S.A. Crate, C.L. Crumley, K. Galvin, H. Lazrus, G. Luber, L. Lucero, A. Oliver-Smith, B. Orlove, S. Strauss, and R. Wilk, "Changing the Atmosphere: Anthropology and Climate Change," *Final Report for the AAA Global Climate Change Task Force* (Arlington, VA: American Anthropological Association, 2014).

6. Simone Athayde, "Introduction: Indigenous People, Dams, and Resistance," *Tipiti: Journal of the Society for Anthropology of Lowland South America* 12 no. 2 (2014): 80–92.

7. Paige West, James Igoe, and Dan Brockington, "Parks and People: The Social Impact of Protected Areas," *Annual Review of Anthropology* 35 (2006): 251–277.

8. Maria Panakhyo and Stacy McGrath, "Ecological Anthropology," in Anthropological Theories: A Guide Prepared by Students for Students (University of Alabama), http://anthropology.ua.edu/cultures/cultures.php?culture=Ecological%20Anthropology

9. Leslie White, "Energy and the Evolution of Culture," in *Anthropological Theory: An Introductory History*. eds. R. Jon McGee and Richard L. Warms (Mountain View, CA: Mayfield Publishing Company, 2000), 249.

10. Julian Steward, "The Patrilineal Band," in *Anthropological Theory: An Introductory History*, eds. R. Jon McGee and Richard L. Warms (Mountain View, CA: Mayfield Publishing Company, 2000), 228–242.

11. Marvin Harris, "The Cultural Ecology of Indian's Sacred Cattle," in *Anthropological Theory: An Introductory History*, eds. R. Jon McGee and Richard L. Warms (Mountain View, CA: Mayfield Publishing Company, 2000), 287.

12. Harold Conklin, *Hanunoo Agriculture. A Report on an Integral System of Shifting Cultivation in the Philippines* (New York, United Nations, 1957).

13. Richard Reed, "Forest Development and the Indian Way," in *Conformity and Conflict: Reading in Cultural Anthropology*, eds. James Spradley and David McCurdy, 105-115 (New York: Pearson, 2011).

14. Darrell A. Posey, *Kayapó Ethnoecology and Culture* (New York: Routledge, 2003).

15. Beth A. Conklin and Laura R. Graham, "The Shifting Middle Ground: Amazonian Indians and Eco-Politics," *American Anthropologist* 97 no. 4 (1995): 695–710.

16. Mac Chapin, "Indigenous Land Use Mapping in Central America," *Yale Forestry and Environmental Science Bulletin* 98 (1995): 195–209.

17. Piers Blaikie, *The Political Economy of Soil Erosion in Developing Countries* (London: Longman, 1985).

18. Melissa Leach and James Fairhead, "Fashioned Forest Pasts, Occluded Histories? International Environmental Analysis in West African Locales," *Development and Change* 31 no. 1 (2000): 35–59.

19. For more on this research see William Balee, *Cultural Forests of the Amazon: A Historical Ecology of People and Their Landscapes* (Tuscaloosa, AL: University of Alabama Press, 2013).

20. William Cronon, "The Trouble with Wilderness: Or, Getting Back to the Wrong Nature," *Environmental History* (1996): 7–28.

21. Ibid., 28.

22. Paige West, James Igoe, and Dan Brockington, "Parks and People: The Social Impact of Protected Areas," *Annual Review of Anthropology* 35 (2006): 251–277.

23. Peter A. Walker and Patrick T. Hurley, "Collaboration Derailed: The Politics of 'Community-Based' Resource Management in Nevada County," *Society and Natural Resources* 17 no. 8 (2004): 735–751.

24. Peter A Walker, "Reconsidering 'Regional' Political Ecologies: Toward a Political Ecology of the Rural American West," *Progress in Human Geography* 27 no. 1 (2003): 7–24.

25. Paul Robbins and Julie T. Sharp, "Producing and Consuming Chemicals: The Moral Economy of the American Lawn," *Economic Geography* 79 no. 4 (2003): 425–451.

26. Andrew P. Vayda and Bradely B. Walters, "Against Political Ecology," *Human Ecology* 27 no. 1 (1999): 167–179.

27. Rachel Harvey and Annette Koh, "Landfill in Paradise: Politics of Waste Management and Environmental Justice in Hawaii," *Anthropology News* 53 no. 8 (2012):1-16.

28. Richard Grant and Martin Oteng-Ababio, "Mapping the Invisible and Real 'African' Economy: Urban E-waste Circuitry," *Urban Geography* 33 (1): 1–21.

29. Barbara Rose Johnston, "An Anthropological Ecology? Struggles to Secure Environmental Quality and Social Justice," *Kroeber Anthropological Society* 101 no. 1 (2013): 3–21.

30. Bruno Latour and Steve Woolgar, *Laboratory Life: The Construction of Scientific Facts* (Princeton University Press, 2013).

31. See for instance Jenny Reardon, "The Human Genome Diversity Project: A Case Study in Coproduction," *Social Studies of Science* 31 no. 3 (2001): 357–388 and Micha Rahder, "But Is It a Basin? Science, Controversy, and Conspiracy in the Fight for Mirador, Guatemala," *Science as Culture* (2015): 1–26.

32. Donna Haraway, *The Companion Species Manifesto: Dogs, People, and Significant Otherness* (New York: Paradigm, 2003).

33. See for instance, Eben, Kirksey, ed. *The Multispecies Salon* (Duke University Press, 2014) and Eduardo Kohn, *How Forests Think: Toward an Anthropology Beyond the Human* (Berkeley, CA, University of California Press, 2013).

34. Gerald F. Murray, "The Domestication of Wood in Haiti: A Case Study in Applied Evolution," *Anthropological Praxis* (1987): 218.

35. S.J. Fiske, et al. "Changing the Atmosphere," 6.

PERFORMANCE

Lauren Miller Griffith, Texas Tech University
lauren.griffith@ttu.edu
https://www.depts.ttu.edu/sasw/People/Griffith.php

Jonathan S. Marion, University of Arkansas
marion@uark.edu
https://fulbright.uark.edu/departments/anthropology/directory/profile.php?uId=marion

LEARNING OBJECTIVES

- Identify cultural performances and performances of culture in various settings.

- Explain the various reasons that anthropologists study performance.

- Describe the role of performance in both reflecting and contributing to social change.

- Define "presentation of self."

- Articulate the relationship between performance and cultural constructions of gender.

- Analyze social conflicts using a theatrical lens.

- Differentiate between descriptive and performative utterances.

- Evaluate the outcomes of performance, especially as they relate to hegemonic discourses.

- Recall framing devices that are used to mark the boundaries of performance.

- Define intertextuality.

It's finally here—after weeks of waiting, your favorite band is playing in concert tonight! Driving in, parking, passing by all the vendors, and getting to your seats is all a swirl of sights, sounds, smells, and textures. Your view is temporarily blocked and then opens up again amidst the jostling bodies all around. You smell the cologne of someone nearby and smoke on someone else, all as you yell over the opening band's tunes to steer your friends to the correct seats. You'd set up two of your friends on a blind date for this concert, Jayden and Dakota, and from their grooming to their outfits to their flirtatious banter, both seem invested. The concert lives up to all your expectations! However, based on all the little cues—from leaning in toward each other to sideways glances—it looks like it was an even better night for Jayden and Dakota.

As you learned in earlier chapters, whether a night out is a "concert" or a "date" (and the appropriate behavior for each) is part of the learned and shared system of ideas and behaviors that comprise culture. The events—sporting events, shows, rituals, dances, speeches, and the like—are clearly cultural performances. At the same time, though, these activities and the interactions they involve are replete with culturally coded and performed nuances such as the lingering eye contact of a successful first date. In other words, there are two types of performances associated with our interactions with others: cultural performances (such as concerts) and performances of culture (such as dating). This chapter looks at both types of performance, exploring the different ways culture is performed and the effects of such performances.

OVERVIEW

In anthropological terms, a performance can be many things at once. It can be artful, reflexive, and consequential while being both traditional and emergent.1 As a result, each performance is unique because of the specific circumstances in which it occurs, including historical, social, economic, political, and personal contexts. Performers' physical and emotional states will influence their performances, as will the conditions in which the performance takes place and the audience to whom the performance is delivered. At the same time, every performance is part of a larger tradition, and the creator, performer(s), and audience are all interacting with a given piece of that larger body of tradition. Performance is consequential because its effects last much longer than the period between the rising and falling of a curtain. The reflexive properties of performance "enable participants to understand, criticize, and even change the worlds in which they live."[2] In other words, performances are much more than just self-referential; they are always informed by and about something.

Despite the importance of performance in our social worlds, it was only in the mid-twentieth century that anthropologists embraced performance as a topic worthy of study. Visual arts received serious attention from anthropologists much earlier, in large part because of Western cultural biases toward the visual *and* because those tangible artifacts lent themselves to cultural categorization and identification. In the 1950s, Milton Singer introduced the idea of **cultural performance**. Singer noted that cultural consultants involved in his fieldwork on Hinduism often took him to see cultural performances when they wanted to explain a particular aspect of that culture.[3] Singer checked his hypotheses about the culture against the formal presentations of it and determined that "these performances could be regarded as the most concrete observable units of Indian culture."[4] He concluded that one could understand the cultural value system of Hinduism by abstracting from repeated observations of the performances. In other words, (1) cultural performances are an ideal unit of study because they reference and encapsulate information about the culture that gave rise to them, and (2) the cultural messages become more accessible with each "sample" of the performances since the researcher can compare the specifics of repeated features of the same "performance."

Singer's observation that analyzing performance could be a useful method for understanding broader cultural values was revolutionary at the time. Today, anthropologists are just as likely to study performance itself—how performances become endowed with meaning and social significance, how cultural knowledge is stored inside performers' bodies.[5] Anthropology's increased openness to treating performance as a worthy area of inquiry reflects a shift from focusing on social structures of society that were presumed to be static to examining the ongoing processes within society that at times maintain the status quo and at other times result in change.[6]

Cultural Performance vs. Performing Culture

When describing the anthropology of performance, two concepts are often confused: performing culture and cultural performance. Though they sound similar, the difference is significant. Richard Schechner, a performance studies scholar whose work frequently overlaps with anthropology, provides a useful distinction between these terms by distinguishing between analyzing something that *is* a performance versus analyzing something *as* a performance.[7] A cultural performance *is* a performance, such as a concert or play. **Performing culture** is an activity that people engage in through their everyday words and actions, which reflect their enculturation and therefore can be studied *as* performances regardless of whether the subjects are aware of their cultural significance.

Mexico's famed ballet *folklorico* is one example of a cultural performance (see Figure 1). In essence, it is an authoritative version of the culture that has been codified and is presented to audiences who generally are expected to accept the interpretation. Cultural performances typically are readily recognizable. Their importance is highlighted by the fact that they take place at specific times and places, have a clear beginning and end, and involve performers who expect to demonstrate excellence.[8]

The umbrella of cultural performances includes many events thought of as performances in the West (e.g., concerts, plays, dances) but also includes activities such as prayers and rituals that westerners would classify as religious practices. That some cultures, particularly in the West, make a distinction between a performance and a religious practice fits with a tendency to see some practices as spurious and others as genuine, one of the reasons anthropologists have

Figure 1: Performance of ballet folklorico in Casa de la Cultura, Puebla, Mexico, 2013.

only recently begun to study performing arts seriously. Singer found that each cultural performance "had a definitely limited time span, or at least a beginning and an end, an organized program of activity, a set of performers, an audience, and a place and occasion of performance."[9] The same is true for religious and secular events. Cultural performances are informed by the norms of one's community and signal one's membership in that community.

Cultural performances contribute to preserving the heritage of a group, and in some cases, they have the same effect as an anthropologist writing in the "ethnographic present" by providing an artificially frozen (in time) representation of culture. For example, among people living along the Costa Chica of Mexico, _artesa_ music and the accompanying dance performed atop an overturned trough retains a strong association with the region's African-descended population.[10] The instruments and rhythms used in this music reflect the African, indigenous, and European cultures that gave rise to these blended communities and thus represent a rich, emergent tradition. In recent years, however, the _artesa_ mostly is no longer performed at weddings, as was traditional, and performers are now paid to represent their culture in artificial settings such as documentaries and cultural fairs.

Performing culture refers to lived traditions that emerge with each new performance of cultural norms—popular sayings, dances, music, everyday practices, and rituals—and it takes shape in the space between tradition and individuality. Using our initial example, the concert Jayden and Dakota attended was a cultural performance while their dating behaviors were examples of performing culture. Obviously, no two dates are identical, but within a given social group there are culturally informed codes for appropriate behavior while on a date and for the many other interactions that commonly occur between people.

EVERYDAY PERFORMANCE

There is a constant tension between **hegemony** and **agency** in our everyday activities. For example, while you choose how you want to dress on a given day, your choice of what to wear is shaped by the social situation. You wear something different at home than you do when going to work, to the beach, to a concert, or on a date. The range of what is considered acceptable attire in different

Figure 2: Professional meeting at a 2017 conference on counterterrorism in Norway.

Figure 3: Skateboarder hanging out at the beach.

social settings is an example of hegemony—for instance, a suit would be expected for a professional conference whereas a bathing suit would be entirely inappropriate (compare, for instance, Figures 2 and 3). An individual's choice within the culturally defined range of appropriate options is an example of how agency—an individual's ability to act according to his or her own will—is constrained by hegemony. Getting dressed is an example of an everyday performance of culture. When Jayden and Dakota paid extra attention to their appearance in anticipation of their date, they demonstrated—performed—their interest in pursuing a romantic relationship.

On the surface, our everyday performances probably seem inconsequential. A single failed performance may lead to an unfulfilling evening but usually does not have long-lasting consequences. However, when we look at patterns of everyday performances, we can learn much about a culture and how members of groups are expected to behave and present themselves to others. The subfield of visual anthropology is based on the notion that "culture can be seen and enacted through visible symbols embedded in behavior, gestures, body movements, and space use."[11]

Presentation of Self

Sociologist Erving Goffman coined the phrase **presentation of self** to refer to management of the impressions others have of us.[12] People adopt particular presentations of self for many reasons. A couple who aspires to be upwardly mobile, for example, may subsist on ramen noodles in the privacy of their apartment while spending conspicuously large amounts of money on fine food and wine in the company of people they want to impress. A political candidate from a very wealthy family might don work clothes and affect a working class accent to appeal to voters from that demographic or make a political appearance at a "working class" bar or pub rather than a country club. In many cases, people are not being intentionally deceptive when they adopt such roles. It is normal to act differently at home, at school, and at work; behavior is based on the social and cultural context of each situation. Goffman thus notes that impression management is at times intentional and at other times is a subconscious response to our enculturation.

Goffman uses theatrical terms to discuss impression management when distinguishing front and back spaces. Front spaces are arenas in which we carefully construct and control the audience's perception of the actors while back spaces are private zones where actors can drop those pretenses (see Figure 4). The front includes the setting—the physical makeup of the stage, including the furniture, décor, and other props, that figuratively, if not literally, set the stage for a social interaction.[13] For

Figure 4: World Under-21 Latin Finalists Stas Nikolaev and Kristina Kozlova competing "front stage" at the Italian Open (4a) and getting what rest they can between rounds "backstage" (4b) at the 2003 Italian Open Dancesport Championships (Cervia, Italy). Photographs by Jonathan S. Marion.

example, a restaurant and a church are both designed to seat tens or even hundreds of people and sometimes serve wine, but they are easily identified by how the seating is arranged, the kind of music played, and the artwork on the walls. Thus, presentations of the self also tend to be defined in part by the physical environment. Waiters adopt their role when they step into the restaurant and step out of those roles when they leave at the end of their shifts.

Another important component of these performances is the **personal front**: aspects of one's costume that are part of the actor's body or worn in close association with it.[14] Clothing, physical characteristics, comportment, and facial expressions all contribute to one's personal front. Some of these traits, such as height, are unlikely to change from one performance to the next. Others, such as a priest's collar, a doctor's white lab coat, a ballroom dancer's dress, and a waiter's convivial smile, can be changed at will (see Figure 5). Changes in the personal front affect the audience's interpretation and understanding of the role played by the individual and their beliefs about the "actor's" sincerity.

The match between the setting and one's personal front helps the audience quickly—and often accurately—understand the roles played by the actors in front of them. But each actor's performance still must live up to the audience's expectations, and a mismatch between expectation and execution can result in the actor being viewed as a failure. Take the example of the college professor. She could be a leading expert in her field with encyclopedic knowledge of the course topic, but if she stutters, speaks too softly, or struggles to answer questions quickly, her students may underestimate her expertise because her performance of an expert failed.

Figure 5a: A priest's collar.

Figure 5b: Doctors' white lab coats.

Figure 5c: National Professional Standard Finalists Mikhail Avdeev and Anastasia Muravyova (United States Dancesport Championships, Orlando, FL, 2008). Photograph by Jonathan S. Marion.

In some roles, the effort to manage an impression is largely invisible to the audience. Imagine, for example, a security guard at a concert. If everything goes well, the security guard will not have to break up any fights or physically remove anyone from the concert. If a fight does break out, a small individual trained in martial arts might be best-suited to diffusing the situation, but security personnel are often large individuals who have an imposing presence, a personal front that matches the public's expectations. A security guard could easily keep an eye on things while sitting still but instead usually stands with arms folded sternly across the chest or walks purposefully around the perimeter to make her presence known. She may make a show of craning her neck for a better view of certain areas even if they are not difficult to see. These overt performances of a security guard's competence are not necessary for the job, but their visibility discourages concert attendees from misbehaving.

Social actors differ in the degree to which they believe in both 1) the social role in question, and 2) their individual ability to performance that specific role. Those who Goffman called "sincere" performers are both confident in their ability to play the role *and* believe in the role itself. A shaman, for example, who believes wholeheartedly that she has been called to heal the members of her community is likely to both believe in the role of a shaman and in her particular ability to fulfill that role. Some begin as sincere performers but later become cynical. Religious roles sometimes fall into this category; the performer loses some degree of sincerity as the religious ceremonies are demystified.[15] Others are cynical in the beginning but grow into their roles, eventually becoming sincere. This is often the case with someone new to a profession. In the beginning, she may feel like a fraud due to lack of experience and worry about being discovered. Over time, the individual's confidence grows until the role feels natural.

Case Study: VH1's "The Pickup Artist"

The popularity of makeover television shows in recent years suggests that there is significant interest in learning to present an idealized version of oneself to others. In 2007, VH1 produced a reality show called "The Pickup Artist" that focused on men who experienced difficulty talking to women or who repeatedly found themselves viewed by women as "just friends" rather than as potential romantic partners. At the beginning of the season, the men were dropped off at a new house in a bus that said "Destination: Manhood" on the front, suggesting that their performance of masculinity was somehow lacking. The show's host was an author and self-proclaimed pickup artist named Mystery who had overcome challenges connecting with women and was there to share his hard-earned knowledge with others. In the initial episode, the men were filmed in a club as they approached women. Oblivious to the cues the women were sending them, all of the contestants blundered through painfully awkward social interactions in which several of the women eventually just walked away. Behind the scenes, Mystery and fellow pickup artists observed and commented on the contestants' attire, their approaches, and their conversation strategies. After diagnosing the contestants' "problems" interacting with women, Mystery taught them specific strategies for things like "opening a set" (initiating a conversation) and "the number close" (securing a woman's phone number). Though presented as a competitive reality show with one contestant ultimately being named "Master Pickup Artist" and receiving $50,000 to invest in his new identity, the show also revealed the level of performance expected within front-space areas such as nightclubs and how they differed from back-space areas such as the communal house, where contestants were (presumably) able to relax without having to micromanage their presentations of self.

Performance of Gender

As you may recall from the Gender and Sexuality chapter, gender is defined by culture rather than by biology. Gender theorist Judith Butler's term "gender performativity" references the idea that gender as a social construct is created through individual performances of gender identity. Butler's key point, published originally in 1990 and expanded in 1993, is that an act is seen as gendered through ongoing, stylized repetitions.[16] In other words, while we all make specific choices—such as how Jayden and Dakota chose to dress for their date—people doing things in patterned ways over time results in certain versions being typified as "male" or "female." Phrases such as "act *like* a man" or "throw *like* a girl" are good examples. Socially, we define certain types of behavior as typical of men and women and culturally code that behavior as a gendered representation. Thus, specific individuals are seen as doing things in a particularly (or stereotypically) masculine or feminine way. How do you know how "men" and "women" are supposed to behave? What makes one way of sitting, standing, or talking a "feminine" one and another a "masculine" one? The answer is that definitions of masculine and feminine vary with the socio-cultural milieus, but in every case, how people commonly do things constitutes gender in everyday life.

In many ways, the notion that gender is created and replicated through patterned behavior is an expansion of Marcel Mauss' classic idea that the very movements of our bodies are culturally learned and performed.[17] Walking and swimming may seem to be natural body movements, but those movements differ in individual cultures and one must learn to walk or swim according to the norms of the culture. We also learn to perform gender. If you showed up to the first day of class and all of the men in the class who had facial hair wore sundresses, you would notice and be surprised or confused. Why? Because, as Butler pointed out, gender is constructed through patterns of activity, and a bearded man in a sundress deviates from the expected pattern of male attire. While this is a particularly obvious example, the mechanism is the same for much more subtle expectations regarding everything from how you walk and talk to your taste in clothing and your hobbies. In Western contexts, for instance, athletic prowess is typically coded as masculine. But as Iris Marion Young noted, it is impossible to throw *like* a girl without learning what that means.[18] The phrase is not meant to refer to the skills of pitcher Mo'ne Davis who, at thirteen years old, became the first female Little League player to appear on the cover of *Sports Illustrated* in August 2014.[19] Young's point, by extension, is twofold: 1) "girls" only throw differently from "boys" insofar as they are taught to throw differently; and 2) what counts as throwing like a girl or a boy is a learned evaluation. Taking the idea a step further, several scholars looked at performance of gender in a variety of sports, including women's bodybuilding, figure skating, and competitive ballroom dancing. In each case, some aspect of femininity is over-performed through blatant makeup and costuming to compensate for the overt physicality of the sport, which is at odds with stereotypical views of femininity.[20]

As anthropologist Margaret Mead first publicized more than 80 years ago, what counts as culturally appropriate conduct for men and women is quite different across cultural settings.[21] More broadly, Serena Nanda provided an updated survey of cross-cultural gender diversity.[22] Two issues are particularly important: 1) the Western concept of binary gender is far from universal (or accurate); and 2) all behaviors are performed within—and hence contingent upon—specific contexts. For example, Nanda's work in India documents the ability to perform a third gender.[23] Similarly, Gilbert Herdt's work among the Sambia in Papua New Guinea counters the idea of sexual orientation as fixed (e.g., heterosexual, bisexual, homosexual) and provides a counter-example in which personal sexuality varies for boys and men by stage of life.[24] Perhaps the most compelling case for performance of gender is the Brazilian *Travesti*, transgendered male prostitutes who, despite having female names, clothing, language, and even bodies achieved through silicone injections and female hormones, identify themselves as men.[25] These cases demonstrate that sexuality is different from gender and that gender, sexual orientation, and sexuality are performed in daily life and at moments of heightened importance such as pride parades.

Case Study: Small Town Beauty Pageants

Oh to be the Milan Melon Queen, the Reynoldsburg Tomato Queen, or even the Circleville Pumpkin Queen, these are the dreams that childhood are made of!

Beauty pageants provide communities with opportunities to articulate the norms of appropriate femininity for the contestants and spectators. Pageant contestants are judged on their ability to perform specific markers of conventional femininity. In local pageants associated with community festivals (i.e., winners do not progress to larger regional and national competitions), contestants are expected to "perform . . . a local or small town version" of this ideal according to performance-studies scholar Heather Williams.[26] In these settings, success is predicated on demonstrating one's poise and confidence as a representative of the community.[27] Those competing in regional, state, and national competitions like *Miss America* often spend years being groomed for competition and developing a stage presence meant to transcend small town ideals of femininity. A striking difference between the national pageants and many local ones is the swimsuit competition in the national pageants. Perhaps local organizers are reticent to objectify young women from their own communities or because of small town conservatism. Anthropologist Robert Lavenda points out that a town may not be seeking to crown the most beautiful contestant and instead seeks the one who will best represent the community and its values.[28] Judges evaluate contestants not on their physical attractiveness per se but on how well their "presentation of self" aligns with the community's views of who they are.

Lavenda identified several characteristics shared by contestants. Though the competitions are generally open to women age 17 to 21, the majority who competed had just finished high school, making them all part of the same cohort leaving childhood and entering adulthood. All had been extremely active in extracurricular activities and were pursuing post-secondary education. Furthermore, because they needed sponsors to compete, the local business community had vetted all in some way. While contestants at the national level have private coaches and train independently for competitions, contestants in local pageants often work together for weeks or months before the festival, learning how to dress, walk on stage, and do hair and makeup. The result is a homogenized presentation of self that fits with the community's expectations, and the ideal contestant represents "a golden mean of accomplishment that appears accessible to all respectable girls of her class in her town and other similar small towns."[29] If the winner chosen does not represent those qualities or behaves counter to the prevailing values of the community, the audience often becomes upset, sometimes alleging corruption in the judging.[30] While the competition is ostensibly about the contestants and their ability to perform a certain ideal of femininity, it also demonstrates "the ability of small towns to produce young women who are bright, attractive, ambitious, and belong—or expect to belong—to a particular social category."[31] At least during the competition, unsuccessful performances of the feminine ideal are pushed out of sight and mind.[32] *This*, the community tries to *show, is what our women are* like.

Social Drama as Performance

Goffman used a theatrical metaphor to analyze how individuals change their presentations of self based on the scenic backdrop—front stage versus backstage. Anthropologist Victor Turner was more interested in the cast of characters and how their actions, especially during times of conflict, mirrored the rise and fall of action in a play.[33] As already noted, everyday life is comprised of a series of performances, but some moments stand out as more dramatic or theatrical than others. When a social interaction goes sufficiently awry, tensions arise, and the social actors involved may want to make sure that others understand precisely how expected social roles were breached. Turner calls these situations "metatheater," and they are most clearly seen in and described as social dramas: "units of aharmonic or disharmonic social process, arising in conflict situations."[34]

A social drama consists of four phases: breach, crisis, redress or remedial procedures, and either reintegration or recognition and legitimation of an irreparable schism.[35] A breach occurs when an individual or subgroup within a society breaks a norm or rule that is sufficiently important to maintenance of social relations. Following the breach, other members of the community may be drawn into the conflict as people begin to take sides. This is the crisis phase of the social drama. Such crises often reignite tensions that have been dormant within the society.

The redressive or remedial procedures used can take a number of forms. It is a reflexive period in which community members take stock of who they are, their communal values, and how they arrived at the conflict. The procedures used during this phase may be private, such as an elder offering sage advice to the parties centrally involved in the conflict. Other procedures are public, such as protests in the town square, formal speeches, and public trials. The Salem witch trials are an example of a public means of redress. This phase can also include payment of reparations or some form of sacrifice.

The final phase takes one of two forms. If the redressive actions were successful, the community will reintegrate and move beyond the schism (at least until another breach occurs). If the redressive actions were not successful, the community will fracture along the lines identified during the crisis phase. In smaller societies characterized by a high degree of mobility, individuals may physically move away from one another. In other groups, the two camps may erect barriers to prevent interactions. Social dramas are important events in communities and can be source material for other kinds of performances such as narrative retellings and commemorative songs and plays, all of which further legitimize the outcome of the social drama.[36]

Case Study: Establishing a New *Capoeira* Group

Capoeira is an Afro-Brazilian martial art that combines music, dance, and acrobatics with improvisational sparring. The traditional bearers of *capoeira* kept it alive despite persecution from the colonial Portuguese government and the Brazilian government until the mid-1930s. Even after that date, it was mostly associated with marginalized segments of the population. However, in the 1970s, several Brazilian *capoeiristas* began demonstrating and teaching their art abroad. This sparked international interest in *capoeira* and demand for teachers in nations such as the United States continues. In many cases, the teachers are apprentices to more established *mestres* (masters) in Brazil and maintain ongoing relationships with them.

While the teachers may continue to operate satellite groups under the primary *mestre's* direction for years, tensions can erupt between a *mestre* in Brazil and the teachers abroad. This is precisely what happened with a group referred to here as *Grupo Cultural Brasileiro*

(GCP). The *mestre* of GCP authorized one of his top students to begin teaching *capoeira* classes in a midwestern U.S. state. Eventually, demand for the classes grew, allowing the teacher to operate classes in two towns in the state, and two of his students were given the opportunity to start classes in new locations. All of the satellite groups were affiliated with the GCP; individuals wore shirts with the GCP logo and the *mestre* periodically visited the United States to give classes to the American students. Unbeknownst to most members of the group, the teacher and *mestre* had a falling out after one of the visits. The *mestre* had asked his teacher for a small sum of money (approximately $2,000) to pay for some repairs on the primary training facility in Brazil. The teacher agreed that it was a worthwhile expenditure but insisted that they had to discuss it with the U.S.-based board of directors before he could send the funds. Feeling that his authority was being slighted, the *mestre* demanded that certain individuals who he viewed as obstacles be removed from the board, and when the teacher explained that this was not possible according to the group's bylaws, the *mestre* demanded that the group stop wearing the GCP logo. This disagreement constituted a breach under Turner's model.

Several weeks later, an emergency board meeting was called to determine the proper course of action. In response, the *mestre* called the teacher's protégés who were already teaching on their own and essentially asked them to take sides. The students were made aware of this crisis when, at one of their weekly classes, they were told to turn their t-shirts inside out so the logo would not show, and thereafter, they were not permitted to wear the shirts.

To resolve the conflict, the board, teacher, and *mestre* considered mediation, and the *mestre* and teacher spent considerable time talking about to various members of the community. These efforts at remediation failed, resulting in a schism. The students in the Midwest convened with the teacher, discussed the group's values, and chose a new name and symbol to represent the group in the *capoeira* community at large. Now, nearly ten years later, the two groups continue to operate independently.

CONSTITUTING SOCIAL REALITY

In many cases, performances produce social realities. Imagine, for example, a political protest song that moves people to action, resulting in overthrow of a government regime. Similarly, performance can provide people with a template for action. For instance, people may model their relationships after ones they observe on television, and famous quotations from films get absorbed into everyday use and language. However, some performances stand out as more likely to shape social reality than others.

Performativity

Many performances are accomplished without words—mime and dance are two obvious examples. Often, though, language is used instrumentally to accomplish a specific task. Many utterances are simply descriptive (e.g., "that was a great concert!") while others are actions that bring about an outcome by virtue of being spoken. To distinguish between utterances that *do* something and those that merely describe, linguist J. L. Austin coined the term **performativity**. For example, compare these sentences:

We hereby bequeath our vast fortune to our darling daughter.
The girl inherited money from her parents when they died.

The first is performative because it causes something to happen; it transfers money between persons. The second is merely descriptive; it shares information that may or may not be factual about an event that occurred independently.

A person making a performative utterance must be genuine in the intent to carry it out and have it ratified by interlocutors—co-participants in the speech event. For example, a mother might say to her son, "I promise we will get ice cream after the dentist appointment." Making such a promise is a performative utterance because it creates a social contract, but her son may or may not believe her based on his prior experience. Likewise, if one makes a bet, the other party must agree to the terms. The bet is only on if the second party agrees.

Performative utterances commonly occur at wedding ceremonies.

Now that you have pledged your mutual vows, I, by virtue of the authority vested in me by the state, declare you to be wed according to the ordinance of the law.

Although wedding ceremonies typically involve numerous performances, such as a procession, songs, and lifting of the veil, the proclamation is the culminating moment in which the two individuals are legally joined in matrimony. Without these words being spoken, the ceremony is incomplete.

In addition to the performative declaration, the proclamation includes another important element: the authority granted by the state to make the declaration. Without this authority, a legal marriage does not occur. So a group of children playing can stage a wedding and say the exact same words and no one is married. In Austin's terminology, the unofficial wedding proclamation is an "unhappy utterance."[37] It is a failed performance because the parties involved did not have sufficient authority to bring the action to reality. A parallel example is a lawyer declaring a defendant guilty, something only a judge or jury (in the correct setting) can declare with authority. The ability of an utterance to shape an individual or a society depends on the words said, the context in which they are said, and the legitimacy and authority of the speaker. Performative utterances occur in many situations and are particularly common in rituals.

Ritual as Performance

Consider a Cuban woman who is experiencing disharmony at home. Her husband is abusive, she struggles to put food on the table, and one of her children left home and is living on the street. To find a solution, she consults a priest of the syncretic religion *Santería*. In the consultation room is an altar with candles, statues of gods and goddesses, and bowls filled with food offerings. The priest is dressed in white, as is customary, and wears several beaded necklaces that correspond to the deities with whom he is most closely associated. To use Goffman's phrasing, the setting and his personal front are congruent, assuring the woman that the consultation is genuine. To perform the divination, the priest tosses cowry shells on the table and asks the woman a series of questions based on what the shells reveal. He listens to her answers, throws the shells again, and fine-tunes his questions until he is able to focus on the crux of her distress. The flow of their dialog is similar to that seen in Western-style psychological counseling, but the ritual specialist performs his expertise using religious paraphernalia.

The Religion chapter introduced the concept of rituals and explained several of their functions, including rites of passage and of intensification. In this section, we call attention to rituals as an area of interest to cultural anthropologists who deal with performances and highlight how performance can be a useful lens for viewing and understanding secular and religious rituals. Obvious examples of rituals that inform anthropologists about a culture are concerts, plays, and religious events, which often portray cultural values and expectations, but rituals are involved in many other kinds of situations, such as trying and sentencing someone accused of a crime in the redressive phase of a social drama. The key here is that rituals are inherently performative. Merely talking about or watching a video recording of one does not *do* anything whereas participating in a ritual makes and marks a social change. Whether stoic or extravagant, a ritual is focused on efficacy rather than entertainment, and its performance gives shape to the social surrounding.

Case Study: Performing Ethnography

Ethnographies are written to engage readers in the lived experience of a particular group, but the reader cannot actually feel what it is like to live in a Ndembu village or smell herbs being prepared for an Afro-Brazilian *Candomblé* ceremony. Consequently, Victor and Edith Turner created a teaching method called "performing ethnography" to help students gain a deeper, kinesthetic understanding of what it is like to participate in the ritual life of another culture.[38] Students prepare for the ritual by reading relevant ethnographies and often meet with anthropologists who have done work with the people who performed it. To prepare for the ritual, the students must seek additional information about the culture so they can understand how to behave appropriately. The process also encourages them to think critically about the presentation of information in ethnographies, especially if gaps in the author's descriptions become apparent. Modeling an experiment after the Turners' example, Dr. Griffith had students perform a Christian American wedding ceremony. Obviously, no single ceremony can be representative of all weddings within that tradition, but the students came away from the experience with a better sense of what it is like to participate in that ritual and how the various roles move the couple from one social status to another. As the Turners pointed out, a serious ritual can be conducted within what they called a "play frame"[39] that negates the action otherwise brought by the ritual. So even though the woman who played the role of minister in the classroom "wedding" was in fact ordained, her words did not marry the individuals. The Turners have also used this method to allow students to better understand rituals such as coming of age ceremonies. Whether one can truly understand what it is like to be an initiate in such an important ritual without firsthand experience is doubtful, but the experience gives students an opportunity to reflect on their feelings as they participate in the rituals, providing the Turners with new hypotheses to explain how and why the rituals bridge childhood and adulthood that can be tested through further fieldwork.[40]

Political Performances

Performances have serious consequences for social reality and are often used to reinforce the status quo. For example, children in the Hitler Youth organization during World War II were encouraged to sing songs related to Germany's supremacy and Hitler's vision for an Aryan nation. Requiring children to give voice to this ideology brought them in line with the goals of those in power. Indeed, many civil rituals are part of such **hegemonic discourses** in which the basic parameters of social thought and action are unquestioningly (and usually invisibly) dictated by those in authority. Singing the national anthem before a sporting event is another example.

On the flipside, performances can be used to resist the status quo. These kinds of performances can be as subtle as a rolling of eyes behind a professor's back or as grand as an outright political uprising. Pete Seeger's song "Bring Them Home," which protested the United States' involvement in the Vietnam War, is a good example. Consider these lyrics: "Show those generals their fallacy . . . They don't have the right weaponry . . . For defense, you need common sense . . . They don't have the right armaments." Those lines provide a clear indication of the singer's political position, but repetition of the chorus "bring them home, bring them home" invites the audience to sing along, echoing and amplifying the singer's message and thus increasing its political force.

BOUNDED PERFORMANCES

Although much of our interaction with others throughout the day involves performing various roles, there are moments of heightened reflexivity that are particularly recognizable as being commonly understood as "performances," such as plays and concerts, which are special because they are marked off from everyday activities. In other words, they are bounded and analyzable. They are also short-lived. Even when such performances are fixed on film or through movement notation (such as Labanotation script, a system for recording dance movements), the interaction and feedback between an audience and the performer(s) happens "in the moment" only once. Because they are known and understood to be bounded, they often serve as moments of heightened consciousness. Jayden and Dakota, introduced at the start of this chapter, paid close attention to their first date because they knew that it was the only first date they could have together. Within such a state of heightened awareness, performers essentially hold a mirror up to society and force audience members to come to terms with themselves—as they are, as they once were, or as they could become.

Training/Rehearsal

Individuals such as shamans who are experts in performing rituals spend years mastering their crafts. Unfortunately, performance scholars have largely focused on final performances and ig-

nored performers' preparations. Scholar Richard Schechner, a pioneer in the study of performance, has advocated for a more holistic study of performance production that includes the training, workshops, rehearsals, warm-ups, performance, cool-down, and aftermath.[41] The steps involved vary according to the culture in which the performance occurs.[42]

Rehearsal and training instill an embodied understanding of the art's form and technique in the performer, and adherence to the forms gives performances their versatility and longevity.[43] Techniques thus serve as a conservative force within a performance genre as each generation

Figure 6: Actor donning mask at a Noh workshop in Copenhagen, Denmark, 2010.

of performers learns to replicate the postures and movements of their predecessors.[44] We do not suggest that performance traditions do not change. Indeed, as individuals master the form and become legitimate bearers of tradition, they have more and more latitude to play with the form and introduce innovations that may, in turn, be reproduced in the future by their protégés.

Some training requires a lifetime. For example, in the Japanese performance of *Noh*—a traditional music and dance performance featuring masked actors (see Figure 6)—training typically begins when an actor is around five years old.[45] Because the actors have, in the process of their training, learned all of the necessary roles, there is little need for a cast to rehearse a drama in its entirety prior to performing it. This kind of training is also seen in classical Indian dance and other forms in which adherence to tradition is the norm. In other cases, audiences expect a continually changing repertoire of pieces that require the cast to rehearse extensively prior to the performance. Ballet dancers, for example, undergo extensive training for a relatively brief career, and the novelty of some performance pieces requires intensive study of new choreography prior to opening night.

The pressure felt by performers during shows are not present during rehearsals, which typically allow for an element of playfulness.[46] Schechner thus likened rehearsals to rites of separation that occur within rituals.[47] In his view, rehearsals are removed in space and time from the rest of society and allow performers to acquire the skills and knowledge needed to create a transformative, liminal experience for themselves and the audience when the performance is given. Thus, the spaces in which training and rehearsals take place are also important. Writing of the ballet studio (see Figure 7), scholar Judith Hamera, who studies performance, noted that "as surely as ballets are made in these spaces, the spaces themselves are remade in the process, becoming, perhaps through the repetition of this epitome of classical technique, a kind of Eden both inside and outside of everyday space and time."[48] This "construction" can be both a concrete process (the floors are scuffed by the dancers' feet and the barres bowed by the weight of novices learning to *plié*) and a metaphorical transformation. The sacrifices of time and energy by the dancers sanctify the space. Even when the rehearsal space is merely a parking lot, empty field, or someone's living room, the actions and intentions of those within the space give it meaning.

Figure 7: Ballet dancers warming up before *Prix de Lausanne*, 2010.

Framing Performance

Imagine sitting down with a group of young children. Their attention is focused on their teacher, who sits at the front of the room. There are many clues that it is story time—the children have moved from their desks to the floor and been told to sit quietly with their hands in their laps. But the unequivocal sign is the teacher saying "Once upon a time, in a land far, far away . . ." This is a familiar formula for people who grew up in American culture. It tells the audience that a fairy tale is about to begin and that the speaker is assuming responsibility for a suitable performance of the tale. With such a simple phrase, the participants in this interaction are cast in specific roles with clearly defined responsibilities. How will the story end? Most of us already know. The protagonist(s) will live "happily ever after." This too is a formulaic phrase, one that signals conclusion of the performance. These are what Richard Bauman calls framing devices: cues that "signify that the ensuing text is a bounded unit which may be objectified."[49]

Such frames are metacommunicative. They offer layered information about how to interpret the ensuing message. Examples of framing devices include codes, figurative language, parallelisms, paralinguistic features, formulas, appeals to tradition, and even disclaimers of performance.[50] Codes are associated with particular types of performances. For example, a performance in which lines includes the words thee and thou signal to listeners that the performance involves religious speech or other old texts such as Shakespearian plays. Figurative language refers to illustrative words and phrases such as similes and metaphors that convey meaning in just a few words. Calling someone "a wolf in sheep's clothing" alludes to a predator masked as prey, and no one familiar with the idiom would imagine this as a reference to a four-legged predator wearing a wool costume. Parallelism is repetition of sounds, words, or phrases used as a memory device or to build momentum. President Obama's repetition of "Yes we can" in his campaign speeches is a good example of this. Paralinguistic features describe how words are delivered, such as an auctioneer's signature speed of delivery. Formulas are stock phrases that give the audience information, such as "once upon a time" indicating that a story is beginning. Appeals to tradition, such as saying "this is how my dad always tells the story," not only frame a performance but place the performance in an intertextual (a more detailed discussion of intertextuality follows) relationship with past performances. Finally, disclaimer of performance is denying that one is competent to perform and calls attention to the fact that a performance is about to occur or just occurred. These devices, used alone or in combination, give the audience the authority to judge the performer and distinguish the performance from the flow of events that preceding and following it.

Meaning Making

Typically, when constructing the meanings of bounded performance events, three primary interests are involved: the author(s), the artist(s), and the audience. In each case, the composition of those groups differs and the meaning of a performance can be quite different. **Polysemy** (derived from the Greek words for "many" and "sign") is used in anthropology to describe settings, situations, and symbols that convey multiple meanings. This is certainly the case for performance events since a single form can be used in a variety of ways depending on the creators' and/or performers' intentions and the audiences' framework for receiving and interpreting the piece.[51] If artists intentionally subvert the author's intentions, the audience could interpret a performance as ironic rather than sincere. Similarly, if an audience fails to understand the author's intent, the message can fall flat or be received quite differently than intended by either the author or the performers.

The author of a performance and the artists who transform the author's vision into a reality often have ambiguous positions in society. They may be admired for their skill and feared for their ability to transform social realities and disrupt the status quo.[52] The author and artist can be the same individual (e.g., an author performing a monologue she wrote) or a group of artists can collectively author a work (e.g., the performance group Pilobolus).[53] Most commonly, an author or authors creates the work and one or more artists perform it. In a ballet, for example, a dancer's role is to carry out faithfully the vision of the choreographer, which may or may not happen. At times, artists in a performance have only a vague sense of who the author is, as when individuals recite folktales or proverbs that have been handed down across generations.

The audience consists of one or more individuals who cooperate with the performer(s) by temporarily suspending the normal communication rule of turn-taking and who gather specifically to observe the performance.[54] Individuals come to a situation with unique background and experiences so the audience does not receive a performance uniformly. Similarly, as part of the context of a performance, the audience participates in constructing its meaning. Audience members evaluate the performance based on the formal features of the genre, holding performers responsible for demonstrating competence in the genre.[55] For example, different criteria are used to evaluate acting in a drama versus a comedy. In in-person settings, artists are often influenced by the audience. A politician, for example, may phrase key points differently depending on the audience or choose particular jokes that will resonate with the demographic at hand in an effort to be judged positively.[56] Adjustments may be made spontaneously in response to the audience's reaction to earlier material.

Linked to the audience, then, is the setting. Experiencing a performance of *Romeo and Juliet* outdoors under a tent is very different from experiencing the same play in a historic theater like The Globe in London (a reproduction of the Elizabethan-era theater where many of William Shakespeare's plays were staged). The setting is important not only for context but for access. Performances in public parks or downtown squares (e.g. Figure 8) are accessible to all while performances at theaters and opera halls (e.g. Figure 9) are limited to people who have time and money to spend on such luxuries. Similarly, and as discussed previously, visual cues in a performance space are often important signals that a performance is occurring. If you see a couple in a park arguing loudly, wildly gesticulating, and drawing bystanders into their conflict, you may have stumbled onto an avant-garde theater production, but the lack of framing (no stage, curtains, or formal audience seats) makes the scene ambiguous. It may be only a couple arguing.

Figure 8: Street performance in Sydney, Australia, 2010.

Figure 9: Dublin Philharmonic performing at the Blumenthal Performing Arts Center in Charlotte, NC, 2009.

Clearly, then, there are many possible outcomes of a performance. Some are staged simply for entertainment, which is an important component of human life. Often, though, there are additional motivations behind the creation and performance. For example, a performance can be used to assert the distinctiveness of a particular ethnic group or to argue for racial harmony in a nation-state. Carla Guerron-Montero described such performances in Panama, which gained its independence from Colombia in 1903.[57] The United States assisted the Panamanian separatist movement and participated in building the Panama Canal shortly thereafter. To distinguish themselves from Colombians and from U.S. citizens in Panama, middle-class intellectuals in Panama have consistently looked to Spain as the legitimate source of their identity. In this romanticized view, the ideal Panamanian is a rural, Hispanic (Spanish and indigenous) peasant, and peasant forms of dress (the *pollera*) and music (the *tipica*) are used to symbolize a unified national identity of pride in being a racial democracy. Along those lines and as performed in numerous everyday actions, Panamanian national discourse holds that mestizo (mixed) identity is normative, and they contrast themselves with other Latin American countries that have racial inequalities. Still, because lived life is always more complex than any single narrative, Afro-Panamanians still contend with discrimination.[58]

Case Study: Theater and Public Health Education

An approach known as Theater of the Oppressed was chiefly promoted by Augusto Boal, who was in turn influenced by Paulo Freire's work on liberator education among oppressed peasants in Brazil. Boal used the term to refer to performances that engaged the audience in a way that transformed its members and influenced them to abolish oppressive conditions in their societies. Though originally conceived as a political action, Theater of the Oppressed has been applied to public education. Performance-studies scholar Dwight Conquergood, for example, spent time in Thailand at the Ban Vinai refugee camp developing a health education program.[59] He started a performance company composed of Hmong refugees that used traditional cultural performances such as proverbs, storytelling, and folksong to produce skits about health problems in the camp. Conquergood wanted to avoid merely coopting local performance traditions and using them to essentially force Western ways of thinking on the refugees, which would establish a hierarchical model of education based on the idea that knowledge can simply be transferred from one who knows to one who does not.[60] He wanted to engage the refugees in a dialog about how they could collectively improve the health conditions of the camp. Early on, the village was threatened by a potential outbreak of rabies, and when instructed to bring their dogs to sites around the camp for vaccination, the refugees did not comply because they did not understand the urgency of the situation or how the vaccines would help. Conquergood's group of actors created a parade in which they dressed up as animals that were important in the Hmong belief system and played music to catch the villagers' attention. When people came to see the parade, the chicken, an animal known for its divinatory powers, shared information about rabies and the importance of vaccinating dogs. The parade was successful in convincing residents to vaccinate their dogs and provided an opportunity for the villagers to give the actors constructive criticism about their performance. Their critiques increased the cultural relevance of future performances and made the villagers more invested in the activities of the theater troupe, further increasing their likelihood of success.

Recontextualized Performances

Established performances (such as a ritual or festival) occur in new and changing contexts. In line with Clifford Geertz's understanding of cultures as "texts," the term intertextuality describes the network of connections between original versions of a performance and cases in which the performance is extracted from its social context and inserted elsewhere. The conventional relationship between text and performance is that "the text is the permanent artifact, hand-written or printed, while the performance is the unique, never-to-be-repeated realization or concretization of the text."[61] In the anthropology of performance, a "text" is a symbolic work (literature, speech, painting, music, films, and other works) that is interpretable by a community. It is the source material, and the relationship between the text and a performance is mediated by many contextual factors, including previous experiences with the text, learning of the lines, rehearsals, directorial license.

Folklorist and anthropologist Richard Bauman asked what storytellers accomplish by "explicitly linking" their tales to prior versions of the source material.[62] In short, Bauman found that linking situates each performance within the web of relationships among performances, which in turn adds to the performer's credibility by demonstrating that the performer is connected in some way to the other performers or at least is knowledgeable of past performances. For example, a man singing a lullaby to his child might preface the song by explaining that it is one his father sang to him and that his father's father sang before him. This places the father in a genealogical relationship with past performers and places the audience, his child, into that genealogy as well.

Alternatively, one can explicitly link a current performance to a prior one to invert what the audience knows about the past performance, as in a parody.[63] In that case, anthropologists refer to how significantly one departs from faithful replication of the original source as the intertextual gap.[64] A direct quotation of another's words, such as a town crier relaying a king's decree, has a narrow intertextual gap while a parody that references an original source to mock it, such as the 2014 film *A Million Ways to Die in the West* or the 1974 film *Blazing Saddles* that both poked fun at Westerns, has a large intertextual gap. Source material taken from one genre and used in another, such as a popular proverb turned into a song lyric, also has a large intertextual gap. Deliberate manipulation of these gaps—the recontextualization of source material—changes their role, significance, and impact in a performance.

Case Study: Intertextuality and the *Coloquio*

Richard Bauman and Pamela Ritch studied a *coloquio* (formal conversation) of a nativity play that has been performed in Mexico as far back as the sixteenth century.[65] Although the play is often associated with the Christmas season, Bauman and Ritch reported witnessing its performance at the culmination of important community events in other seasons as well. The plays are long, often lasting twelve to fourteen hours, and involve a significant number of community members who volunteer their time to act, direct, and produce the spectacle. After parts are assigned, the actors must learn their lines. The words are already familiar to them as they have attended such plays since childhood, and the actors often model their deliveries on presentations they witnessed in the past. Six or seven rehearsals typically precede the formal public performance, and each is a full run-through with no opportunity to stop and rework a scene viewed as poorly done. However, a prompter reads from the script to assist the actors with their lines if necessary, thereby assuring a narrow intertextual gap. When relying on the prompter's cues, the actors echo back the words, reinforcing the narrow gap. One character is an exception. In the written script, the hermit is a pious character. In the performance, however, the hermit is a comic figure. He rarely knows his lines and thus relies on the prompter's cues, but instead of echoing them back faithfully, he intentionally substitutes words for comic effect. He alone is allowed to significantly depart from the script, creating a large intertextual gap that introduces humor into the performance that is absent from the script—and in a way that is impossible to sustain across multiple performances of the play if it were ever "frozen" into the script. A joke, after all, is funny only so many times before becoming boring from repetition.

Performance Communities

Cultural performances are informed by the norms of one's **community of practice** and signal one's membership in the community.[66] Thus, the study of performance is not limited to what happens on a stage or within the limits of Bauman's frames. Rather, studies of performance allow us to see the environment in which the performance occurs as a space in which identity is formed by both accommodating and resisting social norms even as they are being rehearsed and learned.[67] In large, industrialized societies, people often elect to become part of smaller communities of practice around which they build their identities. Each of those communities has its own "folk geography," a term used by performance scholar Judith Hamera to describe the shared knowledge of where to shop for dance-related paraphernalia and which medical practitioners in town best understand dancers' bodies.[68] Folk geographies are all-encompassing. They are global geographies that include historical markers redolent with meaning for the community, the locations of key teachers and everything else a practitioner needs to know to navigate the community.

Sociologist Howard Becker's exploration of "art worlds" highlights how the obvious activity—painting or playing a musical instrument, for example—is contingent on and contextualized by a larger community that provided the materials, training, venues, and audiences for all such art practices. Wulff has extended this concept to the ballet world and by Marion to the ballroom and salsa world.[69] More than simply suggesting that performances happen within communities, the point is that communities emerge and grow around specific performance practices. Indeed, for something to become a genre rather than simply an individual variation, other people must become involved. New styles emerge only when variations find an appreciative audience and then are copied or modified by others. Over time, however, as a style grows in popularity and is shared more widely, broader and deeper cultural elaborations may develop. This has been the case with salsa dancing, which is now both a worldwide phenomenon and a local practice.[70]

Performance in the Age of Globalization

In this age of globalization, communications and interactions among people in vastly different geographical locations have sped up and grown dramatically thanks to ever-faster and more-ubiquitous communication and transportation technologies. Globalization is not a new phenomenon but has greatly intensified in recent decades, creating links between producers and consumers, artists and audiences, which were not possible in the past. And as emphasized in this chapter, performance is a multifaceted phenomenon that touches all aspects of social life. It is particularly relevant to the global media-scape articulated by anthropologist Arjun Appadurai in which many forms of media flow across national borders.[71] Examples of the global media-scape include American teenagers watching Bollywood movies produced in India, a Brazilian telenovela (soap opera) shown in Mozambique, and a Prague newspaper sent to family members living and working in Saudi Arabia. Globalization also helps explain why some performance genres that once were highly localized traditions, such as tango (originally from Argentina) and samba (originally from Brazil), are now internationally recognized, practiced, and celebrated.

In our modern globalized society, many performance genres have come unmoored from their cultural origins. It is one thing to consume such performances as spectators, but it is another to participate in these performance communities, leading to questions of authenticity and appropriation. For example, is it acceptable for a middle-class white American woman to perform an art like *capoeira* (see the preceding case study) that was traditionally associated with poor Afro-Brazilian men? Some in Afro-Brazilian communities view it as acceptable and embrace those willing to dedicate themselves to the art. Others are reluctant to adopt an inclusive philosophy, arguing that Afro-Brazilians endured years of suffering in service of preserving their art and therefore deserve to retain control of its future. Similar debates surround other performance genres with strong connections to ethnicity, such as jazz, blues, hip-hop, and rap.

International interest in local forms of performance also raises questions about intellectual property. For example, the Mbuti people of central Africa's forests believe that song is the appropriate medium for communicating with the forest and alerting it to their needs.[72] Song is also pleasurable for the Mbuti and associated with social harmony.[73] Thus, song in general and the *hindewhu*, a hoot-like sound made with an indigenous musical instrument, in particular play important roles in the worldview of the Mbuti and related groups. Recently, their music has been transported out of the forest and into the mainstream, and anthropologist and ethnomusicologist Steven Feld has traced use of the *hindewhu* to songs by Madonna (*Sanctuary*) and Herbie Hancock (*Watermelon Man*).[74] Hancock apparently developed his song after hearing the *hindewhu* on an ethnomusicology recording released in 1966. When asked about the appropriateness of using this signature sound out of context and without permission, Hancock said "this is a brothers kind of thing," implying that their shared African ancestry allowed him to coopt the Mbuti's musical heritage.[75] The central issue is not whether Hancock's claim to shared heritage justifies his use of the *hindewhu* but whether people like the Mbuti have a right to control the use, reproduction, and alteration of their cultural performances. As world beat music grows in popularity and many indigenous peoples become savvier about protecting their cultural and intellectual rights, these questions will be more pressing.

Another effect of globalization is the rise to new types of performances. For example, many performances are specifically staged for media consumption and distribution, such as photo opportunities arranged by politicians and celebrities. Similarly, some performances no longer exist outside of a media-related state, such as online-only campaigns, protests, and movements. Focusing on the performances regardless of the cultural configuration in which they occur allows anthropologists to more fully understand these emerging forms and practices. All of culture changes constantly, at different rates and in various ways, and performance is no exception. Amid ongoing expansion of modern technologies, the significance of performance in globalized contexts is central to anthropology's ultimate commitment to holistic understanding. As a technology or format becomes commonplace, new options arise as people construct profiles and albums, build social networks across online and mobile applications, and make, post, and share videos. These sites of personal presentation and social action are all sites of cultural performance and performances of culture.

CONCLUSION

The band takes a final bow and exits the stage. The lights come up and people begin streaming out of the auditorium. One performance ends but a multitude of others continues. The security guard continues to present a picture of authority, ensuring orderly behavior. A woman smiles as a man makes a show of opening the car door for her. And Jayden promises to call Dakota sometime next week.

This chapter has highlighted the many different kinds of performance that interest anthropologists. Under anthropology's holistic approach, performance connects to topics from many earlier chapters, including rituals (Religion chapter) and gender (Gender and Sexuality chapter). As we have shown, explicit attention to various performance-based frameworks allows anthropologists to identify the learned and shared patterns of ideas and behaviors that constitute human experience and living. We started the chapter by noting that performance can be many things at once, making it important to so much of human cultural experiences. Cultural performances are the events that most readily fit the Western notion of a performance: clearly defined moments of heightened salience of some feature of a culture's values or social structure. These performances call attention to issues that might otherwise go unnoticed by audience members and consequently can inspire or instigate action. Such performances also can preserve aspects of a culture or facilitate cultural revitalization. Performing culture, on the other hand, refers to the many diverse ways in which individuals both reflect and create cultural norms through daily activities, interactions, and behaviors. Culture does not, indeed cannot, exist simply as an abstract concept. Rather, it arises from the patterned flows of people's lives—their ongoing performances.

Anthropologists who study performance are interested in many of the same topics as other anthropologists, including: gender, religion, rituals, social norms, and conflict. Performance provides an alternative perspective for exploring and understanding those issues. Rather than studying rituals from a structural-functional perspective, for example, anthropologists can focus on performance and thereby better identify and understand theatrical structure and how communities use performance to accomplish the work of rituals. In short, performance anthropologists are interested not only in the products of social life but in the processes underlying it.

(P.S. Good luck Jayden and Dakota!)

DISCUSSION QUESTIONS

1. What is the difference between studying something that *is* performance and studying something *as* a performance? Why is this distinction important?
2. What is the role of performance in reflecting social order and values on the one hand and challenging these and leading to social change on the other? Provide examples of each.
3. Explain the relationship between performance and cultural constructions of gender.
4. How are descriptive and performative utterances different from each other, and what role to each play in verbal performance?
5. What roles do performances play in everyday life, especially as these relate to hegemonic discourses?

GLOSSARY

Agency: An individual's ability to make independent choices and act upon his/her will.

Community of practice: a group of people who engaged in a shared activity or vocation, such as dance or medicine.

Cultural Performance: A performance such as a concert or a play.

Discourse: Widely circulated knowledge within a community.

Hegemonic discourses: Situations in which thoughts and actions are dictated by those in authority.

Hegemony: Power so pervasive that it is rarely acknowledged or even recognized, yet informs everyday actions.

Performativity: Words or actions that cause something to happen.

Performing culture: Everyday words and actions that reflect cultural ideas and can be studied by anthropologists as a means of understanding a culture.

Personal front: Aspects of one's clothing, physical characteristics, comportment, and facial expressions that communicate an impression to others.

Polysemy: Settings, situations, and symbols that convey multiple meanings.

Presentation of self: The management of the impressions others have of us.

Reflexivity: Awareness of how one's own position and perspective impact what is observed and how it is evaluated.

ABOUT THE AUTHORS

Dr. Lauren Miller Griffith is an assistant professor of anthropology at Texas Tech University. Her research agenda focuses on the intersections of performance, tourism, and education in Brazil, Belize, and the USA. Specifically, she focuses on the Afro-Brazilian martial art *capoeira* and how non-Brazilian practitioners use travel to Brazil, the art's homeland, to increase their legitimacy within this genre. Dr. Griffith's current interests include the links between tourism, cultural heritage, and sustainability in Belize. She is particularly interested in how indigenous communities decide whether or not to participate in the growing tourism industry and the long-term effects of these decisions.

Dr. Jonathan S. Marion is an associate professor in the Department of Anthropology and a member of the Gender Studies Steering Committee at the University of Arkansas, and the author of *Ballroom: Culture and Costume in Competitive Dance* (2008), *Visual Research: A Concise Introduction to Thinking Visually* (2013, with Jerome Crowder), and *Ballroom Dance and Glamour* (2014). Currently the President of the Society for Humanistic Anthropology, and a Past-president of the Society of Visual Anthropology, Dr. Marion's ongoing research explores the interrelationships between performance, embodiment, gender, and identity, as well as issues of visual research ethics, theory, and methodology.

NOTES

1. Richard Bauman and Pamela Ritch, "Informing Performance: Producing the *Coloquio* in Tierra Blanca," *Oral Tradition* 9:2 (1994): 255.
2. David M. Guss, *The Festive State: Race, Ethnicity, and Nationalism as Cultural Performance* (Berkeley: University of California Press, 2000), 9.
3. Milton Singer, "The Great Tradition in a Metropolitan Center: Madras," *Journal of American Folklore* (1958): 347–388.
4. Singer, "The Great Tradition in a Metropolitan Center," 351.
5. See Anya Peterson Royce, *Anthropology of the Performing Arts: Artistry, Virtuosity, and Interpretation in Cross-Cultural Perspective* (Walnut Creek, Altamira Press, 2004).
6. Victor Turner, *The Anthropology of Performance* (New York: Paj Publications, 1987).
7. Richard Schechner, *Between Theater and Anthropology* (Philadelphia: University of Pennsylvania Press, 2011).
8. Richard Bauman, *Verbal Art as Performance* (Long Grove: Waveland Press, 1984).

9. Turner, *Anthropology of Performance*, 23.

10. Laura A. Lewis, *Chocolate and Corn Flour: History, Race, and Place in the Making of "Black" Mexico* (Durham, NC: Duke University Press, 2012).

11. Jay Ruby, *Picturing Culture: Explorations of Film and Anthropology* (Chicago, University of Chicago Press, 2000): 240.

12. Erving Goffman, *The Presentation of Self in Everyday Life* (New York, Anchor Books, 1959).

13. Goffman, *Presentation of Self*.

14. Ibid,, 24.

15. Ibid.

16. Judith Butler, *Gender Trouble: Feminism and the Subversion of Identity* (New York: Routledge, 1990); Judith Butler, *Bodies That Matter: On the Discursive Limits of "Sex"* (New York: Routledge, 1993).

17. Marcel Mauss, "Techniques of the Body" *Economy and Society* 2:1 (1973): 70–89.

18. Iris Marion Young, "Throwing Like a Girl: A Phenomenology of Feminine Body Comportment Motility and Spatiality" *Human Studies* 3:2 (1980): 137–156.

19. *Sports Illustrated* August 25 (2014), Cover.

20. Several authors have discussed the relationship between femininity and sport. On bodybuilding, see Anne Bolin, "Muscularity and Femininity: Women Bodybuilders and Women's Bodies in Culturo-Historical Context," in *Fitness as Cultural Phenomenon*, ed. Karina A. E. Volkwein (New York: Waxmann Münster, 1998). On figure skating, see Abigail M. Feder-Kane, "A Radiant Smile from the Lovely Lady," in *Reading Sport: Critical Essays on Power and Presentation*, ed. Susan Birell and Mary G. McDonald (Boston: Northeastern University Press, 2000). On ballroom, see Jonathan S. Marion, *Ballroom: Culture and Costume in Competitive Dance* (Oxford: Berg, 2008) and *Ballroom Dance and Glamour* (London: Bloomsbury, 2014). See also Lisa Disch and Mary Jo Kane, "When a Looker Is Really a Bitch: Lisa Olson, Sport, and the Heterosexual Matrix," in *Reading Sport: Critical Essays on Power and Presentation*, ed. Susan Birell and Mary G. McDonald (Boston: Northeastern University Press, 2000).

21. Margaret Mead, *Sex and Temperament: In Three Primitive Societies* (New York: Perennial, 2001[1935]).

22. Serena Nanda, *Gender Diversity: Crosscultural Variation* (Long Grove: Waveland, 2014).

23. Serena Nanda, *Neither Man nor Woman: The Hijras of India* (New York: Cengage, 1998).

24. Gilbert Herdt, *The Sambia: Ritual, Sexuality, and Change in Papua New Guinea* (New York: Cengage, 2005).

25. Don Kulik, *Travesti: Sex, Gender, and Culture among Brazilian Transgendered Prostitutes* (Chicago: University of Chicago Press, 1998).

26. Heather A. Williams, "Miss Homegrown: The Performance of Food, Festival, and Femininity in Local Queen Pageants" (Ph.D. dissertation, Bowling Green State University, 2009), 3.

27. Ibid.

28. Robert H. Lavenda, "Minnesota Queen Pageants: Play, Fun, and Dead Seriousness in a Festive Mode" Journal of American Folklore (1988): 168–175.

29. Lavenda, "Queen Pageants," 173.

30. Ibid.

31. Ibid., 171.

32. Ibid.

33. Turner, *Anthropology of Performance*.

34. Ibid., 74.

35. Ibid.

36. Ibid.

37. John Langshaw Austin, *How to Do Things with Words* (Oxford: Oxford University Press, 1975).

38. Victor Turner and Edith Turner, "Performing Ethnography," in The Anthropology of Performance, ed. Victor Turner (New York: PAJ Publications, 1987): 139–155.

39. Turner and Turner, "Performing Ethnography," 142.

40. Ibid.

41. Schechner, *Between Theatre and Anthropology*.

42. Bauman and Ritch, "Informing Performance."

43. Royce, *Performing Arts*.

44. Royce, *Performing Arts*, 44.

45. Schechner, *Between Theatre and Anthropology*.

46. Bauman and Ritch, "Informing Performance."

47. Schechner, *Between Theatre and Anthropology*.

48. Judith Hamera, "Performance, Performativity, and Cultural Poiesis in Practices of Everyday Life," in *The Sage Handbook of Performance Studies*, eds. D. Soyini Madison and Judith Hamera, (Thousand Oaks: Sage Publications, Inc., 2006):50–51.

49. Bauman, *Others' Words*, 4.

50. Bauman, *Verbal Art*.

51. See Guss, *Festive State*.

52. Bauman, *Verbal Art.*

53. Royce, *Performing Arts.* For more on Pilobolus, see their website, http://www.pilobolus.com.

54. Karin Barber, "Preliminary Notes on Audiences in Africa," *Africa* 67:3 (1997): 347–362.

55. Bauman and Ritch, "Informing Performance;" Bauman, *Others' Words;* Royce, *Performing Arts.*

56. Alessandro Duranti, "The Voice of the Audience in Contemporary American Political Discourse," *Georgetown University Round Table on Languages and Linguistics* (2003): 114–134.

57. Carla María Guerrón-Montero, "Can't Beat Me Own Drum in Me Own Native Land: Calypso Music and Tourism in the Panamanian Atlantic Coast," *Anthropological Quarterly* 79:4 (2006): 633–663.

58. Guerrón-Montero, "Can't Beat Me Own Drum."

59. Dwight Conquergood, "Health Theatre in a Hmong Refugee Camp: Performance, Communication, and Culture," TDR 32:3 (1988): 174–208.

60. Conquergood, "Health Theatre."

61. Karin Barber, "Text and Performance in Africa," *Oral Tradition* 20:2 (2005): 324.

62. Bauman, *Others' Words,* 2.

63. Ibid.

64. Ibid., 7.

65. Bauman and Ritch, "Informing Performance."

66. Bryant Keith Alexander, "Performing Culture and Cultural Performances in Japan: A Critical (Auto)Ethnographic Travelogue," *Theatre Annual* 55 (2002): 3.

67. Judith Hamera, "Dancing Communities: Performance, Difference, and Connection in the Global City," in *Studies in International Performance,* ed. Janelle Reinelt and Brian Singleton (Houndmills, UK: Palgrave MacMillan, 2011).

68. Hamera, "Dancing Communities," 12.

69. On the ballet world see Helena Wulff, *Ballet Across Borders: Career and Culture in the World of Dancers* (Oxford: Berg, 1998); on the ballroom world see Jonathan S. Marion, *Ballroom: Culture and Costume in Competitive Dance* (Oxford: Berg, 2008); on the salsa world see Jonathan S. Marion, "Contextualizing Content and Conduct in the LA and West Coast Salsa Scenes," in *Salsa World: A Global Dance in Local Contexts,* ed. Sydney Hutchinson. (Philadelphia: Temple University Press, 2013).

70. Sydney Hutchinson, ed., *Salsa World: A Global Dance in Local Contexts* (Philadelphia: Temple University Press, 2013).

71. Arjun Appadurai, *Modernity at Large: Cultural Dimensions of Globalization* (Minneapolis: University of Minnesota Press, 1996).

72. Steven Feld, "Pygmy Pop: A Genealogy of Schizophonic Mimesis" *Yearbook for Traditional Music* (1996): 1–35.

73. Ibid.

74. Ibid.

75. Hancock quoted in Feld, "Pygmy Pop," 5.

MEDIA ANTHROPOLOGY: MEANING, EMBODIMENT, INFRASTRUCTURE, AND ACTIVISM

Bryce Peake, University of Maryland, Baltimore County
bpeake@umbc.edu
http://the-political-ear.com

LEARNING OBJECTIVES

- Describe the history of media anthropology including initial resistance to media as a topic of anthropological study.

- Identify the major categories of media that are studied by anthropologists.

- Explain how anthropologists explore the meaning of media and media experiences including the ways meaning can be shared or contested by individuals and communities.

- Evaluate innovative approaches to media anthropology including autoethnography, photo voice, participatory photography, and fabrication.

- Assess the importance of mechanical and cultural infrastructure for the exchange of ideas.

Media is a word that can be used to describe a set of technologies that connect multiple people at one time to shared content. Media anthropologists study mass communication (broadcast radio and television) and digital media (Internet, streaming, and mobile telephony) with a particular interest in the ways in which media are designed or adapted for use by specific communities or cultural groups. Many research projects focus on **media practices**, the habits or behaviors of the people who produce media, the audiences who interact with media, and everyone in between.

Many classic anthropological concepts are incorporated in studies of media. For example, in her ethnography of Egyptian television soap operas, *Dramas of Nationhood* (2004), Lila Abu-Lughod sought to understand how watching these programs contributed to a shared sense of Egyptian cultural identity. In her ethnography, *Romance on the Global Stage* (2003), Nicole Constable examined how the Internet was transforming ideas about marriage and love by contributing to new kinds of "mail-order bride" economies in which men in the United States could communicate with women thousands of miles away. Utilizing classic ideas about ritual and community life pioneered by Margaret Mead and Bronislaw Malinowski, Tom Boellstorff's book *Coming of Age in Second Life* (2015) explored the ways that people were building realistic communities using virtual reality software like Second Life. Anthropological concepts of ritual, magic, taboo, and organic solidarity can be used effectively to examine the role that media plays in the lives of individuals and communities. Like other specializations in anthropology, studies of media are also organized around a commitment to long-term ethnographic fieldwork and cultural relativism.

This chapter introduces some of the theories, insights, and methodologies of media anthropology. At the heart of media anthropology is the assertion that **media practices**

are not universal. Whether we are discussing how television is viewed, how public relations coordinators negotiate corporate hierarchies, how Facebook statuses are created and circulated, or how cellular towers are built, the local cultural context plays an important role.

A BRIEF HISTORY OF MEDIA ANTHROPOLOGY

Media anthropology has a surprisingly long history. In 1950, Hortense Powdermaker completed the first ethnographic and social scientific study of Hollywood studios. Her book, *Hollywood: The Dream Factory*, preceded by approximately a decade the formation of the academic field of media studies and the theories of mass culture that are popular today. Powdermaker, a student of Franz Boas, was at the forefront of mass communication studies.

Powdermaker's groundbreaking study of media was immediately disavowed by others in the social sciences who believed that media was a topic unworthy of study. "Hollywood as 'Dream Factory' Just Nightmare to Femme Anthropologist," a book review in *Variety* read.[1] A review of the book in the *American Sociological Review* dismissively stated: "The notion, for some time suspect, that previous investigation of a primitive tribe uniquely qualifies a person to study a sophisticated society... is now revealed to be absurd. The anthropological method *here* [in sophisticated society] consists of little more than a series of inane analogies."[2] And so, with the continuation of time, anthropology left the study of mass media to scholars in sociology, political science, and psychology.

Figure 1: Anthropologists have only recently begun ethnographically studying journalists. Here, a Latina journalist working for a conservative, Catholic news outlet interviews a Donald Trump impersonator at a pro-Trump Rally. How, anthropologists might ask, do transnational identities and religion impact perceptions of American politics? Photo by Bryce Peake.

Mass media became a central part of life after World War I and influenced even those cultures that outsiders considered isolated or "primitive." Anthropologists of that era developed two different excuses for avoiding the study of media. The first was the need to distinguish cultural anthropology from journalism. As Elizabeth Bird (2009) wrote, ethnographers were often dismissed as overqualified journalists. Anthropologists who wanted to be seen as scientists (as sociologists often were) wanted to distance themselves as much as possible from mass media, a subject regarded as unserious. Cultural anthropologists also suspected that elitist book and journal editors might dismiss poor ethnographic work as "mere journalism" undeserving of "serious" scholarly consideration. Second, through the 1980s, the discipline of cultural anthropology wanted to distinguish itself from the rising fields of American and British cultural studies, disciplines that had a central interest in interpreting media as "texts" that could reveal cultural values. The cultural studies approach was generally not based on holistic ethnography, which cultural anthropologists continued to see as the defining feature of their profession.[3]

Today, media is a much more mainstream object of analysis in American cultural anthropology and media research also offers a significant career path for many young anthropologists. The company ReD, for example, hires anthropologists as consultants to help telecommunication and media companies innovate new technologies. These anthropologists use social theory and ethnographic methods to help create media technologies for the future. Similarly, major technology companies like Intel and Microsoft employ a number of anthropologists in their artificial intelligence, social media, networked systems, and "Internet of Things" labs. These anthropologists combine corporate work with research, publishing some of the most cutting edge research in the fields of anthropology *and* technology in disciplines like Human Centered Computing. These professionals draw on debates in media anthropology to inform new developments in media technologies, communication and advertising strategies, and culturally-specific programming.

MEANINGFUL MEDIA

What do media anthropologists do to better understand media practices? Media anthropologists typically organize their studies of media in two ways. **First**, they choose a category or type of media: mobile telephones, radio, television, Internet, or others. The choice of media to be studied varies widely between anthropologists. Some media anthropologists work on a topic that crosses multiple technologies (such as radio, which is both broadcast via airwaves and streamed via the internet). Others concern themselves with a particular technology like mobile phones (which play music, allow for phone calls, and support gaming communities) and explore how that single technology contributes to different types of media practices. Some media anthropologists even study the people who study media (such as a study of people who work as advertising researchers, or studies of media scientists in different countries).

Second, media anthropologists locate their ethnographic studies within a particular community. The way media anthropologists

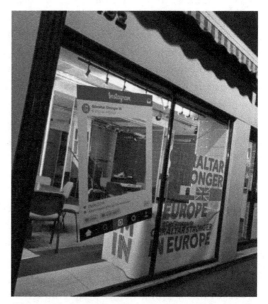

Figure 2: Media anthropologists frequently study the connection between politics and representation. Here, a Brexit information booth sponsored by the Gibraltarian government provides an Instagram frame to pose with. An anthropologist might ask: why do people think Instagram, and photos, are a medium for political participation? Photo by Bryce Peake.

define "community" varies. Some may choose to study a "virtual" community like Tom Boellstorff did in his study of the virtual reality platform Second Life. Others may choose to study how a geographical community, such as a town or a region, uses, adapts, or transforms under the influence of a certain kind of media or technology. This is the approach taken by Lila Abu-Lughod and Nicole Constable in the examples mentioned above. Media anthropologists may also study the ways that mass communication and digital media connect diasporic communities, cultural communities dispersed from their original homelands.

Many media anthropology projects have focused on questions of meaning. **Meaning** refers to the ideas or values that accompany the exchange of information. Historically, some media scientists assumed that the meaning of information was unaffected by its transfer between communities or by the medium of its transfer. In other words, they believed that information would be interpreted the same way regardless of how it was communicated, or who was receiving it. Anthropologists have demonstrated that the reality is much more complex. In her book *Dramas of Nationhood*, Lila Abu-Lughod asked questions about how nationally televised Egyptian soap operas were interpreted by those who watched them. Her research revealed several important insights. First, what soap opera directors and writers *intended* for a television show to mean was not necessarily what communities of watchers *interpreted* the show to mean. Simply put, producers cannot wholly control meaning or the value(s) that will be identified by a group of watchers. Second, different media give different messages or meanings. If the same message is broadcast on radio and television, the histories and cultural associations of these two technologies affects the meaning of the message being conveyed. Televised soap operas were interpreted quite differently, for instance, than the spoken poetry Abu-Lughod had studied in her previous research in Egypt. Third, Abu-Lughod demonstrated that **there is no universal way of consuming media; media consumption is bound to culture**. How Egyptian women participate in listening to or watching soap operas together, the practices of who sits where, of what can or cannot be eaten during a show, or of when a show might be aired, is all bound to the norms and values of the community. These three assertions about meaning are broadly applicable to all cultures and have set the agenda for most academic and professional research in media anthropology.

Unlike other academic fields that study media and meaning, **media anthropologists focus on how producers and audiences share or contest different types of meaning**. Ethnographies by media anthropologists typically focus on the ways producers of media assume, or seek to stimulate, a particular set of feelings in audiences, and how audiences can give feedback to media producers. In his ethnography of advertising agencies in Sri Lanka, for example, Steven Kemper (2001) observed that "when they are able, advertising agencies hire local staff" because they can "think like," and thus sell to, local audiences.[4] In the process, local advertising staff become the audiences they imagine others to be and their work helps to define a new class of consumers who purchase globalized media products. Media production and consumption are interconnected, one creating the conditions for the other.

Many media anthropology projects have focused on mass communication, the process of sending a message to many people in a way that allows the sender complete control over the content of a message—although, as described above, not control over the meaning. This is the definition of **mass communication:** one-to-many communication that privileges the sender and/or owner of the technology that transmits the media. Such a description is not without its challenges. As Francisco Osorio (2005) argues, talking drums like those used in New Guinea not only fit the definition of mass communication—a message sent from one to many that privileges the sender—the talking drums example also reveals the ways in which there is an implicit prioritization of electricity in media anthropology, an assumption that mass communication involves electrical technology. This is ethnocentric given the uneven distribution of electrical infrastructure. Dominic Boyer, an anthropologist who has written ethnographies about both energy infrastructures like electricity and German journalists writing international news, proposed that we move from media anthropology to an "anthropology of mediation."[5] Rather than use a universal definition of what counts as media to the anthropologist, Boyer's term **anthropology of mediation** focuses on the way images, speech, people, and things become socially significant or meaningful as they are communicated. The focus is shifted away from the technology itself, a controversial approach that some have criticized for transforming media anthropology into an "anthropology of everything."

As a result of this proposal for an anthropology of mediation, some anthropologists have started to study the physical human senses that make meaningful interactions with media possible. As Charles Hirschkind (2006) argues for example, the power of a cassette tape sermon in Egypt in "lies not simply in its capacity to disseminate ideas or instill religious ideologies but in its effect on the human sensorium… the soundscape produced through the circulation of this medium animates and sustains a substrate of sensory knowledges and embodied aptitudes."[6] Hirschkind is suggesting that the feeling that Muslim listeners experience while listening to the sermons—rather than the precise meaning or value of the information— is more significant for understanding the appeal of these tapes. This is an example of research that focuses on mediation rather than simply assessing the meaning of the information transferred.

Sensory approaches to mediation present some methodological dilemmas. When media anthropologists study meaning ethnographically they can ask audiences what a particular example of media *means* or what a person finds *meaningful* about it. Anthropologists studying the sensory dimensions of mediation do not have direct access to how audiences *feel* media. We can ask how audiences feel, but describing a feeling involves translating physical sensation into language, a difficult process. To get around this problem, ethnographers of mediation have used innovative approaches to participant-observation that include techniques from psychoanalysis,[7] depth interviews that closely analyze how audiences create meaning rather than what meaning is,[8] and autoethnographic approaches in which the anthropologist explores his or her own personal experiences. These research techniques are used to reduce the gap between what people experience and what they can describe.[9]

Figure 3: Media anthropologists frequently ask how transnational media create a sense of community and change the ways people engage with their environments. At this Indian restaurant on the Mediterranean island of Gozo, restaurant owners have removed a street sign and mounted a TV in its place in order to show Italy playing in a European Union Football Association Cup Match. A family sits and eats. As Mario, the man on the end, explained "It was the only seat to watch the match left in the entire [village]… I would be the only person on the island that didn't [watch it] if I wasn't here." Photo by Bryce Peake.

Debates about the significance of media, mediation, meaning and the senses have occurred primarily in the context of studies of mass communication because mass communication technologies like broadcast radio, television, and cinema are the most globally available. While people in Europe and the United States might speak of the death of older "legacy" media like radio and VHS tapes, these mediums play crucial roles in the lives of peoples in other places. Lynn Stephen (2012), for example, describes how the takeover of a local radio station by a group of women protesters was crucial to their efforts to organize around human rights issues in Oaxaca, Mexico.[10] Brian Larkin (2008) has discussed the economic importance of pirated VHS tapes of recent films in Nigeria, a country in which gross domestic product cannot be easily calculated due to the size of various shadow economies.

While mass communication is a form of one-to-many communication typically broadcast on widely available channels, digital media is a much more personalized many-to-many communication that involves the use of digital signals. In her ethnography of LGBT youth in rural America, Mary Gray (2009) argued that the Internet's more closely controlled access points allowed queer youth to carve out online spaces for their emerging identities. The importance of these online spaces for developing personal identity also meant that it was difficult to distinguish between "online" and "offline" personas. Gray took a meaning-focused approach to understand the ways in which rural LGBT youth create identities and feelings of belongingness in concealed online worlds. Jeffrey Juris (2008) has argued that the Internet interactions allowed anti-corporate, anti-globalization activists in Spain, Indonesia, and the United States to *feel* the threat represented by the Group of Eight summit (a meeting of eight of the largest world economies). These feelings generated a sense of solidarity that was not reducible to language. Both these projects demonstrate the relationship between meaning and feeling that is a part of mass communication.

If digital media has opened up a space for us to think critically about the transformation of mass media and people's relationships with it, so too has digital media opened up new career paths for anthropologists. Increasingly, media anthropologists are taking key positions in technology, advertising, public relations, and broadcasting industries. Dawn Nafus, an ethnographer who works and conducts research in open-source software communities, has led multiple user experience research projects at Intel Labs. Her time is divided between writing academic publications on the anthropology of emerging technologies and doing user testing for Intel's latest innovations in computing and wearable technology.[11]

WHAT MAKES MEDIA POSSIBLE?

Since the 1990s, anthropologists have successfully studied a range of mass communication and digital media, but it is only recently that anthropologists have started studying the technologies that make these forms of connection possible. Broadly speaking, infrastructures are the material technological networks that allow for the exchange of goods, ideas, waste, people, power and finance over space. When used to refer to media, infrastructure includes the pipes, concrete, wires, people, values, electricity, software protocols and other technologies that allow for the movement of information. Brian Larkin (2008), a media anthropologist working in Nigeria, noted that the geographical location of cinemas in the city of Kano was based on the

Figure 4: In Madrid, cables for internet, telephony, and television run alongside the train tracks. Historically, train routes have been principle to media infrastructure. How, media anthropologists ask, does media infrastructure change our understanding and relationship to travel? Photo by Bryce Peake.

colonial requirement that there be a 440 yard buffer zone between white and black populations. This requirement controlled the ways that electrical grids and transportation routes were developed. In this way, various entangled infrastructures are implicated in the forms of taboo, desire, and fantasy shared by members of a society in locations like the movie theater. Similarly, in his ethnography of Brazil's first telecommunication engineers, Gerald Lombardi (1999) describes how engineers "spoke in reverent tones about the selfless dedication of … fellow workers as they fought … to keep Brazil at the forefront of telephonic progress."[12] "Telephonic progress" via infrastructure was an ideal of the Brazilian state and its workers because it was considered "modern" and made Brazil competitive in the eyes of global spectators. It was not phones that made Brazilian engineers feel or describe themselves as modern, but the capacity for making telephony possible.

There are two types of media infrastructure: mechanical infrastructure and cultural infrastructure. **Mechanical Infrastructure** includes the apparatuses that bring networks of technology into existence. **Cultural Infrastructure** refers to the values and beliefs of communities, states, and/or societies that make the imagining of a particular type of network possible. In the foreword to an ethnography on India and the rise of historical archives, Nicholas Dirks (2002) captures the sense of a cultural infrastructure perfectly when he describes how archives *function*, that is how the archive does ideological work, in producing *and* preserving ideas about Indian nationalism. It was the belief in nationalism that made the colonial archive possible as a container of various media—letters and notes, newspapers and telegraphs believed to define the Indian state.

Complicating the study of mechanical infrastructure is the fact that this infrastructure consists of the same technology it uses to run. Information systems, for instance are both made of and run by computers. Typically, an infrastructure is different from a technology. A road is the infrastructure for a car; a pipe is the infrastructure for oil. As Graham and Marvin (2001) argue about the computer, computing is made possible by the electricity that powers the computer, the system of telematics that allow computers to transmit and receive information, and software protocols that delimit a computer's uses. The electricity, the telematics, and the software protocols all rely on computing. What may distinguish the twenty-first century is its reliance on computing as the infrastructure of everything, from oil production to data storage, electricity management to the production of concrete.

For media anthropologists, the ways in which media and communication infrastructure organize everyday life are significant. Mechanical infrastructure affects not only the engineers and bureaucrats who execute and plan projects, but also the millions of people who rely on information exchanged through the infrastructure, drive vehicles through the infrastructure, and whose property rights are often usurped by the construction of infrastructure. At the same time, cultural infrastructure is also important. As Christian Sandvig (2012) describes in his ethnography of building indig-

Figure 5: Media anthropologists frequently use unique methods to better understand how technology users make sense of their use habits. Here, anthropologists with Intel Labs use a pile and sort approach, asking the user to write down meaningful types of data on sticky notes they will then organize. Photo by Bryce Peake.

enous Internet infrastructure on the Santa Ysabel Native American Reservation, anthropological studies of media and communication infrastructure must weave together considerations of both kinds of infrastructure in order to understand how these infrastructures are transformed by cultural values, technological standards, legal regulations, and scientific and engineering techniques. Some anthropologists work professionally designing media technologies or consulting with engineers, bureaucrats, and communities on the construction of media infrastructures. Cathy Baldwin, for example, is an anthropologist at the World Resources Institute Urban Development and Mobility Project. She is known for her research on civil engineering and community participation. Working with communities to maximize various forms of access, Baldwin's career is based on the belief that physical and natural environments should strengthen a community's capacity to stay resilient when afflicted by human-created and natural disasters—particularly climate change.

Practicing Anthropologist: Cathy Baldwin

Cathy Baldwin is an interdisciplinary anthropologist, writer, musician, and consultant who has done anthropological research on city and urban infrastructure, environment, and health.

How did you bring your anthropological training into consultancy work?

My objective was always to be an applied researcher working in policy or think tanks, but I didn't think about how until I graduated. During my doctoral fieldwork, I gave regular feedback to a government minister (Member of Parliament in my fieldwork town) who was working on a program to promote an inclusive British identity. After graduating I did some applied research and a book chapter for a think tank at Oslo University on how non-governmental organizations (NGOs) used information and computing technologies (ICTs) to empower poor communities in developing countries.

What types of collaborators does an anthropologist studying infrastructure encounter?

When doing impact assessments in the infrastructure sector, you work with distressed community members worried about uncertain change, so it's crucial to have a sympathetic, diplomatic manner in order to talk effectively with them. You also need to be able to find ways of communicating social issues to engineers. This can be challenging as it is often unfamiliar territory and beyond their concerns. The most effective solution is to be able to present community concern as it might apply to them and their family members. For instance, "How would your mum feel if...." The policy world is full of people who like findings summarized in short bullet points in non-anthropological language. By the time you are ready with your material to do so, any theory used to underpin an argument that leads to a practical, implementable recommendation has been amalgamated into a point expressed in everyday language. It is still possible to use anthropological ideas at this stage, but they have to be grounded in practical action.

If you could choose one substantial contribution anthropologists can make to both the development and study of city infrastructure, what would it be?

Social anthropologists are well equipped to foresee, understand, and analyze how dynamic social change processes springing from the physical, biophysical or industrial landscape affect communities, and to study how people engage with technologies. These are important skills that can guide the design of projects or structures, and inform strategies adopted to manage the good and bad effects. While I see my colleagues mapping economic, environmental, or physical changes and processes, I can insert the social aspect.

What advice do you have for current anthropology students interested in working on infrastructure, and perhaps media and communications infrastructure, in the future?

Diversify your skill set as much as possible beyond just ethnographic methods as they are just one small option outside academia. Intern at the World Bank in one of its urban programs, or a large engineering consultancy, or an urban development think tank or policy organization. Media and communications infrastructure is a totally separate topic, but there are some urban firms that look at telecommunications infrastructure as well as standard city systems.

ICT4D, or information and communications technologies for development, is an interesting branch of international development where there are studies and NGOs working on practical projects with communities and anthropological input is valued. Also some of the ICT or technology companies such as Microsoft and Intel employ anthropologists to do consumer studies of how people use media and technologies. Genevieve Bell is the most famous employee of Intel, as their in-house corporate anthropologist.

With all infrastructure topics, anthropologists inevitably analyze how people interact with their structures, use infrastructure, what its social and cultural effects are, what values and assumptions inform its design etc. You need to be good at thinking in practical terms about the social and community consequences of hard structures. Understanding dynamic social change processes is also an asset, and how much change is caused by structural as opposed to subjective factors.

I would say that working as an anthropologist outside academia can be very lonely unless you are in a consulting firm that has a special focus on ethnographic methods. At both the civil engineering firm and think tank, I was the only one with my skillset and missed having others to learn directly from. That said, I have enjoyed becoming friendly with economists, civil and environmental engineers, environmental scientists, public health specialists and others. The field attracts nice people with the practical skills to implement things, which I prefer to academic anthropology.

Interview by Bryce Peake

PARTICIPATORY MEDIA AND MEDIA ACTIVISM IN ANTHROPOLOGY

The resurgence of media anthropology in the 1980s and 1990s was heralded by experiments, research, and debates in visual anthropology and ethnographic film surrounding **indigenous media,** media produced by and for indigenous communities often outside of the mainstream commercial market. Portable recording technologies, televisual production, and copy-making technologies made it possible for local communities to use media for cultural expression. People like Eric Michaels (1987), Faye Ginsburg (1991), and Terry Turner (Crocker 1991) used new technologies to help indigenous communities produce media about their local cultures, and the various environmental, legislative, social, and cultural threats they faced. In the Kayapo Video Project, anthropologist Terence Turner understood his role as empowering local Kayapo leaders, who then compiled a compre-

Figure 6: Maltese film makers make a short film celebrating the history of their village. Where indigenous media projects were initially crucial to introducing new technologies to cultural communities, today many communities have robust media infrastructure and channels. Media anthropologists frequently ask how these outlets influence and are influenced by global media industries. Photo by Bryce Peake.

hensive video archive of Kayapo culture, including ceremonies, oral history, ecological knowledge, and mythology, recounted by older members of the community whose knowledge would disappear with their death. As Turner wrote, "in addition to the uses of video self-documentation for education and as a repository of cultural knowledge against losses from death and acculturation, many Kayapo see video as a means of reaching out to non-Kayapo, presenting their culture and way of life in a form that others can understand, respect, and support. They see this as an essential part of their struggle to sustain and defend their society and environment."[13]

For anthropologists, projects like the Kayapo video sparked a debate: do Western inventions like the movie camera endanger or replace indigenous forms of storytelling, or do they empower new forms of cultural creativity and experimentation? How, anthropologists on one side of the debate argued, could technologies used to create the Disney film Fantasia, the American television show Dallas, and other Western televisual and cinematic stories possibly create the complex narrative forms traditionally used for storytelling in other cultures? On the other side of the debate, media anthropologists asked why one would assume that these technologies could not be used in new ways?

Faye Ginsburg is more identified with this debate than any other media anthropologist. Ginsburg described her position in the 1990s: "I am concerned less with the usual focus on the formal qualities of film as text and more with the cultural mediations that occur through film and video works."[14] For Ginsburg, indigenous media constitutes a means for "reproducing and transforming cultural identity among people who have experienced massive political, geographic, and economic disruption," and her work among Australian aboriginal and indigenous media-makers and documentary collaborators is focused on exactly those goals.[15] Ginsburg works with her research subjects on media projects, using media-making as a form

Figure 7: A student in the Off the Beaten Track fieldschool videotapes her edits of an audio ethnography she made with café workers at a local Gozitan cafe. Photo by Bryce Peake.

of fieldwork. The result is an ethnography of the process of media creation and collaboration. Rather than asking how indigenous peoples interpret representations, Ginsburg's work examines how indigenous media producers *create* representations of their and other cultures. Her fieldwork addresses the debate about the limits of Western media technologies, while also pushing video-based media in new directions. Both Ginsburg and Turner's work can be seen as an argument *against* anthropologists who suggest that the use of new technologies to capture indigenous stories or concerns constitutes a form of imperialism. These anthropologists, Turner suggested, hold an outdated and static perception of indigenous groups. Rather than assuming that maintaining traditional modes of communication or storytelling is the only way to safeguard cultural traditions, he suggested that new media technologies can aid indigenous activists in transmitting cultural beliefs into the future.

In addition to documenting traditional cultural beliefs, media technologies can be absorbed into communities in ways that strengthen them. Zeinabu Davis' videowork on Yoruba trance rituals, for example, demonstrates the way in which the meaning of media is not set by the technologies used to create it. For the Yoruba ritual actors who were the subjects of the film, and who watched the film following its production, portable video technologies increased the *ache* (Yoruba for "power of realization") of both trance states and Yoruba communities. According to Yoruba spiritual ideas, images have a presence and can bringing things closer together. The actors believed the video would help grow and sustain the Yoruba community by bringing viewers closer to the spiritual dimensions of the ritual. Meaning, in other words, was not the only source of *meaningfulness* for Davis and her Yoruba partners.

Practicing Anthropologist: Kyle Jones

Kyle Jones is an anthropologist who completed his fieldwork with hip-hop artists in Peru and now works in human-centered design. Below, Kyle talks about applied anthropology and experimental methods:

Your ethnographic fieldwork on hip hop in Peru was supported by the Wenner-Gren Foundation for Anthropology, with some funds dedicated to the *applied* dimensions of your project. What is applied anthropology, and how did it figure into your project?

To me, applied anthropology is about taking the next step in the research process to translate what you've learned into other domains of practice, often toward some kind of solution to a problem someone faces. The Wenner-Gren Foundation's Osmundsen Initiative urges anthropologists to think about the broader social concerns and contributions of their research projects. For my project, I had learned that one of the most important activities for the young people I was working with was putting on various kinds of events, such as concerts or workshops. Despite their obvious passion for hip-hop and motivation to produce events, a lack of funds (among other factors) nearly always proved a significant barrier to their efforts. So what I did was try to support those efforts by facilitating the production of events among each of the three groups I was researching. Led by these different groups in different cities, these events took many different forms, from a series of relatively small concerts, workshops, and competitions spread out over two weeks to large all-day festivals in city plazas. Methodologically, these events dovetailed with the other collaborative and participant-driven methods I was using, and also led to new opportunities for exploring my research topics.

In your ethnographic work, you use some very different methods: photovoice and participatory photography. What are these, and how do you relate them to applied anthropology?

Photovoice is a method used across scholarly, policy, and many other types of research that puts cameras into people's hands so they can make their own representations of their lives and the activities related to your research questions. I similarly engaged in collaborative media production, which included such things as helping to film video clips, playing and recording music, taking promotional photos, promoting and producing events, and designing and circulating imagery. In these things, I played a supporting role, using what resources I had to facilitate the projects of the groups I was researching. These methods are participatory in the sense that they encourage collaborators to get involved in the research process and help bring questions about power in research interactions to the fore. From an epistemological standpoint, these methods might be better termed participant-driven because of how they enable individuals to actively shape the direction of the research through the conscious creation of media (i.e. the research data itself). These methods were also particularly useful in doing research across locales because they can be done remotely via the internet; I could keep up conversations and data creation-collection even when I wasn't in the same city as my interlocutors, including when I was back home in the U.S.

While I did not view them as applied at first because of how they developed in the context of my graduate training, I now see them as a valuable part of my applied/practicing toolkit. Using the media that my collaborators themselves created is a powerful way to tell a story no matter the context of the work. They also entail that element of pushing your work into new domains of practice and problem-solving, while also prompting you to think reflexively. These kinds of methods help in recognizing the power and privileges that you bring as a researcher, but then also entail thinking through how you can translate the resources those things confer (expertise, time, technology, social connections, etc.) to support the efforts of your interlocutors on their own terms.

Research on indigenous media has primarily focused on cultural information and entertainment, but anthropologists have also explored the capacity of indigenous media to contribute to the production of localized science. The Nura Gili Indigenous Programs Unit at the University of New South Wales, for example, has designed software that allows indigenous and Aboriginal communities in Australia to share culture knowledge about astronomy.[16] For many of these groups, astronomic knowledge includes using the sun, moon, and stars for predictive purposes in navigation, time-keeping, seasonal calendars, and food practices. The stars in particular inform sacred law, customs and social structure, such as totem and kinship status and marriage. This knowledge was traditionally passed down through artistic and poetic practices that have since disappeared from some communities. The researchers in the Nura Gili Indigenous Programs Unit are harnessing the power of Microsoft's WorldWide telescope and Rich Interactive Narrative technology to help new generations "reclaim" forms of indigenous knowledge production from archival records and contemporary astronomical data in collaboration with community elders. For these scholars, the project is not simply one of "giving back" to the community; rather, they recognize that indigenous astronomical traditions are underpinned by a philosophy of knowledge that enables a different understanding of how humans relate to the natural world. This knowledge can produce new forms of intercultural understandings about climate and environmental change.

For many of these participatory media projects, the stakes are highly politicized. For those anthropologists working in Australia, Africa, and South America, legacies of colonial violence are still omnipresent. How can anthropologists use their research to not only understand culture, but to also mitigate some of the violent residue of inequality that came from colonialism? This is a key question that undergirds much of this participatory media research. Along with research that addresses that question comes a host of ethical considerations: how should media recordings be stored, who should control the intellectual property developed through media technologies, and who defines the project and how it will be developed. These may seem as though they are only practical questions, but for many media anthropologists engaged in participatory methods they are also research questions. They are also questions about power and fairness. By posing and answering these questions in their projects, media anthropologists doing participatory media methods have contributed to the development of new approaches to ethnography.

Digital media poses several additional ethical issues particularly in terms of protecting the anonymity of research subjects. In her work on the hackers and trolls turned political collective Anonymous, Gabriella Coleman (2014) wrote about the fact that much of her research depended on the anonymity of the hackers with whom she worked. How, she asked, should an anthropologist balance the hacker collective's need for anonymity while still confirming the validity or real identities of research subjects. In the process of researching groups like Anonymous, how should anthropologists try to balance the positive impact of the privacy activism this group engages in with the misogynist, anti-political antics of some members of the group? In other words, what does it mean

for a researcher to "call out" Anonymous on its shortcomings while still protecting the true identities of its members? Similarly, in her ethnography of online dating in Australia, Susan Frohlick found herself needing to "dis-identify" daters who had written particularly offensive or poorly constructed dating profiles. So poorly built, or "uniquely horrible," were these profiles that to describe them as her interviewees did would violate the authors' right to anonymity.[17] Frohlick argued that exploring themes of masculinity and dating were more important to the research than personally identifying individuals with bad dating profiles.

Figure 8: A Gozitan man shoots video and photos inside his village church to send to his parents who now live in Toronto. Media anthropologists are increasingly interested in how the mediation of spirituality is requiring new forms of theological thinking in religious communities. Photo by Bryce Peake.

Ethnographers working with digital and social media in particular, have devised multiple strategies for anonymizing participatory media subjects. Annette Markham (2012), for example, has developed the strategy of **fabrication**. Writing ethnographic work about child sexuality and queer bloggers, Markham urges ethnographers to take the essence of what is being said by people, to combine or rearrange it, and fabricate an ethnographic account that demonstrates the points most relevant for the research. Doing so, she argues, is not new; it is common practice to use direct quotes from research subjects in ethnography even though the quote may be off by a few words because it was heard while spinning pots or cooking or participating in some other activity. Such a practice poses many other ethical questions, and it is this ethical conundrum that Markham says is most important for thinking through methodological and ethical issues in media anthropology.[18] While this fabrication approach is by no means perfect, and is open to criticism, it demonstrates the necessity of ethical considerations when conducting methodological experimentation in media anthropology.

CONCLUSION

Media anthropologists are concerned with many of the classic subjects of cultural anthropology: kinship, religion, mythology, identity, and the transmission of cultural meaning. How, for instance, does media allow people create and maintain kinship ties across large geographical distances? How are religious beliefs transformed as they are communicated through platforms like television and the Internet? How does media contribute to the development of a sense of self or group identities? On the Mediterranean island of Gozo, for example, cellular phones have allowed distant relatives in North America to remain part of the community by participating in the yearly celebrations of village saints. Local Catholic priests in Greece have been forced to consider the spiritual force of religious icons as they are transformed from a statue honored in-person during religious ceremonies into mediated images people see from afar.[19] If the Virgin Mary appears to be weeping in a video, but the statue shows no effect, does it count as a miracle? Rather than answer this question, media anthropologists are interested in why people are concerned with it in the first place.

While class anthropological subjects remain important, media anthropologists are also engaging with new problems and debates while interacting with other academic disciplines such as Media and Communication Studies, Digital Sociology, and New Media Art. For instance, media anthropologists question the assumption that there is a universal media psychology that predicts the ways that people will interpret media. They have pointed out that the impact social media has on individuals is a function of culture, not just political economic conditions.[20] Media anthropologists have even engaged with questions about how basic human ideas about beauty or the passage of time translate into mediums like film and radio.[21]

While grappling with a range of old and new themes, one thing continues to separate media anthropologists from other media scholars: a commitment to long-term, participant-observation based fieldwork. Media anthropologists push the boundaries of what counts as ethnographic research and academic writing, but they continue to rely on deep relationships with people and holistic consideration of the full range of media practices found around the world.

DISCUSSION QUESTIONS

1. What is the difference between interpreting and producing media? How have anthropologists studied these processes differently?
2. How do anthropologists study media consumption, media production, and infrastructure? What different types of approaches did the anthropologists in this chapter use? What sets media anthropologists apart from other types of media scholars?
3. Where do media anthropologists work? What types of topics do they focus on?

GLOSSARY

Cultural infrastructure: the values and beliefs of communities, states, and/or societies that make the imagining of a particular type of network possible

Fabrication: a technique for reporting on research data that involves mixing information provided by various people into a narrative account that demonstrates the point of focus for researchers.

Indigenous media: media produced by and for indigenous communities often outside of the commercial mainstream.

Mass communication: one-to-many communication that privileges the sender and/or owner of the technology that transmits the media

Media: a word that used to describe a set of technologies that connect multiple people at one time to shared content.

Media practices: the habits or behaviors of the people who produce media, the audiences who interact with media, and everyone in between.

Mechanical infrastructure is the apparatuses that bring networks of technology into existence.

Photovoice: a research method that puts cameras into people's hands so they can make their own representations of their lives and the activities.

ABOUT THE AUTHOR

Bryce Peake is an assistant professor of Media & Communication Studies and an affiliate faculty member in Gender + Women's Studies at the University of Maryland, Baltimore County. His current research focuses on masculinity, media, and science in the post-World War II British Mediterranean spaces of Gibraltar and Gozo. He has also published multimodal projects on race in the United States, and been recognized by the American Anthropological Association for his ethnographic photography. Bryce currently runs the *Anthropology, Mediated* workshop on the island of Gozo, a 15 day ethnographic media fieldschool for undergraduates. Prior to arriving at UMBC, Bryce was a Julie & Rocky Dixon Fellow in Graduate Innovation, and worked with anthropologists at Intel Labs to develop a data-tracking application for users living with Tinnitus.

BIBLIOGRAPHY

Abu-Lughod, Lila. *Dramas of Nationhood: The Politics of Television in Europe.* (Chicago: University of Chicago Press, 2004).

Auslander, Mark. "Objects of Kinship." *Transition* 122 (2017): 206–216.

Bird, Elizabeth, ed. *The Anthropology of News and Journalism: Global Perspectives* (Bloomington: Indiana University Press, 2009).

Boellstorff, Tom. *Coming of Age in Second Life: An Anthropologist Explores the Virtually Human* (Princeton, NJ: Princeton University Press, 2015).

Coleman, Gabriella. *Hacker, Hoaxer, Whistleblower, Spy: The Many Faces of Anonymous.* (New York: Verso, 2014).

Constable, Nicole. *Romance on a Global Stage: Pen Pals, Virtual Ethnography, and "Mail Order" Marriages.* (Berkeley: University of California Press, 2003).

Crocker, William H. "Review of The Kayapo; The Kayapo: Out of the Forest." *American Anthropologist* 93 no. 2 (1991): 514–516.

Dirks, Nicholas. "Annals of the Archive: Ethnographic Notes on the Sources of History." In *From the Margins: Historical Anthropology and Its Futures*. Edited by Brian Keith Axel, 47–65. (Durham: Duke University Press, 2002).

Frohlick, Susan. "Fluid Exchanges: The Negotiation of Intimacy between Tourist Women and Local Men in a Transnational Town in Caribbean Costa Rica." *City & Society* 19 no. 1(2007): 139–168.

———"I'm More Sexy Here: Erotic Subjectivities of Female Tourists in the Sexual Paradise of the Costa Rican Caribbean." In *Gendered Mobilities*. Edited by Tanu Priya Uteng and Tim Cresswell, 199–223. (New York: Ashgate, 2008).

Gershon, Ilana. *The Breakup 2.0: Disconnecting over New Media*. (Ithaca: Cornell University Press, 2012).

Ginsburg, Faye. "Indigenous Media: Faustian Contract or Global Village?" *Cultural Anthropology* 6 no. 1 (1991): 92–112.

Graham, Steve, and Simon Marvin. *Splintering Urbanism: Networked Infrastructures, Technological Mobilities and the Urban Condition*. (New York: Routledge, 2001).

Gray, Mary L. *Out in the Country: Youth, Media, and Queer Visibility in Rural America*. (New York: New York University Press, 2009).

Hirschkind, Charles. *The Ethical Soundscape: Cassette Sermons and Islamic Counterpublics*. (New York: Columbia University Press, 2006).

Juris, Jeffrey S. "Performing Politics Image, Embodiment, and Affective Solidarity during Anti-Corporate Globalization Protests." *Ethnography* 9 no. 1(2008): 61–97.

Kemper, Steven. *Buying and Believing: Sri Lankan Advertising and Consumers in a Transnational World*. (Chicago: University Of Chicago Press, 2001).

Larkin, Brian. *Signal and Noise: Media, Infrastructure, and Urban Culture in Nigeria*. Duke University Press Books, 2008).

Lombardi, Gerald S. *Computer Networks, Social Networks and the Future of Brazil*. (New York University, Graduate School of Arts and Science, 1999).

Markham, Annette. "Fabrication as Ethical Practice." *Information, Communication & Society* 15 no. 3 (2012): 334–353.

Michaels, E. *For a Cultural Future: Francis Jupurrurla Makes TV at Yuendumu*. (Australia: Art and Culture Monographs, 1987).

Osorio, Francisco. "Proposal for Anthropology of Mass Media." In *Media Anthropology*. Edited by Eric Rothenbuhler and Mihai Coman, 36–45. (Thousand Oaks, CA: SAGE Publications, 2005.

Peake, Bryce. "Gozo, Mediated." Forthcoming in *OmerTaa: A Journal of Applied Anthropology* (2018): 670–675.

Pidduck, Julianne. "Queer Kinship and Ambivalence: Video Autoethnographies by Jean Carlomusto and Richard Fung." *GLQ: A Journal of Lesbian and Gay Studies* 15 no. 3 (2009): 441–468.

Powdermaker, Hortense. Hollywood: The Dream Factory. (London: Secker and Warburg, 1950).

Sandvig, Christian. "Connection at Ewiiaapaayp Mountain: Indigenous Internet Infrastructure." In *Race after the Internet*. Edited by Lisa Nakamura, 168–200. (New York: Routledge, 2012).

Stephen, Lynn. "Community and Indigenous Radio in Oaxaca: Testimony and Participatory Democracy." In *Radio Fields: Anthropology and Wireless Sound in the 21st Century*. Edited by Lucas Bessire (New York: NYU Press, 2012).

Turner, Terence. *The Kayapo Video Project: A Progress Report*. Unpublished Manuscript, 1990.

Wyatt, Geoffrey. "Dreamtime Astronomy: Development of a New Indigenous Program at Sydney Observatory." *Journal of Astronomical History and Heritage* 17 no. 2 (2014): 195–204.

NOTES

1. The *Variety* headline is cited in Robert Bierstedt, "A Review of Hollywood-The Dream Factory: An Anthropologist Looks at the Movie-Makers," *American Sociological Review* 17 (1951): 124-125.

2. Ibid.

3. Jon Mitchell, *Ambivalent Europeans: Ritual, Memory and the Public Sphere in Malta* (New York: Routledge, 2001), 5.

4. Steven Kemper, *Buying and Believing: Sri Lankan Advertising and Consumers in a Transnational World* (Chicago: University Of Chicago Press, 2001), 27.

5. Dominic Boyer, "From Media Anthropology to the Anthropology of Mediation," in the *SAGE Handbook of Social Anthropology*, ed. Jon Mitchell et al., 411–422 (London: Sage, 2012).

6. Charles Hirschkind, *The Ethical Soundscape: Cassette Sermons and Islamic Counterpublics* (New York: Columbia University Press, 2009), 2.

7. Iain Edgar, *A Guide to Imagework: Imagination-Based Research Methods* (London: Routledge, 2004).

8. Charles Hirschkind, *The Ethical Soundscape: Cassette Sermons and Islamic Counterpublics*.

9. Julianne Pidduck, "Queer Kinship and Ambivalence: Video Autoethnographies by Jean Carlomusto and Richard Fung," GLQ: A Journal of Lesbian and Gay Studies 15 no. 3 (2009): 441–468.

10. Lynn Stephen, "Community and Indigenous Radio in Oaxaca: Testimony and Participatory Democracy," in *Radio Fields: Anthropology and Wireless Sound in the Twenty-First Century*, ed. Lucas Bessire (New York: New York University Press, 2012).

11. See Dawn Nafus, "Patches Don"t Have Gender:' What Is Not Open in Open Source Software," *New Media & Society* 14 no. 4 (2012): 669–683; and Dawn Nafus and Jamie Sherman, "Big Data, Big Questions| This One Does Not Go Up To 11: The Quantified Self Movement as an Alternative Big Data Practice," *International Journal of Communication* 8(2014): 11.

12. Gerald S. Lombardi, *Computer Networks, Social Networks and the Future of Brazil*. PhD dissertation, New York University, 1999), 21.

13. Terence Turner, The Kayapo Video Project: A Progress Report. Unpublished Manuscript (Turner 1990), 1.

14. Faye Ginsburg, "Indigenous Media: Faustian Contract or Global Village?" *Cultural Anthropology* 6(1): 94.

15. Ibid.

16. Geoffrey Wyatt, "Dreamtime Astronomy: Development of a New Indigenous Program at Sydney Observatory," *Journal of Astronomical History and Heritage* 17 no. 2 (2014): 195–204.

17. See Susan Frohlick, "Fluid Exchanges: The Negotiation of Intimacy between Tourist Women and Local Men in a Transnational Town in Caribbean Costa Rica." *City & Society* 19 no. 1(2007): 139–168 and Susan Frohlick "I'm More Sexy Here: Erotic Subjectivities of Female Toursits in the Sexual Paradise of the Costa Rican Caribbean," in *Gendered Mobilities*, ed. Tanu Priya Uteng and Tim Cresswell, 199–223 (New York: Ashgate, 2008).

18. Annette Markham, "Fabrication as Ethical Practice," *Information, Communication & Society* 15 no. 3 (2012): 334–353.

19. See the forthcoming 2018 article by Bryce Peake, "Gozo, Mediated" *Omertaa: A Journal of Applied Anthropology*: 670–675.

20. Ilana Gershon, *The Breakup 2.0: Disconnecting over New Media* (Ithaca: Cornell University Press, 2012).

21. Mark Auslander, "Objects of Kinship," *Transition* 122 (2017): 206–216.

HEALTH AND MEDICINE

Sashur Henninger-Rener, University of LaVerne and the Los Angeles Community College District
sashur.henninger@gmail.com

LEARNING OBJECTIVES

- Define the biocultural perspective and provide examples of how interactions between biology and culture have affected human biology.

- Identify four ethno-etiologies (personalistic, naturalistic, emotionalistic, and biomedical) and describe how each differs in explaining the root cause of illness.

- Explain the significance of faith in healing.

- Examine the relationship between mental health and cultural factors, including stigma, that affect the way people with mental health conditions are perceived.

- Discuss examples of culture-bound syndromes.

- Evaluate the positive and negative effects of biomedical technologies.

What does it mean to be "healthy"? It may seem odd to ask the question, but health is not a universal concept and each culture values different aspects of well-being. At the most basic level, health may be perceived as surviving each day with enough food and water, while other definitions of health may be based on being free of diseases or emotional troubles. Complicating things further is the fact that that each culture has a different causal explanation for disease. For instance, in ancient Greece health was considered to be the product of unbalanced humors or bodily fluids. The four humors included black bile, phlegm, yellow bile, and blood. The ancient Greeks believed that interactions among these humors explained differences not only in health, but in age, gender, and general disposition. Various things could influence the balance of the humors in a person's body including substances believed to be present in the air, changes in diet, or even temperature and weather. An imbalance in the humors was believed to cause diseases, mood problems, and mental illness.[1]

The World Health Organization (WHO) recognizes that the health of individuals and communities is affected by many factors: "where we live, the state of our environment, genetics, our income and education level, and our relationships with friends and family." [2] Research conducted by the WHO suggests that these characteristics play a more significant role in affecting our health than any others, including having access to health care. For this reason, anthropologists who are interested in issues related to health and illness must use a broad holistic perspective that considers the influence of both biology and culture. **Medical anthropology**, a distinct sub-specialty within the discipline of anthropology, investigates human health and health care systems in comparative perspective, considering a wide range of bio-cultural dynamics that affect the well-being of human populations. Medical anthropologists study the perceived causes of illness as well as the techniques and treatments developed in a society to address health concerns. Using cultural relativism and a comparative approach, medical anthropologists seek to understand how ideas about health, illness, and the body are products of particular social and cultural contexts.

ANTHROPOLOGY AND THE BIOCULTURAL PERSPECTIVE

Evolutionary biology is a field of study that investigates the ways that natural processes have shaped the development of life on Earth, producing measurable changes in populations over time. Humans, *Homo sapiens*, are a special case in the discussion of evolution. We are a relatively young species that has been on Earth for only about 195,000 years.[3] Although this may sound like a long time, compared with other animals, humans are newcomers and we have been subject to processes of natural selection and adaptation for less time than many other living things. In that short time period, human lifestyles have changed dramatically. The first humans evolved in Africa and had a foraging lifestyle, living in small, kin-based groups. Today, millions of people live in crowded, fast-paced, and technologically advanced agricultural societies. In evolutionary terms, this change has happened rapidly. The fact that these rapid changes were even possible reveals that human lifestyles are **biocultural**, products of interactions between biology and culture. This has many implications for understanding human health.

The theory of natural selection suggests that in any species there are certain physical or behavioral traits that are **adaptive** and increase the capacity of individuals to survive and reproduce. These adaptive traits will be passed on through generations. Many human traits contributed to the survival of early human communities. A capacity for efficient walking and running, for instance, was important to human survival for thousands of years. However, as cultural change led to new lifestyles, some human characteristics became **maladaptive.**

One example is the obesity epidemic that has emerged all over the world. According to the Center for Disease Control and Prevention, more than one-third of the population of the United States is obese.[4] Obesity is considered to be a "disease of civilization," meaning that it did not exist in early human populations. Taking a biocultural evolutionary approach to human health, we can ask what traits characteristic of early human foraging populations might have encouraged an accumulation of fat in the human body. The answer comes from the evidence of food shortages among foraging populations. In fact, 47 percent of societies that forage experience food shortages at least once per year. Another 24 percent experience a shortage at least every two years.[5] When taking this into account, the ability to retain body fat would have been advantageous for humans in the past. Women with more body fat could give birth to healthy babies and breastfeed them, even in periods of food scarcity. It is also possible that women and men would have viewed body fat as a sign of health and access to resources, choosing sexual partners based on this characteristic. If so, powerful biological and cultural forces would have contributed to genetic traits that led to efficient metabolism and higher body fat.

With the development of agriculture, calories became more easily available while many people in the population became more sedentary. Traits that were once adaptive became maladaptive. The development of cultural preferences for foods high in fat and sugar, such as the "standard American diet" (SAD) is directly associated with obesity. These cultural changes have had a negative impact on health in many places. In Polynesia, for instance, obesity rates were around 15 percent in traditional farming communities, but climbed to over 35 percent as people moved to cities.[6] This is an example of the biocultural nature of many human health challenges.

Another example of this biocultural dynamic is sickle cell anemia, an inherited disease that can be fatal. A person who inherits the sickle cell gene from both parents will have red blood cells with an usual sickle (crescent) shape. These cells cannot carry oxygen as efficiently as normal red blood cells and they are also more likely to form painful and dangerous blood clots. Ordinarily, genetic conditions that make it more difficult for individuals to survive or have children, will become less common in populations over time due to the effects of natural selection. From an evolutionary perspective, one might ask why a deadly genetic condition has remained so common in human populations.

The cultural context is important for answering this question. The sickle cell gene is found most often in human populations in Africa and Southeast Asia where malaria is widespread. Malaria is a mosquito-borne illness that can be deadly to humans. People who have inherited one copy of the sickle cell anemia trait (instead of the two copies that cause sickle cell disease) have resistance to malaria. This is a significant adaptive trait in parts of the world where malaria is widespread. There is some evidence that malaria became a significant threat to human health only after the invention of agriculture. The deforested areas and collections of standing water that characterize agricultural communities also attract the mosquitos that carry disease. [7] In this case, we can see biocultural dynamics in action. Because resistance to malaria is an adaptive trait, the sickle cell gene remained common in populations where malaria is present. In parts of West and Central Africa, up to 25 percent of the population has the sickle cell gene. While sickle cell anemia is still a deadly disease, those who inherit a single copy of the gene have some protection from malaria, itself a deadly threat in many places. This example illustrates the biocultural interaction between genes, pathogens, and culture.

Infectious diseases generally do not have an adaptive function for humans like the examples above, but many infectious diseases are influenced by human cultural systems. Because early human communities consisted of small groups with a foraging lifestyle, viruses and bacteria transmitted from person to person were unlikely to result in large-scale epidemics. Healthy individuals from neighboring groups could simply avoid coming into contact with anyone who was suffering from illness and outbreaks would be naturally contained. [8]

The rapid increase in the size of human communities following the invention of agriculture changed this pattern. Agriculture can support more people per unit of land and, at the same time, agriculturalists need to live in permanent urban settlements in order to care for their crops. In a cyclical way, agriculture provides more food while also requiring that people have sizeable families to do the necessary farm work. Over the course of several thousand years, agricultural communities became increasingly densely populated. This had many implications for local ecology: problems disposing of waste and difficulty accessing clean water. A prime example of the health effects of the transition to urban settlements is cholera, a water-borne illness that spreads through water that has been polluted with human feces. Cholera, which was first detected in urban populations in India, has killed tens of thousands of people throughout history and continues to threaten populations today, particularly in developing countries, where access to clean water is limited, and in places that have experienced natural disasters. [9]

From an adaptive perspective, human beings die from infectious diseases because they do not have immunity to them. Immunity can be built up over time for some diseases, but unfortunately only after the illness or death of many members of a population. [10] When a new infectious disease reaches a population, it can wreak havoc on many people. Historically, several new infectious diseases are known to have been introduced to human populations through contact with livestock. Tuberculosis and smallpox were linked to cattle and influenza to chickens. When humans domesticated animal species, and began to live in close proximity to them, new routes for the transmission of **zoonotic** disease, illnesses that can be passed between humans and animals, were established. [11] Living in cities accelerates the spread of infectious diseases and the scale of outbreaks, but may also contribute to the natural selection of genetic traits that confer resistance to disease. This biocultural evolutionary process has been documented in urban populations where there are genes providing some resistance to leprosy and tuberculosis.[12]

ETHNOMEDICINE

Ethnomedicine is the comparative study of cultural ideas about wellness, illness, and healing. For the majority of our existence, human beings have depended on the resources of the natural environment and on health and healing techniques closely associated with spiritual beliefs. Many such practices, including some herbal remedies and techniques like acupuncture, have been studied scientifically and found to be effective.[13] Others have not necessarily been proven medically effective by external scientific evidence, but continue to be embraced by communities that perceive them to be useful. When considering cultural ideas about health, an important place to start is with **ethno-etiology**: cultural explanations about the underlying causes of health problems.

In the United States the dominant approach to thinking about health is **biomedical**. Illnesses are thought to be the result of specific, identifiable agents. This can include pathogens (viruses or bacteria), malfunction of the body's biochemical processes (conditions such as cancer), or physiological disorders (such as organ failure). In biomedicine as it is practiced in the United States (Western biomedicine), health is defined as the absence of disease or dysfunction, a perspective that notably excludes consideration of social or spiritual well-being. In non-Western contexts biomedical explanations are often viewed as unsatisfactory. In his analysis of ideas about health and illness in non-Western cultures, George Foster (1976) concluded that these ideas could be categorized into two main types of ethno-etiology: personalistic and naturalistic.[14]

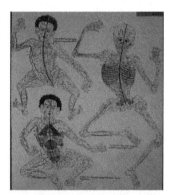

Figure 1: Traditional Tibetan medicine poster.

Ethno-Etiologies: Personalistic and Naturalistic

Personalistic ethno-etiologies view disease as the result of the "active, purposeful intervention of an agent, who may be human (a witch or sorcerer), nonhuman (a ghost, an ancestor, an evil spirit), or supernatural (a deity or other very powerful being)."[15] Illness in this kind of ethno-etiology is viewed as the result of aggression or punishment directed purposefully toward an individual; there is no accident or random chance involved. Practitioners who are consulted to provide treatment are interested in discovering *who* is responsible for the illness—a ghost, an ancestor? No one is particularly interested in discovering *how* the medical condition arose in terms of the anatomy or biology involved. This is because treating the illness will require neutralizing or satisfying a person, or a supernatural entity, and correctly identifying the being who is the root cause of the problem is essential for achieving a cure.

The Heiban Nuba people of southern Sudan provide an interesting example of a personalistic etiology. As described by, S.F. Nadel in the 1940s, the members of this society had a strong belief that illness and other misfortune was the result of witchcraft.

A certain magic, mysteriously appearing in individuals, causes the death or illness of anyone who eats their grain or spills their beer. Even spectacular success, wealth too quickly won, is suspect; for it is the work of a spirit-double, who steals grain or livestock for his human twin. This universe full of malignant forces is reflected in a bewildering array of rituals, fixed and occasional, which mark almost every activity of tribal life.[16]

Because sickness is thought to be caused by spiritual attacks from others in the community, people who become sick seek supernatural solutions. The person consulted is often a **shaman**, a person who specializes in contacting the world of the spirits.

In Heiban Nuba culture, as well as in other societies where shamans exist, the shaman is believed to be capable of entering a trance-like state in order to cross between the ordinary and supernatural realms. While in this state, the shaman can identify the individual responsible for causing the illness and sometimes the spirits can be convinced to cure the disease itself. Shamans are common all around the world and despite the proverbial saying that "prostitution is the oldest profession," shamanism probably is! Shamans are religious and medical practitioners who play important social roles in their communities as healers with a transcendent ability to navigate the spirit world for answers. In addition, the often have a comprehensive knowledge of the local ecology and how to use plants medicinally. They can address illnesses using both natural and supernatural tools.

In **naturalistic** ethno-etiologies, diseases are thought to be the result of natural forces such as "cold, heat, winds, dampness, and above all, by an upset in the balance of the basic body elements."[17] The ancient Greek idea that health results from a balance between the four humors is an example of a naturalistic explanation. The concept of the yin and yang, which represent opposite but complementary energies, is a similar idea from traditional Chinese medicine. Achieving balance or harmony between these two forces is viewed as essential to physical and emotional health. Unlike personalistic explanations, practitioners who treat illness in societies with naturalistic ethno-etiologies are interested in understanding how the medical condition arose so that they can choose therapeutic remedies viewed as most appropriate.

Emotional difficulties can be viewed as the cause of illness in a naturalistic ethno-etiology (an **emotionalistic explanation**). One example of a medical problem associated with emotion is *susto*, an illness recognized by the Mixe, an indigenous group who live in Oaxaca, Mexico, as well as others throughout central America. The symptoms of susto include difficulty sleeping, lack of energy, loss of appetite and sometimes nausea/vomiting and fever. The condition is believed to be a result of a "fright" or shock and, in some cases at least, it is believed to begin with a shock so strong that it disengages the soul from the body.[18] The condition is usually treated with herbal remedies and *barrida* (sweeping) ceremonies designed to repair the harm caused by the shock itself.[19] Although physicians operating within a biomedical ethno-etiology have suggested that susto is a psychiatric illness that in other cultural contexts could be labeled anxiety or depression, in fact susto is does not fit easily into any one Western biomedical category. Those suffering from susto see their condition as a malady that is emotional, spiritual, and physical.[20]

In practice, people assess medical problems using a variety of explanations and in any given society personalistic, naturalistic, or even biomedical explanations may all apply in different situations. It is also important to keep in mind that the line between a medical concern and other kinds of life challenges can be blurry. An illness may be viewed as just one more instance of general misfortune such as crop failure or disappointment in love. Among the Azande in Central Africa, witchcraft is thought to be responsible for almost all misfortune, including illness. E.E. Evans-Pritchard, an anthropologist who studied the Azande of north-central Africa in the 1930s, famously described this logic by describing a situation in which a granary, a building used to store grain, collapsed.

> In Zandeland sometimes an old granary collapses. There is nothing remarkable in this. Every Zande knows that termites eat the supports in course of time and that even the hardest woods decay after years of service. Now a granary is the summerhouse of a Zande homestead and people sit beneath it in the heat of the day and chat or play the African hole-game or work at some craft. Consequently it may happen that there are people sitting beneath the granary when it collapses and they are injured…Now why should these particular people have been sitting under this particular granary at the particular moment when it collapsed? That it should collapse is easily intelligible, but why should it have collapsed at the particular moment when these particular people were sitting beneath it…The Zande knows that the supports were undermined by termites and that people were sitting beneath the granary in order to escape the heat of the sun. But he knows besides why these two events occurred at a precisely similar moment in time and space. It was due to the action of witchcraft. If there had been no witchcraft people would have been sitting under the granary and it would not have fallen on them, or it would have collapsed but the people would not have been sheltering under it at the time. Witchcraft explains the coincidence of these two happenings.[21]

According to this logic, an illness of the body is ultimately caused by the same force as the collapse of the granary: witchcraft. In this case, an appropriate treatment may not even be focused on the body itself. Ideas about health are often inseparable from religious beliefs and general cultural assumptions about misfortune.[22]

Is Western Biomedicine An Ethno-Etiology?

The **biomedical** approach to health strikes many people, particularly residents of the United States, as the best or at least the most "fact-based" approach to medicine. This is largely because Western biomedicine is based on the application of insights from science, particularly biology and chemistry, to the diagnosis and treatment of medical conditions. The effectiveness of biomedical treatments is assessed through rigorous testing using the scientific method and indeed Western biomedicine has produced successful treatments for many dangerous and complex conditions: everything from antibiotics and cures for cancer to organ transplantation.

However, it is important to remember that the biomedical approach is itself embedded in a distinct cultural tradition, just like other ethno-etiologies. Biomedicine, and the scientific disciplines on which it is based, are products of Western history. The earliest Greek physicians Hippocrates (c. 406–370 BC) and Galen (c. 129–c. 200 AD) shaped the development of the biomedical perspective by providing early insights into anatomy, physiology, and the relationship between environment and health. From its origins in ancient Greece and Rome, the knowledge base that matured into contemporary Western biomedicine developed as part of the Scientific Revolution in Europe, slowly maturing into the medical profession recognized today. While the scientific method used in Western biomedicine represents a distinct and powerful "way of knowing" compared to other etiologies, the methods, procedures, and forms of reasoning used in biomedicine are products of Western culture.[23]

In matters of health, as in other aspects of life, ethnocentrism predisposes people to believe that their own culture's traditions are the most effective. People from non-Western cultures do not necessarily agree that Western biomedicine is superior to their own ethno-etiologies. Western culture does not even have a monopoly on the concept of "science." Other cultures recognize their own forms of science separate from the Western tradition and these sciences have histories dating back hundreds or even thousands of years. One example is Traditional Chinese Medicine (TCM), a set of practices developed over more than 2,500 years to address physical complaints holistically through acupuncture, exercise, and herbal remedies. The tenets of Traditional Chinese Medicine are not based on science as it is defined in Western culture, but millions of people, including a growing number of people in the United States and Europe, regard TCM as credible and effective.

Figure 2: The Taiyang bladder meridian, one of several meridians recognized in traditional Chinese medicine. From Shou Hua's Jushikei Hakki, 1716, Tokyo.

Ultimately, all ethno-etiologies are rooted in shared cultural perceptions about the way the world works. Western biomedicine practitioners would correctly observe that the strength of Western biomedicine is derived from use of a scientific method that emphasizes objectively observable facts. However, this this would not be particularly persuasive to someone whose culture uses a different ethno-etiology or whose understanding of the world derives from a different tradition of "science." From a comparative perspective, Western biomedicine may be viewed as one ethno-etiology in a world of many alternatives.

Techniques for Healing

Western biomedicine tends to conceive of the human body as a kind of biological machine. When parts of the machine are damaged, defective, or out of balance, chemical or surgical interventions are the preferred therapeutic responses. Biomedical practitioners, who can be identified by their white coats and stethoscopes, are trained to detect observable or quantifiable symptoms of disease, often through the use of advanced imaging technologies or tests of bodily fluids like blood and urine. Problems detected through these means will be addressed. Other factors known to contribute to wellness, such as the patient's social relationships or emotional state of mind, are considered less relevant for both diagnosis and treatment. Other forms of healing, which derive from non-biomedical ethno-etiologies, reverse this formulation, giving priority to the social and spiritual.

In Traditional Chinese Medicine, the body is thought to be governed by the same forces that animate the universe itself. One of these is *chi* (qi), a vital life force that flows through the body and energizes the body and its organs. Disruptions in the flow or balance of *chi* can lead to a lack of internal harmony and ultimately to health problems so TCM practitioners use treatments designed to unblock or redirect *chi*, including acupuncture, dietary changes, and herbal remedies. This is an example of **humoral healing,** an approach to healing that seeks to treat medical ailments by achieving a balance between the forces or elements of the body.

Communal healing, a second category of medical treatment, directs the combined efforts of the community toward treating illness. In this approach, medical care is a collaboration between multiple people. Among the !Kung (Ju/'hoansi) of the Kalahari Desert in southern Africa, energy known as *n/um* can be channeled by members of the community during a healing ritual and directed toward individuals suffering from illness. Richard Katz, Megan Bisele, and Verna St. Davis (1982) described an example of this kind of ceremony:

> The central event in this tradition is the all-night healing dance. Four times a month on the average, night signals the start of a healing dance. The women sit around the fire, singing and rhythmically clapping. The men, sometimes joined by the women, dance around the singers. As the dance intensifies, *n/um,* or spiritual energy, is activated by the healers, both men and women, but mostly among the dancing men. As *n/um* is activated in them, they begin to *kia,* or experience an enhancement of their consciousness. While experiencing *kia*, they heal all those at the dance.[24]

While communal healing techniques often involve harnessing supernatural forces such as the *num*, it is also true that these rituals help strengthen social bonds between people. Having a strong social and emotional support system is an important element of health in all human cultures.

Faith and the Placebo Effect

Humoral and communal approaches to healing, which from a scientific perspective would seem to have little potential to address the root causes of an illness, present an important question for medical anthropologists. What role does faith play in healing? Sir William Osler, a Canadian physician who was one of the founders of Johns Hopkins Hospital, believed that much of a physician's healing ability derived from his or her ability to inspire patients with a faith that they could be cured.[25] Osler wrote:

> Faith in the Gods or in the Saints cures one, faith in little pills another, suggestion a third, faith in a plain common doctor a fourth…If a poor lass, paralyzed apparently, helpless, bedridden for years, comes to me having worn out in mind, body, and estate a devoted family; if she in a few weeks or less by faith in me, and faith alone, takes up her bed and walks, the Saints of old could not have done more.[26]

In fact, there is a considerable amount of research suggesting that there is a **placebo effect** involved in many different kinds of healing treatments. A placebo effect is a response to treatment that occurs because the person receiving the treatment *believes it will work*, not because the treatment itself is effective.

In Western biomedicine, the placebo effect has been observed in situations in which a patient believes that he or she is receiving a certain drug treatment, but is actually receiving an inactive substance such as water or sugar. [27] Research suggests that the body often responds physiologically to placebos in the same way it would if the drug was real.[28] The simple act of writing a prescription can contribute to the successful recovery of individuals because patients trust that they are on a path that will lead to wellness.[29] If we consider the role of the placebo effect in the examples above, we should consider the possibility that humoral and communal healing are perceived to "work" because the people who receive these remedies have faith in them.

An interesting example of the complexity of the mind-body connection is found in studies of intercessory prayer: prayers made to request healing for another person. In one well-known study, researchers separated patients who had recently undergone heart surgery into two groups, one containing people who know they would be receiving prayers for their recovery and another group who would receive prayers without being aware of it. Those patients who knew they were receiving prayers actually had *more* complications and health problems in the month following surgery.[30] This reflects an interesting relationship between faith and healing. Why did the patients who knew that others were praying for them experience more complications? Perhaps it was because the knowledge that their doctors had asked others to pray for them made patients more stressed, perceiving that their health was at greater risk.

However, it can also be a lack of faith that drives people to look for alternative treatments. In the United States, alternative treatments, some of which are drawn from humoral or communal healing traditions, have become more popular among patients who believe that Western biomedicine is failing them. Cancer research facilities have begun to suggest acupuncture as a treatment for the intense nausea and fatigue caused by chemotherapy and scientific studies suggest that acupuncture can be effective in relieving these symptoms.[31] Marijuana, a drug that has a long recorded history of medical use starting in ancient China, Egypt, and India, has steadily gained acceptance in the United States as a treatment for a variety of ailments ranging from anxiety to Parkinson's disease.[32] As growing numbers of people place their faith in these and other remedies, it is important to recognize that

Figure 3: A botánica store selling herbal folk medicines.

many alternative forms of healing or medicine lack scientific evidence for their efficacy. The results derived from these practices may owe as much to faith as medicine.

MENTAL HEALTH

Unlike other kinds of illnesses, which present relatively consistent symptoms and clear biological evidence, mental health disorders are experienced and treated differently cross-culturally. While the discipline of psychiatry within Western biomedicine applies a disease-framework to explain mental illness, there is a consensus in medical anthropology that mental health conditions are much more complicated than the biological illness model suggests. These illnesses are not simply biological or chemical disorders, but complex responses to the environment, including the web of social and cultural relationships to which individuals are connected.

Medical anthropologists do not believe there are universal categories of mental illness.[33] Instead, individuals may express psychological distress through a variety of physical and emotional symptoms. Arthur Kleinman, a medical anthropologist, has argued that every culture frames mental health concerns differently. The pattern of symptoms associated with mental health conditions vary greatly between cultures. In China, Kleinman discovered that patients suffering from depression did not describe feelings of sadness, but instead complained of boredom, discomfort, feelings of inner pressure, and symptoms of pain, dizziness, and fatigue.[34]

Mental health is closely connected with social and cultural expectations and mental illnesses can arise as a result of pressures and challenges individuals face in particular settings. Rates of depression are higher for refugees, immigrants, and others who have experienced dislocation and loss. A sense of powerlessness also seems to play a role in triggering anxiety and depression, a phenomenon that has been documented in groups ranging from stay-at-home mothers in England to Native Americans affected by poverty and social marginalization.[35]

Schizophrenia, a condition with genetic as well as environmental components, provides another interesting example of cross-cultural variation. Unlike anxiety or depression, there is some consistency in the symptom patterns associated with this condition cross culturally: hallucinations, delusions, and social withdrawal. What differs, however, is the way these symptoms are viewed by the community. In his research in Indonesia, Robert Lemelson discovered that symptoms of schizophrenia are often viewed by Indonesian communities as examples of communication with the spirit world, spirit possession, or the effects of traumatic memories.[36] Documenting the lives of some of these individuals in a film series, he noted that they remained integrated into their communities and had significant responsibilities as members of their families and neighborhoods. People with schizophrenia were not, as often happens in the United States, confined to institutions and many were living with their condition without any biomedical treatments.

In its multi-decade study of schizophrenia in 19 countries, the World Health Organization concluded that societies that were more culturally accepting of symptoms associated with schizophrenia integrated people suffering from the condition into community life more completely. In these cultures, the illness was less severe and people with schizophrenia had a higher quality of life.[37] This finding has been controversial, but suggests that stigma and the resulting social isolation that characterize responses to mental illness in countries like the United States affect the subjective experience of the illness as well as its outcomes.[38]

THE EXPERIENCE OF ILLNESS IN PLACE

Social Construction of Illness

As the above examples demonstrate, cultural attitudes affect how medical conditions will be perceived and how individuals with health problems will be regarded by the wider community. There is a difference, for instance, between a disease, which is a medical condition that can be objectively identified, and an illness, which is the subjective or personal experience of feeling unwell. Illnesses may be caused by disease, but the experience of being sick encompasses more than just the symptoms caused by the disease itself. Illnesses are, at least in part, social constructions: experiences that are given meaning by the relationships between the person who is sick and others.

The course of an illness can worsen for instance, if the dominant society views the sickness as a moral failing. Obesity is an excellent example of the social construction of illness. The condition itself is a result of culturally induced habits and attitudes toward food, but despite this strong cultural component, many people regard obesity as a preventable circumstance, blaming individuals for becoming overweight. This attitude has a long cultural history. Consider for instance the religious connotations within Christianity of "gluttony" as a sin.[39] Such socially constructed **stigma** influences the subjective experience of the illness. Obese women have reported avoiding visits to physicians for fear of judgment and as a result may not receive treatments necessary to help their condition.[40] Peter Attia, a surgeon and medical researcher who delivered a TED Talk on this subject, related the story of an obese woman who had to have her foot amputated, a common result of complications from obesity and diabetes. Even though he was a physician, he judged the woman to be lazy. "If you had just tried even a little bit," he had thought to himself before surgery.

Subsequently, new research revealed that insulin resistance, a precursor to diabetes, often develops as a result of the excess sugars used in many kinds of processed foods consumed commonly in the United States. As Attia observes, high rates of obesity in the United States are a reflection of the types of foods Americans have learned to consume as part of their cultural environment.[41] In addition, the fact that foods that are high in sugars and fats are inexpensive and abundant, while healthier foods are expensive and unavailable in some communities, highlights the economic and social inequalities that contribute to the disease.

The HIV/AIDS virus provides another example of the way that the subjective experience of an illness can be influenced by social attitudes. Research in many countries has shown that people, including healthcare workers, make distinctions between patients who are "innocent" victims of AIDS and those who are viewed as "guilty." People who contracted HIV through sex or intravenous drug use are seen as guilty. The same judgment applies to people who contracted HIV through same-sex relationships in places

Figure 4: AIDS prevention art, Mozambique. The text reads "think of the consequences, change behavior, prevent HIV/AIDS."

where societal disapproval of same-sex relationships exists. People who contracted HIV from blood transfusions, or as babies, are viewed as innocent. The "guilty" HIV patients often find it more difficult to access medical care and are treated with disrespect or indifference in medical settings compared with superior treatment provided to those regarded as "innocent." In the wider community, "guilty" patients suffer from social marginalization and exclusion while "innocent" patients receive greater social acceptance and practical assistance in responding to their needs for support and care.[42]

The stigma that applies to "guilty" patients also ignores the socioeconomic context in which HIV/AIDS spreads. For instance, in Indonesia, poor women can make considerably more money as sex workers than in many other jobs: $10 an hour as a sex worker compared to 20 cents an hour in a factory.[43] In a similar way, poverty and a lack of other choices contribute to a decision to engage in sex work in other societies, including in sub-Saharan Africa where rates of HIV infection are among the highest in the world. Poverty itself is one of the greatest "risk factors" for HIV infection.[44] The clear relationship between poverty, gender, and HIV infection has been the topic of a great deal of research in medical anthropology. One example is Paul Farmer's classic book, *AIDS and Accusation: Haiti and the Geography of Blame* (1992), which was one of the earliest books to critically evaluate the connection between poverty, racism, stigma, and neglect that allowed HIV to infect and kill thousands of Haitians. Projects like this are critical to developing holistic views of the entire cultural, economic, and political context that affects the spread of the virus and attempts to treat the disease. Partners in Health, the non-profit medical organization Paul Farmer helped to found, continues to pursue innovative strategies to prevent and treat diseases like AIDS, strategies that recognize that poverty and social marginalization provide the environment in which the virus flourishes.

Culture-Bound Syndromes

A **culture-bound syndrome** is an illness recognized only within a specific culture. These conditions, which combine emotional or psychological with physical symptoms, are not the result of a disease or any identifiable physiological dysfunction. Instead, culture-bound syndromes are **somatic**, meaning they are physical manifestations of emotional pain. The existence of these conditions demonstrates the profound influence of culture and society on the experience of illness.

Anorexia

Anorexia is considered a culture bound syndrome because of its strong association with cultures that place a high value on thinness as a measure of health and beauty. When we consider concepts of beauty from cultures all over the world, a common view of beauty is one of someone with additional fat. This may be because having additional fat in a place where food is expensive means that one is likely of a higher status. In societies like the United States where food is abundant, it is much more difficult to become thin than it is to become heavy. Although anorexia is a complex condition, medical anthropologists and physicians have observed that it is much more common in Western cultural contexts among people with high socioeconomic status.[45] Anorexia, as a form of self-deprivation, has deep roots in Western culture and for centuries practices of self-denial have been associated with Christian religious traditions. In a contemporary context, anorexia may address a similar, but secular desire to assert self-control, particularly among teenagers.[46]

During her research in Fiji, Anne Becker (2004) noted that young women who were exposed to advertisements and television programs from Western cultures (like the United States and Australia) became self-conscious about their bodies and began to alter their eating habits to emulate the thin ideal they saw on television. Anorexia, which had been unknown in Fiji, became an increasingly common problem.[47] The same pattern has been observed in other societies undergoing "Westernization" through exposure to foreign media and economic changes associated with globalization.[48]

Swallowing Frogs in Brazil

In Brazil, there are several examples of culture-bound syndromes that affect children as well as adults. Women are particularly susceptible to these conditions, which are connected to emotional distress. In parts of Brazil where poverty, unemployment, and poor physical health are common, there are cultural norms that discourage the expression of strong emotions such as anger, grief, or jealousy. Of course, people continue to experience these emotions, but cannot express them openly. Men and women deal with this problem in different ways. Men may choose to drink alcohol heavily, or even to express their anger physically by lashing out at others, including their wives. These are not socially acceptable behaviors for women who instead remark that they must suppress their feelings, an act they describe as having to "swallow frogs" (*engolir sapos*).[49]

Nervos (nerves) is a culture-bound syndrome characterized by symptoms such as headaches, trembling, dizziness, fatigue, stomach pain, tingling of the extremities and even partial paralysis. It is viewed as a result of emotional overload: a state of constant vulnerability to shock. Unexplained wounds on the body may be diagnosed as a different kind of illness known as "blood-boiling bruises." Since emotion is culturally defined as a kind of energy that flows throughout the body, many believe that too much emotion can overwhelm the body, "boiling over" and producing symptoms. A person can become so angry, for instance, that his or her blood spills out from under the skin, creating bruises, or so angry that the blood rises up to create severe headaches, nausea, and dizziness. A third form of culture-bound illness, known as *peito aberto* (open chest) is believed to be occur when a person, most often a woman, is carrying too much emotional weight or suffering. In this situation, the heart expands until the chest becomes spiritually "open." A chest that is "open" is dangerous because rage and anger from other people can enter and make a person sick.[50]

In stressful settings like the communities in impoverished areas of northeastern Brazil, it is common for people to be afflicted with culture-bound illnesses throughout their lives. Individuals can suffer from one condition, or a combination of several. Sufferers may consult *rezadeiras/rezadores*, Catholic faith healers who will treat the condition with prayer, herbal remedies, or healing rituals. Because these practitioners do not distinguish between illnesses of the body and mind, they treat the symptoms holistically as evidence of personal turmoil. This approach to addressing these illnesses is consistent with cultural views that it is the suppression of emotion itself that has caused the physical problems.

BIOMEDICAL TECHNOLOGIES

In the history of human health, technology is an essential topic. Medical technologies have transformed human life. They have increased life expectancy rates, lowered child mortality rates, and are used to intervene in and often cure thousands of diseases. Of course, these accomplishments come with many cultural consequences. Successful efforts to intervene in the body biologically also have implications for cultural values and the social organization of communities, as demonstrated by the examples below.

Antibiotics and Immunizations

Infectious diseases caused by viruses and bacteria have taken an enormous toll on human populations for thousands of years. During recurring epidemics, tens of thousands of people have died from outbreaks of diseases like measles, the flu, or bubonic plague. The Black Death, a pandemic outbreak of plague that spread across Europe and Eurasia from 1346–1353 AD, killed as many as 200 million people, as much as a third of the European population. Penicillin, discovered in 1928 and mass produced for the first time in the early 1940s, was a turning point in the human fight against bacterial infections. Called a "wonder drug" by Time magazine, Penicillin became available at a time when bacterial infections were frequently fatal; the drug was glorified as a cure-all.[51] An important factor to consider about the introduction of antibiotics is the change to an understanding of illness that was increasingly scientific and technical. Before science could provide cures, personalistic and naturalistic ethno-etiologies identified various root causes for sickness, but the invention of antibiotics contributed to a strengthening of the Western biomedical paradigm as well as a new era of profitability for the pharmaceutical industry.

The effects of antibiotics have not been completely positive in all parts of the world. Along with other technological advances in areas such as sanitation and access to clean water, antibiotics contributed to an **epidemiological transition** characterized by a sharp drop in mortality rates, particularly among children. In many countries, the immediate effect was an increase in the human population as well as a shift in the kinds of diseases that were most prevalent. In wealthy countries, for instance, chronic conditions like heart disease or cancer have replaced bacterial infections as leading causes of death and the average lifespan has lengthened. In developing countries, the outcome has been mixed. Millions of lives have been saved by the availability of antibiotics, but high poverty and lack of access to regular medical care mean that many children who now survive the immediate dangers of infection during infancy succumb later in childhood to malnutrition, dehydration, or other ailments.[52]

Figure 5: Women and children waiting to enter a medical clinic in Somalia. The clinic is open 2 days each week and treats 400–500 people each day.

Another difficulty is the fact that many kinds of infections have become untreatable as a result of bacterial resistance. Medical anthropologists are concerned with the increase in rates of infectious diseases like tuberculosis and malaria that cannot be treated with many existing antibiotics. According to the World Health Organization, there are nearly 500,000 cases of drug resistant tuberculosis each year.[53] New research is now focused on drug resistance, as well as the social and cultural components of this resistance such as the relationship between poverty and the spread of resistant strains of bacteria.

Immunizations that can provide immunity against viral diseases have also transformed human health. The eradication of the smallpox virus in 1977 following a concerted global effort to vaccinate a large percentage of the world's population is one example of the success of this biotechnology. Before the development of the vaccine, the virus was killing 1–2 million people each year.[54] Today, vaccines exist for many of the world's most dangerous viral diseases, but providing access to vaccines remains a challenge. The polio virus has been eliminated from most of the world following several decades of near universal vaccination, but the disease has made a comeback in a handful of countries, including Afghanistan, Nigeria, and Pakistan, where weak governments, inadequate healthcare systems, or war have made vaccinating children impossible. This example highlights the global inequalities that still exist in access to basic medical care.

Because viruses have the ability to mutate and to jump between animals and people, human populations around the world also face the constant threat of new viral diseases. Influenza has been responsible for millions of deaths. In 1918, a pandemic of the H1N1 flu infected 500 million people, killing nearly 5 percent of the human population.[55] Not all influenza strains are that deadly, but it remains a dangerous illness and one that vaccines can only partially address.[56] Each year, the strains of the influenza virus placed in the annual "flu shot" are based on predictions about the strains that will be most common. Because the virus mutates frequently and is influenced by interactions between human and animal populations, there is always uncertainty about future forms of the virus.[57]

Reproductive Technologies

Today, the idea of "contraception" is linked to the technology of hormone-based birth control. "The pill" as we now know it, was not available in the United States until 1960, but attempts to both prevent or bring about pregnancy through technology date back to the earliest human communities. Techniques used to control the birthrate are an important subject for medical anthropologists because they have significant cultural implications.

Many cultures use natural forms of birth control practices to influence the spacing of births. Among the !Kung, for instance, babies are breastfed for many months or even years, which hormonally suppress fertility and decrease the number of pregnancies a woman can have in her lifetime. In Enga, New Guinea, men and women do not live with one another following a birth, another practice that increases the time between pregnancies.[58] In contrast, cultures where there are social or religious reasons for avoiding birth control, including natural birth spacing methods, have higher birth rates. In the United States, the Comstock Act passed in 1873 banned contraception and even the distribution of information about contraception.

Although the Comstock Act is a thing of the past, efforts in the United States to limit access to birth control and related medical services like abortion are ongoing. Many medical anthropologists study the ways in which access to reproductive technologies is affected by cultural values. Laury Oaks (2003) has investigated the way in which activists on both sides of the abortion debate attempt to culturally define the idea of "risk" as it relates to women's health. She notes that in the 1990s anti-abortion activists in the United States circulated misleading medical material suggesting that abortion increases rates of breast cancer. Although this claim was medically false, it was persuasive to many people and contributed to doubts about whether abortion posed a health risk to women, a concern that strengthened efforts to limit access to the procedure.[59]

Other forms of reproductive technology have emerged from the desire to increase fertility. The world of "assisted reproduction," which includes technologies such as in vitro fertilization and surrogate pregnancy, has been the subject of many anthropological investigations. Marcia Inhorn, a medical anthropologist, has written several books about the growing popularity of in vitro fertilization in the Middle East. Her book, *The New Arab Man* (2012), explores the way in which infertility disrupts traditional notions of Arab masculinity that are based on fatherhood and she explores the ways that couples navigate conflicting cultural messages about the importance of parenthood and religious disapproval of assisted fertility.[60]

CONCLUSION

As the global population becomes larger, it is increasingly challenging to address the health needs of the world's population. Today, 1 in 8 people in the world do not have access to adequate nutrition, the most basic element of good health.[61] More than half the human population lives in an urban environment where infectious diseases can spread rapidly, sparking pandemics. Many of these cities include dense concentrations of poverty and healthcare systems that are not adequate to meet demand. [62] Globalization, a process that connects cultures through trade, tourism, and migration, contributes to the spread of pathogens that negatively affect human health and exacerbates political and economic inequalities that make the provision of healthcare more difficult.

Human health is complex and these are daunting challenges, but medical anthropologists have a unique perspective to contribute to finding solutions. Medical anthropology offers a holistic perspective on human evolutionary and biocultural adaptations as well as insights into the relationship between health and culture. As anthropologists study the ways people think about health and illness and the socioeconomic and cultural dynamics that affect the provision of health services, there is a potential to develop new methods for improving the health and quality of life for people all over the world.

DISCUSSION QUESTIONS

1. This chapter describes several examples of diseases that result from interactions between biology and culture such as obesity. Why is it important to consider cultural factors that contribute to illness rather than placing blame on individuals? What are some other examples of illnesses that have cultural as well as biological causes?
2. Many cultures have ethno-etiologies that provide explanations for illness that are not based in science. From a biomedical perspective, the non-scientific medical treatments provided in these cultures have a low likelihood of success. Despite this, people tend to believe that the treatments are working. Why do you think people tend to be satisfied with the effectiveness of the treatments they receive?
3. How does poverty influence the health of populations around the world? Do you see this in your own community? Who should be responsible for addressing health care needs in impoverished communities?

GLOSSARY

Adaptive: traits that increase the capacity of individuals to survive and reproduce.

Biocultural evolution: describes the interactions between biology and culture that have influenced human evolution.

Biomedical: an approach to medicine that is based on the application of insights from science, particularly biology and chemistry.

Communal healing: an approach to healing that directs the combined efforts of the community toward treating illness.

Culture-bound syndrome: an illness recognized only within a specific culture.

Emotionalistic explanation: suggests that illnesses are caused by strong emotions such as fright, anger, or grief; this is an example of a naturalistic ethno-etiology.

Epidemiological transition: the sharp drop in mortality rates, particularly among children, that occurs in a society as a result of improved sanitation and access to healthcare.

Ethno-etiology: cultural explanations about the underlying causes of health problems.

Ethnomedicine: the comparative study of cultural ideas about wellness, illness, and healing.

Humoral healing: an approach to healing that seeks to treat medical ailments by achieving a balance between the forces, or elements, of the body

Maladaptive: traits that decrease the capacity of individuals to survive and reproduce.

Medical anthropology: a distinct sub-specialty within the discipline of anthropology that investigates human health and health care systems in comparative perspective.

Naturalistic ethno-etiology: views disease as the result of natural forces such as cold, heat, winds, or an upset in the balance of the basic body elements.

Personalistic ethno-etiology: views disease as the result of the actions of human or supernatural beings.

Placebo effect: a response to treatment that occurs because the person receiving the treatment *believes it will work*, not because the treatment itself is effective.

Shaman: a person who specializes in contacting the world of the spirits.

Somatic: symptoms that are physical manifestations of emotional pain.

Zoonotic: diseases that have origins in animals and are transmitted to humans.

ABOUT THE AUTHOR

Sashur Henninger-Rener is an anthropologist with research in the fields of comparative religion and psychological anthropology. She received a Master of Arts from Columbia University in the City of New York in Anthropology and has since been researching and teaching. Currently, Sashur is teaching with The University of LaVerne and the Los Angeles Community College District in the fields of Cultural and Biological Anthropology. In her free time, Sashur enjoys traveling the world, visiting archaeological and cultural sites along the way. She and her husband are actively involved in animal rescuing, hoping to eventually found their own animal rescue for animals that are waiting to find homes.

NOTES

1. Jermone Gilbert, *Humors, Hormones, and Neurosecretions* (New York: State University of New York Press, 1962).
2. World Health Organization, "Health Impact Assessment," http://www.who.int/hia/evidence/doh/en/.
3. Sally McBrearty and Allison Brooks, "The Revolution That Wasn't: A New Interpretation of the Origin of Modern Humans," *Journal of Human Evolution* 39 (1999), 453–563.
4. U.S. Center for Disease Control and Prevention, "Adult Obesity Facts," http://www.cdc.gov/obesity/data/adult.html.
5. Marjorie G. Whiting, *A Cross Cultural Nutrition Survey* (Cambridge, MA: Harvard School of Public Health, 1968).
6. Ian A.M. Prior, "The Price of Civilization," *Nutrition Today* 6 no. 4 (1971): 2–11.
7. Steven Connor, "Deadly malaria may have risen with the spread of agriculture," *National Geographic*, http://news.nationalgeographic.com/news/2001/06/0625_wiresmalaria.html.
8. Jared Diamond, "The Arrow of Disease," *Discover Magazine*, October 1992. http://discovermagazine.com/1992/oct/thearrowofdiseas137.

9. World Health Organization, "Cholera," http://www.who.int/mediacentre/factsheets/fs107/en/.

10. George J. Armelagos and John R. Dewey, "Evolutionary Response to Human Infectious Disease," *BioScience*, 25(1970): 271–275.

11. William McNeill, *Plagues and People* (New York: Doubleday, 1976).

12. Ian Barnes, Anna Duda, Oliver Pybus, Mark G. Thomas. Ancient Urbanisation Predicts Genetic Resistance To Tuberculosis," *Evolution* 65 no. 3 (2011): 842–848.

13. George T. Lewith, *Acupuncture: Its Place in Western Medical Science* (United Kingdom: Merlin Press, 1998).

14. George M. Foster, "Disease Etiologies in Non-Western Medical Systems,"
American Anthropologist 78 no 4 (1976): 773–782.

15. Ibid., 775

16. S.F. Nadel, *The Nuba: An Anthropological Study of the Hill Tribes in Kordofan* (Oxford: Oxford University Press, 1947), 173.

17. Foster, "Disease Etiologies in Non-Western Medical Systems," 775.

18. A.J. Rubel, "The Epidemiology of a Folk Illness: Susto in Hispanic America," *Ethnology*
3 (1964): 268–283.

19. Robert T. Trotter II, "Susto: The Context of Community Morbidity Patterns," *Ethnology* 21 no. 3 (1982): 215–226.

20. Frank J. Lipp, "The Study of Disease in Relation to Culture: The Susto Complexe Among the Mixe of Oaxaco," *Dialectical Anthropology* 12 no. 4 (1987): 435–442.

21. E.E. Evans-Pritchard, *Witchcraft, Oracles and Magic Among the Azande* (Oxford: Oxford University Press, 1937), 70.

22. Leonard B. Glick, "Medicine as an Ethnographic Category: The Gimi of the New Guinea Highlands," *Ethnology* 6 (1967): 31–56.

23. Elliott Mishler, "Viewpoint: Critical Perspectives on the Biomedical Model," in
E. Mishler, L.A. Rhodes, S. Hauser, R. Liem, S. Osherson, and N. Waxler, eds.
Social Contexts of Health, Illness, and Patient Care (Cambridge, UK: Cambridge University Press).

24. Richard Katz, Megan Biesele, and Verna St. Davis, *Healing Makes Our Hearts Happy: Spirituality and Cultural Transformation among the Kalahari Ju/ 'hoansi* (Rochester VS, Inner Traditions, 1982), 34.

25. Michael Bliss, *William Osler: A Life in Medicine* (Oxford: Oxford University Press, 1999), 276.

26. William Osler, "The Faith That Heals," *British Medical Journal* 1 (1910): 1470–1472.

27. Cara Feinberg, "The Placebo Phenomenon," *Harvard Magazine* http://harvardmagazine.com/2013/01/the-placebo-phenomenon.

28. Ted J. Kaptchuk, and Franklin G. Miller, "Placebo Effects in Medicine," *New England Journal of Medicine* 373 (2015):8–9.

29. Robert Bud, "Antibiotics: From Germophobia to the Carefree Life and Back Again," in *Medicating Modern America: Prescription Drugs in History*, ed. Andrea Tone and Elizabeth Siegel Watkins (New York: New York University Press, 2007).

30. H. Benson, J.A. Dusek, J.B. Sherwood, P. Lam, C.F. Bethea, and W. Carpenter, "Study of the Therapeutic Effects of Intercessory Prayer (STEP) in Cardiac Bypass Patients: A Multicenter Randomized Trial of Uncertainty and Certainty of Receiving Intercessory Prayer," *American Heart Journal* 151 (2006):934–942.

31. National Cancer Institute, "Acupuncture," http://www.cancer.gov/cancertopics/pdq/cam/acupuncture/healthprofessional/page5.

32. Mira Taow, "The Religious and Medicinal Uses of Cannabis in China, India, and Tibet," *Journal of Psychoactive Drugs* 13(1981): 23–24.

33. Marsella, A. and White, G., eds. *Cultural Conceptions of Mental Health and Therapy* (Dordrecht, Netherlands: D. Reidel, 1982).

34. Dominic T.S. Lee, Joan Kleinman, and Arthur Kleinman, "Rethinking Depression: An Ethnographic Study of the Experiences of Depression Among Chinese," *Harvard Review of Psychiatry* 15 no 1 (2007):1–8.

35. Arthur Kleinman, *Rethinking Psychiatry: From Cultural Category to Personal Experience* (New York: The Free Press, 1988).

36. Robert Lemelson and L.K. Suryani, "Cultural Formulation of Psychiatric Diagnoses: The Spirits, Penyakit Ngeb and the Social Suppression of Memory: A Complex Clinical Case from Bali," *Culture, Medicine and Psychiatry* 30 no. 3 (2006): 389–413.

37. For more information about these studies, see J. Leff et al., "The International Pilot Study of Schizophrenia: Five-Year Follow-Up Findings," *Psychological Medicine* 22 (1992):131–45; A. Jablensky et al., "Schizophrenia: Manifestations, Incidence and Course in Different Cultures: A World Health Organization Ten-Country Study," *Psychological Medicine Monograph Supplement* 20(1992); N. Sartorius et al., "Early Manifestations and First-Contact Incidence of Schizophrenia in Different Cultures," *Psychological Medicine* 16 (1986):909–28.

38. Bernice A. Pescosolido, Jack K. Martin, Sigrun Olafsdottir, J. Scott Long, Karen Kafadar, and Tait R. Medina, "The Theory of Industrial Society and Cultural Schemata: Does the 'Cultural Myth of Stigma' Underlie the WHO Schizophrenia Paradox?," *American Journal of Sociology* 121 no. 3 (2015): 783–825.

39. Collean Barry, Victoria Bresscall, Kelly D. Brownell, and Mark Schlesinger, "Obesity Metaphors: How Beliefs about Obesity Affect Support for Public Policy," The Milbank Quarterly 87 (2009): 7–47.

40. Peter Conrad and Kristen K. Barker, "The Social Construction of Illness: Key Insights and Policy Implications," *Journal of Health and Social Behavior,* 51(2010): s57-s79.

41. Peter Attia, "Is the Obesity Crisis Hiding a Bigger Problem?," *TEDMED Talks* April 2013 Retrieved from https://www.ted.com/talks/peter_attia_what_if_we_re_wrong_about_diabetes.

42. Anish P. Mahajan, Jennifer N. Sayles, Vishal A. Patel, Robert H. Remien, Daniel Ortiz, Greg Szekeres, and Thomas J. Coates, "Stigma in the HIV/AIDS Epidemic: A review of the Literature and Recommendations for the Way Forward," AIDS 22 supp. 2 (2008): S67-S79.

43. Elizabeth Pisani, "Sex, Drugs, & HIV: Let's Get Rational," *TED Talks* February 2010. http://www.ted.com/talks/elizabeth_pisani_sex_drugs_and_hiv_let_s_get_rational_1#t-1011824.

44. United Nations, "Poverty and AIDS: What's Really Driving the Epidemic?" http://www.unfpa.org/conversations/facts.html.

45. Maria Makino, Koji Tsuboi, and Lorraine Dennerstein, "Prevalence of Eating Disorders: A Comparison of Western and Non-Western Countries," Medscape General Medicine 6 no. 3 (2004):49.

46. Joan Jacobs Brumberg, *Fasting girls: The Emergence of Anorexia Nervosa as a Modern Disease* (Cambridge, MA: Harvard University Press, 1988).

47. Anne E. Becker, "Television, Disordered Eating, and Young Women in Fiji: Negotiating Body Image and Identity during Rapid Social Change" *Culture, Medicine and Psychiatry, 28* no. 4 (2004):533–559.

48. Sing Lee, "Reconsidering the Status of Anorexia Nervosa as a Western Culture-Bound Syndrome," *Social Science & Medicine* 42 no. 1 (1996): 21–34.

49. L.A. Rebhun, "Swallowing Frogs: Anger and Illness in Northeast Brazil," Medical Anthropology Quarterly 8 no. 4 (1994):360–382.

50. Ibid., 369–371

51. Robert Bud, "Antibiotics: From Germophobia to the Carefree Life and Back Again."

52. Nancy Scheper Hughes, *Death Without Weeping: The Violence of Everyday Life in Brazil* (Berkeley: University of California Press, 1989).

53. World Health Organization, "Antimicrobial Resistance," http://www.who.int/mediacentre/factsheets/fs194/en/.

54. David *Koplow, Smallpox: The Fight to Eradicate a Global Scourge (Berkeley: University of California Press, 2003).*

55. Jeffery K. Taubenberger, David Baltimore, Peter C. Doherty, Howard Markel, David M. Morens, Robert G. Webster, and Ian A. Wilson, "Reconstruction of the 1918 Influenza Virus: Unexpected Rewards from the Past," mBio 3 no. 5 (2012).

56. Jeffrey Taubenberger and David Morens, "1918 influenza: The Mother of All Pandemics," *Emerging Infectious Diseases,* 12 (2006).

57. Suzanne Clancy, "Genetics of the Influenza Virus," *Nature Education,* 1(2008): 83.

58. For more about these and other examples, see Carol P. MacCormack, *Ethnography of Fertility and Birth* (New York: Academic Press, 1982).

59. Laury Oaks, "The Social Politics of Health Risk Warning: Competing Claims about the Link between Abortion and Breast Cancer," in *Risk, Culture, and Health Inequality: Shifting Perceptions of Danger and Blame,* eds. Barbara Herr Harthorn and Laury Oaks (Westport, CT: Praeger, 2003).

60. Marcia C. Inhorn, The New Arab Man: Emergent Masculinities, Technologies, and Islam in the Middle East (Princeton, NJ: Princeton University Press, 2012).

61. Food and Agriculture Organization of the United Nations, "The Multiple Dimensions of Food Security," http://www.fao.org/docrep/018/i3458e/i3458e.pdf.

62. World Health Organization, "Urbanization and Health," *Bulletin of the World Health Organization,* 88(2010): 241–320.

Seeing Like an Anthropologist: Anthropology in Practice

Logan Cochrane, Vanier Scholar, University of British Columbia
logan.cochrane@gmail.com
http://www.logancochrane.com

LEARNING OBJECTIVES

- Identify ways in which "seeing like an anthropologist" differs from the approach to local cultures used by international development agencies.

- Explain why "harmful traditional practices" are prioritized for change by development agencies and describe how negative attitudes toward these practices can be examples of "bad for them, okay for us."

- Assess the reasons why anthropological perspectives and techniques tend to have a limited impact on the design or goals of international development projects.

What does it mean to see and hear what others do not see and hear and how can that unique information be practically applied? The lack of a simple answer is fitting to anthropology because the work of anthropologists often demonstrates that simplistic explanations are, at best, only part of the complex stories of human culture. In this chapter, I provide examples of how the ability to see and hear is applied in practice and how these skills add value in a socio-cultural anthropology setting associated with international development. In particular, I shed light on the potential challenges of practicing anthropology within non-governmental organizations. Given the ethic of confidentiality in anthropology, I omit details about the country, organization, and ethnic groups as much as possible and instead focus on the processes involved.

Although an education in anthropology stresses the importance of confidentiality and the potentially dire consequences of drawing attention to individuals and communities, it probably does not truly sink in until you conduct your first fieldwork and "subjects" turn into human beings with names, families, and feelings. One of the greatest ethical challenges anthropologists face in writing about individuals and communities is the additional attention drawn to them when the intention of the anthropologist is to highlight a concern that extends beyond specific individuals and communities and can thus have negative consequences. Take, for example, an assessment I conducted of a national safety net program that took place in a limited number of communities.[1] If the individuals and communities participating had been explicitly identified or could be identified, they may have experienced negative political consequences such as a loss of government-provided social services or their jobs. Instead, the anonymity of the individuals and communities was protected, and the concerns and challenges were identified in a way that protected those who graciously and generously contributed their time and ideas to the research process. Complete anonymity is not always desirable, needed, or possible but is always an important consideration for anthropologists.

Throughout the last ten years, I have worked for non-governmental organizations—about five years in Eastern Africa and shorter periods in Asia and the Middle East—as a volunteer, employee, and consultant with community-based groups and national and international organizations. In this chapter, I explore one of those experiences to convey a sense of what "seeing like an anthropologist" means by analyzing an effort to eliminate **food taboos** by a nongovernmental international development organization. This chapter was inspired by the work of political scientist and anthropologist James C. Scott, particularly his *Seeing Like a State* (1998). I shift the focus inward onto anthropology as a practice and a way of seeing.[2]

ANTHROPOLOGY AND DEVELOPMENT

Socio-cultural anthropology is best understood by its primary approach to data collection: participant observation. This key component of ethnographic research involves long-term engagement, living with and learning from a cultural community different from one's own. In listening, learning about, and seeing the world from the perspectives of others, anthropologists draw on the idea of cultural relativism. This is in contrast to ethnocentrism, the belief that one's own culture, cultural values, and societal organization are true, right, and proper and that others' are erroneous to some degree. Cultural relativism posits that cultural practices and ideas must be understood within their contexts.

In the past, some anthropologists participated in the "development" activities of colonial governments, and individual anthropologists and the discipline as a whole were rightly criticized for their roles in the injustices that resulted. While working in Afghanistan in 2013, I encountered anthropologists who were engaged in activities in the name of "development" that could be defined as neo-colonial in that they supported militaries by analyzing cultural communities with the goal of finding ways to weaken them and foster unequal and unfair relationships (**cultural imperialism**). Anthropological engagement is not always benevolent or neutral. As a result, anthropologists are encouraged to engage in self-reflection—to examine their roles, engagements, practices, and objectives critically, known as reflexivity.

Varying degrees of criticism of the nature, objectives, and embedded assumptions of international development continue. Some have called on international development practitioners to significantly reform their activities to make them more effective, while others have expressed more radical criticisms, including the view that provision of aid causes greater impoverishment and should end.[3] It is essential when deconstructing development, as a concept and an activity, to ask why, when, how, and for whom the development is intended and who it excludes. It also requires identifying the power dynamics and motivations involved. Anthropological tools and ways of seeing are important means by which to answer these questions.[4]

"HARMFUL TRADITIONAL PRACTICES"

My interaction with the project discussed in this chapter was limited in duration and I had specific tasks related to program evaluation and impact assessment. I interacted with management staff based in the international head office as well as the national head office, who provided me with background information about the region and clarified expectations before visiting the project area. The project itself was not primarily geared toward ending "harmful traditional practices," but included a component related to addressing gender inequality and practices that negatively impact women. Reflecting back on those discussions, it appears that staff and donors who were located furthest from the area of the project had the greatest interest in these "harmful traditional practices." Based on their emphasis, it is clear that foreign and exotic practices had an appeal that basic and shared needs did not. For example, those who were more distanced from the people the project sought to support were particularly interested in "female genital mutilation," exchange marriages, and seemingly irrational and bizarre food taboos.

On the other hand, within almost every community in the project area, both men and women were primarily concerned about the lack of clean drinking water and healthcare options. Unfortunately, these concerns attracted little attention from outsiders.[5] In fact, many governmental agencies funding international development have explicitly restricted their funding such that water infrastructure is not an allowable project expense, including the governmental donor for the project in which I was involved. The reason for this is rarely explicitly stated, however informal discussions with development agency personnel cite high costs and sustainability as concerns. Abu-Lughod's (2013) research on western perceptions of Muslim women, and broadly on conceptualizing "others" and their needs, provides insight into how prioritization of needs often takes place based upon assumptions, not reality.

"**Harmful traditional practices**" are an odd collection of practices that range from tattooing and scarification to exchange marriages, forced marriages and marriages wherein a woman who is widowed becomes the wife of her deceased husband's brother. "Harmful traditional practices" also include acts typically considered criminal activity throughout much of the world, such as abduction and unlawful confinement. A national committee in Ethiopia, for example, listed 162 "harmful traditional practices."[6] While many of these practices are illegal and generally agreed to be abuses of human rights, some have parallel practices that are legal in the countries in which international organizations are based, such as tattooing and scarification. Numerous examples of "bad for them, okay for us" could be made. Each practice, its context, laws, and discourse requires contextualization beyond the scope of this chapter. However, useful examples of deconstructions of one frequently discussed practice, female genital mutilation, have been made by Russell-Robinson (1997), James (1998), Obermeyer (1999), Ahmadu and Shweder (2009) and Londono (2009).

The project staff identified a number of "harmful traditional practices" they believed ought to be stopped; however, I will only explore one of them: a collection of food taboos that were believed to negatively affect the nutrition of women. In particular, there was a focus on one specific food taboo: the restriction of women from eating eggs, which was the only food taboo mentioned in every report provided by the organization.

I learned from the project proposal that there were "cultural taboos" forbidding women from eating eggs and milk.[7] To address this, the project would improve their access and provide training on the nutritional value of these products. An initial assessment report stated that this taboo was not only about prohibiting the consumption of eggs, but also poultry. However, it later became clear that the restriction was only on eating eggs and meat from a specific breed of chicken that was raised in a woman's own home or in the home of her in-laws. The organization advocated that this practice was negatively affecting women and infants because sources of already limited nutrition were being restricted, particularly an important source of vitamin A, which is a common micronutrient deficiency amongst the population. While eggs were a primary focus, other internal organizational reports provided different information: women and children also did not eat goat meat, animals that had been hunted, or any dairy products.

The consumption of these products was believed to cause illness and bring about the death of an in-law, hence the prohibition. Several years into the project it was reported that a significant change in child nutrition had occurred and the report suggested that training and education programs discouraging food taboos were the reason for this shift. A detailed gender report, conducted halfway through the project, suggested that women and girls were still not generally allowed to eat chicken meat and eggs, but provided some case studies of positive change. This particular report pointed to the mother-in-law as the person who instituted the prohibition of chicken meat and eggs, while most reports simply said the prohibition was "cultural" amongst this ethnic group or due to community misconceptions. After five years of work, the project continued to actively engage in activities aiming at addressing the "misconceptions" and "traditional practices" of not eating eggs or drinking milk.

One report, finalized a few years into the project, mentioned significant resistance to project activities encouraging the consumption of eggs and chicken meat. The "harmful traditional practice" was described as a "serious taboo," and a "deeply rooted belief." This report referenced another organization that was working to "prove the taboo is wrong" and had fostered remarkable change. Meeting with management staff in the national head office, I heard the same general story: there are cultural taboos forbidding women and girls from eating some foods, and specifically eggs. Staff permanently based in the project area repeated this information.

However, throughout the years of the project very little was understood about this particular practice. The food taboo was identified and a few potential, sometimes conflicting, reasons were given. No one appeared to have taken the time to understand why these food taboos existed. When I later explored this question, a staff member who had lived and worked within the region for almost two decades remarked, "I have not had a chance to know about this." This is one of the challenges anthropologists face in working within non-governmental organizations: often the difficulties communities face are assumed to be a result of ignorance and the "solution" is presented as a straightforward, often technical, activity such as education. I believe the lack of understanding of these practices was not due to insurmountable barriers, but a lack of inquiry into the "why," "how," "when," and other questions that make cultural practices understandable. The ability to ask these kinds of questions, I argue, is a skill built into the anthropological way of seeing. For those familiar with "schemes to improve the human condition," as Scott put it, the lack of interest in asking questions would not be surprising. Organizations tend to identify a problem, propose a solution, and plan evidence-based activities to achieve an objective. For many in the international development sector, finding out why these taboos exist is not particularly important. Rather they believe it is most important to stop those practices deemed (by them) to be harmful.

WE NEVER ASKED ABOUT IT BEFORE

The historian Eugen Weber wrote that "when one looks for different things, one *sees* different things."[8] He was referring to seeing within a text; I believe the same applies to other kinds of observation. Anthropologists fundamentally view the world through a unique lens, and their ability to see what others do not is fostered through anthropological methodologies, approaches, and ideas. The physical reality is the same; the lens is different. Likewise, professionals in non-governmental organizations—management staff, economists, medical professionals, and development experts—bring their particular training, their lenses, to the problems, often focusing on different kinds of information they respectively view as important. In other words, our individual perspectives alter what we see.

The ethical challenge for anthropologists working in international development is that often the donors, organizations and projects operate without detailed sociocultural information. As a result, many anthropologists end up advocating for significant shifts in how the sector operates. For example, in designing a project, the proposed activities are often outlined before the baseline assessments of community needs are conducted. When the project is approved, and budget is set, it is difficult to completely adjust the focus and plan based on new knowledge of community needs. Anthropologists working on these projects often find themselves in the challenging space of advocating for new approaches, such as funding structures based on needs, rather than donor priorities, and flexibility in programming as opposed to carrying out the set activities that are outlined in program plans.

In the case of the food taboos identified within this development project, diverse ways of seeing were evident in the reports, in which medical perspectives focused on the impacts of the nutritional content of the foods, gender specialists were most concerned with the abuse of women's rights, planners identified how behavior changes could occur and be integrated into the project using evidence-based measures, and economists paid attention to the potential income women could generate by producing poultry and selling eggs. Despite the passing of years and even the identification of some strong resistance by people in the communities, the food taboos were consistently presented as cultural issues or misconceptions that best practices and evidence-based behavior-change approaches could eliminate. The plan was to "raise awareness," hold "community-based dialogues," "facilitate exchange visits" with communities in which such taboos were not practiced, and provide nutritional education. On paper, the plan sounded good. The diverse activities would reinforce the message of behavior change with each offering unique insight and thus having a compounding effect in achieving the desired objective. The activities had previously been shown to be successful in a range of settings. For the project staff, all required information appeared to have been gathered.

My work began with spending time with the people in their communities and asking them about the food taboos—what they actually were and why they existed—and the community members provided detailed and insightful information. When I talked to the field staff about it, they reported that they had never asked the people in the communities those questions. That might sound like a case of neglect, but I view it is the logical outcome of one way of seeing. When a problematic practice has been identified and the organization has experience with activities that have changed such behavior, why do the details matter? From that perspective, the tedious task of collecting such data would waste valuable resources, time, and effort. It is important, at this juncture, to shed some light on the systemic nature of seeing from technical perspectives of this sort, which are common in the organizational cultures of international development programs and their staff members. It is not limited to international development workers—national and local organizations often present the same narratives about "bad" cultural taboos that can be eliminated by providing education about nutrition and empowering women.

SEEING LIKE AN ANTHROPOLOGIST

When I started my work in the program, I had no previous experience with the ethnic group that practiced the food taboos and had never been in the region. I was sent to visit a number of communities as part of an assessment unrelated to food taboos and to conduct gender-separated focus group discussions and individual interviews. In the first community I visited, the adult men made no mention of food taboos but the women did, and what they said was at odds with the project reports. They said that the restrictions applied only to adult married women and were, as one of the official reports had noted, limited to a specific local breed of chicken raised in specific households. I made note of the comments and went on with my tasks. In the second community, I interviewed religious leaders from two Christian sects who also mentioned the food taboos, describing them as examples of common practices of witchcraft. In the third and fourth communities, I had lengthy discussions exploring the context that no one had asked about until then: What in fact were the food taboos? Why did the taboos exist? What reinforced them as an ongoing practice? How did people view the practices and what were the consequences of not following them? The staff members who had been working with the communities were amazed at the valuable information gathered by simply asking the questions.

Community members made a number of important clarifications, some of which aligned with what was presented in reports and some did not. The details of these taboos were not uniform in all communities, however they shared some trends. For example, once a woman married a number of restrictions began, which included the prohibition of eating eggs and chicken meat, although only those that were produced from local breeds of chicken and only those raised within her household or the household of her in-laws. The restrictions did not apply to children or unmarried girls, nor did they apply to other breeds of chickens. Additionally, women could eat eggs and chicken meat as long as it was from a different source, such as eggs from a neighbor's chicken. In some communities, this also applied to the meat of hunted animals and milk. Women who did consume the prohibited products were believed to suffer from illnesses, such as swelling and itching, or even to cause the death of one of their in-laws. One project activity instructed women to bring the eggs they were forbidden to eat to the project staff, who then cooked the eggs and told the women to eat. The response of some women was outright refusal, some ate and then induced vomiting, while others followed the instructions and ate without strong objection. Reactions such as these suggested that there was more to the prohibition than a simple misconception.

I WILL NOT EAT IT UNTIL I DIE

Elders in the communities explained that food taboos were one of a series of interconnected restrictions on behaviors, some identified by the project as harmful but not connected to the food taboos. In addition to food taboos, the restrictions included limitations on what women can touch and places they could enter while menstruating, a prohibition against a wife eating from the first harvest of the season until after her husband does, and rules preventing a wife from drinking from a newly prepared batch of alcoholic drink until after her husband does. Project workers had identified many of these practices, but understood them to be isolated from each other as separate traditions. The elders' view of the practices as linked suggested that they needed to be understood as manifestations of something larger.

I found that the communities' narratives differed but the information and specific rules were consistent. The food taboos were, in fact, a small part of a detailed belief system that influenced many components of everyday life. There had been, perhaps two generations ago, a respected leader from their ethnic group who had supernatural traits. His name was Gumzanjela, and he guided the community and held a role akin to religious leadership. Although Gumzanjela had passed on, he continued to be present in the community. His presence, described as his spirit, influenced what happened, could bring about illness, and could be called on when seeking cures. Some believed that Gumzanjela was a person; others believed that he had always been a supernatural being. Regardless, belief in Gumzanjela was a serious matter; people believed in him, believed his regulations were true, and had witnessed repercussions of failing to follow them. Gumzanjela had established the food taboos and restrictions for women. One of the many stories told about him was that his first child was born holding a leaf of a specific plant that was thereafter used as a cure for spiritual illnesses. Treatment of illness was a common theme in recollections of Gumzanjela and was a primary reason people continued to seek his help. Disobeying Gumzanjela was said to result in curses, sometimes on the one who violated a rule and other times on a relative such as the in-laws cited in the food taboos. The curses ranged from relatively minor ailments such as severe itching or swelling to the death of an in-law.

In addition to prohibiting a number of behaviors for women, Gumzanjela had imparted specific directions for people to follow, often built on his teachings, that were delivered via spiritual mediums in the community who communicated with Gumzanjela. For example, Gumzanjela had prescribed a cure that involved cutting off the claw of a chicken and placing it in the belly button of the person needing treatment. The claw was left there for one week, and the person could not bathe during that time. At the end of the week, the claw was removed and the person bathed. Only the person being treated could eat the chicken from which the cutting was taken.

In each community, there were well-known practitioner spirit-mediums, both male and female, to whom people go to connect with Gumzanjela. They sought various forms of support or requested that curses be placed on someone. The seeker could be given specific instructions to do certain things or to refrain from doing certain things. Payments and sacrifices were sometimes required, and occasionally Gumzanjela called for lengthy spiritual events during the night in which rites were performed and/or sacrifices were made.

One of the project reports had referred to the food taboos as being deeply rooted and, in context, it is easy to understand why that was the case. The specific food taboos were components of a much larger belief system; they were integral activities required by the communities' religious traditions and thus taken very seriously. They were, as one member of the community noted, part of the "law of Gumzanjela."

A brief analogy demonstrates the gravity of this point. Imagine that the people in the project communities were followers of Judaism or Islam, religions that prohibit consumption of a number of foods, including pork.[9] An international development organization and its external staff members might identify a protein deficiency that could be resolved by people consuming pork and view the taboo against it as a harmful traditional practice that should be eliminated through education about its nutritional value. Additionally, disadvantaged members of society could be encouraged to raise and sell pigs to generate income. Because Islam and Judaism are major recognized religions with millions of followers, it might seem absurd to try to convince them to eat pork based on nutritional and economic grounds. But the law of Gumzanjela is also a belief system and is as important to the communities in the project as Islam and Judaism are to their followers. The project had failed to recognize that the food taboos were part of a comprehensive belief system and that the organization had made demands that directly confronted culturally important beliefs and values. As a result, the project activities were viewed as an affront to their religious traditions and to the righteous, respected man from whom the laws had come and his living spirit.

I asked a group of men if a person could continue to believe in Gumzanjela and not practice the food taboo regarding chicken and eggs. No, they said, it was not possible. They added forcefully, "I believe in Gumzanjela. I have seen the effects; no cure works except from Gumzanjela." They explained that there "is no cure from the medical professionals; only Gumzanjela can cure these illnesses." Women thoroughly embraced these beliefs as well. Several years into the project, for example, a woman stated that she would "not eat it [the eggs] until I die." Her response reflected the strength of her personal beliefs despite the project's efforts. The majority of the community members interviewed agreed that belief in Gumzanjela was correct and that they must follow the system set out. Gumzanjela was present in their lives and in their homes and affected their lives daily. They experienced it and knew it to be true.

Some members of the community had "left Gumzanjela" and practiced a different faith, either Christianity or Islam. A primary reason for their leaving Gumzanjela and abandoning the food taboos, they explained, was the theology of their new faith. The women ate eggs, disregarded the menstruation rules, and sought medical help from local clinics rather than cures from spiritual practitioners. Abandoning the taboos required abandoning the greater belief system, a religious conversion either to a new theology or to a rejection of faith (at least theoretically; I did not encounter any community members who rejected faith altogether).

AN ISOLATED CASE?

Is this particular project unique or is the narrow vision of practitioners common in international development? Another project in which I was involved was run by an agricultural organization that was promoting changes in planting methodologies aimed at increasing yields. The farmers recognized that the new planting method increased yields but did not adopt it. A primary reason for that failure was a different way of thinking about what is important in an agricultural livelihood—the organization was promoting short-term gains and the farmers were prioritizing long-term sustainability of the soil. Another international organization and its donors were confident that child malnutrition in a region was the product of lack of knowledge about the nutritional value of consuming a diversity of foods to reduce micronutrient deficiencies, and they developed a series of educational projects to address the problem. But after spending time with members of the community, they realized that a lack of diversity in their diets was due largely to having few options, primarily because of poverty, and that the malnutrition was associated with seasonal food shortages and could not be alleviated through education. The activities of these projects appeared beneficial, but did not address the actual problems; instead, they were designed based on assumptions about both the problems and the solutions and failed to value contextualized, ethnographic information.

Technical approaches too often exclude the socio-political context in which they are applied and, consequently, entirely miss the politicized nature of the project and its activities. A vocational training effort I worked with in the Middle East, for example, failed, not because the need for education was misunderstood, but because the socio-political context in which it took place was neglected; the poor quality of existing educational systems was not addressed because improving the quality of the education provided was not an objective. Similarly, in the evaluation of the social safety net mentioned at the outset, the political nature of the implementation of the project was not adequately recognized by the international funding agencies.[10] Thus, the experience explored in this chapter is not uncommon, and it is clear that the anthropological way of seeing allows broader issues to come into view—cultural, social, and political—which can then be incorporated into the project goals and activities. These are areas that relatively technical approaches and evaluations tend to miss.

REFLECTIONS

What, then, do socio-cultural anthropologists do? There is no single answer to this question. There are, however, skills that anthropologists acquire that unveil unique ways of seeing and listening that can be applied to many different settings. Some anthropologists use these skills to facilitate the creation of policies that are more inclusive and multicultural, some engage with poorly understood subcultures, and others enhance the effectiveness of marketing of consumer goods. This chapter illustrates how I used the anthropological way of seeing to contextualize development actions, actors, and the people for whom the "development" was being done and explores the ethical challenges faced by anthropologists when working in the international development sector and within non-governmental organizations.

In general, I have found that many people working in international development organizations have not yet recognized the value of asking people why they do what they do. From the anthropologist's point of view, understanding why a practice occurs is not merely an act of inquiry; it is also a means of demonstrating respect for people and their knowledge and taking time to listen, learn, and see. The typical approach of development practitioners implicitly and explicitly conveys a lack of respect for the culture, values, and ideas of the people the projects seek to support.

The respect inherent to the anthropologist's view is based on cultural relativity, which guides the inquiry process. Judgment is withheld to understand the relative context of the practices in question. Far too frequently staff of development organizations judge based on their assumptions and do not see value in investigating further. That limited vision is a barrier to their success. It is essential, in seeing like an anthropologist, to be willing to understand other people's perspectives and respect their ideas. As an anthropologist, I am not required to believe in Gumzanjela. However, my training and education prepare me to understand and to begin to see the world from a perspective founded in that belief. My ability and willingness to see reality from perspectives other than my own are essential skills—the ability to see what some people do not see and hear what some people do not hear. Anthropology can connect the activities of international development efforts to cultural values so they work together instead of against each other. The identification of the comprehensive belief system in which the food taboos were embedded, for example, opened up new avenues for practical, culturally respectful solutions to the problem of poor nutrition for women and children.

The story of the development organization's efforts is purposely left unfinished. Did the community resist? Did the organization change its activities? Was a different learning and inquiry-based culture supported within the organization? Did belief in Gumzanjela continue? Did the organization succeed in changing specific behaviors? How did the community navigate the external pressure? Did individuals mostly succumb to the project's advocacy or did they find ways to deflect, redirect, and mislead the external advocates? As I hope this chapter has conveyed, people's responses to efforts to change them are complex. Anthropologists play an important role by extending an organization's vision so that its programs and activities can better align with the realities of the people for whom they are designed and implemented.

DISCUSSION QUESTIONS

1. The international development professionals described in this chapter were determined to eliminate the food taboos associated with the "law of Gumzanjela," but Cochrane points out that these rules were part of a larger belief system. Are there situations in which it is acceptable to try to alter a group's cultural values in order to promote changes in health, nutrition, or women's rights? Or, do you think it is inappropriate for outsiders to demand change? Do you think it is possible to achieve goals, such as improved nutrition, without pressuring groups to change their values and beliefs?

2. Cochrane provides several examples of situations in which anthropological perspectives and methods led to the discovery of important information about local communities that development professionals did not have. However, the lack of knowledge about local cultures that characterizes many development projects is not caused simply by a lack of anthropological expertise. What other factors mentioned in this chapter contribute to a mismatch between the needs of local people and the goals of international development projects?

GLOSSARY

Cultural imperialism: attempts to impose unequal and unfair relationships between members of different societies.

Food taboos: cultural rules against the preparation and/or consumption of certain foods.

Harmful traditional practices: behaviors that are viewed as ordinary and acceptable by members of a local community, but appear to be destructive or even criminal to outsiders.

ABOUT THE AUTHOR

Logan Cochrane is a Vanier Scholar at the University of British Columbia (Okanagan). For the last twelve years he has worked overseas, including in Afghanistan, Benin, Burundi, the Democratic Republic of Congo, Ethiopia, Tanzania and Uganda. Logan has worked as a consultant with clients that have included Management Sciences for Health, Save the Children, The Liaison Office, UNICEF and UNAIDS.

BIBLIOGRAPHY

Abu-Lughod, Lila. *Do Muslim Women Need Saving?* Cambridge, MA: Harvard University Press, 2013.

Ahmadu, Fuambai. S. and Shweder, Richard. A. "Disputing the Myth of the Sexual Dysfunction of Circumcised Women." *Anthropology Today* 25 no. 6 (2009):14-17.

Robert Chambers. *Provocations for Development.* Warwickshire, UK: Practical Action Publishing, 2012.

Cochrane, L. and Tamiru, Y. "Ethiopia's Productive Safety Net Program: Power, Politics and Practice." *Journal of International Development.* 28 no. 5 (2016):649-665.

Escobar, Arturo. *Encountering Development: The Making and Unmaking of the Third World.* Princeton, NJ: Princeton University Press, 1994.

Farmer, Paul. *Infections and Inequalities.* Berkeley: University of California Press, 2001.

Green, Duncan. *From Poverty to Power.* Oxford, UK: Oxfam, 2012.

Illich, Ivan. "Development as Planned Poverty." In *The Post-Development Reader*, edited by M. Rahnama and V. Bawtree, 94-102. London: Zed Books, 1997.

James, Stanlie. M. "Shades of Othering: Reflections on Female Circumcision/Genital Mutilation." *Signs.* 23 no. 4 (1998):1031-1048.

Lock, Margaret. "Afterward: Seeing Like an Anthropologist." In *Troubling Natural Categories*, edited by N. Adelson, L. Butt and K. Kielmann, 209-222. Montreal: McGill-Queen's University Press, 2013.

McGovern, Mike. "Popular Development Economics—An Anthropologist Among the Mandarins." *Perspective on Politics* 9 no. 2 (2011):345-355.

Moyo, Dambisa. *Dead Aid. Why Aid is Not Working and How There is Another Way for Africa.* New York: Farrar, Strauss & Giroux, 2009.

NCTPE [National Committee on Traditional Practices of Ethiopia]. *Old Beyond Imaging Ethiopia – Harmful Traditional Practices*. Addis Ababa, Ethiopia: National Committee on Traditional Practices of Ethiopia, 2003.

Obermeyer, Carla. M. "Female Genital Surgeries: The Known, the Unknown, and the Unknowable." *Medical Anthropology Quarterly* 13 (1999):79-106.

Russell-Robinson, Joyce. "African Female Circumcision and the Missionary Mentality." *A Journal of Opinion* 25 (1997):54-57.

Scott, James. C. *Seeing Like a State: How Certain Schemes to Improve the Human Condition Have Failed*. New Haven, CT: Yale University Press, 1998.

Sulkin, Carlos. D. Londono. "Anthropology, Liberalism and Female Genital Cutting." *Anthropology Today* 25 no. 6 (2009):17-19.

Weber, Eugen. *Peasants into Frenchman: The Modernization of Rural France, 1870-1914*. Stanford: Stanford University Press, 1976.

NOTES

1. See Logan Cochrane and Y. Tamiru, "Ethiopia's Productive Safety Net Program: Power, Politics and Practice," *Journal of International Development* 28 no. 5 (2016):649-665.

2. I cannot claim to be the first to write about "seeing like an anthropologist;" others have done so, including Lock (2013), though with slightly different objectives.

3. Those who have called on international development practitioners to reform their activities include Robert Chambers (2012), Paul Farmer (2001), and Duncan Green (2012). A more radical critique suggesting that the provision of aid causes greater impoverishment can be found in Arturo Escobar (1994) and Ivan Illich (1997). Dambisa Moyo (2009) has called for an end to international development projects.

4. Those interested in an anthropological perspective of the views of other development actors can read McGovern's (2011) article on the works of Collier.

5. I use the term outsiders to refer to those external to the communities, either as non-members or as those not living within or near that particular location, and am not referring only to international staff.

6. NCTPE, National Committee on Traditional Practices of Ethiopia, 2003

7. The project proposal and reports mentioned in this chapter are internal organizational reports not available to the public. The purpose of the reports is to inform programming, which differs from academic research articles that are made available to the public (although not always open access). While these practices appear quite different, there are some similarities: organizations publish publicly available reports on their work based on the totality of the data collected, but these reports do not include all of the information that they have. Similarly, not all data collected by academic researchers is made available to the public nor is it all published, rather a selection of that data is published in academic article and books.

8. Eugen Weber, 1976, *Peasants into Frenchman: The Modernization of Rural France, 1870-1914*. Stanford University Press: Stanford University Press, x.

9. Leviticus 11:7–8: "And the pig, because it parts the hoof and is cloven-footed but does not chew the cud, is unclean for you. You shall not eat any of their flesh and you shall not touch their carcasses; they are unclean for you." Quran 2:173: "He [God] has only forbidden to you dead animals, blood, the flesh of swine and that which has been dedicated to other than God."

10. Cochrane and Tamiru, "Ethiopia's Productive Safety Net Program."

PUBLIC ANTHROPOLOGY

Robert Borofsky, Hawaii Pacific University, Center for a Public Anthropology
borofsky@hpu.edu
http://www.publicanthropology.org/

LEARNING OBJECTIVES

- Explain how the structure of academic careers, topical specialization, and writing styles contribute to difficulty with communicating findings from academic anthropology to a wider public.

- Identify examples of anthropological research that has contributed to the public good.

- Define public anthropology and distinguish it from academic anthropology and applied anthropology.

- Assess the factors that contribute to a desire for public engagement in anthropology as well as the obstacles to this engagement.

- Evaluate the ways in which accountability, transparency, collaboration, and the goal of benefitting others could contribute to reframing anthropology.

- Discuss actions that can be taken by anthropologists to facilitate social change.

As an example of public anthropology (following the model of the Kahn Academy), Dr. Borofsky has created short 10–15 minute videos on key topics in anthropology for introductory students. All 28 videos are available from the *Perspectives: An Open Introduction to Cultural Anthropology* website.

INTRODUCTION

Was Julie Andrews right when (in the Sound of Music) she sang, "Let's start at the very beginning, a very good place to start?" Should authors follow her advice in writing textbook chapters by, at the beginning, explaining the organization of the chapter so readers will know what to expect and be able to follow the chapter's themes clearly? I cannot sing Do Re Me half as well as Julie Andrews. But I will try to follow her suggestion.

This chapter begins with an outline of its organization—which topics follow others plus a little "secret." After this introduction, the chapter turns to (**a**) two puzzles stemming from anthropology's interactions with the broader public. It next (**b**) discusses how we might best define public anthropology given that different people interpret it in different ways, especially in respect to the field's ambiguous overlapping with applied anthropology. Building on these points, the chapter then turns to (**c**) public anthropology's four main strategies for enhancing the discipline's credibility with the broader public. The chapter concludes with (**d**) a section on facilitating change—guides for those who want to help transform people's lives for the better. Even without Julie Andrews singing, I trust this sounds interesting. **The chapter asks important questions and offers thoughtful answers that, I hope, will draw you into reflecting on the challenges public anthropology faces as well as how it seeks to encourage anthropology to better serve the common good.**

Before beginning, however, I should share a secret. You will see throughout this chapter—as in most anthropological articles and books—a host of references in numbered footnotes. You might ask why anthropologists are intent on citing colleagues extensively, especially when it is off-putting to students and the broader public. Seeing all the references with only a limited sense of who is being referred to and what they mean can be intimidating. Anthropologists use these references to show colleagues that they "know what they are talking about." It demonstrates that they are familiar with key literature relating to a topic. The citations also serve another purpose. They reinforce the discipline. The more anthropologists cite each other, the more they convey that anthropology is an important discipline with important things to say—just look at all the people and articles being cited. But intriguingly, many anthropologists only discuss the references in passing—usually for a sentence or two—just enough to show they are familiar with them.

As a result, these citations should be taken with a grain of salt. They involve anthropologists conveying, to each other, their intellectual mettle, their academic competence. Skip over them if they do not seem interesting. Do not let them intimidate you. Why do I use them? Simply stated, I am writing not only for you—a student reading this text—but also for colleagues who may review this chapter as well. They may be interested in exploring further some of the provocative things I say so I need to let them see my sources.

Why do I bold certain passages? I do this for three reasons.

1. **It highlights key points in each section so the chapter is easier for you to read. Either before or after a bolded passage, there is additional material that amplifies the bolded text. This allows you to separate the key points from additional material that discusses and/or explains the central points being made.**
2. **If you are in a rush, you can skim the chapter's main themes by focusing on the bolded passages. You will get the main ideas but not the details and explanations that clarify the bolded points.**
3. **You can use the bolded passages to review the chapter once you have read it. Go back through the bolded points and see if you remember the chapter's key themes. If you come across a point about which you are unclear, simply read the neighboring text to clarify what the bolded passage is about.**

TWO PUZZLES

Turning to the chapter's key themes, let's start by exploring two puzzles. The first puzzle: By the time you reach this chapter, I hope you see how exciting anthropology can be. It deals with all sorts of intriguing questions about the human condition—how humans and their societies have evolved through time, what life is like in unfamiliar places, what human differences suggest about our commonalities, and how understanding them may facilitate better human relations. **And yet, most of the widely read, popular books that deal with anthropological issues—books that win prominent prizes and are bestsellers—tend to be written by non-anthropologists. Why is that?**

The second puzzle: Anthropologists have done much good in the world—not only helping to enrich human understanding of our past and present but also facilitating concrete changes that improve people's lives. **Yet anthropology's positive efforts have not often been highlighted in the world's newspapers or other media outlets. Again, why?**

Starting with the first puzzle, why non-anthropologists tend to write the bestselling anthropologically oriented books, let me offer three examples. Reading this textbook, you can see that books on the evolution of human societies, including how the West (meaning Western Europe, Canada, and the United States) became more developed than the "Rest" (i.e., non-Western societies), are standard anthropological fare. Many anthropologists have written about these topics. But only one book has become wildly popular: **Jared Diamond's *Guns, Germs, and Steel: The Fates of Human Societies*** (1997). The book won the 1998 Pulitzer Prize for General Non-Fiction, was the subject of a well-received PBS National Geographic special, and remained on the *New York Times* bestseller list for almost four years. Diamond studied anthropology as an undergraduate but obtained a doctoral degree in physiology. Starting out as a professor of physiology at University of California, Los Angeles, he is now a professor of geography.

Katherine Boo's *Behind the Beautiful Forevers: Life, Death, and Hope in a Mumbai Undercity* (2012) is an insightful ethnography of life in an Indian slum. It provides a vivid sense of how people, despite overwhelming difficulties, not only are able to survive but at times are filled with hope for a better life. In the tradition of the best ethnographies, the book allows readers to understand and appreciate how the main characters navigate their lives through conditions that might surprise, and perhaps shock, some. *Behind the Beautiful Forevers* won the 2012 National Book Award for nonfiction and the *Los Angeles Times* Book Award and has been a *New York Times* bestseller. While Boo spent a number of years studying the people of Annawadi (a Mumbai slum near the airport), she is not an anthropologist. She is an investigative journalist, formerly of the *Washington Post* and now a writer for the *New Yorker*.

Anne Fadiman's *The Spirit Catches You and You Fall Down* (1997) is a detailed, extended case study in medical anthropology that documents the miscommunications that developed between a Laotian refugee Hmong family and the medical staff of a Merced, California, hospital treating the family's epileptic daughter, Lia. It offers a nuanced, sensitive ethnographic account of the problems well-intentioned people face when they talk past one another. As the *New Yorker* observed, "Fadiman describes with extraordinary skill the colliding worlds of Western medicine and Hmong culture."[1] The book has received numerous honors, including the National Book Critics Circle Award for General Nonfiction and the *Los Angeles Times* Book Prize for Current Interest, and almost one million copies have been sold. (Sales of most anthropology books are around 2,000 copies). Fadiman refers to anthropologists but is not one herself. When she wrote the book, she was a journalist and editor. She is now a writer in residence at Yale University.

There is no doubt that anthropologists would like to be read and recognized by audiences beyond the discipline. Such an accomplishment means more than just selling lots of books; it means having a public impact that stretches beyond the university.

Some anthropologists have been popular authors, most prominently, perhaps, Margaret Mead. Her 1928 book, *Coming of Age in Samoa*, which compared sexual experiences of Samoan girls with those of American girls, sold hundreds of thousands of copies. But such anthropologists are relatively rare today. Clifford Geertz won the National Book Critics Circle Award for Criticism in 1988 and Robert Levy was a finalist for the National Book Award in 1974, but neither book sold particularly well beyond academia. Recently, another anthropologist, David Kertzer, won the Pulitzer Prize. But his book, *The Pope and Mussolini: The Secret History of Pius XI and the Rise of Fascism in Europe,* is, as its subtitle suggests, focused on details of European history, a topic outside the anthropological mainstream.

My point is this: Few anthropologists writing on anthropological themes today are widely read beyond the discipline. **The anthropology-oriented books that are best sellers and win promi-**

nent awards tend to be written by non-anthropologists, and when an anthropologist writes an award-winning book, it tends to be on a less-anthropological subject.

What gives? Clearly, anthropologists have the skill and interest to write for the broader public. **I suggest, in part, that it is a matter of priorities.** Many anthropologists would enjoy a large, public audience (A survey in the *Chronicle Review* in 2016 indicated that 83 percent of the *Chronicle* subscribers sampled believed that academics should do more to shape public debate.)[2] For most junior professors, however, an even higher priority is promotion and tenure. To achieve these, they must demonstrate to their faculty review committee that they can produce serious, professional work. A key marker, if not the key marker, of significant professional work is the degree to which academic colleagues cite one's publications in their publications. It is often referred to as an author's intellectual impact.

While there are other standards for assessing promotion and tenure, committees tend to fall back on cited publications in assessing a faculty member's achievements because clear metrics exist for the degree to which colleagues cite one's work. All committee members have to do is log on to Google Scholar, for example, and type the individual's name in quotes. (It also helps to include the author's discipline since Google Scholar does not differentiate between two scholars with the same name.) Until recently, there were no metrics for assessing an author's citations in the public press. Almost by default, then, anthropologists seeking promotion needed to demonstrate their competence through academic citation-oriented metrics.

There is also the matter of maintaining appearances. Promotion committees often encourage anthropologists to conform to certain professional standards. Mary Douglas, a famous British anthropologist, in a book entitled *Purity and Danger* (1966) emphasized social structures (including anthropology departments) "are armed with articulate, conscious powers to protect the system; the inarticulate, unstructured areas . . . provoke others to demand that ambiguity be reduced."[3] For some, seeking to speak to nonacademic audiences challenges academic practice. It creates ambiguity regarding who anthropologists should be writing for and to what end. Anthropologists usually need to be of high status to challenge academic practice in this manner safely. (Note that Margaret Mead, who was world famous, never held a senior academic position at a prominent university though, intriguingly, many universities asked her to speak at them.)

Moreover, anthropologists tend to focus on fairly specialized topics. In 1980, Eric Wolf wrote a famous editorial in the *New York Times*, stating "they divide and subdivide, and call it anthropology."[4] He was objecting to anthropology's tendency to turn from broad, holistic analyses to more limited, specialized ones. As part of their academic training, anthropologists usually learn to focus on narrow, specialized subjects. It enhances their status because, with a narrow niched subject, faculty members can be familiar with most of the associated professional literature. That is more difficult with a broad topic. While the books by Diamond, Boo, and Fadiman all deal with specialized topics, their authors are masters at showing how their topics fit into broader concerns that interest a range of readers. Many anthropologists, unfortunately, are not experienced in writing in this manner.

I face this issue as editor of the California Series in Public Anthropology. The series encourages scholars in a number of disciplines to write about major social concerns in ways that help the broader public understand and address them. Two presidents (Mikhail Gorbachev and Bill Clinton) and three Nobel laureates (Amartya Sen, Jody Williams, and Mikhail Gorbachev) have contributed to the series as authors of books or forwards. Given its prestige, many anthropologists are eager to write for the series, but it is often a struggle for them to write for broad audiences in exciting ways. Given their desire for promotion and tenure, it is often a bridge too far.

There is another often-unstated reason that I describe later in this chapter but want to briefly touch on here. **It relates to cultural hegemony, a term associated with the Italian Antonio Gramsci.** We might define cultural hegemony as the means by which a dominant group or perspective orders various beliefs, explanations, values, and worldviews so that they seem to be not only the norm—the expected way to behave—but also justify the status quo as natural and beneficial, thereby leaving the dominant group in control. **Essentially, it is a means of dominating without having to apply overt power or violence.**

An example of such cultural hegemony is the *New York Times'* review of **Robert and Sarah LeVine's *Do Parents Matter?*** The book's theme—that American parents should be less tense in raising their children—should attract a relatively broad range of readers, which presumably is why it was reviewed in the *New York Times Book Review* (2016).[5] The problem is that the LeVines were not able to step outside of an academic writing style to show the relevance of their ideas to a broad audience. Let me quote from part of the review:

> Firm takeaways . . . are rare, though, peppered inside a dizzying survey of firsthand experiences and other studies: on toilet training, eating patterns, tantrums . . . It's not that any one culture has it figured out, but that practices "vary much too widely across cultures for us to accept uncritically the supposition that the mental health of American children is being put at risk by 'insensitive' infant care."

> . . . The LeVines have deep understandings of cultural contexts, allowing them to offer how-to-style pieces of advice: Co-sleeping makes life easier for parents and does not inhibit child development; a "skin-to-skin style of infant care" can foster more compliant children. But a combination of endlessly complicated cultural contexts and the limits of in-field research make these conclusions less than useful for Western readers. Toilet training is easier when conducted outdoors or on dirt floors. Compliance is more achievable when the child is put to work at age 6.

> Most frustrating of all: "We don't have all the evidence needed to settle the question of whether the parental practices described in this book inflict harm on adult mental health." Someone should do that research and write a book about it. I would read it.

The LeVines are senior anthropologists who need not worry about tenure/promotion review committees. Their book addresses a significant topic. While attempting to write for a wider audience. They were not able to move outside the academic styles of presentation with which they were familiar and comfortable. Instead, they remained within the cultural hegemonic framings of anthropology and the academy.

The same pattern can be seen in the rise of internet sites associated with anthropology. In principle, the changing media landscape should widen readers' interests, presenting them with a rich wealth of information. But more frequently than not, readers focus on websites that fit their existing interests and often remain within their own intellectual "bubbles." One sees this with anthropological efforts to reach a broader public with websites such as Sapiens and Anthrodendum, which seek to make anthropological insights available to a wide audience. But the way they frame the issues, choose topics to cover, and present the information limit their readership.

In brief, despite a desire to reach wider audiences, we see the difficulty even senior anthropologists have in escaping the hegemonic frameworks of their discipline and academia. They are uneasy operating too far outside their comfort zones, too far outside the frameworks they have grown accustomed to as scholars.

Let's turn to the second puzzle—why anthropologists tend not to be more recognized for helping others and nourishing the common good. Again, we will consider three examples. The first concerns individuals faced with arbitrary bureaucratic demands. In 1978, six elderly Native American women from the Bannock and Shoshoni tribes in Idaho were accused by a local social services agency of fraud and required to pay $2,000 each in restitution. The fraud accusation was based on the belief that these women had misled the U.S. government about their incomes and, hence, their eligibility for Supplementary Security Income support. Anthropologist Barbara Joans acted as an expert witness for the women in court. She emphasized that the women had an imperfect grasp of English and, as a result, a limited understanding of government regulations. Joans "concluded that the social services personnel and the Indian women were operating at different levels of English and cultural understanding . . . [consequently] the women would not have been able to comprehend what was expected of them."[6] The judge agreed with Joans' conclusion and decided that, henceforth, "social services personnel would have to use an interpreter when they went to the reservation to explain programs and their requirements."[7] The women did not lose their government benefits.

The second example involves a study of a government program—the Experimental Technology Incentive Program (ETIP) set up by the U.S. Department of Commerce[8] that sought to stimulate innovation among American companies. Gerald Britain, an anthropologist, spent more than two years observing the program and provided an in-depth evaluation of its effectiveness. Britain suggested that, despite its good intentions, the program was caught in a structural bind. Companies had little incentive to follow through on the program's suggestions and had their own priorities. Moreover, the program had a high rate of staff turnover, which meant that its projects were often erratically supervised. What ultimately proved the program's undoing was its inability to spend all of the funds allocated to it. Its surplus of roughly $2 million brought the program to the notice of prominent administrators, and, after a brief investigation, the Commerce Department terminated the program. Through his fieldwork, Britain was able to explain why a government program might fail despite its value and good intentions.

The third example concerns the Vicos Project, which is often praised within the discipline as an important effort by anthropologists to assist with third world development. In 1952, guided by Alan Holmberg, Cornell University leased "Vicos," a Peruvian highland hacienda (farm) with roughly 1,800 Quechua-speaking residents, to conduct agricultural experiments. "Between 1952 and 1957 Holmberg, with colleagues and students, initiated a set of social, economic, and agrarian changes . . . By the end of a second lease in 1962, sufficient political pressure had been brought to bear . . . to force the sale of Vicos to its people."[9] Despite this positive result, some have challenged the project's overall success. According to Paul Doughty, who participated in the project and revisited Vicos years later, "In the decades since the end of the project [officially in 1966], the community experienced numerous successes as well as failures as an independent community. Its attempts to diversify the economic base were often thwarted [by others] and the farming enterprise was affected by plant diseases [and] bad market prices . . . For several years from 1974–80, self-serving government manipulations left the people in the community confused, corrupted their leadership, and eroded their confidence."[10] Still, Doughty concluded that the Vicosinos had "altered their society from one of denigrated serfdom and subordination to become an autonomous community of Quechua highlanders fending for themselves on a par with others in Peru's complex and uncertain milieu."[11]

Many other examples like these demonstrate anthropology's ability to empower people and facilitate good, but they often go unnoticed by the broader public. Why? Let me suggest four reasons. You are welcome to add others.

First is the complexity of change. Consider the U.S. Civil Rights Movement. It led to two major laws that have helped transform American society: the Civil Rights Acts of 1964 and the Voting Rights Act of 1965. They were a long time coming—a century, in fact, after passage of the Thirteenth Amendment in 1865 (formally ending slavery). It is difficult to pinpoint one event that led to their passage. Part of the impetus for the Voting Rights Act stemmed from the violence faced by black marchers, including Dr. Martin Luther King, Jr., in Selma. Without the organizing of Dr. King and the Southern Christian Leadership Conference (SCLC), the actions of the National Association for the Advancement of Colored People (NAACP) and the Student Nonviolent Coordinating Committee (SNCC), the rise of television that allowed millions to witness the violence of Selma, the political skills of President Lyndon Johnson, and a coalition of liberal Democratic and Republican legislators, the bills would never have passed. With so many involved, it is hard to specify one event or person that was the tipping point that led to their passage.

Anthropologists played a role in the Civil Rights Movement. Before World War II, Franz Boas and Margaret Mead emphasized that changing social environments could lead to significant behavioral changes. In 1939, Hortense Powdermaker wrote an insightful ethnography of black life in Mississippi that dealt with economic and political barriers that limited black success. **Even though Boas, Mead, and Powdermaker helped develop the intellectual framework for the 1964 and 1965 laws, they are rarely mentioned in relation to the Civil Rights Movement because they were not directly involved in the events that led to the bills' passage.**

A second factor was noted by Shirley Fiske, who described anthropologists as frequently working from the bottom up. Anthropologists are not highlighted as key change agents because they do their work away from the political spotlight, slowly chipping away at the problem. Regarding anthropological work on climate change, Fiske writes:

> Anthropologists have been involved at every step, from the formation of interagency committees in the 1990s, to membership on the National Academy of Sciences studies, to contemporary efforts to insert the social and power dimensions into concepts like "vulnerability assessment" that are building blocks of the National Climate Assessments required by statute. It is not just one person, but the continuing insertion of the "bottom up" approach.[12]

Anthropologists often provide important data regarding what happens "on the ground," but those who actually make changes usually get the credit. In terms of the 1964 and 1965 laws, the spotlight was focused on the major political figures involved—Martin Luther King and President Lyndon Johnson.

A third factor relates to anthropologists working in "third world" settings studying the less powerful on the margins of Western society. President Obama's mother, Ann Dunham, was an anthropologist who conducted valuable fieldwork in Indonesia, but to the broader public, the main value of her work was that she took her son along with her, broadening his international perspective. Helping six elderly Bannock and Shoshoni women is valuable. The Vicosinos who gained control over their land appreciated Cornell's efforts. But such efforts usually do not draw much attention outside of anthropology.

Fourth, given the everyday onrush of information, references to anthropologists in the news media rapidly fade from the spotlight. Ann Kingsolver, an anthropologist at University of Kentucky, was cited in an *Economist* article on Appalachia in 2015, but the *Economist* provided its readers with many other articles on the United States as well. With a host of new articles the following week, she became just one voice among many for the month.[13]

For this situation to change, anthropologists need to demonstrate the good they do on an ongoing basis. Presently, the benefits they bring appear to be episodic—a bit here, a bit there. For the public to take greater notice, the discipline as a whole rather than a few individuals must consistently demonstrate how anthropology nourishes the common good. Sadly, it does not do that yet.

I hope that the preceding discussion has helped to unravel the two noted puzzles—why the most popular anthropological works today tend to be written by non-anthropologists and why anthropological efforts to do good are often less recognized by the broader public than they might be. **Many anthropologists wish to be publicly recognized outside the discipline, but both overt and covert frameworks reinforce the status quo.** Facilitating change will involve refocusing the discipline away from the specialized interests and academic priorities that dominate it now and toward work that directly benefits society more broadly, that serves the common good.

I make this point about structural constraints and hegemonic frameworks before defining public anthropology for an important reason. While anthropologists are often eager to push their ideas and deeds out to the broader public, they tend to pass over the need to address the subtle but significant covert obstacles they face.

In the next section, you will see how different anthropologists perceive public anthropology and how concern for public engagement has varied over time. I leave the tricky part—how anthropologists might overcome the structural constraints limiting public engagement—until later.

DEFINING PUBLIC ANTHROPOLOGY

Let me offer a brief definition of public anthropology: Public anthropology focuses on the interface between anthropology as an academic discipline and the broader public that supports and, ideally, finds much value in it. This works as a definition you can recite to others. It emphasizes the role the public plays in supporting anthropology as well as that anthropology is not an academic island unto itself. Still, it does not address certain subtleties.

Public anthropology has gone from a term I created in the 1990s as a name for the California Series I edit to a term that now has more than 100,000 links in Google Search. I coined the term because it represented a goal of the series: addressing public problems in public ways. Public, in this sense, contrasted with academic styles of presentation. As phrased in the front matter of early books in the series, "the California Series in Public Anthropology emphasizes the anthropologist's role as an engaged intellectual. It continues anthropology's commitment to being an ethnographic witness, to describing in human terms how life is lived beyond the borders of many readers' experiences. But it also adds a commitment through ethnography to reframing the terms of public debate—transforming received, accepted understandings of social issues with new insights, new framings."[14]

Public anthropology has taken on added significance since the series began. It has become an institutionalized part of the discipline. There is an Institute of Public Anthropology at California State University Fresno, a public anthropology lecture series at University of Waterloo, a public anthropology post-doctoral fellowship at the Field Museum, a master's program in public anthropology at American University, a faculty focus in public anthropology at Tufts University, a public anthropology review section and a public anthropology editor at *American Anthropologist*, a master's degree in public issue anthropology at University of Guelph, a doctoral program in *antropología de orientación publica* at *Universidad Autonoma de Madrid* in Spain, and a public anthropology category for posts at *Savage Minds*. Courses dealing with public anthropology are taught at a number of North American schools.

Different groups use the term in somewhat different ways. In the master's program in public anthropology at American University, for example, students "explore the workings of culture, power, and history in everyday life and acquire skills in critical inquiry, problem solving, and public communication." A Tufts University web page states that "Public anthropology includes both civic engagement and public scholarship . . . in which we address audiences beyond academia. It is a publicly engaged anthropology at the intersection of theory and practice, of intellectual and ethical concerns, of the global and the local." The Public Issue Anthropology program at University of Guelph explores "the interface between anthropological knowledge and issues crucial to governance, public discourse, livelihoods, [and] civil society." The *American Anthropologist*'s review section highlights "anthropology of general interest to a wide audience" (an earlier version of the section's purpose suggested its articles were aimed at nonacademic audiences).

In recent decades, other terms have arisen that cover some of the same intellectual territory. Let me offer a sampling. Thomas Hylland Erikson stated that "*Engaging Anthropology* takes an unflinching look at why the discipline has not gained the popularity and respect it deserves."[15] Kay Warren wrote, in an article entitled "Perils and Promises of Engaged Anthropology," that engagement involves "investigations that consider such issues as social justice . . . [and] globalization's impacts."[16] *Practicing anthropology* works "to understand and help people around the world." It adds, "we also turn up in places you might not expect to find us, including the fields of agriculture, computer science, law enforcement forensics, and more."[17] *Activist anthropology*, according to the University of Texas Anthropology Department, is "predicated on the idea that we need not choose between first rate scholarship on the one hand and carefully considered political engagement on the other." Charles Hale stated that there need not be a "contradiction between active political commitment to resolving a problem and rigorous scholarly research on that problem."[18]

Despite the florescence of terms, public anthropology remains the preferred one. If we use a Google search as a rough standard, public anthropology (as previously noted) generates more than 100,000 links. There are roughly 38,000 for practicing anthropology, 10,000 for engaging anthropology, and 4,000 for activist anthropology. **Why have these other terms not replaced public anthropology? I am not sure. But I suspect it derives from the fact that the other terms are not as institutionalized, not as embedded in the discipline's social structures as public anthropology.** They are not associated with programs, lecture series, and book series as public anthropology is.

PUTTING PRESENT CONCERNS IN PERSPECTIVE

It is important to place public anthropology's current popularity in historical perspective. Readers should note that anthropology has not always been as isolated from the general public as it seems today. James Frazer's *The Golden Bough*, Margaret Mead's *Coming of Age in Samoa*, and Ruth Benedict's *Patterns of Culture* engaged a wide range of readers outside the academy in stimulating and important ways during the first half of the twentieth century. In the 1930s, 1940s, and early 1950s, anthropologists often played prominent roles in public arenas. In May 1936, for example, Franz Boas appeared on the cover of *Time Magazine*, which referred to Boas' *The Mind of Primitive Man* as the "Magna Carta of self-respect" for non-Western peoples. Margaret Mead was a cultural icon. During the 1950s, she was the most widely known and respected anthropologist in the world. Upon her death in 1978, tributes came not only from the president of the United States but from the secretary-general of the United Nations. In 1979, she was posthumously awarded the United States' highest civilian honor, the Presidential Medal of Freedom.

Why did anthropology become less publicly engaged? Basically, an academic trend that had been building since the early 1900s came to dominate the discipline. By the late 1960s, anthropology had very much embraced the academy (or university), and the academy had very much embraced anthropology. The founders of anthropology in the mid to late 1800s resided outside universities, either as private scholars (e.g., Henry Lewis Morgan) or as government employees (e.g., James Mooney and John Wesley Powell). But with the rise of universities as centers of learning in the late 1800s—for anthropology, it started with Franz Boas becoming a professor of anthropology in 1899 at Columbia University—more and more anthropologists became associated with academic settings.

What is striking about anthropology's early years is how few anthropologists there were. The American Anthropological Association had 306 members in 1910 and 666 in 1930. "Some elders of our tribe," George Stocking noted, "can recall an age when most anthropologists knew each other personally, and [conferences] could be held . . . in one meeting hall of modest size."[19] This means that anthropologists who wrote books had to write for wider audiences if they wanted anyone to publish them. The anthropology market was too small to attract major publishers. Here's how Raymond Firth phrased it regarding his ethnography of Tikopia, a Polynesian island in the South Pacific:

> In writing *We, The Tikopia*...I had to cater for a nonspecialist readership... in the mid-thirties [1930s], the name Tikopia would be completely meaningless to the outside world . . . I believe then as now that . . . anthropology by its very nature ought to have a wider appeal than its tiny specialist market indicated. I had been supported in this view by the enthusiastic response to my public lectures and broadcasting talks to schools. So I tried to broaden the interest of the material—opening of the book "reads like a novel" as a friend remarked—without sacrificing the scientific rigor of its exposition."[20]

A key turning point in this process was the expansion of student enrollments at American universities in the 1960s associated with the post-World-War-II baby boom. This led to expansion in the number of anthropology departments and, consequently, in student anthropology majors. This meant teachers no longer had to write primarily for public audiences if they wanted to be published. They could write their books solely for students taking anthropology courses. This trend continues today with further expansion of the discipline. The American Anthropological Association now has more than 10,000 members, and academically oriented publishers find it profitable to focus solely on classroom sales for anthropology books.

Especially striking, relative to Firth's work in the 1930s, is how anthropologists frame their work today. Current works often have a "turned inward" quality. Seeking a broader public is less of a priority. As Andrew Abbott noted, "Since professionals draw their self-esteem more from their own world than from the public's [today] . . . The front-line service [i.e., engagement with the public] that is both their fundamental task and their basis for legitimacy becomes the province of low-status colleagues and para-professionals."[21] One sees this in the tendency for large introductory classes to be taught by lower-status adjuncts, for example. High-status full professors tend to teach small advanced courses in their specialties.

Drawing on Mary Douglas once more, we might frame the effort to keep the broader public at bay—while accepting its funding—in terms of purity and pollution. Moving beyond the academic pale makes faculty impure—it "pollutes" them (Margaret Mead's failure to gain a prominent university position is a prime example). The pure remain comfortably ensconced within anthropology departments producing work that few read outside the discipline.

PUBLIC ANTHROPOLOGY'S RELATION TO APPLIED ANTHROPOLOGY

A question commonly raised about public anthropology is how it differs from applied anthropology. In answering, let me start with a personal anecdote. After I coined the term public anthropology, I was under pressure to demarcate how it differed from applied anthropology, which surprised me. I wondered why various academics felt a need to make a clear delineation between ambiguously defined fields as if they could differentiate between them as one does with cars (e.g., Fords versus Hondas) or baseball teams (e.g. the Boston Red Sox versus the New York Yankees). I understand the desire for clarity but personally feel uneasy making precise delineations between the fields. What follows is a suggestive sense of how they differ—no more.

Perhaps the best way to differentiate public and applied anthropology is by understanding the different contexts in which they developed. Applied anthropology has its roots in late nineteenth century American and British colonialism. The focus was on understanding how various indigenous groups lived in order to govern them more effectively. E.E. Evans-Pritchard's famous studies of the Nuer, for example, were financed by the British government of Anglo-Egyptian Sudan to understand why the Nuer were opposing colonial rule. The American Bureau of Ethnology had a similar aim. It sponsored precedent-setting studies by Cushing, Dorsey, Stevenson, and Mooney to understand the dynamics of certain North American Indian tribes and how they were changing under American domination.

In 1941, a group of anthropologists formally established the Society for Applied Anthropology "to promote the investigation of the principles of human behavior and the application of these principles to contemporary issues and problems." The society's opening statement in its journal noted that "*Applied Anthropology* is designed not only for scientists, but even more for those concerned with putting plans into operation, administrators, psychiatrists, social workers, and all those who as part of their responsibility have to take action on problems of human relations." Today, the society's website repeats the first sentence ("to promote the investigation of") and then continues: "The society is unique among professional associations in membership and purpose, representing the interests of professionals in a wide range of settings—academia, business, law, health and medicine, government, etc. The unifying factor is a commitment to making an impact on the quality of life in the world." In a recent review of the field, Trotter, Schensul, and Kostick wrote that applied anthropology tended to have a pragmatic, practical orientation motivated by two concerns: "One is to produce research that has straightforward findings that can be used for direct interventions or implications that can lead to recommendations for policy change . . . The other is to test and improve anthropological theory through devising experiments in sociocultural interventions or policy changes."[22]

Public anthropology grew out of a different context. I coined the term to give an upbeat, positive name to the California book series I was developing in the late 1990s. Why did I not employ applied anthropology in the series title? Partly because it was already widely used. I wanted something new, something different, that could catch people's attention. Another reason was that applied anthropology no longer had the same innovative "buzz" that it had in the 1940s, 1950s, and 1960s. It had become part of the established order.

The tension between applied and public anthropology became clear when, soon after publishing an article on public anthropology in *Anthropology News*, an applied anthropologist, Merrill Singer, wrote an article entitled "Why I Am Not a Public Anthropologist" (2000). He offered a two-fold critique of public anthropology: (1) it ignored work applied anthropologists had done to date in this field and (2) it could lead to a two-tier system in which public anthropologists became the high-status theoreticians while applied anthropologists became lower-status grunts in charge of addressing concrete, practical problems.[23] If the author had read what I had written prior to publishing his piece, he would have seen that I did not mean to disparage applied anthropology. **Why, I wondered, was there not room for both of us—whatever we called ourselves?** Certainly there were many people and many problems needing urgent attention. It puzzled me that some academics wanted to argue over definitions and status given all the problems of the world.

THE UPS AND DOWNS OF PUBLIC ENGAGEMENT

Rather than being drawn into what Sigmund Freud called "the narcissism of small differences" (related groups arguing over small differences to differentiate their identities), I prefer to step back and look at a bigger picture. **Since at least the founding of the Bureau of Ethnology in 1879 under John Wesley Powell, American anthropologists have sought to address the problems of various groups of people.** Prominent in those early years was the work of James Mooney, who described the ghost dance, a religion sweeping Indian tribes of the American West in 1889 and 1890 in response to American domination. He also provided vivid details about a cavalry massacre of more than 200 Sioux at Wounded Knee on December 29, 1890. **The commitment to social engagement continued into the twentieth century even as anthropology became institutionalized as an academic field within universities.** Franz Boas was very much an activist. He opposed racist theories popular in the United States and Europe during the 1930s. Anthropologists, moreover, were actively involved in the Allied war effort during World War II. The well regarded anthropologist Cora DuBois served with the Office of Strategic Services, for example. She was awarded the Army's Exceptional Civilian Award as well as the Order of the Crown by Thailand.

Margaret Mead noted that anthropologists coming out of the war years realized "their skills could be applied fruitfully to problems affecting modern societies and the deliberations of national governments and nation states."[24] One of the highlights of this post-World-War-II period was the Coordinated Investigation of Micronesian Anthropology (CIMA), which represented "the largest research effort in the history of American anthropology" and involved roughly 10 percent of the American anthropological profession conducting fieldwork for the U.S. Navy in Micronesia (which the Navy had a mandate to administer).[25] In the 1960s, anthropologists such as Marvin Harris and Marshall Sahlins played prominent roles in establishing the first "teach-ins"—activist public discussions held at universities—opposing the Vietnam War. They wrote prominent pieces in widely read publications such as *The Nation* and *Dissent*.

In the late 1980s, public engagement was once again popular in the discipline. In 1972, 88 percent of new PhDs were employed in academic settings and just 12 percent were employed in nonacademic settings. But in 1988, 54 percent were employed in nonacademic settings.[26] This change in the job market both symbolized and encouraged increased engagement with those outside the discipline.

And yet, each time these efforts languished. The efforts of Boas, Harris, and Sahlins are still remembered, but their efforts are not that frequently emulated today. The CIMA Navy project is a distant memory, known mostly through a book that documented it. In 1997, 71 percent of new Ph.D.s were hired for academically related positions and 29 percent for nonacademic positions.[27]

TAKING STOCK OF WHERE WE ARE AND WHERE WE ARE HEADING

Let me highlight three summarizing points relating to the preceding sections. First, despite the institutionalized structures and hegemonic frameworks limiting public outreach (noted in the opening section), public engagement seems to repeatedly return to excite the discipline. Why? Victor Turner's concept of anti-structure suggests an answer. Turner highlights "two alternative 'models' for human relations. One involves society as a structured, differentiated, and often hierarchical system of politico-legal-economic positions."[28] The other, termed anti-structure, opposes society's formal structures, emphasizing instead alternative, less conforming orientations. He writes that "there would seem to be—if one can use such a controversial term—a human 'need' to participate in both modalities."[29] Public engagement is not precisely the same as Turner's anti-structure. Still, it emphasizes a different form of accountability from standard academic practice. It reaches out to others beyond the discipline. It supports a different style of prose. It focuses on actively addressing the world's problems.

Since they are ensconced in departmental structures, one might suggest many anthropologists periodically long for greater social engagement and public recognition. They tire of the narrow, inward-looking academic structures that pervade the discipline. They reach out, seeking to engage the public on its own terms, not theirs. **But their efforts usually do not last —they lack structural support that would allow them to be more than momentary bursts of enthusiasm.** In this context, anthropologists' attempts are temporary transformations, momentary defiances, of the established order. With time, anthropologists mostly return to the professional grind centered on academic standards of accountability and pursuing their separate interests in their separate ways.

Second, applied anthropology has an ambiguous relationship with mainstream academic anthropology. On the one hand, applied anthropologists might feel proud that they have resisted the academic structures of the discipline—perhaps better than any other group in the discipline's history. They now have their own formal society (Society for Applied Anthropology), annual meetings, and their own journal (*Human Organization*), and applied anthropology is seen as a major disciplinary subfield (along with cultural anthropology, archaeology, biological anthropology, and linguistics).

On the other hand, applied anthropology has succeeded by adopting certain academic structures. Despite determined effort to engage outside the academy, a sizable number of applied anthropologists hold university positions. There are at least two reasons for this. First, to become a certified applied anthropologist, one needs a graduate degree. The field can only intellectually reproduce if a sizable number of applied anthropologists remain at universities to train new generations of applied anthropologists. Second, given that applied anthropology is now very much a part of the discipline, anthropology departments are a prime source of paid positions so many of the applied anthropologists who attend the society's annual meeting and publish in its journal are academics. They give the meeting and journal an academic feel while, at the same time, espousing to be different from mainstream anthropology.

Third, if public anthropology is not to befall the fate of such trends, it must reflect on how it can reframe certain academic structures. Might I suggest this brings us back to Julie Andrews? If we want public anthropology to make a difference in people's lives, we need to start at the beginning—with the underlying structures of the discipline that repeatedly limit public engagement. To effectively address public problems, we need to address them on the public's terms, not our own. That means not simply listing a set of academic studies that others should attend to and follow—as one might offer to academics. It means rethinking what anthropology does and how it does it. It is within this context that readers can perceive public anthropology's revolutionary intent. Public anthropology seeks to revise key academic structures. It seeks to transform the structures that prevent anthropology from becoming more interdisciplinary, more publicly engaged, more focused on helping others.

Cultural hegemony, you will recall, is a term associated with Antonio Gramsci, a prominent Italian communist. (He spent more than ten years in prison because of his opposition to Mussolini and fascism.) **In relation to anthropology, cultural hegemony refers to the themes previously discussed—the focus on publishing academically oriented books that enhance one's professional career and the reward system that makes deviance from academic standards dangerous for those who wish to be promoted. The term refers not only to helping maintain the status quo but to making it seem as if the status quo is a reasonable, appropriate way to behave. My point is this: If we want to change the discipline and the broader academic structures that support it, we must perceive the hegemonic constraints that limit social engagement in the discipline.**

The next question is how to facilitate such change. The following section offers suggestive strategies. **With the first two strategies, the hope is that anthropology can become a more credible discipline in the public's eyes by improving its accountability standards and providing greater transparency regarding how certain results are achieved.**

The third strategy is based on the idea that anthropology works best when it involves collaboration with others. Anthropologists need to work with other groups, other organizations, to facilitate significant change. **Anthropologists need the power and resources those organizations provide. Addressing the larger society's concerns regarding accountability and transparency offers a means by which to reach out to others—since many beyond academia are interested in facilitating precisely those changes within the academy.**

The fourth strategy suggests anthropology can further its credibility by focusing on helping others instead of mainly striving not to harm them—the discipline's current ethic. Anthropologists' efforts to help others have, as previously noted, been well-intended but episodic. They have occurred irregularly rather than representing a broad disciplinary effort. Anthropologists should strive, as best they can, to help the people who help them in their research.

Let me share another secret with you. These strategies may be a bit too bold for some anthropologists who, ensconced in traditional academic ways, have grown comfortable with the status quo. They might long for greater public recognition but are not necessarily be eager to change. **If you are interested in exploring anthropology beyond the introductory level, these strategies offer a way for you to participate in changing the discipline for the better and, through that change, the broader world as well.**

A FRAMEWORK FOR RESHAPING THE DISCIPLINE

This section sets out in detail the four strategies for reframing the discipline. A later section invites you to grapple with ways to facilitate social change.

(1) Accountability—Moving beyond judging faculty members by the number of academic papers they publish to judging them by whether what they have written helps others rather than just their careers. Anthropologists tend to assess the intellectual quality of their colleagues by the published works they produce. According to Deborah Rhode's *In Pursuit of Knowledge: Scholars, Status, and Academic Culture*, "Because academic reputation and rewards are increasingly dependent on publication, faculty have incentives to churn out tomes that will advance their careers regardless of whether they will also advance knowledge."[30] She notes a report by the Carnegie Foundation that more than a third of faculty members surveyed believed that their published works were mostly assessed in terms of quantity rather than quality (at schools with doctoral programs, more than 50 percent of the faculty members held that view).[31]

Instead of focusing on quantitative calculations of accountability, such as publishing a certain number of articles per year (or books every few years), I suggest that accountability would be better assessed in more pragmatic terms: How socially significant is the problem being addressed? To what degree does the author successfully address it? What impact does the author's published work about this problem have outside the academy?

The vast majority of funding for anthropological research comes from nonacademic agencies and foundations. A key criterion for funding is that the research must be valuable for a relatively broad public rather than only a few individuals. The National Science Foundation (NSF), for example, requires that all proposals and final reports specify the "broader impacts" of the research, which NSF defines as encompassing "the potential to benefit society and contribute to the achievement of specific, desired, societal outcomes" and written "insofar as possible, [to] be understandable to a scientifically . . . literate lay reader."[32] The National Institutes of Health (NIH) Office of Behavioral and Social Sciences Research affirms that "realizing the full potential of our Nation's investment in health research requires that science inform both practice and policy . . . we can stimulate relevant and usable research that is informed by the needs of end users whether they are healthy individuals, patients, practitioners, community leaders, or policymakers."[33] Paralleling these perspectives, the United Kingdom's Research Councils UK (RCUK) stresses a commitment to "supporting and rewarding researchers to engage with the public."[34]

Despite affirmation of these standards by funders, many anthropologists still opt for academic standards that focus on the number of academic colleagues who cite their work. They also focus on who obtains research funding. British anthropologist Adam Kuper has suggested that "The [grant] review process rewards people who can write good proposals even if they failed to deliver on earlier grants. Few foundations evaluate the research they fund . . . The best credential for a fellowship is a previous fellowship. And landing a grant usually wins you more kudos than getting out the results of your research."[35] In other words, the path to success often lies in claiming to advance knowledge rather than in demonstrating that you have.

The primary value of focusing on outcomes is that outcomes can be assessed fairly directly. Do the results effectively address the problem? Do they contribute to building coherent, cumulative knowledge that can be used beyond the discipline to address real problems? Do they improve other people's lives?

Take Abhijit Banerjee and Esther Duflo's *Poor Economics* as an example. The authors systematically identified approaches that work best for particular problems. For example, they compared programs for preventing malaria and asked which program had a better chance of being used in a group of villages—malaria nets given away free to villagers or malaria nets that villagers had to partly pay for and hence had an incentive to use properly? Rather than assuming the answer, they compared randomized groups in several locales using various levels of financial support provided for acquiring the nets. Based on that information, they were able to draw conclusions regarding the best way to distribute the nets in a range of locales to fight malaria effectively. They found that (a) all of the villagers accepted free nets but, as the price went up, fewer did, and (b) there was no difference in use of the nets based on whether the villagers paid for them.[36] Apparently, people valued the nets regardless of how they got them—because they helped fight malaria.

The Nobel-winning author Robert Solow described *Poor Economics* as follows: "Abhijit Banerjee and Esther Duflo are allergic to grand generalizations about the secret of economic development. Instead they appeal to many local observations and experiments to explore how poor people in poor countries actually cope with their poverty."[37] This represents anthropology at its best. By comparing the effectiveness of different approaches, anthropologists can develop a comprehensive understanding of how to address a problem in a particular context.

When advocating for this sense of accountability, it is important not to get caught up in academic rhetoric concerning objectivity. As the social sciences moved into universities in the late 1800s, objectivity in the social sciences took on a different meaning. It came to refer to avoiding politically charged topics that might upset the political and financial elites who often helped fund and direct universities. Mary Furner, in *Advocacy and Objectivity: A Crisis in the Professionalization of American Social Science, 1865–1905*, described how professionalization changed what it meant to study a social issue.

> The professionalization process altered the mission of social science [within universities]. Only rarely [as the twentieth century proceeded] did professional social scientists do what no one else was better qualified to do [and what they had done decades earlier]: bring expert skill and knowledge to bear on cosmic questions pertaining to the society as a whole. Instead, studies and findings tended to be internal, recommendations hedged with qualifiers, analyses couched in jargon that was unintelligible to the average citizen. . . . The academic professionals, having retreated to the security of technical expertise, left to journalists and politicians the original mission—the comprehensive assessment of industrial society—that had fostered the professionalization of social sciences.[38]

Objectivity does not lie in avoiding certain politically charged topics. The issue is not whether an individual has an "agenda"—one could suggest that everyone has biases of one sort or another. Being a "disinterested professional" does not mean being uninterested in the world outside one's laboratory. **It means putting the larger society's interests ahead of one's own personal interests or the interests of those for whom one works. Objectivity derives from open, public analyses of divergent accounts. We know an account is more objective—more credible, more scientific—after various individuals, whatever their personal biases, independently confirm the claims made. The opposition is not between objectivity and advocacy; it is between claiming objectivity and substantiating it.** Anthropologists who claim to act in a disinterested manner with no hint of social advocacy are not necessarily being objective. Objectivity comes from others confirming one's data. If the data cannot be confirmed, it is critical to understand how and why this limits the claims one can make.

(2) Transparency—Moving beyond highlighting conclusions that attract attention to allowing others to understand how these conclusions were reached.

Lancet, one of the world's leading medical journals, reported in 2014 that perhaps $200,000,000,000 (that is, 200 billion dollars), which constitutes about 85 percent of all global research spending, is likely wasted on poorly designed and poorly reported research studies. Since this is a rather shocking figure, let me offer the actual words from *The Lancet*. Macleod et al. report:

> Global biomedical and public health research involves billions of dollars and millions of people . . . Although this vast enterprise has led to substantial health improvements, many more gains are possible if the waste and inefficiency in the ways that biomedical research is chosen, designed, done, analysed, regulated, managed, disseminated, and reported can be addressed. In 2009, Chalmers and Glasziou . . . estimated that the cumulative effect was that about 85 percent of research investment—equating to $200 billion of the investment in 2010—is wasted.[39]

In a related article, Glasziou stated that "research publication can both communicate and miscommunicate. Unless research is adequately reported, the time and resources invested in the conduct of research is[sic] wasted . . . Adequate reports of research should clearly describe which questions were addressed and why, what was done, what was shown, and what the findings mean. However, substantial failures occur in each of these elements." [40] Related to this point, the *Economist* reported that "half of clinical trials do not have their results published . . . Proportionally, the worst culprits are government and academia."[41]

In an article entitled "Many Psychology Findings Not as Strong as Claimed," in the *New York Times,* Benedict Carey reported:

> The past several years have been bruising ones for the credibility of the social sciences. A star social psychologist was caught fabricating data, leading to more than 50 retracted papers. A top journal published a study supporting the existence of ESP that was widely criticized. The journal *Science* [one of the world's leading journals] pulled a political science paper on the effect of gay canvassers on voters' behavior because of concerns about faked data. Now, a painstaking years long effort to reproduce 100 studies published in three leading psychology journals has found that more than half of the findings did not hold up when retested.[42]

These studies make clear there is a real need for transparency in research so others can properly review, assess, and, if possible, confirm important studies. Two hundred billion dollars is a lot of money to spend on questionable research.

Let me offer two examples of the importance of increased transparency in anthropology. First, there is heated debate over whether the Yanomami (living in the Amazon region between Brazil and Venezuela) were once particularly violent and, in frequent wars, killed numerous opponents. Because some have viewed the Yanomami as exemplifying tendencies of "early man," an incorrect assumption in my view, the issue has drawn worldwide attention regarding just how violent "early man" was. The issue also carried serious political implications for the Yanomami. If they were indeed as violent as some had portrayed them, the Brazilian government felt they should be broken up into several small reserves rather than be permitted a large single reserve that would help prevent gold miners from entering the Yanomami's territory. (After considerable debate, a large single reserve was established in 1992.)

Though much has been written on the topic, **reliable data are needed to assess the Yanomami's level of violence accurately.** All we have are ambiguous anecdotal assessments and suggestive statistics that might or might not be valid. The argument revolves around data reported by Chagnon in a famous article in *Science* (1988).[43] But these data have not been made public making it impossible to confirm them. Chagnon indicates he has "never published data that would enable someone to determine who specifically was a 'killer,' his name, his village, his age, how many wives he had, and how many offspring. In short, the data needed to make the criticism that Fry makes [questioning the validity of Chagnon's statistics] cannot be gleaned from my published data."[44] If Chagnon will not release his data so others can confirm them, readers might wonder if new research might be conducted. The problem is that the Yanomami have since been pacified. Readers might think, therefore, that anthropologists would just drop the debate, admitting it is unresolvable until Chagnon makes his data public. But that has not happened. Anthropologists continue to get into heated arguments over the topic. Just ask one of your teachers who specializes in lowland South America about this and see how she or he responds.

The second example is Herrnstein and Murray's widely discussed book, *The Bell Curve* (1994), which suggested that differences in intelligence among "races" (as they defined them) performed differently on certain IQ tests. From this debatable proposition, the authors implied that whites appeared to be more successful economically than blacks because whites were more intelligent.

Needless to say, the book caused a stir in the press. Early reviews, drawing on the statistical analyses the authors provided, were generally positive. Nicholas Lemann noted a key reason for the positive reviews: "The ordinary routine of neutral reviewers having a month or two to go over the book with care did not occur . . . The [initial] debate . . . was conducted in the mass media by people with no independent ability to assess the book." Early reviewers had to base their reviews on the statistics provided by Herrnstein and Murray, "It was not until late 1995 that the most damaging criticism of *The Bell Curve* began to appear, . . . ***The Bell Curve*, it turns out, is full of mistakes ranging from sloppy reasoning to mis-citations of sources to outright mathematical errors."** [45]

In other words, without the ability to carefully analyze the data supporting an author's conclusions, allowing others to confirm the author's assertions, the social and medical sciences cannot produce credible results on which the public may rely. Without transparency, it is mostly people offering suggestive but unproven uncertain possibilities.

Are you puzzled by why the Center for a Public Anthropology is not the Center for Public Anthropology? Do you know what the phrase "a public" refers to? It emphasizes making anthropology's dynamics more public, embedding the focus on transparency in the name of the center.

(3) Collaborating with others—Moving beyond working alone to working with others to facilitate significant change. Working on their own, anthropologists rarely have the power to bring significant social change. To be effective, they usually need the energy, resources, and momentum generated by larger organizations that have the ability to mobilize people and persist in a project through time. **Stated succinctly: *Public anthropology works best when it collaborates with others.***

Before providing examples of anthropological collaboration, let me discuss three points to place both the strategy and the examples in context. First, **the key to getting readers to take note of what one writes often lies less in what is disclosed than in to whom the information is disclosed. Anthropologists should target their information to those most interested in it while being sure to present it in a form that these interested parties can readily use. The value of targeted transparency— providing institutions with truthful public information they need to discredit the claims of competitors—is that there is a ready group of individuals committed to publicizing it.** When reporting on where foreign aid does (and does not) work, for example, anthropologists could focus on reporting the information to organizations that compete financially with ones that wastefully spend aid grants.

Second, targeted transparency makes clear why anthropologists need to reach beyond policymakers to other constituencies in presenting their information. Providing information solely to policymakers (who then use it at their discretion) can be a dangerous tango. To have credibility—to really speak truth to power—cultural anthropologists cannot be pawns of the powerful. With their academic appointments and tenured positions, anthropologists can be respected, independent critics. Yes, anthropologists should collaborate—both formally and informally—with a range of social and political institutions. But anthropologists need to retain a certain independence so their information and insights are not buried by those seeking to maintain the status quo. Simply reporting information back to those who fund one's research or pay one's salary means important information is unlikely to ever become public. Anthropologists need to reach out to others who will use their information and build on it to facilitate change.

Third, if you accept my point regarding cultural hegemony—the structural and cultural constraints that limit the discipline's public engagement— then collaborating with those outside the discipline offers a way to overcome such constraints. Since many outside the academy are concerned about higher education's limited accountability and transparency, collaborating with outside groups offers a means by which to address these problems.

My first example of anthropological collaboration is Partners in Health (PIH), a nonprofit organization that builds medical support programs on communities' existing structures and uses community personnel as staff. Two of the medical doctors who founded the organization, Paul Farmer and Jim Yong Kim, both have PhDs in anthropology. According to its website, PIH's mission is to "provide a preferential option for the poor in health care. By establishing long-term relationships with sister organizations based in settings of poverty, Partners In Health strives to achieve two overarching goals: to bring the benefits of modern medical science to those most in need of them and to serve as an antidote to despair."

Collaboration is central to PIH's organization, as the *Catalogue of Philanthropy* notes:

> Health programs should involve community members at all levels of assessment, design, implementation, and evaluation. Community health workers may be family members, friends, or even patients who provide health education, refer people who are ill to a clinic, or deliver medicines and social support to patients in their homes. Community health workers do not supplant the work of doctors or nurses; rather, they are a vital interface between the clinic and the community . . . PIH doesn't tell the communities we serve what they need— they tell us.[46]

PIH perceives community health workers as critical partners in a patient's care:

> For nearly three decades, PIH has hired and trained community health workers to help patients faced with . . . challenges receive care. Our 12,000 community health workers around the world visit patients at home, assess their health, and link them with clinics and hospitals.

> In Haiti, where PIH's community health worker program originated, they are called *accompagnateurs* to emphasize the importance of accompanying people in their journey through sickness and back to health.

Living in the communities where they work, community health workers are trusted and welcomed into patients' homes to provide high-quality services for a wide range of health problems. A patient beginning treatment for tuberculosis, for example, is paired with a health worker who visits every day to supervise treatment and ensure the patient takes medications regularly and correctly. For people living with HIV or other chronic diseases, this support enables them to live longer and healthier lives.[47]

In brief, PIH emphasizes community collaboration in extending its effectiveness as a health care provider. The *accompagnateurs* are key partners in treating patients.

Another example of working with others is the Center for a Public Anthropology's collaboration with Altmetric.com on the Metrics Project. Working together, we provide metrics on anthropological articles and books highlighted in the world's major news outlets, thereby broadening the metrics used to assess a faculty member's intellectual work. **By offering clear metrics of public engagement to both deans and department chairs, we hope to support anthropologists becoming more publicly engaged—thereby addressing the first puzzle noted at the beginning of the chapter.**

It would be impossible for the Center to gather the data needed for the Metrics Project, which are collected using digital object identifiers (DOIs) of articles and books to search for references in media around the world. Altmetric is proficient in gathering these data in the social sciences; the center is not. But Altmetric tends to work with librarians, the Center with social science chairs and deans. With the Metrics Project, the Center broadens the reach of Altmetric's work.

A third example is the Center's work with members of the U.S. Congress. Until recently, relatively few researchers—approximately 11 percent—complied with the NSF requirement to submit project outcome reports following completion of their research to report the benefits of their work. Working with student volunteers, the Center brought this problem to the attention of members of Congress, who in turn raised the issue with NSF. Over a four-month period, completion of the benefit reports rose to roughly 80 percent. Obviously, the Center could not facilitate greater completion of the project outcome reports on its own. Congress was not aware of the problem until the Center and students brought it to light. Working together, the Center and congressional members were able to raise the percentage of NSF project outcome reports substantially.

(4) Benefiting others—Moving beyond "doing no harm" to demonstrating how anthropology actually benefits others. Presently, the American Anthropological Association's code of ethics (2012) focuses on "doing no harm." What happens, however, when—as occurs at many fieldwork sites—the people the anthropologist is studying are suffering from a range of maladies? Do anthropologists leave the people be because they are not the source of the maladies or do they try to help the people who are helping them with their research?

The agencies that fund anthropological research are entitled to ask whether it is enough for anthropologists receiving grants to "repay" the funding agency and, more generally, the larger society by affirming that they did no harm to anyone in spending the thousands of dollars given them. Or should the funding agency expect a more positive response—that the anthropologists actually sought to address a problem that would benefit a group of people in some helpful way?

Contrary to popular belief, the Hippocratic Oath that medical students affirm on becoming doctors does not primarily focus on "do no harm." The original phrasing of the oath in Epidemics, I,II states that, "As to disease make a habit of two things—help, or at least, to do no harm." The phrase "first, do no harm" likely derives from Thomas Inman, a nineteenth century house surgeon. Why anthropologists should focus on "do no harm" in their code of ethics—rather than on helping others—is an interesting question.

Anthropology's "do no harm" standard is both out of date and somewhat self-serving. It is drawn from a period in the late 1800s and early 1900s when anthropologists sought to differentiate themselves from missionaries and colonial administrators who sought to reshape indigenous societies. Anthropologists did not try to remake these societies; they consciously tried to avoid changing them. But this context no longer holds. The "do no harm" ethic is now self-serving in that it allows anthropologists to skirt certain moral dilemmas and obligations. When you ask people for help–such as in your research–you are usually expected to return the favor in some form at some time. That reciprocity is a key principle of social relations (articulated in an anthropological classic, *The Gift*, by Marcel Mauss in 1925.

Returning for a moment to the Yanomami, there have been questions over the years about whether the unconfirmed reports of their violence harmed the Yanomami. Focusing on this question has allowed anthropologists to side-step a critical concern: What tangible benefits have come to the Yanomami for helping a host of anthropologists in their research over several decades? Chagnon made well over a million dollars from his various books and movies. Other anthropologists have not made as much, but their publications have allowed them to gain promotions and salary increases that put their standard of living well above the average American's. Mostly they supplied the Yanomami with minor goods and guns. Only a few individuals, such as Bruce Albert, sought to address the critical health problems decimating the Yanomami highlighted in Kopenawa and Albert's *The Falling Sky (2013)*.

Rather than focusing on not harming others, which can be interpreted in various ways by people with different agendas, anthropologists might focus on helping the people who help them in tangible ways, which would certainly enhance indigenous groups' perceptions of anthropologists. It would also enhance public perceptions of anthropological endeavors—presenting them not as self-serving exercises in career building but as mutually beneficial efforts in understanding and helping others.

FACILITATING SOCIAL CHANGE

The preceding strategies are aimed at improving how the public perceives anthropology—especially in terms of anthropology's credibility and value. In this section, we turn to specific ways anthropologists could facilitate change. The standard model for anthropologists is to be hired by companies or government agencies interested in helping others—in the role of consultants, cultural intermediaries, or researchers. The suggestions presented here are somewhat different. They offer alternative approaches that anthropologists might pursue. They are meant to offer additional possibilities.

(1) If you accept my point regarding how cultural hegemonic structures shape resistance to change, then collaborating with others beyond the academy is critical. What is needed are the staying power and resources that large organizations provide. Given concerns in the broader society about accountability and transparency in higher education, anthropologists have a means for reaching out to various public groups. The value of targeted transparency—providing key institutions with truthful public information needed to discredit the claims of competitors—is that there are groups ready to publicizing the information anthropologists provide. We see this particularly in the next two strategies—conceptualizing important issues and exposés.

(2) **Conceptualizing important issues: At its core, anthropology embodies comparison. By comparing one group to another, anthropology allows people to step outside their parochial perspectives. It provides frameworks that voters, politicians, officials, and activists can use to conceptualize a problem and take effective action to address it.** Here is an example.

Based on comparative work in Pakistan and Norway, Norwegian anthropologist Fredrik Barth wrote that "**Contrary to what is still a widely shared view, I [have] argued that ethnic groups are not groups formed on the basis of shared culture, but rather the formation of groups on the basis of differences of culture . . . The contrast between 'us' and 'others' is what is embedded in the organization of ethnicity.**"[48] He asserted that there are few clear, distinct cultural boundaries. Rather, a range of continuous variation exists across a geographic area. Oppositions make cultural distinctions come alive. Barth suggests that behind many cultural conflicts—such as the bitter tensions between Arabs and Christians, Ukrainians and Russians, Sunni and Shiite Arabs—are "ethnic entrepreneurs."

> **The conflicts we see today are the work mainly of middle echelon politicians who use the politics of cultural difference to further their ambitions for leadership**. This is tempting to them because in ethnic identities they see a potential constituency, so to speak, waiting for them, and all they need to find is the key to set the process in motion. Leaders seek these constituencies and mobilize them by making select, contrastive cultural differences more salient, and . . . by linking them to grievances and injustices . . . They engage in confrontational politics.[49]

To reduce ethnic conflict, Barth suggests bringing how these political entrepreneurs work into the open. Rather than letting these entrepreneurs emphasize group differences, we should focus on people's common ground.

> We need to reduce the saliency of . . . particular differences, and draw [people's] attention to all the other crisscrossing differences and the joint interests they have. We want to create arenas, specifically for negotiations, where one can work from common interests and move outward . . . You don't start with opposed constituencies and try to bring them together. You start with the common ground. You ask what the shared interests between the parties are. Then you negotiate to expand that common ground.[50]

In a sense, this is what Boas did in his work on race—and is why *Time* magazine recognized him. **Anthropologists can conceptualize new ways to solve serious public problems. Through their clarity, documentation, and power, they can draw politicians, key decision-makers, and the larger public to give them serious consideration. It involves the power of ideas to reframe and clarify problems so as to facilitate effective action. But to do so, anthropologists must collaborate with others and target their insights to those who are most willing to use them effectively.** They cannot simply speak out, expecting others to listen, as occurs in their classes. Anthropologists need to identify the individuals and organizations that can take advantage of their innovative framings and strive to insure that those individuals and organizations make use of them.

Could you apply Barth's insight to help reduce racial and social tensions at your university? If so, how? If not, why not?

(3) **Exposés—Effectively speaking truth to power.** There is an excitement in challenging authority, especially when you can expose illegal or inappropriate activity. There is less excitement in what

frequently follows. You are often ignored. Not every exposé makes headlines. Moreover, those that do are often forgotten in the onslaught of later news. **In announcing an exposé, the question is how you can get others to recognize it and take action to address it. Let's explore two case studies.**

Nancy Scheper-Hughes, an anthropologist at UC Berkeley, used her ethnographic skills to facilitate the trial of the first person ever convicted of organ trafficking. The following report appeared in *Bloomberg Business*.

> A New York man admitted to brokering black-market sales of human kidneys to three Americans, becoming the first person convicted in the U.S. of organ trafficking. Levy Izhak Rosenbaum, 60, pleaded guilty today to three counts of organ trafficking and one count of conspiracy in federal court in Trenton, New Jersey. He said three ailing people in New Jersey paid him a total of $410,000 to arrange the sale of kidneys from healthy donors and an undercover FBI agent paid him $10,000. A 1984 U.S. law bans the sale of human organs.[51]

Interestingly, most of the news reports did not mention the role Scheper-Hughes played. However, Wikipedia in its description of "Operation Bid Rig," the New Jersey political corruption scandal based on an FBI "sting operation," noted that "anthropologist and organ trade expert Nancy Scheper-Hughes claimed that she had informed the FBI that Rosenbaum was 'a major figure' in international organ smuggling."[52] Quoting Scheper-Hughes:

> I went to the media, to CBS, to *60 Minutes*, and then to *48 Hours*, which did send an investigative reporter, Avi Cohan, to meet me in Israel where we spoke to patients who had had 'undercover' transplants at hospitals in NYC, Philadelphia, the Bay Area, and Los Angeles. CBS decided not to do the exposé. I was stumped. No one wanted to accuse surgeons, or prevent a suffering patient from getting a transplant, even with an illegally procured kidney from a displaced person from abroad.[53]

Thus, it took several more years for the New Jersey FBI office to arrest Rosenbaum in 2009 as part of a much larger organized crime sting. Because Rosenbaum was involved in another case that was more important from the FBI's perspective, the agents finally followed up on Scheper-Hughes' information.

A second exposé continues to make world news—Edward Snowden leaking classified government documents about the activities of the U.S. National Security Agency (NSA). Wikipedia summarizes the case:

> On May 20, 2013, Snowden flew to Hong Kong after leaving his job at an NSA facility in Hawaii and in early June he revealed thousands of classified NSA documents to journalists Glenn Greenwald, Laura Poitras, and Ewen MacAskill. Snowden came to international attention after stories based on the material appeared in *The Guardian* and the *Washington Post*. Further disclosures were made by other newspapers, including *Der Spiegel* and the *New York Times*.

> It was revealed that the NSA was harvesting millions of email and instant messaging contact lists, searching email content, tracking and mapping the location of cell phones, and undermining attempts at encryption via Bullrun and that the agency was using cookies to

"piggyback" on the same tools used by internet advertisers "to pinpoint targets for government hacking and to bolster surveillance. The NSA was shown to be "secretly" tapping into Yahoo and Google data centers to collect information from "hundreds of millions" of account holders worldwide by tapping undersea cables using the MUSCULAR surveillance program.[54]

It might seem obvious that Snowden's whistleblowing would garner wide public attention since it involved explosive documentation on the degree to which the NSA was collecting information most people thought was private. **What is less known is that the *Washington Post* published related information in articles by Dana Priest and William Arkin before Snowden's disclosures. They reported:**

> Nine years after the terrorist attacks of 2001, the United States is assembling a vast domestic intelligence apparatus to collect information about Americans using the FBI, local police, state homeland security offices, and military criminal investigators. The system, by far the largest and most technologically sophisticated in the nation's history, collects, stores, and analyzes information about thousands of U.S. citizens and residents, many of whom have not been accused of any wrongdoing.[55]

The disclosure, entitled "Monitoring America," was turned into a PBS *Frontline* report, "Top Secret America." The Department of Homeland Security, the authors note:

> provides local agencies a daily flow of information bulletins. These reports are meant to inform agencies about possible terror threats. But some officials say they deliver a never-ending stream of information that is vague, alarmist, and often useless. "It's like a garage in your house you keep throwing junk into until you can't park your car in it," says Michael Downing, deputy chief of counterterrorism and special operations for the Los Angeles Police Department.[56]

The disclosures by Snowden and Priest/Arkin differ in emphasis. Priest/Arkin focused solely on data collected in the United States while Snowden focused on a global surveillance program. Snowden's disclosures violated national security laws; Priest and Arkin did not, though presumably they made a number of NSA officials uncomfortable. They were suggesting that a vast amount of secret information was being collected that was mostly useless. It might be suggested that Snowden was simply expanding their analysis. The results of these exposés are interesting. Edward Snowden is forced to live in Moscow since, if he returns to the United States, he will be tried and likely imprisoned. Dana Priest holds the Knight Chair in Public Affairs Journalism at the University of Maryland.

Why the dramatic difference in these two exposés? One key reason is that Priest and Arkin are journalists who played by the accepted rules and did not violate any laws. The agencies involved knew what they were going to announce and apparently did not strenuously object. After a big splash, their report was mostly forgotten. Hence, there was no need for the NSA to react. **But as soon as Snowden made his disclosures, he not only attracted worldwide attention but created a number of international incidents with U.S. allies such as Germany, which accused the United States of violating its citizens' privacy. Leaking secret information as well as the conflicts created with American allies made Snowden an international outlaw forced to live beyond the reach of the U.S. judicial system. Because he did not play by the accepted rules, he**

garnered more attention and had a much greater impact than Priest and Arkin.

If you were to speak out as a public anthropologist—speak truth to power—what type of exposé would you try to make? How would you go about doing it? What do you think the personal cost, if any, might be?

(4) **Writing narratives with impact.** When discussing the first puzzle in the chapter's section, I emphasized that non-anthropologists tend to write the most popular anthropology-oriented books. It is not that anthropologists cannot write for broader audiences. Rather, they operate within academic contexts that discourage such writing. That said, some anthropologists, focusing on books used in course adoptions, do rather well financially. Chagnon's introductory ethnography on the Yanomami, for example, has run through five editions and sold well over a million copies. Part of what makes the book successful is that teachers can use a set of vivid ethnographic videos that make the book's descriptions come alive.

Chagnon also depicts his interactions with the Yanomami in a lively manner, portraying himself as an Indian Jones type figure. To my knowledge, no other anthropologist has ever discussed how particular members of the tribe being studied purposely sought to kill them (with a gun in Chagnon's case). Such incidents might have happened to other anthropologists, but they have never bragged about them as Chagnon has done. Anthropologists generally take pride in displaying tolerance toward people who are different from themselves, showing respect for those with whom they live and work while conducting their research. Chagnon moved in the opposite direction, giving a dramatic, and at times pejorative, flair to his depictions of the Yanomami.

Yet many undergraduates enjoy Chagnon's book. It brings out their prejudices—emphasizing Amazonian Indians as exotic "savages." This was not necessarily Chagnon's intent. He wanted to stress that the Yanomami were just as barbaric as Americans—no more, no less. But that is not what students tend to take away from his book. They take away their superiority to the Yanomami. **What does one do with a popular ethnography such as Chagnon's? While it offers a detailed description of an Amazonian group, it also goes against an anthropological tenet of describing people studied in fairly favorable terms. What would you do?**

Most anthropologists resist the notion that they produce works of fiction. They do not compose their ethnographies out of thin air—as many suspect Carlos Castaneda did in *The Teachings of Don Juan*. Most anthropological ethnographies sell around 2,000 copies—a pittance compared to the millions of books Castaneda has sold. It is not always clear where facts leave off and fiction begins in some colleagues' accounts. Anthropologists claim they are objective; they claim they present accurate accounts. But few visit the field sites of other anthropologists to test this assumption. It makes for better relations with colleagues if they do not.

You have read many books. Some have excited you; others have not. If you were to write a popular anthropology book that involved a sense of professional scholarship, what topic would you select if you wanted to sell a hundred thousand copies (and gain 10 percent of the selling price)? How would you write to capture students' attention without moving too far into fiction or demeaning those with whom you worked?

Let us review what I have discussed and see whether you recall key ideas made in each section. We started this chapter with (a) two puzzles stemming from anthropology's interactions with the broader public. I then turned to (b) describing public anthropology especially varying perceptions of it and its relation to applied anthropology. Next, I discussed (c) four of the field's central strategies for transforming anthropology in order to enhance its credibility with the larger public. Finally, I explored

(d) suggested ways to facilitate change. In this chapter, I have sought to help you not only understand the problems public anthropology addresses but also consider effective ways for anthropologists to reach out to the public. Did you get these points or did you keel over with boredom? Did some of the points seem relevant to you?

CONCLUDING QUESTIONS

First, in an earlier section, I highlighted the Center for a Public Anthropology's work with Altmetric. **Please look over the** website **and explore the data it presents. Do you think it will prove effective in broadening the standards for promotion by highlighting faculty publications in the world's media? If so, why? If not, why not?**

Second, below is an account of how introductory students like yourself, working with the Center for a Public Anthropology in coordination with key Brazilian groups facilitated the return of blood samples taken from the Yanomami in the late 1960s. **What strategies highlighted in this chapter do you think proved effective in this effort? I counted four. How many do you find in this account? How would you draw media outlets to this story so it will reach the broader public?**

> As an example of public anthropology (following the model of the Kahn Academy), Dr. Borofsky has created short 10–15 minute videos on key topics in anthropology for introductory students. All 28 videos are available from the *Perspectives: An Open Introduction to Cultural Anthropology* website.

CENTER FOR A PUBLIC ANTHROPOLOGY PROJECT: HOW THE BLOOD CAME BACK TO THE YANOMAMI

More information about this project along with the full set of references can be found on the Center for Public Anthropology website. Students and instructors are welcome to participate in the Community Action Project.

STAGE ONE: The issue seemed fairly straightforward—before it became a question of legal liability. Initially, one's perspective on returning the blood to the Yanomami came down to where you stood on a continuum between advocating for science and advocating for indigenous rights. At stake were blood samples collected from the Yanomami during the late 1960s by an American research team that included James Neel, a geneticist, and Napoleon Chagnon, an anthropologist. [S1-a] Unbeknownst to the Yanomami, the blood samples were subsequently stored at a number of American institutions, most prominently Pennsylvania State University. The Yanomami only discovered this fact following the publication of Patrick Tierney's *Darkness in El Dorado* (2000).

Figure 1: Yanomami Portrait by Claudia Andujar. All rights reserved.

Tierney wrote the Yanomami blood samples were stored "in an old refrigerator at Penn State University." [S1-b]

For the Yanomami, this was deeply upsetting. Some Yanomami felt they should be compensated better than they had been since the samples were helping researchers' in their careers. But many more felt it was a religious sacrilege to retain, rather than return, the samples so they could be properly disposed of in accord with Yanomami tradition. [S1-c]

The Yanomami had been promised that their blood samples would be used to learn more about the diseases ravaging them. [S1-d] (They were collected, it should be noted, in the midst of a measles epidemic.) Unfortunately, this did not occur. A few researchers used the samples for their personal research. But judging from the publications produced over the more than forty years the samples were stored at various institutions, they were not widely studied, nor were they ever used in a way that directly benefitted the Yanomami. Hence, what appeared to be a conflict between science and indigenous rights was, for the first few years at least, mostly a conflict between those who wanted to save the samples for some vague, future use (such as the Human Genome Project) and the Yanomami who wanted the blood returned for religious reasons.

But the frame of reference changed significantly when, to help resolve the dispute, lawyers became involved. The focus then turned to a question of legal liability and the fear of being sued.

STAGE TWO: Davi Kopenawa, a prominent Yanomami leader in Brazil, first learned about his relatives' blood samples being stored in the United States from Bruce Albert during a conversation about Tierney's book. The Pro Yanomami Commission (CCPY), working with Kopenawa, brought the matter to the federal attorneys of the MPF (Federal Public Ministry) residing in Roraima (the state where most Yanomami lived in Brazil) as well as in Brasila, Brazil's capitol. In 2002, Deputy Attorney Ela Wiecko

Figure 2: Davi Kopenawa. Photo by Claudia Andujar. All rights reserved.

Volkmer de Castilho corresponded with Dr. Kenneth Weiss, who was storing Pennsylvania State University's samples. [S2-a] Subsequently, Albert wrote Weiss, including a note from Kopenawa. [S2-b] Paralleling this correspondence, key Yanomami wrote letters to the Indian Resource Center in Washington D.C. [S2-c] Little resulted from this correspondence. In 2005, Deputy Attorney of Brazil Mauricio Frabretti, wrote to Weiss [S2-d] as well as Dean Susan Welsh of Penn State [S2-e] and Binghamton University's Vice President for Research, Dr. Gerald Sonnenfeld. [S2-d] Once more, little happened. Welch's response emphasized the considerable problems preventing Penn State from returning the blood. [S2-e]

STAGE THREE: Penn State's response turned more positive in 2006, following the involvement of the Center for a Public Anthropology working in collaboration with students from across North America. Emails from these students to Weiss had little effect. [S3-a] But a formal letter to Pennsylvania State University's President, Dr. Graham Spanier, from the Center combined with student letters supported by scores of other students [S3-b] had a positive impact. One need only contrast Provost Dr. Rodney Erickson's reply to these letters [S3-c] with Welch's reply to Fabretti to see the difference.

Figure 3: Photo by Victor Englebert. All rights reserved.

At roughly this same time, Dr. Joseph Fraumeni, a director within the National Cancer Institute (NCI), in correspondence with Deputy Attorney Fabretti, indicated that the Institute was "willing to return the [blood] specimens to Yanomami representatives." [S3-d] Knowing this, Provost Erickson suggested that Pennsylvania State University's transfer of the blood "could ideally take place at the same time and under the same circumstances" as the NCI's. [S3-c]

But what seemed reasonable at first, became problematic. While Dr. Fraumenini's assistant, Dr. Karen Pitt, made a significant effort to facilitate the return of the samples, others—at NCI, at Pennsylvania State University, and in Brazil—obstructed the process, at times spreading false rumors.

STAGE FOUR: It remained unclear for several years who or what was delaying the return of the blood samples. American lawyers insisted on a formal legal agreement waiving all liability and warranties on their part related to the blood. The Brazilians, puzzled by this insistence and not sure what they were consenting to, hesitated to sign such an agreement. The Deputy Attorney of Brazil, Mr. Antonio Morimoto, suggested that the blood samples simply be turned over to the Brazilian Embassy in Washington, D.C. [S4-a] But Pennsylvania State University and the National Cancer Institute refused. The fact that the blood samples were going to be ritually disposed of soon after being returned to the Yanomami, [Globo video S5-c3] and this was part of the final agreement [S5-b1a 2.4] was irrelevant to the NCI's lawyer. She insisted an agreement waiving liability be signed before the samples could be returned. The final transfer agreement held NCI "harmless with respect to any action arising from the use of Samples prior . . . to [the] transfer." [S5-b1a, 2.3]

For several years, there was a standoff. On one side, Pennsylvania State University and NCI insisted they wanted to return the blood and, on the other, the Brazilian government insisted it wanted the blood returned. But they could never agree on how it would be done.

Given this situation, those wanting the blood returned had only one option—to pressure the parties involved to come to some agreement. In the United States, the Center for a Public Anthropology repeatedly contacted key figures involved, assisted Deputy Attorney Morimoto [S4-b] (as well as Bruce Albert) in their efforts when possible, and sought to attract media attention. [S4-c1, S4-c2, S4-c3, S4-c4, S4-c5, S4-c6, S4-c7, S4-c8, S4-c9] On the Brazilian side, returning the blood samples became a priority for the Hutukara Yanomami Association (HAY), a Yanomami NGO (non-governmental organization) created in 2004 with CCPY assistance, and partner organizations, especially the Instituto Socioambiental (ISA), which absorbed CCPY in 2007. Davi Kopen-

Figure 4: Photo by Victor Englebert. All rights reserved.

awa, HAY's president, played a key role in keeping the issue alive, encouraging articles in Brazilian, French, and British media. [S4-c1, S4-c2, S4-c3, S4-c4, S4-c5, S4-c6, S4-c7, S4-c8, S4-c9]

STAGE FIVE: Ultimately, the Brazilian pressure was key. Through multiple meetings with the Federal Public Ministry's (MPF's) attorneys, ISA learned, quoting ISA's skilled lawyer, Ana Paula Caldeira Souto Maior: that "new Brazilian government agencies were brought to the case due to the requirements made by the contacted American institutions . . . [relating to] a Biological Material Transfer Agreement. Besides the Foreign Ministry, ANVISA [Brazil's FDA equivalent], and the AGU [the Attorney General of Brazil] were also involved [because of American concerns over] . . . the safety conditions and the final destination of the samples." Finally, "MPF was able to solve the bureaucratic obstacles on the Brazilian side and, through clarifying conversations with the American Institutions, felt able to sign the Agreement for the return the samples insisted upon by the Americans."

In April 2015, Pennsylvania State University returned their blood samples: 2693 vials. These samples included those that had been stored at Binghamton University. In September 2015, the National Cancer Institute returned their samples: 474 vials. Readers can peruse, if they wish, the formal transfer agreements. [S5-a, S5-b1, S5-b1a, S5-b2]

The transfer of the samples back to the Yanomami was highlighted in the Brazilian media [S5-c1, S5-c2, S5-c3, S5-c4, S5-c5, S5-c6, S5-c7], Brazilian government reports [S5-d1, S5-d2, S5-d3] and British media. [S5-e]

Figure 5: Photo by Victor Englebert.

It should be noted that none of the rumored dangers emphasized by the transfer's opponents—which made the transfers into such a complicated legal matter—ever came to pass, either in terms of spreading disease or the Yanomami suing the American institutions. Instead, the return of the blood samples was a deeply moving moment for many Yanomami. One can listen to Davi Kopenawa's comments regarding the return of the samples in a video. [S5-c4]

The return of the blood samples also represents an important moment for American anthropology. Countering various criticisms lodged against the discipline in print [S5-f] and in film [S5-g], the return of the blood constitutes a clear case of American anthropologists helping the Yanomami – on Yanomami terms, not on their own. It portrays American anthropology in a much more positive light vis-à-vis the Yanomami than has been the case in recent years.

ABOUT THE AUTHOR

Robert Borofsky is Professor of Anthropology at Hawaii Pacific University. A distinguished scholar, he has authored or edited six books as well as published articles in the discipline's leading journals. Dr. Borofsky is editor of the Public Anthropology Book Series published by University of California Press, Director of the Center for a Public Anthropology, and webmaster of the http://www. publicanthropology.org and http://www.publicanthropology.net

websites. Selected publications include: *Making History* (1987), *Assessing Cultural Anthropology* (1994), *Remembrance of Pacific Pasts* (2000), and *The Yanomami: The Fierce Controversy and What We Can Learn From It* (2005).

BIBLIOGRAPHY

Barth, Fredrick. "Ethnicity and the Concept of Culture." Program on Nonviolent Sanctions and Cultural Survival Seminar Synopses. Paper presented to the Conference "Rethinking Culture," Harvard University, 1995.

Bloomberg Business. "Kidney Broker Pleads Guilty in First U.S. Organ Trafficking Prosecution." *Bloomberg Business.* October 27, 2011. http://www.bloomberg.com/news/articles/2011-10-27/kidney-broker-pleads-guilty-in-first-u-s-organ-trafficking-prosecution.

Catalogue for Philanthropy. "Partners in Health: A Non Profit Corporation." http://www.philanthropydirectory.org/charity/partners-health-nonprofit-corporation

Doughty, Paul L. "Ending Serfdom in Peru: The Struggle for Land and Freedom in Vicos." In *Contemporary Cultures and Societies of Latin America*, edited by Dwight B. Heath, 225–243. Prospect Heights, IL: Waveland Press, 2002.

Douglas, Mary. *Purity and Danger: An Analysis of Pollution and Taboo.* New York: Routledge, 1966.

Erwin, Alexander. *Applied Anthropology: Tools and Perspectives for Contemporary Practice.* New York: Pearson, 2005.

Firth, Raymond. "An Appraisal of Modern Social Anthropology." *Annual Review of Anthropology* 4 (1975):1–25.

Fiske, Shirley J. "Global Climate Change from the Bottom Up." In *Applying Anthropology in the Global Village*, edited by Christina Wasson, Mary Odell Butler, and Jacqueline Copeland-Carson, 143–172. Walnut Creek, CA: Left Coast Press, 2012.

Givens, David, Patsy Evans, and Timothy Jablonski. "American Anthropological Association Survey of Anthropology PhDs." http://www.americananthro.org/LearnAndTeach/ResourceDetail.aspx?ItemNumber=1499

Glasziou, Paul. "Reducing Waste from Incomplete or Unusable Reports of Biomedical Research." *Lancet* 383 no. 9913 (2014):267–276.

Hale, Charles R. "What is Activist Research?" *Social Science Research Council*, 2, no. 1–2 (2001):13–15.

Kiste, Robert C. and Mac Marshall. *American Anthropology in Micronesia: An Assessment.* Honolulu: University of Hawaii Press, 1999.

Kuper, Adam. "Anthropology." *Times Literary Supplement.* March 30, 2009.

Lemann, Nicholas. "The Bell Curve Flattened," *Slate*, January 18, 1997. http://www.slate.com/articles/briefing/articles/1997/01/the_bell_curve_flattened.html.

Lock, Margaret. *Twice Dead: Organ Transplants and the Reinvention of Death.* Berkeley, CA: University of California Press, 2001.

Macleod, M. R., Susan Michie, Ian Roberts, Ulrich Dirnagl, Iain Chalmers, John P. A. Ioannidis, Rustam Al-Shahi Salman, An-Wen Chan, and Paul Glasziou. "Biomedical Research: Increasing Value, Reducing Waste." *Lancet* 383 no. 9912 (2014):101–104.

Mead, Margaret. "Changing Styles of Anthropological Work," *Annual Review of Anthropology* 2 (1973):1–2.

Miklikowska, Marta and Douglas Fry. "Natural Born Nonkillers: A Critique of the Killers-Have-More-Kids Idea." In *Nonkilling Psychology*, edited by Daniel Christie and Joan Evan Pim. Honolulu: Center for Global Nonkilling, 2012.

National Association for the Practice of Anthropology, "The Practice of Anthropology." http://practicinganthropology.org/practicing-anthro/

National Institutes of Health, Office of Behavioral and Social Sciences. "The Contribution of Behavioral and Social Sciences Research to Improving the Health of the Nation." https://obssr.od.nih.gov/wp-content/uploads/2016/09/OBSSR_Prospectus_2007.pdf

National Science Foundation. "Grant Proposal Guide: Chapter III—NSF Proposal Processing and Review: A. Review Criteria." http://www.nsf.gov/pubs/2004/nsf042/3.htm.

Priest, Dana and William M. Arkin. "Monitoring America." *Washington Post*, December 19, 2010. http://projects.washingtonpost.com/top-secret-america/articles/monitoring-america.

Research Councils United Kingdom. "Embedding Public Engagement in Research," www.rcuk.ac.uk/pe/embedding.

Salzstein, Dan. "Chill Out, Mom and Dad." *The New York Times*, September 4, 2016, BR23.

Scheper-Hughes, Nancy. "The Rosenbaum Kidney Trafficking Gang." *Counterpunch*. November 30, 2011. http://www.counterpunch.org/2011/11/30/the-rosenbaum-kidney-trafficking-gang.

Singer, Merrill. "Why I Am Not a Public Anthropologist." *Anthropology News* 41 no. 6 (2000):6–7.

Stocking, George W. "Ideas and Institutions in American Anthropology: Thoughts Toward a History of the Interwar Years." In *Selected Papers from the American Anthropologist, 1921–1945*, edited by George W. Stocking, 1–50. Washington, DC: American Anthropological Association, 1976.

Trotter, Robert, Jean Schensul, and Kristin Kostick. "Theories and Methods in Applied Anthropology." In *Handbook of Methods in Cultural Anthropology*, edited by H. Russell Bernard and Clarence Gravlee, 661–693. New York: Rowman & Littlefield, 2015.

Warren, Kay B. "Perils and Promises of Engaged Anthropology: Historical Transitions and Ethnographic Dilemmas." In *Engaged Observer: Anthropology, Advocacy, and Activism*, edited by Victoria Sanford and Asale Angel-Agani, 213–227. New Brunswick, NJ: Rutgers University Press, 2006.

Wikipedia. "Edward Snowden." https://en.wikipedia.org/wiki/Edward_Snowden.

Wikipedia. "Operation Bid Rig." https://en.wikipedia.org/wiki/Operation_Bid_Rig.

Wolf, Eric. "They Divide and Subdivide, and Call It Anthropology." *The New York Times*, November 30, 1980: E9.

NOTES

1. Anne Fadiman, *The Spirit Catches You and You Fall Down* (New York: Farrar, Straus, and Giroux, 1997), front matter.
2. Chronicle of Higher Education, "Academics Should Do More to Shape Public Debate," *The Chronicle Review*, November 11, 2016, B9.
3. Mary Douglas, *Purity and Danger: An Analysis of Pollution and Taboo* (New York: Routledge, 1966), 123.
4. Eric Wolf, "They Divide and Subdivide, and Call It Anthropology," *The New York Times*, November 30, 1980, E9.
5. Dan Salzstein, "Chill Out, Mom and Dad," *The New York Times*, September 4, 2016, BR23.
6. Alexander Erwin, *Applied Anthropology: Tools and Perspectives for Contemporary Practice* (New York: Pearson, 2005), 149.
7. Ibid.
8. Ibid., 102–104.
9. Tom Greaves, Ralph Bolton, and Florencia Zapata, *Vicos and Beyond: A Half Century of Applying Anthropology in Peru* (Lanham MD: AltaMira Press, 2010), viii.
10. Paul L. Doughty, "Ending Serfdom in Peru: The Struggle for Land and Freedom in Vicos," in *Contemporary Cultures and Societies of Latin America*, ed. Dwight B. Heath (Prospect Heights, IL: Waveland Press, 2002), 238.
11. Ibid., 239.
12. Shirley J. Fiske, "Global Climate Change from the Bottom Up," in *Applying Anthropology in the Global Village*, ed. Christina Wasson, Mary Odell Butler, and Jacqueline Copeland-Carson (Walnut Creek, CA: Left Coast Press, 2012), 162.
13. "The Fifty Years War: What Has Changed Since the Federal Government Went to War in the Hollows," *The Economist*, May 21, 2015.
14. Margaret Lock, *Twice Dead: Organ Transplants and the Reinvention of Death* (Berkeley, CA: University of California Press, 2001), front matter.
15. Thomas Hylland Erikson, *Engaging Anthropology: The Case of a Public Presence* (New York: Berg, 2006), back cover.
16. Kay B. Warren, "Perils and Promises of Engaged Anthropology: Historical Transitions and Ethnographic Dilemmas," in *Engaged Observer: Anthropology, Advocacy, and Activism*, ed. Victoria Sanford and Asale Angel-Agani (New Brunswick, NJ: Rutgers University Press, 2006), 213.
17. National Association for the Practice of Anthropology, "The Practice of Anthropology." http://practicinganthropology.org/practicing-anthro/
18. Charles R. Hale, "What is Activist Research?" *Social Science Research Council*, 2, no. 1–2 (2001):13–15. www.utexas.edu/cola/anthropology/_files/PDF/Hale.pdf.
19. George W. Stocking, "Ideas and Institutions in American Anthropology: Thoughts toward a History of the Interwar Years," in *Selected Papers from the American Anthropologist, 1921–1945*, ed. George W. Stocking (Washington, DC: American Anthropological Association, 1976), 1.
20. Raymond Firth, "An Appraisal of Modern Social Anthropology," *Annual Review of Anthropology* 4 (1975):4.

21. Andrew Abbott, *The System of Professions: An Essay on the Division of Expert Labor* (Chicago: University of Chicago Press, 1988), 119.

22. Robert Trotter, Jean Schensul, and Kristin Kostick., "Theories and Methods in Applied Anthropology," in *Handbook of Methods in Cultural Anthropology*, ed. H. Russell Bernard and Clarence Gravlee (New York: Rowman & Littlefield, 2015), 661.

23. Merrill Singer, "Why I Am Not a Public Anthropologist," *Anthropology News* 41 no. 6 (2000):6–7.

24. Margaret Mead, "Changing Styles of Anthropological Work," *Annual Review of Anthropology* 2 (1973):1–2.

25. Robert C. Kiste and Mac Marshall, *American Anthropology in Micronesia: An Assessment* (Honolulu: University of Hawaii Press, 1999), front book flap.

26. David Givens, Patsy Evans, and Timothy Jablonski, *American Anthropological Association Survey of Anthropology PhDs*, http://www.americananthro.org/LearnAndTeach/ResourceDetail.aspx?ItemNumber=1499

27. Ibid.

28. Victor Turner, *The Ritual Process: Structure and Anti-Structure* (Chicago: University of Chicago Press, 1969), 96.

29. Ibid., 203.

30. Deborah L. Rhode, *In Pursuit of Knowledge: Scholars, Status, and Academic Culture* (Stanford, CA: Stanford University Press, 2006), 11.

31. Ibid., 46.

32. National Science Foundation, *Grant Proposal Guide: Chapter III—NSF Proposal Processing and Review*. A. Review Criteria. www.nsf.gov/pubs/2004/nsf042/3.htm.

33. National Institutes of Health, Office of Behavioral and Social Sciences, https://obssr.od.nih.gov/pdf/OBSSR_Prospectus.pdf.

34. Research Councils United Kingdom, "Embedding Public Engagement in Research," www.rcuk.ac.uk/pe/embedding.

35. Adam Kuper, "Anthropology," *Times Literary Supplement*, March 30, 2009, 23.

36. Abhijit V. Banerjee and Esther Duflo, *Poor Economics: A Radical Rethinking of the Way to Fight Global Poverty* (New York: Public Affairs, 2011) 49–50, 57–58.

37. Ibid., back cover.

38. Mary Furner, *Advocacy and Objectivity: A Crisis in the Professionalization of American Social Science, 1865–1905* (Lexington, KY: University of Kentucky Press, 1975), 324.

39. M. R. Macleod, Susan Michie, Ian Roberts, Ulrich Dirnagl, Iain Chalmers, John P. A. Ioannidis, Rustam Al-Shahi Salman, An-Wen Chan, and Paul Glasziou, "Biomedical Research: Increasing Value, Reducing Waste." *Lancet* 383 no. 9912 (2014):101.

40. Paul Glasziou, "Reducing Waste from Incomplete or Unusable Reports of Biomedical Research." *Lancet* 383 no. 9913 (2014):267.

41. "Tested and Found Wanting," *The Economist*, November 5, 2016.

42. Benedict Carey, "Many Psychology Findings Not as Strong as Claimed, Study Says," *New York Times*, August 27, 2015.

43. Napoleon A. Chagnon, "Life Histories, Blood Revenge, and Warfare in a Tribal Population" *Science* 239 no. 4843 (1988): 985–992.

44. Marta Miklikowska and Douglas Fry, "Natural Born Nonkillers: A Critique of the Killers-Have-More-Kids Idea." In *Nonkilling Psychology*, edited by Daniel Christie and Joan Evan Pim (Honolulu: Center for Global Nonkilling, 2012), 61.

45. Nicholas Lemann, "The Bell Curve Flattened," *Slate*, January 18, http://www.slate.com/articles/briefing/articles/1997/01/the_bell_curve_flattened.html.

46. Catalogue for Philanthropy, "Partners in Health: A Non Profit Corporation," http://www.philanthropydirectory.org/charity/partners-health-nonprofit-corporation

47. The Partners in Health approach and mission are described in http://www.pih.org/pages/our-mission; http://www.pih.org/pages/our-principles; and http://www.pih.org/priority-programs/community-health-workers.

48. Fredrick Barth, "Ethnicity and the Concept of Culture." Program on Nonviolent Sanctions and Cultural Survival Seminar Synopses Paper presented to the Conference "Rethinking Culture," Harvard University, 1995, 1.

49. Ibid., 7.

50. Ibid., 8.

51. "Kidney Broker Pleads Guilty in First U.S. Organ Trafficking Prosecution, *Bloomberg Business*, October 27, 2011, http://www.bloomberg.com/news/articles/2011-10-27/kidney-broker-pleads-guilty-in-first-u-s-organ-trafficking-prosecution.

52. "Operation Bid Rig," *Wikipedia*, https://en.wikipedia.org/wiki/Operation_Bid_Rig.

53. Nancy Scheper-Hughes, "The Rosenbaum Kidney Trafficking Gang," *Counterpunch*, November 30, 2011, www.counterpunch.org/2011/11/30/the-rosenbaum-kidney-trafficking-gang.

54. "Edward Snowden," *Wikipedia*, https://en.wikipedia.org/wiki/Edward_Snowden.

55. Dana Priest and William M. Arkin, "Monitoring America." *Washington Post*, December 19, 2010, http://projects.washingtonpost.com/top-secret-america/articles/monitoring-america.

56. Ibid.

APPENDIX: TEACHING RESOURCES

VIDEO PRESENTATIONS

By Robert Borofsky, Hawaii Pacific University, Center for a Public Anthropology

These videos have been included in the teaching resources for *Perspectives: An Open Introduction to Cultural Anthropology* with permission from Dr. Borofsky and may be used for educational purposes by instructors and students.

Video Title	Length
Defining Anthropology - Lecture 1	12:52
Defining Anthropology - Lecture 2	7:02
Historical Trends - Lecture 1	10:33
Historical Trends - Lecture 2	11:23
Historical Trends - Lecture 3	10:54
Historical Trends - Lecture 4	10:26
Political Economy - Lecture 1	9:42
Political Economy - Lecture 2	12:35
Political Economy - Lecture 3	8:48
Political Economy - Lecture 4	8:35
Political Economy - Lecture 5	9:44
Political Economy - Lecture 6	10:24
Ethics - Lecture 1	13:26
Ethics - Lecture 2	16:57
Informants - Lecture 1	18:20
Informants - Lecture 2	15:19
Anthropology's Value - Lecture 1	11:26
Anthropology's Value - Lecture 2	17:13
Anthropology's Value - Lecture 3	14:21
Anthropology's Value - Lecture 4	
Public Anthropology - Lecture 1	12:16
Public Anthropology - Lecture 2	17:39
Religion - Lecture 1	15:20
Religion - Lecture 2	14:45
Religion - Lecture 3	12:14

ANTHROPOLOGY IN OUR MOMENT IN HISTORY: INTERVIEW WITH PHILIPPE BOURGOIS

Robert Borofsky, Hawaii Pacific University, Center for a Public Anthropology
borofsky@hpu.edu
http://www.publicanthropology.org/

How did you become an anthropologist?

Discovering anthropology for me was like falling in love. I was a freshman in college and I knew nothing about the subject. I didn't have a major. I took one of those big introductory classes in a large lecture hall because I was curious, but I didn't really have any idea what anthropology might be.

The very first lecture blew my mind. It was by an old-style style anthropologist talking about his fieldwork in the Amazon. He introduced us to the Yanomami, an indigenous people who were at the center of a huge anthropological debate about the nature of violence at the time: How much of human violence is cultural? How much of it is at the essence of human nature? How much of it is imposed by larger historical and economic forces? The teacher described to us their "shaman" who sniff hallucinogenic drugs to communicate with spirits and to protect their village from sickness and attack by neighbors. The Yanomami shaman are the Amazonian equivalent to our philosophers, scientists, doctors and religious or political officials. I couldn't believe what I was hearing. Here is an academic discipline that sends its practitioners around the world to immerse themselves in utterly unfamiliar, foreign cultures in order to explore the meaning of human existence.

I adored the class even with all its old-fashioned faults—it did, after all, "exoticize" indigenous people as if they were not our contemporaries but lived in a bubble, oblivious to the effects of global power relations and colonial conquest. The teacher did alert us, however, to the contemporary invasion of non-indigenous settlers, miners and cattle barons who were—and still are—destroying indigenous ways of life all around the world. I quickly signed up to major in anthropology.

What do you find special about anthropology?

There are a few things that I think are magical about anthropology but, what I like best is our methodology of "participant-observation ethnography", our insight on "cultural relativism" and our multi-disciplinarity. Our methodology is extraordinarily powerful but simple. To put it commonsensically, it is the technique of deep "hanging out" in a setting to attempt to see the world through the eyes of the people or society you want to find out about. You engage with people in a friendly, empathetic way, and participate in their daily life activities so as to avoid distorting interactions or calling excessive attention to yourself. This allows you to break through appearances and simultaneously experience emotionally and document rationally life in that setting. We have developed strategies of note-taking, tape-recording and, most importantly, of self-reflexive skepticism. You have to learn to be careful not to see only what you want to see and not to confuse the way you want the world to be with the way the world really is. You try to figure out how things really work by being aware of your own biases.

Participant-observation methodology forces you to break through the barriers of status that limit people's lives: economic class, race and ethnicity, gender, and social conventions—to name a few. Anthropology tells you: "Go out there and explore the world; open your mind to all kinds of different perspectives and settings—or take a long close critical look at your own society. Treat your own culture and its common senses as if you were an outsider confronting the bizarre logic of an exotic people for the first time. You discover that there is nothing more normal or right about your culture than anyone else's culture."

Anthropology pushes you to dare to break through, what we have called the "intimate apartheids" (Bourgois and Schonberg 2007) that confine us to our narrow little segregated worlds that we find most comfortable. Too often these intimate apartheids turn us into ethnocentric, or even racist individuals, who think so highly of ourselves and our way of being that we end up disrespecting and mistreating anyone who is different from us.

Respect for others is a related core value of anthropology and is reflected in our core value of cultural relativism which is not a theory, but simply a heuristic device, (a technique) that enables us to learn about others without being blinded by prejudgments. In a nutshell, cultural relativism declares that cultures are not good or bad; they all have a logic. Our job as anthropologists—and indeed as human beings—is not to judge culture along righteous moral lines, but to find out how its internal logic makes it operate. Often the first reaction of people confronted with something different is, "Ewww gross!" simply because it is different from what they are used to and what they consider to be normal, or moral, or the proper way to do things.

Anthropology tells us to throw out our preconceptions and biases and recognize our own culture's brain-washing and instead become aware of why people do things, because those different ways of doing things inevitably have a meaning and a logic to them. All people everywhere are convinced that they too are moral, good, and normal in the same way we think we are moral, good—and for the most part normal. No matter how horrific/crazy/cool/mean or beautiful a cultural practice may appear to be at first, our job as anthropologists is to jump into its logic to see how it makes sense to the people engaging in that practice. It is this combination of participant-observation ethnography and cultural relativism that can make anthropology powerfully anti-racist, self-critical and alert to power inequalities and disparate life chances across the world, and in our own society—or even in our own families!

Finally, anthropology is also an unusual field of study because it spans the scientific boundaries that divide academic disciplines. We include multiple subfields—cultural anthropology, archeology, linguistics, biological anthropology, and medical anthropology —that transcend the academic gulfs between the humanities, the social sciences, and the natural sciences. I happen to be a cultural (sometimes called a social) anthropologist and also a medical anthropologist. The questions important to me draw from theories and methods from both the humanities and the social sciences. Furthermore, as a medical anthropologist concerned about HIV, addiction and violence I find myself in dialogue with laboratory scientists and epidemiologists who operate with very different (primarily quantitative) definitions of facts and who are often initially unfamiliar with, and sometimes fail to recognize, the value of qualitative anthropological research.

Anthropology makes you realize that academic disciplines are like cultures. They each have their logics and insights, as well as their blinders and biases. Anthropology has a long history of melding together different epistemologies—that is to say different techniques of understanding the world. We read widely in philosophy, literature, history, economics, art, architecture, poetry, biology, law—you name it. This makes our theoretical approaches to understanding why the world is the way it is especially innovative.

What do you like best about anthropology?

Conducting fieldwork is the best part of being an anthropologist. I think I am happiest when I'm in the middle of a participant-observation ethnographic fieldwork project. Some mornings I have to pinch myself when I wake up. It seems like a dream that I am paid to spend my time in so many different, interesting—sometimes scary—settings and with such compelling people to learn from and about them.

Much of my work has been in the U.S. inner city. These are settings beset by social inequality, poverty, violence and substance abuse. As part of my fieldwork, for example, I lived for almost five years in a rundown tenement apartment building in East Harlem, New York with my family, right when the crack and HIV epidemics hit. I watched many of my friends and neighbors get swept off their feet by crack, and some died of AIDS. I befriended a network of crack dealers operating on my block and they invited me into their homes. I wrote a book about how they and their families made sense of their world and struggled to survive (Bourgois 2003). I also became a medical anthropologist to try to contribute usefully to policy and advocacy in the field of public health and HIV prevention.

My neighbors and friends were suffering real poverty. Most were unemployed, struggling with addiction, and engaging in violence. There was a great deal of gun violence. The mid-1980s through the early 1990s were a dangerous and stressful era on U.S. inner city streets. But on another level, it was an exciting and fun moment of history to be in East Harlem. It was the birth of hip-hop and rap. People were eager to talk, full of hope and the illusions of going from rags to riches. I tried to make their suffering, struggle, and dreams less invisible and more humanely comprehensible to the rest of America.

I wanted readers of my book to understand the historical tragedy of inner city poverty, the effects of de-industrialization, racist segregation and the loss of jobs. The economy was in shambles, because of the disappearance of factory jobs to lower wage, countries that repressed unions and human rights. The global narcotics industry flooded in to this devastated economic vacuum overwhelming all of us. These were "structural forces" that were badly managed by U.S. politicians and misunderstood by the press. The young men and women I befriended could not find legal jobs that would pay enough money to feed a single individual—let alone their families and loved ones. Schools were not working; abandoned buildings were going up in flames, and crack offered a seductive promise of sudden, easy access to the American Dream: Get rich quick through risky entrepreneurship.

Setting up a crack house at that time was not so different from founding a high-tech start-up company today except that your product was illegal and you had no access to loans from banks, or to legal protection for enforcing contracts. You had to rely on your wits or brute force to start your business, stay alive and keep off of drugs. At that moment in history, politicians and the press vilified crack dealers as public enemies, but in fact, they were the logical product of powerful social and political forces that trapped them into a destructive, violent relationship with their community. More often than not they ended up as victims themselves, becoming addicts and spending the rest of their lives rotating through prison, because this was the moment when mass incarceration was taking hold of the United States.

Since that time, I've done similar fieldwork in other inner city settings. I co-authored a book on homeless heroin injectors and crack smokers, called *Righteous Dopefiend,* with a student, Jeff Schonberg, who is also a great photographer (Bourgois and Schonberg 2009). Jeff is now an anthropology professor at San Francisco State University. We combined the documentary and aesthetic/emotional effects of photography with the analytical tools of anthropology to convey the human suffering of homelessness, social inequality, and addiction. We also critiqued the dysfunctional effects of the war on drugs and offered practical solutions such as harm reduction and "housing-first" interventions and diversified medical treatment options—including opiate prescription—for indigent addicts.

What was your first fieldwork as a student?

My first fieldwork was in Central America among the Miskitu Indians in Nicaragua. They are an extraordinary people who were at the center of a terrible cold war conflict in the 1980s. A populist leftisat revolution had triumphed in Nicaragua overthrowing a brutal, U.S.-supported dictatorship that had been in power for forty years. I literally jumped on a bus heading for Nicaragua and presented myself at the New Agrarian Reform Office saying, "I'm an anthropologist. I'd like to work for your socialist experiment." They replied, "Oh, you're a gringo [i.e. from the United States] anthropologist. You must like indigenous people." This is the stereotype of anthropologists. And frankly it is largely true, cultural relativism guides anthropologists to respect indigenous cultures. The revolutionaries sent me out to Miskitu territory in the jungle along Nicaragua's Atlantic coast, and I took a leave-of-absence from graduate school. That is how I found myself among the Miskitu Indians in revolutionary Nicaragua in 1979-1980 instead of in school. Unfortunately the revolutionary leaders were just as racist against the indigenous minorities in their country as the right wing dictator had been before them. The Miskitu people were excited about the revolution, but they wanted to retain control over their culture, language, land, and natural resources and rebelled against the revolutionary central government's racism. Unfortunately the CIA stepped in to manipulate the conflict because of its Cold War era anti-communist obsession and flooded the Miskitu territory with AK-47 machine guns. A bloody civil war erupted.

The revolutionary leadership in Nicaragua failed to recognize that the cultural demands of the Miskitu were just as legitimate as the economic demands of the poor, Latino non-indigenous population for whom they had fought and overthrown the dictatorship. Most Latino Nicaraguans viewed the Indians as being from a "lower cultural level." But again, cultural relativism tells us there is no such thing as a lower cultural level. There are simply different ways of organizing society. All cultural forms are legitimate in their own social uniqueness. The Miskitu conflict made me realize that anthropology can have a very important role to play in changing the world for the better.

Several anthropologists with whom I was working in the agrarian reform ministry co-authored a report and published a book calling for the decolonization of the Miskitu territory and the establishment of an autonomous local government of indigenous regional autonomy (Philippe Bourgois and Jorge Grunberg 1981). The revolutionaries could not understand our anthropological perspective. Instead they pursued a hard line against the Miskitu and repressed everyone demanding cultural rights. I was thrown out of the country and returned to graduate school. Four years later, the revolutionary government realized that its policy had backfired, and it granted regional political autonomy to the Miskitu territory. They invited me back to Nicaragua in 1985 to evaluate their experiment in autonomous indigenous territorial and political rights. Unfortunately the Nicaraguan revolution foundered three years later—that often happens to populist revolutions. The regional autonomy they initiated, however, is still an interesting model for indigenous people around the world and has a great deal of potential.

Have others benefited from your work?

My commitment to engaging with urgent contemporary social and political problems has taught me that it is important not to think we have all the answers, know the truth, or even ask the right questions. We have to be careful about taking ourselves too seriously as anthropologists. The crack dealers I had befriended in East Harlem came to the book opening party for *In Search of Respect Selling Crack in El Barrio* hosted by Cambridge University Press. They received copies of the book and liked the fact that their words were published to make a complex theoretical and policy analysis of de-industrialization, racism, and gender power relations. Nevertheless, one of the most violent, main characters in the book insightfully poked fun at me, "Oh Felipe you make us sound like such sensitive crack dealers." Another one resisted the linearity of my argument about the impact of structural forces on the neighborhood and his life, "I don't blame nobody but me, myself and I for the bad I've done."

I still keep in touch with several of the main characters in the book and I asked my best friend from the scene, whom I called Primo, if he minded if I could publish a follow-up article about his addiction to heroin (Bourgois 2000). He was ashamed of being a heroin user and I didn't want to embarrass him or violate his privacy. He looked at me in a super hesitant and pained way. I thought, "Oh no! He's going to tell me I can't publish this!" Instead, he said, "I don't mean to disrespect you... but you can write whatever you want to write. No nobody reads the shit you write—at least not no one that I know."

It made me realize that we have to be humble as academics. Our anthropological publications only reach a small section of college-educated people. My books on the inner city, for example, are mostly read by college students. That is frustrating on some level. But college students are at a turning point in their lives. They can open their minds up to new perspectives and transform their ways of thinking in ways that can alter the course of their lives and the future of their society.

Some of the readers of my books in college classes send me feedback through email. I also occasionally get letters from prisoners who somehow gained access to my books through crummy, underfunded prison libraries. Sometimes they tell me they see themselves or their parents reflected in the pages of *In Search of Respect* and in *Righteous Dopefiend*: "I was always so angry at my [violent or addicted or neglectful] father—or my mother—but now I can begin to understand what was going on . . ."

Working in public health on HIV prevention as an anthropologist has also been rewarding but challenging, especially with the government wasting so much money on locking people up, which simples makes the problem of violence, addiction, and unemployment worse. But frankly, we need to figure out how to reach more people more broadly and more effectively. That is where future generations can help with the explosion of digital technology and social media. The new technology offers new ways of communicating anthropological insights. It is very effective to show images and display audio at the same time that you present on anthropological analysis. It can render off-limits places and problems more humanely visible or it can help set the individual experience of viewers in the larger context of our moment in history.

Remember, an anthropologist can study almost anything. You can enter the world of stockbrokers or crack dealers, doctors or homeless heroin injectors, indigenous hunter-gatherers or suburban commuters and shed light on what gets taken for granted but may actually be problematic, urgent or complex or is simply beautiful and inspiring. New access to online technologies gives anthropology greater potential to address the urgent questions of our contemporary moment in history and reach wider audiences. But, we still have to figure out how to use these platforms effectively. We have to be wary of becoming inadvertent pornographers or manipulators of the truth like reality TV shows. I think anthropology should be at the forefront of the digital communication tide and it will be the new generation that embraces these new possibilities. Digital technology has already transformed public health and politics and most nefariously big business is enslaving us to it and monopolizing online access. It is up to the new generation to wrench back its potential.

Any Closing Thoughts?

I want to end by saying that ethnographic fieldwork and theoretical analysis can help us understand the invisible negative effects of power, domination, and social inequalities. Actions that seem immoral or look horrendous—behaviors that seem to be pathological—may often be imposed on individuals by larger structural forces—harsh economic conditions, environmental assaults, repressive public policies, and discriminatory social hierarchies—that constrain the lives of the individuals we study ethnographically. In some sense we are all trapped into doing the things that we do. This is certainly the case for addiction, HIV and the violence surrounding drug distribution and mass incarceration. Anthropology's ethnographic method gives us intimate access to people's daily lives while simultaneously allowing us to grasp the bigger picture. The challenge is to use anthropology's critical tools to recognize the burning issues of our moment in history and go out into the world to change some corner of it for the better—or at least try to help stop it from imploding.

BIBLIOGRAPHY

Bourgois, Philippe., and Jeff Schonberg. "Intimate Apartheid: Ethnic Dimensions of Habitus among Homeless Heroin Injectors." *Ethnography* 8 no. 1(2007): 7–31.

Bourgois, Philippe. "Disciplining Addictions: The Bio-Politics of Methadone and Heroin in the United States." *Culture, Medicine and Psychiatry* 24 no. 2(2000): 165–195.

Bourgois, Philippe. *In Search of Respect: Selling Crack in El Barrio.* New York: Cambridge University Press, 2003.

Bourgois, Philippe, and Jeff Schonberg. *Righteous Dopefiend.* Berkeley: University of California Press, 2009.

Philippe Bourgois, and Jorge Grunberg. "Informe de Una Investigacion Rural En La Costa Atlantica Norte." In *La Mosquitia En La Revolucion.* Jaime Wheelock Roman, ed. Pp. 89–149. Managua: Centro de investigacion y estudios de la reforma agraria [CIERA], Colección Blas Real Espinales, 1981.

CAN ANTHROPOLOGY SAVE THE WORLD?

Nancy Scheper-Hughes, University of California, Berkeley

We are living in difficult times, facing out of control, escalating wars in the Middle East for which we are partially to blame and destructive political wars at home. We are a divided nation within a profoundly divided world despite globalization and its allegedly democratizing effects. The gap between North and South, Middle East and Mid-West, between haves and have-nots has become a chasm making all of us less free and less safe.[1]

Two weeks ago, I was giving lectures in Rome and Prague on the plight of political refugees in detention and deportation camps cropping up in Europe. It was a sobering visit, as many countries including Poland, the Czech Republic, Hungary and Denmark were taking moves to build walls and to reject the waves of refugees fleeing wars and drought in Syria, Iraq, Afghanistan, and Pakistan and crushing poverty in Somalia. It is the largest migration of people in Europe since World War II. Smugglers are legion and they defraud frightened refugees of their money and even of their kidneys, demanded in exchange for basic necessities. One of the smugglers involved in this shady business is a human trafficker who I have run into before named Boris Wolfman. Indeed as the old adage goes, "man is wolf to man."

In Prague hate, rather than love was in the air driven by a new nationalism and popular calls for rights to cultural, racial, and religious homogeneity. Czech police began pulling refugees off trains and wrote numbers on their arms with felt-tip pens, a creepy (rather than creeping) xenophobia, Islamophobia, and a re-emerging anti-Semitism within the country. In the beautiful historical center of Prague, resisters began to plaster the walls and windows of certain hotels, museums, and restaurants with posters announcing: "Hate Free Zone" as if this was the exception. This could happen to us. At the DOX Centre for Contemporary Art, where I gave my lectures, I found it difficult to talk about human trafficking in a way that would jibe with the art exhibition on the Soul of Money. While humans and animals might have souls, I was pretty sure that money did not.

The trip to Prague was painful because I was born in 1944 into a Czech immigrant family growing up in Williamsburg, Brooklyn when it was still a slum and "Holocaust haunted." Eastern European Catholics and Hassidic Jews lived side by side but mostly in silence about our histories. What could we say? Meanwhile, the public health department periodically appeared to shoot educational films about the East River rats and garbage on our streets and in our tenements. Today these same buildings that have survived are worth a fortune.

My older brother and I were the first in our large extended family to go to college. I didn't quite get the hang of it and I dropped out of Queens College (City University of New York) twice, first to join the Peace Corps in 1964-1966, and then, after an abortive return to Queens College, I dropped out to go South to the Civil Rights Movement in Selma, Alabama in 1967-1968 in part to memorialize and to replace one of my classmates, Andrew Goodman, who was killed with two other rights workers during Mississippi Summer in 1964. I joined SNCC, the Student Nonviolent Coordinating Committee, as one of the last two white civil rights workers under the auspices of the Lowndes County Black Panthers and the Black Power Movement.

Thanks to an undergraduate mentor at Queens College, CUNY, Hortense Powdermaker, the author of an anthropological memoir, *Stranger and Friend: The Life of an Anthropologist*, I followed her

1

to Berkeley in 1969 where Powdermaker had retired to work on her last anthropological research project, youth culture. I was invited to be her research assistant while completing my B.A. at U.C. Berkeley and going on to get my doctorate in Cultural and Medical Anthropology.

I chose the life of an anthropologist, because it was a field so open, so free, that it allowed one to be a freethinker, to think outside the box, as my colleague Laura Nader puts it. So let me suggest based on my life as a dedicated anthropologist and obsessive fieldworker some rules to live by. I'll call these rules "Operation Instructions for the New Generation of Anthropologists."

Operating Instruction: Rules to Live By

Rule 1: Everything in life is an Experiment. There are no winners and no losers. There's just a precious amount of time to live.

Rule 2: Work is essential, but it should not be an obsession. Peter Maurin, a French peasant philosopher who lived on the margins of New York City wrote in his book, *Easy Essays*: "There's always work, there's just not always **paid** work." He added: "The world would be better off if people tried to become better. And people would become better if they stopped trying to become better-off."

Rule 3: Drop Out—Take a Break! Gap years are important before jumping into the fray. Join the Peace Corps or go on a road trip or cross the country by bicycle (as Professor Harley Shaken does each summer). Find work as you go along. Carry a paperback copy of Mark Sundeen's book: *The Man who Quit Money.*

Rule 4: Be disciplined, that is, be a disciple. Find someone wise, or smart, or creative and follow him or her. Seek out people who are doers and thinkers, artists and artisans, philosophers, innovators and inventors, authors and scholars, political leaders, surgeons and country doctors. I've had so many mentors in my life I'd be here until tomorrow morning and would not get to the end of the list that includes former professors, colleagues, collaborators as well as people whose writings changed my life or way of thinking: Ivan Illich, Oliver Sacks, the Irish poet Seamus Heaney, the anti-apartheid lawyer Albie Sachs, and the Italian radical psychiatrist Franco Basaglia. The forensic pathologist Claude Snow gave me the courage to refashion myself as a cultural medical forensic anthropologist. My students have taught how to teach and how to write, while my companions in the field— hundreds of them—have been my lifelong teachers. Alfred Kroeber, the founding father this department, always answered the question, occupation: as student of humanity.

Rule 5: Be inspired by others. Everyone doesn't have to be a leader. I've been an intellectual heretic for most of my life and I don't often seek to lead. When I do I often find it uncomfortable. I'd rather be commenting *sotto voce* from the sidelines, a trickster, of sorts. Mario Savio inspired me when he was an awkward and extremely shy student at Queens College. But he had a soul on fire. In 1963 I followed Mario— who then called himself Bob Savio and 38 other Queens College students who traveled by bus from New York City to Guerreo, Mexico to work with local activists on building schools, and working in hospitals and public clinics. A local newspaper in New York City announced our project in unflattering terms: "QC Students Invade Mexico to Help Peons." Our bus tickets were two feet long and it took us a week to arrive in Guerrero. After crossing the border, we traveled by *Flecha Roja* through desolate desert areas. Bob Savio and several guys were assigned to work in Taxco. Three of us were sent to Chilpancingo where no one knew quite what to do with us. In letters home, I wrote that that racism toward indigenous communities was rampant. I began to wonder why we had come and what we could possibly accomplish.

We heard rumors that Bob Savio was stirring up a storm in the beautiful post-colonial city of Taxco, doing what we had hoped to do, advocating for social justice among the rural and indigenous communities. So Marsha Steinberg and I left Igula and Chilpancingo to see what was going on in Taxco and if we could lend a hand. But by the time we arrived Bob had returned to the U.S. The sole survivor of his group, Kevin Donavan, told us that Bob and the local Catholic Bishop didn't get along and that Bob had been ordered to leave the country.

Kevin was in awe of Savio and told us of Bob's transformation, as he emerged, chrysalis-like, into a powerful speaker and organizer who had participated in demonstration by indigenous people protesting their inhumane treatment by landowners. The local Bishop was so flummoxed by Savio that he sent Bob and his team packing. I was amazed at the story of the man who we knew as almost incapable of carrying on a conversation, a profound stutterer who had no Spanish to speak of. How had he managed to reach people across language, class, and culture? The Savio we knew was a modest, solitary fellow. We couldn't fathom how Bob had managed to stir up so much trouble and what it was that he could have possibly conveyed to indigenous Nahunta speakers. He was "inspired" was all that his buddy could tell us.

Bob moved to California and enrolled in U.C. Berkeley where he changed his name to Mario and in December 1964 Mario jumped on top of that car and he let freedom ring. He said those unforgettable words: "There is a time when the operation of the machine becomes so odious, makes you so sick at heart, that you can't take part; you can't even **passively** take part, and so you've got to put your bodies upon the gears and upon the wheels, upon the levers, upon all the apparatus, and you've got to make it stop. And you've got to indicate to the people who run it, to the people who own it, that unless you're free, the machine will be prevented from working at all!"

Rule 6: Admit to Errors and Correct Them. Our Berkeley anthropology founding father, A L Kroeber, made a huge mistake following the death from tuberculosis of the Yahi Indian known as Ishi. He sent his brain in a bottle with cotton and formaldehyde to a racist physical anthropologist working at the Smithsonian Institution. Kroeber never spoke of Ishi again. He could not stand it, he wrote, acknowledging the genocide that preceded Ishi's living in what was then the Lowie Museum as a custodian and a spectacle — the last wild Indian. But he helped his wife to write the book he could never have written himself: *Ishi in Two Worlds—The Last Wild American Indian*. First published in 1961, the book names what actually happened in California beginning with the Gold Rush, in chapters with titles: A Dying People; The Long Concealment, and The Yahi Disappear.

Rule 7: Engage in dialogue those with whom you most disagree. Cross those aisles. In my work on human trafficking, I've had to work with an Afrikaner cop who spoke rudely about his Zulu assistant and in Israel I worked with a military man and Zionist forensic pathologist. In both cases, we changed each other as well as got some good work done. In April 2015, I got to meet up close a man who I had lambasted, in an article entitled "Can God Forgive Jorge Bergoglio?," of being a poor choice for the Pope who would replace the dogmatic Rottweiler of the Vatican, Pope Benedict XVI. Bergoglio, I argued, was a weak protector of Argentine people, ordinary people, and priests and nuns when he was the principal head of the Jesuits in Argentina during the Dirty War. I had accumulated a lot of evidence that he had led leftist-leaning men and women dedicated to liberation theology which the Argentine junta targeted as Marxist insurrection. My article was sardonic, suggesting that God could, after all, forgive any sin, no matter how grave, but first, the penitent needed to acknowledge their fault, to confess it, to do penance and to create a new social contract.

When I received an invitation to present my work on human trafficking in the Vatican it came with a Xerox copy of a handwritten note by Pope Francis saying that "organs trafficking" would be part of the plenary session held inside the Vatican and I was to be "it," that is the only participant invited to speak on the topic. Of course, I expected it was a mistake and that as soon as I arrived I would be banned from entering the Santa Marta residence where we would be housed during the conference, on the same floor where Pope Francis had his simple two-room apartment. I died a dozen deaths on entering the lunchroom to find Pope Francis sitting a few tables from mine. On meeting Papa Francisco after the first three days at a special Papal audience, I stood at the very end of the reception line carrying a Spanish translation of my book, *Death Without Weeping*, with a long inscription, and paperclips marking the pages I hoped he might possibly read that linked the hunger and death of angel babies of the Alto do Cruzeiro, Brazil to the Vatican's ban on contraception and abortion. As I awkwardly knelt to kiss his papal ring I begged him: "Remember the women!" Papa Francisco pulled me up on my feet. Of course, he wore no papal ring, and no pink papal slippers either. From the floor I could see that his shoes were black and scruffy. The bodyguards in tuxedos rushed up to grab the books and articles I had brought to the Pope. He pushed them aside and nodding his head he said. "Pray for me." *What a lesson in humility.*

Rule 8: Humor is Mandatory. Our iconic humorist, the late Alan Dundes, is no longer with us. He was often criticized for making politically incorrect jokes. But Professor Dundes held nothing to be too sacred, taboo, or even too disgusting to be a source of humor. He said that sacred cows made the best hamburgers. He saw jokes as Geiger counters of the spirit— as expressions of deep-seated social anxieties and conflicts. When I was writing my book *Death Without Weeping* on mother love and child death in Brazil, Alan mischievously stuffed a reprint of his analysis of "Dead Baby" jokes in my campus mailbox. I was shocked at first, but then I sat down to read the article and found his analysis sobering and insightful. He argued that these offensive jokes were an unconscious cultural expression of American ambivalence toward babies, a kind of fallout from the sexual revolution that had produced a new generation of adults who wanted sex without babies.

Alan knew that "folklore" had the capacity to act as a force for evil as well as for good, as his book on the Blood Libel Legend—as a history and projection of centuries of anti-Semitism powerfully demonstrated. Ironically, Dundes, who was Jewish, was accused of anti-Semitism by conservative American Jews who asked for his dismissal in 1988 following an article he wrote about German jokes set in Auschwitz that had been published in Harper's Magazine. The subject outraged Alan's accusers. Likely, they had not read his analysis. Alan saw these jokes—offensive as they were—as keeping alive the memory of Auschwitz in the German collective consciousness. Comedy and tragedy were two sides of the same coin and black humor—even Auschwitz jokes—albeit culturally insensitive and inadequate—allowed Germans to come to terms with the unimaginable horrors that occurred at German death camps. The jokes were an *acknowledgement* of, rather than a *denial* of the tragic history of the Holocaust.

Rule 9: Beware political correctness—be self-critical, be sensitive but be honest and openly expressive. Resist censorship and even worse self-censorship.

Rule 10: Flexibility as needed: All rules can be amended or suspended.

In two days, I fly to Recife and Timbauba in Northeast Brazil to work with 120 community health agents with middle school educations who are the first and often the only responders to the needs of pregnant women infected by the Zika virus, which carries the threat of severe birth defects and is complicated by Brazilian laws that still prohibit abortion. The public health crisis is occurring during the near collapse of the Brazilian economy and the real threat of a coup d'etat against the Workers

Party President Dilma Rousseff whose impeachment by Brazil's congress was an attempt to avoid corruption charges against themselves.

We are facing another kind of populist coup d'etat in the United States. And you, dear class of 2016, are walking into a booby-trapped terrain, a world not of your making, and ill-equipped, you might think, with little more than a degree in anthropology. But never more was that degree more valuable and more needed. First of all we need to erect real intellectual barriers against xenophobia, the dangerous fear and hatred of strangers.

Xenophilia

I think we have a little known secret in anthropology. The opposite of xenophobia would be *xenophilia*, a term that barely exists on the internet except with reference to certain botanical species that seem to adjust to cohabiting with alien plants. Taking that botanical metaphor, xenophilia is not so much the love of difference as freedom from the fear of difference, and a healthy curiosity and desire to understand strangers who anthropologists have always seen as precious repositories of human knowledge. Can anthropologists—cultural, biological, medical, linguistic and archaeological—deploy our deep commitment to human and biological diversity to resist the forces of hate, fear and xenophobia?

Anthropologists are restless and nomadic people. We are a tribe of hunters and gatherers of human artifacts, human cultures, life ways, and human values. Anthropology requires us to become intimate with the people we want to understand—getting inside their skin, standing in their shoes kind of thing. Ethnography is an art form, a work of translation, that demands all the senses—the observant eye, the attentive ear, a keen sense of smell, touch, and a sense of taste—a "gusto" (in Portuguese) that carries a double valence—a taste not only for new foods and spicy condiments, strong drinks—but also a taste for the sentient life through which a "society" is embodied—catching its sense of time and timing, its movements and gestures, its patterns of work, play, and devotion, its sense of humor and its sense of justice, its sense of dignity.

Anthropology also requires strength, valor, and courage. Pierre Bourdieu called anthropology a combat sport, an extreme sport as well as a tough and rigorous discipline. Anthropologists are the Green Berets of the social sciences. Archaeology teaches not only a deep appreciation and reverence for the past and for "small things forgotten," as Jim Deetz described historical archeology. It teaches students not to be afraid of getting one's hands dirty, to get down in the dirt, and to commit yourself, body and mind. Susan Sontag called anthropology a "heroic" profession—one that required brains and strength, sensitivity and guts. It was not just a job, not just a profession. It was, she said, one of those very few rare and true vocations.

You, the next generation of anthropologists are the ones in which your professors have invested their hopes and their trust. We need your intelligence, your initiative, your risk-taking, and your energy. We look to you as the next generation of "loyal rebels"—loyal to what anthropology has taught you: to value diversity; to embrace and enjoy (not just tolerate) human difference; to be open to the wisdom of strangers and resolute in refusing any proposals that denigrate other ways of living and being in the world. You are the heirs to a great tradition of anthropology. May it give you the courage to work in the service of all humankind and be conservative protectors of all the creatures and plants and bio-diversity that sustains Mother Earth. May you be wise and strong and steadfast in building a better world than the one you have inherited.

NOTES

1. This text was prepared as a commencement address and was delivered at the Department of Anthropology graduation ceremony at the University of California, Berkeley, May 19, 2016.

ENVISIONING A MORE PUBLIC ANTHROPOLOGY:
INTERVIEW WITH FREDRIK BARTH

Robert Borofsky, Hawaii Pacific University, Center for a Public Anthropology
borofsky@hpu.edu
http://www.publicanthropology.org/

Fredrik Barth: Let me begin with a general preamble to our conversation. Since anthropology draws on the ethnography of the whole world—as it must and should—it has a unique potential to supplement Western science and Western humanism. It can contribute broadly to human thought, to human imagination.

Robert Borofsky: You are referring to anthropology's role in broadening people's perspectives?

FB: Yes, to opening up windows of human reflection on the human condition in radically new directions, that people have never really imagined. Certainly anthropology has not been very good at doing this, at shaping an image of the diversity of how people live. But nonetheless, something is there and we must cultivate it and harvest it much more actively.

RB: Why do you think anthropology has not succeeded in this goal?

FB: Well as far as American anthropologists and American anthropology are concerned, and this probably will not be popular, I think one difficulty is the emphasis that American anthropologists have placed on an evolutionary perspective. It's a fine perspective for some purposes, but it gives a license for others to say, "How interesting, how great, yes, if I was interested in the past I would listen to you, but I'm interested in the present." It shunts anthropology off to the side when what we should do is speak about issues now and the human condition now. We should consider the issues people presently engage with. Implicit in this is a view that democratic societies need a wide and public discussion of ideas.

RB: Let's talk more about anthropology's role in this regard.

FB: I think it's very important that if we want influence in the world, we should speak up about issues that are important to others, not just ourselves. Even more important than voting, though that is important, is presenting a view, a voice, on issues because that may influence public policy. One should, of course, realize the difficulties here. But speaking out is much better than only responding to the packages that the political system presents. That is part of being a citizen—finding the occasions and the places where you can have public influence.

RB: What forms do you think a more publicly-engaged anthropology might take?

FB: I think it important that we enter into as many discourses as possible that are already going on where there is an audience that is already engaged and knowledgeable. What we want to do is find ways of bringing something additional into public conversations that are already going onthereby subverting the established position and contributing something that may catch people's attention.

RB: Can you provide a concrete example?

FB: One example is Unni Wikan's work on the new immigrants of Europe. Here is an issue that lots of people were thinking about, talking about, and in fact being quite confused about. The main discussion of Norwegian immigration policy focused on how many immigrants we should let in? Unni was allowed a two-minute statement on Norwegian public television on the topic: She said we

1

should be talking about what are we doing for the welfare of those who are here already rather than focusing on those who might come. With this intervention, she helped redefined the entire discourse on the subject. It led to people voicing their concern about what was happening inside Norway and to developing programs that could be critiqued and argued about. It broke a political silence about the issue.

RB: A more publicly-engaged anthropology in this sense, then, would be directly engaging in public discourses about public problems.

FB: It would try to find ways of reframing publicly-articulated issues. To do this, however, you need some kind of cultural capital so that people will say, "listen, this may be important."

RB: How do you gain such capital?

FB: You need to speak out but speak out carefully, with limited purposes in every case – not to grab the microphone to give a lecture on anthropology, but to formulate something that really pricks people's attention regarding one aspect of the problem. Rather than disrupting the conversation that's going on, you become a part of it. If you are too ambitious, and feel this is your one chance to speak out, then you start lecturing others. You become irrelevant to what is going on in the conversation. We need to develop an ability to focus and make our points relevant to others' concerns.

RB: Would you say that there is more of this sort of public engagement, by academics, in Europe or America?

FB: There is more of an audience for it in Europe because people are more prepared to believe that academics have cultural capital. There is the idea that academics are competent to address the world's problems. Many countries, both in Eastern and Western Europe, have cabinet ministers who are professors, not just professors of political science, but professors of other subjects as well: humanists, historians and scientists. It affirms that academics are thoughtful people to be listened to while in America academics tend to be looked down upon as impractical intellectuals.

RB: To what might you attribute this dynamic of American intellectual life?

FB: Brad Shore (at Emory University) once commented to me that his neighbors felt sorry for him because he do not make as much money as they did. Here is a very crude measurement of private influence and judgment. But, of course, it is reciprocal. Many anthropologists think going public is less than respectable. The public does not respect us so we do not respect them. If you want to speak to the public effectively, you have to respect them.

RB: Where in Europe do you see an active intellectual tradition, among anthropologists, that contrasts with the one in America?

FB: I guess the place where there is the most of this is in France. I think it used to be in England – Malinowski was fashionable and his seminars were famous. Intellectuals in England talked about him. In France, of course, Levi-Strauss has been very famous. But other French anthropologists also have followings and public visibility. It thus becomes interesting for a French reading public to know what French anthropologists are saying about the issues of the day. Also in India, in Mexico, in Brazil, and perhaps in Scandinavia, there is more public interest in this way than in the U.S.

RB: What specific steps might be taken to draw American anthropologists into such public engagements?

FB: The image that comes to mind is of American anthropologists, like penguins on the edge of an ice sheet afraid that something in the water will eat them. They stand on the ice and push and push each other until one falls in, and then they see what happens to him. If nothing bad happens, then they might be willing to dive in, too. I do think many people would like to have some input, and if they see that it's possible, they would jump. But they must do it individually.

I think one of the difficulties that's hidden somewhere in this syndrome, is that there is in America, because of the media hype that one is used to, a sense that you have to be tactical. You can't speak as a free spirit, you can't afford to be self-critical and honest. You must find some way of projecting some facile image, and take a tactical position, or else you will be totally ineffective. And this is contrary to academic quality and intellectual integrity. I think the way we see it constantly is in the roles played by ecologists and political scientists. When they speak on public television, they are hung up in the tactical game of trying to manipulate audiences instead of speaking honestly. They hold back things that they know are relevant but seem politically incorrect or critical of their own constituencies. At times there seems to be almost a pre-set agenda. We shall touch on these things and not on those because they are contrary to American interests. Let's not talk too clearly about them, let's position ourselves in ways that don't raise ugly issues.

I think it is important to speak out in contexts that are not made up only of anthropologists. I should speak to historians and political scientists who say things about the clash of civilizations. But I would not lay out the problem as an anthropological issue. I would try to disturb and subvert their frames of reference by undermining one or more of the premises on which they base their arguments, showing how it does not make sense from a broader perspective.

RB: Could you give an example?

FB: Well I presume that's what Boas did long ago. Boas addressed something that everybody was concerned with—race—and had a specific point he wanted to make. He had professional research supporting his position regarding the cultural, rather than genetic, basis of behavior which was highly relevant to other people who weren't anthropologists.

Perhaps the whole controversy around Samuel Huntington's *Clash of Civilizations* is a lost opportunity. Instead of piling abuse on Huntington for what he said, we might have undermined particular positions presented in a careful scholarly way that other scholars would take note of.

Dr. Gro Harlem Brundtland (the former Director-General of the World Health Organization) was on a United Nations commission regarding the environment and coined the idea of "sustainability." Her idea was not all that well thought out at the time. Still, it changed the frame of reference. It replaced the optimistic sense that we will invent our way out of our environmental problems to asking what we can so as not to reduce options for future generations.

One final example: I've just written an op-ed for the main Oslo newspaper on the university's function. There have been committees that have tried to plan and redesign universities so that they are more responsive to the specific needs of contemporary society, to make them more accountable. What I did was to say, look here, we must not forget that the university's first task is to produce competently trained personnel for a changing world. It is not simply offering skills for today but preparing these students for the world they will find themselves in tomorrow. The point, I am saying, is to suggest new ways of looking at problems.

RB: What type of response, would you hope for, from your op-ed piece?

FB: I would hope that more of those who engage in the university debate will start saying: But the issue is not only how some established kind of knowledge or competency can be deployed in society but rather how we must secure a place where creativity and imagination can flourish for the future. We must train people who are intellectually awake. Disciplines are breaking down. We must be able to be creative as an academic community to cope with a changing world. I would hope the government's department of education, which is in charge of universities, would review plans for reorganizing the university from a different perspective. My colleagues might also start using this argument in the defense of more money for research, more advanced training, more investment in post-doctoral students rather than simply addressing the problem as others have framed it—of being accountable.

I would not mind if I were called to argue this with others. Others might say that they have certain priorities that must be taken care of, and I would then have to show how they could be better taken care of in the way I suggested. They might well challenge me. They might examine my arguments and find points that are factually distorted, incomplete, partial, or where the logic failed. But the discussion would change—we would be arguing over facts and logic from a shared position. Yes, we all want universities to train professionals in a better way, yes we want them to be more publicly responsible and so on. We would be arguing about different ways to approach the problem that would not follow the political packaging and rhetoric of the moment.

INTERVIEW WITH CAROLYN NORDSTROM

Robert Borofsky, Hawaii Pacific University, Center for a Public Anthropology
borofsky@hpu.edu
http://www.publicanthropology.org/

Robert Borofsky: Where would you like to begin?

Carolyn Nordstrom: I'll start with what I was thinking about this morning. As I was walking my dog, I was reflecting on what makes anthropology so cool. I thought about all the definitions I know, the introductory texts I have read, and the various things anthropologists converse about.

All of a sudden, I thought: Wait a minute. When I think about what's in my heart, what is it that anthropology offers to others as well as myself? I realized I needed to go back to the Enlightenment of the 1700s. The Enlightenment asserted that the world was logical, that it was linear. It portrayed people as objective, as rational. Building on this perspective, various sciences categorized, classified, and boxed people and things in the world. Our theoretical systems are based on the rational nature of existence and the rationality of people. This perspective has produced many important innovations—engineering, harnessing electricity and energy sources, medical breakthroughs.

But you know what? A whole lot of the world is defined by chaos theory. Humans are anything but fully rational beings. We create incredibly noble values. We create things that bring me to tears. I see things in the world that are so moving. But this creativity is far from being logical, far from being rational.

We are this hot bed of rationality and irrationality all mixed together like a fine stew. We're logical as well as mystical and magical, we're absurd as well as practical. We are all these things, often at the same time. We don't merely live in contradictions; we embrace them. We at times deny them; we frequently argue over them. Still we embed them in our lives.

Anthropology opens these dynamics to us. It lets us touch these realities. I often ask my classes "How many textbooks have you read in your life that you loved and remembered?" The most anyone has ever answered is five, the average is one or a couple. I know it's painful for some academics to hear. Textbooks teach us important "stuff." But they don't often touch the reality of how we live our lives. Anthropology gives us tools to touch the heartbeat of humanity. I think that's anthropology's gift to the world.

Education in the West draws strongly on this model of logical, rational reality. We keep applying it over and over again in systematic, ordered ways. It would be better to ask: How can we apply models of rationality in irrational ways? The world is embracing digital and virtual realities, globalization, chaos and quantum theory, and multidimensional solutions to pressing issues. People today are breaking down many boundaries of what we take to be ourselves, our genders, our nations. Anthropology is well positioned to help us understand this changing, fluid world.

Robert: Could you share with students why you become an anthropologist?

Carolyn: Why wouldn't you become an anthropologist? You can go anywhere, study any issue. You are not bound to only follow it through the lens of politics and political science, or the highs and lows of economics. Your explorations can range from the offices of elites to the most remote locations on earth. You can ask any question. You can study borders and their breakdowns simultaneously. You can study traditions amid change. You can study how people love and kill at the same time. You can do research and work anywhere in the world. No other discipline lets me do that.

Robert: What particularly excites you about anthropology?

Carolyn: Obviously, the big question is what does it mean to be human? That's fascinating. I grew up a world where everything had its "place." People were from places and things were put in "appropriate" places. One thing was in one place and not in another. We're now entering an era where we're able to move beyond this framework.

It's exhilarating because this new era is still uncharted, un-mapped. We are creating it as we go along. We know place is important; but things are also unplaced. How do you intellectually deal with holding both of those ideas in your head at the same time? It is this realization regarding migrant flows, cultural flows, and virtual flows that is reformulating how we think about place and how place affects us. We are studying something that is very much in motion.

For example, clothes are symbols. They involve values, which are full of stereotypes, morals, joys, and a range of other emotions. When I see people, if they're wearing clothes like mine, I often feel a certain kind of affinity. I make certain kinds of judgments. I can tell you what I have on and what particular place I'm in at the moment. But how does this information get all mixed together in today's flows? Just sitting here looking at what I have on, my clothes are a product of work from numerous countries. Clothes, indeed goods in general, flow from place to place and thus are "multi-place" and yet, at the same time, exist in very specific places.

How do we understand global financial flows? How do we understand the changing lives of people? How do we understand the experiences of Syrians, for example, given the horrors many of them are living through? What's home for them? What's family? What's safety? How do they understand humanity and security as they travel from Syria into Turkey and across Europe often faced with grave dangers?

Another topic I find fascinating is "invisibility." The world's full of things that we can see and others we are trained "not to see"—things that societies try to keep hidden from public awareness. Anthropology offers vibrant approaches for investigating and bringing to light these "made-invisible" realities, as I call them, so we are better able to forge solutions to problems that have seemed insurmountable in the past. What really goes on at the frontlines of wars, and in the elite command bunkers—and what impact does war leave in its stead? Why did Wall Street crash; what stories aren't they telling us? What's it really like to be a kid living on the street—in a rich urban city, in an impoverished shanty, or in a natural disaster? Governing institutions seldom ask the kids, making their stories, their perceptions, invisible to the public realm. In sheer objective fact it makes good sense to include children representatives on city councils, national committees, development programs, and United Nations assemblies addressing children's issues—but the idea seems ludicrous to cultures whose adults define only adults as capable of making fully informed and morally responsible decisions.

Understanding creativity is equally important to me. How do societies, advancements, beliefs get created: how do we produce social change, values, cultural ideas, innovation, new senses of ourselves? How do we create new worlds? How do we create answers to our questions?

Robert: You did fieldwork in war zones. What was that like?

Carolyn: I had no intention of studying war or violence. I was a medical anthropologist doing my graduate research in Sri Lanka, a country then often seen as one of Asia's tropical paradises. It was one of two countries in the world that had very high health standards for a relatively lower GDP—and this in a country facing both the spectrum of illnesses associated with urban educated life, and tropical diseases in developing regions. It was anomalous because a strong link exists globally between lower economic rankings/lower health indices. Sri Lanka had created a very successfully health system, and I was intrigued to find out how.

In the midst of this research, I realized that as a student, and even as a medical anthropologist, I had never seen a definition of "illness." I had seen thousands of definitions of different kinds of illnesses, but not of what defined the very core phenomenon of illness itself. So I started looking into what people viewed as illness.

This led me to devoting three months in Sri Lanka asking people—from urban to rural areas, doctors to patients, young to old—"What is illness?" I got some very intriguing answers. They were not what I expected. But they made sense. It changed my perspective, and helped shed light on bigger issues like why some aspects of medicine simply aren't able to achieve desired results. I realized if we asked questions like this, we could provide better health care to people. We often seem to be treating things that people do not see as illness and not treating things that they do, or ignoring aspects of treatment patients deem important while focusing on some they find alienating.

In the middle this fieldwork, severe rioting erupted nationwide in Sri Lanka. In seven short days, one-sixth of the entire country was destroyed. Thousands died. I was in the middle of this weeklong massive slaughter; there was no escaping it. I got caught in places where entire city blocks were in flames, every building and vehicle set on fire. People were massacred in the streets, pulled from their homes, cars, and businesses and beaten to death or set on fire. I found I needed to try to make sense of what I saw: both for my own peace and mind, and to try to help correct many of the misconceptions in explanations of political and civil violence.

I had been taught about the exhilaration and glory of war all my life – in school, by public media, through books. Societies create myths about war that are widely believed. But there was nothing attractive about what I saw, nothing glorious. Seeing a body chopped up into pieces isn't nice or wonderful. There's no glory in burning people to death. If we show that reality, how horribly it affects everybody—victims, witnesses, and perpetrators alike—people might do a lot less of it.

I wondered why people killed each other like this? It lacked any ultimate sense. Why would someone drive a nail into someone else's head? Why would someone see children, unarmed women, harmless grandfathers as dangerous—to be killed? This is not the exception, but the norm: today globally 90 percent of the casualties of political violence are non-combatant civilians. I began to ponder what violence involves. What motivates people to act in this way?

It's important to stress that I also saw some amazing acts of altruism in the midst of this violence. People risked their lives in the middle of these riots for complete strangers. I witnessed the full spectrum of humanity, seeing extremes we normally do not see in our lives. It became obvious that what is portrayed in texts, media, and movies about such violence only scratched the surface, and generally presented "facts" that, as I wrote in one book, are 180 degrees the opposite of what really takes place in war.

This unexpected event in my life changed the direction of my research for decades to follow: for caught in the middle of this violence and seeking ways to survive it, I realized we needed a much better understanding of the dynamics behind how humans create and react to violence like this.

Robert: Students in my introductory anthropology class enjoy reading your book, *Global Outlaws*. How did you come to study the illegal global interchanges you discuss?

Carolyn: After studying political violence on several continents for more than fifteen years after Sri Lanka, I was pretty burned out with dealing with such traumas. Through the years I had collected lots of data on large smuggling systems running through war zones. I realized delving into this allowed me to continue working with war and peace while giving me a respite from the frontlines violence.

People in societies at war need smugglers because governing, financial, and economic institutions are impaired, support services are interrupted, legal systems break down, and trade routes, industry, agriculture, etc. are disrupted. People can't get what they need to survive, from food and medicines to weapons and technology. I kept seeing a lot of the same international "players" wherever I traveled in the world—the same arms merchants, the same vendors of critical necessities, the same smugglers. I thought what's going on here; how does smuggling, how does the extra-legal in general, operate?

Such inquiries lead to questions on a bigger level: how do these extra-legal economies surrounding smuggling and politics affect global economies in general? It's impossible to have wars without it; and as I later learned it's impossible to do business today at all without some extra-legal activities. But there is little written about it.

Around this time, people were talking about blood diamonds, and I thought this might be a good place to begin studying illegal economies "on the ground"—where it's all taking place. I started in the center of Angola during one of the worst periods of the country's civil war. It quickly became obvious that smuggling didn't just involve diamonds and weapons. It involved a vast range of things—clothing, food, petroleum, computers, medical equipment, building supplies, vehicles, cooper wire, paint, pharmaceuticals, agricultural tools and seeds, lights, industrial supplies, textbooks, clean water—anything and everything that could transported.

This extra-legal trade is profoundly international: goods come in from and go out to countries all over the world. And it is essential: the legal markets in any warzone I've been in are not able to provide anywhere close to what the country's population needs to survive. A small proportion of all smuggling is devoted to military supplies, the majority of it brings in survival and development supplies for the whole country, or carries out valuable resources (gold, diamonds, oil, timber, fish, etc.).

Smugglers seldom match the common media stereotypes of violence: young male adults (bearded, clad in leather jackets, and disenfranchised from society). Curiously, most smugglers are pretty peaceful people. Many see themselves are regular businesspeople. Some are considered noble by societies caught in war: people bringing in essential medicines, food, communications equipment, clothing, tools to make a survival living, ad infinitum. As true as the classic of "blood diamond for weapons of war exchange" is as an icon of horrendous violence, suffering, and war-profiteering—it is equally true that smuggling often involves getting critical necessities to the front lines, saving people's lives.

Since I found goods from all over the world in the middle of a remote warzone, I decided to follow how everything from massive Mercedes transport trucks to pocket-able diamonds got in and out of a country or, on a broader scale, in and out of a region where there was so much disruption, and ultimately traverses intercontinentally. How do the things that people need or want get across borders? Across continents? Across oceans? Expensive cameras, Nike shoes, elephants, high-tech products, mega-tons of fish and tomatoes, airplanes, scissors. A whole universe of essential supplies, raw resources, and luxury goods travel outside the law. All flowing in and out of Angola, of all warzones—and because many of these raw resources and goods went to, or came from, peacetime nations around the world—in and out of all virtually all countries.

World Bank, United Nations, and government indices at that time stated only 10% of Angola's economy was legal. 90 percent was what I call extra-legal: including informal, illicit, illegal, and unrecorded. Following extra-legal linkages globally, it became obvious that perhaps half the global economy—including both wartime and peacetime nations – involves extra-legality.

Yet there are no formal economic indices that calculate the impact of extra-legal goods, monies, and exchange on legal economies, on government and financial stability, or for development. There are no formal methodologies to research, track, analyze, and deal with extra-legal activities; no formal ways to even determine their size with any precision. The repercussions are dramatic: Angola's development policies, like all nations, focus on the legal realm only. But if 90 percent of the country's economy wasn't legal coming out of war—how can any development projects that deal with only 10 percent of reality work?

Because these flows in and out of Angola link across countries worldwider—so too do the repercussions. To study this, I followed extra-legal routes, across borders, along payment and laundering systems, and then globally. I traveled to a number of ports, first in Africa, and then globally (e.g. Rotterdam, Singapore, Long Beach USA) to look at how goods were entering and leaving; and also traveled on a freighter internationally.

We don't really understand economies if we don't understand their smuggling networks. It's fascinating. Perhaps a third or up to a half of the world's economy taken in total is moving across borders extra-legally in all kinds of ways and we don't know how to formally chart it. There are formal analyses for GDP, but none for what I call XGDP (extra-legal gross domestic product). What does this say about our economic analyses? We—government institutions, economic and development organizations, academics, alike—don't fully understand the vast world of smuggling and the extra-legal, yet it's critical to our survival.

Robert: Yes, you make a good point. Turning to another topic, if I may, what advice would you give introductory students thinking about majoring in anthropology?

Carolyn: I can tell you what I tell my introductory classes. I tell them anthropology is one discipline where you can study how various aspects of our lives and worlds are linked together. Anthropology is a global study not only in what it explores but also in how it thinks about issues. It looks at the big picturer—not just at a single country, for example, but also at cross-cultural, international interactions. We take seriously not only understanding other cultures but the ways in which they fit together with one another to make the world we live in. We're interested in what takes us from human to humanity.

Anthropology values both the local and global perspectives. In the twenty-first century, businesses, medical schools, and NGOs are discovering that their policies do not work if they do not understand larger cross-cultural issues, the bigger picture that ties things together. Yet at the same time they need to understand on-the-ground daily realities: What are the rationalities and irrationalities that humans display in different contexts and at different times? What are the hopes, fears and dreams that drive people forward? How do these dynamics fit into the way we perceive governance, development, legality; shape our ideas of self, belonging, emotions, human potential; influence our definitions of good and bad, success or failure, possible or impossible?

One of the things that delights us in anthropology at my university is the fact that our anthropology graduates are equally competitive in getting in medical schools and choice business jobs as those coming from the traditional medical and business majors. Our students are very successful going into development, policy, planning, and innovation work—whether local or international—and people love them because they hit the ground running with cultural sensitivities and valuable field training. They have knowledge that isn't necessarily being taught in some of the others disciplines: they know how to cross intellectual as well as physical borders; link the micro to the macro; weave together seemingly different aspects of life to better understand societies, to problem-solve, and to gain a better understanding of why people act as they do.

Anthropology is well prepared to address future advances. For example, if I were to work in the civilian Space X program founded by Elon Musk, I'd want to be an anthropologist. The technical aspects are critical, of course—but technology has no meaning apart from the heartbeat of humanity that animates it. It would be fascinating to explore what goals and hopes guide the people involved in long-term space flight. What facilitates space travel, ensuring it doesn't totally disrupt the travelers – mentally and physically? What social bonds and human interactivity do people require, do societies wherever they are in space, depend on? What is human intelligence, as we increasingly turn technological control over to artificial intelligence—and what is not/human as people and digital technologies merge in more extensive and complex ways?

What other discipline studies such diverse topics—from smuggling to violence and altruism, from creativity to space travel, from local family interactions to global dynamics, from the changing definitions of what it means to be human to the vibrant ethnographies of lives being lived – and then weaves these together in groundbreaking ways?

Robert: Thank you for sharing your thoughts today. It is an exciting and inspiring vision of anthropology.

IMAGE CREDITS

Many of the images used in this book appear with permission of the copyright holder. None of the figures in this book should be assumed to be in the public domain or creative commons licensed unless otherwise noted in the original image information.

The Development of Anthropological Ideas

No images in this chapter.

The Culture Concept

Figure 1: Public domain image from Gulliver's Travels in Lilliput and Brobdingnag by John Lang. London: T.C. and E.C. Jack, 1908.

Figure 2: Public domain image from https://commons.wikimedia.org/wiki/File:JamesGeorgeFrazer.jpg

Figure 3: Public domain image from *Anthropology: An Introduction to the Study of Man and Civilization* by E.B. Tylor 1904. https://commons.wikimedia.org/wiki/File:Anthropology;_an_introduction_to_the_study_of_man_and_civilization_(1896)_(14760690736).jpg

Figure 4: Public domain image from London School of Economics Library Collections Public domain.

Figure 5: Photograph of Franz Boas is from the public domain collection of the Canadian Museum of Civilization, Negative 79-796.

Figure 6: Photograph of Ruth Benedict is public domain from the Library of Congress. https://en.wikipedia.org/wiki/Ruth_Benedict#/media/File:Ruth_Benedict.jpg

Figure 7: Image of Yanomami mother and child by Cmacauley https://commons.wikimedia.org/wiki/File:Yanomami_Woman_%26_Child.jpg

Figure 8: Photo courtesy of Emily Cowall.

Figure 9: Photo courtesy of Priscilla Medeiros.

Doing Fieldwork: Methods in Cultural Anthropology

Figure 1: Photo by Katie Nelson, 2001.

Figure 2: Photo by Katie Nelson, 2001.

Figure 3: Photo by Katie Nelson, 2001.

Figure 4: Image of Bronislaw Malinowski is public domain from the London School of Economics Library Collections. https://en.wikipedia.org/wiki/Bronis%C5%82aw_Malinowski#/media/File:Wmalinowski_trobriand_isles_1918.jpg

Figure 5: Image reproduced from Benjamin Lee Whorf, "Science and Linguistics." *MIT Technology Review*: 42 (1940).

Figure 6: Chart courtesy of Katie Nelson.

Figure 7: Photograph courtesy of Katie Nelson.

Language

Figure 1: Illustration by MegSmith from https://commons.wikimedia.org/wiki/File:Tract.gif

Figure 2: Chimpanzee photo from The Green Parent, https://www.flickr.com/photos/thegreenparent/6943988092/in/photolist-bzBKJC-zDUYsp-7SB2Ti-a1dNpR-o9XYFt-QHJxws-5V3K9S-6GGsaB-24BHdf-8PxP51-4bTFt1-g8HhXg-bVPhdX-g8HHEV-djgDGX-g9Fokm-3oyJyK-djgDNk-6aYFFn-7MEHY8-dbzPCy-g8GRG8-4wg2PA-7UHWGR-g8HSif-bymeE7-g8HGUA-g9G1iF-3oDcjJ-ppg5zK-g8Jjm6-g8HneV-9fb4op-7MEHYk-7UMhkQ-g8GKPh-L478z-cV3zFW-g8GU42-5oXTdK-4wF5Nb-g8HoqU-poYJLp-g8Hfyu-ppg5Fr-g8H6Gw-nxDiWa-4TzY8N-q3C5FL-nQ4JKS

Figure 3: Photograph courtesy of James Kim.

Figure 4: Photograph from Cultural Survival and Make Peace Productions

Figure 5: Photograph courtesy of Linda Light.

Subsistence

Figure 1: The carrying capacity image collage contains work by Andreas Lederer. https://et.wikipedia.org/wiki/Hatsad and Dennis Jarvis https://commons.wikimedia.org/wiki/File:Agriculture_in_Vietnam_with_farmers.jpg

Figure 2: Includes public domain image from https://commons.wikimedia.org/wiki/File:Fishing_Katcha_Valai.JPG and https://commons.wikimedia.org/wiki/File:Fish_Farm_Site.jpg

Figure 3: Woolly mammoth figure contains images from https://et.wikipedia.org/wiki/Hatsad by Andreas Lederer and https://commons.wikimedia.org/wiki/File:Woolly_mammoth.jpg by By Flying Puffin.

Figure 4: Maasai herd by ILRI/Lieve Lynen from https://www.flickr.com/photos/ilri/12170593993/in/photostream

Figure 5: Bean plant image by Perry Quan from https://www.flickr.com/photos/pquan/6066910690

Figure 6: A culinary shoe pot from Oaxaca, Mexico. Courtesy of the Burke Museum of Natural History and Culture, Catalog Number 2009-117/536. All rights reserved.

Figure 7: Clay Cooking Pots in the Republic of Suriname. Courtesy of Karina Noriega. All rights reserved.

Figure 8: Illustration by Nicolle Rager Fuller, National Science Foundation, https://www.nsf.gov/news/news_images.jsp?cntn_id=104207

Figure 9: Commodity chain figure includes images from Adam C. Baker https://commons.wikimedia.org/wiki/File:ElSalvadorfairtradecoffee.jpg and Brian Johnson and Dane Kantner https://www.flickr.com/photos/danebrian/7798861630 and M.O. Stevens https://commons.wikimedia.org/wiki/File:Coffee_beans_at_Longbottom_-_Hillsboro,_Oregon.JPG and Hao Xing https://pl.wikipedia.org/wiki/Plik:Employees_work_inside_the_Starbucks_at_the_Taj_Mahal_Palace_hotel_in_south_Mumbai,_India.jpg

Figure 10: Photo courtesy of Isaac Shearn

Economics

Figure 1: Image by Thelmadatter https://commons.wikimedia.org/wiki/File:MasaMetate.JPG

Figure 2: Sorting coffee beans image from https://commons.wikimedia.org/wiki/File:Coffee_beans_being_sorted_and_pulped.jpg by http://flickr.com/photos/rohsstreetcafe/380885309

Figure 3:Image is public domain from https://commons.wikimedia.org/wiki/File:Chipata_-_roadside_clothes_vendors.JPG

Figure 4: Image from Bronislaw Malinowski, *Argonauts of the Western Pacific* (Routledge & Kegan Paul, 1978[1922]), plate xvi. From https://commons.wikimedia.org/wiki/File:Malinowski_mwali_plate_xvi.png

Figure 5: From the Institute for Money, Technology and Financial Inclusion https://www.flickr.com/photos/imtfi/5868331010/in/photostream/

Figure 6: Tea workers image by Shankar S. https://www.flickr.com/photos/shankaronline/7168516257

Figure 7: Image courtesy of Sarah Lyon

Political Anthropology: A Cross-Cultural Comparison

Figure 1: Age grades and age set, based on Sengree in Peoples of Africa is reproduced with permission of Kendall Hunt Publishing Company from *Cultural Anthropology: A Concise Introduction* by Paul McDowell.

Figure 2: Bilateral Cross-Cousin Marriage from Yanomamo is reproduced with permission of Kendall Hunt Publishing Company from *Cultural Anthropology: A Concise Introduction* by Paul McDowell.

Figure 3: Segmentary :Lineage Model is reproduced with permission of Kendall Hunt Publishing Company from *Cultural Anthropology: A Concise Introduction* by Paul McDowell.

Figure 4: Conical Clan Design of Chiefdom is reproduced with permission of Kendall Hunt Publishing Company from *Cultural Anthropology: A Concise Introduction* by Paul McDowell.

Figure 5: Matrilateral Cross-Cousin Marriage is reproduced from is reproduced with permission of Kendall Hunt Publishing Company from *Cultural Anthropology: A Concise Introduction* by Paul McDowell.

Figure 6: Image courtesy of Paul McDowell.

Family and Marriage

Figure 1: Courtesy of Laura Tubelle de González.
Figure 2: Courtesy of Thomas McIlwraith.
Figure 3: Courtesy of Thomas McIlwraith.
Figure 4: Courtesy of Thomas McIlwraith.
Figure 5: Courtesy of Laura Tubelle de González.
Figure 6: Courtesy of Mary Kay Gilliland.

Race and Ethnicity

Figure 1: Photo by Mike Graham https://www.flickr.com/photos/mike626/10980456

Figure 2: Illustration from *Systema Naturae*, Carolus Linnaeus, https://commons.wikimedia.org/wiki/File:Systema_Naturae_Plate_IV.jpg

Figure 3: Image is from Anthro Palomar https://commons.wikimedia.org/wiki/File:Map_of_blood_group_o.gif

Figure 4: Image from NMI Portal https://commons.wikimedia.org/wiki/File:Worldwide_prevalence_of_lactose_intolerance_in_recent_populations.jpg

Figure 5: Image from UN Women https://www.flickr.com/photos/unwomen/22766182427

Figure 6: Image from https://en.wikipedia.org/wiki/Jiichir%C5%8D_Matsumoto#/media/ File:Jiichiro_Matsumoto.JPG

Figure 7: Image courtesy of Laura Gonzalez.

Figure 8: Image courtesy of Justin Garcia.

Gender and Sexuality

Figure 1: Image from Sharma Pictures Publication, 174, Princess Street, Bombay-2. India.

Figure 2: Image from Sharma Pictures Publication, 174, Princess Street, Bombay-2. India.

Figure 3: Image courtesy of Carol Mukhopadhyay, 2010.

Figure 4: Image courtesy of Carol Mukhopadhyay, 2010.

Figure 5: Photograph by Ajay Tallam, 2007. https://commons.wikimedia.org/wiki/File:Men_not_ allowed.jpg.

Figure 6: Photograph by Carol Mukhopadhyay, 1989.

Figure 7: Photograph by Carol Mukhopadhyay, 1989.

Figure 8: Image is from ca. 1405 manuscript "Bellifortis," by Kyeser von Eichstadt https://commons.wikimedia.org/wiki/File:Chastity_belt_Bellifortis.jpg

Figure 9: Photograph by Takeaway, 2005. https://commons.wikimedia.org/wiki/File:Amphoe_ omkoi_lahu_people.jpg.

Figure 10: Photograph by Tami Blumenfield, 2002.

Figure 11: Photograph by Tami Blumenfield, 2002.

Figure 12: Photograph by lecercle, 2009. https://www.flickr.com/photos/lecercle/3707261938.

Figure 13: Photograph by Carol Mukhopadhyay, Tanzania, 2010.

Figure 14: Photograph by Carol Mukhopadhyay, Tanzania, 2010.

Figure 15: Photograph by Carol Mukhopadhyay, 2008.

Figure 16: Photograph by Carol Mukhopadhyay, Tanzania, 2010.

Figure 17: Photograph by Francis Hannaway. https://en.wikipedia.org/wiki/File:Basankusu_ collecting_firewood_by_Francis_Hannaway.jpg.

Figure 18: Photograph by Tami Blumenfield, 2002.

Figure 19: Reproduced with permission.

Figure 20: Image courtesy of Carol Mukhopadhyay.

Figure 21: Image courtesy of Tami Blumenfield.

Figure 22: Image courtesy of Susan Harper.

Figure 23: Image courtesy of Abby Gondek.

Religion

Figure 1: Image by Matthias Kabel https://commons.wikimedia.org/wiki/File:Venus_von_ Willendorf_01.png
MatthiasKabel

Figure 2: Photograph by HTO https://commons.wikimedia.org/wiki/File:Paintings_from_the_ Chauvet_cave_(museum_replica).jpg

Figure 3: Public domain image from https://commons.wikimedia.org/wiki/File:Taksin_Memorial_ Spirit_House.jpg

Figure 4: Public domain image from https://commons.wikimedia.org/wiki/File:Nikko_Toshogu_ Outer_Torii_M3032.jpg

Figure 5: Photograph by Christopher Hogue Thompson https://commons.wikimedia.org/wiki/File:Pentecost_Land_Diving.JPG

Globalization

Figure 1: Image from David and Paulina https://www.flickr.com/photos/davidandpaulina/
Figure 2: Photographs by Jonathan S. Marion. All rights reserved.
Figure 3: Photograph by Lovisa Selander https://commons.wikimedia.org/wiki/File:Fishing_boat_Lake_Poopo.jpg
Figure 4: Photograph by André Mellagi https://www.flickr.com/photos/mellagi/
Figure 5: Photograph by Jerome W. Crowder. All rights reserved.
Figure 6: Photograph courtesy of Lauren Miller Griffith.
Figure 7: Photography courtesy of Jonathan S. Marion.

Culture and Sustainability: Environmental Anthropology in the Anthropocene

Figure 1: Photo by Adalberto H. Vega from https://commons.wikimedia.org/wiki/File:Cop%C3%A1n_Ballcourt.jpg
Figure 2: Photo by Himalayan Academy Publications, Kapaa, Kauai, Hawaii. https://commons.wikimedia.org/wiki/File:CowHA.jpg
Figure 3: Image by Christian Palmer.
Figure 4: Image by Christian Palmer.
Figure 5: Image by Christian Palmer.
Figure 6: Image by Christian Palmer.

Performance

Figure 1: Photograph by Mariana Rodriguez Guttierrez https://commons.wikimedia.org/wiki/File:Ballet_Folkl%C3%B3rico_en_la_Casa_de_la_Cultura.JPG
Figure 2: Photograph by George C. Marshall European Center for Security Studies https://www.flickr.com/photos/gcmcphotos/with/31874211260/
Figure 3: Photograph from https://pixabay.com/en/man-sitting-back-skateboard-steps-1030859/
Figure 4a: Photograph by Jonathan S. Marion. All rights reserved.
Figure 4b: Photograph by Jonathan S. Marion. All rights reserved.
Figure 5a: Photograph from https://pixabay.com/p-873830/
Figure 5b: Photograph by National Cancer Institute https://commons.wikimedia.org/wiki/File:Doctor_consults_with_patient_(4).jpg
Figure 5c: Photograph by Jonathan S. Marion. All rights reserved.
Figure 6: Photograph by Insho Impressions https://www.flickr.com/photos/insho/
Figure 7: Photograph by Fanny https://commons.wikimedia.org/wiki/File:Exercises_at_the_barre,_Prix_de_Lausanne_2010-2.jpg
Figure 8: Image by Zhu https://www.flickr.com/photos/xiaozhuli/5326211113/
Figure 9: Photograph by Derek Gleeson https://commons.wikimedia.org/wiki/File:Dublin_Philharmonic_Orchestra_performing_Tchaikovsky's_Symphony_No_4_in_Charlotte,_North_Carolina.jpg
Figure 10: Photograph courtesy of Lauren Miller Griffith.

Figure 11: Photograph courtesy of Jonathan S. Marion.

Media Anthropology: Meaning, Embodiment, Infrastructure, and Activism

Figure 1: Photograph by Bryce Peake. Licensed CC BY-SA.
Figure 2: Photograph by Bryce Peake. Licensed CC BY-SA.
Figure 3: Photograph by Bryce Peake. Licensed CC BY-SA.
Figure 4: Photograph by Bryce Peake. Licensed CC BY-SA.
Figure 5: Photograph by Bryce Peake. Licensed CC BY-SA.
Figure 6: Photograph by Bryce Peake. Licensed CC BY-SA.
Figure 7: Photograph by Bryce Peake. Licensed CC BY-SA.
Figure 8: Photography Bryce Peake. Licensed CC BY-SA.

Health and Medicine

Figure 1: Photograph by Mlogic https://commons.wikimedia.org/wiki/File:Ancient_Tibetan_Medicine_Poster.jpg
Figure 2: Public domain image from
https://commons.wikimedia.org/wiki/File:Hua_t08.jpg
Figure 3: Photograph by Sgerbic
https://commons.wikimedia.org/wiki/File:Botanica_store_close_up.JPG
Figure 4: Photograph by Ton Rulkens
https://commons.wikimedia.org/wiki/File:AIDS_awareness_in_Machaze_district_(4513750269).jpg
Figure 5: Photograph by African Union Mission in Somalia (AMISOM) https://www.flickr.com/photos/au_unistphotostream/with/10418757505/

Seeing Like an Anthropologist

Figure 1: Image courtesy of Logan Cochrane

Public Anthropology

Figure 1: All rights reserved. Claudia Andujar 1 (black and white)
Figure 2: Davi Kopenawa. All rights reserved. Claudia Andujar
Figure 3: All rights reserved. Victor Englebert
Figure 4: All rights reserved. Victor Englebert
Figure 5: All rights reserved. Victor Englebert
Figure 6: Image by Robert Borofsky

CPSIA information can be obtained
at www.ICGtesting.com
Printed in the USA
BVHW060256060220
571512BV00012B/348